Gower
Handbook
of Project
Management

SECOND EDITION

GOWER
HANDBOOK
OF PROJECT
MANAGEMENT

SECOND EDITION

Edited by
Dennis Lock

Gower

First published 1987 by Gower Technical Press Ltd
as Project Management Handbook

Second edition published by
Gower Publishing
Gower House
Croft Road
Aldershot
Hampshire GU11 3HR
England

Gower
Old Post Road
Brookfield
Vermont 05036
USA

British Library Cataloguing in Publication Data

Gower Handbook of Project Management. –
2Rev.ed
I. Lock, Dennis
658.404

ISBN 0–566–07391–9

Library of Congress Cataloging-in-Publication Data

Gower handbook of project management / edited by Dennis Lock. — 2nd
    ed.
        p.   cm.
    Rev. ed. of: Project management handbook.
    Includes index.
    ISBN 0–566–07391–9 : $99.95
        1. Industrial project management—Handbooks, manuals, etc.
    I. Lock, Dennis.   II. Project management handbook.
T56.8.P776   1994
658.4′04—dc20   93–11068
                                                            CIP

Typeset in 10 point Cheltenham by
Raven Typesetters, Ellesmere Port, S. Wirral
and printed in Great Britain by
Hartnolls Limited, Bodmin.

Contents

views on the benefits of formal risk management processes — Choosing the most effective level of analysis — Issues beyond project duration risk management — Further reading — Acknowledgements

PART SEVEN   MANAGING PROGRESS AND PERFORMANCE

Figures

Notes on Contributors

Peter Baily is a former senior lecturer in business studies at the Polytechnic of Wales. He started as a telecommunications mechanic and later worked in machine tool manufacturing and textile industries as buyer, materials controller, chief buyer and assistant to company secretary. Mr Baily worked with the Business Education Council as a Board member and has been chief examiner for the Institute of Purchasing and Supply. He has addressed conferences and contributed to courses in Europe, America and the Far East, and has written many articles and several books, including *Purchasing Systems and Records* (Gower, 1991) and *Purchasing and Supply Management* (Chapman & Hall, 1987).

Colin Beaumont has over 30 years' experience in the freight forwarding industry including a period of 8 years working in the Middle East on major projects. His current post as divisional manager at BIFA includes management responsibility for policy on all surface modes of transport, quality assurance, and production of the monthly newsletter BIFALINK. He visits Brussels regularly to represent the industry on customs related matters.

John Butterworth has been successively credit manager and executive director of International Factors Ltd. As director, his main responsibility was credit risk management. In 1986, Mr Butterworth joined the Royal Bank of Scotland plc to set up a new invoice factoring subsidiary Roy Scott Factors Ltd, of which he is Managing Director.

Robert L. Carter OBE is Emeritus Professor of Insurance Studies, Nottingham University. Before his academic career, Dr Carter was with the Norwich Union and was assistant insurance manager with the Dunlop Company plc. He is the author of *Economics and Insurance* (2nd edn, P. H. Press, 1979), *Reinsurance* (2nd edn, Kluwer, 1983) and *Theft in the Market* (Institute of Economic Affairs, 1976). Among books of which he is joint author are *Success in Insurance* (Murray, 1984) and *Handbook of Risk Management* (Kluwer, 1974, plus subsequent updates). He is chief editor of *Handbook of Insurance* (Kluwer, 1990, updatable) and, in addition to contributing to many other books and journals, has prepared tuition courses for the Chartered Insurance Institute, of which he is a Fellow.

Chris Chapman is Professor of Management Science and a former Head of the Department of Accounting and Management Science at the University of Southampton. His academic and consulting activities span more than twenty years, with particular emphasis on decisions concerned with risk and uncertainty. He has developed methods which are now used on important oil industry projects all over the world. Professor Chapman holds a BASc degree in engineering (Toronto), an MSc in operational research (Birmingham) and a PhD in economics and econometrics (Southampton). He is a very experienced speaker and is co-author of a number of management books and papers.

Bob Chilton has had many years of project experience with the consulting engineers Merz and McLellan, finally becoming head of their management services group. As coordinating engineer, he has been responsible for projects in India and Brazil, as well as for several projects in the UK. Mr Chilton is a Chartered Engineer and a Member of the Institution of Mechanical Engineers.

Eric Cowell is an environmental consultant whose varied career has embraced ecological advisory work in many parts of the world. Previously he held research appointments with government, agricultural, educational and pharmaceutical organizations, followed by a succession of positions spanning many years with a major oil company. Mr Cowell has been involved, for example, in the ecological evaluation of many of the world's most serious oil spills. He has written over 100 papers on environmental issues as well as editing three scientific textbooks. In addition to his own consultancy company, BH Environmental Services, Mr Cowell is also the director of a recording company that, among other specialized output, has produced a number of sound tracks for environmental videos and training cassettes for industry.

Kim Godwin has gained a wide range of experience in all aspects of the supply chain, since graduating from Imperial College in 1978. He initially joined Smiths Industries plc, working in purchasing, materials, and eventually production management roles with the industrial and aerospace markets. From there he joined S C Johnson Wax to develop logistics and distribution managements skills in FMCG, before joining Sony Broadcast International in 1990 with responsibility for European procurement and logistics. He is an active member of the Chartered Institute of Purchasing & Supply and, besides contributing to many conferences, has served on the Board of Management and as Chairman of the Logistics Committee.

F. L. Harrison is Director of Operations in the largest public sector direct labour organization in Western Europe. He has been concerned with project management for many years, having worked for the National Coal Board, Cementation Ltd, ICI and Imperial Oil of Canada. His experience also includes ten years at a business school, teaching and acting as a consultant to a variety of manufacturing and public sector organizations. Mr Harrison is the author of numerous papers on management, planning and control and of *Advanced Project Management*, the third edition of which was published by Gower in 1992.

K&H Project Systems, now part of InterSoftware®, launched the UK's first computer-based project management information system in 1963. Drawing on some 30 years' experience in project planning, 4c was launched in 1992. This, the company's sixteenth system, is designed to work with industry-standard database products, runs on a very wide variety of hardware options, and can plan, analyse and monitor every aspect of a project. The company's products are used worldwide, in industries ranging from aerospace and defence to banking and insurance.

0. P. Kharbanda, who spent many years in teaching and industry in the US, Britain and India, now runs his own consultancy advising clients across a wide range of industries in many parts of the world. He is a Fellow of the Institution of Chemical Engineers, a visiting professor, and regular leader of seminars on corporate planning, cost estimating, project management and communication skills. Dr Kharbanda has contributed hundreds of articles to technical and scientific journals and newspapers, and has written or participated in many management books.

Dennis Lock is a freelance writer. His early career began with a Higher National Certificate in Applied Physics and an appointment as an electronics engineer with the General Electric Company. His subsequent management experience has been successful, and exceptionally wide, in industries ranging from electronics to heavy machine tools and mining engineering. He is a Fellow of the Institute of Management Services and a Member of the Institute of Management. Mr Lock has carried out lecturing and consultancy assignments in the UK and overseas, and he has written or edited many successful management books.

Lucas Management Systems are the world's largest suppliers of project management software, with 50 offices in 27 countries around the world. For the last 15 years the **Artemis** range of software, which runs on all major hardware platforms, has been recognized as the *de facto* standard in many industries.

Peter Marsh, principal of Peter Marsh Associates (contract consultants) qualified as a solicitor, now retired, and has an honours degree in management sciences. He was chief contracts officer of the National Coal Board before becoming central contracts manager for AEI (and then GEC). He later joined STC as manager, contract administration, subsequently becoming projects manager for their Submarine Cable Division. Mr Marsh then held a number of senior appointments with companies in the George Wimpey group, which included commercial director of British Smelter Construction, director of business development for George Wimpey International and a director of Wimpey Major Projects. He is the author of *Contract Negotiation Handbook* (2nd edn, 1984) and

Contracting for Engineering and Construction Projects (3rd edn, 1988), both published by Gower.

NatWest Markets is the Corporate and Investment Banking division of National Westminster Bank Plc. NatWest Markets spans corporate banking, treasury, securities, investment, corporate banking and advisory services on a global basis. NatWest Markets is one of the leading project finance banks with a worldwide client base and specialist teams dedicated to energy and natural resources, transport, power generation, telecommunications and advisory services.

Jim Pearce is Technical Resources Manager of the Training Division of The Royal Society for the Prevention of Accidents. He has worked in the chemical industry both in production, pilot plant and training activities, before becoming the fire and safety officer for a multi-disciplined research and development centre.

David Ross is a director and consultant with Kildrummy Technologies Limited. Previously he was with BP International, responsible (in their Project Systems Division) for the development of microcomputer based project management systems and with preparation of project policies and procedures manuals. His early career started in manufacturing with an engineering apprenticeship, and included five years with Westland Aircraft and Massey-Ferguson respectively. He then spent fifteen years with Seltrust Engineering Limited (a subsidiary of BP Minerals International) which included work both in the UK headquarters and in Africa, particularly related to copper mining projects in Zambia, where he worked for three years with responsibility for the planning and cost control of operations both above and below ground.

The late **Ernest A. Stallworthy** was for many years a management consultant with his own company, Dolphin Project Management Services. He was previously a manager responsible for the cost control of large-scale projects in the petrochemical industry. He was a Fellow of the Association of Cost Engineers, a member of the American Association of Cost Engineers and co-author (with Dr Kharbanda) of numerous books on management.

A. G. Simms first worked in the telecommunications industry on the early development of electronic telephone exchanges. He then lectured on statistics and operations research at Woolwich and Leicester Polytechnics, and at the Cranfield Institute of Technology. He was also a visiting lecturer at the Administrative Staff College, Henley and the Royal Institute of Public Administration. From 1966 until recently Mr Simms was a Principal Scientific Officer at the Building Research Establishment. He was a founder member of the Networks Study Group of the Operational Research Society, and Chairman of the British Standards Institution's committee responsible for the *Glossary of Symbols and Terms Used in Project Network Analysis*.

Lionel Edwin Stebbing is the Senior Partner and Principal Consultant of Stebbing and Partners International. He has more than 30 years' worldwide experience in quality management. This experience has included the development and application of quality management systems in major capital plant projects, manufacturing companies, service industries and small companies, together with the development and presentation of quality-related training courses and seminars. He is one of the leading presenters of Quality Management Assessor/ Auditor training courses. Additionally, Mr Stebbing is a Fellow of the Institute of Quality Assurance and a Vice President of its Council, a Fellow of the Quality Society of Australasia and a Senior Member of the American Society for Quality Control. He is also the author of many publications on quality matters, including the books *Quality Assurance: the route to efficiency and competitiveness* now in its third edition and *Quality Management in the Service Industry*, both published by Ellis Horwood Limited, Chichester. He is also a registered lead assessor under the UK National Registration Scheme for Assessors of Quality Systems.

David Warby is principal of Director Power, a consultancy which specializes in providing director and general management business skills to industrial companies. After reading mechanical engineering at King's College, London, Mr Warby trained with the Metropolitan Vickers Electrical Company, where his first appointment was on the installation and commissioning of turbo alternators. He joined AEI-John Thompson at Berkeley power station at the start of the civil nuclear programme and became deputy resident engineer, subsequently taking a similar post with the Nuclear Power Group at Oldbury power station. In 1966 he joined Jordan Engineering (Bristol) Limited where, as Chief Executive, he helped that company to become an established leader in its field, with a thirtyfold growth over 20 years. In 1990 he established his own firm, Director Power, to apply his experience of small and medium industrial business. Mr Warby is a Fellow of the Institution of Mechanical Engineers. He has a keen interest in management, corporate and European matters and has published numerous papers on project management, safety, contract administration and quality assurance.

Edmund J. Young is a senior lecturer in engineering management at the Elton Mayo School of Management, University of South Australia. A graduate of four disciplines (civil engineering, industrial management, economics and educational administration) he worked first for six years as a civil engineer on design and investigations with the Australian Government. His next six years were spent with a large Australian company, Concrete Industries (Monier), as field and project engineer, project manager and, finally, as executive engineer responsible for management training, working in several Australian states and in South-East Asia before taking up full-time academic teaching in management. He has been a visiting lecturer in engineering or production management at the Universities of Newcastle-upon-Tyne and Bradford in England, and at the University of Missouri-Rolla, USA. In 1992 he was appointed a visiting professor in engineering management at Portland State University, Oregon, USA. Mr Young is a Fellow of both the Institution of Engineers, Australia and the Australian Institute of Management, as well as being a Member of the Institute of Management (UK) and of the American Society for Engineering Management. *xxi*

Preface

The *Project Management Handbook* was created for practising managers, trainee managers, engineers and other professional people involved in projects. We determined that the book should provide a source of instruction and reference that readers would appreciate as authoritative, comprehensive and practical. Six years after publication of the successful first edition we have revised and expanded the original work to ensure that it will continue to fulfil those aims. The result is this completely updated, improved and enlarged edition.

All chapters retained from the first edition have been revised or rewritten to ensure that they reflect current practice and legislation. The increasing influence of the European Community, for example, has meant making several changes. Many chapters now end with lists of books or articles for further reading, which will be of interest and help to those who wish to delve more deeply into specialist subjects

The sequence of chapters has been changed slightly, but the most significant feature of this new edition is its increased size and scope. Eight new chapters deal with project management politics, the impact of Europe, project investment appraisal, materials planning, risk management, fast tracking, safe working, and environmental responsibility. Two new appendices are associated with the important work of INTERNET and its flourishing British affiliate, the Association of Project Managers.

This Handbook has been written by over twenty individuals and organizations. All the contributors were chosen because of their special experience and talent in relation to each subject and we have been fortunate in being able to assemble such a strong team.

I must acknowledge my gratitude to all those who have written the chapters and to the individuals and professional organizations who have helped in other ways. I am grateful also to reviewers of the first edition; while I was obviously *xxiii* pleased and encouraged to read their favourable comments and conclusions, this new edition has benefited from their criticisms and suggestions.

This preface gives me an opportunity to remark on the role of women in project management. It is unfortunate that industrial project management remains a male-dominated profession. In the UK, for example, women account for less than 1 per cent of members of The Association of Project Managers. I hope very much that this will not always be the case. Masculine pronouns are used generally throughout this book, but only for convenience: they should be read as applying equally to men and to women.

I want to end by remembering David Barrett, Managing Director of K&H Project Systems until his fatal flying accident. David was a pioneer developer of powerful project management software systems. I profited from the use of his products and from his advice during my own early management career, when introducing multi-project scheduling and control techniques into companies in Britain and the US. In later years David contributed chapters to various Gower books, and Chapters 18, 23 and 24 of this Handbook are based on chapters which he wrote for the first edition.

Dennis Lock

St Albans

Part One

PROJECT MANAGEMENT AND ITS ORGANIZATION

1 The Nature and Purpose of Project Management

Dennis Lock

Projects have been part of the human scene since civilization started, yet the practice of project management is, on the historical timescale, almost brand new. Only in the last couple of decades has the subject appeared to any extent in management literature. Current budgeting and planning methods are all relatively recent. Perhaps the reason for emphasis on project management is that it is concerned with the management of resources, including the most expensive resource of all – namely the human resource. It is no longer the case that a few thousand slaves can be deployed to build some architectural extravagance regardless of their welfare and safety. Everything now depends on getting things done on time and within cost budgets. Moreover, there is competition. If one contractor fails to meet his obligations or targets, no doubt twenty others will be ready to jump in to take his place when the next job comes up. Management has been described as 'getting results through people'. Change that to 'achieving project goals with the resources available' and you have a succinct definition of project management, the resources being time, space, money, materials, equipment, information and people.

CHARACTERISTICS OF PROJECTS

Any sales engineer working for a company which sells products from a catalogue, off its shelves, will know that his job is to dissuade the customer from asking for anything not listed in the catalogue and standard price list. If the sales engineer achieves a full order quota on the basis of accepting a number of 'specials', the production management will probably be quite upset at the resulting disruption to their batched manufacturing programme and the inevitable cost penalties. Project work is exactly opposite. Everything is special and 'one-off' or in very small quantities. Designs are new and usually unproven. Every industrial or commercial project is a risk venture. The job of the contractor is to identify the

3

risks and, through his project management, contain them.

In this book, many project management techniques and practices are described. Their application will depend on the size and type of project, and upon the relative priorities which are assigned to the cost, time and performance objectives. Three broad categories of project can be identified, each with its own characteristics and demands upon project management methods.

Manufacturing projects

Included in the category of manufacturing projects are specially designed and built machines or equipment ordered to some unique customer specification. Typically these involve original design work, possibly prototype testing, and then manufacture, assembly and testing or commissioning in a factory with subsequent delivery and installation at the customer's premises. Apart from possible installation and commissioning work, most of the contractor's work is carried out completely under his own control on his own premises and with his own management in command. The job has probably been sold for a fixed price with a target profit in mind. There will be a promised delivery date, and there should be a set of unambiguous data which defines the required project.

Development projects for new products fit into this classification, since they are carried out with internal resources using the company's own management. Development projects differ in management emphasis because there is no direct profit objective, but they still require definition of timescale, expected performance and cost budget limits.

Manufacturing projects need the project management techniques of definition, cost estimates and budgetary control and timescale planning and control (although small manufacturing projects may not need the application of network analysis and the more sophisticated forms of resource scheduling which are described in later chapters). Communication problems are not likely to arise, and the project manager should be able to monitor progress easily and obtain access to line managers for the purpose of getting deficiencies corrected.

The situation becomes more complicated when more than one big contractor is engaged on the project in a joint venture organization, in which case the project more readily fits into the next category.

Civil engineering, construction, petrochemical, mining and other projects requiring external organization

Projects which aim to establish buildings or operating plant at some site remote from the contractor's offices, or which require substantial participation of other contractors in joint ventureship, need more attention to the problems of organization and communication. It will almost certainly be necessary to prepare and issue a formal set of project administrative procedures, and to set up a management team at the site.

Assuming that projects in this category are likely to be bigger and more expensive than simple manufacturing projects, financial management to provide and control the flow of funds will need expert professional attention, while the contracts between participating companies will be more difficult to draft and agree.

The more expensive, the longer the duration and the more complicated the organization, the more the project will be likely to benefit from the sensible application of modern sophisticated planning, scheduling and cost control techniques (almost certainly using computers).

Management projects

The categories of project described so far are the obvious cases which spring to mind whenever the words 'project management' are uttered. But all companies, whatever the nature of their business, encounter project management problems at some time. A company engaged in flow or batch production will be vitally interested whenever a production facility is modernized or reorganized, and project management techniques will be needed to ensure efficient installation and start-up of the new plant. Even a commercial company with no manufacturing base at all must exercise efficient project management when it enlarges or moves its offices. Under these circumstances, where there is probably little project management experience resident within the company, the employment of an external project manager or managing contractor is the sensible practice.

Project management techniques find their application in many situations far removed from the obvious industrial project scene, helping to manage changes of premises, new installations, refurbishment or maintenance of existing plant and facilities, company relocations and so on. Although scientific research projects may be too innovative and experimental to allow the definition of objectives, without which project management is unable to operate properly, setting up the research facilities in the first place will probably take less time and stand less chance of exceeding budgets if the principles of project management are applied.

Another kind of project which needs formal management of budgets and timescale is the systems development and implementation work seen when a team of internal or external specialists is engaged to investigate administrative or accounting procedures, suggest and develop alternative (improved) methods, and then implement them. In fact, the name 'project manager' is sometimes applied to the head of a team responsible for designing a special computer system application for a commercial user.

Most managers working in industry or commerce need the expertise of a project manager at some time during their working lives.

OBJECTIVES

The objectives of project management can be condensed under three headings. A successful project is one which has been finished on time, within its cost budgets and to a technical or performance standard which satisfies the end user.

Timescale

Provided that quality standards and design are satisfactory, it is a fairly safe assumption that projects which finish on time are likely to meet their other objectives, whereas projects that finish late overrun their budgets and cause customer resentment and other problems. Controlling the timescale must be a top priority for any project manager. There is no shortage of management techniques available to help in this quest. While it is true that strikes, failures by other contractors and unavoidable design errors are all hurdles to be overcome, nevertheless careful attention to timescale planning and progress control are essential if a project is to stand any chance of success.

A project costs money during every day, working or non-working, weekday or weekend day, from day one of the programme right through until final payment has been received from the customer. These costs arise from the obvious 'direct' cost elements of bought-out materials and all the man-hours expended in design and production activities. There are also the costs of management and adminis-tration to be borne. Accommodation is another big cost factor in many projects, with all kinds of problems for future work schedules and subsequent projects if the work is not finished and cleared away on time. Other costs include the notional cost of money used or tied up in the project. This can include the obvious interest charges from banks or other sources for large projects with special financing, but it also includes the cost of money invested in work in progress. And work in progress does not only include the obvious work carried on in the factory or on a construction site, but it also encompasses all the costs of engineering and drawing which are buried in designs and drawings in progress or awaiting production or construction use.

Delays on a large project can amount to additional costs of thousands of pounds per day. If work is not finished, the contractor is unable to issue invoices or claim progress payments. And there can be the final ignominy of cost penalties in contracts which contain clauses providing the customer with the sanction of penalty payments for each day or each week by which the contractor fails to meet his delivery obligation.

Every project manager must ensure that his project is efficiently and sensibly planned and scheduled from the start, and that critical tasks are identified. Control has then to be applied to keep the work on time, if necessary by putting additional effort into critical jobs which are at risk of running late. Such control has to embrace all areas of the project and all subcontractors and vendors of equipment. If the contractor makes it clear from the start that he expects all participants to meet their delivery and work schedule commitments, and then proceeds to monitor progress closely, he stands a better chance of success. It is no good waiting until a supplier fails to deliver goods at the appropriate time, or being surprised that a specialist design subcontractor asks for more time to complete drawings. Only by a constant process of checking achievement against a series of intermediate, planned criteria or events can timely completion be assured. And the project manager should have rooted in his mind, if not actually displayed in his office, the axiom 'TIME IS MONEY'.

Project costs

For many industrial projects cost control will be seen as an essential part of managing for profit or, in other words, safeguarding the planned margin between total project costs and the sales revenue achieved. Many projects, however, are not conducted for profit. As a generalization, it is safer to say that the purpose of cost control is to contain costs within the level of expenditure which has been authorized (the project budget).

The actual process of cost control is, unlike timescale control, not always a straightforward procedure. Whereas, if a job runs late, managers or supervisors can take steps to expedite the work, it is more difficult directly to control costs. The process of containing costs within budgets is more a matter of applying sound control principles before any money is committed.

Cost control starts with careful definition of the scope of work for which funds are to be committed. For all but the smallest venture, this is followed by division of the whole project into a number of more easily manageable parts (known universally as the work breakdown process). Each part of the work becomes a 'work package', to be cost estimated, budgeted and (subsequently) cost controlled.

Some projects, such as those for pure research, where results are impossible to predict, are of course less amenable to cost control against measured performance. However, it is rare to find any project for which unlimited funds are available. Some attempt has to be made to set and authorize budgets and review expenditure regularly. If the work cannot be broken down into definable work packages with predetermined performance targets, a common alternative is to review past and future expenditure at regular intervals (perhaps quarterly or annually), assess results to date, and then reappraise the project before voting funds allowing the work to continue for a further period.

The control of labour costs, including professional man-hours, is largely one of controlling the timescale. If progress is maintained on schedule with the planned workforce, then no serious cost problem should arise.

The control of material and equipment costs is exercised before orders are placed, through the procedure of obtaining competitive quotations and by comparing quotations for similar items in a rational and orderly fashion. Formal procedures for the approval of expenditure commitments are essential, so that a responsible manager or organization examines each significant item before issuing the purchase order. If equipment orders committed exceed the amount budgeted, then no amount of work can undo the damage. It will simply be too late to recover the over-expenditure.

There are project managers who believe that because they have good cost coding and work breakdown systems, possibly backed up by computers, that the resulting detailed reports constitute good cost control. They are mistaken. Cost reporting is not cost control. The purpose of accurate and detailed cost reporting is to provide early warning of dangerous trends, giving sufficient time for corrective action. But corrective action can, as already stated, only consist of rigorous progress control and formal vetting and approval of purchase commitments before they are made.

Other important factors in cost control concern the intrinsic costs of the project design. These are mentioned in the next section.

Performance

If a project is delivered on time and within budget the contractor will be well pleased. The customer should also be pleased, unless the finished result is below his functional or aesthetic requirements. This is not a technical textbook, and cannot deal with the intricacies of conceptual and detailed engineering which must be the jealously guarded capability of every reputable and competent contractor within each industrial field. There are, however, sound engineering management principles which fall within the scope of project management generally, and without which all the project objectives will be put at risk.

The first and obvious step in attaining the required performance is to define, from the outset, exactly what that performance is to be. Engineering then proceeds along guidelines which correspond with the cost and timescale objectives. All three objectives are interlocked, and the conduct and progress of engineering has to be managed to make sure that the design standards and concepts keep on the chosen track. Variations and modifications are inevitable in a large contract: these must be subjected to definition, vetting, approval and control along with the mainstream activities.

Some companies pride themselves upon their technical excellence. Pride in a company's products can be a wonderful motivating force. Care has to be taken, however, not to produce a result which far exceeds the requirements. There is a useful motto in this respect for engineering managers: 'Don't let the *best* be the enemy of the *good*!' Firms have been known to lose potential orders because their fundamental engineering standards were too good, and too costly to achieve. Sometimes their methods were actually wasteful: why use stainless steel where mild steel would do, and why use 50mm plate thickness when all the competitors would use the (perfectly adequate) thickness of 25mm? These are areas where companies can benefit from the common-sense techniques of value engineering and value analysis. A sensible company will involve the project manager and managers from the engineering and fulfilment divisions in pre-design meetings which aim to eliminate unnecessarily wasteful procedures, and to arrive at designs which, while functional, are practicable to produce.

Quality assurance is a vital function in the achievement of performance and, rightly, has a chapter of its own later in this book. As with control over time and costs, quality assurance must extend over all concerned with project fulfilment, whether they are working in the contractor's own factory, producing goods or equipment for supply through vendors, or carrying out construction, installation or erection on site.

THE PROJECT MANAGER

The role of the project manager, and the organization of project management is discussed at length in the following chapters. It is, however, useful to reflect here

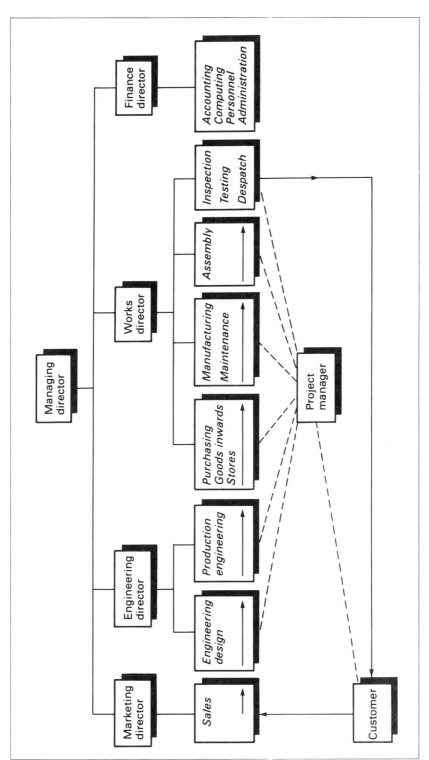

Figure 1.1 Example of organization for a manufacturing project

Without the project manager, this diagram illustrates an example of a manufacturing organization suitable for handling small batch production. When the output is, instead, large one-off special projects, the addition of a project manager is necessary to coordinate all activities and ensure that the project work flows smoothly within proper cost and time constraints.

Stage in project management	Method	See chapter
0 Feasibility	A preliminary stage, before project management involvement, in which appraisals are carried out to ensure that the project will be viable technically and economically, and that funds can be made available	15
1 Definition of objectives		
— scope	Solution or feasibility engineering by potential contractors, often in consultation with the client	9
— costs	Evaluation of the proposed engineering solution as accurately as possible (given the limited amount of design information available) to arrive at provisional cost estimates. The project may have to be sold against such preliminary estimates	12
— timescale	An assessment of the project duration and its key dates, based mainly upon past experience of similar projects rather than on detailed planning. A simple bar chart may be produced or a network, but there is insufficient information or time available at this pre-contract stage to allow detailed planning	16
2 Arrange funding	The client, having decided that he wants to proceed with a contract, has to ensure that funds are arranged or are available from his own resources. Preliminary cash flow forecasts are necessary.	11
3 Agree the objectives	The successful contractor, by entering into a contract with the client, has accepted his commitments and agreed to the project objectives	4 5 6 7
4 Work breakdown	The project is divided into a set of manageable tasks, known as work packages. Each work package is a mini-project, with its own objectives of scope, cost and timescale. Work packages are chosen so that they fit together into hierarchical (or family tree) fashion to constitute the entire project.	12
5 Work schedule	Bar charts or network diagrams are used to show all project activities in a logical sequence. Network notation is best suited to this process, but bar charts are acceptable for very small jobs.	16 17
	The duration of each activity is estimated, and the overall project timescale is calculated, together with the identification of all critical activities. The logic is re-examined if the timescale is too long.	17
	The resources needed for the project are calculated and scheduled, using a computer for all but the very smallest projects.	18

Figure 1.2 Stages of project management

Stage in project management	Method	See chapter
6 Set the cost budgets	Re-estimate the project costs, in the detail afforded by the work breakdown and work schedule. Reconcile the new estimate with that used for the contract commitment, and take practical steps to limit the expenditure if this is initially estimated to exceed the total budget objective. Then set the work package budgets accordingly.	12 13
7 Work implementation	Set up the project organization. Write and issue administrative procedures (unless standard). Issue an order authorizing work to start. Issue detailed task lists and assign tasks to individuals. Set up purchasing arrangements. Identify and buy all long-lead purchased items.	3 19 20
8 Review the objectives	Reviewing the initial objectives is a continuous function of the project management team to ensure that any threat to them is acted upon promptly. Special attention must be paid to any proposals for project variations, to assess their likely effect on the overall scope, final costs and timescale.	9 13
9 Work follow-up	Expedite materials. Monitor, report and predict costs. Set up and carry out effective quality assurance procedures, to follow through until all work has been finished. Monitor work against key events or quantities, as appropriate. Ensure that personnel are well organized and motivated. Conduct progress meetings and report to the client and to the contractor's own management.	21 13 31 28 30 28
10 Close down	Assemble, summarize and archive a historical record of the project, showing final costs and scope of work, together with a technical description supported by as-built drawings. Include test certificates, calculations and copies of operating and maintenance manuals. This stage can be regarded as the final part of project definition, which started with the definition of objectives, and (now) finishes with the objectives as they were actually achieved.	9

Figure 1.2 (*concluded*)

on the emergence of project management as a distinct management specialization. Large projects seem to demand more complex organizations these days, and we tend to marvel at the greatness and stamina of engineering giants such as Telford and Brunel, who personally directed all aspects of their projects. There now exist project managers with no direct responsibility for engineering, whose role is co-ordination and administration. It is to these administrative, co-ordinating and control functions and techniques that this book is addressed.

At its simplest, the need for the separate role of a project manager is seen in an engineering company faced with producing special one-off products which are large in relation to its total production capacity, and which involve several departments. Whereas normal batch production is handled adequately by the existing production management, the larger project needs an independent co-ordinating eye to see the whole picture and keep everything controlled and co-ordinated. This concept is illustrated in Figure 1.1. The ordinary organization of a factory contains no individual who can devote time, or has the authority to oversee all phases of the project. In industries such as construction, the need for project management is more apparent, and does not need further amplification.

TECHNIQUES OF PROJECT MANAGEMENT

This book contains much advice and explanation in the use of a number of management and commercial practices and techniques for project management. The armoury of such management tools is extensive and expanding. The choice of techniques, sometimes available on a selection of computers, is often a matter of personal preference. It is, however, necessary to be clear about the sequence in which the techniques should be used, and to know what they can and what they cannot achieve.

The sequence and choice of techniques

Faced with having to plan and control a large project, the inexperienced manager might well feel overfaced by the number of apparently conflicting and insoluble problems. Many decisions have to be made, and procedures established. The situation is, in some respects, analogous to the solution of a mathematical problem containing several unknown quantities. The way out of the dilemma is to use a logical method for eliminating the unknown quantities one at a time. The problem is then made manageable.

Please now refer to Figure 1.2. This shows the principal stages of project management, and provides a 'directory' to the chapters in this book which deal with the appropriate practices.

INTERNET AND THE ASSOCIATION OF PROJECT MANAGERS

The profession of project management is represented by the International Association of Project Management (INTERNET). Its corporate member in the UK is the Association of Project Managers, and further information is available from their secretariat at: The Association of Project Managers, 85 Oxford Road, High Wycombe, Buckinghamshire HP11 2DX. Membership of the Association, which arranges seminars and meetings and publishes the magazine *Project* and the *International Journal of Project Management*, is a good way for project managers to meet other project managers and to maintain current awareness of modern techniques, practices and available computer systems.

2 Project Organization

Edmund J. Young

The Chinese philosopher Confucius once stated, 'The beginning of learning starts with the precise meaning of words'. Unfortunately, the fields of management in general and project management in particular are plagued by the problem of semantics. There are a number of different meanings of such terms as 'management', 'project management', 'project organization', 'project teams', etc., and at present there is no general agreement or consensus of views on the precise definitions of these words.

DEFINING 'ORGANIZATION'

While the term 'project' is more readily definable in terms of such attributes as a complete sequence of tasks that has a definite start and finish, an identifiable goal and entity, and an integrated system of complex but interdependent relationships, the term 'organization' has several meanings. Consider the term 'global project organization'. While the English author Harrison (1992) refers to it as 'the arrangement and relationships between client company, contractor and subcontractor organizations and their respective project managers who are all involved in undertaking a project in a particular environment', American authors Davis and Lawrence (1977) refer to it as meaning the arrangement and interrelationships of projects on a global or worldwide scale. So it is a matter of taking a point of view on what precisely one means by the various terms, and more importantly, on what is generally accepted in project practice.

The term 'organization' has four different, but related meanings, as follows:

1 The systematic arrangement or division of work, activities or tasks between individuals and groups with the necessary allocation of duties and responsibilities among them to achieve common objectives.
2 A cohesive social group with formal relationships between members who combine together to achieve common goals, for example, a football club, a political party, a pressure group, etc.

3 The total aggregation of human and material resources that can be distinguished as a separate entity purposely combined together to achieve specific objectives, for example, a company, a government department, a construction project, etc.
4 The structure of authority and responsibility relationships in a cohesive social system that is a separate entity purposely set up to achieve specific objectives.

The relationships between these four definitions can be stated as follows: to achieve the objectives required in Organization 2 or 3 entails Organization 1 (involving arrangement or division of work), which in turn requires a structure of authority and responsibility that is Organization 4.

Thus, organizations have specific objectives, a formal structure of authority with some persons in leadership roles and others in subordinate roles, division of work which entails specialization by members in various activities or functions, a formal system of communications, and generally a set of formal procedures and customs that distinguish them from other social entities. Social scientists, from the German sociologist Max Weber early this century to today, called these features the attributes of 'bureaucracy' but it is difficult to see how organizations could continue to exist without possessing these attributes to some degree. The direct antithesis of 'organization' is disorganization, chaos and anarchy. In project organization, accomplishment of the specific project in the most economical, efficient and effective manner within the constraints of time, budget and performance or quality standards is the prime objective.

ROLE OF THE PROJECT MANAGER

The problem of semantics relates also to defining the role of project manager. In practice, while all may be designated 'project managers', roles may vary considerably from one who is strictly a project monitor or expediter, through one who oversees or who exercises broad supervision over a project, to one who exercises total authority and accepts full responsibility for the execution of the project. The common element in defining the role of the project manager is that it relates to acceptance of managerial responsibility for certain aspects of the project. This managerial responsibility entails responsibility for planning, organizing, co-ordinating, staffing, leading, major decision making, motivating personnel, monitoring and controlling operations on the project.

The varying roles can be seen in Figure 2.1 which depicts simply three organizations involved in the undertaking of a typical construction project. Organization meanings 2 and 3 are implied here.

There is Organization A – the principal, customer or client, who wants the project and is prepared to pay for it. If Organization A does not have the resources and expertise to carry out such tasks as feasibility studies, planning, design, preparation of the necessary contract documents and general supervision of project execution, then it engages Organization B to undertake these activities for a fee. Organization B may be an architectural firm, engineering *15*

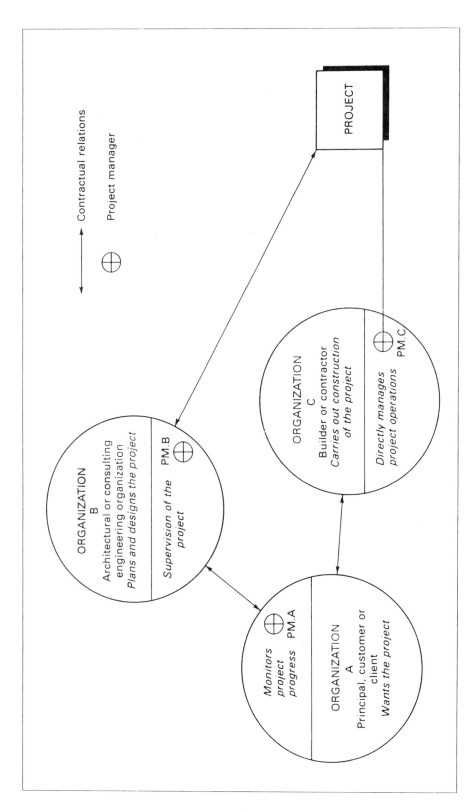

Figure 2.1 Project manager roles

Different roles of the project managers in three organizations involved in a construction project.

consultant, or a firm specializing in project management, depending on the nature and scope of the project. Organization B is the second party involved and there is a contractual relation between Organizations A and B.

But to execute the project, a third party, Organization C – the builder or contractor – with the necessary human and material resources, constructional experience and expertise, must be involved. Either by tendering or by negotiation a contractual relation is established between the principal or customer, Organization A, and the contractor or seller, Organization C. Organization B then acts on behalf of Organization A to supervise the project to be carried out by Organization C. This is a typical situation where three parties are involved in a construction project. But if Organization A was of such size and possessed all the resources to plan, design, supervise and construct the project by itself, then there would be no need for Organizations B and C. Likewise, if Organization A had the resources and expertise to plan, design and supervise the project only, then Organization B would not be needed. The arrangement of work to undertake the project is dependent upon the availability of resources, specialization of functions between organizations and their roles, nature of the project and the environment.

The project depicted by the organization in Figure 2.1 could be of such importance and complexity that each of the three organizations would need to appoint its own project manager. The roles of these project managers will not be identical, owing to the division of work and responsibilities, and to the particular roles and functions of the different organizations. For reference, we can designate these project managers as PM.A, PM.B and PM.C (for organizations A, B and C, respectively).

PM.A's role would be more of a monitor, progress chaser, reporter and expediter. PM.A's duty would be to keep the top management of Organization A informed on progress, expenditure, and likely delays on the project. He may approve progress payments by his organization for work satisfactorily completed by Organization C on the recommendation of the representative from Organization B. Public relations for the project may be handled by PM.A. His top management has delegated the responsibility for the project to him to oversee. He is the key person to contact in his own organization on all matters relating to the project.

PM.B's role would be more comprehensive insofar as it involves preparation of feasibility studies, advising the customer or client on best choice, planning, design, preparation of contract documents, analysis and recommendation of tenders, contract administration, checking quality and progress, and exercising general supervision over the project. In the investigation stage, PM.B may be involved with contacting and negotiation with local authorities.

PM.C's role is the one most directly involved with the actual execution of the project. This involves detailed planning, daily decision making, organizing, co-ordinating, directing and supervising personnel, and controlling human and material resources in actually carrying out the project. Although not shown in Figure 2.1, he may be involved in the negotiation and supervision of sub-contractors, and in dealing with suppliers and local authorities whose co-operation is necessary in implementing the project.

The role of the person designated as the 'project manager' would depend, therefore, on the arrangement of work and role of the organization employing him in relation to the project. The focus of his duties and responsibilities is on the project.

The roles of the project manager can be viewed in terms of:

1 *Externally* – to others outside his own organization, or to inter-organizational relationships, and
2 *Internally* – to members within his own organization, or to intra-organizational relationships.

Externally, the project manager has to deal with the customer or client organization, subcontractors, suppliers of materials and equipment, local authorities and other organizations which could affect the project. Of these, the customer is the most important.

The project manager–customer relationship

One of the main reasons for the appointment of a project manager by an employer is the wish of top management to delegate the responsibility for monitoring, co-ordinating, supervising or managing the project from start to finish to one person – the project manager. In doing so, he becomes the key person whom the customer can contact on progress, complaints, taking corrective action, changes of plans or delays on the project. The project manager is in the key role for communications on the project. Both top management of his own organization and the customer would consider him the main contact person on development or progress.

The project manager is also the organization's representative for the project to the customer and others externally. He is the firm's chief spokesman and main negotiator on all matters relating to the project. For the project manager in a consulting engineering organization (like PM.B in Figure 2.1) he has also the responsibility to advise the client or customer on best courses of action, costs of changes to plans, and to make recommendations on approval of progress payments to the contractor. Such services imply professional liability on the part of the consulting organization which can be more than the straight principal–contractor contractual relationship.

The project manager's relationships within his own organization

Having recognized that there could be a number of different responsibilities that a project manager could assume, five major classes of responsibility can be identified, as follows:

1 Project expediter, monitor or reporter.
2 Project planner.
3 Project co-ordinator.

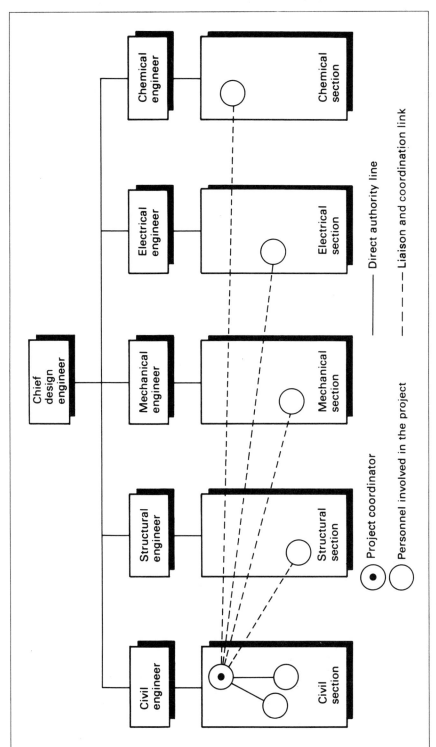

Figure 2.2 Project coordinator in a design engineering organization

Example of a project coordinator based (in this case) in a civil engineering department with direct responsibility for the work in his own section and with liaison and coordination responsibilities with all other sectors.

Legend within figure:

Chief design engineer

Civil engineer — Structural engineer — Mechanical engineer — Electrical engineer — Chemical engineer

Civil section — Structural section — Mechanical section — Electrical section — Chemical section

——— Direct authority line

– – – Liaison and coordination link

⊙ Project coordinator

○ Personnel involved in the project

4 Project supervisor or controller.
5 Project manager, administrator or director.

Wearne (1973) recognized nine degrees of relative project responsibility but the above simplified classification makes for easier identification in practice. Depending on the situation, it is possible for one person to assume one, several or all of these responsibilities. In Figure 2.1 PM.A assumed role 1, whereas PM.B carried out roles 2 and 4. PM.C assumed role 5 for his own organization.

The role of the project co-ordinator (3) is more restricted in liaison and co-ordination with personnel outside his own department. Figure 2.2 shows an engineering design organization in which the project co-ordinator in the civil section co-ordinates the efforts of personnel in the other sections working on the same project. He is not allowed to exercise direct authority over these other personnel, but has instead to use more persuasion and other means of influencing them in carrying out their part of the project. At most, he can call co-ordination meetings to ensure that everyone involved reports progress and integrates effort.

The project co-ordinator has been delegated this task of co-ordination by senior management or by his superior (the chief civil engineer) on the basis that the major portion of the project is a civil engineering one, but requires inputs from the other engineering functions. Any conflict between personnel has to be taken up to the section engineers and ultimately to the chief design engineer for resolution. Within the civil section the project co-ordinator may be directly in charge of subordinates who, together, make up his own project team within the section. Then there exists line (direct) authority between the project co-ordinator and members of his own project team.

Figure 2.2 also shows the arrangement common to most organizations, which is functional organization (organization according to main functions or similar groups of activities). All civil engineering activities, all mechanical activities, and so on, are grouped together in their respective sections, with each headed by its appropriate specialist engineer. If, for example, the civil section had several large projects which were wholly or predominantly civil, it might be convenient to appoint project managers or officers with responsibility for each of these projects. This would become a form of project organization within the functional department.

Pure project team organization

The pure project team or 'projectized organization' is depicted in Figure 2.3, which shows the structure for an engineering construction project. Here the division of duties and responsibilities of personnel directly under the project manager and his assistant are according to main functions (which comprise civil and mechanical design, construction, transport, purchasing, etc.). The project manager exercises full authority and control.

Line and staff organization

The prime tasks or functions of the enterprise are to design and construct the

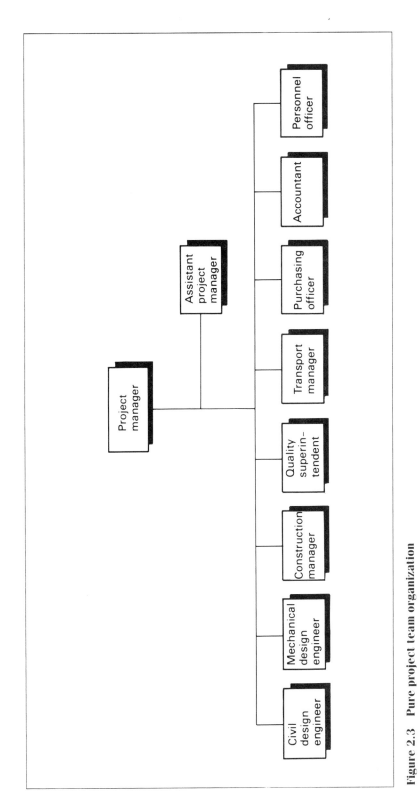

Figure 2.3 Pure project team organization

Organization in which the project manager is in total charge of the project.

project. While the transport, purchasing, accounting and personnel activities are all a necessary part of the total set of operations, these sections are not directly involved with the prime tasks of design and construction. They are more in support or 'staff' roles. Their roles are to assist, aid, render counsel and advice, and to service the 'line' activities. The quality superintendent is in a more controlling role but is still considered as more a 'staff' function. While all the subordinates under the project manager are in line relationship to him, the organization is also one of 'line and staff'. Thus, Figure 2.3 which depicts a pure project team organization is really one that shows both line and staff relationships with some personnel performing line functions of design and construction, and other personnel rendering service, aid, counsel or support to those in the 'line'. A distinguishing feature of this pure project organization is that the total efforts of all personnel involved are concentrated solely on the project. This is also the oldest form of project organization. It was used by the ancient Egyptians, Chinese and Romans to build pyramids, walls, canals and roads.

Matrix organization

In the early 1960s the concept of 'project management' was promoted by the US Defence Department and the aerospace industry as a new form of managerial organization. The term 'matrix management' was conceived and applied to both client and contractor organizations in the United States. This raises the issue of whether there are different organizational relationships in different industries. We have considered the pure project organization, which is common on large-scale building and construction projects, and the line and staff organization which is formed from a functional organization. The pure project organization is usually part of a broader line and staff-functional structure of the total enterprise. Where the project is of a small size and does not warrant accounting and personnel departments set up under the project manager (as shown by Figure 2.3) then it is usual to have 'staff' roles advising and assisting the project manager and his team from outside the project team structure.

A matrix form of organization is depicted in Figure 2.4 which shows the functional organizations with engineering, production and other functional managers in charge of their respective departments with vertical lines of authority, and project managers A, B and C in charge of projects A, B and C respectively also exercising equal authority (shown by lateral or horizontal lines) with the functional managers.

This is a situation in which personnel in the functional departments could be responsible to two or more superiors. The diagram shows only the simple case, with a single person in each department allocated to one project (like the engineers X, Y and Z, allocated to projects A, B and C respectively). The situation would become more complicated if (for example) engineer Z were also to be assigned to work on project A. Or, suppose that project managers A, B and C all required the services of engineer Y. The result is a multiple command system which appears to violate the age-old principle of one man, one boss (unity of command).

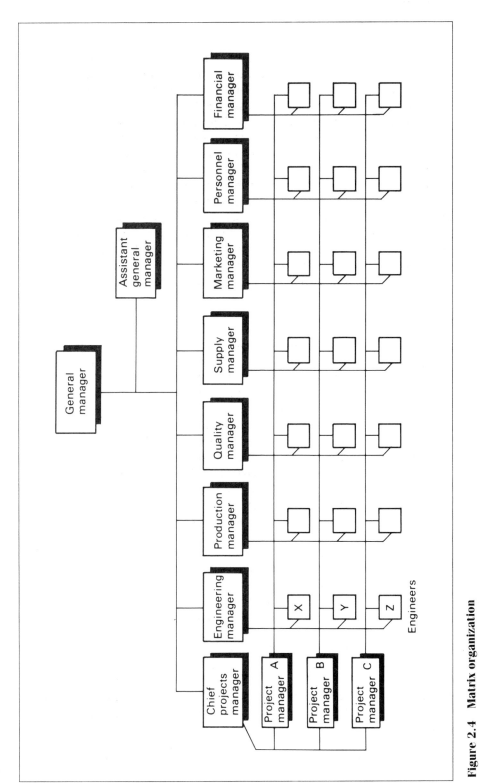

Figure 2.4 Matrix organization

Project managers exercise equal (lateral) authority with functional managers.

Figure 2.4 depicts the situation where a chief projects manager heads all the project managers A, B and C. This has the advantage that the span of control is reduced – the number of direct subordinates to the general manager is nine (assistant general manager, chief projects manager and seven functional managers). Without the chief projects manager, the three project managers would have to report directly to the general manager. The appointment of a chief projects manager enables more projects to be undertaken, with improved co-ordination between projects, and it allows consultation between the chief projects manager and the functional managers in order to settle any differences on project matters.

This matrix form of organization was a 'spin off' from the US aerospace industry during the 1960s, and many organizations in various industries from manufacturing, consulting, construction, service to educational have adopted it with varying success (Kingdon, 1973; Davis and Lawrence, 1977; and Knight, 1977). Shannon (1972) maintained that the concept of dual or multiple authority relationships stemmed from the 'functional foremanship' theory of the American pioneer of scientific management, F. W. Taylor, with the basic difference that Taylor did not conceive it as applying to management of a project.

The matrix organization can be one of two forms: shifting or fixed. In the shifting matrix (widely used in the American aerospace industry), personnel in functional departments were shifted between projects depending on the work load and project cycle. In the fixed matrix, personnel in functional departments are always assigned to the same project managers whatever the project. In the fixed matrix a project manager would be responsible for managing the projects in successive series; for example, projects P, Q and R would follow each other under the guidance and control of the same project manager. In the shifting matrix the personnel assigned to the project team are disbanded when the project is finished.

The concept of a project team can apply also within the matrix, where it relates to personnel in functional departments who work directly under the project manager in a team, group or task force. These personnel may either stay within their own departments or they can be grouped together and placed under the charge of the project manager in a place chosen for the duration of the project. But, in these cases, each person has two or more bosses – the project manager(s) and his usual functional manager.

In manufacturing industry, the concept of product manager is used to relate to the responsibility for conception, development, manufacturing, marketing and servicing of a particular product. Here, the matrix of Figure 2.4 still applies, but with the difference that the project managers are replaced by the product managers. In Figure 2.4 both line and staff personnel are used by the product managers to undertake project work. The matrix can also be developed in other dimensions, like services (Kerzner, 1979 and Cleland and King, 1983).

The basic organization structures of line, line and functional, line and staff, or a combination of these can be identified irrespective of the industry being considered. The *project* organization (whether in the form of pure project organization or of project groupings within functional departments) focuses

24

attention on the project. The *matrix* organization combines functional structure with a project (or product) organization overlay.

It should be noted that there are two other types of organization, namely committee organization (not relevant for consideration here) and military style general staff organization (described later in this chapter).

MATRIX VERSUS THE PURE PROJECT ORGANIZATION

Matrix advantages

Those who advocate the matrix claim a number of advantages for this type of organization. It permits project managers to focus attention on all stages of the project from start to finish while operating in the traditional functional structure. It allows greater flexibility and so is more adaptable to changes in technology in that personnel can be readily transferred to different projects as in the shifting matrix. This facilitates balancing of workloads between the demands of all the projects being undertaken.

Better communications are maintained between all parties (especially with customers) as well as better utilization of resources. Because the matrix can be considered as an overlay on the functional structure the benefit of functional specialization in maintaining a high standard of technical excellence is another advantage. With the fixed matrix, functional personnel are likely to be more motivated because of continuity of projects whereas with the pure project organization (and to some extent with the shifting matrix) motivation and morale can decline as each project approaches completion.

Matrix disadvantages

A prime disadvantage of the matrix is that it is a more complex form of organization to operate. This is mainly due to its dual or multiple command structure with functional personnel being subjected to the authority of both their functional and project managers. It may lead to role ambiguity and conflict of interests. Cleland and King (1983) maintained that there can be a separation of responsibility in the sense that the project manager assumes responsibility for project planning, determination of project objectives, scheduling and budgeting while the functional manager assumes responsibility for the method of work and assignment of personnel.

Such division and clarification of responsibilities can be assisted by the use of a linear responsibility chart (LRC) – or linear responsibility matrix (LRM) – as developed originally by the American consultant Serge Birn. Responsibility is divided into primary responsibility and support responsibility, similar to line and staff responsibilities (Cleland and Kocaoglu, 1981). A useful variation of Birn's chart (used in Australia) is shown in Figure 2.5.

Using the linear matrix, the Americans found it easier to solve the problem of 'violation of command' (or multiple command), as was foreseen by Fayol (1949) in

Activity code	Activity	Project manager	Civil design	Structural design	Mechanical design	Electrical design	Chemical design	Investigation engineer	Surveyor	Estimating engineer	Contracts engineer	Cost engineer
2.14	Develop cost report formats	A					I					P
2.15	Review purchasing order	R								I	P	
2.16	Review and approve budget	A	S	S	S	S	S		S			P
2.17	Monitor project costs	R										C
2.18	Prepare cost reports		P	P	P	P	P		P			
2.19	Analysis of cost reports	R										P

Personnel responsibilities

P = primary responsibility
S = secondary responsibility
C = coordination responsibility
R = review required
A = approval required
I = input required

Figure 2.5 A linear responsibility matrix chart (From E. Young, in D. Samson (ed), *Management for Engineers*, 1989)

Taylor's original fundamental organization, which reared its head again in the matrix organization. They suggested that functional managers should be responsible for work methods, functional staff specialist services and functional component costing, leaving the project managers with responsibilty for overall project planning, co-ordination, scheduling, total costing, and overall monitoring and control. Some organizations appoint a general project co-ordinating manager, to whom the various project managers report and to whom senior management delegate responsibility for sorting out any difficulties or conflict resolution with the functional managers.

In practice, it is difficult to separate the method of work from the time and cost aspects. Where highly talented or specialized functional personnel are involved, it is more likely for functional managers to give preference to these personnel for their own important jobs rather than allowing them to be used on project work. Thus conflict of interests can easily arise, and this involves conflict of loyalties.

Another disadvantage is the higher overhead costs involved in setting up project managers and the system of communications. Davis and Lawrence (1977) saw the problem of the delicate balance of power in the matrix form with tendencies to anarchy, power struggles, slowness of decision making, 'groupitis', and even collapse during business decline. They maintained that the three reasons for operation of the matrix form were due to: (a) outside pressure for dual focus; (b) pressures for high information-processing capacity; and (c) pressures for shared resources.

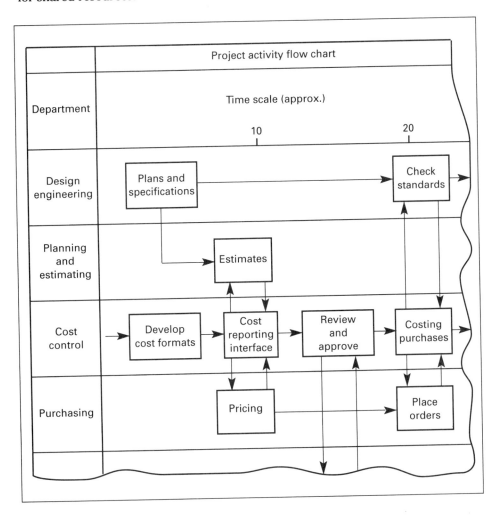

Figure 2.6 Project activity flowchart (from E. Young, in D. Samson (ed.), *Management for Engineers*, 1989)

Operating the matrix

To use the matrix, personnel must be properly trained in understanding the concept, principles involved and the techniques of operation. Lines of authority and responsibility must be clearly defined, and any subdivision of responsibilities clearly allocated. This is where the linear responsibility chart can be an invaluable tool. The objectives and functions must be clearly stated for all components of the project, and the work breakdown structure and work package concepts are useful aids in this regard. Clear guidelines on incentives, loyalties and promotional opportunities for functional personnel need to be stated.

Another useful chart to assist project organization is the project activity flow chart, which is really a combined organization and scheduling chart. An example is given in Figure 2.6. The chart shows the various project activities, plotted on a linear horizontal timescale and positioned vertically in relation to departments or functional responsibilities.

The system of communications between all personnel must be established early, with provision made for constant consultation as the project progresses.

The roles of each person must be clarified at the beginning with procedures established for resolution of role ambiguities or conflicts should they arise. The appointment of a chief projects manager to co-ordinate the various projects, to avoid duplication of resources, and to help resolution of conflicts between the various project managers and the functional managers is a useful device to aid the operation of the matrix although it means higher costs. On the other hand, such an appointment would reduce the span of control of the general manager while adding another level to the organization.

The project managers can also be viewed as a form of 'mini-general managers' and appointment to such roles is often considered good training for future promotion to general or top management roles.

While many favour the matrix organization in certain situations and some like Stickney and Johnson (1983) view it as an effective means of delegation, others like Sinclair (1984) are sceptical on whether such a form of organization is really necessary in many situations.

Pure project advantages

The pure project or projectized organization has the clear advantage of simplicity, with the project manager in complete control of the project and exercising total authority over all personnel involved. Functional specialization is clearly demarcated and this permits a high level of technical competence. There is no confusion over line and staff roles and the chain of command is clear and direct.

Pure project disadvantages

On the other hand, the pure project form has some disadvantages. It may be more applicable to large-scale projects which can command the range of specializations necessary. There may be unbalanced work loads due to variations in demand for resources in the project cycle and this makes for employment instability. The level of technical expertise may not be as high as in the functional organization in the parent enterprise of which this project organization is only a part. The morale and motivation of the project team members may decline as a project approaches completion because the organization is dismantled once the project is completed.

Matrix versus pure project

In weighing the use of the matrix versus the pure project team organization, the advantages and disadvantages of each must be considered in light of the nature, scope and size of the project, the relative costs of each in terms of expected benefits, and the particular environment in which the project is to be undertaken. As an example of the environmental factor, a matrix organization is more likely to be successfully implemented in a sophisticated aerospace company in a technologically advanced country than on a construction project in an under-developed country where pure project team organization is the norm.

Bear in mind that the matrix organization is usually applicable at middle management level and is normally imposed on an existing functional organization structure. It is seldom applicable at the top managerial level. It is also rarely used at lower management levels without difficulties and much training.

PROJECT ORGANIZATION WITH MORE COMPLEX ARRANGEMENTS

The organizations of many projects involve more than just one contractor in undertaking the project. Subcontractors are employed to undertake specialized work which requires skills, expertise and resources not normally possessed by the main contractor but who, in turn, is still held accountable for their work by the principal or customer. Two or more contractors may combine together in a temporary partnership just to undertake a project forming a joint venture or consortium. Specialist consultants may be used by not only the principal but also the contractor to advise and render services on certain aspects of the project. Finally, the organization of international projects requires consideration of special factors affecting organizational arrangements.

Joint venture organizations

Joint ventures are undertaken for large-scale complex projects where their accomplishment requires the use of skills and resources beyond that possessed by one contractor organization. Two or more firms may form a temporary partnership whereby each firm sees advantages in utilizing the skills and resources of the other in order to secure the contract and so mutually profit from the project. There may be forced partnership situations where governments in certain countries or organizations stipulate that a joint venture with certain firms known for some special expertise be included in the partnership. A common form of joint venture is where an overseas firm joins with a local firm in undertaking a project whereby both the expertise of the overseas organization and the knowledge, experience and facilities of the local organization are combined. The term 'strategic alliance' is sometimes used nowadays to describe such joint ventures.

Like ordinary partnerships, there may be major and minor partners, or equal partners but the difference is that the joint venture partnership exists only to undertake the project. On completion of the project the joint venture partnership is dissolved. In forming joint ventures the most important document is the joint venture agreement which sets out the rights and obligations of each partner, sharing of profits or losses, provisions for default by any partner and especially should one partner drop out or go bankrupt during the course of the project. A common hazard of joint ventures is when one partner decides to withdraw from the project due to factors outside of the venture. Poor quality work and delays on the part of one partner could adversely affect the whole project, and responsibilities and obligations for such should be clearly defined in the agreement.

Figure 2.7 depicts a joint venture organization structure for a project whereby a management committee comprising representatives from the various partners is made responsible for policy decisions on the project. The project manager is the chief executive officer and is totally responsible for the project. The organization is of the pure project team form, with subordinate personnel drawn from the personnel of the partner organizations but whose time and efforts are solely devoted to the project. The project manager may be chosen from the major partner or from whomever the joint partners deem most capable and experienced for the job.

Subcontractor organization

Subcontractors are in contractual relation to the main or prime contractor with whom the principal or customer must deal. In the tender documents the principal may designate certain nominated subcontractors to be included in undertaking the project. The principal may approve or reject any subcontractor prior to start, but during the course of the project the main contractor has the responsibility for all work undertaken by the subcontractors.

Figure 2.8 depicts the situation whereby the project manager in the prime contractor organization has delegated the task of co-ordination and supervision of the various subcontractors to a contracts manager on a large construction project. Unlike the joint venture the subcontractors are not partners on the project but are in a similar contractual relationship as between the prime contractor and themselves to that between the principal and the prime contractor. Thus they operate as separate entities rather than as a joint entity. Where the principal has a consulting engineer or superintendent acting on his behalf then dealings on any unsatisfactory work by the subcontractors must be through the prime contractor by the engineer or superintendent. Payments for work completed are made direct to the subcontractor by the prime contractor and not by the principal. The project manager of the prime contractor is responsible for all negotiations with

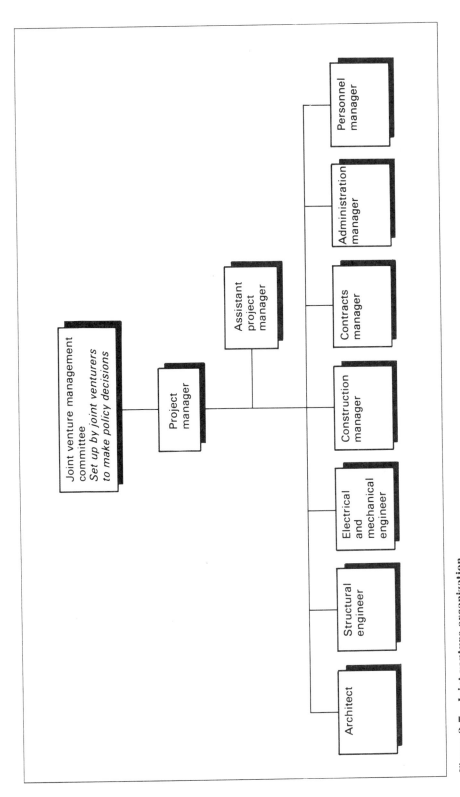

Figure 2.7 Joint venture organization

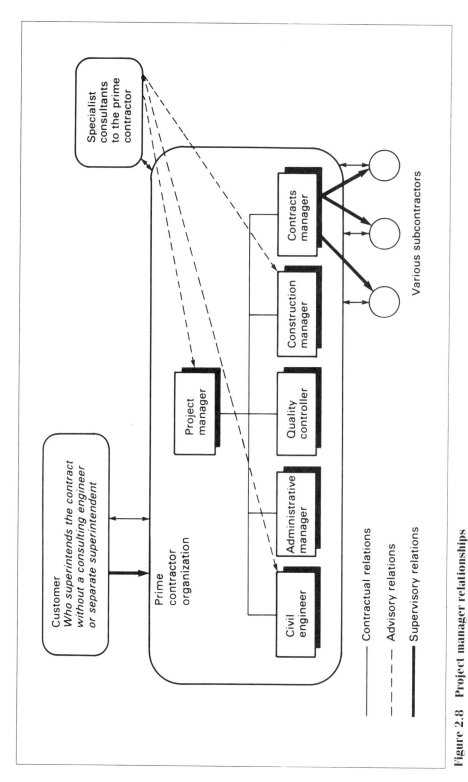

Figure 2.8 Project manager relationships

The project manager's relationships with customer, specialist consultants and subcontractors.

Customer
Who superintends the contract without a consulting engineer or separate superintendent

Prime contractor organization

Specialist consultants to the prime contractor

Civil engineer

Administrative manager

Project manager

Quality controller

Construction manager

Contracts manager

Various subcontractors

——— Contractual relations

– – – Advisory relations

━━━ Supervisory relations

the subcontractors, making agreements on their schedule of work and what part they contribute to the total project.

Organization with specialist consultants

Specialist consultants may be employed at two levels: first, to the principal or customer, and secondly, to the contractor. It is preferable for the principal to have a single prime consultant whether an architectural firm or an engineering consultant to be responsible for all consulting work, to design and supervise the project. Employing too many consultants would result in lack of unity of direction and co-ordination. The prime or major consultant can integrate and co-ordinate the work of the other consultants. This comes back to the situation depicted in Figure 2.1. Usually this is the level where most specialist consultants such as geologists, environmentalists, biologists, etc. (depending on the nature of the project) are used, especially in the planning and design stages of the project.

On some projects the contractor may require specialist advice and services on matters under his responsibility and not that of the consulting engineer. For a construction project, specialist consultants like work study, safety, ergonomics, and materials handling experts may be employed. In a manufacturing project, outside specialists like management consultants and consulting metallurgists may be employed to advise on the most economical production organization and processes or usage of certain metals. Figure 2.8 shows the situation where the specialist consultants may be used to advise the project manager, civil engineer and construction manager of the prime contractor. This example also shows where the principal or customer plans, designs and superintends the contract implying that he has personnel under a project manager in his organization who can carry out such functions.

ORGANIZATION OF INTERNATIONAL PROJECTS

Organization of international projects or 'off-shore' project organization, like joint venturing, is increasing due to increasing project size and complexity, and to the drive for expansion and greater profitability. Most projects undertaken are of the pure project team organizational form but increasing use is made of the matrix, especially with the third dimension of area or regional managers where several projects may be undertaken in a geographical area or region.

Joint ventures (or strategic alliances) are favoured for international projects whereby the overseas firm joins temporarily with the local firm to undertake the project. But in international projects the following special factors need to be considered:

1 *Local incentive and assistance* – which refer to what inducements the host country offers to undertake the project and what assistance the local government provides to assist the project. The search for greater profits, providing greater employment opportunities and assisting economic development, combined with provision of infrastructure facilities and tax-   *33*

free inducements may all attract the organization to undertake the project in another country.

2 *Language barriers and local customs* – in some countries the language barrier may pose some difficulties in that interpreters are needed, instructions have to be accurately relayed and local customs may restrict certain operations as well as impose constraints on project personnel on and off the job.

3 *Culture of the country of operations* – allied to (2) is the culture of the local people. It may be that traditions are such that quality, tempo and standards of operations acceptable to one country are not applicable to another. This makes for different styles of supervision and control. In many countries the Western notions of worker participation and participative democracy among personnel is entirely foreign to workers who are used to authoritarian styles of leadership and management.

4 *Logistics problems* – which relate to the transportation and storage of materials and equipment especially from overseas to the site of the project. The cost, protection and security may vary with the particular country.

5 *Personnel problems* – which relate to the availability of skilled personnel, industrial relation setting, training and safety procedures.

6 *Organization of project work* – methods may vary with different countries and so the division of work may require a different organization structure. In underdeveloped countries where labour costs are low and machines are expensive to operate and maintain, the organization of work would be different to that for developed countries.

Generally a pure project team organization structure is favoured for most project work but for high technology industries (like aerospace and electronic components manufacturing) operating internationally, the combination of line and staff with matrix organization is being increasingly used.

General staff organization for international operations

The general staff organization, first developed by the Prussian military in the late nineteenth century, has since been mastered and perfected for widespread use in all military forces. James D. Mooney (1947) saw its usefulness during military service in the Second World War and subsequently suggested its adoption by General Motors Corporation, particularly for planning, co-ordinating and controlling overseas projects from a centralized office.

Figure 2.9 shows an organization chart in which a military general staff organization has been adapted for an Australian construction engineering company which operates on a global basis, with projects in Australia, New Zealand, the Pacific islands, South-east Asia, America and Europe.

In addition to the normal line and staff form, the general staff organization involves the use of a top-level, continuously meeting, committee. This committee comprises top-level staff officers – the general staff group – headed by a chief of staff. These top staff officers are responsible for their own specialized staff officers. The general staff group will:

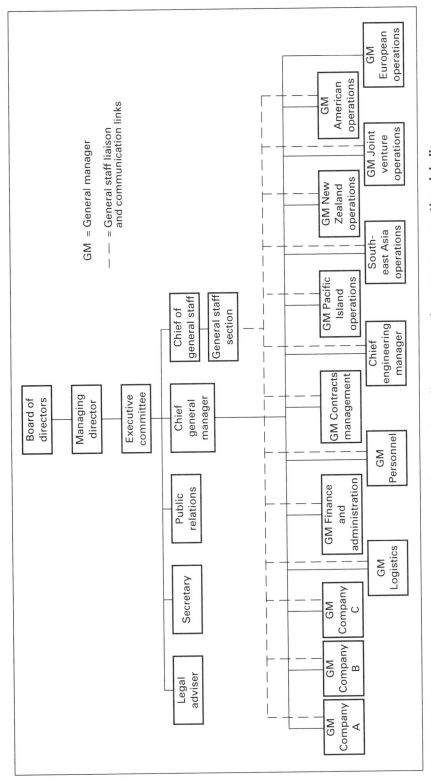

Figure 2.9 Military general staff organization applied to an Australian construction company operating globally.

GM = General manager

— — — = General staff liaison and communication links

Board of directors

Managing director

Executive committee

Chief general manager

Legal adviser

Secretary

Public relations

Chief of general staff

General staff section

GM Company A

GM Company B

GM Company C

GM Logistics

GM Finance and administration

GM Personnel

GM Contracts management

Chief engineering manager

GM Pacific Island operations

South-east Asia operations

GM New Zealand operations

GM Joint venture operations

GM American operations

GM European operations

1 Handle all details of staff work.
2 Assist in the formulation of strategies and long-range plans.
3 Co-ordinate the various staff services.
4 Assist in issuing instructions and directions.
5 Oversee, supervise and control the various arms of the organization.

This form of organization is seldom mentioned in non-military books on organization. This writer has taught officers and engineers of the Australian Army, and officers of a US Army Corps of Engineers and has found that, although there are differences between the military and civilian organization forms, the concept and application of the general staff organization is practically universal. Please refer to military textbooks for more information on general staff organization.

ORGANIZATION AS A MEANS TO AN END

Project organization aims to achieve successful accomplishment of the project. Without proper and logical organization there would be inefficiency, waste, and possibly chaos and delays on the project. Without systematic organization there would be poor quality and performance, and cost over-runs. Without effective organization, the efforts of personnel are duplicated and conflicts and frustration occur. The purpose of project organization is clear – to achieve the project in the most efficient, economical and effective manner. As an American engineer, Russell Robb, a pioneer of organization theory observed; 'Organization is but a means to an end; it provides a method.' The end is the successful completion of the project.

REFERENCES AND FURTHER READING

Babcock, D. L., *Managing Engineering and Technology*, Prentice Hall, Englewood Cliffs, 1991.

Cleland, D. I. and King, W. R., *Systems Analysis and Project Management*, 3rd edn, McGraw-Hill, New York, 1983.

Cleland, D. I. and Kocaoglu, D. F., *Engineering Management*, McGraw-Hill, New York, 1981.

Davis, S. M. and Lawrence, P. R., *Matrix*, Addison-Wesley, Reading, Mass., 1977.

Dibner, D. R., *Joint Venture for Architects and Engineers*, McGraw-Hill, New York, 1972.

Harrison, F. L., *Advanced Project Management*, 3rd edn, Gower, Aldershot, 1992.

Kerzner, H., *Project Management: A Systems Approach to Planning, Scheduling and Controlling*, Van Nostrand Reinhold, New York, 1979.

Kingdon, D. R., *Matrix Organisations*, Tavistock, London, 1973.

Knight, K. (ed.), *Matrix Management*, Gower, Aldershot, 1977.

Mooney, J. D., *Principles of Organization*, Harper & Row, New York, 1947.

Purtell, M. L., 'Problems in administering overseas projects', *Issues in Engineering*, **108**, (E12), April 1982, 140–4.

Samson, D. (ed.), *Management for Engineers*, Longman Cheshire, Melbourne, 1989 (see Chapter 15, E. Young, 'Engineering Project Management').

Shannon, R. E., 'Matrix management structures', *Industrial Engineering*, **4**, (3), March 1972, 26–9.

Sinclair, J. M., 'Is the matrix really necessary?', *Project Management Journal*, **15**, (1), March 1984, 49–52.

Stickney, F. A. and Johnston, W. R., 'Delegation and a sharing of authority by the project manager', *Project Management Quarterly*, **14**, (1), March 1983, 42–53.

Tatum, C. B., 'New matrix organisation for the construction manager', *Issues in Engineering*, **107**, (E14), October 1981, 255–67.

Taylor, W. J. and Watling, T. F., *Successful Project Management*, Business Books, London, 1970.

Wearne, S. H., *Principles of Engineering Organisation*, Edward Arnold, London, 1973.

3 Establishing a Project Organization

O. P. Kharbanda and E. A. Stallworthy

Of the three categories of project dealt with in this handbook, it is probable that civil engineering and construction projects, where a substantial part of the work is carried out on site, are the most complex in terms of project organization. This chapter therefore deals with the project organization appropriate to such complex projects, in order to present a comprehensive view of the possible requirements. Various aspects of the organization outlined will, however, be relevant to the other two categories of project.

Before coming to consider project organization in any detail it should be set into context. There will always be a *promoter* of the project, who could be the owner, 'employer', sponsor or user, but hereafter referred to as the 'owner'. Once the owner has decided to proceed with a project he always has first to establish feasibility and then ensure that the necessary funds are available. When a decision has been taken to proceed, a project manager should be appointed. It is indeed implicit in the concept of project management that a project manager be appointed by the owner at a very early stage to 'manage' the project. This is illustrated in Figure 3.1. Once a project has been defined and is in preparation the project manager should become involved and it is he who will ensure that the project organization appropriate to the project is set up. Part of his responsibility must be to consider the facilities available to him and assess what help he needs.

As he begins work the project manager has a variety of choices. That choice will be determined to some extent by his own capability or (more often) by his own judgement of his capability – which might well be at fault. The choices are as follows:

1 Do it all within his own company.
2 Seek the services of a consultant.
3 Seek the services of a contractor.
4 Seek the services of both consultant and contractor.

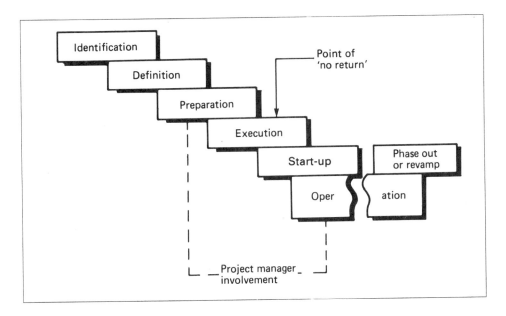

Figure 3.1   Project development

This diagram highlights the basic steps in project development. As time passes the commitment grows, and once the point of no return has been reached it costs more to cancel than to complete.

THE THREE PARTIES TO A PROJECT

Since alternative 4 is the most complex, it is that which will be developed and reviewed. This means that at least three separate parties can be involved in a project. These are: (a) owner (b) consultant and (c) contractor. Their specific functions can well vary from case to case. No two projects are ever the same, even when they may appear to be. Each and every project is unique and so, therefore, are the roles of these three parties. Parties other than these three can be involved in the project, but they will not be directly involved in the project organization. For instance, a process used in the project may be licensed, so the process licensor has an involvement, or finance may be secured from outside, so that a bank has an involvement, but these companies or organizations do not participate in the project directly. They do not become involved in the project organization. It is true, however, that the project organization has to take account of their existence.

In the concept of project management being developed here the three key participants have three distinct and separate roles to play, thus:

- The owner — oversees and pays
- The consultant — advises
- The contractor — does the job.

39

The potential relationship between these parties is illustrated in Figure 3.2. It is proposed to consider the project organization which should be set up on the assumption that what is often called a 'managing contractor' is appointed (although the term 'contractor' will continue to be used). It then becomes his responsibility to set up a large part of the necessary project organization. However, the owner will still have to set up an organization of his own, which must be interrelated with the organization set up by the contractor. Both should have a project manager. Were the owner to decide to 'go it alone', then his project manager would have to establish a project organization such as is later outlined as part of his own project management facilities.

THE ROLE OF THE CONSULTANT

Of the three parties directly involved, the consultant occupies a separate and

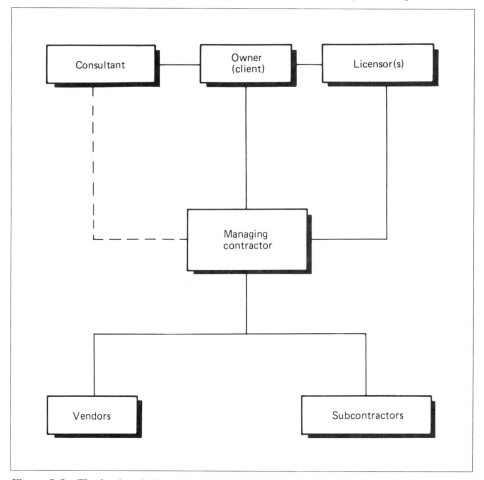

Figure 3.2   The basic relationship

Here we see the relationship between the various parties involved in a project as it develops.

special position. He will advise the owner on the development of the project and its organization. A consultant can be employed at various phases of project development and his degree of involvement will always depend on the needs of the owner. If the owner has previous experience, then his involvement may well be minimal or he may not be needed at all. But for the inexperienced owner he can be a most valuable asset.

To set project organization in the context of project development, Figure 3.3 illustrates all the phases through which a project will pass from identification onwards. It will be seen that the consultant can contribute to all the phases indicated with the exception of Phase 3. The degree of consultant involvement will depend upon the resources of the owner. It is recommended that a project

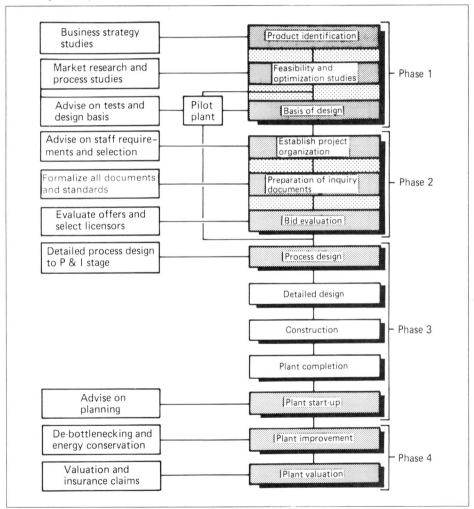

Figure 3.3   The role of the consultant

The steps in project development where the consultant can and should have a role are emphasized (developed from data provided by Trichem Consultants Limited, London).

organization be set up when Phase 2 is entered, but it can only be in outline at that point, since decisions have still to be taken with respect to the involvement of outside parties.

THE CONTRACTOR

When a contractor is used the project manager appointed by that contractor should be made responsible, within the contractor's organization, for every aspect of the project. This is what one such contractor says of the project manager:

He is responsible for every aspect of the job from inception to completion. He is responsible for every service required to carry out the work: planning, scheduling,

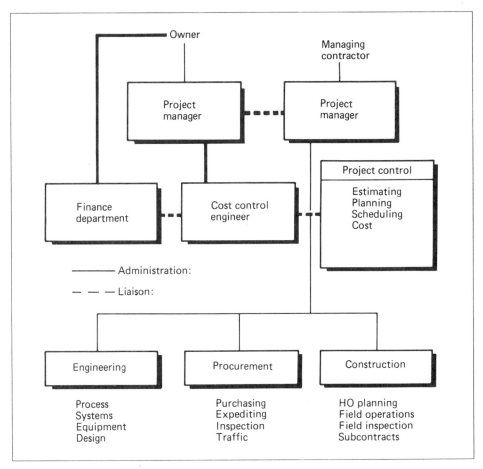

Figure 3.4   The project team

The chart shows in light rule a typical project team (with acknowledgements to the M. W. Kellogg Company, Houston). Added in heavy rule are the key functions that afford the owner control.

costing, designing, engineering, purchasing, inspection, shipping, construction and commissioning. And he is responsible to you, our client. He is your direct contact. And you will know him personally. His position calls for wide experience, broad knowledge of every group within the organization, the ability to control progress and make decisions.

However, the owner still has certain responsibilities which cannot be delegated to the contractor. These are effected through his own project manager. The organizational set-up to achieve this is illustrated in Figure 3.4. From this diagram it can be seen that the owner and the contractor should be mutually supportive. This is indeed the way in which the relationship is seen by the contractor, since the layout shown in Figure 3.4 has been copied faithfully from a brochure illustrating the project team as proposed by one such contractor. The inter-relationship shown in light rule is from the brochure. The heavy rule has been added to the chart as originally prepared and its purpose is explained below.

There is no doubt that this method of working both alongside and in parallel, just like a team of horses 'in harness', is highly successful and should therefore be completely acceptable to all the parties involved. How does it work? To quote once again from a brochure issued by a contractor:

The project control team [refer to Figure 3.4] under the direction of the project manager sets the control guidelines for the project. On major projects a project control manager heads the project control team. Each supervisor within the engineering, procurement and construction areas is involved in the development of the project controls which affect his area of work. Thereafter, the supervisor is responsible for the execution of the project within the control plans and budget established for his area of work. The project manager, the project control manager and project control team constantly monitor performance, making adjustments as may be required to plans as they may affect the interfaces between the speciality groups.

It is very clear that this contractor knows the road that has to be followed. But the owner also has a role to play and this is demonstrated in Figure 3.4. It is the 'heavy rule' addition to the original organigram produced by the contractor. Two key functions should be exercised by the owner, both functions that he should have or should establish within his own organization. These are the functions performed by the finance department and the cost control engineer. They will have to work alongside the managing contractor's personnel day in, day out for the next three years – or however long it takes not only to bring the project to completion and commission it, but to pay the very last invoice. They will still be busy when the contractor's team has packed up, left the site and gone off on the next project.

APPOINTING A CONTRACTOR

In the project organization broadly outlined in Figure 3.4 a fundamental role is played by the contractor. Hence in order to establish a project organization, once the decision has been taken to proceed, a contractor has to be appointed. It is here that a consultant (see Figure 3.2) may be called in to help. In order to appoint a contractor, bid documents will have to be prepared and issued. For the

43

purposes of illustration it is assumed that the project has three main construction areas:

1. The process units, or manufacturing units.
2. Derivative production units.
3. Offsites, utilities and general facilities.

The particular approach adopted must depend upon the circumstances, but in Figure 3.5 a logic diagram is presented of the events that could lead to the appointment of a contractor. Great care is needed in the drafting of the bid documents, so that both the project specification and conditions of contract (subjects dealt with elsewhere in this handbook) are right in terms of scope. Another aspect of vital importance, which also affects both the project specification and the conditions of contract, is the financial arrangements, which are a specific element in the logic diagram, Figure 3.5. Once the bid documents have been prepared and are ready for issue, they have to be sent out to selected contractors under cover of an enquiry letter.

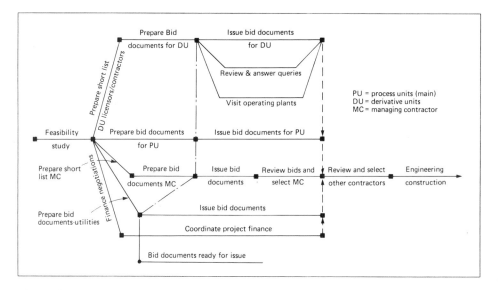

Figure 3.5 Logic diagram – bid document preparation and contractor selection

Outline of a typical plan for getting an approved project 'on the way' (data provided by Trichem Consultants Limited, London).

The primary enclosure with the enquiry letter will be the project specification. It is this document (which can be anything from a few pages to hundreds, even thousands, of pages long) that defines the 'work' that the contractor will be required to do, in cooperation with the owner and other third parties. While it is the project specification which is of prime and continuing interest to all those involved in the project, it has to be put into context. That is the function of the conditions of contract. They define the situation – the relationship of the various parties to the work to be done as described in the project specification, and also to one another in legalistic terms.

Choosing the contractor

When the various offers are received in response to the enquiry, a choice has to be made. The selection criteria include:

- Quality of personnel nominated to carry out the project, with special emphasis on the project manager.
- Cost incentive and liability arrangements proposed.
- Local currency content of the project cost and the total investment required for the project.
- Loan terms.
- Project organization and relationship with local subcontractors.
- Workload of office where the design engineering will be carried out.
- Quality and contents of the technical proposal.
- Contractor's recent experience in the design and construction of similar projects.
- Appreciation and knowledge of local conditions at the job site.
- Ability to provide the owner with technical support services.
- Schedule for project completion.

The above criteria are not listed in order of importance. While the price is significant (for example), it is only one of three financial considerations. The contractors selected to bid should have been chosen on the basis of their past performance, but what now matters is their *present* competence. This means that the specific personnel put forward to form the project team are of crucial importance. Within the project team it is the project manager and his qualifications that need the most careful appraisal.

COMMUNICATIONS – THE KEY

Once the contractor has been appointed, a working relationship has to be established between the owner and the contractor, and then between the contractor and the construction site, the subcontractors and others involved in the project. This is the responsibility of the contractor, but he should work closely with the owner in order to define the requirements of the project and its boundaries. This involves process decisions, fixing design standards, material supply, financing, transport and shipping, site conditions, subcontractor services, and the parameters of performance and reliability.

In order to ensure that all possible activities involved in the project have been dealt with and the duties of the several parties properly defined, it is usual for the contractor, in cooperation with the owner, to set down and then issue what is called a project coordination procedure. This document will give all the *45* information relevant to the administration and management of the project including the organization, planning and control procedures to be used in order to complete the project successfully. A checklist is used to assist in the development of such a procedure and this is presented at the end of this chapter. All items are of importance and they should be reviewed one by one, the necessary information being written, reviewed and agreed with the interested parties.

A fundamental element in the operation of the procedures once implemented is the ability to communicate. These days a wide range of facilities are available, including the postal system, telephone and telex facilities, data transmission via computer and telephone and the like. These should be reviewed and the appropriate facilities provided, keeping in mind the site location and its possible problems. A courier service is often the most efficient means of transferring the substantial volumes of paperwork that have to be moved between the various offices and the site, especially when the latter is in a remote location not well served with modern communication facilities.

THE OWNER'S ORGANIZATION

Figure 3.4 outlines not only the key elements in the contractor's organization, but also those called for within the organization of the owner. The owner should provide a project manager, with engineers to support him, a cost control engineer, with support staff and financial facilities. These latter should already be in existence, but specific arrangements are called for to coordinate the activities of the finance department in relation to the project.

The finance department is going to be responsible for authorizing payment against the budget provided for the project. This role is centred in the accountant, who has two different functions. One is the regulating function of audit that requires him to ensure the correctness of the accounts processed and paid. The other function, that of management accountant, requires him to monitor the financial progress of the project. While in this he has many areas of common interest with the cost control engineer, their objectives will be different.

The cost coding system

The financial control exercised by both the accountant and the cost control engineer is achieved by means of what are called 'controllable items'. These are the separate cost items into which a total project budget is broken down for the purposes of cost control and financial administration. This calls for the use of what is called a 'code of accounts' or a 'cost code'.

In establishing the project organization, a cost coding system must be available for all cost analysis. Normally, such a code should be set up for the specific project, although it may correspond to some degree with an existing system employed in the finance department. In order to satisfy the requirement that the code identifies controllable items, it is usually, if not always, prudent to ensure that it can be used to label every part of the project work breakdown structure, which is relevant to all other areas of planning and control. Ideally, the code should be logical and hierarchical, so that each code can be seen to be related to its particular place in the work breakdown structure.

It often happens that the organization with main responsibility for managing a project is forced to use a code of accounts which is alien to its usual practice and which may even be illogical and unsuited to project control purposes. This can happen, for example, when a client insists that his contractor uses the client's own system for collecting and reporting all costs in regular progress reports and in references on invoices. Fortunately, with the availability of database management information systems, it is relatively simple to satisfy such wishes, while still using the preferred system for actual control. The computer can be used to translate codes from one system to the other, and to provide the essential cross-references that this practice requires.

Whatever its source, the code of accounts is an essential and integral part of the project organization.

Project control

The purpose of the project organization established by the owner is to give him real and effective *control* of the project. To achieve this, the owner must:

1 Give the project manager *total* responsibility for the entire project: design, engineering, procurement and construction. He should produce a monthly project cost control report.
2 Provide a cost engineering function to operate at the job site, responsible to the owner's project manager and headed by a senior project cost engineer.
3 Ensure that the finance department works in close liaison with the cost engineering function, while maintaining their own normal expenditure records and a cumulative commitment record.

The primary duty of the cost engineering function will be to establish the exact position of the total project in its 'controllable segments', from month to month, comparing actual progress with target progress. The finance department will check that the information provided in the project cost control report is in line with accounting records. They should also, in line with their standard procedures, check that all invoices for materials and services are duly authorized and that all materials are properly controlled and accounted for.

The audit function

The audit function does not appear on the outline project organization but it is an essential element and makes a material contribution to project management. The owner should have or should employ accountants to act as an internal audit group. This group should examine both the financial and related operations of both the owner and contractor. The internal audit group would, at the very beginning and thereafter at intervals, examine the accounting policies of both parties with their

47

related systems and procedures. It is their task to diagnose weaknesses in the project organization as set up and then make recommendations for any necessary improvements to the system, specifically to protect the money being employed. This is for the benefit of those working on the project as well as for those whose money is being used. It protects those working on the project from accusations of fraud or the misuse of funds, or of giving undue advantage to companies or to persons. A formal report should be prepared by the accountants each time a review is undertaken, setting out the audit findings and the recommended corrective action. This should be followed by the discipline of receiving formal written assurance from the parties concerned within a stated period (say three months) that the recommended corrective actions have in fact been implemented. Weaknesses not remedied to the auditor's satisfaction should be reported to the project manager for the owner, for his further action.

The scope of such internal audits should not be limited to financial or accounting matters. With technical help from a consultant, auditors can and should review a wide range of routine activities carried out by the contractor and his subcontractors, particularly in relation to work assessment in the field. In the UK this latter work is carried out by quantity surveyors. For instance, contract letting procedures should involve competitive tendering, secret bidding and a proper comparison of offers. These are typical instances where an audit of the arrangements being made within the project organization can be of real help. A proper internal audit system will always make a serious contribution to project management, bringing increased and more effective discipline to the contracting process.

THE CONTRACTOR'S ORGANIZATION

The contractor brought in to handle a project on the behalf of the owner will have an established company organization. Within that the contractor will provide a project organization designed to provide the services required for the specific project. There are several ways in which a contractor can be organized, but the two most common are called the matrix and the team organizations, as have been discussed in Chapter 2.

The organizational matrix

Within any organization there are bound to be certain conflicts of interest and this fact should be recognized, because it cannot be resolved. When a new project is introduced into the contractor's organization, it immediately begins to compete for services with the other projects already in hand. This conflict becomes manifest as soon as a project team is formed to handle a project. Such a team will be drawn from a number of different disciplines within the organization, as illustrated in Figure 3.6. There will be a variety of design disciplines, each of which requires separate coordination and supervision for proper management and the administration of the particular design function. However, there is also a need for the close integration of the specific project requirements with the several design disciplines. This is achieved through the projects manager, who has a team of project managers (or engineers) who are responsible for individual projects. This concept is presented in Figure 3.6, each project engineer (five are shown) being responsible for a project. The requirements of the projects will differ in terms of the services they need, and such variation is indicated in the chart. Ideally, the resources of the design function should match the requirements of the project groups, with a slight reserve of capacity, but that never happens in practice. This leads to competition for services, which competition – and hence conflict – should be resolved by consultation between the various department heads.

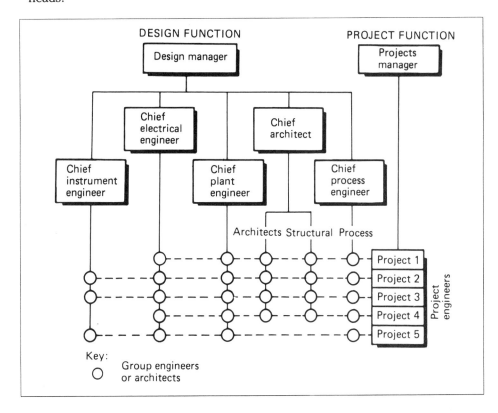

Figure 3.6   Organization chart for the design group

This chart demonstrates the manner in which the design department should be grouped under section leaders in order to integrate with the project management function. While the design department is necessarily internally streamed and managed in accordance with the several disciplines involved, the external integration is on a project basis.

THE PRINCIPLE OF ACCOUNTABILITY

If these organizational concepts are to be expressed in management terms, then the project manager (whether one considers the project manager working for the owner or the project manager working for the contractor) is accountable to his   *49* senior management for the project. An obligation is thereby placed, in the first instance, on the project manager to carry the project to a successful conclusion. But the usual problem is that while the project manager is held accountable, he is often not given the authority to discharge his obligation to management properly. Once made accountable he should have both the right and also the duty to make those decisions and to take those actions which he judges necessary within the scope of his responsibility without needing to seek prior approval from his superiors.

All too often there is a certain reluctance in this respect, from two sides. Senior management is reluctant to leave important decisions to the project group, whilst, within the contracting organization, the managers responsible for specialist functions such as design think that theirs should be the last word. The project manager may recommend, but *not* direct and instruct.

It is indeed true that limits of authority have to be established and must be established in relation to certain decisions. These decisions will involve factors and circumstances outside the scope and direct knowledge of the project manager, so that a measure of direction and control *must* in such circumstances be retained by senior management. A common instance in this context is in relation to money. Limits may well be placed on the project manager with respect to expenditure, despite the fact that blanket financial approval has been given to the project as a whole. Orders over a certain value, for instance, may well be referred to senior management for final approval before placing.

Care should be taken to see that these limits on the authority of the project manager do not inhibit him from discharging his responsibilities. It is here that the owner, rather than the contractor, may err. The owner is more likely to be setting up a project organization specifically for the project in hand and perhaps, even, for the first time. Contractors, inevitably, will have walked the road before and found by experience the constraints and restraints appropriate to the circumstances. The owner, however, especially if he lacks experience, may be over-restrictive. The best approach is to draw up all the guide lines, as part of the project organization. Each person in a position of authority should be given a mandate. This should take the form of a written description, brief but explicit and positive, describing the basic objectives of the position, together with some detail of the activities considered implicit in the mandate. Not only should such documents be prepared, but the owner should seek to see the 'mandate' of the project manager, and perhaps other key personnel, appointed by the contractor to run the project.

MANAGEMENT BY EXCEPTION

The project organization to be set up consists of two separate entities, one within the owner organization and the other within the contractor organization. The responsibilities of the personnel employed should be built around the principle of 'management by exception'. This is a long-established management principle, which implies that policies are established and plans are laid. In the context of a project the plans should be outlined in the project specification, together with the related project estimate and planning schedules. From then on, all that should be discussed are the deviations from those agreed policies and plans. If management by exception is to be successful there are four basic requirements which will have to be fulfilled. They are:

1 There must be a detailed, timed plan.
2 There must be the ability to delegate.
3 There must be confidence and trust placed in subordinates.
4 There must be a proper system of *management information*.

There are a number of separate areas for delegation in the project organization that has been outlined above. First, the owner has delegated to the contractor the obligation to complete the project in accordance with the agreed plan. This plan will cover at least two key aspects of the project: cost and time.

For such delegation to be possible there must therefore be a project programme and a project estimate, which will become an integral part of the management information system. The term management information is intended to cover the various reports relating to both the physical and financial status of the project, which will provide the information needed at the successive levels of management on both sides to enable them to make the appropriate decisions. In all these reports there must be continuous comparison between the initial agreed programme and estimate and the current expectations. This reporting system is therefore an essential element within the project organization. Its details are dealt with in later parts of this handbook.

Management needs to know the *deviations* from the plan once it has been agreed, for management by exception to be effective. It is the deviations, and only the deviations, that will call for managerial direction and action. It is therefore such deviations that form the substance of the various reports and the level that they reach within the management organization will depend upon their significance and magnitude in relation to the project as a whole.

Good administration will result in only the essential information being provided. This means that data has to be edited, reviewed and condensed before reports are prepared. Of course, all such reports should be accurate, complete and up to date. Above all, reports at one level should not include data which is more properly the concern of subordinates at a lower level. While the senior executives are entitled to ask for and receive specific information on any subject, excessive demands of this nature tend to undermine the concept of delegation. Then the basic principle around which the project organization should have been built, that of management by exception, would have been destroyed.

Project liaison

It has already been stated that the basic need within a project organization is the ability to communicate and the coordination procedure is designed to facilitate such communication. Both the owner and the contractor will be setting up project organizations which match at the top, as illustrated in Figure 3.4. This enables the *51*

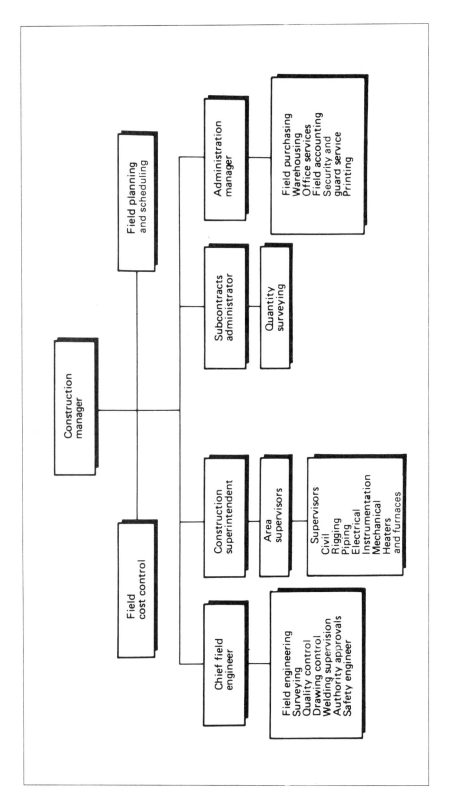

Figure 3.7 Typical construction site organization

The number of personnel covered by this organigram will vary according to the size and complexity of the project.

two opposite parties to liaise on equal terms at each level. The administration established in accordance with the co-ordination procedure should ensure that the appropriate records are maintained, that all data is readily accessible and that those involved in the project are always informed of that which concerns them.

SITE ADMINISTRATION

A good, experienced, strong and comprehensive site organization with sound administrative techniques is the best insurance possible against the multitude of problems that will arise once work begins on site. The contractor should not be allowed to skimp his efforts in this direction, which he may well be tempted to do if he is being remunerated via a fixed fee. A typical site organization is presented in Figure 3.7 and of the many facets of site organization and administration highlighted by this organigram, the following are probably the most significant:

1 Site planning.
2 Site cost control.
3 Control of subcontracts.
4 Quality control.
5 Industrial relations.

Site planning

The process of site planning involves manpower resource scheduling, progress reporting and the assessment of the particular site requirements. The most practical and economic construction method has to be selected, and due regard must be given to specific factors such as temporary work areas and site access. Safe working conditions have to be established, first aid facilities have to be provided and it is necessary to make provision for certain comforts (a place to eat, rest rooms, changing rooms, etc.). On a remote site, housing may also be required. Transport is needed, not only to and from the site, but also all over the site, both horizontally and vertically. Communication facilities are essential and, apart from telex, it may be necessary to provide portable radios. There should also be a site postal system.

Co-operation is required from the shipping department to ensure the timely delivery of heavy and difficult loads. What are termed 'heavy lifts' require the provision on site of very expensive, specialized lifting equipment and personnel. It is therefore usual to establish a 'heavy lift' programme in order to bring all such work together and minimize the length of time such costly equipment is on site. This may involve traffic problems not only on or near the site but also hundreds of miles away. It may be necessary to make arrangements for movement of loads under police escort, routes will have to be carefully planned, obstacles on the route removed and later replaced.

Site cost control

All site costs, including the delivery of materials to site, should be closely monitored by the site cost engineer. It will be his task to prepare statements on the commitments and forecasts in relation to construction costs, including all the subcontracts, for inclusion in the overall project progress reports.

Site subcontracts

While it is possible for the contractor to carry out some of the work on site by 'direct labour', that is, by people in his own direct employment, there will always be a considerable volume of work that is subcontracted to specialist contractors. The preferred approach for completely effective project cost control is for *all* work on site to be carried out by a series of subcontractors. With respect to the administration of such contracts, which are usually for a combination of materials and services, such administration is usually separate from the purchasing organization handling materials. This is because the type of contract and the methods of assessing the value of work done for payment are very different.

The site contracts will normally be let one by one over a substantial period of time (probably over a period of at least two years with a project of any substance). As the contracts are let, their work content becomes gradually more predictable, because detailed design is progressing, and this allows for a change in the form of contract. Early contracts may well be let using a form of contract that employs a schedule of rates or some other form of cost reimbursement, while it should be possible to let the later contracts on a fixed price basis. The contract organization should therefore establish procedures which allow this.

Quality control

All the work on site should be quality controlled. This is most important and the appropriate personnel should be incorporated in the site organization with the relevant systems. Of the various aspects of quality control probably the most important is the quality control of site welding. There has to be detailed preparation for this, with the drawing up of welding procedures, the testing and certification of welders, the non-destructive testing of this work as it is done in accordance with the relevant specifications. All this requires not only the most meticulous supervision but proper administration of the related documentation, so that if necessary it can be later demonstrated that all is in order.

Industrial relations

Last, but not least, there is the matter of industrial relations, often hiding behind the cryptic letters IR. It is a subject kept well in the background but of supreme importance in relation to the successful execution of work on site. It is an area of possible confrontation, with two opposing parties each seeking their own ends. It is regrettable that such is the case, but it is a situation that seems to exist in most parts of the world these days. The problems will be different, dependent upon which country the project is being built in, but they will always be there. In the developed countries it is usual to tread warily, keeping in close touch with the unions at both local and national level. In the developing countries the problem may be very different: that, for instance, of training a completely ignorant, locally recruited workforce, or of satisfying the demands of expatriate personnel. Provision will have to be made within the site organization for the appropriate facilities according to location, but above all it has to be recognized that the person or persons appointed to look after industrial relations *must* have relevant experience and be competent negotiators.

DOCUMENTING THE ESTABLISHED ORGANIZATION AND ITS PROCEDURES

For all projects of significant size it is customary and appropriate to compile and issue a project co-ordination procedure document. The use of a checklist is invaluable in helping to ensure that the document is comprehensive, practical and logically structured. A typical checklist follows.

Checklist for the contents of a project coordination procedure document

1 Introduction

- 1:1   Objective of document
- 1:2   Scope of work
- 1:3   Terms used

2 General policy

- 2:1   Relationship between parties
- 2:2   Facilities and information from owner

3 Coordination with owner

- 3:1   Project description
- 3:2   Project references and addresses
- 3:3   Correspondence to and from owner
- 3:4   Minutes of meeting with owner
- 3:5   Contractor's progress reports
- 3:6   Project programme
- 3:7   Approvals by owner
- 3:8   Change notice procedure
- 3:9   Code of accounts (cost code)

14:3   Start-up procedures
14:4   Vendor services
14:5   Performance tests
14:6   Guarantees and penalties

15 Spares

15:1   Initial spares
15:2   Capital spares
15:3   Running spares

FURTHER READING

Burgess, R. A. and White, G., *Building Construction and Project Management*, Construction Press, London, 1979. (A sound foundation for the new project manager. Simple figures are presented for complex ideas. Intended for an international readership, it contains little reference to national standards.)

Kerzner, H., *Project Management for Executives*, Van Nostrand, New York, 1982. (This book is based on experience in the author's consulting practice and his seminars on the subject worldwide. Real-life case studies are included.)

Kharbanda, O. P., Stallworthy, E. A. and Williams, L. F., *Project Cost Control in Action*, 2nd edn, Gower, 1987.*

Snowdon, M., *Management of Engineering Projects*, Newnes Butterworth, London, 1977. (A sensible little book, which presents the management and engineering aspects of maximizing the value of capital investment.)

Stallworthy, E. A. and Kharbanda, O. P., *Total Project Management*, Gower, Aldershot, 1983.*

Taylor, W. J. and Watling, T. F., *Successful Project Management*, Business Books, London, 1970. (A practical, down-to-earth treatment, with an excellent grasp of the financial and strategic considerations in project management.)

---

* The figures used to illustrate this chapter have been taken from the two books marked with an asterisk in the above list.

4 The Politics of Project Management

David J. Warby

'Politics is the art of the possible' is a well-used phrase. The implication is that political objectives are seldom reached without compromise. Perhaps the realities of political life dictate that politicians have to accept the utilitarian view of 'the greatest good for the greatest number'. Project management is also concerned with the possible, relying on management science, management skills and technology to reach its objectives. Among the management skills required, political skills may sometimes be the critical factor for success. Even when they are not the dominant feature of a project, politics, at all levels, will play a part.

THE NETWORK

Consider the parties involved in any project. The obvious players are those concerned with its physical implementation – the owner (probably with a project team including external professionals for execution, and a separate team for operation), a main contractor (who may have project partners), many sub-contractors, sub-subcontractors, and equipment and service suppliers.

Most projects will be subject to some external regulatory control and will require approvals at certain key stages. In some cases this will even mean obtaining approval from the national government (in the UK, perhaps a parliamentary bill). The most frequent requirements are for planning, environmental, and technical approvals.

The process of consultation with the appropriate authorities has to begin at the very earliest project definition stage, and might continue in an iterative fashion as the practicalities are balanced. An example of this is the design of process plants where (for UK projects) consultation with Her Majesty's Inspectorate of Pollution regarding emission limits is advisable as early as possible. This can alter the previously assumed process parameters. Redesign could be required, for example, to meet criteria determined by the Environmental Protection Act; this change will cost less if it is made before other commitments and more detailed design aspects are firmed up.

On the financial side, others will be involved apart from the project owner. These could include financial partners who are not directly concerned with the project execution or operation. Almost certainly there will be project funding provided by banks or other financial sources in addition to the basic project investors. There might be bondsmen guaranteeing performance. In some cases, government assistance may be needed (typically in export or regional development programmmes). Within the European Community, this might well bring the European Commission into play, either as a source of funds, or in a regulatory role overseeing the disbursement of funds that might be thought to contravene Community competition policy.

The people involved will have a profound effect on the project's outcome. There will be those concerned with its execution and eventual operation. At all levels they need to be correctly motivated. For the team involved with the execution, a fundamental difficulty associated with projects is that of working on a transient task with a finite period. To those engaged on a temporary basis, progress to a successful project completion might mean dismissal at its end and loss of earnings. The permanent people face the challenges of building temporary teams for the project, managing the changing demands and resources over the implementation programme, and motivating the majority who will not be employed on the project after the completion of their task.

Outside the project, there are those who will be affected by it. Typically these include various members of the local community, who might look upon the project from widely differing standpoints. Some could see the project as an opportunity for material benefit; others as an intrusion and a threat. Special interest groups might also have an influence, perhaps in terms of environmental or archaeological concerns.

In the case of a project which is built to make a saleable product, those involved or affected include the potential customers. The success of the project will depend ultimately on the customers' acceptance of the product. A great deal of positive or negative influence can be exerted on the future market by the project organization's conduct and communications to the outside world during the course of the project.

With such a complex network of relationships, the importance of the political management of a project, large or small, is obvious. Figure 4.1 presents a typical set of relationships in diagrammatic form. Politics, according to the *Oxford English Dictionary*, is 'the science and art of government'. The role of the project manager lies very close to this definition.

PROJECT BASICS

A project is a cycle of activities with the purpose of supplying, within definite starting and completion dates, a unique product, service, or set of information to a specified quality and cost. For all projects there will be comparable steps in the

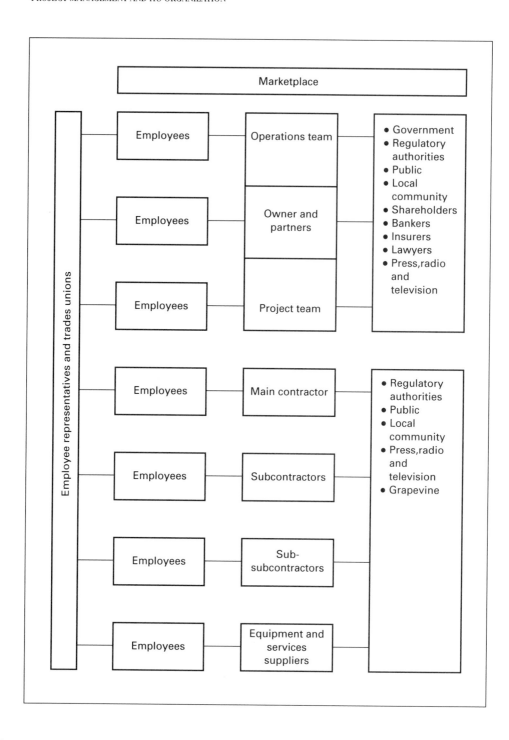

Figure 4.1   Project relationships

Phase	Activity	Political needs
Definition	Setting objectives	Review all political constraints
		Test opinion with all parties that are vital to success
Concept	Outline specification	Consult regulators
	Market research	Test market acceptance
	Research and development	
	Preliminary technical and commercial assessment	Consult financiers/local bodies
	Preliminary specification and design	Confirm with regulators
	Capital proposal	
		Confirm with financiers
Evaluation	Corporate policy assessment	Review external and internal effects of the project against corporate objectives
	Technical and commercial assessment	Consult internally. Confirm with all external parties
	Raising capital	Present the reviews, consultations and confirmed conclusion
Decision	Contract strategy assessment	Review political risk issues with own employees, suppliers and local people. Consult trades unions
	Contract type assessment	Select to minimize risk
	Decision to proceed	Information memorandum to all parties involved at this stage
Redefinition	Final specification and design	Confirm with regulators
	Production method planning	Minimize political risk
Preproduction	Supplier appraisal	Review any political risks
	Bid package preparation/issue	Consider political risks
	Supplier bids/evaluations	
	Final negotiations and costings	Confirm contract strategy with selected suppliers
	Project report for authorization	Report on all political issues and plans to handle them
Authorization	Review project report	Confirm project strategy with all concerned
	Confirm decision to proceed	Issue information release
		Decide on information policy and methods for the project
Execution	Information for production	Establish the project team with the necessary consultation. Brief employees and suppliers regularly on policy and progress
	Production	Minimize risk from political problems by avoiding key contracts with risk-associated suppliers
	Installation	Apply contract strategy. Brief employees regularly. Consult trades unions and local bodies. Have informal get togethers
	Commissioning	Inform and consult the local community
Operation		Inform and consult local community regularly

Figure 4.2   The project cycle and politics

project cycle, regardless of the eventual product. These steps, the project activities, and possible political needs are tabulated in Figure 4.2.

Politics and project success

Nowhere is the influence of politics more apparent than in the winning of projects. Factors essential to companies in achieving success against competition are credibility in performance, political acceptability, price and technical quality. Even assuming that competing tenders are made on a comparable basis (a big assumption), there is still all to play for and much which is typically influenced by political and other factors.

Credibility should have been established in the supplier assessment. There will inevitably be shades of acceptability in any assessment. In marginal decisions, doubts cast on performance or, in contrast, proof of past successes can sway a decision one way or the other. The political influence in such circumstances cannot be brought to bear at short notice, and requires a consistent policy of positive and honest communication.

Political acceptability is a comparable issue. This sort of acceptability operates at all levels – inter-departmental, inter-company, local, regional, and national. The wise project manager will identify apparent 'no-go' areas (and some which may not be so apparent) and decide whether it is possible to solve the impasse. If so, the political solution must be the prelude to any further decisions. If no solution seems possible, cutting losses may be the right action. Many abortive bids and unsuccessful projects have their roots in this dilemma.

The cost of a project (and, therefore, its price) can be affected in many political ways. In addition to varying contract requirements between competitors these can include the availability of financial subsidies and the terms available for contract finance and insurances. Differences in financial support are particularly apparent in international trade, where in many cases it is impossible to win projects without financial support, in one form or another. This requires government participation with industry. For most industrial nations this is recognized as an essential part of government policy. Because of this there are international agreements, particularly within the European Community, that set out to regulate the extent of such support.

Technical performance is a topic where precise specification and objective assessment should eliminate anything but rational decisions. The reality is different. Even the most simple products, with comprehensive specifications that are not capable of misinterpretation, can give rise to subjective margins of choice. These are affected by political and personal pressures. The power of consistent positive communications makes the difference, even in the face of facts and figures. This is not always to condemn the decision maker in such circumstances – we all reach decisions in this way from time to time.

The importance of winning

In the international field, the importance of winning can be clearly demonstrated.

The benefit to the nation's economy from exports is clear. In practical terms it has been shown that, for a typical engineering capital goods project, there is a 'multiplier effect' from the primary contract to secondary contracts for goods and services. This 'multiplier' has been quantified in separate studies as around 1.8 – in effect nearly doubling the value accruing to the economy from the initial contract. The benefits spread throughout the country, with typically around 5 000 companies undertaking work. Project value is not finite. The requirement for spares and continuing technical support continues for decades in many cases.

THE PROFESSIONALS

The full-time politicians and civil servants in central government are the most clearly defined of the political operators. Their role in projects can be crucial, and a proper understanding of the organizations and systems involved is an essential skill for any manager. A great deal of authority is also devolved to local government and government agencies. For project managers in the UK an understanding of the European Community as well as the British government systems is also vital.

The British governmental system

The most accessible part of the government system is the local constituency member of Parliament, minister or backbencher. Your Member of Parliament (MP) will be available for advice and other help at local surgeries, through the constituency office or by mail. Your elected representative will know all the lines of responsibility and the names of contacts to the centres of influence and decision. This representative should always be the first port of call.

Influence on policy can be exercised in a number of ways. The main component of influence must be reliable, relevant and properly presented information. Members of Parliament have limited time and resources; they need the assistance of good material if they are to do their job effectively. Your issue will be just one of many, which will range over a variety of topics. It might be best to communicate the information to your own MP, or to the suggested contact elsewhere in Parliament. Face to face is always the best, if possible. The other centres of influence apart from the constituency MP are the special parliamentary interest groups, select committees, and the civil servants in the relevant ministries.

The special interest groups each comprise all party representation, drawn from both the House of Lords and the House of Commons. These are *ad hoc* groups of members who have volunteered an interest in topics such as construction. Presenting a point of view is often effectively done to an invited group over an informal lunch or buffet supper.

The all party select committees are very powerful bodies and, while not as accessible as the special interest groups, are an invaluable forum for specialized issues. Initial submissions in this case are best made in writing. The permanent civil servants are naturally the repositories of the depth of knowledge in   *65* specialized areas, and they represent the continuity in politics, even though they must carry out the policies of the current government. They are the means of access to the highest levels of detailed decision making. For effective action, material must be well presented and argued with supporting facts.

While we are told that a week is a long time in politics, a year is not a long time in setting and agreeing policy. If political influence is to bring results it must be conducted on a continuing basis. Regular contact and communication must precede the day when urgent response is needed.

The European Community

The relative geographical remoteness of Brussels, Strasbourg and Luxembourg should not obscure the very immediate presence of the European Community institutions in the daily conduct of business in Britain. Your Member of the European Parliament (MEP) may not have the same familiarity as your Westminster representative (there are only 81 MEPs for the UK, giving roughly eight times the constituents per member compared with a Westminster MP), and the business of the European Parliament is conducted outside the UK. Nevertheless, the future is being determined on many important issues in the European Parliament, and interests can only be represented if they are clearly conveyed to the MEPs, who are available to constituents (generally by appointment) in their constituencies when they are not working abroad.

The conduct of Community politics is very different from UK domestic politics, largely because of the power of the European Commission. The Commission comprises unelected civil servants, who formulate policy and initiate legislation. They will usually (but are not obliged to) consult parties likely to be affected by the proposals. These proposals are passed to the Council, and the Council must consult the European Parliament for its opinions and amendments, which are then returned to the Commission for consideration. The Commission may adopt the amendments, in which case it will pass the revised proposal back to the Council, which must again consult the European Parliament. Subject to any further opinions and amendments the Council will adopt the proposal as a Directive, which will in due course be translated into the national laws of each member state.

The Commission operates through Directorates-General (DGs), of which there were 23 by the end of 1992. Each covers a different area of policy, has a Commissioner responsible for its work, and has a 'Cabinet' of six or more permanent administrators with secretarial support. The main Commission personnel are career civil servants from the member states, and are known as 'services'. These 'services' are the best points of contact for information and influence. The DGs handle a vast budget which is spread over a colossal range of activities. Access to the 'services' and their masters is quite straightforward, by post, telephone or visit (subject to availability). On this last point, the Commission is a super-bureaucracy, and the routine is frequently the master of the man.

A final comment on EC matters. The legislation that attracts so much criticism for its intrusions on our previous ways is far reaching and important to the conduct of business in many areas of project management. While constraints may be imposed by this legislation, it can also be seen as a potential for defence against unlawful business actions, if fully understood and used through the British or European courts. The impact of Europe on project management is discussed in greater detail in Chapter 10.

PROJECT POLITICS

The sophistication of some project planning and control systems and the technical complexities of many projects tend to obscure some simple underlying management truths. Out of a long experience of projects large and small, successful and not so successful, emerge seven common rules that stand for all:

1　Recognize the project as a separate undertaking.
2　Define the objectives of the project clearly.
3　Appoint a project manager and give him the necessary authority.
4　Make an appropriate project organization structure.
5　Set contract conditions that support the project objectives.
6　Apply suitable systems to report, and allow correction of, quality, time and cost.
7　Ensure that all parties with common interests are brought together regularly.

None of these seven rules can be separated from political considerations. The first four are frequently the source of deep-seated organizational problems.

Organizations

Recognizing the existence of a major project as a separate undertaking is no problem. For many smaller ventures, particularly in organizations not regularly working in the project mode, the setting of objectives for a unique and non-repetitive task can result in conflict if the separate nature is not recognized. The lack of definition of project objectives in sufficient detail and with sufficient accuracy can cause mistaken policies. The rule is: 'define, then redefine' – and then communicate.

Having recognized the project as such, the appointment of a project manager is critical. The correct human qualities and abilities are those of general management, rather than those of the technical specialist. The project manager will be in need of those political skills that come from sensitivity to surrounding issues, and an ability to deal with people.

Without authority, the project manager's task is made very difficult. However, most project managers have to perform without the full authority that they really need, primarily because of the limitations of their organizations in a multi-project environment. Where this situation exists, the project manager will have to share people and other resources, and thus will not have complete control of the project team.

This raises the matter of the project organization structure. Most projects will require a team that largely replicates the pyramidal, functional structure of the main company, with the necessary capabilities in the technical, production, and finance/administration areas. For the project manager in charge of a full-time team with all the necessary functional capability, for as long as the project demands, there will be no basic organizational problem. The owner, the main contractor, and the larger subcontractors on a major project may well have such dedicated task forces. However, in many companies this will not be the case.

All but the largest organizations usually have to compromise on the project team, because of the unavailability of people, or the cost. Typically, a company will have a number of concurrent projects, all with demands on the same skill resources. The usual solution is to operate a matrix organization, setting up the required number of pyramidal project teams, but with the members of those teams being allocated on a shared, part-time basis from the main organization's departments (see Chapter 2). This immediately introduces two split authorities: the authority of the departmental manager; and the authority of the various project managers that use the people on a shared basis. This is a fundamentally unsatisfactory way of working, but is the best of the options available in most cases.

For the project manager, the situation demands political skills to secure the resources needed in the face of competition from his colleagues, and without absolute authority. The main contractor will look at the resources of the subcontractors and their sub-subcontractors, recognizing this potential difficulty. Using political skills and commercial pressures, the main contractor will make sure that if there is a risk of shortage of total resources, it will be on someone else's project.

Style and people

Rules 5, 6 and 7 relate to the political style of project management. Contract conditions are a cornerstone in the project strategy and are increasingly becoming a source of dispute in a litigious world. The contract type chosen is a fundamental indicator of the management style to be adopted. The range is enormous, even within the UK, and even more so throughout the rest of the world, although the influence of British contracts is widespread.

The most frequent sources of contractual dispute and difficulty are the responsibilities for specification and design, the timely issue of information, post-contract changes in the client's requirements, and coordination difficulties between contractors. All can lead to additional costs, payment disputes and delays to the work. The contract conditions will signal the owner's objectives clearly in the provisions for a proper balance of responsibility between the parties for these key activities. There may be supplementary documents that give other messages: for example, the arrangements for employee relations and welfare, and contact between the management teams of all parties.

The planning and reporting systems specified for a project will also set the tone for problem solving. All systems should have the facility to allow correction of deviations. The best of systems will not be proof against all possibilities, and the solution of problems that threaten a project will be a true test of the political sense of the parties involved. The hard line contractual approach can keep all the issues clear, and place responsibility fairly and squarely on the party with the immediate problem. But this might be at the expense of greater costs and problems to many others than if a collaborative approach had been adopted. These additional costs will inevitably be the source of argument (and possibly litigation). A collaborative approach to problem solving may blur the issues at times and cost the innocent party more, but it could secure the project objectives with less overall cost – a good test of 'the art of the possible'.

Project success is only achieved through people. Some projects hit technical or financial problems that threaten their completion. Such problems are only resolved through the exceptional efforts of people. On the more routine level, the daily conduct of project work requires a close identification of common interests. With all the parties involved, each pursuing their own limited objectives, the common self-interest (and how that relates to the project) is a crucial motivator. Of many options that have been tried, experience shows that probably the most effective method is regular meetings between the owner, the main contractor and the most senior management representatives of all the subcontractors. Provided that the necessary authority is vested in all those attending, and that there is a climate of positive action, problems can be identified and responsibility accepted for resolution – whether by owner, main contractor or subcontractor.

The senior management commitment that this process will demonstrate needs to be conveyed by the individual managers to their organizations. Typically this might be done by regular briefings of all concerned, stressing the part they have to play and the interrelationships with others.

Where installation is involved, the daily problems require prompt solutions, and do not lend themselves to routine meetings. Willing people, who understand the situation and the need for action, are the only answer. The pressures of installation sites and the absence of ready support from base pose special problems for site personnel. A way of building relationships to the benefit of daily life in these circumstances is to hold informal after-hours get-togethers, with some refreshments. In a relaxed atmosphere, people will resolve problems that might otherwise develop into big issues. A beer a day could save a delay – and avoid a writ.

CONCLUSION

Project management is concerned with achieving objectives. Projects are executed through the efforts and abilities of people. Difficulties will arise in the course of the project, and threaten the objectives. The resolution of these difficulties will almost certainly have to be achieved through the people involved. The routine execution of the work, and the resolution of difficulties along the way will require compromise and the exercise of political skills at all levels, working through and with those people.

The complete project objectives may not always be achieved, but correct political judgement will bring in an acceptable result. It is no benefit to have right of way, but be killed on a zebra crossing!

FURTHER READING

Brussels can you hear me?, Department of Trade and Industry, Victoria Street, London SW1H OET.

Jay, A., *Management and Macchiavelli*, Hodder & Stoughton, London, 1967.

Kliem, Ralph L., and Ludin, Irwin S., *The People Side of Project Management*, Gower, Aldershot, 1992.

The Times Guide to the House of Commons, Harper Collins, London.

Vacher's Parliamentary Companion, A. S. Kerswill Ltd, 113 High Street, Berkhampstead (updated quarterly).

Part Two
CONTRACT ADMINISTRATION

5 Contract Law

Peter Marsh

The purpose of this chapter is to provide a brief outline and layman's guide to English contract law as it applies between commercial organizations. It is in no way intended to replace the need for legal consultation in cases of difficulty or dispute but rather to suggest ways in which such cases can be avoided. If however such problems do occur then it is essential that professional legal advice should be sought at the earliest opportunity and before action has been taken which can be prejudicial to the company's rights.

CONTRACT FORMATION

There are four essential elements for a binding contract to be formed between two companies. These are:

1 The intention to be legally bound.
2 Consideration.
3 Offer.
4 Acceptance.

The intention to be legally bound

Although this requirement exists it is of little practical importance as the courts have consistently held that between commercial organizations such a requirement can be assumed. Only if the parties have expressly stated in their agreement that it is not intended to be legally binding will the requirement take effect; then courts will hold that such an agreement is not binding. The agreement becomes a mere 'gentleman's agreement', not enforceable at law.

Consideration

Consideration is a highly technical doctrine which is peculiar to English law. It requires, in general, that an act or promise of one party must have been given in exchange for the act or promise of the other in order for a binding contract to exist. Normally no problem with the doctrine will arise since a commercial contract will be one under which the seller or contractor undertakes to provide goods or services in return for payment by the purchaser. But the doctrine may play a part in the following three instances which are of practical significance and deserve mention.

Standing offers

A purchasing organization (such as a local authority) may consider that it will require a list of items over say a 12-month period without being certain of its specific needs. It will therefore invite tenders from suppliers indicating its likely requirements and notify those who have been successful that their tenders have been accepted for particular items. From time to time the authority will then call-off from those firms concerned the items they want and pay for these at the tendered prices. The question then arises as to whether or not the 'acceptance' of the firm's tender creates a contract since at that stage there would appear to have been no consideration provided by the authority.

The answer as so often is that it all depends on the wording used in the documents concerned, in particular as to whether or not the authority has actually promised to do anything. If, for example, the authority had stated in their enquiry that they would buy their requirements only from the firms whose tenders they accepted then this might be considered by the courts as sufficient consideration to support the promise made by the supplier to supply at the prices specified in his tender. The importance of the distinction is that if no contract exists then, while the supplier must fulfil any orders which the authority places on him so long as his offer remains open, he is free to withdraw that offer at any time (and clearly would do if, for example, there was an unexpected increase in his costs). If, however, a contract does exist, then he must meet any orders which the authority may place on him during the period for which the contract remains in force.

Options

A case analogous to standing offers is that of an option. An example is provided by the tenderer who declares 'I will maintain the validity of my offer for a period of 60 days'. It has long been an established principle of English law that an undertaking to keep an offer open for acceptance is not legally binding, owing to the absence of any consideration. This can be particularly troublesome to a main contractor who has submitted his bid on the basis of prices provided by subcontractors only to find, when he is awarded the contract, that the sub-contractors have withdrawn their offers.

In order to protect himself against that situation the main contractor would have had to create some consideration, however small, in order to establish a contract between himself and the subcontractor that the bid will remain open for acceptance for the specified period. It has been suggested that such consider-ation could be the supply of the contract documentation to the tenderer at his request. This would, of course, need to be stated in form of the invitation to tender.

Settlement of claims

It is important in an agreement for the settlement of a claim to recognize that there must be consideration for an undertaking by one party to waive rights which he has against the other. Since consideration need not be adequate, and can have a merely nominal value, it would appear that the withdrawal of a counterclaim which was unlikely to succeed would be treated by the courts as consideration, but it needs to be expressed as such in the settlement documentation.

In an agreement for the settlement of a claim it is important, however, to recognize that there must be consideration if a small sum is to be accepted in place of a larger liquidated amount. The case of *Tiny Engineering* v. *Anode Knitting Machine Company* (decided in 1986) is a good modern example of the general rule. In that case a commission of 10 per cent had been agreed between the parties but later a disagreement arose. After negotiations the invoice for 10 per cent was amended to 5 per cent, initialled and endorsed 'accepted in full and final settlement' by the plaintiff's negotiator. The plaintiff then sued for the balance and won the Court of Appeal, holding that there had been no consideration for the promise to accept the smaller sum.

Offer

It is necessary to distinguish between an 'offer' and an 'invitation to treat'. An offer in law is both an indication of the terms upon which a party is willing to contract and an expression of willingness to do so if an acceptance is given of those terms. An 'invitation to treat' (of which the classic example is the display of goods in a shop window) is an indication of the terms upon which the seller is willing to do business, but not that he would accept any offer which was made. The commercial significance of this distinction is that an order made on the basis of a price list is not a binding contract until the order has been accepted by the seller, unless there are some special terms contained within the price list which would clearly indicate to the contrary.

As stated in the previous section an offer can be withdrawn at any time unless there is a separate contract under which it is to be kept open. However, withdrawal of the offer (revocation, as it is termed) is only effective when it has been communicated to the person to whom the offer was made. Accordingly if the offer is accepted prior to the receipt of the notice of revocation, then a valid contract exists and the purported revocation is of no effect.

Acceptance

An acceptance of an offer only becomes effective when it has been communicated to the person having made the offer. If the offer prescribes the form or manner in which the acceptance is to be made then the acceptance must be made in that manner, or in a way which is at least as beneficial to the party making the offer.

Since the last century the rule has been that the contract is complete when the acceptance is posted (properly stamped and addressed) even if the letter is never in fact received, although it is, of course, open to the person making the offer to state that he will not be bound until he actually receives the acceptance.

In instances where acceptance is by telex the general rule is different and acceptance is when the telex message is received. It would appear that receipt here means at the telex machine of the party making the offer, even if it has not been read, although it is not clear that this would necessarily apply if the telex was received out of business hours (because, for example, of time differences between the UK and overseas).

The principal difficulty with acceptance is that in order for a binding contract to be formed the acceptance must be in the same terms as the offer. In very many instances this is not the case. What purports, therefore, to be an acceptance is in fact a counteroffer which it is open to the other party to accept or reject. The issues which then arise are, first, whether or not a contract exists at all and, secondly, if a contract does exist, then on what terms? This problem is often referred to as 'the battle of the forms' since it most commonly arises between buyer and seller, each of whom is seeking to ensure that the contract is placed on his own standard terms and conditions.

In arriving at a solution to this problem the first essential point to be understood is that in English law:

> an offer falls to be interpreted not subjectively by reference to what has actually passed through the mind of the offeror, but objectively by reference to the interpretation which a reasonable man in the shoes of the offeree would place on the offer. It is an equally well-established principle that ordinarily an offer, when unequivocally accepted according to its precise terms, will give rise to a legally binding agreement as soon as acceptance is communicated to the offeror in the manner contemplated by the offer, and cannot thereafter be revoked without the consent of the other party (per the Court of Appeal in the case of *Centro-Provincial Estates* v. *Merchants Investors Assurance Company* (1983)).

The practical result of this is that evidence of the party's subjective intentions in the matter is irrelevant. The test to be applied is the objective one of a reasonable observer. The second point is that nothing less than unequivocal acceptance will do. A response which raises questions (or, even more significantly, seeks to amend the terms of the offer in some way), even if it purports to be an acceptance, will be considered as a counter-offer, which puts an end to the original offer and itself counts as an offer which is up to the original offeror to accept or reject.

In ordinary purchasing practice the sequence of events could be:

1 The buyer issues an enquiry.
2 The seller sends a quotation with his conditions of sale.

3   The buyer issues an order with his conditions of purchase.

At that stage no contract exists assuming (as is almost certainly the case) that the seller's and buyer's conditions do not coincide. It is therefore what happens next which is vital. There are many possibilities of which three will be considered:

1   Nothing is done to resolve the conflict in terms, but in due course the goods are delivered and accepted by the buyer. By delivering the goods the seller would be considered to have accepted the buyer's terms, unless there were documents accompanying the delivery which amounted to a counter-offer. The important point is that up until that time it is most probable that there is no contract between the parties at all although both may believe that there is.
2   The supplier returns the buyer's acknowledgement slip which is sent with the order and which refers to the order being accepted on the buyer's conditions. In that event there is a contract on the buyer's conditions.
3   The supplier returns the buyer's acknowledgement slip as requested but under cover of a letter which refers back to his original quotation. If the covering letter does not specifically refer to the seller's conditions of contract then the answer would very probably be, as happened in the leading case of *Butler Machine Tool Co. Ltd* v. *Ex-Cell-O Corporation* (1979), that the court would consider the reference to the quotation as limited only to the price and identity of the goods and therefore of no contractual effect. The result would be again a contract on the buyer's conditions. If, however, the covering letter does refer specifically to the seller's conditions of sale then the position would be that this would constitute in law a counter-offer which the buyer could either accept or reject. If as is quite likely in practice there is no further reference to the terms of the contract, then there would be no contract between the parties until such time as the buyer had acted in some manner which constituted acceptance (for example by issuing a delivery schedule).

The general rule would seem to be, then, that the battle of forms is usually won by the party who fired the last shot. 'He is the man who puts forward the latest terms and conditions: and, if these are not objected to by the other party, then he may be taken to have agreed to them' per Lord Denning in the *Butler* case.

Letters of intent

Like many other expressions in common commercial use, letters of intent have no distinct legal meaning. In order, therefore, to determine what the parties meant when issuing and acting upon a letter of intent it is necessary to examine what happened. As was said in a recent judgement 'everything depends on the circumstances of the particular case'. It is difficult, therefore, to lay down any general rules but the following are offered as guidance:

1   Generally, a letter of intent does not give rise to any legal obligation on the part of the person issuing it nor on the part of the recipient. It is simply an expression of intentions.

2   If, however, it is clear from the facts of the case that the purchaser in issuing the letter of intent did mean to be bound and for the other party to act on the letter of intent as if it were an order, then the mere use of the expression 'letter of intent' will not avoid that conclusion. In a recent case after having telephoned an order and given an order number the purchaser sent the supplier a letter which among other things stated '[the suppliers] should accept in the meantime this correspondence as our letter of intent to purchase the items previously specified herein'. It was held that a binding contract existed.

3   Although the letter of intent may not amount to a binding promise to award the contract for the works concerned it may amount to a contract for the preliminary work to which the letter refers. Frequently the letter of intent will ask the supplier to proceed in the meantime with tooling, certain design work or the purchase of long-lead items and these instructions will amount to a promise to pay for such work.

4   If the facts of the case are such that the letter of intent is just a stage in the negotiating process, but nevertheless acts as an encouragement to the supplier to proceed with the contract work while negotiations continue, and he does so proceed with the full knowledge and indeed participation of the purchaser (for example, in inspection), then, if no contract is ever con-cluded because the parties never reach agreement on terms, the supplier will be entitled to be paid on a *quantum meruit* basis for the value of the work performed. The problem for the buyer in those circumstances is that if no contract is ever concluded, then he has none of the contractual rights which he would otherwise possess. So if the supplier is late in making delivery, the buyer cannot claim damages for delay.

CONTRACT TERMS

The contract price

If a lump sum quotation is submitted and accepted for the carrying out of certain work or for the supply of specified goods, then it is the contractor's/supplier's obligation to complete his contract and without additional payment, even if the carrying out of the work becomes more difficult or entails work beyond that which the contractor/supplier originally contemplated – unless the contract specifically provides otherwise or there was misrepresentation on the part of the purchaser. In an old case involving a lump sum contract to build a house, flooring was omitted from the specification and it was held that the contractor must put it in without additional payment as it was clearly indispensably necessary in order to complete the house.

Because the word 'estimate' is used it does not mean that the contractor is not bound by the figure which he submits. It depends on the facts and generally in the building trade 'estimates' are in practice treated as quotations which, if accepted, become lump sum contracts.

The price is not always agreed at the time when the order is placed. If it is left to be agreed between the parties at a later date and they fail to agree, then the contract may be invalid for lack of certainty. However, if the goods have been delivered to and accepted by the purchaser then the court will almost certainly hold that the buyer must pay a reasonable price for them.

In times of inflation many contracts are placed on the basis that the contract price will be varied in accordance with a price variation clause or formula. In general such escalation clauses have been construed strictly by the courts in deciding on whether or not a particular increase in costs was included within their provisions. Thus where an escalation clause allowed a contractor to recover the additional costs arising from 'binding national awards' and a national award was made which included an element for a voluntary bonus scheme, the House of Lords held that this was not part of a binding national award and the increased cost to the contractor of complying with that part of the award could not be passed on to the employer. However, it is equally clear that if a contract provides for escalation to be calculated in accordance with a price variation formula, then the contractor is entitled to be paid in accordance with the terms of that formula irrespective of the amount of his actual increase in costs.

Passing of property

The general rules as to the passing of property are laid down in the Sale of Goods Act 1979 and may be summarized as follows.

Section 16 provides that property in unascertained goods only passes when they have been ascertained. Unascertained goods are those which are generic (for example, 100 tonnes of coffee beans), not yet built, or forming part of larger bulk. In general goods will become ascertained when they have been irrevocably attached to the contract, so that those goods and no others become the subject of the contract.

Section 17 provides that if goods are specific or ascertained then the property in them passes to the buyer when the parties to the contract intend it to be passed. There are then in s. 18 set out a number of rules which apply if the parties have been unwise or careless enough not to specify their intentions in the contract for sale. Of these the first and most important is that, if the goods are specific and in a deliverable state, then the property passes when the contract is made and it is immaterial if the time of payment or delivery or both are postponed.

The fact that the property in the goods has passed to the buyer but he has not yet paid for them leaves the seller in a vulnerable situation in the event of the buyer ultimately defaulting and becoming bankrupt or going into liquidation. For this reason reservation of title, or as they are often today referred to as *Romalpa* clauses (after the name of the leading case on the subject) have become popular.

The legal effect of any clause will depend on the specific way in which it is drafted and the decided cases on the subject have to date left the law in a state of some uncertainty. However, the following is a guide to the current position:

1 Where the goods are still in the buyer's possession the seller will be entitled to recover the goods. If the clause so provides, this right will enable the seller to recover not only the contract price but all sums due to the seller – the so-called all sums clause. This is particularly important where the seller is making regular deliveries. It means that the property in the goods which were the subject of the first delivery will not pass to the buyer until all subsequent deliveries have been paid for.

2 The buyer will be able to pass a good title to a third party under s. 25(1) of the Sale of Goods Act and s. 9 of the Factors Act if the third party bought in good faith and without notice of the retention of title clause. If the clause provides that the purchaser holds the goods as bailee for the seller and is under a fiduciary duty to account to the seller for the proceeds of the sale, the seller may be able to recover such proceeds, provided that they can be identified.

3 If the goods have been used in the manufacture of other products and mixed with other goods, the seller would appear to have no right to recover possession or to receive any part of the proceeds of sale unless he had registered a charge under the Companies Act.

Passing of risk

One reason for the importance of the clause relating to the passing of property is that, unless a contract for the sale of goods provides otherwise, the risk in the goods passes at the same time as the property does. Whoever is the owner of the goods takes the risk of their being lost or damaged (possibly in transit). If, therefore, the seller introduces a reservation of title clause which is effective, so that property does not pass until he is paid, he would be wise also to introduce a clause providing that the risk in the goods passes to the buyer at some earlier point such as when the goods are despatched.

Buyers also need to consider the question of the risk in goods when they wish for property to pass to them while the goods are still in the course of manufacture because they have made part payment. They should provide expressly that the risk remains with the seller until at least despatch, and that the seller insures accordingly.

Delivery

In one of the more old-fashioned clauses, the Sale of Goods Act s. 29(2) provides that the place of delivery for specific goods is the seller's place of business. It is, of course, open to the parties to make other provisions, and if the seller is required to make delivery to the buyer's premises, then he discharges his obligations if he delivers the goods there without negligence to a person apparently having authority to receive them.

It is also provided in the Act that delivery to a carrier is presumed to be delivery to the buyer, but this will only be so if the seller has made a reasonable contract of carriage on the buyer's behalf. In the case of *Thomas Young and Sons Ltd* v. *Hobson and Partners* (1949) electric engines were sent by rail unsecured at owner's risk. The engines were damaged in transit. The buyer was held to be justified in refusing to accept delivery, as he would have had no remedy against the carrier, and the seller should have sent the engines at carrier's risk (which would have meant that they would have been inspected and required to have been secured).

Time for completion

In a contract for building or civil engineering works, and probably also a contract for the supply and installation/erection of electrical or mechanical plant, time is not of the essence unless the contract provides otherwise. In a commercial contract for the sale of goods however, time will generally be of the essence unless the contract provides to the contrary. The significance of time being of the essence is that if the supplier is late, even by a single day in completing delivery, then the buyer is entitled to cancel the contract and reject the goods. The buyer will also be entitled to claim for damages. If time is not of the essence, failure to complete on time is still a breach of contract for which the purchaser is entitled to claim damages.

It is normal in construction and similar forms of contract to provide that the contractor is entitled to an extension of time if he is delayed either by the act/ default of the employer or some other mitigating circumstance. There are two possible approaches to the drafting of an extension of time clause:

1 One approach is to list in detail all the events which could possibly entitle the contractor to an extension of time. An extreme example of this in the UK is the standard form of building contract known as JCT80, which manages to list some 14 clauses.
2 The other approach is to provide that the contractor is entitled to an extension of time if he is delayed by any act or omission of the purchaser, or by any industrial dispute, or by reason of any circumstances beyond the contractor's reasonable control. This is the approach adopted in the Standard Conditions of Contract for Electrical and Mechanical Engineering Works in the UK, known as MF/1. It is suggested that this second approach is the preferred method of drafting.

One phrase which should in any event be avoided is '*force majeure*', unless its meaning is given within the clause so that it becomes simply a form of shorthand. The term has no definite meaning in English law and has caused the courts problems of interpretation on the few occasions when it has come before them. In French law, from which the term came, *force majeure* is defined very strictly as being an event 'which was unforeseeable, irresistible, rendered performance of the contract impossible and was external to the contractor'.

If this terminology were applied in English law, then few events would qualify.   *81*

It is clearly much narrower than the standard English phraseology of 'industrial disputes or other causes beyond the contractor's reasonable control'. It would probably mean that the court would not be giving effect to the real intention of the parties in using the term. It is this uncertainty as to how the term would be interpreted that makes the use of 'force majeure' in an English contract so undesirable unless its meaning is clearly defined.

Damages

The object of an award in damages is to place the injured party in the same position financially as he would have been had the contract been properly performed, provided that the losses are not too remote.

Essentially the rule on remoteness is that the loss or damage which is recoverable is that which the parties could reasonably have contemplated at the time when the contract was made would be incurred from the breach in question. They could reasonably have contemplated a loss either because it would normally follow and arise naturally given that event, or because it should have been anticipated having regard to what was known to the parties at the time when the contract was made. Thus if a piece of equipment is delivered late, which it is obvious the buyer intends to put into immediate use, then the supplier will be liable for the losses which the buyer incurs as a result of such delayed delivery, provided that such losses are such as the supplier could reasonably have expected when he entered into the contract would follow from the delay. They would not therefore include exceptionally high profits which the buyer anticipated the machine would earn unless when issuing the enquiry the buyer had brought that fact to the seller's attention.

Because of the difficulties and uncertainties surrounding the issue of what level of damages a purchaser will be entitled to if works are completed late, the contract will often contain a clause specifying the damages which can be recovered. In commercial practice such a clause is often referred to as a penalty clause but legally there is a sharp distinction to be made between penalties and liquidated damages.

Liquidated damages are a genuine pre-estimate of the sum which the buyer considers would be lost in the event of the works being delayed, or, if he considers that would be excessive, some lesser amount. In practice such a clause nearly always contains a limit of liability although there is no legal need for this.

Usually the damages are expressed either as a sum or as a percentage of the contract price payable per week of delay up to a specified limit. The question as to the purchaser's rights if the works are still not complete after the limit has expired has been much debated. In the MF/1 conditions (to which reference was made earlier) there is provision for the purchaser in such circumstances to give notice either requiring the contractor to complete or terminating the contract with the right to recover damages up to a limit stated in the appendix to the contract.

Certainly, since the contractor is still in breach of contract during the further period of delay after expiry of the specified limit, there should be some additional remedy available to the purchaser, and there should be a continuing incentive on the contractor to complete the works.

A penalty, as distinct from liquidated damages, is a sum which is greater than any loss that the purchaser at the time of contract could reasonably anticipate suffering. It is included in an attempt to compel the contractor to complete on time. One of the most common situations in which a clause will be considered to be a penalty is if it makes the same sum payable on the occurrence of one of several events and the loss which the purchaser could suffer on one of these would be trifling in comparison with the amount of the penalty.

With a true liquidated damages clause it is irrevelant whether the actual loss suffered by the purchaser is greater or less than the amount of liquidated damages. Whatever the level of the purchaser's actual losses, he can only recover the amount of the liquidated damages – neither more nor less. For this reason, it has been suggested that the clause could be caught under the Unfair Contract Terms Act 1977 and be subject to the test of reasonableness; however, there is no decision which confirms this view and it is not universally shared.

If the sum is classified by the courts as a penalty then the clause is void and the penalty is irrecoverable by legal action. However, this does not alter the fact that the contractor is late and in breach of contract, so he will still be liable for damages calculated under the normal rules. It makes no difference what the clause is called in the contract – the only question to be answered is whether or not it was a genuine pre-estimate.

Quality and performance

The issues of quality and performance are central to the carrying out of commercial contracts. The obligations of the seller and the rights of the buyer, as set out in the Sale of Goods Act, cover three broad areas:

1 *Description and sample* Under the Sale of Goods Act goods must correspond to description and the bulk must correspond to sample. From our point of view the most important consequence of these provisions is that the goods must correspond to the specification. In the older cases which have come before the courts there have been a number of examples where the goods have not exactly corresponded with the specification and the courts have held that the purchaser was accordingly entitled to reject them. As an example, a case in 1921 (*Moore and Co.* v. *Landauer*) allowed the buyer to reject tins of fruit because they came packed in 24 tins to the box instead of 30. Whether that case would be followed today is uncertain (unless the deviation made a significant difference to the buyer) because the buyer's motive in seeking to reject has often been to avoid what, by the time of delivery, has become an unprofitable bargain. This aspect was commented upon by the House of Lords in *Reardon Smith* v. *Hansen Tangen* in 1976.

2 *Merchantable quality* Where a seller sells goods in the course of business a condition is implied that the goods shall be of merchantable quality. 83

Section 14(6) of the Act defines goods as being of merchantable quality if they are 'fit for the purpose or purposes for which goods of that kind are commonly bought as it is reasonable to expect having regard to any description applied to them, the price (if relevant) and all other relevant circumstances'.

Where goods are perfectly usable for one of the main purposes for which goods of that type are commonly bought, then the goods will be regarded as being of merchantable quality. If there is one particular purpose for which they are not suitable and that is the purpose which the buyer had in mind, then it is up to the buyer to specify that purpose so that he is protected under s. 14(3) of the Sale of Goods Act.

Even minor defects may make goods unmerchantable if they affect the purpose for which the goods are required – for example the comfort, reliability and appearance of a new car.

When goods are sold at varying qualities and this is reflected in their market price, then, if the actual price paid is commensurate with the quality in fact supplied, the goods will be considered to be of merchantable quality. Where goods are for resale, this will be so even if the contract price was in fact higher than would normally be paid for goods of that quality, provided they can be resold at a price which is not substantially less than the contract price.

There are two exceptions in the Act to the requirement as to merchantable quality. The first of these relates to defects specifically drawn to the buyer's attention. The second exception arises if the buyer examines the goods prior to contract and there are defects which that examination ought to reveal. If, therefore, the buyer is offered the opportunity of inspecting goods and does so, he must be careful to ensure that his examination is thorough enough. If it is only cursory (for example, looking at barrels from the outside only instead of examining them more closely) the buyer will lose his rights under this clause.

3 *Fitness for purpose* Under s. 14 of the Act, if the buyer, expressly or by implication, makes known to the seller the purpose for which he requires the goods, then there is an implied condition of fitness for purpose, unless circumstances show that the buyer did not rely on, or it would be unreasonable for him to rely on, the skill and judgement of the seller. In some situations the purpose for which the goods are required will be obvious. In others, however, there may be difficulties either because the buyer has a particular purpose in mind for an item which is of general application or because the goods in question have more than one use and again the buyer has only one which he has selected.

If the goods have more than one use, they must be suitable for all that range of uses. If feeding stuffs for animals are being supplied, for example, they must be suitable for all animals unless, perhaps, they would be unsuitable for some especially rare species and the buyer had failed to make known to the seller that it was that particular species for which the feed was required. So, where pails were sold which were suitable for all normal purposes, including export, but could not stand the intense heat when left standing stacked six high on a Kuwait dockside, it was decided that the seller was not liable (*Aswan Engineering Company* v. *Lupidine Ltd*).

Payment

Unless the parties otherwise agree, time is not of the essence as regards the time for payment. Delays in payment by the buyer do not, therefore, automatically give the right to the seller to terminate the contract. This point is of particular importance where the contract provides for stage payments. If the purchaser defaults on a single stage payment then whether or not the supplier or contractor has a right to terminate will depend on the size of the breach in relation to the contract as a whole and the likelihood of the breach being repeated. Because of the general uncertainty of the supplier's rights in this type of situation, it is important from the supplier's viewpoint that he should include express provisions in the contract covering his rights should the purchaser default on payment.

Interest on delayed payments can only be claimed by the supplier if the right was expressly included in the contract conditions. There is no general implied right to recover interest for delay in payment. It is important to note that inclusion of right to recover interest must be within the documentation forming part of the contract. Reference to it only on the invoice will not be effective unless the invoice is a part of the contract. It will only be so if the invoice constitutes the seller's acceptance of the buyer's order. In all other circumstances the invoice is a demand for payment under the terms of an existing contract and the rule is clear that once a contract has been made the terms can only be varied by mutual agreement and not by the unilateral act of one of the parties.

The contract should set out expressly the event or events on the happening of which the supplier or contractor is entitled to receive payment. It is one point on which the basic rules implied by law differ as between contracts for the sale of goods and contracts for services. Under a contract for the sale of goods, s.28 of the Sale of Goods Act provides that, unless otherwise agreed, delivery of the goods and payment of the price are concurrent conditions. With a contract for services the general rule is that services are to be performed first and payment is only due when the whole of the services have been completed. So where there was a contract for the installation of a central heating system the contractor was only entitled to be paid when the work had been completed; that is to say, when the system had been made to work effectively.

Guarantees and exclusion clauses

For commercial reasons it has long been the practice of suppliers and contractors to limit their liabilities in damages for the supply of defective goods or for the carrying out of defective work. This practice even extends to excluding such liabilities altogether, offering the purchaser in return some limited undertaking to make good defects which arise within a specified period. At one time, under the general principle of freedom of contract, English law allowed the parties to make a contract on more or less any terms they chose, ignoring the reality of life that such freedom could be totally illusory if there was a significant difference in the bargaining power of the parties. In order to provide some rough kind of justice, particularly in cases where one of the parties was a domestic purchaser, the courts did on occasions strain the construction of exclusion clauses beyond any normal interpretation of the words, so as to be able to find that the clause did not cover the issue in question. They also invented the doctrine of fundamental breach, which was to the effect that there were fundamental obligations under a contract that it was impossible to exclude, such as that in selling a car it had to be capable of self-propulsion. All that has now been swept away by a combination of decisions of the House of Lords and the passing of the Unfair Contract Terms Act.

First, the House of Lords in the *Photo Production* v. *Securicor Ltd* case ruled that exclusion clauses in commercial contracts between businessmen were to be interpreted in accordance with the natural meaning of the words used and no strained constructions were to be applied. The doctrine of fundamental breach was firmly rejected. It was for the parties to decide how the risks involved were to be apportioned between them and if the meaning of the clause was clear the courts would not interfere. If there were any doubt as to the meaning then the court would approach the problem of construction of the clause by looking at who was in the strongest position (usually by way of insurance) to accept the risk involved.

Secondly, the Unfair Contract Terms Act has outlawed certain exclusion provisions and made others subject to the test of 'reasonableness'. Dealing only with commercial contracts the most significant provisions of the Act are:

1 Liability for death or personal injury due to negligence cannot be excluded or restricted by any contract term. In the case of other loss or damage due to negligence, liability can only be restricted or excluded if the contract term satisfied the test of reasonableness.
2 The seller's implied undertakings under the Sale of Goods Act in respect of conformity of the goods with description or sample, or as to their quality or fitness for purpose, can only be excluded or restricted by a contract term if it satisfies the test of reasonableness.

There are five guidelines in the Act to be taken into account in deciding on whether or not a term is reasonable and the onus is on the party seeking to rely on the exclusion provision to show that the clause is reasonable having regard only to what was known (or ought reasonably to have been known) to the parties at the time when the contract was made. The guidelines are:

1 The strength of the bargaining positions of the parties relative to each other
2 Whether the purchaser received an inducement to agree to the term or could have entered into a similar contract with someone else without such a term.

3 Whether the purchaser knew, or ought reasonably to have known, the existence of the term.
4 Whether it was reasonable at the time of contract to expect that it would be practicable to comply with the term.
5 Whether the goods were manufactured, processed or adapted to the special order of the customer.

There have been a number of cases before the courts where the test of 'reasonableness' has been at issue. Although it has to be stressed that each case must be considered on its own facts, it is suggested that the following are the more important points which the court will take into account:

1 Whether or not the buyer has sought to negotiate on the terms of the clause, or had the opportunity to do so.
2 The possibility of the risk being insured against by the person providing the service without materially affecting the price.
3 The level of the loss which would be suffered by the purchaser and the difficulty of the task being undertaken. The higher the level of the foreseeable loss and the easier the task, the less likely is it that an exemption or limitation clause will be considered reasonable.
4 A clause totally excluding liability is more likely to be held unreasonable than one which only partially excludes liability.

Finally, if the clause restricts liability to a specified sum, then two additional guidelines become relevant:

1 The resources available to the supplier to meet the liability.
2 How far it was open to the supplier to cover himself by insurance.

On the first point it is not yet clear whose resources are to be taken into account when the supplier is part of a larger group. Is it just those of the subsidiary, or does it extend to those of the group?

VITIATING FACTORS

Mistake

The law has traditionally divided mistake into three categories:

1 *Common mistake* If the parties both make the same mistake, as to, say, the suitability of the goods for a certain purpose, then they are still bound by the contract they have made. Only in the rare type of case in which the goods have later been found to have been destroyed, or even never to have existed, will the court declare the contract to be void.
2 *Mutual mistake* In common parlance, the parties are simply at cross

87

purposes. The courts then apply the objective test of the reasonable person, and ask if he would say that the parties had reached a binding agreement.

3 *Unilateral mistake* This is where only one party has made a mistake, the other being well aware of the error since he himself is not mistaken. Usually these ones are cases of sharp practice, if not downright fraud. If the subject matter of the mistake is a crucial part of the bargain then the courts have ruled that the contract is void.

Misrepresentation

A representation is a statement of fact made by one party to the contract to the other before the contract is made, which induces the person to whom it is made to enter into the contract, but is not itself a term of the contract. A misrepresentation is a representation which turns out not to be true. In general, silence is not a misrepresentation except in cases requiring utmost good faith, such as insurance.

The law on misrepresentation has been developed both by the courts and by Parliament. In the briefest of outline there are four alternatives to be considered:

1 *Fraudulent misrepresentation* This is where the misrepresentation is made knowingly or without caring whether it is true or false. The remedy is both damages and recision.

2 *Negligent misrepresentation* A statement which is made carelessly during the course of negotiations by one side and is relied on by the other can be the subject of an action for damages. If the seller held himself out as an expert giving advice on some crucial aspect of the sale, and if that advice were given negligently and acted upon by the purchaser, then this would be the type of situation in which the purchaser could claim damages.

3 *Misrepresentation Act 1967, s. 2.2(1)* This gives a statutory right to claim for damages for misrepresentation which is negligent. The curious part of this provision is that it reverses the normal burden of proof once the falsity has been established, so that the person making the representation must then prove that he was not negligent.

4 *Innocent misrepresentation* This is where the person making the representation honestly and reasonably believes it to be true. The remedy is that the other party can rescind the contract and claim an indemnity against those losses which he suffered necessarily from entering into the contract but not damages. However, under the Misrepresentation Act s. 2(2) the court now has the discretionary power to award that the contract shall be continued and damages awarded to the party to whom the representation was made to compensate them for being obliged to continue with the contract.

Frustration

English law has always placed a very restricted interpretation on the doctrine of frustration. For it to apply there must have been an unforeseen event occurring after the contract, beyond the control of both parties, which makes further performance of the contract impossible. If the contract can still be performed, although only in a more expensive way, then it is not frustrated.

CONTRACT LAW, JURISDICTION AND ENFORCEMENT

The proper law of the contract

Where a contract is entered into with a company overseas, or is for work to be performed overseas, then it is important that the contract should state the law by which the conclusion or performance of the contract is to be governed.

As a result of the Contracts (Applicable Law) Act 1990, which gave effect to the Rome convention, the English rules as to the law by which a contract is to be governed have been amended. Those rules are now as summarized below:

1   The court will give effect to the choice made by the parties.
    The only exception is if the parties choose a law with which the contract has no connection, and all other choices point to the law of another country: then the choice does not prejudice the application of the mandatory rules of that other country. The reason behind this exception is clear. The parties cannot choose a law so as to get round mandatory provisions (for example, the Unfair Contract Terms Act in a case where the contract is to be performed in England).
2   If there is no choice by the parties, then the applicable law will be that of the country in which the party who is responsible for the performance characteristic of the contract had his head office at the time when the contract was made. The performance characteristic of a sales contract is the supply of goods, so that the law would be that of the country in which the seller had his head office (or, if the contract was made by a branch office, the country in which the branch office was situated).
3   It is only the manner of performance (for example, the detail of the method to be used to examine goods) that will now be governed by the law of the place of performance.
4   The material validity of the contract will be governed by 'putative law' (which is that law that would apply if the contract were valid).

Although the Contracts (Applicable Law) Act results from a convention agreed between the EC member states, the Act is now part of English law and applies to any contract in which there is a choice of law between different countries.

Jurisdiction

Again, it is highly desirable that the contract should state which court or arbitration tribunal is to have jurisdiction and it is to be noted that this question is quite separate from that of the proper law of the contract. Thus a case can be held in England with the court applying a foreign law. Since, however, this requires proof of that law through expert witnesses, the costs and time involved are considerable and the position is one to be avoided if possible.

Enforcement

This is perhaps the biggest problem for the English company where the other party to the contract is situated abroad with all his assets outside the jurisdiction of the English courts. An award by an English arbitration tribunal may be capable of being directly enforced if the other country is a signatory to the Convention on the Recognition and Enforcement of Foreign Arbitral Awards – the so-called New York Convention, or the Geneva Convention of 1927. With countries not signatory to these conventions enforcement may be difficult and in some instances impossible, particularly if the foreign territory is strongly nationalistic or under an autocratic government and the dispute involves a state organization or government department.

PRIVITY OF CONTRACT AND NEGLIGENCE

Privity of contract

The general rule of English law is that a contract can confer rights and duties only on the parties to the contract. This means *inter alia* that there is no contractual right for an employer to take action directly against a subcontractor for defective work. Nor equally is there generally any right by a subcontractor to claim against the employer for the value of work done.

At one time there was considerable interest in the extent to which a subcontractor was protected by the terms of the main contract, and by the terms of the taking-over certificate issued by the employer to the main contractor, against claims made against him by the employer in tort. Such claims were generally for defects in the subcontractor's work and would now be classified as claims for economic loss and, as such, not recoverable in tort (see the next section under the heading 'Negligence'). Nevertheless it is still the case that a subcontractor can take the benefit of a clause in the main contract which defines the 'contractual setting' and negates any duty of care which the subcontractor might otherwise owe to the employer. An example of such a clause exists in Clause 36.9 of Form MF/1,

Negligence

In July 1990 in the case of *Murphy* v. *Brentwood District Council* the House of Lords departed from its own previous decision in *Anns* v. *Merton London Borough Council* and over-ruled a number of earlier decisions of the Court of Appeal. Essentially the House of Lords returned the tort of negligence to its grass roots.

Damage is a necessary ingredient in the tort of negligence and the kind of damage which will normally support a claim in negligence is limited to physical injury to the plaintiff or physical damage to property other than that to the property which is the subject of the negligence itself. Damage to the property which is the subject of the negligence itself merely makes the thing which has been built or supplied less valuable and is properly to be classified as economic loss. Such loss is recoverable in negligence only if there is a special relationship between the parties in which the plaintiff placed reliance upon the defendant in the making of statements or the giving of advice and the defendant was aware of this.

If, therefore, under normal circumstances work is done or goods supplied, the contractor or supplier will be liable to the employer or purchaser in contract for the proper quality of his work. But he will have no liability to any third party (including a subsequent purchaser) for defects in his work which make it simply less valuable than it would have been had it been built or manufactured correctly. He will only be liable to the third party in negligence for either physical injury or damage to other property of the third party which is caused by his defective work.

It follows that the previous cases in which a subcontractor has been held to owe a duty of care to an employer in respect of the quality of his work can no longer be relied upon. The liability of the subcontractor in negligence is almost certainly limited to cases in which he has given negligent advice outside of any contractual relationship.

As a result of this reversal of the previously accepted legal liabilities of subcontractors there is an increasing trend towards requiring subcontractors (in particular specialist firms undertaking design) to enter into collateral warranties with the employer. Under the terms of such warranties the employer would have a direct remedy in contract against the subcontractor for faulty workmanship, materials or design, so avoiding the employer being left without any effective remedy if the main contractor went into liquidation. As regards subsequent purchasers it may be possible to protect their position as against the main contractor by an assignment of the employer's rights.

Professional services

The professional person rendering a service, such as a doctor, lawyer, accountant, engineer, architect or surveyor, is in a different position from a supplier or contractor. His duty is to exercise reasonable care and to show such skill as may reasonably be expected of an ordinarily competent person exercising that particular profession. Unless the terms of contract provide otherwise, the professional person does not (unlike the contractor or supplier) guarantee the achievement of a particular result and such a term will not be implied into his contract as a matter of law, but only as a matter of fact if this is justified according to the facts of a particular case. One such case was where a consulting engineer was employed by a package deal contractor to design a building suitable for a particular purpose.

The only exception to this rule is where a professional person is responsible for the supply of an article. If, for example, a dentist were to supply a set of dentures   *91* then, in respect of that supply, his liability would be equated to that of a supplier of goods. But, in fitting the new dentures, the dentist's obligation would be that of using reasonable skill and care.

FURTHER READING

Davies, F. R., *Contract*, 6th edn, Sweet & Maxwell, London, 1991.

Duxbury, R., *Contract Law*, 2nd edn, Sweet & Maxwell, London, 1991. (A concise paperback.)

Uff, J., *Construction Law*, 5th edn, Sweet & Maxwell, London, 1991.

6 Contracts and Payment Structures

Peter Marsh

There are three main ways in which the contract price may be expressed or calculated:

1 Lump sum.
2 Schedule of rates or remeasurement.
3 Cost reimbursement.

These different ways are not necessarily mutually exclusive. Thus the above-ground element of a building contract may be on a lump sum basis while the foundations are subject to remeasurement; the supply portion of a plant contract may be a lump sum, while the installation of the plant is on cost reimbursement; a contract for a complex chemical plant may be on cost reimbursement but with the overheads and profit margin compounded as a lump sum.

The choice of which way to ask the contractor to price the work will depend very largely on the amount of information regarding the job, and the conditions under which it will be carried out, which the buyer can provide to the contractor in the time available for tendering.

LUMP SUM

From the purchaser's point of view the ideal is a firm lump sum. It establishes the amount of his commitment in advance, it provides the maximum incentive to the contractor to complete the work on time, and it reduces to a minimum the amount of administrative work involved after the contract has been let. But these benefits will be obtained only if it has been possible for the contractor to tender realistically. Any marked divergence between the contract price and the actual cost of doing the work may not only lose the purchaser the benefits he expected but, worse, may endanger or destroy the effectiveness of the contract as a means of achieving management's overall objectives.

In addition to the general information needed by a tenderer, in order to bid on a lump sum basis answers to the following questions must also be found, either from the prospective purchaser or from the contractor's own organization:

1   Material quantities and specifications. These may be in the form of drawings from which the estimator can himself take off quantities.
2   Tolerances permitted and any special finishes required.
3   Labour hours and trades both for shop production and on site. This means that decisions on methods of production/construction affecting labour quantities and skills must have been made.
4   Description and quantities of bought-out items. This requires decisions to have been taken on, for example, sizes, capacities, and horsepowers.
5   Types of production or constructional plant which will be utilized both in the shops and on site, and the times or periods involved.
6   Where design is significant, and is not included as an overhead, the amount of design work involved.
7   The site organization which will be needed and for what period.
8   Overtime to be worked in shops and on site.
9   Time when the work is to be carried out.
10 Factors which will affect labour productivity on site – climatic conditions, religious holidays, nationality of labour to be employed.
11 Geographical and climatic factors as they affect civil, building or mechanical and electrical site work. These would include rainfall, presence of corrosive salts liable to attack steelwork, humidity, dust, availability of fresh water, general local facilities, supply of clean aggregates.
12 Local material availability: cement in proper condition and in the right quantities to meet programme, port off-loading and transport facilities including any heavy load restrictions on roads or bridges.
13 General local amenities and workshop facilities.

This is a formidable list. It confirms the need for the purchaser to be able to give complete and accurate information before a firm lump sum price can be tendered. It also indicates the time and cost in which the contractor is involved in lump sum tendering. What must be remembered is that every time a tenderer guesses, he may guess wrong, and every wrong guess costs someone money. Moreover, that someone, if the tenderer is to stay in business, can in the long run only be the employer, whether on that particular contract or another.

Just as the contractor's problem on lump sum tendering is to assess the risks involved, so the employer's problem is the time which it will take him to give the information necessary to reduce those risks to reasonable proportions. Some element of risk there will always be; that is in the very nature of contracting itself.

The problem of information against time arises particularly on contracts for building and civil engineering work where the employer is normally, though not necessarily, responsible for design, and two of the main factors affecting design are both largely outside the designer's control. These are, first, the nature of the subsoil and, second, the detailed requirements of the specialist contractors and subcontractors for plant and services. Increasingly, these latter form a major part of most building or civil engineering projects. If the start of construction were to be delayed until exhaustive bore-hole research had been carried out and detailed designs for the plant and services prepared, the element of uncertainty could of course be minimized. Managements, however, are not normally prepared to accept delays of this sort so that it becomes necessary to find some way in which the risks inherent in these unknowns can properly be shared between contractor and employer and a start made on the project.

SCHEDULE OF RATES OR BILL OF APPROXIMATE QUANTITIES

This leads to the schedule of rates or bills of approximate quantity method of pricing under which a schedule or bill is prepared, covering each of the items which it is anticipated may be met during the course of construction, for example excavation, concreting, brickwork, etc. These items are then priced by the contractor and he is paid at those rates for the amount of work actually carried out, irrespective of the quantity shown against the item in the schedule or bill. The problem has, however, always existed of where the change in the quantity from the estimated to the actual is such that it affects the contractor's method of working, perhaps a change to hand from machine work. It was expressly provided in the 5th edition of the ICE conditions clause 56(2) that the contractor is entitled to an adjustment of the rate if there is a change in quantities which makes the rate 'unreasonable or inapplicable', and there is no minimum percentage change required. This provision has been retained in the 6th edition of the ICE conditions.

In pricing a contract in this way a contractor has to estimate the quantity and cost of the labour, materials, and plant which will be required to execute the given quantity of work. Since the largest elements are labour and plant, the assessment of productivity is a vital part of the estimating process. This in turn is closely related to the physical conditions under which the work will be carried out – for example, the time of year – and to the possibility of carrying out the work in a planned way with a reasonable degree of continuity – for example, drawings arriving on site well in advance of the commencement of construction of the work to which they relate. The importance of these points will be referred to again when discussing variations and claims.

As regards specialist subcontractors' work, these items are made the subject of prime cost or provisional sums. An amount is included by the employer in the bill which represents his best estimate of the cost of the item. When the subcontract is placed (after the main contract has been let) that sum is deleted and replaced by the amount of the subcontract. When tendering himself, the main contractor is only required to tender the margin he wants for handling the subcontractor, usually expressed as a percentage plus any sum he wants for attendance on the subcontractor, like providing scaffolding, storage, etc.

COST REIMBURSEMENT

With many industrial projects today, speed in getting work carried out is   *95* regarded as more vital than lowest initial capital cost. Moreover, apparent cost advantages at tendering stage may be lost by the time final settlement is reached on the payment of claims. On the other hand, simple cost reimbursement provides no incentive to the contractor to minimize costs, nor any penalty should he fail. Indeed the reverse is true. Most contractors in fact dislike straight cost plus because of the inefficiencies which it may breed within their own company. Costs can so easily be charged to cost-plus jobs if no other home can be found for them!

Various types of incentive, target cost or cooperative forms of contract have been devised, therefore, as a means of combining the flexibility and speed associated with cost reimbursement with a strong measure of cost discipline and an incentive to efficiency and economy. All these forms of contract have certain features in common:

1 The principle of design and construction in parallel as opposed to in series.
2 The early establishment of a target estimate either as a definite sum or on civil or building work as rates in an approximate bill of quantities, against which the work can be remeasured.
3 The recording of the actual costs incurred and their comparison with the final target cost. This is the original target cost adjusted to take account of authorized variations.
4 The sharing between employer and contractor of the difference between 2 and 3.
5 The payment of a management fee in addition to cost which may either be part of the comparison or paid quite separately as a lump sum or a percentage of the target estimate.

How the final contract price is arrived at under the conventional, and the target or incentive form of contract, can best be illustrated by the comparison in Figure 6.1.

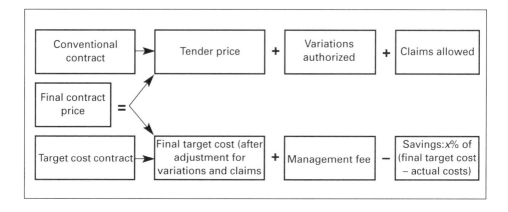

Figure 6.1 Final price comparison between conventional and target price contracts

Two points need particular attention at the negotiating stage. First, the over-run, if any, above a defined ceiling should be borne wholly by the contractor. This ceiling may be the target itself or more likely the target plus a certain margin, the extent of which will reflect the unknowns inherent in the contract. Secondly, in the assessment of the target cost it is essential that the target should be built up from the component elements of labour, materials, plant, etc., which the contractor can be expected to use on the job, and has regard to the construction or manufacturing methods which it is anticipated that the contractor will adopt. It is not just a question of selecting 'average' competitive rates, but of seeing that they are tailored to the job in question and reflect its particular circumstances. The target must, however, contain a contingency margin which is sufficient to ensure that, provided the contractor uses proper efficiency, the target remains at all times credible to beat. The aim should be to set a target which ought to be beaten by a low margin, say 10 per cent.

If time is particularly vital, it is possible to build in an additional incentive by varying the share of the savings accruing to the contractor according to the extent to which the contract is completed early or late. This may be done as under:

Period in weeks by which contract is finished before or after target completion date	Contractor's % share of savings
−6	90
−4	75
−2	60
0	50
+2	35
+4	20
+6	nil

With this type of scheme, while the contractor is given an incentive to complete early, he is at the same time encouraged to achieve that result by greater efficiency and productivity, rather than by excessive overtime.

The target method is not, however, suitable in all cases where time is vital. Sometimes, because information is lacking, it may not be possible to establish the target, and it may be necessary to place the contract initially on a cost reimbursement basis with the intention of firming up the price into a lump sum at a later date. Also, to administer a target cost contract effectively imposes a substantial burden on the employer and may require the services of outside quantity surveyors, thus pushing up the total cost by the amount of their fees. This applies with certain contracts for complex chemical plants. In this type of case the contract price may have to be broken down and dealt with as set out below.

Design

This is usually paid for on a man-time basis, the unit of time – hour, day, week,   *97* month, or even year – being selected to suit the individual contract. To the actual wages or salaries of the draughtsmen or engineers the contractor will add his designer's overhead. The following points need watching when considering these rates:

1 In respect of which classes of staff are they payable? This may be only actual engineers or draughtsmen or may extend through bills of material clerks to clerks, typists, and the like. Obviously this alters substantially the allowance for overheads; the smaller the chargeable base the higher the overhead.

2 Are the overheads included in the rates the whole of the company's overheads, or only those related to design? Practice differs on this according to whether the firm's normal selling unit is design time or not. If it is, then normally all overheads (other than possibly those relating purely to construction or procurement) will be charged against design.

3 The above two points have a tremendous effect on the overhead as a percentage. The swing can be as much as from 75 to 300 per cent.

4 Do the rates include:

   (a) Overtime?
   (b) Travelling and subsistence?
   (c) Telex, cables, and telephone calls?
   (d) Printing and reproduction costs?

   Or are these chargeable at net cost?

5 Do the same rates apply to subcontract design?

6 The rates may be expressed as so many pence or pounds per time unit, in which event they are usually based on an average of the salaries of the designers expected to be employed or as the actual wages plus percentage.

Obviously from the employer's point of view the more elements which can be properly made the subject of lump sums the better; particularly if the job is going out to competition. It is extremely difficult to compare either percentages or hourly rates; percentages because these have no validity by themselves but only when related to a base, and it cannot be assumed that the base will be the same for all firms; hourly rates because these have no validity unless one is in a position to assess the real value to be placed on the work which will be turned out in an hour, and quite simply one is not.

Thus firm A may offer design at £25 an hour, firm B at £30 an hour. But by themselves these figures mean nothing. Firm A may take 50 000 man-hours and produce a design which costs £4 m to build. Firm B may take only 35 000 man-hours and their scheme result in a final price of £3.7 m. The same sort of reasoning applies to labour rates for construction or erection work.

Procurement

This is usually paid for as a percentage of the value of materials purchased after deduction of trade but not cash discounts. It includes purchasing, expediting, and inspection. Again one needs to check that travel and subsistence, which may be high, are included.

Materials

Net price after deduction of trade but not cash discounts. The total value of discounts can be very substantial, particularly on items such as motors, valves, pipework, and so on, and should not be regarded as the estimator's contingency.

Site supervision, UK contracts

This may be negotiated as a lump sum, or a weekly rate. It will include:

1 Salaries, allowances, and charges, National Health Insurance – for example, for site supervisory staff.
2 Site huttage.
3 General services – for example, telephone, lighting.
4 General site transport.
5 Consumables.
6 Canteen.

Erection labour, UK contracts

Charges for erection labour on a per hour basis will normally include:

1 Wages and allowances – for example, subsistence and radius allowance, condition money, etc.
2 Bonus.
3 National Health Insurance, holiday with pay, redundancy fund payment, etc.
4 Common law insurance.
5 Hand tools.

Care needs to be taken in dealing with the non-productive element of overtime. This will affect only a small proportion of the overhead charges related to wages.

Site supervision overseas

On overseas contracts the indirect charges for supervisory staff may easily amount to 150–200 per cent of the person's payroll costs. Such charges may include:

1 Provision of accommodation, its maintenance and services costs, such as charges for electricity and water which are often substantially higher than in the UK.
2 A car and its running/maintenance costs. Although, depending on the

territory, petrol may be cheaper than in the UK, maintenance and depreciation may be very high due to unfavourable climatic conditions and the poor state of the roads.

3 Food allowance.

4 Air fares to and from the UK.

Practice on housing and food varies both from company to company and according to the size of the supervisory team.

On projects involving only a small team some firms pay a fixed allowance per day leaving it to the person to find his own accommodation and food. This is often preferred by the supervisory staff since it leaves them free to choose their own standard of living and sometimes to form local 'liaisons'. It does, however, weaken the company's control and may lead to staff living and behaving in a manner which lowers the firm's reputation.

With larger contracts it would be normal for the company either to set up a camp containing shopping, laundering and recreational facilities in addition to the accommodation or select itself the accommodation for its staff according to their grades. In remote areas or where there is no suitable expatriate type accommodation, there is no alternative and the company must totally establish its own facilities, often including drinking water, sewerage, catering facilities, cottage hospital, etc.

A further complication is caused on long-term contracts by the need to offer at least senior staff married contracts. There are then the problems of children's education, either paying fees for a local English/American school if there is one or, if not, providing a school with a teacher for juniors and paying at least part of boarding school fees for older children. While bachelors can be accommodated in flats or barrack-type blocks on site, families need houses. If suitable ones do not exist locally then prefabricated ones, air-conditioned and complete with all services, must be provided. Shopping and medical and recreational facilities will need to be expanded to cater for the needs of spouses and children or additional allowances paid to allow use to be made by families of local facilities which are normally expensive. Air fares to the UK for mid-term leave and for children at boarding school for at least one holiday per year with parents need to be included.

Finally if the overseas territory imposes income tax there may be the vexed question of taxation to be considered, and the following issues will arise:

1 Is there a double taxation convention between the overseas territory and the UK? If so what are its terms?

2 On what basis will the individual be charged tax in the overseas territory – on his living allowance only or total earnings as assessed by the local tax authorities?

3 Does an exit visa from the territory depend on the issue of a tax clearance certificate?

100 Although firms often take the line that while giving general answers an individual's tax affairs are his own business, they inevitably get drawn into the problem since the individual who goes to work overseas is only interested in the net remuneration package.

To the extent that a contractor is able to utilize locally recruited administrative and professional staff then the costs of supervision will necessarily be reduced by the allowances for housing, accommodation, air fares, etc., although in territories in which such staff of an appropriate calibre are available base salaries are not likely to differ widely from those in the UK. Depending, however, on the nationality of such staff, problems may arise in terms of differences in social and religious habits and customs and these will be accentuated if both the expatriate and local staff are required, because of the site's isolation, to live as well as work together.

Overseas erection and construction labour

On overseas contracts construction and erection labour will be either local or recruited from third national countries: for example, in the Gulf States and Saudi Arabia, labour including skilled tradesmen will come from either India, Pakistan or the Philippines. Different considerations, all of which affect pricing, apply to the employment of local as opposed to third national labour and may briefly be summarized as follows:

Third national labour

1 Recruited through a labour contractor in the country of origin on a one- or two-year contract.
2 Trade testing normally carried out in country of origin.
3 Payment includes recruitment fee and return air fare.
4 Wages are generally subject to control of the government of origin.
5 Accommodation and food must be provided.
6 Work permits and visas are usually restricted to employment by the contractor and the person must return to his country of origin on termination of his contract.

In practice at the time of writing the employment of third nationals on the above basis has had the effect of largely protecting the contractor against escalation or labour disturbances but has also meant that he lacks flexibility in being able to hire and fire. Labour costs become in effect semi-fixed instead of a variable, which could have a serious impact if the work programme becomes subject to changes or delays outside the contractor's control. Productivity becomes largely a function of the number of persons on the site relative to the available quantity of work.

Local labour.   In general it is not recommended that contractors working overseas should directly employ local construction/erection labour for the following reasons:

1 Local labour laws which can be tough in their theoretical provisions will be strictly enforced against an expatriate contractor and complying with them to the letter in terms of working hours, redundancy payments, bonuses, etc. will be expensive. Local contractors however have a way of getting round these provisions or at least minimizing their cost impact.
2 Local working and amenity practices will be unfamiliar to the expatriate contractor and even when he does become aware of them they will be difficult for him to apply, which again will cost the contractor money.
3 Trade testing and qualifications may not exist.
4 The problem of language.
5 Local contractors will already have an established network of relationships with government and union officials, client's inspectors, etc. and also with sources of reliable labour which an expatriate firm on its own will never achieve.

The only circumstances under which an expatriate firm can successfully employ any quantity of local labour is if it has formed a joint venture with an established local contractor and matters related to the employment of local labour and dealing with local officialdom are made the responsibility of the local partner who is obliged therefore to take an active interest in the partnership.

Constructional plant

There will normally be a schedule of weekly hire rates. The following points need covering:

1 Do the rates include any element of profit?
2 Are they tied to a number of hours?
3 Do they include for drivers?
4 Do they include fuel, lubricants, spares, maintenance? There is a danger of paying twice.
5 Do they include charges for transport to and from site? These are often heavy.
6 Where the plant belongs to the contractor what allowance has been made for depreciation and what residual value has been assumed?

On overseas projects, unless exemption is granted by the government, a problem may arise regarding import duties. First, even though the plant is only being imported temporarily, duty may be payable on certain types of plant or on particular makes in order to protect local industry or exclusive dealer arrangements. Even if this is not the case, duty or a bond in lieu may have to be deposited (which is in theory returnable on that item of plant being re-exported but is forfeit if the plant is sold in that country). Unfortunately, in practice temporary importation procedures tend to be so drawn-out that in desperation to get moving the contractor will pay the import duty and hope to recover it. The actual practice of temporary importation in the territory in question needs to be carefully examined both by the contractor and by the employer's negotiator.

Management overheads and profit

These are preferably treated as a lump sum which can be made the subject of competitive tender. Sometimes, depending on the information available, it may be possible to include in this lump sum the design element and even perhaps the site supervision, leaving only the direct materials, subcontract, and labour costs to be either reimbursable or negotiated during the contract period.

MANAGEMENT CONTRACTING

Management contracting covers a number of possible contractual arrangements between client and contractor. These are discussed in a useful guide to the whole subject, *Management Contracting*, published by the Construction Industry Research and Information Association (Report number 100). There is also a standard form of project management contract, prepared by Fédération Internationale des Ingénieurs-Conseils, Lausanne (FIDIC) and also one prepared by the Joint Contracts Tribunal for the Building Industry (JCT).

Management contractor – agent or principal?

The question is whether the management contractor, when entering into contracts with others for supplying equipment or services, is doing so as an agent for and on behalf of the client or as a principal. To put the matter another way, who takes the risk of the supplier's default, and who is ultimately liable to the supplier for payment – the client or the management contractor?

Responsibility for results

The issue here is whether the management contractor is basically providing professional services and is liable only for his own negligence, or is acting as a contractor responsible for the achievement of an end result.

The problem is that what the employer is really purchasing from the management contractor is the benefit of his skills in contract administration and coordination. While it is reasonable that he should be made strictly liable for any defects in the works or any delay to their completion which result from his failure to fulfil those duties, he cannot sensibly be held responsible for a fault by a subcontractor (usually referred to as a 'works contractor') which the management contractor could not prevent. Any attempt to make him so responsible would negate the concept of management contracting.

If, in addition to his responsibilities for contract administration and co-ordination, the management contractor is made responsible for design, then such responsibility should carry with it the strict liability of a contractor – not the more restricted liability of a consulting engineer or architect for professional negligence.

Back-to-back agreements

The extent to which it is practical for the management contractor to enter into back-to-back agreements with the subcontractors and suppliers will depend in part on the nature of the works and in part on the willingness of the client to pay an acceptable level of profit. The more integrated the plant, the more difficult it will be to break into major packages and only if it can be packaged in that way can the management contractor reasonably expect to obtain back-to-back cover. As an example, an electrical supply system could be purchased as separate units (switchgear, transformers, cables, motors, etc.) and be coordinated by the management contractor. Alternatively it could be purchased as a total system from one subcontractor. If there is one system subcontractor, then he can be expected to accept broadly the same terms for payment and warranty liability as the management contractor, whose risk is then mainly limited to the interface risk between the electrical subcontract package and the other subcontract packages (mechanical, building and civil works, etc.).

If, however, the management contractor has to place purchase orders for individual items himself, then there is bound to be a gap between his contract conditions with the client and those which he can place on the supplier (for example, the supplier is only likely to accept a 12-months' warranty period ex-works or FOB whereas the management contractor's own liability to the client for warranty may not start until the acceptance of the total project, which could be many months or even years later).

Obviously this will not be a problem for the management contractor if he is acting as agent and buying for and on behalf of the client, since it is assumed that his only liabilities for warranties will be co-extensive with those he obtains from the suppliers. But it does become a major issue if he is buying as principal and is giving his own overall warranty. Naturally it has to be someone's problem and in the agent case it is that of the client. He can finish up with as many different warranty periods as there are suppliers, and most of these warranties will have expired before the project is commissioned. But the difference in the management contractor's risk is, or should be, reflected in his fees.

There is often a halfway house, where the management contractor does not accept the responsibility for ensuring the making good of defects or other defaults by a works contractor but has a right to recover the costs from the employer if, in the event, he cannot recover these from the defaulting works contractor and the management contractor has not himself been to blame. This is essentially the position under the JCT form of contract.

The route for payments

Do payments to the subcontractors and suppliers pass through the management contractor's books, or do they go direct from the client? If they go through the management contractor he will be able to increase his profits by taking advantage of the period of time for which he can hold payments received from the client before passing them on to the supplier or subcontractor. As an example, if it is assumed that the period of retention is 30 days, and if payments average £2 000 000 a month over a year, then with short-term interest rates at 1 per cent the management contractor can add £20 000 interest to his earnings. At the same time, unless he has subcontractors and suppliers on 'pay when paid' terms, he does have the ultimate contractual liability to them for payment.

If the payments do not pass through the management contractor's books, and he only certifies the amounts which are due to subcontractors and suppliers, then this removes from him both the opportunity to increase his profits and his potential liability for any default in payment by the client.

TERMS OF PAYMENT

Policy considerations

Terms of payment are a matter on which the commercial/technical and financial sides of the employer's business may find themselves pulling in opposite directions. The employer may attain the best commercial and technical result if he offers to the tenderers terms of payment which, while providing the employer with reasonable contractual safeguards, impose the minimum strain on the contractor's financial resources. By so doing the employer will:

1 Avoid having to restrict the tender list to large firms possessing the resources to finance the contract, whose overheads and prices will be higher than those of smaller companies. (This assumes of course that such smaller companies are otherwise technically and commercially competent to carry out the work.)
2 Ensure that the tenderers do not have to inflate their tender prices by financing charges. In many instances the rate of interest which the contractor has to pay when borrowing will be higher than that paid by the employer.
3 Give encouragement to, and be able to take advantage of, firms possessing technical initiative who would otherwise be held back from expanding by lack of liquid cash.
4 Minimize the risk of being saddled with a contractor who has insufficient cash with which to carry out the contract and of having, therefore, either to support the contractor financially or terminate the contract.

On the other hand, to offer such terms means that the employer has to finance the work in progress and tie up his own capital in advance of obtaining any return on his investment. Particularly with a project such as a new factory or power plant, it would impose the least strain on the employer's financial resources if he could avoid having to pay anything at all until the project is earning money, and make the payments wholly out of revenue. With very major contracts of this type overseas, particularly in the underdeveloped countries, buying on credit in this way is not a matter of choice but of necessity. The authorities or companies *105* concerned are not in a position to do anything else. As usual, however, the price which a customer pays for credit is high. Even with preferentially low interest rates for exports, the cost to the purchaser of the financing charges on a long-term credit contract may easily amount to a third of the 'cash' selling price.

The factors related to cash flow and contract risk/profitability on both home and international contracts were analysed by Roland B. Neo in *International Construction Contracting* (1976). However, only construction contracts under which payment is related broadly to the value of work carried out were considered and on overseas contracts the effect of having to provide bonds cashable by the purchaser on demand was not taken into account, a factor which seriously diminishes the author's conclusions on risk assessment.

On civil engineering and building contracts carried out in the UK either under the ICE or JCT forms or some major customer's adaptation of these, the contractor is paid monthly for the value of work done and materials delivered to site for incorporation into the permanent works in the preceding month, less a percentage for retention money: the relationship of the contractor's expenditure related to payments received is broadly illustrated in Figure 6.2. The shape of the expenditure curve will be affected by the labour/material ratio and the proportion of the work to be undertaken by nominated subcontractors. The higher the ratio of labour to material the steeper the expenditure curve as the less the contractor will be able to benefit from delaying payment to suppliers. Equally the higher the proportion of nominated suppliers and subcontractors who can demand payment be made to them of the amount certified by the engineer/architect within x days of certification, again the less room the main contractor has to delay payment.

Roland Neo mentions but does not take account of two other actions which a main contractor can take to improve cash flow: over-measurement in the early months of the contract; and front-end loading by artificially increasing the value of the rates for the work to be carried out early. These practices are common both in the UK and more especially overseas and, unless carried to excess, the engineer or quantity surveyor will often turn a blind eye to them as being a matter of custom and practice. Indeed during a time of high or sharply rising inflation, if the contract is subject to contract price adjustment they can work to the contractor's disadvantage by diminishing the amount of escalation recovered relative to that incurred.

The other factor which may materially affect cash flow is the extent of variation orders issued by the architect/engineer which are not covered by rates and prices contained within bills of quantity and the time taken to get such rates and prices agreed. Although payment for such variations will normally be made on interim certificates on a provisional basis, the amount certified will inevitably be conservative.

But the major factors in determining the cost to the contractor of financing the contract are:

1 Time between execution of work and the receipt of payment as the contract proceeds.

2 Time taken to settle the final account and release the final portion of the retention money.

The example in Figure 6.2 is based on the following assumptions:

1 50 per cent of the contractor's expenditure relates to staff, labour and plant which must be paid for in the month in which it is incurred.
2 20 per cent is represented by the contractor's own subcontractors on 90-day credit.
3 30 per cent is represented by nominated suppliers/subcontractors on a 30-day credit.
4 Certificates are issued by the engineer within 14 days of the end of the month in which the work is carried out and payment is made by the employer 30 days later.
5 Retention is 10 per cent, 5 per cent to be released on the issue of the certificate of practical completion and 5 per cent at the end of the 12-months' defects liability period. In practice the final account is not settled until 6 months after the end of the contract and includes settlement of claims equal to 5 per cent of the contractor's costs.
6 The contract work is substantially carried out according to programme.

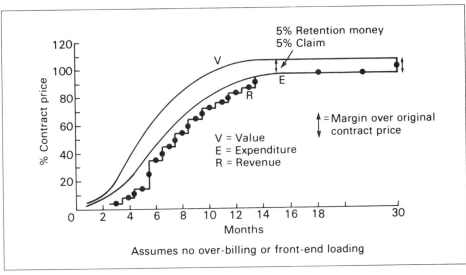

Figure 6.2 Contractor's expenditure in relation to payments received

It will be seen that the contract is funded by the contractor to the extent of 16.6 per cent of the contract sum for one year which at 10 per cent p.a. interest represents an interest charge of about 1.7 per cent against profit. Had completion of the contract been seriously delayed, then the position would have been significantly worse since the contractor's preliminaries would have continued at broadly the same rate regardless of progress and the same would to an extent apply to plant costs.

On overseas construction contracts for which the contractor can expect to receive a down payment of say 10 per cent of the contract price then it might be expected that the amount of 'capital lock-up', to use Neo's term, would be less; indeed that is his suggestion. Whether, however, this is the case in practice will depend on the following factors:

1 The amount of the contractor's initial expense for such items as ECGD premiums, bonding charges and agents' fees which are payable on contract signature. These may easily amount to 10 per cent of the contract price.
2 Mobilization costs in the overseas territory (e.g. setting up the site establishment, importation of plant, and whether these are paid as a separate item from the down payment), are deemed to be covered by the down payment or amortized over the billed rates and recovered pro rata to progress. Only if they are paid as a separate item is the contractor's cash flow likely to be other than negative particularly on any contract such as road construction which is plant-intensive.
3 Delays in certification and payment either deliberate or the result of bureaucratic inefficiency. This applies especially to payments for escalation or variations. Certification delays may be mitigated if the contract is being supervised by international consultants but those for payment can usually only be reduced by personal attention being given to each person in the chain of required signatures to ensure that your piece of paper is moved ahead of others.
4 Delays in the release of retention monies usually due to the unwillingness of overseas clients to take the responsibility of releasing their hold over the contractor.

Although not directly affecting the cash flow situation of the individual contract, the contractor's financial position as a whole will be materially influenced by any on-demand bonds which he is required to put up under the terms of the overseas contract. The value of these will be regarded by his bank as liabilities when deciding on the extent of the facilities they are prepared to make available to him. A contract of say £20 million on which the amount of bonding averaged 15 per cent could therefore reduce the contractor's overdraft limit by £3 million.

Typical revenue and expenditure curves for a medium-sized civil engineering contract overseas are given in Figure 6.3. It will be seen that the interest charges against profit amount to 35 per cent, again assuming an interest rate of 15 per cent. The periods for certification and payment have, however, been increased to 30 and 60 days respectively.

For plant and equipment contracts it has been traditional within the UK for payments only to be made against the value of materials delivered to site, so that the burden of the financing costs during manufacture has fallen entirely on the contractor. Continental practice has, however, for a long time been to make payments in stages during manufacture and this practice appears to be spreading within the UK.

In the author's view objection can reasonably be taken to the principle of

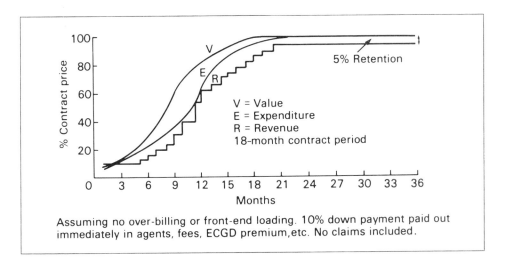

Figure 6.3   Revenue and expenditure curves for overseas contract

expecting the contractor wholly to finance the work either up to delivery or to the commencement of site erection. First, it imposes on many companies a substantial and continuing strain on their cash flow position. This is particularly so when the company is seeking to expand or to take contracts of longer duration. Secondly, it is against the national interest in that it puts such firms at a disadvantage when competing against continental companies who would normally expect in their domestic market to be paid as much as 30 per cent of the contract price with order. Clearly such companies do not have to include within their overheads for the financing of work in progress; their money is turned over faster, capital employed is reduced, and they can invest more, for example, in development and new machinery. These are formidable advantages.

So far as retentions are concerned, the purchaser is obviously sensible to withhold an appropriate percentage of the purchase price until he is satisfied that the plant is working properly and has met its guarantees. Provided that the retention moneys are considered in this way and not as a form of finance for the purchaser then the contractor can have no reasonable objection to them.

To sum up, provided the employer can possibly afford to do so he is likely to get the best bargain if he, rather than the contractor, largely finances the contract. By so doing he will also be acting in the national interest and indirectly therefore in his own, by assisting British companies to compete abroad on level terms.

Contractual safeguards

In order to safeguard the interests of both parties the contract should:

1   Define precisely the events against which payment becomes due.
2   Relate those events to the achievement of some particular objective.

3 State the amount due at each stage or provide a mechanism by which such amount can be determined.
4 Establish a time limit within which payment must be made.
5 Provide the contractor with an effective remedy should the employer default in payment.
6 Provide the employer with means by which he can obtain or recover the value of payments made before completion should the contractor default and be unable to complete.

Definition of events (1 and 2)

Where the contract includes for the issue by the nominated engineer of certificates, then provided the criteria for these have been properly established no problem should arise unless for any reason, other than the contractor's default, the issue of a certificate is delayed. To cover this possibility two provisions are required:

1 The certificate must be issued within a stated time of an application which the contractor was entitled to make.
2 If issue of the certificate is delayed because the event itself is delayed, that is guarantee tests cannot be held because the employer's other work is not ready, then after a suitable time interval the contractor must become entitled to the payment. The same applies in relation to delayed delivery because of non-readiness of the employer to receive the goods.

If, however, entitlement to payment is to be determined solely by reference to an event, for example delivery of the goods FOB, together with relevant shipping documents, then it is important if misunderstandings are to be avoided to ensure that the event is clearly described and that it is kept simple.

It is desirable to avoid multiple requirements wherever possible, since it will often be found in practice that one of them takes much longer to comply with than the others.

From the employer's point of view it is inadvisable for payment to be related solely to time, for example six months after placing the order, unless this is qualified by a requirement as to the progress which must also have been achieved. This can be done very simply by providing that the engineer must be satisfied that progress is to programme, or, if not, then he can reduce the amount to be paid.

Alternatively, if the work is being controlled through network analysis, values can be allocated to certain key activities, and the contract can provide that payment of these sums will be made as those activities are completed. Properly planned, the linking together of payment and programme in this way can be most effective.

A problem which can arise on the sums due on commercial operation or take-over is that often the contractor has carried out all but a small amount of the work involved but, because there is still some work outstanding, the engineer is unwilling to issue his certificate, so that retention money to the value of very many times the outstanding work continues to be withheld. Provided what has still to be done does not significantly affect the operation of the works, there is no reason why the engineer should not issue the certificate with an appropriate endorsement and release the retention money, apart from whatever he considers appropriate to retain in order to ensure satisfactory completion of the outstanding work. This is specifically provided for in Model Form *A* conditions (clause 34(ii)).

Determination of amount due (3)

Only rarely will the contract state a definite sum to be paid at the various stages of completion; usually it will refer only to percentages, for example:

10   per cent with order.
80   per cent on delivery.
 5   per cent on take over.
 5   per cent on final acceptance.

As with any percentage, it is important that no ambiguity should arise as to the base to which it relates. On supply and erection contracts there are broadly two possibilities:

1   All percentages relate to the contract price as a whole.
2   The percentages due on delivery are calculated on the contract value of the materials delivered (excluding therefore the erection and commissioning element of the price), and those elements are paid for separately as the work is carried out. In that event the 80 per cent payment might be expressed in the contract as 80 per cent of the value of materials delivered to and work executed on site (see, for example, condition 31(ii) of the Model Form *A* conditions).

The contract should also clearly establish the method of payment for variations and price escalation.

Variations

It is suggested that variations should be paid without any down payment and that the down payment is recovered therefore only against the original value of the contract. Retention money, however, would normally be deducted from the value of the variations executed.

Escalation

If the contract is subject to contract price adjustment then it is essential to establish the data necessary for the calculation of the amount of escalation due on the variation, unless for simplicity the price for the variation can be settled on a   *111* fixed price basis. Payment for escalation, it is proposed, should be made with each monthly certificate at 100 per cent of the value properly claimed. There seems no justification for involving escalation payments with either the recovery of any down payment or percentage deductions for retention.

Care, however, needs to be taken in the contract drafting, particularly in respect of the use of the term 'contract price'. If the contract price is defined as 'the sum named in the contract subject to such additions thereto or deductions therefrom as may be made under any provisions of the contract' and the term contract price is then used in the payments clause without qualification, it could be argued that both down payment and retention provisions apply to variations and escalation alike. It is preferable to set out separately the payment terms for both these items so that no ambiguity can arise. In fact the ICE and JCT conditions retention is withheld from payments made for escalation and the argument for doing this in relation to the ICE conditions is that the contractual entitlement to any payment for escalation is derived from the payments clause 60(2) and the amounts certified by the engineer under this clause are subject to retention.

Time limit for payment (4 and 5)

No one likes paying bills before they are obliged to do so. The accountants for big companies have been quick to see the money which can be saved by not paying their creditors until the last day for payment (unless a discount for cash has been offered). The short-term investment of daily cash balances can make a useful contribution to company profits. The administrative procedures of large organizations, both public and private, can of themselves impose substantial delays in the money actually being paid. Main contractors, to protect their own position, have developed the habit of only paying subcontractors on 'as and when' terms, that is when they themselves have been paid by the employer.

All this emphasizes the need for the contract conditions to lay down a clear time limit within which payment should be made, which is practical in the circumstances of the contract. It is better to lay down a rather longer time initially, which stands a reasonable chance of being kept, than to include the standard 28-day clause knowing that it is unlikely to be honoured and to be faced with the inevitable bickering which follows.

Should payment not be made within the prescribed time, the contractor's normal remedy (which in practice is seldom applied) is to claim interest, or, in an extreme case, to stop work.

Recovery of payments made (6)

Where payments are made in advance of delivery to site the two rights which an employer will usually seek to have included are:

1 A bond to be lodged for not less than the amount of the down payment. The making of the payment and the lodging of the bond should take place at the same time, and the contractor should check that the time limits for doing

both are the same. Cases have been known in which the time for lodging the bond ran from acceptance of the contractor's tender, while the time for making the down payment ran from the signature of the formal contract.

2   That where progress payments are made during manufacture:

   (a) plant to the value of the payment made is identified, becomes the property of the purchaser and is marked as such;
   (b) such plant remains, however, at the sole risk of the contractor and is insured by him accordingly.

Retention money

Reference has already been made to the principle that retention moneys should be considered by the employer as a contractual safeguard, not as a cheap form of finance. The fixing of the level of retention money should take this into account so that no higher amount is retained than is reasonably necessary. Where the works are completed and taken over in sections these retention moneys should be released on a sectional basis.

The higher cost to the contractor of retention moneys on many plant contracts lies in the 5 or 10 per cent retained during the defects liability period.

It is to the contractor's advantage, therefore, to press strongly for the release of the final retention after take over against, if necessary, a bank guarantee. Nor is it considered that the employer's contractual interests would be harmed by such action.

REFERENCES AND FURTHER READING

Cox, P. A. (ed.), *Civil Engineering Project Procedure in the EC*, Thomas Telford, London, 1991.

Marsh, P. D. V., *Contract Negotiation Handbook*, 2nd edn, Gower, Aldershot, 1984.

Marsh, P. D. V., *Contracting for Engineering and Construction Projects*, 3rd edn, Gower, Aldershot, 1988.

Morgan, M. O'C. and Roulston, F. R., *The Foundations of Engineering Contracts*, Spon, London, 1989.

Neo, Roland B., *International Construction Contracting*, Gower, Epping, 1976.

Smith, N. J. and Wearne, S. H., *Construction Contract Arrangements in EC Countries*, European Construction Institute, Loughborough, 1993.

Stallworthy, E. A. and Kharbanda, O. P., *Guide to Project Implementation*, Institution of Chemical Engineers, London, 1986.

Wearne, S. H., 'Engineering contracts' in Dennis Lock (ed), *Handbook of Engineering Management*, 2nd edn, Butterworth-Heinemann, Oxford, 1993.

7 Contract Administration

Peter Marsh

This chapter deals briefly with two aspects of contract administration, namely, contract variations and the arbitration of disputes.

VARIATIONS IN PRICE AND TIME

Variations may be described, not unfairly, as the cancer of contracting. In quantity their cumulative effect can operate to destroy the best of contracts: the habit of ordering them is in itself a disease. What causes this disease? The causes are many but the principal ones may be summarized as follows:

1 *Inadequate allowance for thinking time.* It is distressing but true that many managements are still not convinced that progress is being made unless holes are being dug on site or plant manufactured.
2 *Inadequate specifications.* One finds a great reluctance amongst people to be completely specific as to what they require, as to the services which the employer will himself provide or the actual conditions under which the work will be carried out.
3 *Insufficient attention paid* as to whether what the tenderer is offering is in fact precisely what the purchaser wants to buy. The tendency to say 'That's a matter of detail we can sort out later.'
4 *Lack of discipline.* In the matter of variations it is often far easier to say 'Yes, while we are about it we might as well have that done' than to say firmly 'No, it's not necessary.'
5 *Improvements to avoid obsolescence.* With the rapid rate of technical change taking place today any major plant is likely to be out of date in some respects long before it is completed. There is always the temptation to try to avoid this by incorporating improvements in the design.
6 *Genuinely unforeseeable circumstances.* It would be idle to pretend that no variation is ever justified. There will be times when conditions do arise when it is essential to vary the works – for instance, the existence of unsuspected drains or cables which have to be diverted.

What is often not fully appreciated is the effect which even quite a simple change of specification can have on a contractor. This may involve him in:

1 Design work which because of the change is now abortive.
2 Additional design work including studying the consequential effect of the variation on a number of drawings.
3 Cancellation of, or modification to, orders already placed on his own works or on outside suppliers.
4 The placing of new orders.
5 Delay and/or rephasing of the manufacturing programme to accommodate the variation.
6 Delay in delivery of material to site due to action under 3 above.
7 Rephasing of site works or concentration of work into a shorter period with consequent additional overtime costs and loss of productivity.
8 Extending the period to the contract.

It follows from the above list that unless the variation is ordered very early indeed

Additions	Deductions
1 Works or bought-out cost of the new item.	Works or bought-out cost of the item to be replaced
2 Percentage for overheads and profit related to works or bought-out costs.	Percentage for overheads and profit related to works or bought-out costs.
3 Man-hour costs for installation of new item.	Man-hour costs for installation of the item to be replaced.
4 Percentage overheads and profit related to installation costs.	Percentage overheads and profit related to the installation costs.
5 Charges for additional design work including overheads and profit necessary to incorporate new item.	Charges for any detailed design work which will no longer be required including related overheads and profit.
6 Design, labour, and material costs and related overheads and profit on any consequential modifications or alterations to the remainder of the plant, including study of drawings to determine whether any such are necessary.	
7 Cancellation charges payable to outside supplier or costs of any work actually carried out in contractor's works.	

Figure 7.1 Balancing cost factors of a contract variation

Ignoring possible effects on timescale, the listings compare factors which are taken into account when considering the costs of a variation which requires that one or more items of equipment are to be deleted from the specification and replaced by other items.

in the contract, the assessment of the effect of the variation either in terms of cost or time is not easy. Consider first the question of the assessment of the change in the contract price for a plant due, say, to the deletion from the specification of one item and the substitution of another.

The listing in Figure 7.1 represents the direct financial balance between the item originally included and that now ordered as a variation. It takes no account of the factor of time. Taken in isolation this is correct, unless the single variation itself is so significant that it does have an immediate effect on the overall programme. It also takes no account of the double administrative cost effect on the contractor of having to go through the same operation twice. The contractor's staff, whose services are recovered for under the estimate as a percentage of prime cost, will have been involved to some extent on the item already in estimating and procurement, but under this listing the contractor would recover for such services only once for the new item. Again, if it is only one item, few contractors would seriously quarrel with this, accepting it as one of the hazards of contracting. The trouble starts when it is not one variation but a series of variations, when the programme is affected, and when the time spent by the contractor's head office staff starts to become totally disproportionate to the value of the contract. Under these circumstances the employer must expect that the contractor will seek to recover additionally for:

1 Abortive time spent by head office staff not otherwise directly charged to the contract.
2 Prolongation of the contract period on site – for example, hire of huts, supervisors' salaries.
3 Loss of productivity and overtime working due to changes in the programme.

It is easy enough to set down the basis on which single variations should be priced in the manner which has been done above. It is often, however, another matter actually to negotiate the alteration in price. The purchaser will be thinking the contractor is trying to take him for a ride, but may additionally be genuinely unappreciative of what trouble and cost his simple instruction has caused. He will also be acutely aware that he cannot get competitive quotations. The contractor may be anxious to recover some of the ground he lost in post-tender negotiations. Neither side is likely to be in the mood for concessions, but the purchaser will probably be in the weaker bargaining position.

Partially for this reason attempts are sometimes made to establish in advance the main tender rates on which variations can be calculated. It is possible to do this for civil engineering or building work or for structural steel or pipework, although the value of doing so seems questionable. This is because in putting forward his rates the contractor must make certain assumptions regarding the quantity and complexity of work which will be involved, the plant required, and so on, and as to whether it will be convenient to do the work in parallel with or as an extension of existing work of the same nature; or whether it will be something quite separate for which perhaps plant and a gang of people must be specially brought to site. For this reason, and also because it is difficult to take rates for the purpose only of pricing variations into account in deciding on the award of the contract, the tenderers have every incentive to assume the worst conditions and price accordingly.

In general, therefore, it would seem preferable from the purchaser's point of view, despite the difficulties involved, to negotiate when the occasion arises and on the facts of the particular variation without being tied in advance. The contractor may, however, press, for quite a different reason, for at least the overhead percentages and margins to be fixed and stated in the contract.

It is often assumed that contractors welcome variations in that they can use them to recoup any losses they may have made on the main contract or at least improve their overall rate of recovery on the job. While, as explained above, the contractor may be placed in a favourable negotiating position when it comes to settling a price for the variation, it has also been pointed out that the cumulative effect of a number of variations on his contract programme can be extremely serious and result in disruptions of work, loss of productivity and so on. These losses, while real, may often be difficult for him to quantify or to claim from the employer. In any event he is likely to be involved in protracted claims negotiations which are both time- and cost-consuming in themselves and may well be detrimental to his chances of obtaining further business from the employer concerned.

For this reason some contractors seek to put forward as part of their tender, rates or percentage charges for different classes of work which may be involved in handling variations – for example, design – which are deliberately so high as to be penal. In this way the contractor seeks to utilize the contract as a means of disciplining the employer's engineers.

While obviously such an arrangement can be open to abuse, there does seem considerable merit in any system of pricing which will bring home to those responsible for administering contracts the real cost involved in having frequent changes of mind. Accordingly a system of differential pricing for work as a variation as compared with the same work under the main contract seems justified. If as a result variations become a luxury which can be afforded but rarely, then so much the better. It might also help to avoid the other practice of including an allowance within the original tender for the 'messing about' which, from past and often bitter experience, the contractor knows that he is likely to receive with certain clients.

A vital factor in the successful control of variations is the timing of price negotiations. Only too often, because of the pressure for physical progress with the work and the complexities in assessing the price change, instructions are given to the contractor to make the change, with the alteration in price to be negotiated later.

Ideally the sequence of events should be:

1 Purchaser decides that a particular variation would be desirable.
2 Contractor is instructed to assess the effect of the proposed variation in terms of:

(a) price;
(b) time; and
(c) performance.

3 Contractor submits his proposals under the above three headings.
4 Purchaser decides whether he can afford the variation taking all factors into account.
5 If purchaser decides to proceed with the variation, then he negotiates amendments to price, time for completion and specification.
6 Purchaser issues formal variation order in writing, using a standard serially numbered form.
7 Contractor proceeds with the work.

This seems a long series of steps; the temptation is there to go straight ahead and tell the contractor to start work. Indeed there will be genuine emergencies when it is necessary to do just that and tidy up the paper work afterwards. But in doing so, not only is any possible negotiating advantage lost, but also any curb on the enthusiasm of the purchaser's staff to make variations is removed and financial control of the contract is made impossible. Except in the case of a real emergency it should be made difficult to make variations.

However, while it may be possible at the time to assess the direct effect of the individual variation on the contract price and time for completion, it is much more difficult to assess the indirect or consequential effect. With one variation this may be small, but as the number of variation orders grows so do the consequential effects increase, often at a much faster rate.

While therefore, ideally, one should treat each variation order separately and assess finally its effect on the contract price and time before it is issued, there are occasions when it is just not practicable to do this. In order to retain as much control as possible in these circumstances it may be necessary to divide the negotiation of variations into two stages:

1 The assessment of the direct effect of the variation.
2 The assessment of the consequential effect of the variation on the contract price and the overall time of completion.

Stage 1 should be completed for each variation order before it is issued. Stage 2 cannot be completed until the design has been finally frozen. At that point the cumulative effect of the variation orders can be reassessed and any necessary adjustments to the contract price and programme made. Obviously the earlier the design-freeze date, and so the final contract value and programme, can be established the better for both parties. What is vital, however, to do at the time is to record and agree with the contractor the facts on which the stage 2 negotiations will be based. There is no excuse for there not being accurate records of, for example, the time plant was on site and the periods during which it could not fully be utilized.

118   Not all variations relate to the physical content of the works. The employer may

wish either to speed up completion or to slow it down, or possibly to put the contract into suspense. Any such actions are bound to have a serious effect on the contract price.

The simplest case is probably trying to speed up completion. Time may be bought by:

1 Working additional overtime or at weekends.
2 Putting on an additional shift.
3 Offering suppliers or subcontractors a bonus to deliver or finish earlier.

By such methods small improvements can be obtained fairly easily. But above quite a low level the law of diminishing returns starts to operate and it becomes more and more expensive to purchase smaller and smaller improvements. Once a certain level has been passed the productivity value starts to drop rapidly, and on double shifting the productive effort may be 25 per cent or more below normal. Moreover, the longer one tries to continue with excessive overtime or double shifting, the lower the return one obtains for the increased expenditure.

As regards pricing, provided the make-up of the labour charges already included within the contract is known, this presents no real difficulty. For site work the make-up will normally comprise:

1 Basic wage which may in these days bear no relation at all to the so-called basic wage agreed nationally between the union and the employer's federation concerned.
2 Bonus often related to productivity.
3 Condition money which may cover such things as working in dirty conditions, wearing rubber boots, etc.
4 Subsistence allowance for people lodging away from home or radius allowance for those living within a certain distance from the site.
5 Travelling time.
6 Allowance for overtime. It is virtually impossible today to obtain site labour without a guarantee of a certain number of hours' overtime a week.
7 National Health Insurance, holidays with pay and common law insurance, all of which bear a direct relationship to wages costs.

To these the contractor will add his charges for supervision, small tools and consumables and other erection on-costs including normally a margin to cover his head-office erection department.

One important point to ensure, when negotiating an addition to cover for extra overtime, is that where such an addition is to be charged on a percentage basis, such percentage is charged only on those costs which are directly proportional to wages, or alternatively that the percentage is adjusted to take account of the non-variable items. Item 4 in the above list, for example, is a flat weekly charge which will not alter.

Slowing down a job is rather more difficult, in that it will involve the contractor being engaged for a longer time on the contract and will therefore tie up his *119* resources for a longer period, so reducing his potential earning capacity over that period. For this reason the contractor may reasonably claim under the following headings:

1 Charges for plant, huts, etc., retained on site for an extended time.
2 Salaries and overheads of supervisory staff so retained.
3 Some additional charge for wages costs due to less productive work.
4 Additional costs for any work which is now to be carried out under different and more arduous conditions, for example excavation to be carried out in the winter instead of the summer.
5 If the contract is on a fixed price basis an addition to cover:

(a) any increase likely to be met in the extended period;
(b) the proportionately more serious effect which increases occurring earlier in the contract period will have, over the allowance made for these when the estimate was prepared: for example, 40 per cent of the contract work may now be carried out after the date when a wages award will take effect, instead of the 25 per cent on which the estimate was based.

6 Additional interest charges due to retention moneys being outstanding for a longer period.

Where the contract is put into suspense, consideration will need to be given by the buyer to the following points:

1 Should the contractor's site organization plant, huts, etc., be removed from the site? Obviously, if all or any part of it remains, the contractor is going to want to be paid for it. On the other hand the costs of taking it away and then re-establishing it may also be heavy. The buyer must weigh up the advantages of each course, taking into account the likely period for the suspension.
2 Work partially completed on site must be properly protected; loose items not yet incorporated or built into the works must be identified, labelled or marked, and properly stored. If the contractor's organization is being removed from the site then the responsibility for such storage and safe custody will vest in the purchaser.
3 Items in course of manufacture or not yet despatched must be similarly treated. In this case, however, they should remain at the risk of the contractor; this needs making clear explicitly; also the buyer will want to make sure that the contractor has insured the items against all insurable risks.
4 The contractor will seek to ensure that he is not prejudiced by the suspension as regards the time when payments under the contract should be made. Thus if the contract provides for retention money to be released on completion, and completion is delayed as a result of the works being suspended, he will want to be paid the retention moneys relating to work

already executed not later than the date by which they would originally have been released. This is reasonable, and certain standard conditions of contract do make provision for this. It is also reasonable to make payments on account of work partially completed in the contractor's shops but not yet delivered or ready for delivery, provided that it has been identified as the purchaser's property. The buyer will want to make sure that such parts are correctly marked and so on, and that they are covered by all-risks insurance.

5   From the buyer's point of view it also seems reasonable that he should not as a result of the suspension lose the rights he may have in respect of any defects which may occur in the works after they have been finally completed. In other words, payment of retention moneys in respect of the partially completed job must be without prejudice to the defects liability period, which should only start to run after the actual completion of the job. Where, of course, equipment which suffers natural deterioration no matter what care is taken is stored for any period, this must be subject to the contractor's right to inspect and make good the results of any such deterioration at the buyer's expense.

Variations on overseas contracts

Variations, unless they are of a minor nature which can be accommodated within existing resources and the contract programme, are even more troublesome when the contract is being executed several thousand miles from the contractor's home base.

First, there is the problem that the design or planning for the variation may have to be referred back to the UK or personnel sent out from the UK specially to site for that purpose which all takes time and costs money.

Secondly, the contractor's site organization and facilities will have been geared to the contract as it is known and will lack the flexibility for adjustment which is possible within the UK. A major variation will therefore have that much greater impact on the economic utilization of existing resources – plant and labour may have to be retained even if there is no immediate use for them – and additional resources of a different character which may be required will take time to make available.

Thirdly, as has been indicated earlier, the high cost of retaining supervisory staff on site is that much higher because of the expenses of housing, feeding, etc., so that the labour costs associated with the variation will be substantially increased.

DISPUTES AND ARBITRATION

Technical disputes and law

It is still widely believed that in arbitration the arbitrator is free from the need to follow legal principles and to apply what is sometimes referred to as 'palm-tree' justice: that is to say, to decide the case on what he considers to be its merits. In reality this is not so and the arbitrator is bound to comply with the established principles of law, otherwise his award may be subsequently challenged in the courts.

It has been claimed that arbitration is both cheaper and quicker than resorting to the courts. In practice today this is not so. Both are expensive and both are subject to extensive delays. Perhaps the only real two advantages of arbitration are that:

1 It is private.
2 Where the matter in issue is technical, then an arbitrator can be appointed who has the necessary expertise to appreciate the technicalities involved.

However, the nature of any dispute will not, of course, be known at the time when the contract is drafted.

General dissatisfaction with both arbitration and litigation as a means for settling disputes has led to the development of ADR (Alternative Dispute Resolution) procedures. These can take many forms, but essentially they are non-binding procedures in which a neutral person seeks to assist in bringing the parties together, so that they can arrive at a settlement. These procedures offer substantial time and cost savings and, because of their flexibility, can allow non-legal factors (for example, the maintenance of future business relationships) to enter into the settlement process. However, they are only likely to be successful if both sides become convinced that it is in their best interests to settle.

Arbitration or settlement

The advantages of settling a dispute rather than allowing it to go to arbitration are substantial. Indeed, the very threat of taking proceedings is often sufficient to force a settlement. While proceedings in arbitration are private, which may be a definite advantage for the parties, there is no guarantee that in the end they will be speedier or cost less than taking the issue to court. One thing is certain: the arbitration proceedings will tie up one's own staff to a significant extent in the preparation of evidence, so that they cannot be used for any more productive purpose.

Then there is the problem of 'discovery of the documents' (as lawyers refer to it), which involves the collections of all files and papers relevant to the case and their disclosure to the other party. Estimating papers, inter-office memoranda, general correspondence, even private diaries will all have to be disclosed if they are relevant. Generally, only documents passing between a party and his lawyer will be privileged. On a major contract the documents to be disclosed could run into many hundreds of pages. The party concerned will, of course, need to scrutinize them himself before 'making discovery' to see what they are going to reveal.

Arbitration is not, then, a process to be embarked upon lightly in the belief that it is a quick and simple way of resolving a dispute.

8 Insurance

R. L. Carter

All the types of project dealt with in this book are exposed to the risk of uncertain events, which may cause loss of or damage to property, death or bodily injury, environmental damage, financial losses owing to delays in completion, and so on. Such losses may directly affect the responsible individual or organization, or give rise to a legal liability to compensate others. Some of those risks can be managed through the purchase of insurance, although the insurers (insurance companies and Lloyds of London) are reluctant to provide insurance if:

1 The particular type of loss-producing event is virtually certain to occur and/ or is not fortuitous so far as the insured is concerned.
2 The insurer does not have access to a large number of similar risks.
3 Past loss experience does not provide a reliable guide to the future.
4 There is a possibility that the insured may benefit from the insured event occurring.

So, for example, insurance is not normally available for business risks of a speculative nature which, therefore, must be handled in other ways. For example, foreign exchange futures contracts can be used to hedge against the potential impact of foreign exchange rate fluctuations on the costs and revenues of overseas projects.

The fact that a risk can be insured does not mean, however, that it should be insured. Insurance is only one of the ways in which risks can be handled.

RISK MANAGEMENT AND INSURANCE

If risks are to be managed efficiently, they must first be identified. This requires in-depth knowledge of the nature of the risks and the hazards associated with different types of projects. Various techniques can be used to assist in this task, and these may be undertaken either in-house or by outside risk management specialists.

Only after risks have been identified is it possible to evaluate the potential loss frequencies and severities, and thus both the expected and the maximum aggregate amount of the losses that may occur. Not only is such information required for deciding how risks shall be managed, but also failure to identify a risk may leave the firm exposed to severe, hidden threats to its financial viability and the possibility of prosecution if an accident arises therefrom. The basic approaches to the management of risks are through physical loss control and financial loss control.

Physical loss control

Physical loss control involves taking measures to reduce the probability of loss-producing events occurring and/or the potential size of losses. Loss control is a specialized field of management, but two points merit mention here:

1 Most countries have extensive legislation covering such matters as the safety of employees, consumers and members of the public, product safety, pollution or other damage to the environment and so on. Failure to comply with statutory regulations might be a criminal offence which could lead to the prosecution of directors, managers, supervisors, employees, contractors, designers or other responsible persons and, in any event, would strengthen the case of an employee or third party claiming compensation for any injuries sustained as the result thereof. The trend worldwide is for legislatures and courts to impose more onerous liabilities on those who cause injury or damage, so that a major accident involving personal injury, or damage, or both could lead to an award of damages of catastrophic proportions.
2 Measures to improve safety are often the most cost effective way of handling a risk, particularly when the occurrence of some event might cause prolonged interruption of work on a project, perhaps on the order of the responsible authority.

Financial loss control

Financial loss control involves taking measures to finance the losses that do occur, so that the cost of losses which could cause severe financial strain are spread over a longer period, thereby smoothing out the profit performance of the firm. The measures may be either *ex ante, ex post* or concurrent with the time of the loss. They may also either involve the firm absorbing the loss itself, or transferring the risk to another party.

Risk transfer

Insurance is the most common form of risk transfer. It is simply a contractual arrangement whereby an insurer, in return for the payment of a predetermined premium, undertakes to meet the cost of any loss which the policyholder may incur due to some specified uncertain event occurring during the period of the insurance. It is a form of *ex ante* risk financing in that usually the premium, or a major part of it, is payable at the inception of the insurance.

The transfer of risks also frequently forms part of the contractual arrangements for major projects. Particularly hazardous jobs may be subcontracted to specialists. Also, responsibilities for injury or damage arising out of the performance of the works may be allocated between the contracting parties through the inclusion in the contract of 'hold harmless' and similar clauses.

Risk retention

Risks not transferred will be retained within the organization. Losses which are too small to have any significant impact on cash flows and liquidity may be absorbed as part of the current operating costs, but if larger losses are to be retained their costs will need to be spread over a longer time. Provision may be made in advance by setting aside readily realizable assets to create an internal contingency fund to finance future losses: this is often called 'self-insurance', though there is no transfer of risk outside the firm. (Most large industrial, commercial and construction groups have taken 'self-insurance' a stage further by forming their own 'captive' insurance companies to insure or reinsure part of their risks.) The alternative method of financing large losses is to try to arrange guaranteed lines of credit to be made available if required, so that the cost of any loss can be spread over the future.

Insurance versus risk retention

The choice as to the methods employed for the financing of risks is constrained by statute and contract conditions. Most countries have compulsory insurance legislation which requires persons and corporate bodies that undertake certain activities to effect insurance with an authorized insurer. In Britain, for example, owners of vehicles used on a public highway must effect third party insurance, and employers must insure against their liability for injury to employees. Some countries have far more extensive compulsory insurance regulations. An obligation to insure certain risks is also a common feature of leases, debenture deeds, construction and other contracts.

Even if there were complete freedom of choice in the handling of risks, the choice between risk transfer and retention would still depend upon various factors, including the firm's corporate objectives, its management style and attitudes to risk, its financial situation, and tax considerations. Consequently it is impossible to say precisely what risks should or should not be insured. However, as a general rule insurance should be effected only for those risks with a low frequency of occurrence and a potential high severity of loss which could cause financial strain. To insure high frequency/low severity risks is to indulge in a 'pound-swapping' exercise in which each year premiums charged will exceed losses recovered because the insurer needs to cover the costs of handling a large number of small claims. Most insurable risks are of a type where losses may vary *125* from low value/high frequency to high value/low frequency. Then instead of fully insuring, it is usually more economic to insure subject to a deductible amount so that the policyholder pays the first £x of every loss, so excluding small losses from the insurance. If a deductible is fixed at a relatively large sum, it may be wise to arrange an aggregate limit to the total loss payable by the policyholder in any one year.

CONTRACTUAL RESPONSIBILITIES

When decisions are being taken regarding insurance, the interests of various people and organizations need to be taken into account, notably:

1 The parties to the contracts associated with the project.
2 The employees of all of those contracting parties.
3 Members of the public.
4 The owners of surrounding land, buildings and plant, including coastal, river, and other water authorities, and so forth.

There may be a large number of organizations and contracts associated with a single project. For example, a harbour board may arrange for consulting engineers to design a new dock, and for the construction to be undertaken by a main contractor, who may place part of the work with subcontractors: then each contractor may place contracts for the purchase of materials, the hiring of plant, and so on with several suppliers. The legal rights, responsibilities and liabilities of each of the contracting parties for any injury, damage, impairment of the environment or other infringement of property rights, arising out of the perform- ance of the project, including their liabilities to injured employees or members of the public, and any contractual obligations to pay compensation for delayed or unsatisfactory completion of the works, would be determined according to the terms of their respective contracts and the laws of tort.

As noted above, the contracts may include conditions:

1 Imposing on one of the parties a liability for losses arising out of the performance of the contract, including possibly losses for which he other- wise would have no legal responsibility.
2 Requiring one party to indemnify the other for any liability the latter may incur towards third parties for bodily injury, damage to property or other losses they may sustain due to the performance of the contract.
3 Requiring one party to insure against such losses for the protection of both.

Such provisions form part of all the standard forms of contract used for construc- tion and engineering projects (e.g. in Britain, the RIBA, JCT, ICE, FAS, ACA, EB/ BEAMA, IMechE/IEE, CPA and, for government contracts, the GC/Works/1 (Edition 3) Conditions of Contract). Therefore, one of the first steps for anyone engaged in project management should be to examine the terms of any contracts *126* into which his organization enters, paying particular attention to the options that may be exercised under, or amendments that may be made to, the standard forms of contract. It is necessary to check:

1. What are the organization's responsibilities for any losses which may flow from loss-producing events that may occur during the carrying out of the project?
2. What obligations, if any, are imposed on the organization to effect insurance and the scope and terms thereof?
3. Whether any other party is required to effect insurance, and if so whether the insurance arranged is satisfactory in regard to the scope of cover, sums insured, period of insurance, and the financial standing of the insurer(s).

It is normal for insurance policies to contain a condition relieving the insurer of any liability which the policyholder has accepted under the terms of any contract, for which he otherwise would not be responsible. Therefore, when any insurance is being arranged it is essential that the insurer is informed of any liabilities which the policyholder may have accepted, or any rights which he may have waived, under the terms of any contract. Insurers are well aware of the terms of standard industry contracts, and are prepared to provide cover accordingly: when necessary, the insurance can be arranged in the joint names of the parties.

THE BENEFITS OF INSURANCE

A well-designed insurance programme provides a number of benefits to all who may be involved in the carrying out of a project.

It will provide a guarantee that if some loss-producing event does occur, funds will be available to meet the resulting losses. Thus a contractor has the assurance that he is protected against any contractual liability he may incur for material loss, damage or injury under the terms of his contract, even if the loss was caused by a subcontractor, provided the latter had either effected the required insurances or had been included in the contractor's own insurance arrangements. Equally an employer knows that if, say, his property is destroyed, or if he becomes liable to compensate some third party injured during the course of the work, he will not be dependent upon the contractor being in a financial position to indemnify him or to rebuild the damaged property. Also, if during the course of any particular contract a major loss should occur, the cost to a contractor or an employer will not fall wholly on either that contract, or on the profits for the year in which it occurs.

TYPES OF INSURABLE RISK

The risks for which insurance is available fall into six main classes:

1. *Property insurances*, covering loss of or damage to buildings, work in progress, furniture, plant, machinery, materials and other property, caused by fire, explosion, riot, storm, flood, theft and other perils.
2. *Transportation insurances*, covering loss of or damage to land vehicles, 127

mobile plant, railway rolling stock, aircraft, ships, other vessels and goods in transit, and liabilities arising from the use of vehicles, aircraft and ships.

3 *Liability insurances*, covering legal liabilities to compensate third parties for bodily injury, damage to property, financial losses, or infringement of property rights, due to accidents occurring in the course of business, including products liability, professional negligence, pollution and employer's liability for injury to employees (or workers' compensation in some countries).

4 *Pecuniary insurances*, covering credit, embezzlement by employees, suretyship, legal expenses, and miscellaneous financial losses, including losses arising from business interruption.

5 *Personal accident, sickness and medical expenses insurances.*

6 *Life annuity and pensions insurances.*

Often, several classes of insurance are packaged together in one insurance contract (as in the case of motor insurance, which may cover third party liability as well as fire, theft and accidental damage to the insured vehicles). Insurances may be arranged to cover losses caused by specified perils, or be on an 'all risks' basis covering loss from any cause, other than losses specifically excluded from the insurance.

Although a checklist of the types of insurance available is useful when considering insurance needs, the danger is that by concentrating on the types of risks listed some unusual risk(s) may be overlooked.

LIMITS TO COVER PROVIDED

The amount of insurance provided by most policies normally is limited in amount.

Apart from life and personal accident policies which undertake to pay a stated, guaranteed sum if the insured event occurs, all other classes of insurance are subject to the principle of indemnity, which basically limits the amount recoverable from the insurer to the financial loss incurred by the policyholder at the time of loss. So a liability policy will indemnify the policyholder for damages which he is legally liable to pay to a third party, plus any costs awarded and costs incurred in defending the action with the insurer's consent. Provision frequently is made under property insurances for the principle of indemnity to be amended, so that the insurer accepts liability for the full cost of repairing, replacing or rebuilding damaged property (without making any deduction for wear, tear and depreciation), plus costs of: removing debris; professional fees incurred in the rebuilding or replacement; and additional building costs incurred in complying with planning authority regulations.

Normally the insurer also limits his liability in respect of any one loss or a series of losses in any one period of insurance. In the case of property insurances the insurer's maximum liability for any one loss is limited to the sum(s) insured on the item(s) involved, and in the event of a claim, the sum insured is reduced by the amount paid unless an additional premium is paid to reinstate the full sum insured. Liability policies are made subject to limits of indemnity: the nature of those limits depends on the type of risk insured but may include a limit on the amount payable in respect of all claims arising out of a single loss-producing event plus an aggregate limit on losses occurring in any one year. Business interruption insurances are made subject to both a sum insured and a limit to the period of interruption for which a claim will be paid.

If the amount of cover available in the event of a loss is not to prove inadequate, it is essential that the basis of the cover is fully understood and the limits negotiated are adequate not just at inception but to cover the eventual cost of settling a loss at some future date. Therefore, when fixing sums insured or limits of indemnity, allowance must be made for future inflation. Most property insurances are subject to the so-called condition of average which reduces the amount payable by the insurer if the sum insured is less than the full value of the property at the time of loss.

Care must also be exercised in arranging the scope of cover for liability insurances in regard to:

1 The basis of the contract: that is, whether the cover is on a 'losses occurring' or the more restrictive 'claims made' basis.
2 The territorial limits to the insurance. Even though the insurance may provide for accidents occurring abroad, a jurisdiction clause may require any action to be brought in a UK court.

The whole area of the basis of cover, sums insured and limits of indemnity is one on which expert advice is necessary.

INSURANCE FOR PROJECTS

The insurance needs of the various parties involved in any project vary according to both the nature of the project and, as explained above, the terms of the various contracts involved. In every case each party will need such basic insurances as third party insurance for motor vehicles and mobile plant used on a public highway; employers' liability insurance; property insurances for its own property, etc. Also in every case architects, consulting engineers, surveyors and anyone else engaged in design or supervision work will need to ensure that their professional liability insurance is adequate to cover any liability that may arise in connection with the contract in question. Attention will now be focused upon the specific forms of insurance associated with different types of project.

CIVIL ENGINEERING AND OTHER CONSTRUCTION PROJECTS

The following specially designed forms of insurance policy are available to cover the contractual responsibilities of the various parties to construction projects:

1 Contract works policies to cover physical loss or damage to the contract works, including temporary works, materials and plant owned or hired by the contractor, during the construction period.

2 Public liability insurance to cover the contractor's legal liability to third parties for injury or damage to their property arising out of the contract work caused during the period of insurance.

3 Professional indemnity insurance to cover the legal liability of a contractor, architect, consulting engineer or other professional for injury or damage arising from a breach of professional duty.

4 Employers' liability insurance to cover the contractor's legal liability for injury sustained by employees arising out of and in the course of their employment.

5 Decennial (latent defects) insurance.

6 Various forms of insurance to cover consequential losses of a contractor, owner/purchaser or developer, including Joint Contracts Tribunal for the Building Industry (JCT) 21.2.1 and 22D losses.

7 Performance and other bonds.

Arranging the insurance

In every case the insurer(s) must be supplied with all of the material facts (i.e. those facts which could influence the underwriter's decisions) regarding the contract, including the relevant plans and technical data. Insurers retain their own consulting engineers and they normally wish both to carry out a site survey and receive periodical reports as the work progresses. Although it is not the function of insurers to interfere in the way a job is to be performed, they may wish to recommend additional safety measures.

In the case of large projects it is usually advantageous to employ an insurance broker who specializes in construction insurances. The broker will assemble the information required, arrange for the insurance survey, and after having negotiated terms with the leading underwriter, will then place the insurance with a number of insurers, each of whom will be separately liable for the share it writes.

Contract works policies are issued to contractors on an annual basis whereby all contracts undertaken that are below an agreed monetary limit are automatically insured (though care must be taken to ensure that if a contract is subject to any special features details must be supplied to the insurer(s) and their agreement obtained). The alternative is to arrange a separate policy for individual contracts. For very large contracts involving a consortium of contractors, with each contractor having a number of subcontractors, it is usually more satisfactory for the employer to arrange an 'umbrella' policy covering all the parties involved. When only one main contractor is involved, although the employer may still effect an insurance on the contract works, it is usually preferable that the contractor should be responsible for doing so: he can ensure that it fits in with his normal insurance arrangements and that it covers his contractual responsibilities and liabilities.

Contract works

The 'all risks' insurance

This cover may be defined as follows: the insurers will indemnify the insured in respect of loss of or damage to any of the property described in the Schedule arising from any cause whatsoever (except as hereinafter provided) occurring during the period of insurance. All forms of loss or damage are covered, subject to a number of exceptions noted below. Although the insurer will normally settle any claim by monetary payment, it may elect to repair, reinstate or replace any lost or damaged property.

The property insured

This will typically be defined as:

1 the works and temporary works erected or executed in performance of the contract and materials for use in connection therewith;
2 construction plant, tools, equipment, temporary buildings, and any other property;

all belonging to the insured or for which they are responsible and not otherwise insured by or on behalf of the insured, while on or adjacent to the contract or in transit thereto and therefrom anywhere in (the territorial limits). The cover is extended to include:

1 Architects, surveyors, consulting engineers, legal and other professional fees necessarily and reasonably incurred in the reinstatement of the insured property consequent upon loss or damage (though not fees incurred in preparing a claim.)
2 Additional reinstatement costs incurred in complying with building or other regulations in accordance with a notice served following damage to the contract works.
3 Debris removal and propping-up costs consequent upon an insured loss. No cover is provided for the cost of fees incurred in preparing a claim.

Cover may also be arranged for such items as:

1 Costs necessarily incurred in rewriting or redrawing plans, drawings or other contract documents following loss or damage, subject to an agreed monetary limit.
2 Hire plant: cover for indemnity to plant owners, negligent breakdown of plant, continuing hire charges and so on, in accordance with the Construction Plant-hire Association (CPA) conditions of hire.
3 Costs of recovering plant which has been immobilized (for example in soft ground) other than because of breakdown.

Exclusions

It is not possible to list here in detail the normal exclusions to the property insured and the losses covered, but the main exclusions are:

1   Waterborne or airborne vessels and craft.
2   Motor vehicles other than construction plant.
3   Cash, bank notes, cheques, stamps, deeds, bills of exchange, etc.
4   Property of the employer existing at the commencement of the contract.
5   Property for which the contractor is relieved of responsibility by the contract conditions.
6   Damage to any part of the permanent works after practical completion (i.e. after having been taken over by the employer) or upon partial possession by the owner or occupier, other than for any loss or damage which is the responsibility of the contractor during any specified maintenance period or defects liability period.
7   Loss or damage due to wear, tear, rust, mildew or deterioration.
8   Fault or defect in design, material or workmanship, but damage to other property resulting therefrom is usually covered.
9   Damage to plant caused by breakdown, its self-explosion or derangement, but consequential damage to other parts of the plant or other property is covered.
10 Loss or damage caused by nuclear risks, sonic boom, war, civil war, requisition and nationalization, and in Northern Ireland, by civil commotion and malicious damage.
11 Delay or non-completion penalties, and other consequential losses.

A policy may contain other limitations or exclusions, such as the exclusion of testing and commissioning, and losses solely due to cessation of work. In every case exclusions will need to be examined in relation to individual contract circumstances.

Excesses

It is normal for insurers to require the insured to pay at least the first £250 of each and every claim, and some large contractors accept substantially larger excesses.

Period of insurance

This should be the same as the period of construction and maintenance, with provision for it to be extended if the contract is not completed on time.

The sum insured

This should be based on the estimated contract price, plus any professional fees, debris removal and the value of temporary works and buildings, plant, equipment, etc., which are to be insured.

Provision will also need to be made for inflation during the construction period, extended to allow for reinstatement of major damage to the works. Various methods are in use to allow for this, including cost escalation clauses that provide for an increase in cover (usually 20–25 per cent) above the selected sum insured.

Liability insurance

The parties to construction contracts need insurance to cover their legal liability for injury or damage to the property of (a) employees and (b) other third parties.

Employers' liability

The policy covers the insured's legal liability for bodily injury (including death, disease or illness) caused to any employee arising out of and in the course of employment within the territorial limits. The definition of an 'employee' includes labour masters, labour-only subcontractors, and the drivers or operators of hire plant. The territorial limits are restricted to the UK, including off-shore installations; cover for injuries sustained elsewhere may be restricted to commercial visits only.

Public liability

A typical policy wording would set out the cover as follows:

> The insurer will indemnify the insured during the period of insurance in respect of all sums which the insured shall become legally liable to pay for:
> 1   accidental bodily injury to any person; or
> 2   accidental loss of or damage to property;
> arising out of the performance of the contract described in the Schedule.

The insurance extends to include (a) costs and expenses awarded against the insured; and (b) costs and expenses incurred with the consent of the insurers in resisting a claim. A limit of indemnity is applied to the aggregate cost of all claims arising from one occurrence but normally the cover is unlimited over the period of insurance. When product liability is included the cover may be subject to a limit over the period of insurance. It is vital that any limit is sufficiently high to cover all possible claims, bearing in mind the nature of the contract, the site and its surroundings, and the size of awards for personal injury.

Exclusions

The normal main exclusions are:

1   Liability to persons under a contract of service with the insured for injuries or disease arising out of and in the course of their employment.

2 Liability arising from the ownership or use of road vehicles other than construction plant.
3 Liability arising from the ownership or use of locomotives, waterborne vessels, aircraft and steam pressure vessels.
4 Liability arising from defective designs, specifications, the giving of advice or other professional services.
5 Loss of or damage to property belonging to or under the control of the insured, or the contract works.
6 Liability arising out of any contract or agreement, unless the insured would have been liable notwithstanding such contract or agreement.
7 Liability arising from pollution or contamination unless caused by a sudden, identifiable, unintended and unexpected incident. No cover is provided for pollution caused by gradual release of pollutants, though there is a very limited market for such cover but with relatively low limits of indemnity.

Policies issued to contractors may have other exclusions, such as: vibration and weakening of support, demolition risks; tunnelling; dam construction; use of explosives; bridges and viaducts; and so on. If cover is required against either such special risks or any of the normal exclusions, an additional premium usually will be payable.

Territorial limits

Care must be taken to ensure that the territorial limits stated in the policy are sufficiently wide to embrace the insured's area of activity. If work is conducted abroad, the policy should cover not only actions brought against the insured in a UK court but also in the courts of the country where the injury or damage occurs, and preferably worldwide.

The insured

The definition of the insured must be sufficiently wide to protect all of the parties needing to be indemnified under the policy according to the contract terms. So an insurance effected by a contractor may need to be extended to indemnify the employer and possibly subcontractors too. The trade or business of each of the insured must be stated in the policy.

Professional indemnity

Architects, consulting engineers and other professionals, and contractors who provide a 'design and build' service, need to effect a separate professional liability insurance. Although the insurance will cover any legal liability for damage to property or bodily injury arising out of any negligent act, error or omission in the supply of professional services, usually the insurance is mainly to provide cover against financial economic losses.

134   Policies are usually on a 'claims made' basis that restricts the cover to claims brought against the insured during each period of insurance, so creating problems with (for example) latent defects which may become apparent many years hence. In the case of partnerships, cover will need to be arranged for not only existing partners but also for incoming and outgoing partners, with run-off liability for the latter. When a firm acts as part of a consortium, provision will need to be made to cover that risk. Also if it is required to enter into collateral warranties special arrangements will need to be made with the professional indemnity insurer.

As with other liability insurances, the cover is subject to limits of indemnity and territorial limits.

Decennial (latent defects) insurance

This insurance originated in France but is now common in many parts of Europe and the Middle East. A few insurers are prepared to write it in the UK. The insurance is issued for a period of ten (or fewer) years running from the time of practical completion of a building; once effected it is non-cancellable. It provides cover against physical damage to the insured premises directly caused by an inherent defect in design, materials or construction, including damage caused by subsidence, heave or landslip, occurring during the period of insurance. The insurance can also be extended to include the cost of replacing defective waterproofing and damage to other parts of the premises caused by failure of the waterproofing envelope. The existence of such an insurance avoids the expense and uncertainty of having to sue the contractor and/or professional firms if a latent defect is discovered after the end of the maintenance period.

Excluded from the insurance is damage caused by or arising from: fire or other perils that normally would be insured under a fire policy; alterations, additions or modifications to the premises; inadequate maintenance; and exceeding designed floor loadings. The insurance is also subject to a (usually substantial) excess.

An important feature of the insurance, which must be arranged before the inception of a construction project, is technical control. The insurer needs to be assured that the structure is designed and constructed to reasonable standards and is suitable for the proposed usage. Therefore, an independent technical control bureau is employed by the insurer to exercise a constant monitoring of the project, including frequent site visits.

The person who effects the insurance is referred to as the policyholder until practical completion, when the cover commences in the name of the insured. However, as the owners or tenants may not be known at the commencement of the project, the insured would be described as the owner(s) of the freehold or leasehold interest in the premises, or any person who acquires such an interest, during the period of insurance, whose name is advised to and agreed by the insurer.

The insurance may be arranged either for the full value of the premises, with provision for inflation during the period of insurance, or on a first-loss basis to cover the maximum expected loss.

JCT Contract clause 21.2.1 insurance

When clause 21.2.1 of the JCT form of contract, or similar clauses in other contracts, are invoked the insurance will need to be specially arranged, either as an extension to the contractor's public liability insurance or as a separate policy. Even if a premium and other terms cannot be agreed with insurers before the contract commences, temporary insurance should be obtained from the start of the works.

The objective of the clause is to protect the employer:

1 against any liability he may incur for damage to adjoining property; and
2 for damage to his own property not forming part of the contract works, including consequential losses (damage to the contract works would be covered under the contract works policy);

which he cannot recover under the indemnity clause of the contract because the damage is not due to any negligence on the part of the contractor or his subcontractors.

The insurance has to be arranged in the joint names of the contractor and employer, though the indemnity applies solely to the employer. As the employer will be indemnified either under the contractor's public liability policy (if the damage is due to the contractor's negligence) or under the clause 21.2.1 insurance, it is highly desirable that both insurances should be placed with the same insurer(s) to avoid any problems in the event of a dispute as to the cause of the damage.

The cover provided follows the wording of the relevant contract clause, but because it is not limited to accidental damage, the insurance will be subject to the specific exclusion of damage which can reasonably be foreseen to be inevitable. It will not cover damage due to errors or omissions in the designing of the works which would be the responsibility of the designer and fall under his professional indemnity insurance.

Sole responsibility for deciding upon the limit of indemnity under the insurance falls upon the employer.

Consequential loss insurances

Loss or damage to the contract works or plant, which may cause delay in the completion of a project, may result in consequential financial losses to various parties. For example, a contractor may incur a trading loss or increased expenditure, or be liable to pay the employer liquidated damages for delayed completion; and a developer may incur a loss of interest due to delayed sale of the property, or the loss of rent from prospective tenants. Various forms of insurance are available to cover such losses, though the cover would be restricted to losses following damage or loss caused by specified perils.

Performance and other bonds

Contractors may be required to supply various forms of bonds which, though technically not insurance contracts, can be supplied by insurance companies. So, for example, a performance bond provides a guarantee to an employer that if the contractor fails to fulfil his contractual obligations, the surety (the insurer) will be obliged to do so. A bid or tender bond guarantees that if the employer accepts a bid and the contractor fails to perform the work, the surety will meet the cost to the employer of having again to put the work out to tender.

Policy conditions

There are three conditions common to all policies which it is vital that the insured should observe:

1　Any change in the material facts existing at the date of the policy must be notified immediately to the insurers in writing.
2　All reasonable measures must be taken to prevent accidents and, if an accident does occur, to minimize the loss.
3　Immediate notification must be given to the insurers upon receiving notice of any claim or accident, and all of the provisions regarding claims must be observed, such as passing on writs, summons, etc., supplying information, providing assistance, giving insurers access to the site, and so forth.

Failure to comply with any of the above conditions may result in the insured being unable to recover under the policy for losses incurred. Therefore, the insurance arrangements must be administered efficiently and steps taken to ensure that there is good communication between the site management and the individual responsible for insurance administration. The employer will need to ensure that the required insurances are kept in force and that the conditions are observed.

MANUFACTURING PROJECTS

The insurances needed in connection with the erection and commissioning of a new plant are much the same as for construction projects. The standard forms of contract for the supply and installation of plant and machinery (e.g. the EB/BEAMA and the IMechE/IEE forms of contract) contain similar clauses to those in construction contracts in respect of (a) the liabilities of contractors and sub-contractors for loss or damage to the contract works and for third party injury and damage; and (b) their obligations to insure. Therefore, engineering insurers offer 'all risks' contract works insurances similar in scope to the insurances described above.

The remarks regarding the arranging of construction insurances equally apply to engineering projects. Usually contractors maintain annual 'all risks' and liability policies to cover all contracts undertaken up to a predetermined limit, but for *137* large projects special arrangements may be made by either the contractor(s) or the purchaser.

Transit risks

Engineering projects often involve moving valuable plant and machinery from the manufacturer's premises to the site by road, rail and possibly by sea or air. Therefore, besides the site insurances, cover is also required for transit risks. During transit sensitive plant and machinery may suffer latent damage which may not become apparent until its erection and testing has reached an advanced stage, when it may be difficult to prove that the damage occurred during transit, particularly if the shipper or carrier has been given a clean receipt. Therefore, both the transit and erection insurances ideally should be placed with the same insurer(s), possibly under the same policy.

Engineering all risks insurance

Even if under the terms of the contract the contractor is only responsible for loss or damage to the contract works by specified perils, normally 'all risks' insurance is arranged. It needs to provide for loss or damage:

1   From the time of unloading on site, during the period of erection and testing, until a taking-over certificate is issued.
2   During the contract maintenance period.

Besides covering the contract works, temporary buildings, construction plant, equipment, etc., can be included in the insurance. The policy exclusions (including excesses) and other conditions are similar to those applicable to contract works policies, but two points are worth noting:

1   The wording of the exclusion of mechanical and electrical breakdown of plant (but not damage resulting therefrom) occurring either during commissioning or during the maintenance period and caused by defective workmanship, materials or design, needs to be studied carefully. In its strictest form it could mean that not only are the insurers not responsible for repairing or replacing the defective part itself, but also that they accept no liability for the costs of gaining access to the defective part and re-assembling after the rectification of the fault and repair of the damage. Such access costs could be the most expensive part of the work involved. In the case of export contracts there is the possibility too that part of the plant may need to be returned to the manufacturer's works for repair, so that substantial shipping costs may be incurred. It may be possible to reach agreement with the insurers for at least the costs of gaining access for rectification of the fault and repairing the resulting damage to be shared.
2   The insurance provided for the maintenance period needs to be tailored to meet the contractor's liabilities under the terms of the contract. In its

narrowest form the insurance will only cover damage to the plant while the contractor is on the site to carry out his obligations under the contract. Usually such 'visits risk' insurance is insufficient to cover the contractor's contractual responsibilities and liabilities, and a wider form of insurance is necessary.

The same considerations apply to the fixing of sums insured, and territorial limits for the 'all risks' insurance as for contract works insurances. Likewise purchasers, consulting engineers, contractors and subcontractors need to make the same sort of arrangements for the insurance of their liabilities to third parties for bodily injury or damage to property which may arise out of the performance of the contract as in the case of construction contracts.

Other aspects of manufacturing projects

When, instead of commissioning consultants and contractors to design, supply and erect new plant, a firm undertakes the work itself, it will need to make special insurance arrangements. 'All risks' insurance can be purchased to cover both installation of new plant, and major resiting operations of existing plant, during both installation and test running of the plant. In every case, arrangements need to be made to extend existing property insurances to cover new buildings and plant from the time that they are taken over from contractors, and other insurers may need to be informed of the new developments so that business interruption, engineering, employers', public and products liability, and any other relevant policies are extended to cover the new products/operations.

Finally, engineering insurers offer comprehensive inspection and testing services covering the design, erection and commissioning of new plant.

OTHER PROJECTS

It is impossible to deal with all of the other types of project included in this book. It must suffice to say that:

1   Care must be taken to identify all of the risks associated with the project.
2   The firm's insurance arrangements must be reviewed to ensure that they adequately cover any responsibilities and liabilities it has accepted under any contract, not forgetting that existing policies will probably contain an exclusion of any liability accepted under contract unless the insurer's agreement is obtained.
3   Special insurances are available to cover certain types of project.

An example of such a special form of insurance is that available for exhibitors covering both material damage and public liability risks. It might also be desirable to extend the firm's business interruption policy to include cover for loss of profits on anticipated orders if, due to the operation of an insured peril, the exhibition either cannot take place or is brought to an abrupt end.

FURTHER READING

Association of Insurance and Risk Managers in Industry and Commerce (ed.), *Company Insurance Handbook*, 2nd edn, Gower, Aldershot, 1984.

Bunni, N. G., *Construction Insurance*, Elsevier, London and New York, 1986.

Carter, R. L. (chief ed.), *Handbook of Insurance*, Kluwer, Kingston upon Thames, 1990 (updated).

Carter, R. L. and Crockford, G. N., *Handbook of Risk Management*, Kluwer, Kingston upon Thames, 1974 (updated).

Diacon, S. R. and Carter, R. L., *Success in Insurance*, 3rd edn, John Murray, London, 1992.

Eaglestone, F. N. and Smyth, C., *Insurance under the ICE Conditions*, George Goodwin, London, 1985.

Hickson, R. J., *Construction Insurance: Management and Claims*, E. & F. N. Spon, London, 1987.

Levine, M. and Wood, J., *Construction Insurance and UK Construction Contracts*, Lloyds of London Press, London, 1991.

Wright, J. D., *Construction Insurance*, Study Course 650, Distance Learning Division, Chartered Insurance Institute, Sevenoaks, 1991.

9 Project Definition

Dennis Lock

If project management can be summarized as managing resources so as to achieve the three objectives of performance, timely completion and containment of costs within budgets, then project definition is the process of ensuring that these objectives are clearly set out before any work starts. Too often, projects are finished months, even years later than their promised dates, costing millions of pounds more than the original estimates, and with the technical content quite different from that envisaged at the outset. Project fulfilment will always be a risk undertaking, but careful definition will at least remove those risks which are preventable through careful planning and forethought.

THE PROJECT SPECIFICATION

The project specification is (or should be) the document which contains all the elements, technical and commercial, of the project definition. Starting from the first client enquiry to the contractor, and following through all the various technical and sales discussions between the parties involved in the establishment of a contract, a large volume of data is amassed for any project of significant size. This information must be recorded faithfully, its interpretation has to be clear and uniformly appreciated by both client and contractor and, most important of all, this information has to be communicated through the project manager to all participants to ensure that the project is carried out in the manner intended by the client and the original sales team.

During the sales negotiations for any major project, and in the formulation of the sales proposal document, it is customary for the contractor to invest a considerable amount of initial engineering design. Often working with the client, the contractor's sales engineers come to understand the client's technical requirements, suggest or recommend one or more particular solutions, and then develop a solution into a fully cost-estimated, defined and timed proposal. This process is sometimes, appropriately, termed 'solution engineering'.

Solution engineering will invariably require the participation of senior *141* technical people, usually from within and outside the sales engineering department. In fact, it is never good practice to isolate this activity from the organization's 'mainstream' engineering and project fulfilment departments, even in a company big enough to afford a sales engineering department containing all the essential skills. Solution engineering is best conducted as a consultative process. The optimum results for both the contractor and the client are more likely to be achieved if people who are going to manage the actual design and manufacture or construction are involved from the outset in the project definition and the proposed solution.

Many companies involve their client's engineers throughout the solution engineering phase, and some even carry out their main project design engineering in collaboration with the client's engineers in a process known as simultaneous engineering. This applies particularly where the contractor is designing and building special purpose machinery that the client will buy to make his own new product: simultaneous design work on the machine and its workpiece should result in a product that is easier and more economical to make.

In some cases it may be possible to arrange that the senior sales engineer responsible for most of the solution engineering on a project transfers to the main engineering department when the project becomes live, even to take over as project manager. That is an excellent way of ensuring continuity of method and purpose but it is, of course, not usually practicable. In any case, formal documentation in the shape of a well-produced project specification is the only safe way to to define the project so that the project manager knows exactly what has to be done.

Some typical contents of a project specification are now described: actual formats of such documents will obviously vary according to company styles and project requirements but all must include functional, financial and timescale sections if the project is to be defined properly.

Functional definition

The most obvious elements of functional definition are the quantitative data expressing performance. These might be the output rate and production tolerances of a machine, together with its capacities, power requirements, foundations, dimensions, control methods, types of fixtures and jigs, and so on. Alternatively, the project might be a construction venture, in which case the functional aspects are expressed in terms of dimensions, layout, architectural style, standards of accommodation, lighting, heating, environmental control, and many other factors. All functional details are expressed by means of schematic or outline drawings, data sheets, and other engineering documents. All this is very obvious, and should not come as a surprise to any reader who has ever worked in an engineering company. Unfortunately, companies quite often get the initial definition wrong, either by error or by omission. One of the worst phrases with which a contractor can confront his client is 'unforeseen difficulties' when trying to make excuses for failure. Often, the difficulties should have been avoided by giving more thought to the original specification.

The environment into which the project is going to be delivered or constructed is a vital factor to be examined. For a civil or construction project (for example), is the territory subject to earthquakes, subsidence, excessive humidity, high or low temperature extremes, hurricanes, torrential rain, dust, blown sand, destructive pests or other natural hazards? Are there good road, rail, sea and air communications? What materials handling equipment already exists at the site and what must be provided additionally? What are the power supply standards? In addition to the natural conditions, man-made regulations are also important. Governments impose all kinds of statutory conditions concerning health and safety and working regulations, and there are also likely to be local technical standards which differ from those used in the home country of the contractor.

Each project has its own set of rules, and every contractor has his own particular bank of experience from which to cope with these problems. Sensible contractors develop standard checklists which can be used to try and ensure that no important item is forgotten. Figure 9.1 is an example, taken from the mining industry, of a checklist used by engineers during the early stages of a new project. Obviously the application of this example is specific to one industry, but each contractor should be able to establish a checklist which has particular use for his own field of activity.

Establishing the project ground rules can be a time-consuming business. They include some items which have to be sorted out between the client and the contractor after the contract has been signed, but before serious work can really get started. Such things as drawing numbering standards, the types of drawing sheets to be used (the clients', the contractors', or entirely new sheets for a joint venture?) and some technical principles have to be defined. One machine tool specialist developed a standard network diagram to serve the purpose of checklist and control document for carrying out these preliminaries. While these preliminary investigations cost money in terms of engineering man-hours, they are more significant in relation to the elapsed time taken up in getting answers to the questions posed. Against all the usually accepted commercial rules, it may be worth a contractor's while to commit *limited* resources to these preliminary tasks before an order is received. The risk is relatively small compared to the size of the eventual project, since the work level is right at the front, low end of the familiar 'S' curve or resource build-up, and the reward can be a gain of several weeks or months on the overall timescale. Figure 9.2 shows the standard preliminary network which was indeed put into action before receipt of an order by a major American machine tool company.

Financial and commercial definition

The financial and commercial aspects of the specification are based upon the cost estimates, expanded into prices, terms of payment, and all other contractual conditions. These factors are described in Chapters 6 and 12.

Timescale and delivery promises

It might be thought (and some textbooks might say) that projects are given *143*

Project site

Availability of utilities (power, water, sewerage, etc.)
Local taxes
Import restrictions
Political restraints on purchasing sources
Statutory or mandatory local regulations relating to labour and environmental
    controls
Site accessibility by road, rail, air, sea
Site conditions – seismicity tectonics
Climatic conditions (temperature, humidity, precipitation, wind direction and force,
    sunshine, dust, barometric pressure)
Site plans and survey
Soil investigation and foundation requirements
Local manufacturing facilities
Sources of materials, manpower and construction equipment
Transportation, insurance, etc.
Access restrictions (e.g. low bridges)

Contractual and commercial

How firm are proposals?
Client's priorities (time/money/quality)
Termination points and responsibility
Client's cost expectations/budget available
Client's programme requirements
General contract matters
Scope of work envisaged:
– Full detailed design or basic design only?
– Procurement responsibility – ourselves, client or other?
– Construction responsibility – ourselves, client or managing contractor?
How accurate are existing estimates (ball park, comparative?)
Check below-the-line estimate items with the checklist in the estimating manual
How is project to be financed?
Any restraints on purchasing owing to financing requirements?

Initial design and technical definition

Flowsheets
Layouts
Urgent specifications for long-delivery purchases
Identify other critical jobs
Are further investigations necessary?
Is further information required from the client?
Process parameters
Design parameters
Design standards, drawing sheets, etc.
Engineering standards
Is information from previous similar projects available for retrieval and use?

Figure 9.1   Project definition checklist

This example was developed by a mining engineering company for use in the early stages of
a project or potential project.

Organization

Names, addresses, telephone and telex numbers of participants and nominated
  project representatives for correspondence
Communication methods available (telephone, telex, mail, couriers, facsimile, etc.)
Work breakdown
Sectional responsibilities for project management, specialist functions,
  procurement, construction
Manpower resources
Organization chart

Programme

Timescale targets
Are targets realistic?
Have long-delivery items been considered in target dates?
Transport time expected to site
Initial bar chart or network

Control techniques and procedures

Methods and management tools involved
Site capability for handling techniques (e.g. Is computer available?)
Procedures for updating the programme and updating frequency
Methods for expediting and programme control
Methods for cost control
Transportation procedures to be used
Arrangements for project meetings
Arrangements for site visits
Design approvals
Drawing approvals
Purchasing approvals
– enquiry specifications
– bid evaluations and choice of vendors
– authority for placing orders and for committing costs
Purchasing procedures
– arrangements for paying vendors' invoices
– inspection arrangements
Numbering systems to be used on this project – as specified by the client, or our
  usual standards?
Distribution of documents, who gets what and how many copies?
Define all procedures by issuing project standing instructions

Figure 9.1 (concluded)

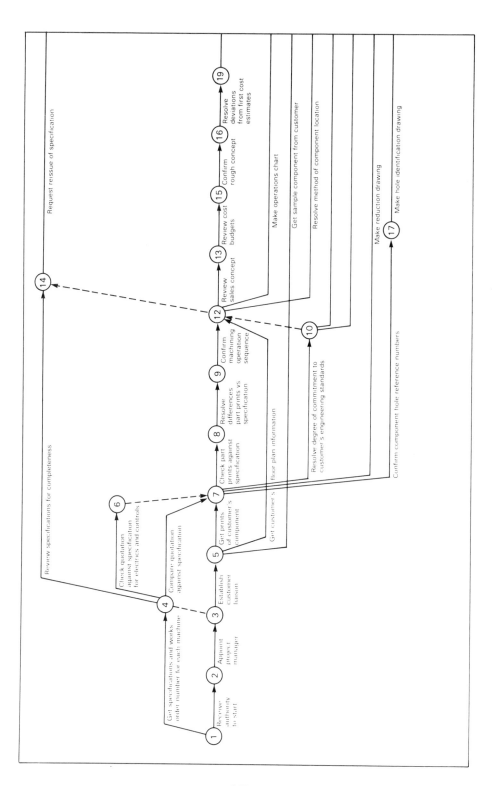

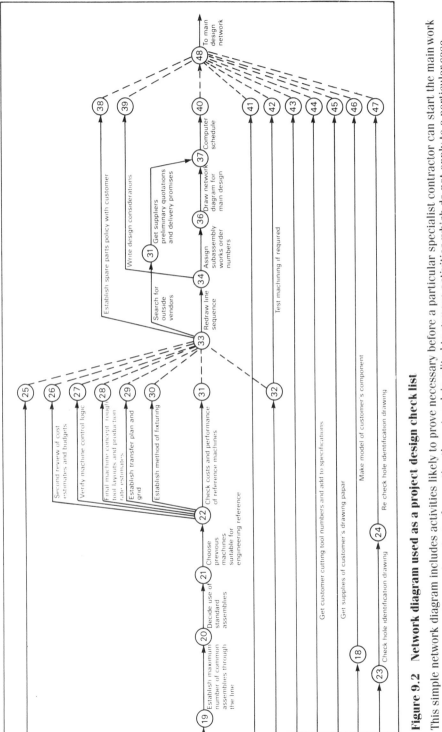

Figure 9.2 Network diagram used as a project design check list

This simple network diagram includes activities likely to prove necessary before a particular specialist contractor can start the main work of design on heavy machine tool projects. In practice the network is edited to remove activities which do not apply to a particular case. Since most of the activities consume time rather than any considerable amount of design manpower, the company sometimes allows these activities to be carried out before a contract is signed with the customer. Although a small cost risk is thereby acccepted, the reward is to gain several weeks on the overall programme.

delivery date promises on the basis of sophisticated planning using critical path networks and other detailed considerations. Real life can be quite different from this ideal. When the contract is signed there is usually no information upon which to base detailed planning of any sort. The dates promised are far more likely to be based on the contractor's expert judgement. If a company has built a number of hospitals, for example, of different sizes and on sites of varying degrees of difficulty, it should be able to gauge a new sales opportunity by comparison with one or more of its earlier projects, where the overall timescales are recorded in their records. What happens in practice is that projects are sold with the technical and cost/price details calculated with some care, and with the timescale promises made on a 'broad brush' basis. This does not mean that the delivery promises are not valid, and it implies no sense of impropriety or dishonesty. The company is simply using its experience to make a reasoned judgement. The purpose of all the detailed project management and planning and scheduling which must follow is to ensure that the reasonable promises made at the outset are fulfilled in practice.

The detailed network diagrams and other schedules produced later may quite possibly indicate that the initial promises are too optimistic. In such cases the network logic has to be re-examined to change working methods and sequences to make sure that the dates are met. The sequence of timescale definition is, for practical purposes, seen as follows:

1 Delivery promises made on the basis of reasoned judgement, possibly assisted by the drawing of very simple bar charts.
2 The preparation of detailed schedules, made with the objective of achieving the dates already promised by the sales and higher management team.
3 The revision of detailed schedules, in the event that they predict a project duration which is unacceptable, but certainly not carrying out such revision simply by making impossible reductions in the estimates for activity durations – timescale shortening can only be planned by rearranging the logical working sequence in a practical way.
4 The subsequent updating of schedules as work proceeds in order that they remain valid and workable as actual results and progress are substituted.

Project schedules typically provide some events which stand out from the others as 'milestones' or 'key events' as denoting completion of important phases of the project. Some of these milestones will be related to the various promises made in the original proposals, and as such the original project specification defines the timing of the more important project phases and sets the total framework for the critical path planning.

Publishing the first issue of the project specification

Ideally, when the authorization is received for a project to proceed there should be a logical and orderly handover from the contractor's sales organization to the departments responsible for carrying out the work. If the project manager has been involved in the sales engineering activities or, better still, has transferred from the function of leading the sales or solution engineering process, then so much the better. The important objective at this stage is to ensure that all the objectives are set out in the specification so that there is minimum risk of their misinterpretation.

The project specification is not usually a document which has been written in a day or two at the end of the selling operation. It is more likely to be a compilation of various documents which have accumulated over a period of discussions and negotiations with the client. Most specifications are centred around a main document that contains a descriptive text, which is supported by various separate specifications, schedules and drawings. Some of these documents will have undergone several changes during solution engineering and commercial discussions.

In order to be able to define the specification in all respects, therefore, it must contain a contents list giving the reference number, title, date and correct revision number of every document that forms part of the specification. It follows that, should it be necessary to revise and reissue any of the documents listed, the specification contents list must itself be updated and reissued to show the correct revision number of the documents affected. The serial and revision numbers of the contents list therefore identify the specification and its correct revision status.

As the accurate definition of work and contract terms depends so much on having the correct document numbers and revision numbers, it is relevant now to discuss briefly some aspects of document numbering.

Numbering systems within the specification

It is assumed that the contractor will use a general document numbering system which is dictated either by his normal practice, or (alternatively) by the demands of the client. The subject of numbering systems is discussed elsewhere in this book, especially with relevance to cost coding and work breakdown packages, but care should be taken to keep the systems as simple as possible, avoiding the need for numbers containing great numbers of digits. Such numbers irritate and confuse those who have to work with them, and they are often designed by systems or computer engineers in the (mistaken) belief that they will afford great benefits of detailed cost analysis and effective control.

Starting with the project number itself, this can form the prefix to all drawing and cost code reference numbers in a well-regulated system. One good idea is to start with the last two digits of the year, and then allocate a serial number. Thus, the tenth project started by a contractor in the year 1997 might be numbered 97010. If the project splits nicely into two or more main parts, rather than complicating the numbers by adding subcodes a block of numbers can be used in a series: for example the supply of five special machines, all different, but all comprising one project, could be covered by allocating number 97010 for the main project, with 97011, 97012, 97013, 97014 and 97015 as the subproject numbers for the separate machines. Main assembly codes and, within them, subassembly codes can then be suffixed.

149

If the main specification is given the number 97010SPEC (for example) the revision number at the time of start-up must also be given in any works order or project procedure authorization. If (again for example) the specification is issued at revision 4, then its contents list is also at revision 4. Thus the specification issue number should automatically define the issue or revision number of all constituent documents, since all these document serial and revision numbers are listed in the contents list.

MODIFICATIONS, VARIATIONS AND OTHER CHANGES

Production of the project specification at start-up is only one stage in project definition. As work is done, so client-generated changes, production difficulties, alternative methods chosen for expediency and essential engineering changes for reasons of safety or performance assurance can all lead to divergence from the details contained in the first active issue of the project specification.

It is good practice to highlight the items which have changed in any document at each revision. This will be a familiar practice to engineers working with drawings, where the details of changes are listed in tables on the borders of the drawings, while the relevant revision numbers are used to annotate the actual drawing changes by placing them in triangles adjacent to the altered dimensions or views. This practice can be extended to the specification itself, with the revision numbers entered in the margins alongside the paragraphs which differ from earlier issues. One company uses the simple device of ruling a vertical line in the margin against items which have changed at the first revision, two parallel vertical lines for those affected at the second revision, three parallel lines for the third revision, and so on. The project manager, and anyone else interested, can see where the text changes have taken place and get an accurate picture of how the technical and commercial specification has been developed with the customer.

At any stage in a project, each participant who is working to documented instructions must be clear that he or she has the correct issue of the document. This may or may not be the latest issue (for example, it is possible for more than one batch of components to be in production at the same time which must be built to different issues of the same drawing because some are for prototype use while others are being made for project stocks for use on later assemblies). And so, the concept of the master record index or build schedule has developed. This document, which is an amplification of the original contents list in the project specification, lists all production documents needed by number, description and revision number. Where more than one main assembly or batch of equipment is being produced, and where these are built to different designs owing to changes, then there must be a build schedule or master record index for each situation.

The control of changes is a very important aspect of project management and formalized procedures are developed in all well-run companies to deal with them. For more on the subject of contract variations which affect the project definition, see Chapters 7 and 12. Procedures for controlling the introduction of

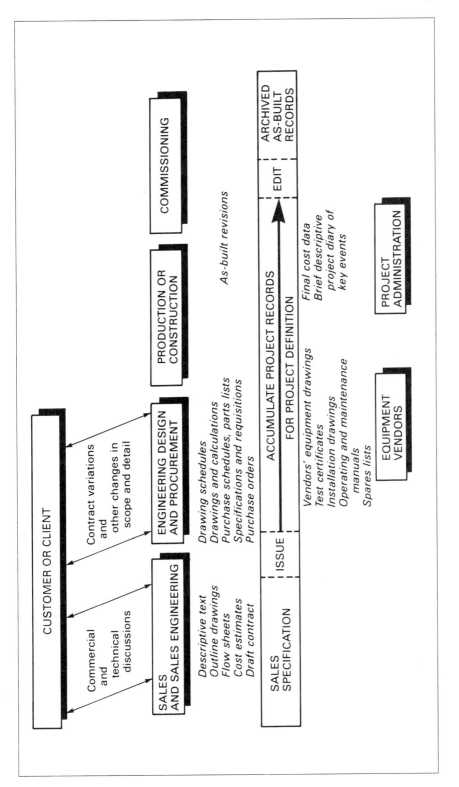

Figure 9.3 Stages of project definition

The sales specification is only the first stage in defining the project. The process of definition is not complete until as-built records are safely archived for future retrieval.

changes arising from various reasons during the progress of a project are given in Chapter 28.

DEFINING THE PROJECT 'AS-BUILT'

In Figure 9.3 a sequence of stages is depicted which shows that a project cannot be fully defined until it has been finished. Changes to engineering drawings may be necessary right up to the very last stages of commissioning. Vendors' drawings, operating manuals, test certificates and results, spares lists and the specifications against which the equipment was purchased all form part of the project records. This information has to be assembled and kept in order that the contractor is able to fulfil later commitments to the client if rectification work is needed, or if the client needs operating advice or later extensions to the project. The contractor is obliged to make sure that he knows and retains in archives all information needed to define the project as-built.

When the project started, final costs were available only in the form of estimates. When the project has been finished, the actual costs should be known. These, if recorded, are valuable data towards the comparative cost estimating of similar projects to be undertaken in the future.

Some companies arrange that a concise 'project diary' is filed with the archives, describing briefly the scope and course of the project, together with any key events and particular problems, difficulties or successes. Coupled with the filing of contractual documents, calculations and other engineering data, such a diary can be invaluable should disputes arise between client and contractor concerning plant operation or safety, or any other contractual matter. When it is borne in mind that the active life of some built projects is sufficiently long for problems to arise several years after initial completion, the need for careful historical definition is very important. Project managers come and go. If a serious defect arises which gives rise to a claim for damages, the contractor organization will be in a stronger position to mount a fair defence if his records are properly archived in a readily readable and retrievable form.

10 The Impact of Europe on Project Management

David J. Warby

The Single Market is a reality, 42 years after the initial vision of a European community by Robert Schumann, the French foreign minister. Great Britain has been a member of the European Community since 1973 although, for many people and businesses, the implications have been understood slowly. The effects of the legal changes already implemented and those further contemplated will have an accelerating impact. This will be particularly noticeable in the management of large projects.

The profound changes with the European Community and the Single Market seem set to be extended through additional membership. Formal applications for full membership of the Community have been submitted by Austria, Sweden, Turkey, Malta, Cyprus, Finland, Hungary, Czechoslovakia, and Poland. The first step is likely to be the addition of six of the seven EFTA nations: Austria, Finland, Iceland, Norway, Sweden and Lichtenstein (Switzerland having decided to remain outside). These six will observe all the Single Market laws but retain border controls, external non-EC tariffs, and their own social and fiscal policies. With their full participation in the free trade agreements, this will form the European Economic Area, increasing the market to some 380 million people.

The upheavals in the former Soviet Union and Eastern Europe have unexpectedly broadened the scope and potential for unification throughout Europe. The Community already plays a significant role in certain areas, specifically with the PHARE programme for the reconstruction of the Polish and Hungarian economies which, in 1992, had a budget of ECU 1000 000 000 to provide assistance through consultancy services. There are plans to expand this aid to the former Soviet and other East European nations. Indications that they wish to apply for membership of the Community have been received from Estonia, Latvia, Lithuania, Romania and Bulgaria. The specific and limited objectives of the early Community are now much modified, and 'Europe' is less precise a definition than customarily used in this context.

A NEW ERA

The Community's purpose in establishing the Single Market was to give all the citizens of member states the right to the 'four fundamental freedoms', anywhere within the Community:

1   to live where they choose;
2   to work where they choose;
3   to set up in business to trade in goods and services; and
4   to trade in capital.

These ambitious criteria have required laws which necessarily curtail certain previous freedoms in order to permit the wider freedoms. An immediate example is that of public procurement, where public (and some private) purchasers are required to operate their buying practices in ways that open up their business to all companies in all member states.

The Single Market legislation has three fundamental parts – the removal of physical, technical, and fiscal barriers to free trade. The Cecchini Report (1988) concluded that full implementation of the Single Market will produce a 5 per cent economic gain, increasing to 7 per cent when the correct macro-economic policies are in place. This will be accompanied by a 6 per cent fall in prices and a 5 million increase in employment. When fully operational, these laws seek to make doing business in Birmingham no different or more difficult than in Bremen, Bordeaux, or Barcelona. The reality will always be less perfect, but the essential conditions now exist for this to be possible. For project managers, the legal issues that will be of most importance are public procurement, technical harmonization, competition policy, and the free movement of labour and the professions.

A brief history of the European Community

In the post 1945 years, Cold War tensions, and the issue of the economic recovery of Federal Germany as a defence against the Russian threat were at the centre of policy for the American, British and French governments. There were looming economic difficulties with the European steel industries because of rising output and falling demand. At the request of his American and British counterparts, Robert Schumann was given an urgent assignment to reintegrate Federal Germany into the Western community. Efforts to face a Soviet threat, to avoid future conflicts between the countries that had fought each other so often, and to solve the problems of the European coal and steel industries found a common cause. The Schumann Declaration of May 1950 opens: 'World peace cannot be safeguarded without the making of creative efforts proportionate to the dangers which threaten it.' With this imperative, the declaration set out four principles for 'France ... to rebuild Europe ... inviting Germany to play its part':

1   Rivalry between France and Germany would be eliminated. The venture would be open to other European nations sharing the same objectives.

2 Immediate action would focus on a limited but decisive target, Franco-German coal and steel production, which would be placed under a common high authority.

3 The merging of economic interests would raise the standard of living and pave the way for the establishment of an economic community.

4 The high authority's decisions would be binding. Its members would be independent figures, jointly appointed. Its decisions would be enforceable.

This declaration led to an intergovernmental conference being convened by France in Paris the following month, with the three Benelux countries and Italy responding to the invitations. The conference refined and developed the plan, adding a council of ministers, a parliamentary assembly and a court of justice. This structure is still the basis of the present European Community. The details were incorporated in the Treaty of Paris to establish the European Coal and Steel Community (ECSC), signed in April 1951 by France, Germany, Italy, Holland, Belgium, and Luxembourg.

The possibilities of further economic cooperation were recognized, and in 1957 the same signatories completed the Treaty of Rome to establish the European Economic Community. Cooperation in nuclear energy was covered at the same date by a further Treaty establishing the European Atomic Energy Community (EURATOM).

Britain signed the Treaty of Rome on 1 January 1973. Denmark and Ireland joined on the same date, with Greece (1981), Portugal and Spain (1986) as subsequent additions.

THE SINGLE MARKET

The legislation to complete the Single Market became fully effective on 1 January 1993. This is in the form of 282 directives, issued by the European Commission. They are binding upon the member states as to the result to be achieved within a stated period, but leaving the detailed implementation to national legislators.

The completion into national laws was required prior to 1 January 1993. The summary of the legislative programme is shown in Figure 10.1. Not all the directives listed in Figure 10.1 will affect projects, at least not directly. The area of most familiarity for those in project management is Part II, and the summaries given later in this chapter identify the key issues.

Great Britain stood aloof from the Treaty of Paris and the birth of the Community with the formation of the ECSC in 1951, had its application to join the developing European Economic Community vetoed in 1963, and eventually became a member in 1973.

The thinking in recent years within the Commission has identified fundamental practical and political changes that are seen as necessary for the full implementation of the Single Market, and the vision of Europe from Brussels. These involve the sovereignty of member states, with common economic, monetary, foreign, defence and social policies. The European Economic Community (ECC) has been retitled the European Community (EC), underlining the far reaching nature *155*

PART I: THE REMOVAL OF PHYSICAL BARRIERS	Number of directives
1 Control of goods	
1.1 Various controls	10
1.2 Veterinary and phytosanitary controls	82
2 Control of individuals	8
PART II: THE REMOVAL OF TECHNICAL BARRIERS	
1 Free movement of goods	
1.1 New approach to technical harmonization and standards policy	11
1.2 Sectoral proposals	67
2 Public procurement	6
3 Free movement for labour and the professions	13
4 Common market for services	
4.1 Financial services	24
4.2 Transport	11
4.3 New technologies and services	5
5 Capital movements	3
6 Creation of suitable conditions for industrial cooperation	
6.1 Company law	7
6.2 Intellectual and industrial property	8
6.3 Taxation	5
PART III: THE REMOVAL OF FISCAL BARRIERS	
1 VAT and excise duties	22
Total	282

Figure 10.1   The Single Market legislation directives

of the plans, beyond the original economic objectives. The 'federal Europe' argument rages. The basic economic objectives are not disputed, however, and the debate about how far political changes are essential for their proper working should not obscure the vital and urgent need to react to the new commercial world.

The competitive arena

The new trading freedom within the Community has changed the project scene for ever. The United Kingdom has a long history of trading outside its borders, and has built an industrial capability for the design and execution of capital 156 projects of all types and sizes throughout the world, but this trade was founded on the protected markets of the Empire. In the same timescale as the development of the European Community, the former Empire nations, now independent, have established new trading patterns with other suppliers. UK overseas project activity has steadily declined in the face of competition from all over the world.

The Single Market adds another dimension to the competitive pressure on UK companies, and demands new attitudes. Great Britain can no longer be seen as a 'home' market, where the only competition is from other British companies. The UK is now just part of a market without commercial frontiers. This brings the competitors from all the other member states to our doors – but gives free access for UK companies to their markets in return.

The scope of projects as they will be performed in the EC is immense. While the traditional large construction projects will tend to be those that spring to mind at first, large projects also take place in telecommunications, information technology, aerospace, defence, transport and scientific research. At lower levels the range is almost infinite.

Strategies

The first decision that an organization has to make in pursuing its market is to decide the geographical limits of its activities. For some it will be the local operations, close enough to be served on a daily travel basis. Beyond that lie regional, national, and international levels of organization. Balanced against those choices will be the questions of size, capability and credibility.

It is apparent that international operations cannot be effectively undertaken without local knowledge, skills and connections. These can be provided by:

- joint ventures for specific projects;
- permanent joint ventures;
- setting up new local companies and recruiting local nationals; and
- acquiring existing local businesses.

In the run up to 1993 all of these approaches have been adopted by virtually all the member states. The single project joint venture is the simplest and there were already many instances before the 1993 threshold (for example, the second Severn crossing with Laing and GTM–Europe of France which, in turn, resulted in the introduction of Italian steel fabricators through GTM–Europe, and demonstrates a likely pattern).

A significant number of cross-border acquisitions have taken place, and continue to do so, establishing a new pattern of industrial ownership. In 1991 the pattern of these transactions in the field of project management and construction showed the position summarized in Figure 10.2. This trend is likely to continue, with the control of international operations falling to progressively fewer companies. Non-EC nations are facing the problem by setting up European subsidiaries.

The ability to win projects will depend as always on the ability to assemble a comprehensive package of concept, finance, technical expertise, credibility, and *157*

Nation	Inward acquisitions	Outward acquisitions	Outward inward ratio
France	40	120	3.0
Germany	51	63	1.2
United Kingdom	49	56	1.1
Netherlands	40	51	1.3
Italy	9	21	2.3
Spain	65	12	0.2
Belgium	47	6	0.1
Luxembourg	7	0	0.0
			———
Totals	308	329	
Average ratio			1.1

Figure 10.2 European Community cross-border company purchases in the construction industries to 1991 (Source: Twist, 1992)

resources that meets the competitive demands of the market. Competition for projects is likely to become intense, because of the importance to the company of winning and, in the case of large projects, the local and national interest. Government support and intervention is supposed to be regulated as part of the process of creating 'a level playing field'. In many cases government co-operation is inseparable from success, and this is an area which will be watched carefully as the full market matures.

One part of the effective response to project demands is the capability of companies to offer the necessary resources and competitiveness. The enlarged market will enable the leading organizations to benefit by increasing their resources (at the expense of weaker competitors) and benefit from economies of scale and specialization. This will apply to project-based businesses at main contractor, lead contractor, subcontractor and equipment supplier levels.

While the legislative programme for the Single Market was completed for the end of 1992 deadline, full implementation of the laws in all member states will not take place immediately, giving some nations leeway on account of particular problems. It is also a probability that the enforcement will vary from state to state. The European Court of Justice has extensive powers to punish breaches of the law but the practicability of policing all the transactions that will take place must be questionable. One European industrialist was heard to remark 'What level playing field? This is not a game. This is war!'

STANDARDS, TESTING AND CERTIFICATION

Individual national standards will be progressively eliminated, so that a product that meets the relevant standard can be sold in any member state. This will be achieved by:

- Preventing new technical barriers to trade being introduced, through the requirement to notify the Commission of any new technical regulations that are envisaged. The Commission and any member state can object if the regulation would act as a barrier to trade.
- The introduction of European standards and common rules. These will be produced through the European standards bodies CEN, CENELEC, and ETSI which work with national standards bodies and governments. Under the 'new approach to technical harmonization and standards', essential requirements are laid down by directives for health, safety, consumer protection and the environment. The technical requirements to comply with these directives are then developed as European standards. Products that meet these standards must carry the 'CE' mark, and no member state can refuse access to the market of such a product on technical grounds.
- Testing, certification and inspection under the 'new approach' directives will only have to be carried out once, rather than (as in the past) often having to be repeated for each nation's requirements. To make this possible, common criteria for assessing the competence of national test and certification bodies are being developed.

Approved bodies

Approved bodies (sometimes called notified bodies) are those who meet the criteria for competence set out in the relevant directive and have been notified to the European Commission. They will be the approved bodies for the testing, certification or inspection of products or systems. In the United Kingdom they will be expected to comply with the EN45000 series of European standards. A relevant accreditation will normally be taken as evidence of compliance with the criteria.

Technical cooperation between the approved bodies in different member states will be fostered by the European Organization for Testing and Certi-fication. The thrust will be to avoid challenges to the acceptability of CE-marked products, and to help meet special requirements for certification in addition to the CE mark.

Testing and the accreditation of testing laboratories

In the United Kingdom, laboratory accreditation is undertaken by the National Measurement Accreditation Service (NAMAS), operated by the National Physical Laboratory. The concept of accreditation is gaining wide acceptance in the other Community nations, and nearly all the 18 countries of the EC and EFTA have laboratory accreditation systems in operation or under development. A network of agreements for the mutual recognition of test results is developing. The purpose of these agreements is to recognize the equivalence of the accreditation systems. The adoption of European standards on the basic oper-ation of calibration and test laboratories, and for their accreditation will help. These standards, EN45001, EN45002 and EN45003, were published as identically worded British standards in the BS7500 series in 1989.

Certification and the accreditation of certification bodies

In the United Kingdom accreditation of certification bodies is given by the Secretary of State for Trade and Industry, on the advice of the National Accreditation Council for Certification Bodies (NACCB) which assesses certification bodies against the EN 45000 series. Accredited certification bodies are entitled to use the NACCB mark, the national quality 'tick'. Mutual recognition of national accreditation systems is beginning to develop in the Community along similar lines to the United Kingdom.

The assessment of a firm's quality systems in the United Kingdom is generally to BS5750, which is identical to the European standard EN29000 series and the international ISO9000 series. Quality Assurance systems are not widely adopted in the rest of the Community, although the adoption of BS5750 as a European standard is likely to make the concept more widely understood and used. In France a new national body, AFAQ, has been set up to coordinate third party certification of firms against EN29000.

For the time being, possession of a BS5750 compliance will not give UK companies automatic access to customers in other Community countries. Similarly, UK purchasers who demand BS5750 compliance from their suppliers will not be able to buy from companies in other Community countries who are unable to offer the equivalent, without breaching their own rules.

Product certification is common in other European countries, and in the United Kingdom is best represented by the BSI's 'kitemark'. The 'kitemark' certifies that a product has been manufactured to comply with a specific product standard by a company with a quality system that conforms to BS5750. Because of the low incidence of formal quality systems in other countries, product certification is frequently done by tests on sample products, some element of assessment of production methods, and follow-up checks on products and factory inspection.

Inspection bodies

With the adoption of the EN45000 series of standards, inspection bodies are now eligible for accreditation by the Secretary of State for Trade and Industry on the advice of the NACCB. Progress with mutual recognition between the other member states has not commenced, and the distinction between inspection, testing and certification is less clearly defined. In Germany for example, TUV (Technischer Uberwachungs-Verein) operates as separate organizations, which are described as test laboratories, inspection bodies, and certification bodies.

PUBLIC PROCUREMENT DIRECTIVES

The reform of public procurement was recognized by the EC heads of government as one of their top five priorities. The Commission has comprehensive objectives in this field. They are:

1 To stop government intervention, and to have purchasing done on commercial, not political grounds.

2 To create competition:

(a) allowing the economies of world-scale production;

(b) eliminating discriminatory national rules and protecting purchasers from political influence by ensuring the publicity of all transactions; and

(c) preventing monopolies.

3 To create a 'transparent' market by ensuring that:

(a) information on forthcoming contracts is published;

(b) purchasers specify in a way that is accessible to all;

(c) product specifications are against published standards.

The complete programme of public purchasing rules covers five areas. The term 'public' has been given a very wide definition with the drafting of the Utilities Directive, which will bring the operations of energy, water, transport and telecommunications within similar rules. This brings a large number of private undertakings into the net.

A simplified summary of the five directives follows. This sets out the main provisions, but not the detailed procedures that are required of both purchasers and suppliers. The financial limits given applied at the time of writing (early 1993).

Public Supplies Directive

The Public Supplies Directive covers the sale, hiring and leasing of goods to central, regional and local government and similar bodies (such as the UK National Health Service, education, fire, police authorities and comparable bodies in the other EC and EFTA countries). All contracts above the threshold values of ECU 134 000 (for central government) or ECU 200 000 (for regional and local government) are subject to the rules.

The rules lay down stringent requirements for advertising of contract requirements, the qualification of suppliers, contract award procedures, and contract award criteria.

Public Works Directive

The Public Works Directive covers contracts for construction or civil engineering works for the same bodies as the Supplies Directive. All contracts above a threshold value of ECU 5 000 000 are subject to the rules, and if work is divided up into several packages, the aggregate value is used to determine the threshold.

Similar rules to those in the Supplies Directive exist for the administration of tendering and contract award.

Public Services Directive

This directive deals with the purchasing of services by the entities covered by the Supplies and Works Directives. Contracts above the threshold value of *161*

ECU 134 000 (for central government) and ECU 200 000 (for regional and local government) are covered. Scheduled to come into force in mid-1993, the directive divides services into three categories.

Category 1 services (priority services)

These are likely to be the maintenance and repair of equipment, land transport and courier services, air transport services of passengers and freight, transport of mail by air and land (except rail), telecommunications, certain financial services, computer and computer-related services, some research and development, accounting, auditing and book-keeping, market research, management consulting and related services, architectural, engineering planning and related scientific and technical services, advertising, building cleaning and property management, publishing and printing, and sewage, refuse disposal and sanitation services.

Category 2 services

These are likely to be hotel, restaurant, rail transport, water transport, auxiliary transport, and some financial, legal, personnel, security, educational, health, recreational, cultural, and sporting services not covered by Category 1.

Category 3 services

This category is for those services which are impractical to cover by the directive.

Compliance Directive

This directive deals with the arrangements to ensure compliance with the Supplies, Works, and Services Directives and provides for:

- the setting up of national systems to review allegations of the infringement of the rules;
- the national bodies operating these systems to have powers to set aside unlawful decisions (if contracts have not been awarded), or to award damages; and
- the Commission to ask member states for an explanation of any 'clear and manifest infringement'.

Regulation is left to member states, with the ultimate ability of the Commission to take action against a member state in the European Court of Justice.

Utilities Directive

162   This directive widens the scope of the Community's public purchasing rules, by

covering some private sector bodies, where they have 'special or exclusive rights'. Four sectors which are excluded from the Public Supplies and Public Works Directives are energy, water, transport and telecommunications. Purchasing of supplies, works and services in these sectors is covered by the Utilities Directive. The following activities are covered by the rules:

- Production, transport, or distribution of drinking water.
- Production, transport, or distribution of electricity.
- Transport or distribution of gas.
- Exploration for, and extraction of, oil or gas.
- Exploration for, and extraction of, coal and other solid fuels.
- Contracting entities in the field of railway services.
- Contracting entities in the field of urban railway, tramway, trolley bus, or bus services.
- Contracting entities in the field of airport facilities.
- Contracting entities in the field of maritime or inland port or other terminal facilities.
- Operation of telecommunications networks or the provision of telecommunications services.

The rules cover public contracting entities in the public sector. Private sector bodies will be covered if they have 'special or exclusive rights', and if they:

- provide or operate a network producing or distributing drinking water, electricity, gas or heat;
- exploit a geographical area to explore for, or extract, oil, gas, coal or other solid fuel;
- provide terminal facilities to carriers by air, sea, or inland waterways; or
- provide or operate one or more public telecommunications services.

Bodies which supply water, gas, or electricity to the relevant networks will also be covered, unless their production is not covered by the directive and is a small part of their turnover.

The definition of services is very similar to that of the Public Services Directive.

Contract thresholds for this directive are:

- ECU 600 000 for telecommunications supplies and services.
- ECU 400 000 for supplies and services in other sectors.
- ECU 5 000 000 for works.

The rules provide for similar requirements for advertising, qualification of suppliers, contract award procedures, and contract award criteria as the Public Supplies and Works Directives, but with some more flexibility.

Remedies

To ensure compliance with the Utilities Directive, member states have two alternative systems from which they may choose:

1 They may follow the arrangements that exist under the Compliance Directive for the Public Sector.
2 Alternatively they may choose to have the power to impose a purchasing systems audit on certain, or on all, contracting parties. This would be as an alternative to the possible suspension of award procedures or the setting aside of decisions. The review body would have the power to order compensation if a confirmed infringement is not corrected. In claims for damages, tendering costs will be deemed to be 1 per cent of the contract value, unless proved to be higher.

Transitional arrangements exist for Spain (where this directive comes into force on 1 January 1996) and for Portugal and Greece (where the effective date is 1 January 1998).

COMPETITION POLICY

A fundamental principle of the Treaty of Rome is that the Community should set up a system ensuring that competition in the Single Market is not distorted. The essential requirements are set out in Articles 85 and 86 of the Treaty.

Article 85 (1) prohibits agreements between firms which may affect trade between member states, and have as their objective the prevention of the distortion of competition within the common market. In particular, the fixing of prices, sharing of markets or discriminating against third parties are strictly precluded. Such agreements are void and unenforceable, and the parties involved are liable to substantial fines by the Commission. Third parties are able to seek injunctive or other remedies in their national courts. The scope of this article is limited to actions that have an appreciable effect on trade, and involve firms with an aggregate turnover of more than ECU 200 000 000 and a market share of more than 5 per cent.

Article 86 prohibits the abuse by one or more firms of a dominant position, where this may affect trade between member states. This might be by predatory pricing, limiting production, refusal to supply, or the imposition of discriminatory trading terms. There are no provisions for exemption from these prohibitions.

Article 90 extends the principles of Articles 85 and 86 to the operation of public enterprises, and to firms that have been granted exclusive rights by a member state.

Articles 92, 93, and 94 regulate the application of state subsidies. Briefly, these state that governments must notify the Commission of aid proposals, and these are considered on the criterion of whether the aid will contribute to the agreed Community objectives. The Commission issues its decision, if necessary after consulting all member states.

These provisions have been invoked regularly since their enactment and are likely to be a feature of trading in the Single Market with its unique competition policy.

WORKING IN THE SINGLE MARKET

Nationals of member states have the right to seek and take up work in any EC country, provided that they comply with the laws on employment, and have a valid passport or national identity card. They are entitled to the same treatment as nationals of that country in matters of pay, working conditions, training, income tax, social security and trade union rights. In practical terms, many jobs will require specific proof of professional qualifications, skills or vocational training.

The professions

Freedom of movement for the professions is provided for by a number of directives. Eight directives provide specific arrangements for doctors, nurses, dentists, veterinary surgeons, midwives, architects and pharmacists. Directive 89/48/EEC lists the professions regulated by law (for example, solicitor, patent agent and so forth) and those regulated by professional association (such as chartered engineer, chartered accountant, etc.). The law adopts the principle of mutual recognition of qualifications, subject to two safeguards. These are that additional requirements may be imposed if the person's length of education and training is shorter or the content different from that specified by the country to which they wish to move.

Vocational skills

Work on vocational skills is being carried out in Berlin at the European Centre for the Development of Vocational Training (CEDEFOP) to establish the comparability of vocational qualifications. Sectors so far covered include the construction industry and electrotechnology. EC legislation exists to require that member states recognize qualifications and experience obtained elsewhere in the Community. Member states must also issue certificates of experience which in turn must be recognized by other member states in place of their own national qualifications. Directive 64/427 covers certificates of experience for self-employed work in manufacturing, processing, repair and construction.

Health and safety

The Single European Act of 1986 introduced to the Treaty of Rome new provisions for health and safety. The responsibilities for employers and employees are analogous to those provided by the Health and Safety at Work Act 1974. It covers assessment of risks, introduction of preventive measures, provision of information, safety training, and consultation with workers' representatives.

Product safety will be defined by the 'new approach to technical harmonization *165* and standards', whose essential requirements lay down a level of health and safety to which products have to conform.

THE PRACTICALITIES

The twelve countries of the EC are on a unique road with the Single Market. Their relative economic strengths and stages of industrial and social development vary considerably. The objective is an open market for the member states, with free competition, all for the common good. The Schumann Declaration of 1950 may be seen in history as one of the world's great political visions and, amazingly, in 43 years has been translated into a close model of the original concept.

Full implementation of the Single Market will take some time, as transitional arrangements are completed, and the practice of new laws is tested. As all this happens, additional participants will join, initially to form the European Economic Area, and subsequently, full members will probably be admitted. This has already created one of the world-scale markets, and looks set to grow.

For British project managers, it is a situation filled with opportunities and threats: access to the enlarged market provides a colossal opportunity, but many of the existing obstacles to doing business in other EC countries will remain. The converse is true: the UK offers a very open market for foreign competitors. Acquisition of UK public companies by foreign bidders presents no basic problems, whereas for British companies to acquire public companies in some EC countries is virtually impossible. Control will influence the placing of contracts that are not in the public domain.

Fog in the channel – Europe cut off

This apocryphal newspaper headline has, in the past, typified the British feeling about Europe. The British are an island people. History has given good reason to be grateful for this natural fact. However, while insularity has its strengths, with modern transport and communications, and world-scale industries, physical separation from our neighbours must be seen in a different light. The English Channel means that a journey to a continental client from the UK is a significant task, but for our continental competitors it is often a modest car trip. The centre of business activity in the Single Market must lie somewhere well east of the continental coast. With contact in the market being crucial, the United Kingdom's businessmen are going to have to adopt strategies that overcome this physical disadvantage.

The opportunities for strengthening industry through increased economies of scale are crucial in a world that increasingly operates on a global basis. The United Kingdom has insufficient home demand to support many industrial sectors at competitive world class and, without the former Empire markets, needs to look to its new home market – The European Single Market – and beyond to the rest of Europe. The best of British companies have already understood this and acted effectively.

Project managers will have to recognize new constraints on their actions, as well as the opportunities that are presented by the wider scope of the new market. The directives discussed will be of immediate relevance. Inevitably, observance of the law will vary, and enforcement may prove a Pyrrhic victory for the plaintiff, with damages being a poor substitute for lost business. However, the history of actions by the Commission through the European Court of Justice demonstrate that the laws affecting the conduct of the Single Market will progressively bring about the planned free trade. The most important influences on success will be the actions to establish local connections. Just as 'walking the job' is necessary to learn the facts, so living and working at the critical location of influence is the only way to do business – which is the start and finish of project management. Those 'Spanish practices' exist everywhere – in Manchester as well as Madrid.

USEFUL ORGANIZATIONS FOR FURTHER INFORMATION

The European Commission, 200 Rue de la Loi, 1049 Brussels.
  Telephone: 010–322 235 1111
  The Commission has information offices in London, Belfast, Cardiff, and Edinburgh

The European Parliament UK Information Office, 2 Queen Anne's Gate, London SW1H 9AA.
  Telephone: 071–222 0411

The Department of Trade and Industry, 1–19 Victoria Street
  London SW1H OET.
  Telephone: 071–215 5000
  Also at regional offices throughout the United Kingdom

European Information Centres
  A network established by the European Commission to provide information to small and medium-sized enterprises on research and development, finance, training, public contracts, market intelligence and community contracts. They are frequently located at Chambers of Commerce. See local telephone directories.

European Documentation Centres
  These contain substantial collections of EC documentation. They are mostly based in university libraries. Though mainly intended for academic research, they allow public access and provide an information service to the wider community. See local telephone directories.

REFERENCES AND FURTHER READING

Cecchini, Paolo, *Research on the cost of non-Europe*, HMSO Books, Brussels, 1988.

Croner's Europe, Croner, Kingston upon Thames (updated monthly).

Twist, D. R., 'A main contractor's response to the European market', Conference paper from 'Project management in the Single European Market', Institution of Mechanical Engineers, 19 May 1992.

Vacher's European companion and consultants' register, A. S. Kerswill Ltd, 113 High Street, Berkhampstead, Hertfordshire HP4 2DJ, UK (updated quarterly)

Part Three
ACCOUNTING AND FINANCE

11 Financing the Project*

National Westminster Bank plc

Project finance has developed over a number of years and the term has acquired several different, and sometimes rather specialized, meanings. For the purpose of this chapter the term 'project finance' will be used in its broadest sense, meaning the arrangement of adequate funds to finance the development and construction of a specific major project.

The particular way in which finance is arranged will depend upon the type of development and will vary from project to project. For example, the scheme needed for an infrastructure project in a developed industrialized country will differ from that required in a lesser developed country and both of these will be different from the type of financing arrangements appropriate to the development of a natural resource such as a mine or an oilfield.

In some projects the sponsors will undertake full responsibility for arranging the financial package, leaving the contractor to produce the technical response to the tender invitation. In others the sponsor will require the contractor to produce a technical proposal supported by a full financial proposal. Whichever approach is adopted, there is a wide variety of financial options available. These might include, for example, capital issues, commercial borrowing, export credits, bilateral and multilateral aid.

This chapter describes some of the options available and the ways in which a bank can provide professional advice and arrange the necessary financing. Intended as a guide to the types of funding and financial services which are available from banks and other lending institutions, the chapter starts from the point where a project's viability has been established (at least to the borrower's satisfaction) and the decision has been made that the project should be financed from external sources.

* © National Westminster Bank plc.

SOME PROJECT FINANCING SITUATIONS

Projects in developed countries

There is a long history of arranging finance for projects in the developed countries. Project sponsors are usually well experienced in the traditional methods such as utilizing funds raised by taxation, the subscription of equity by private investors, the issue of capital bonds and the arrangement of loans against an acceptable security. However, the enormous increase in development costs in recent years has placed many projects, even in developed nations, outside the scope of the traditional methods and project sponsors and contractors increasingly are required to design alternative financing schemes.

Financial assistance is available, for example, from many governments as part of their internal programmes of industrial and social development, and these can provide a useful source of project funds. Again, many projects, which at one time might have been considered the responsibility of the public sector, are now beyond the resources of that sector and are being considered for privatization. While this is an important concept it must not be assumed that privatization will relieve the public sector of all its financial responsibilities towards a project. Many of the projects which might be suggested for privatization are provided for the public good and as such it is inevitable that they will have continuing environmental, social and infrastructural implications which will remain the concern of governments and for which governments will retain at least partial financial responsibility.

To summarize, therefore, while it remains important to understand the conventional methods of financing projects in the developed countries, it is also necessary to examine some of the alternatives that are now available.

Projects in developing countries

Most important projects in developing countries are in the public sector. If finance is required for these projects, the sponsor will usually be the government and the project will also probably be part of a larger scheme contained within, say, a national economic or development plan.

Few projects of this kind can be assessed in conventional balance sheet terms and it will be impossible for lenders, other than the World Bank and similar development agencies, to determine whether a project is viable within the context of the national plan as a whole. The lending institution will often have to content itself with an examination of the social and political situation within the borrowing country and the ability of the economy to generate sufficient foreign earnings to repay the loan. It will also consider the extent of its existing exposure to the borrowing country. If it is satisfied with all these factors it may be prepared to lend against the guarantee of the government of the borrower.

This is not to suggest, however, that project financing in the developing nations fits neatly within specific categories. Some projects may be part self-financing and part government sponsored, while others may involve the participation of large corporations, possibly in partnership with a government entity. Furthermore, the project itself may qualify for funds from a wide variety of sources including commercial banks, export credit agencies, development agencies, bilateral aid, or indeed any combination of these. Such considerations make it necessary to examine all the available methods of funding so that the sponsor can obtain the best mix of financing facilities; both sponsors and contractors may wish to call upon an experienced international bank to assess the alternatives and recommend the best solution.

Projects for the development of natural resources

Many projects for the development of natural resources are undertaken by large corporations whose financial position is often sufficient to enable them to undertake the projects, backed by the strength of their own balance sheets. However, the cost of some projects is now so great that these same corporations are becoming increasingly unwilling to make disproportionate financial commitments towards one particular project and are seeking other means of arranging the necessary finance.

In order to meet this requirement, the technique of 'limited recourse financing' has been developed so that the financial commitment and the risks associated with a project can be shared between the project sponsor and the lending institution, the lender's recourse for repayment being limited primarily to revenues from the project itself. Projects in the energy, mining and other natural resource industries are particularly suitable for such treatment. Limited recourse financing is discussed in more detail later in this chapter.

THE ROLE OF THE FINANCIAL ADVISER

Project sponsors do not always have the resources to identify and evaluate the variety of financing options that are available. Independent financial advisers may therefore play an important part by identifying those alternatives, in helping to prepare a financial plan and in coordinating the implementation of the eventual financing package. Project sponsors will turn to the international banks in seeking this advice and the adviser's task will include the consideration of both non-financial and financial factors.

Non-financial factors

Non-financial factors relate to the interrelationship between the project originator (who will probably also be the paymaster) the executing authority and the project manager. It will be most important to recognize the respective roles of these three entities and to make sure that the arrangements between them are such that there is no delay in the execution of the project because of misunderstanding or poor communications. For example:

173

1 *The statutory framework* The need to ensure that the project will not be disrupted because of statutory requirements, financial constraints or foreign exchange problems.

2 *The status of the project sponsor* As a borrower, the sponsor's:

(a) past experience of borrowing;
(b) ability to administer debt;
(c) legal position regarding state and federal authorities; and
(d) method of funding.

3 *The contractual framework*

(a) whether the project will be conducted on a turnkey basis or under the management of the sponsor;
(b) the position and responsibility of the main contractor and sub-contractors; and
(c) the terms of supply and offtake contracts.

Financial factors

On the financial side the adviser's task will be to recommend the way in which the project can be financed in a manner which will be of maximum benefit in terms of total financing cost, economy and ease of execution. The following are some of the factors that the adviser will consider:

1 *Advice on the project's financial structure* The adviser will:

(a) give advice on the level of borrowing which the project can support with different equity structures;
(b) recommend the optimum mix between different types and sources of funding; and
(c) provide advice on the structure of an appropriate security package for offshore loans, export credits and any local currency facilities.

The adviser may also need to provide advice on taxation issues, and on the use of appropriate Treasury products to hedge against interest rate risks.

2 *Negotiation with potential lenders* The adviser will assist with:

(a) the selection of, and approaches to, potential lenders in the international Eurocurrency market;
(b) Negotiations of credit terms with export credit agencies; and
(c) the obtaining of possible aid allocations or loans from governments and from such agencies as the World Bank, the European Investment Bank and the European Bank for Reconstruction and Development.

3 *Evaluation of financing proposals submitted in support of contractors' bids* It will be necessary for the project to obtain the best and most flexible terms available from concessionary and commercial sources in terms of interest rates, maturities, repayment schedules and currency options. A bank will apply computer-based techniques involving discounted cash flow (or

present value) analysis to the various financing proposals, so as to present an evaluation of the alternatives (see Chapter 15).

4 *Choice of currency* There are superficial attractions to borrowing in a currency which carries a low interest rate (such as the yen or Swiss franc) but the lower interest costs might be offset by movements in the exchange rate over the borrowing term. This, when it comes to repaying the loans, could mean that borrowing in a low-interest currency is no cheaper overall than borrowing in a higher-interest currency.

FUNDING METHODS

There are a number of alternative ways in which project finance packages can be assembled and some of the sources of funds which are available and some of the techniques that are used in deploying those funds are described below.

Eurocurrency market

Substantial funds can be raised in the Eurocurrency market either through borrowing from a number of individual banks, or through a syndicated loan from a group of banks. Such loans are available in many of the main currencies (although Eurodollar loans predominate) and are usually arranged at a margin of interest above a floating indicator rate, such as LIBOR (London Interbank offered Rate).

The terms of a Eurocurrency loan can be designed to give a great deal of flexibility. For example, it is possible to incorporate a multi-currency option which gives the borrower the right to switch part or all of the loan in any fully convertible currency (e.g. US dollars, pounds sterling or Deutschmarks). Currency and interest rate 'swaps' may be combined with a Eurocurrency loan to provide additional benefits. For example, if a loan has been put in place on a US dollar floating rate basis, it may be possible at a later date to convert the loan into fixed rate debt in another hard currency (say, yen or Swiss francs) through a technique involving interest rate and currency swaps which, when combined with long-dated currency exchange risk protection, can achieve savings in interest costs and a hedge against currency exposure. Borrowers of fixed interest export credits may find themselves well placed to offer loans to this market when there is an appropriate level of concessionality in the fixed rate.

If the size of the Eurocurrency loan is such that it will be necessary to syndicate it amongst a number of banks, the choice of a bank to lead the syndication (the lead manager) will be an important matter. It will be the lead manager (in liaison, if appropriate, with the financial adviser) who will be responsible for preparing an Information Memorandum and inviting other banks to participate in the loan. It will also be the lead manager's responsibility subsequently to negotiate a loan agreement acceptable to all parties. It is therefore essential that the bank appointed as lead manager should enjoy the confidence of the banking community.

Export credits

Most industrialized nations have government-supported export credit agencies which provide short- and medium-term export credit insurance and guarantee schemes which, subject to certain conditions, are readily available to exporters. In addition, subsidized finance on medium- and long-term credit is generally available to support the export of capital goods and services.

The terms upon which the majority of the industrialized nations make export credits available are arranged in accordance with agreements made under the auspices of the Organization for Economic Cooperation and Development (OECD).

These agreements are intended to prevent harmful competition and are known as the 'consensus terms'. Twenty-four nations accept the consensus terms, including the members of the European Economic Community, Japan, United States, Canada, Switzerland and the Scandinavian countries. A few countries which are not members of the OECD (Brazil, for example) have their own credit schemes which operate outside the agreed terms.

Interest rates under the consensus terms are offered at standardized fixed rates. These rates are dependent on the economic rating of the country of the borrower and on the currency of the loan. Importing countries are divided into three categories:

1 relatively rich;
2 intermediate; and
3 relatively poor.

The interest rates applicable to categories 1 and 2 countries are the commercial interest reference rates, which change each month and depend on the currency and term of the loan. The interest rate for category 3 is the lower of the consensus SDR (special drawing rights) based rate (which is reviewed every six months) and the commercial interest reference rate for the relevant currency.

Although at a first glance the consensus rates might not appear particularly attractive when viewed in isolation against market rates, there are the following inherent advantages in opting for this type of financing which are not always available in the more conventional forms of borrowing:

1 Interest fixed at a rate that is probably lower than the prevailing commercial rate.
2 A maturity period that is longer than that normally associated with commercial fixed interest lending.
3 A grace period on repayment covering the construction or supply phase.
4 Progress payments covering the construction phase.

Export credits are normally available for up to 85 per cent of the value of the export portion of the contract. The actual funding is frequently routed through commercial banks and, where there is a shortfall between the export credit element and the contract value, the banks may be willing to lend the shortfall or 'front end' element in the form of a commercial Eurocurrency loan, subject to market conditions.

Export credits are made available as either buyer credits or supplier credits. In the case of supplier credits, the exporter sells on deferred payment terms while borrowing from a commercial bank to finance the agreed payment period. The export credit or insurance agency will normally insure the exporter against political risks together with some of the commercial risks relating to the buyer and will provide a guarantee of repayment to the lending bank. In the case of buyer credits, the loan is made to the overseas buyer and the exporter receives direct payment from the lending bank on the instructions of the buyer. The bank which grants the loan is the beneficiary of the guarantee issued by the export credit or insurance agency.

It is usual for export credit agencies to match terms offered by other agencies in order to ensure that a potential exporter from the country in question is not placed at a competitive disadvantage. It is therefore important that the project sponsor should consider the strategy to be adopted in respect of export credits at the earliest possible stage.

The capital markets

The international bond markets in Europe, the United States and the Far East each offer to borrowers of undoubted strength the advantage of fixed and variable rate funding in a wide range of currencies and maturities. The markets are relatively free from regulation and offer enormous flexibility. Bonds are generally issued for up to 20 years, depending upon the currency, and in amounts per issue of up to US$100 million. International bonds are issued outside the country of residence of the issuer and, while the majority of issues have been in US dollars, Swiss francs, Deutschmarks or pounds sterling, more limited markets are available in Canadian dollars, French francs, Australian dollars and European currency units. Bonds offer the borrower flexibility at a cost that can be below that of a conventional syndicated loan.

The advantages of these markets therefore include savings in financing costs, the availability of long-dated maturities and fixed interest rates, flexibility and the fact that the markets attract non-bank investors and thereby widen the funding sources available to the borrower.

Multilateral aid

Multilateral aid funds are those made available by subscribing countries to such development agencies as the World Bank and the Asian Development Bank. These funds are on-lent, normally on concessionary terms, in support of developmental projects in those countries which are members of the development agencies. The governments of these member countries will maintain contact with the development agencies and will decide a list of priorities for using aid funds. A project which the government considers suitable for development aid support *177* will be submitted to the appropriate agency who will undertake an assessment of the viability and acceptability of the project. If support is agreed the agency will require the project sponsor to act as buyer and to invite tenders on an international competitive basis.

For projects in Central and Eastern Europe an important source of funds is the European Bank for Reconstruction and Development. This multinational institution was formed in 1991 with the objective of fostering the transition of the Central and Eastern European countries towards market-oriented economies.

Bilateral aid

Bilateral aid is provided on a direct country-to-country basis. The governments of the developed countries operate their own individual bilateral aid programmes, the policies and objectives of which differ and which have been developed as a result of discussions between donor and recipient nations. Each donor country has established its own organization; in West Germany for example, the Kreditanstalt für Wiederaufbau (KfW) and in Japan the Overseas Economic Cooperation Fund (OECF). The United Kingdom's aid programme is administered by the Overseas Development Administration (ODA).

The ODA is responsible for allocating funds between recipient countries and, in consultation with those countries, for selecting viable and worthwhile projects. United Kingdom industrial and commercial interests are taken into account and the acceptance of UK goods and services can sometimes be a condition of the provision of aid.

A small portion of United Kingdom bilateral aid funds is set aside each year for 'Aid and Trade Provision' (ATP). This is a fund which is available to support British firms tendering for projects in developing countries where Britain does not normally provide aid or where an allocation is already committed. Usually aid allocated under ATP is made available in association with export credits to enable UK exporters to match aid-assisted bids made by foreign competitors; this technique is sometimes known as 'mixed credit'.

The United Kingdom's bilateral aid is also distributed indirectly through the Commonwealth Development Corporation (CDC). This is an investment institution supported by loans from the aid programme and by self-generated funds. The purpose of the CDC is to assist in the economic development of lesser developed countries and, while its support is not necessarily tied to British goods, CDC requires that UK suppliers should be allowed an equal chance of tendering alongside other international contractors.

Leasing, forfaiting and confirming

These are financing techniques which limit the contingent liability on either the buyer or the seller and in some circumstances could usefully be introduced as part of a financing package.

Leasing

Leasing is based upon the concept that profit is generated by the use of an asset and not by its ownership. Under a leasing agreement the goods remain the property of the leasing company (the lessor) to whom the user (the lessee) will pay a rental. The lessor will often be able to make use of local taxation allowances and grants, the benefits of these allowances being reflected in the rental calculation, and it is therefore usually advantageous for a leasing facility to be arranged in the country of the overseas client.

Forfeiting and confirming

Exporters who wish to offer medium-term credit in support of their exports but wish to avoid the consequential recourse liability, might consider either forfaiting or confirming. Both methods involve the provision by a bank of fixed interest funding against the purchase of the supplier's bills of exchange. In the case of forfaiting, the financing will be at commercial rates of interest and will require the guarantee of an acceptable bank in the importing country. In the case of confirming, the finance will be at export credit rates and the guarantees will be provided by the export credit agency.

Bonds and guarantees

A bond or guarantee is a document issued on behalf of an exporter to a buyer by a third party, for example a bank, whereby the latter indemnifies the buyer against the failure of the supplier to comply with the obligations of a contract. There are many types of bonds and guarantees of which the following are the most common.

Tender bond

A bond provided by a bank to the buyer providing compensation, usually on demand, in the event that a supplier declines to enter into a contract in conformity with the bid that has been put forward.

Advance payment guarantee

A bond given to the overseas buyer in the amount of the advance payment and which will remain valid until progress on the contract equates to the amount of the advance payment.

Performance bond

A bond provided by a bank or an insurance company to the buyer providing compensation in the event that the contract is not completed or the goods supplied do not perform within the agreed specifications.

LIMITED RECOURSE FINANCE

A project sponsor may wish to limit his obligations to lenders and to restrict the *179* lenders' interest and repayment rights solely to the assets and revenue of the project. This section describes a lending technique known as limited recourse project finance, which goes some way to satisfy this requirement.

The advantages and disadvantages of limited recourse finance

Some of the advantages of limited recourse finance are:

1 Certain projects demand a degree of financial commitment beyond the resources of the asset owner and limited recourse financing is one means of obtaining the level of finance required.
2 Project sponsors may wish to reduce the extent of their financial exposure, either because of the technical nature of the project or of its particular location, or because of the uncertainty of future price levels.
3 The repayment of the financing may be tailored to reflect the actual performance of the project.
4 Constraints on the debt/equity ratios of a sponsor may be overcome by the creation of a credit structure which will give favourable balance sheet treatment to obligations and the associated debt.
5 Any security pledged in support of the financing can be isolated from the borrower's other assets, thereby avoiding the impact of cross-default clauses on other borrowings, should the project fail.

Some of the disadvantages of this type of financing are:

1 The interest cost may be higher than for a normal corporate or sovereign financing to reflect the additional risks the lender is asked to accept.
2 Other charges sought by the lender may be higher to reflect the greater complexity of the loan structure.
3 Project revenues may be locked-in to the project during the term of the financing.

Risk sharing

For purposes of explanation, the issues discussed in the following paragraphs relate particularly to petroleum projects. However, the principles can be applied to other resource industries, to processing projects and to other types of project that have an identifiable future revenue stream. The risks involved fall into three broad categories.

Technical

The extent to which lenders will accept technical risk will depend upon the sponsor's own technical evaluation of the project and upon a review by an independent consultant. Such a review would cover:

1 Geological and geophysical features and field delineation.

2 Calculation of proved and probable reserves and estimation of recovery factors.
3 The feasibility of the development programme.
4 The adequacy of the proposed production and transportation facilities and a consideration of any untried technological features.

Economic

Lenders will usually undertake:

1 An appraisal of the capital expenditure budget as proposed by the operator.
2 An assessment of anticipated operating costs.
3 A market study to assist in forecasting future prices.

Political

Political considerations can be divided into fiscal and non-fiscal, both of which may have a direct or indirect impact on cash flow:

1 Fiscal, including taxes, royalties, miscellaneous provisions and allowances, and exchange controls.
2 Non-fiscal, including regulations concerning field developments and production.

Normally, lenders will be able to obtain appropriate consents, undertakings and assurances from government that new or amended regulations will not be introduced which will affect their rights to obtain repayment of the debt.

Historical considerations

The willingness of international banks to assume risks in project financings has increased steadily in line with their familiarity with those risks and their ability to understand and assess them. For example, in the first major North Sea financing, banks were willing to assume (only) the reservoir risk – that is the risk of whether the oil was actually in place, regardless of technical or economic recoverability and that only after completion of the field facilities had taken place. In some more recent North Sea financings, banks have assumed all technical and economic risks on a proportion of the loan from the outset.

The terms of each financing will reflect not only the characteristics of the development itself but also the prevailing economic conditions and the future outlook for the industry as forecast by both lenders and borrowers. The bank invited to create a loan structure will be anxious to meet the defined objectives as expressed by the borrower, but it is vitally important, for successful syndication, to ensure that the structure devised for the project represents the banking market's attitude towards risk sharing.

Completion risk

Many projects, particularly offshore oil fields, have inherent production and development problems. For this reason lenders usually retain recourse to the sponsors until physical completion has taken place as defined by a completion test. Following a completion test, debt service may be a function solely of the revenues generated by the continued operation of the project. The terms of a completion test will always be tailored to meet the characteristics of each project, but in the case of an offshore oilfield, for example, will require evidence of:

1 completion of the physical facilities in accordance with the development plan;
2 cumulative production of a specified quantity of crude oil;
3 average daily production of a specified quantity of crude oil from a given number of wells over a specified period; and (if appropriate)
4 the efficiency of operation of a water and/or gas injection programme.

A completion test for a coal mining project would be similar in nature but would place rather more emphasis on the successful progress of the associated infrastructure development, such as roads, railways and coal distribution facilities. The completion test will usually be undertaken by an independent consultant acting on behalf of the lenders.

Cover ratio

A loan may be designed in such a way that once a completion test has been satisfied, lenders will assume some, or all, of the technical and economic risks of a project. However, in most cases, the amount of the resultant non-recourse loan will be limited by reference to recoverable reserves and future revenues. Customarily the revenue will be expressed in net present value terms and will take account of operating expenses, royalties and taxes. The discount factor used in this calculation will usually be related to the market view on interest rates during the life of the loan. The ratio between this revenue and the amount of the loan is the cover ratio. This ratio will have to be satisfied, for example:

1 At the time of drawdown of the non-recourse loan.
2 At the time of conversion of any part of the loan from recourse to non-recourse.
3 Following any repayment of principal.

The actual cover ratio to be maintained will be negotiated between lender and borrower and will reflect the perceived economic and technical viability of the development. In typical petroleum development financings, cover ratios of outstanding loan to future revenues have ranged from 1:1.5 to 1:2.0 over the loan life.

The calculation of the cover ratio will usually be performed either by an independent consultant for the lenders, or by the borrower, but with the lenders having the right to call for an independent audit in the event of disagreement, and to impose their own assumptions in such areas as future market price for the product. Depending on the circumstances, the revenue that will be calculated is that accruing over either the full life of the reserves, or the loan life. In calculating future revenues it will be necessary to estimate:

1 likely production levels of the remaining proven reserves;
2 future prices;
3 government royalties;
4 operating expenses;
5 taxation; and
6 any other project costs.

In the case of coal or gas projects (which unlike oil do not have large open markets), the lenders, when evaluating the revenue stream, would wish to be assured that firm sales contracts, probably with a fixed floor price, had been signed with first-class purchasers.

Repayment profile

Banks will view the proposed repayment profile as extremely important in assessing the acceptability of project risks. The repayment arrangements on project financings are normally set to balance two requirements:

1 The borrower's desire to achieve a reasonably long maturity with perhaps a fairly even repayment schedule and to retain a portion of the revenue.
2 The lenders' wish to avoid undue extension of the loan period, with a consequent increase in the risks being assumed, and to protect themselves against a deterioration in production or some disaster occurring during the life of the loan.

It is therefore likely that lenders will require a combination of the following repayment provisions:

1 The dedication of a specified percentage of available revenues from the preceding period on each repayment date.
2 A minimum repayment schedule over the life of the loan, with a provision that if repayments at the specified dedication percentage fail to maintain that schedule, the percentage may be increased up to 100 per cent while the shortfall exists.
3 A requirement that the dedication percentage should also be increased up to 100 per cent in the event that the cover ratios cease to be satisfied. (It is also possible to provide for a reduction in the dedication percentage if the ratios improve significantly – subject to an overall minimum repayment schedule.)

Whatever repayment arrangements are built into the loan agreement, lenders will require that a significant volume of proven reserves remain to be lifted after the expected final maturity of the loan.

Other considerations

Amount of project loan

The amount of a project loan will depend on the requirements of the sponsors and would typically be up to 70–80 per cent of development costs. In each case, the prime consideration will be the magnitude of the future revenue available for debt service.

Abandonment

Lenders have normally been willing to allow sponsors to cease production and abandon the project once production becomes uneconomic, for example once total costs of production in any period have not been covered by the proceeds of sale. In circumstances of abandonment the lenders will normally (of course) have the right to exercise their security.

Interest-rate premium

In order to compensate for the additional risks being assumed by lenders, they will usually seek a premium above the normal margin payable by the sponsors on a straightforward corporate or sovereign credit. The size of the premium will depend on the risks being assumed and the length of the loan.

FURTHER READING AND INFORMATION

Development Forum – Business Edition, twice monthly, from United Nations, CH 1211, Geneva 10, Switzerland (includes *Monthly Operational Summary of World Bank and Inter-American Bank*).

The Courier, bi-monthly from EEC Commission, Rue de la Loi 200, 1049 Brussels, Belgium. (Information about the European Development Fund.)

Britain's Aid Programme and Overseas Development. Six editions a year. Obtainable from Information Department, Overseas Development Administration, Eland House, Stag Place, London SW1E 5DH.

ECGD Services, Export Credits Guarantee Department, PO Box 2200, 2 Exchange Tower, Harbour Exchange Square, London, E14 9GS.

Export Intelligence Service. An information service for UK exporters. Obtainable from British Overseas Trade Board, Lime Grove, Eastcote, Ruislip, Middlesex HA4 8SG.

ACKNOWLEDGEMENT

This chapter was originally written by Michael Bull and Keith Savage (both formerly senior managers at the International Banking Division of National Westminster Bank). It has been revised for this edition by Peter Phillips, Director of Project Finance, NatWest Markets.

12 Cost Estimating

David Ross

Accurate cost estimates form the bedrock upon which all aspects of project pricing, budgeting and cost control are built. This chapter explains the various categories of cost estimates that the project manager is likely to encounter, outlines the principles for their compilation, and examines some of the procedures associated with computer-based techniques. The examples quoted are taken from projects in the mining, minerals and petrochemicals industries although the principles and techniques can be applied to virtually all organizations involved with project work. The practices described illustrate how the application of sensible work breakdowns, the use of a logical code of accounts and the employment of checklists, all act as practical aids in achieving estimates without avoidable omissions and with the degree of accuracy relevant to their purpose.

Together with the development of: project strategy, economic studies, resource planning and scheduling, cost estimating is a vital front-end project activity that should not be abbreviated. A casual approach is likely to lead to later mistakes in the management of the project, which could prove costly to the owner and associated groups.

THE NATURE OF COST ESTIMATES

Cost estimates prepared by the client or project purchaser (referred to from now on as the owner) are likely to be concerned with the life-cycle costs of the project. This ensures that the overall economic viability can be assessed in advance as part of the project appraisal techniques, and hence that the projected investment is likely to prove worthwhile.

The owner's cost estimate will be objective; embracing the pre-project, active project and post-project phases. The owner will need to estimate for:

1 capital costs;
2 operating and maintenance costs;

3   plant and equipment replacement costs;
4   working capital requirements; and
5   end-of-life costs.

Other estimates, although outside the scope of this chapter, will be the amount of revenue generated by the project from product sales.

Capital costs

A potential contractor preparing to tender for a project is likely to be concerned mainly with the initial capital cost estimates for the project rather than the subsequent operating costs. Capital costs include the acquisition of fixed assets together with the associated costs of bringing the fixed assets to an operational level.

Acquisition costs

Acquisition costs include supply, packing and transport (including any import duties, port charges and the like), construction, installation and commissioning charges associated with the permanent works.

Associated costs

Associated costs include engineering design, project management, construction management, contractors' preliminary and general costs, strategic and initial spares, consultancy services and temporary installations which will not form a part of the permanent works and charges for energy consumed (air, water, power, gas, etc.). Associated costs also include the following, where these are directly attributable to the capital project:

1   interest on finance;
2   fees on dedicated loans;
3   legal fees;
4   owner charges and overhead expenses;
5   land acquisition or rental; and
6   insurance.

Operating costs

Operating costs may include provision for maintenance costs, but will normally exclude the costs of replacing plant. Typically included are operating labour, materials, energy, plant and equipment maintenance costs, engineering services and other routine service costs which the owner must meet to successfully manage and operate the plant that has resulted from the capital project.

Plant and equipment replacement costs

Replacement costs include for the replacement of the fixed assets. These embrace costs for the replacement of worn-out assets on a like-for-like basis together with any enhancements to the fixed assets. Replacement costs include the supply, transportation, installation and commissioning of replacement equipment together with any down time costs associated with loss of production and/or profits.

Working capital costs

That part of a company's total capital which is tied-up in stocks, work in progress, and the provision of credit to customers is the working capital. It is equal to the total value of all stocks, customers' debts and cash, less the amount owing to suppliers.

End-of-life costs

End-of-life costs (also known as abandonment costs) are all costs associated with the decommissioning of the fixed assets at the end of the project life, less any monies received from the sale of the assets. These costs include dismantling, disposal and land reclamation, together with costs associated with health, safety or environmental considerations.

ESTIMATING QUALITY

A contractor preparing to tender for a project will need the most accurate estimates possible, given the quality of the information available, in order that his senior management have the best possible basis upon which to set their pricing (taking into account all the current forces of the market and competition).

There may be instances where the owner's and contractor's expectations are in opposition. The owner is concerned with preparing an objective and comprehensive cost estimate which will satisfy the company's financial criteria for investment. For example these criteria may include: net present value (NPV), discounted cash flow (DCF), payback, project sensitivities to shifts in either capital and/or operating costs and/or revenue from sales, and so on (see Chapter 15). Alternatively, the contractor will be seeking to satisfy the owners' technical specification while simultaneously maximizing contribution to profit and over-head at the owner's expense.

While recognizing that an owner and a contractor need cost estimates for different reasons, similar principles apply to the compilation procedures in both cases. Where it is necessary to assume a viewpoint in this chapter, then the role of the owner has been used since this is likely to encompass a broader and more complex view of project costs over all phases.

Owing to the complexity and duration of many projects it will be necessary to repeat cost estimates at various stages in the project life as definition becomes more precise. Efforts will be made to keep financial exposure to a minimum in the early development of the project until scope definition improves to the extent that important decisions having a significant financial impact on the owner can be taken with greater knowledge and confidence. To satisfy this phased approach it is desirable to establish criteria against which cost estimates can be prepared and later independently classified in respect to accuracy. The estimating criteria needed for phased classifications will need to be established to suit the particular business. Some typical technical definition classifications are described below.

Ball park estimates

Initial cost estimates prepared from scant information are sometimes referred to as 'ball park estimates'.

A ball park estimate can best be illustrated as a type of inspired guess which an experienced estimator can make with little information. For example, there may be no access to detail drawings, quotations for equipment, or any other data other than his own intuition and broad knowledge of the size of the task, together with an idea of the costs experienced with projects of a similar size and scope in the past. The usefulness of ball park estimates is obviously limited. They have an application in the pre-tender period, and will help the contractor to decide whether or not he has the resources available which would make him want to tender. The financial standing of the potential customer (i.e. his potential ability to meet payments) is one of the factors which the contractor will consider at the pre-tender stage, and knowledge of the ball park extent of total costs will prove useful. The benefit to the owner is that the initial project economics can be tested, and decisions made on whether or not to investigate the project in more detail.

Pre-development cost estimates

Engineering design may be only 5–10 per cent complete. Criteria which satisfy the needs of the cost estimate may include:

1 Pre-development study and report completed and scope developed.
2 First relevant programme prepared (which may be a bar chart).
3 Main statutory requirements known.
4 Preliminary budget-type quotations sought for significant or for unfamiliar equipment items or any unusual construction requirements.

After inclusion of a contingency, the upper accuracy limit could be as high as +50 per cent. A typical accuracy rating would be −20 to +40 per cent. An estimate of this type would be suitable for the first application for funds to advance the project through the next phase.

Feasibility cost estimates

Engineering design may be in the order of 10–15 per cent complete. To prepare a cost estimate the following criteria may need to be satisfied:

1 Feasibility study completed in draft form.
2 Process flow sheet frozen.
3 Engineering plans developed, preliminary plant and building arrangements prepared, utilities requirement defined, layouts and general arrangements completed together with piping and instrument diagrams. All major equipment specified and budget quotations obtained.
4 Preliminary take-off for bulk materials completed.
5 Significant site, environmental and geotechnical data evaluated.
6 Project and contract strategy established.
7 Preliminary critical path network programme agreed.
8 Capital contributions by, or to, public authorities, utility companies, etc., established.

After inclusion of a contingency allowance the upper accuracy limit could be as high as +30 per cent. A typical accuracy rating would be −10 to +25 per cent. An estimate of this type would be suitable for application to full project sanction or alternatively would allow:

1 Review of an existing project estimate to establish any significant trends and to rerun economic evaluations.
2 Identification of long delivery items and facilities for procurement.
3 Approval of further funds for continued project activity.

Definitive cost estimates

Engineering design would be at least 30 per cent complete. To prepare a definitive cost estimate the following criteria would need to be satisfied:

1 Detailed engineering by the main contractor (or others) substantially complete so that procurement can be advanced to the extent where vendors' firm prices and deliveries are known.
2 Contracts critical to the achievement of the programme are awarded and preliminary prices obtained on the remaining contracts.
3 Detailed network programmes developed and agreed.

Where a lump sum bid covering a defined scope has been received, and after detailed evaluation has been judged acceptable, then this would qualify as a definitive cost estimate. After inclusion of a contingency allowance, the upper accuracy boundary should not exceed +15 per cent. A typical accuracy rating would be −7 to +10 per cent. Estimates of this type are suitable for full-scale review of the project cost estimates to establish any further significant trends, and to rerun economic evaluations. They also provide an opportunity for the owner to affirm commitment to the total project development.

In-project cost estimates

There may be occasions when it would be prudent to prepare a re-estimate of the project even when capital spending is well advanced. Normally the cost control function as applied to the project is sufficient for all cost estimating needs insofar as the project is effectively re-estimated at each cost report. However, there may be instances when an independent assessment is required, say, for the corporate board. This usually applies if a project has experienced considerable scope change, or alternatively, the project economics are considered marginal.

PROJECT RISK MANAGEMENT

An important developing technique in recent years has been associated with the concept of risk management. Project risk management is all about how project owners, or project managers, can choose between options, and how they can optimize their chances of achieving the declared objectives.

Risk analysis is usually carried out at the front end of a project (although special studies are often conducted during the life of projects). Pre-project risk analysis is carried out at the definition stage to ensure that properly considered targets have been set. In other words, ensuring that targets have been optimized and have a reasonable chance of being achieved. The benefits of risk analysis are most readily apparent in the early stages of the project because the results can exert the greatest influence at this time on its future direction. This can lead to schedule, cost and economic savings.

Project risk management techniques should, therefore, be of concern to those responsible for compiling project cost estimates. The subject is dealt with in Chapter 25.

COST DATA COLLECTION

Current cost data

The quality of cost data available to the estimator will depend upon the degree of project scope definition. For international contracts involving local costs in unfamiliar territories or countries, it will be necessary to obtain local cost data on a more formalized basis. This may necessitate preparing preliminary bills of quantity and contract scope definitions for issue to local contractors in order to obtain pricing details. Other cost collection methods will include written quotations received from potential suppliers in response to enquiries, order of magnitude costs elicited over the telephone, and so forth.

Cost data bank

A comprehensive and up-to-date cost data bank, preferably located on a computer database, provides a powerful tool for building cost estimates. The data bank should clearly separate capital, operating/maintenance, replacement, working capital and end-of-life cost entries. It is desirable that cost data is coded so that rapid access can be achieved. A code of accounts convention will assist in this respect. Cost information will need to include such details as:

1   A precise definition of the cost record.
2   The date ruling for price details.
3   The source of the information, supplier details, location, etc.
4   Actual/estimated costs, purchase order number, etc.

At the conclusion of a project, actual cost information should be recovered and stored in the cost data bank for application to future projects.

When employing historic cost data, it is essential that the composition of any bulk material cost rates is clearly defined. For example, a cost rate for imported steel may need to include all or some of the following elements:

1   Price ex works.
2   Packing and transport to port.
3   Ocean freight costs.
4   Special rates for heavy lifts.
5   Import duties and sales tax provisions.
6   Inland freight costs to site.
7   Handling and storage at site.

Similarly, equipment prices of each item will require a precise definition of the contents of each item. When applied to a specific project, historic costs will need to be updated selectively to a ruling base date to ensure uniformity across all the estimates. This must be done before any calculation of escalation/inflation rates applicable to the life of the project.

ESTIMATING INTERFACES

Planning and cost control

Cost rates are compiled with costs relating to a particular point in time or base date. In order to make provision for escalation expected during the life of the project it will be necessary to spread the base date cost estimate over the programme. This task can be simplified to an extent if the project programme is developed around the work breakdown structure or code of accounts. Reference to a coding structure will also help to ensure that the network is comprehensive in respect to all the items in the cost estimate.

After the decision to proceed with the project, cost control measures will be needed to ensure that the project is completed within its authorized budget. For this reason it is important to bear in mind the future needs of the cost control function when the estimates are compiled. As with the task of planning the project, the business of relating cost estimates to elements for cost control is simplified by the use of a logical and well-ordered work breakdown into work packages, built around a comprehensive code of accounts. When the intended project work breakdown structure is agreed, the cost estimate should be compiled by work package. This will help to avoid the need for wholesale restructuring of either planning or cost control data when the project goes live. Unnecessary work of this nature is wasteful of time, prone to error, and not in the best interest of efficient project management.

Work breakdown structure (WBS)

A work breakdown structure is unique for each project. It subdivides the total work scope into a logical series of smaller tasks. Typically, it is a hierarchical structure including up to five or six levels for complex projects. The top level comprises the overall project. Lower levels are progressive subdivisions of the project and will be defined to suit the needs of the project.

The lowest level of the WBS will contain the work packages. These incorporate the detailed cost information needed to control the project. For example, this will include: budget costs, committed costs, expended costs, estimate of costs remaining, etc. All of the costs elements included in a work package will be cross-referenced to the particular code of accounts convention used by the owner company. The project cost estimate is therefore the primary source of cost data needed for each work package. For more information on work breakdown structures refer to Chapter 13.

Cost code of account conventions (CCA)

Unlike the WBS, which is unique to the project, a CCA convention is usually a standard applied to accounting methods within the company. Given time and usage the standard CCA can therefore become a very comprehensive document. Sometimes this can provide a useful checklist to test the completeness of the project cost estimate.

Cost code of account conventions will vary according to the needs of the company. For example, a typical code could include the following structure:

Geographic	Discipline	Classification	Finance
[Code]	[Code]	[Code]	[Code]

In more detail, each code is further subdivided, for example:

- The geographic code might include:

    01 mine
    02 open pit

03 concentrator
04 smelter
nn and so on

- Typical discipline codes are:
  01 Site preparation
  02 Civil and structural
  03 Mechanical plant and equipment
  nn and so on

- The classification code might include:

  10 Supply
  20 Freight
  30 Import duties and taxes
  40 installation and testing
  nn and so on

- Typical finance codes are:

  AU Australian dollar
  GB UK pounds
  US US dollar
  nn and so on

For some projects it may be necessary to define the source of funding: for example, ECGD funding, owner funding, and so forth. In this case the finance code can be extended to incorporate a funding source code letter or number.

At the time of preparing the initial project cost estimate, the project strategy and contracting strategy may still be in the formulation stage. It might therefore not be possible to define the project WBS. The cost estimate will thus be compiled by individual item and coded against the CCA convention. This will provide a comprehensive framework for compiling the estimate, which can later be summarized into the particular work breakdown structure developed for the project.

It is possible to recover actual project costs against both the WBS and CCA structures. Insofar as the CCA is usually an enduring company standard, the CCA actual costs will prove particularly useful when estimating costs for subsequent projects. Applying the same discipline to both the planning and cost control functions encourages a unified approach to the successful control of the project.

Project and contract strategy

The project and contract strategy will have a major influence on the cost estimate. It may be a requirement, for example, that the cost estimate recognizes sources of finance, high-risk contracts or technology, procurement policy and so forth. It will be useful to note some aspects of project and contract strategy. Clearly the actual strategy developed will depend upon the particular business, but could include the following topics.

Management

How will the project be managed? Joint venture, partnerships, owner as operator?

Finance

How will the project be financed? Owner/joint venture/partner sources, bank-financed loans?

International policy

For projects of an international nature what will be the procurement and contracting policy – local or imported or both?

Project team

Having split the work up into a number of suitable contract packages, does the owner's project team have the capacity to manage one or more of the main contractors, or is it necessary to appoint a managing contractor as its agent?

Control and types of contract

How closely does the owner's project team wish to exercise control over the work of contractors?

Definition and types of contract

How well defined is the scope of work? Poor early definition may result in inefficient working, delay and overspending. Will the project definition and technology (mature or innovative) allow lump sum type contracts in preference to cost plus or measured work?

Risk

In general the concept of fairness should operate. However, as with insurance there is a premium to be paid for passing on risks to the contractor, who may even then not have sufficient substance to bear those risks. As a consequence the project team may opt to retain the risk itself.

Compatibility

What other contracts, or other owner company project team investments, will be undertaken concurrently? Industrial relations problems may arise if parallel contracting operations, close enough to interact, are implemented using different forms of contract.

Some, or indeed all, of the factors listed above will influence the composition of the project cost estimate, provisions for contingency, and so forth.

ESTIMATING METHODS

Estimating instructions

Before starting to compile cost estimates for a project, it is useful to develop estimating instructions or guidelines. These should be issued to groups participating in the compilation of the estimate and should include:

1 The project title (and case number if appropriate).
2 Technical scope definition including engineering design, drawings, equipment lists and so forth.
3 Project and contract strategy, if available.
4 Estimate base date.
5 Estimate currency.
6 Estimate exchange rates to be used.
7 Principal unit cost rates (bulk materials) to be used and their composition.
8 Escalation/inflation rates to be used.
9 Work breakdown structure and code of accounts conventions.
10 Project programme.

Formal issue of the estimating instructions, including any later revisions, will help to ensure the consistency of the cost estimate and hence its accuracy and scope. In their widest context cost estimates will need to embrace total life-cycle costs including:

1 Capital costs.
2 Operating and maintenance costs.
3 Replacement costs.
4 Working capital costs.
5 End-of-life (or de-commissioning) costs.

These estimates should be prepared to a base date with separate provisions for future escalation and currency fluctuations, to create the 'money-of-the-day' values.

The base case

In many instances a project can present a number of possible scenarios (for example, different sized process plants, throughputs, locations, project strategies, etc.). In this instance it would be usual to nominate the most likely outcome as the so-called base case against which other options would be measured.

In an estimating context the base case would comprise the most detailed cost estimate. Alternative case studies may be expressed as partial cost estimates defining cost movements (either increases or reductions) versus the base. Alternatively, computer-based systems allow the estimator to define the base case in detail: after saving the data this estimate can then be used as a template from which the alternative cases are compiled.

Factoring methods

In those instances where in-house actual cost information is available for a similar project, or alternatively where there is a paucity of scope information, then factoring techniques may be considered for cost estimates completed in the pre-development phase.

Factoring techniques utilize historical project cost information, which is escalated to an estimate base date using factors that take account of:

1 Escalation/inflation rates apparent between the historic cost data and the new project base date.
2 Variations in scope between the historic cost and the new project.
3 Variations in location between the historic cost and the new project. Location factors may attempt to recognize technical, economic, environmental, social and political factors.
4 Variations in project/contract strategy and/or operating philosophy between the historic data and the new project.

After factoring the historic costs to a common base date, separate allowances will be made for:

1 Items unique to the new project and not available in the historic data.
2 Escalation/inflation over the period from the project base date to commissioning, including any allowances that are to be made for estimated fluctuations in currency exchange rates.
3 Contingency provisions.

Detailed and factor methods

In certain estimates it may be practical to employ a combination of detailed and factored methods. Under these circumstances, the individual high-cost components will be estimated in detail with factor methods used to calculate the low-cost bulk items, usually taken as a percentage of the high-cost elements. Separate provisions would then be made for escalation and contingency allowances.

Detailed methods

To satisfy the requirements of feasibility or definitive estimates, detailed estimating methods should be used. This will necessitate subdividing the estimate into cost items which can later be grouped into work packages for the purpose of project control.

The estimator will need to interpret process flow sheets, general arrangement drawings, detailed drawings, bulk material take-off and the like. Engineering designs created using computer-aided techniques (CAD or CAE) will be suitable for rapid generation and revision of material take-off. For the major high-cost items of equipment, it is usual to obtain faxed/written quotations from the potential suppliers.

Computer-based systems which can extend quantity and rate data into base source cost and project currency equivalents will hasten the compilation of the cost estimate. Systems that can also access a library of bulk material commodity rates are particularly beneficial, insofar as rate data are consistent and less prone to error. Commodity rates held in a database can be rapidly modified at a later date if this proves necessary in the light of improved information. Careful consideration will always need to be given to the compilation of bulk material cost rates.

Pareto

A useful technique to apply to all cost estimates comes from the Italian economist Vilfredo Pareto. Stated briefly, Pareto's rule helps to focus on items having the most influence by identifying the vital few from the trivial many. Typically 20 per cent of causes result in 80 per cent of the problem. In an estimating context it is useful sometimes to rank cost items in their order of magnitude starting with the most expensive down to the least expensive. The estimator then concentrates on the accuracy of the top 20 per cent of the estimate items that are likely to contribute 80 per cent of the total estimated cost of the project. Using a computer-based spreadsheet or database should allow the cost items to be ranked easily in order of magnitude.

MONEY-OF-THE-DAY PROVISIONS

After the cost estimates have been prepared against a single defined base date, it will be necessary to assess the effects of future inflation over the planned life of the project. This establishes 'money-of-the-day' values relevant to dates in the future when the money will actually be spent. In cases of projects involving several foreign currencies, it may also be policy to make some provision for currency fluctuations measured against the defined project currency.

Escalation

Escalation rates have to be determined relevant to the inflation expected for each currency involved. It may be necessary to adopt different escalation rates for different kinds of project work, especially for different disciplines (civil, mechanical, electrical, etc.).

Escalation provisions can be allocated as a total amount for the project, or subdivided by discipline, or (in more detail) by individual item. When the project proceeds to the construction phase, it will be desirable to show the allocated escalation against each individual work pack, to ensure a like-for-like comparison of actual costs against those estimated.

Escalation provisions should be related to the forecast value of work done (and, therefore, to the value of work remaining). Using the project schedule, escalation amounts are calculated from the project base date for each currency, and according to the value of work done. The results are grouped into periods (months, quarters, half-years, etc.).

Cost estimates should be prepared on a computer-based system, spreadsheet or database, enabling escalation provisions to be assigned against each work package. These provisions can later be assigned against purchase orders, contracts and authorizations for expenditure. It will also be possible to alter escalation rate provisions with respect to time. For example, escalation assumptions might state: assume 5 per cent per annum for non-imported components for the period January 1993 to December 1993, then use 7.5 per cent p.a. for the period January 1994 to August 1994 and so forth.

Currency exchange rates for multi-currency estimates

For international projects the cost estimate is likely to comprise a number of different source currencies. It is usual to nominate a common currency in which costs can be summarized; this is known as the 'project currency'. All costs should be estimated in the currency of origin or anticipated payment, referred to as the 'source currency'.

By identifying the source currency applicable to each work package it will be possible to subdivide the cost estimate into its constituent currencies. It will then be possible to make provision for anticipated currency fluctuations.

Currency fluctuations have to be predicted over the life of the project. All fluctuations should be stated with reference to the starting project base date for each individual currency. For example, assume a project currency of US dollars and a particular item, or work pack, is to be paid for in pounds sterling. The estimator will then define the likely changes over the period from the project base date in a simple table (see Figure 12.1).

Such forecasts are perhaps speculative, although there may be hard evidence to suggest that some provision for currency fluctuations is relevant for the project. Once agreed forecasts have been tabulated, these can be used to adjust the

Period	Forecast rate
January 1993 (base date) to December 1993	1.95
January 1994 to December 1994	1.9
January 1995 to December 1995	1.8
January 1996 to December 1996	1.85

Figure 12.1   Example of a project exchange rate forecast for use in cost estimating (values are fictitious and for illustration only).

values of work scheduled to be done (or equipment scheduled to be purchased), according to the relevant payment periods. In other words, the project cash flow plan can be used for this purpose, and is itself modified as a result.

Computer-based cost estimates will be able to calculate exchange rate fluctuations for each work package, similar to the approach adopted for escalation allowances.

In summary, each cost item, or work pack, will include the base cost, escalation provision and currency fluctuation provision, all relevant to the point in time when the work is completed. This constitutes the money-of-the-day value for the particular item.

CONTINGENCIES

There are wide-ranging and differing concepts about contingency allowances. A traditional view is that contingency is an event for which an allowance is made to cover unforeseen errors and omissions. Other concepts will attempt to quantify risks associated with the project and the accuracy of the estimates: for example, stating that by the addition of a quantifiable 'allowance' to the cost estimates there is (say) a 60 per cent chance that the estimated costs will prove sufficient to complete the project. By adding further allowances in the form of 'comfort money', the probability of completing the project within the revised, higher-cost estimate is further increased (to 80 per cent, for example). The amount of comfort money to be added is obviously a matter of judgement – in fact a management decision. In all cases where such additions are made, clear definition of the terminology is a prerequisite. For more information on risk techniques refer to Chapter 25.

Returning to the traditional approach, contingency allowances can be defined as: financial provisions intended to cover items of work which will have to be performed, or elements of cost which will be incurred, and which are considered to be within the scope of the project covered by the estimate, but are not specifically defined or foreseen at the time the estimate is compiled. The actual provisions that are included in the estimate require a blend of experience, historical data, and knowledge of the current commercial conditions applied to a technical understanding of the project.

In order to avoid confusion in the later requirements of cost control after project go-ahead, it is necessary to define three further components of contingency allowances. These are estimate contingency; budget contingency; and forecast contingency.

Estimate contingency

These provisions specifically exclude any change in scope to the project that would later be the subject of a project variation. Insofar as contingency provisions are intended for those items that are unforeseen, or not specifically defined, then the provisions may be retained as a single lump sum. However, if the rationale of determining contingency provisions allows for calculations on either a discipline or commodity basis, then the contingency total will be apportioned in like manner. The estimate contingency sum included in the cost estimate prior to project approval is not related to its usage or allocation after sanction during the execution of the project.

Budget and forecast contingency

These terms are associated with cost control as opposed to estimating. Budget contingency is the sum, usually the same in value as the estimate contingency, included in the control budget after project go-ahead. It is allocated by the project manager for whatever purpose is deemed appropriate. In some company conventions the contingency sum is apportioned into elements. For example, this could include the main contingency sum under the control of the project manager, together with a separate amount held by the owner to use at his discretion.

Forecast contingency allowances are quite separate from budget contingency allowances as they are concerned with provisions against future costs not yet committed to the project. At the start of the project the forecast contingency sum is likely to be the same as the original budget contingency. As the project develops, the unknown element diminishes, with a consequent reduction in the forecast contingency.

CASH FLOW

Cash flow statements can be interpreted and presented in a variety of ways. The concepts are, however, simple.

Cash outflow is the expenditure of money needed to fulfil all aspects of the project. The cash outflow statement has to be phased to agree with the timing of payments, so that the organization providing the project funding can be given a forecast, not only of how much has to be paid, but when. A cash outflow statement cannot be prepared without the benefit of a detailed cost estimate and a project programme.

Cash inflow statements are more relevant to the operating phase of the project, when the facility has been commissioned and is earning money for the owner. A full cash flow statement balances these inflows against the outflows to arrive at net figures for each period considered, and the results can either be inflows (profit) or outflows (loss).

In calculating a project cash (out)flow statement, the project manager must ensure that all costs are taken into account, suitably augmented for escalation and currency fluctuations to arrive at money-of-the-day values. These are related to the forecast values of work done, as derived from the project programme. Material and equipment costs, for example, are timed to fall into the periods when their invoices are expected to fall due for payment. Likewise, equipment being purchased against contracts which allow progress payments will result in each progress payment estimate being scheduled in the appropriate cash flow period. The person making the cash flow table uses his judgement to allow for the normal delays which occur in commerce in the payment of invoices, so that an *201*

XYZ PROJECTS LIMITED — Project No. 1005-85
Cash Flow Schedule for: FERTILIZER PLANT — Client: Beanz - Talk inc — Issue date: Dec 1992

QUARTERLY PERIODS - ALL FIGURES ARE DOLLARS × 1000

COST ITEM	COST CODE	1993 Q1	1993 Q2	1993 Q3	1993 Q4	1994 Q1	1994 Q2	1994 Q3	1994 Q4	1995 Q1	1995 Q2	1995 Q3	1995 Q4	TOTAL BUDGETS
ENGINEERING														
Design	A105	10	20	50	100	100	80	60	20	5				445
Support	A110			2	2	5	5	4	4	4	3	2		31
Commissioning	A200									1	2	2	1	6
Project management	A600	4	5	7	8	8	8	8	8	6	4	2		68
EQUIPMENT PURCHASES														
Main plant	B110				400		500	400	1100	400	200	10		3010
Furnaces	B150							200	250					450
Ventilation	B175						20		20		20			60
Electrical	B200					5	20	25	60	40	10	2		162
Piping and valves	B300				10	5	5	10	15	20	5			70
Steel	B400				80	100	100	100	30	100				410
Cranes	B500			50		100			100		50			300
Other	B900	2	1	4	1	1	5	25	1	2	4	2		48
CONSTRUCTION														
Plant hire	C100			1	2	10	10	8	6	4	2			43
Roads	C150			4	6	10	20	15	10	2				67
External lighting	C200				2	2	4	1	1	1				11
Main building -Labour	C300 / C325				10	30	100	150	200	400	200	50	5	1145
Main building -Materials	C350			12	20	20	80	100	50	20	30			335
Stores building -Labour	C400 / C425				5	10	15	15	15	20	10	2	1	94
Stores building -Materials	C450				2	5	15	15	5	10	2	1		55
-Racking	C460										10			10
-Fork trucks	C470											120		120
CONTINGENCY SUMS					20	10	5	20	50	20	10	5	2	142
ESCALATION PROVISION						16	50	58	97	106	56	20		404
QUARTERLY TOTALS		16	26	131	668	337	1042	1214	2042	1161	618	220	11	7486

Figure 12.2 A cash outflow forecast for a project

This illustrates a spreadsheet-based cash outflow forecast of a project's capital costs. A real project is likely to contain more detail, in which case the use of a computer system will provide more flexibility and greater facility.

invoice for £100 000 payable for goods scheduled for delivery in March, might be shown as a cash outflow of £100 000 in April, where the contract terms are 30 days. These delays in payments, sometimes called the 'payments pipeline', can be of considerable duration on large international contracts. Cash flow schedules derive their timing from the project plan. If the plan incorporates a resource schedule, then this can be a useful aid in developing a project cash flow forecast. For more information on resource scheduling techniques refer to Chapter 18.

The scope of the cash flow statement needs to be defined. Is it, for example, intended to include operating costs, revenue from sales, tax, and so forth? An example of a cash flow statement is given in Figure 12.2. This is limited to the capital cost outflow.

ESTIMATING WITH AND WITHOUT A COMPUTER

Estimating systems may be either computer-based or manual although with the plethora of good quality computing packages now available it is very desirable for the system to be computer-based. The longer-term benefits of investing in a computing system will far outweigh the initial costs.

Computer-based systems can be either desktop-based, for single or multi-user applications, or mini/mainframe. To minimize error, systems will benefit by using standard coding, such as code of account conventions, wherever possible.

Computer-based systems

The choice of system will be influenced by the information technology strategy employed by the company. There may be instances where a central mainframe computer is the ideal solution, although current evidence would suggest that desktop systems are generally favoured due to their flexibility. Desktop applications will allow either independent or multi-user shared operations, minimizing the risk of system failures, and can also be used in portable mode, office or remote site.

The precise features of an estimating system will depend upon the nature of the business. Some aspects to be considered include the following:

1   Estimates derived by factoring historical costs held in a data bank.
2   Estimates built up in detail for individual work packages.
3   Combinations of both of these.

Other features to be included in the estimating system might be:

4   Definition of the project base date.
5   Multiple currency provisions and their conversion to the common currency used throughout the project, using the relevant exchange rate facilities.
6   A library of cost rates for bulk materials.
7   A library of the cost code of account conventions.
8   Extension of quantity data into cost equivalents from standard cost rates.   *203*

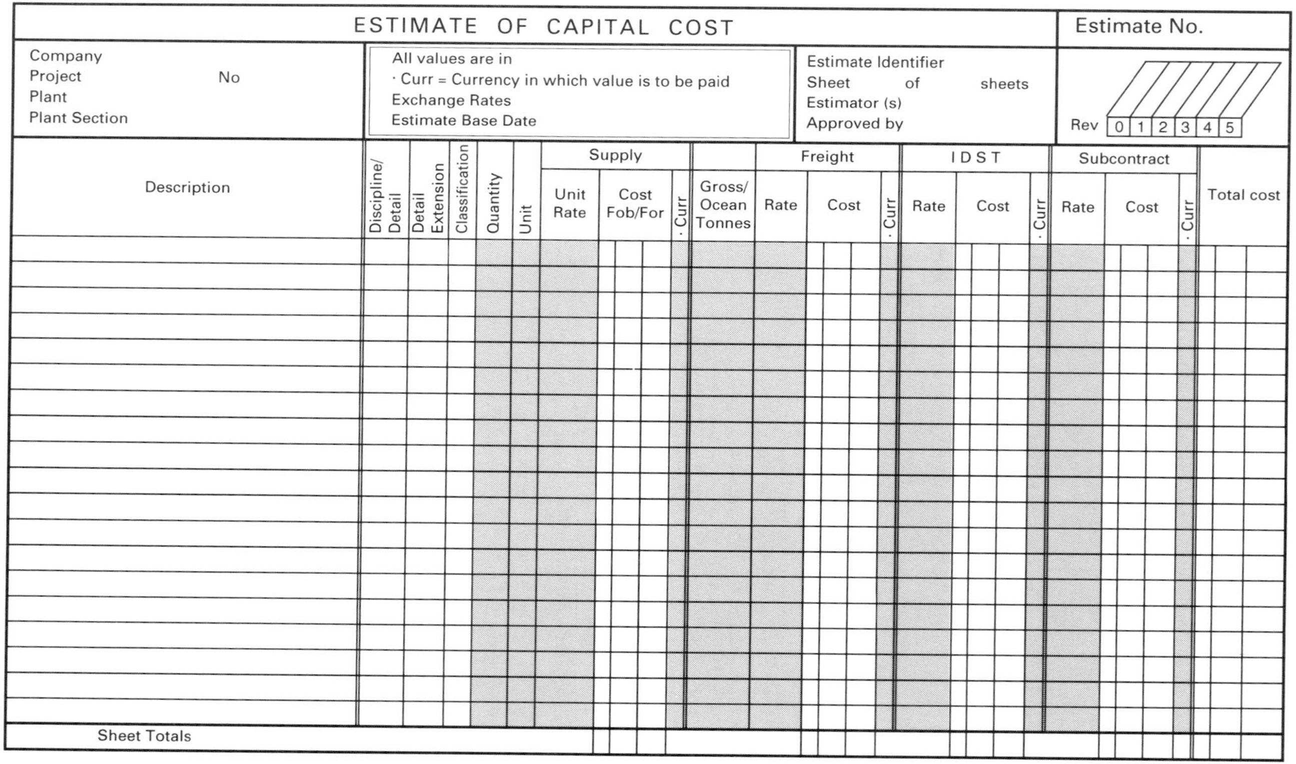

Figure 12.3 Estimating form for capital equipment

This is an example of a form suitable for listing and estimating major items of equipment to be purchased for a project.

204

WORK FUNCTION (See note 1)	DESCRIPTION	UNIT	HOURS EACH	NO. OFF	MANHOURS BY GRADE								TOTAL HOURS	METHOD % (See note 2)	LINE NO
					11	21	22	31	41	51	52	61			
	MANAGEMENT INFORMATION SYSTEM **ESTIMATE OF MANHOURS** DEPARTMENT DETAILS														
	DRAUGHTING THIS SECTION TO BE COMPLETED BY ENGINEERING DEPARTMENTS ONLY (See note 3)														
1 1	Flowsheets Single line diagrams	Dwgs			–	–	–					–			1
1 2	Studies Schematic diagrams Panel layouts	Dwgs			–	–	–					–			2
1 3	General arrangement & layouts Piping arrangements Power layouts – Ints. plot plans	Dwgs			–	–	–					–			3
1 4	Details Isometrics - Hook ups Lighting & small power	Dwgs			–	–	–					–			4
1 5	Reinforcement schedules Supports - Ints. indexes Cable & termination schedules	Dwgs			–	–	–					–			5
1 6	Architectural	Dwgs			–	–	–					–			6
1 7	Other SEL drawings	Dwgs			–	–	–					–			7
					–	–	–	–	–	–	–	–			8
1 9	Other drawing office work (See note 4) including supervision				–	–						–		*	9
	ENGINEERING THIS SECTION TO BE COMPLETED BY ENGINEERING DEPARTMENTS ONLY (Depts. 41 - 46 Inc.)														
2 9	Engineering supervision & dept. supervision (See note 5)								–	–	–			*	10
	GENERAL THIS SECTION TO BE COMPLETED BY ALL NON-ENGINEERING DEPARTMENTS														
9 9 9	Totally unclassified & default for reconciliations only													*	11
	GRAND TOTAL BY GRADE														12
	GRADE TOTAL AS % OF GRAND TOTAL														

Notes

PROJECT			PROJECT No.			
Senior Engineer	Chief Engineer Department manager		PLANT			
			DEPARTMENT			
Date			EST/CV	REV	SHT	OF

Figure 12.4   Estimating form for engineering man-hours

This form allows clerical collation of estimated man-hours for the engineering and draughting of a project. The forms are assembled in batches, one for each discipline (civil, structural, mechanical, piping, electrical, process control, general office). The total engineering estimate is assembled on another of these forms, used as a summary sheet.

9   Allocation of cost estimates to the project timescale.
10 Automatic allocation of escalation and exchange rate provisions to generate money-of-the-day estimates.
11 Generation of both detailed and summary reports for analysis of the estimate.
12 Provision for selective factorization of the estimate from later, more up-to-date information.
13 A facility to rework estimates to different base dates and timescales.

Standard features now available in low cost, proprietary spreadsheet system applications, will meet many of the requirements needed for building cost estimates. Where the methodology is already well established, there may be some benefits in building an estimating system within a commercial database application. The advantage here is that the estimating discipline can be built into the software code, thus discouraging non-conformance in estimating technique.

Manual systems

Manual systems can be enhanced by the use of standard forms together with an accompanying definitive procedure. An example form is illustrated in Figure 12.3. Careful attention should be paid to the design of forms supporting a manual system to minimize error. Another example of form design relating to the estimation of design hours, is shown in Figure 12.4.

An obvious drawback with manual systems is that change is more difficult to accommodate. Last-minute adjustments to exchange rate assumptions, alterations in scope, recompilation of bulk material cost rates and the like cannot be easily accommodated.

FURTHER READING

Kharbanda, O. P. and Stallworthy, E. A., *Capital Cost Estimating for the Process Industries*, Butterworth Scientific, Guildford, 1989.

Stewart, R., *Cost Estimating*, 2nd edn, Wiley, New York, 1991.

13 Cost Control

David Ross

Effective control of project costs is an obvious requirement within the total project management function. It is important to the client, and to the contractor. The emphasis of cost risk between buyer and contractor must depend on the type of contract (e.g. fixed price, cost-plus, etc.). Whatever the contract type, it is in the best interests of all concerned that costs are contained within pre-planned (i.e. budgeted) and authorized limits. Even with a fixed price arrangement the buyer is faced with risk when excessive costs arise, since the contractor, at best, may be inclined to cut corners and try to skimp, while, at worst, his financial viability could be brought into question as a result of the substantial losses that he must incur. This chapter examines some aspects of cost collection and control, including the viewpoints of the project buyer (i.e. the eventual owner) and the contractor.

OVERALL CONTROL OF PROJECT COSTS

For the owner company it will be important to establish authority levels at which financial commitments can be made. The nature of these authority levels will depend on the size of the owner company and the nature of its organization, but they will typically be based upon some sort of hierarchical structure. Thus, there will be levels of authority set that can:

1 Sanction the use of funds.
2 Approve authorizations for expenditure (AFEs) for specific items or work packages.
3 Authorize contract conditions.
4 Specify individual levels of authority, usually according to rank or status.

Authority to sanction funds

As an example of an hierarchically based structure of authorizing levels, a large   *207* owner organization might assign the following limits of authority on its management:

1	Chief executive of subsidiary company principally responsible for buying the project	– up to £5m.
2	Group managing director	– up to £10m.
3	Main board of subsidiary	– up to £20m.
4	Main group board	– over £20m.

Authorizations for expenditure

After the sanctioning of funds by the appropriate authority, and particularly if the project is being funded by a number of partners, it will be necessary to establish a formal system of authorizations for expenditure (known as AFEs for short). This system allows all partners providing the funding to be kept informed of their current financial commitments on the project. Normally the total sum approved for expenditure through AFEs will never be allowed to exceed the amount of funds sanctioned. Thus it is necessary to arrange that every significant contract or purchase order commitment is subject to AFE approval in advance of the actual commitment being made.

Contract committee authority

With the current movement for cultural change, the role of the central committee is not as fashionable as was previously the case. However, assuming that a committee exists for the consideration and approval of contracts, this committee's involvement would only be invoked for purchase order commitments or for new third party contracts that exceeded some predetermined financial commitment level. Such a committee's duty might also include the approval (or rejection) of overall strategies for contracts. Contract committee approvals are primarily concerned with technical and commercial aspects, and could include:

1 Approval of project contract strategy.
2 Approval of lists of bidders.
3 Approval to award a contract or purchase order.

An advantage of the committee approach is that the collective 'pooled wisdom' is essentially there in support of the project manager and his decisions, and will therefore be accountable for the same, together with the project manager. This is also crucial to the control of the project as it is at this time when the critical cost control decisions are taken.

Individual authority levels

208 After each AFE has been approved, there will be individual levels of authority, at

which various members of management are able to commit expenditure within the constraints of overall funds sanctioned, AFE levels, and the dictates of the contract committee. A large multinational company might, for example, sub-divide individual authority levels on the basis of:

1 Approval of indents and purchase orders.
2 Authority to place orders and contracts with third parties.
3 Authority to approve payments to third parties.
4 Authority to approve expenses, travel requisitions and the like.

Within each of these categories various levels could apply, for example:

1	General manager	– unlimited within authorized funding
2	Divisional manager	– up to £5m.
3	Departmental manager	– up to £3m.
4	Project manager	– up to £2m.
5	Resident engineer	– up to £500 000

and so on down the line.

A small contracting company might take the view that their project manager has absolute authority to commit company funds. In any event, the recognition and definition of individual and collective levels of authority is an important criterion before funds are committed on a project. Although at first glance a formal authority level structure might appear to be cumbersome and time consuming, it is an essential feature of project cost control for the larger business, because it ensures that every aspect of the project is considered before expenditure is committed and not after (when it would be too late to exercise any control). Summing up, it is vital that the sanctioning process considers essentials such as project finances, risk factors, relevance to company (rather than project) strategy, and so forth. The procedures are also supportive to the project manager in those cases where the manager's assessment of a particular situation is endorsed through a consensus process involving a group.

CONTRACT STRATEGY IN RELATION TO PROJECT CONTROL

After recognition of the overall requirements, another key aspect of project control is the development of the project contract strategy. The strategy seeks to define the number, scope and types of contract that should be used. These considerations are important to the owner and to the contractor responding to an invitation to bid. The arguments also apply to contracts for work to be done by other (third) parties. Some of the major factors to be taken into account are:

1 *Management* Does the owner have sufficient management resource or expertise to undertake the project, or will it be necessary to appoint a managing contractor?
2 *Control* How closely does the owner wish to exercise control over the contractor?

Basis for paying the contractor	Type of contract	Owner's degree of project control needed	Project definition required	Contractor's risk	Contractor's motivation
Performance {	— Turnkey — Lump sum — Bill of quantities and scheduled rates	least	highest	highest	highest
	— Target price				
Time {	— Fee plus reimbursable daywork rates — Cost plus	highest	least	least	least

Figure 13.1 Relationship between type of contract and control emphasis

Choice of the type of contract greatly affects the way in which project control and risk will be apportioned between the contractor and the owner of the project.

3 *Definition*   How well is the scope of work defined?
4 *Risk*   How is risk to be apportioned between the owner and the contractor?
5 *Motivation*   How best can the contractor, and subcontractors, be motivated by contract terms to work for the benefit of the project team?

These factors can be summarized and explained in outline by the comparative table in Figure 13.1. The owner will need to exert maximum control over the contractor for cost-plus contracts, and least control for fixed-price or turnkey contracts.

THE CONTROL BUDGET

The control budget is the yardstick against which all subsequent cost actions are measured. It is approved by the project manager and will be closely related to the funding sanctioned by the owner's corporate group. To facilitate control of the project it will need to be subdivided into smaller, manageable elements. The main control tool for subdividing the project will be the project work breakdown structure (WBS) together with the company code of accounts. It is desirable that the original project cost estimate sanctioned by the approving authority will have been subdivided in this manner.

Work breakdown structure (WBS)

The project WBS subdivides the total project (or multiple jobs) into a logical series of smaller tasks. Typically, it is an hierarchical structure of up to five or six levels for complex projects. The top level will be the overall project. Lower levels will be progressive subdivisions of the project and will be defined to suit the needs of the project. For example, a workload comprising a number of jobs could typically include the following:

Level 1   Overall workload
Level 2   Jobs by site location
Level 3   Jobs by type (fee earning, overhead, etc.)
Level 4   Individual jobs
Level 5   Work packages

The work packages, at level 5 in the example, will contain the detailed cost information for each job. For example, this will include: budget costs, committed costs, expended costs, estimate to complete costs, etc. For cost reporting, and control purposes, the costs held at work pack level can be 'rolled-up' through the WBS and summarized at (say) level 1, or level 2 if required.

To achieve the necessary control each work pack, will have:

1   a defined scope;
2   single responsibility;

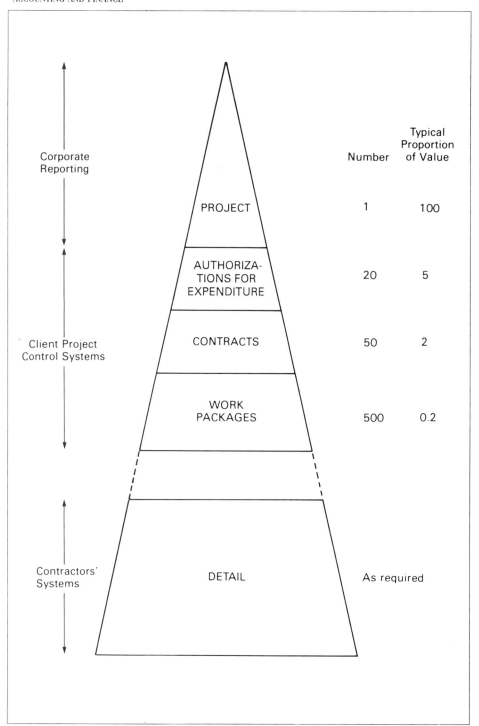

Figure 13.2   Work breakdown structure for a large civil engineering or construction
212   **project.**

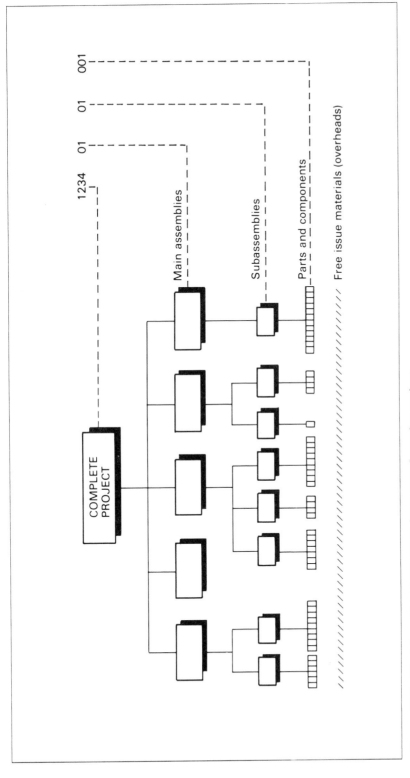

Figure 13.3 Work breakdown structure for a manufacturing project

This hierarchical or 'family tree' breakdown is typical of many manufacturing projects. Sometimes known as 'goes into the charts', the version here is very simplified. The complete project might be, for example, a transfer machinery line, built against a works order numbered 1234. Each main assembly is a machine along the line (milling, drilling, etc.) numbered – 01 upwards. Then there are the subassemblies (heads, fixtures, transfer sections) which have their own identifying numbers. And so on down to the individual parts and components. The numbering system can be used for cost accounting and estimating, and for the drawing numbering system.

213

3   a measurable programme; and
4   a defined cost budget.

The manner in which the WBS is developed is unique to the project and will be influenced by the project and contracting strategy. Work packages will also be subdivided into cost elements based upon the standard code of account conventions used by the owner.

WBS, and code of account conventions, can be simple or complex depending upon the particular project(s). Figure 13.2 illustrates the concept for large, international projects. Here the work breakdown is concerned also with authorizations for expenditure, sometimes referred to as 'AFEs'. The AFE document is needed when the project is being financed by a number of partners or joint ventures. The document signals the approval of the partners to enter into financial commitments as defined in the authorization-for-expenditure document. Each AFE may be divided into one or more contracts as defined in the project contract strategy. It is not usual to subdivide a contract when seeking approval for an authorization for expenditure. In this way, the project can be summarized into both authorization-for-expenditure format, to allow control and reporting to the partners, plus individual-contract format, which is more commonly used for project management control of the project.

At the simplest level, a WBS can be likened to the division of tasks represented by a manufacturing 'goes into' chart (see Figure 13.3). This chart shows how the work breakdown and cost coding structures are related. In the manufacturing environment such correlation can be extremely useful, especially if the manufacturing drawings can also be numbered to correspond with the coding. Companies using these techniques find them essential for the standardization of designs across different projects or works orders, and it is far easier to retrieve information from past projects for use on future work, whether this is design information or cost data. At the level of Figure 13.3, the situation is applicable to the manufacturer supplying equipment to the larger projects with which this chapter is principally concerned.

Cost code of accounts (CCA)

Work packages will be subdivided by code of accounts, so that it should be possible also to prepare cost summaries according to the specialist disciplines working on the project, or by any other subdivision suggested by the accounts coding structure as required by project management. For further details on CCA conventions, refer to Chapter 12.

Money-of-the-day provisions

The control budget will need to be expressed in money-of-the-day terms. This means that it has to include provisions for escalation and, where different currencies are involved in international projects, allowances for fluctuations in exchange rates. Since like must always be compared with like, it will be

214

necessary to include similar allowances when considering or reporting committed costs, estimate to complete, and estimated final costs.

When, inevitably, changes are made to the project scope, these will need to be properly evaluated and authorized through a formal change (or variation) order procedure, with the resulting changes in money-of-the-day costs added to the control budget after approval.

Contingency provisions

A contingency sum should be included in the control budget; this is termed the 'budget contingency'. It is intended to cover work or expenditure which would be considered to lie within the scope of the project as sanctioned, but where such work cannot be defined, or even foreseen, at the time the budget is compiled.

Contingency sums can be set aside in a separate part of the budget, to be allocated to relevant AFE areas by the project manager as the project proceeds and the actual contingencies arise. This allocation has to be carried out on a debit/balancing credit basis in order that the total amount of the control budget remains unchanged. The application (draw down) of contingency sums after final sanction would normally be at the discretion of the project manager for whatever purpose is deemed appropriate by him. All such draw downs should be explained in the regular project reports.

It should be noted that budget contingency sums are held in the control budget for work not foreseen at the time the budget was compiled. However, actual commitments and/or expenditures (although originally deemed to be a contingency) will not normally be allocated against a contingency account. Rather, they will always be charged to the appropriate work package/cost code as defined by the type of work. Contingency provisions for future unknowns are termed 'forecast contingency', and will be specified as an 'estimate to complete' cost. Refer to the section entitled 'predicting trends and overspends' for details on forecast contingency.

DEFINITIONS OF COST CONTROL TERMS

Before proceeding to describe cost control methods, it will be useful to list and define some of the terms used. These are typically used in reports and their clear understanding is essential to the correct interpretation of those reports.

Committed costs

Committed costs represent the total value of all work and expenses contained in contracts and purchase orders awarded to third parties. In the case of reimbursable or measured work contracts, committed costs are calculated in respect of the defined scope of work as at contract completion.

For control purposes, costs must be regarded as being committed after the approval of the relevant control document. In large companies this can be a two- *215* tiered structure where indents (covering either one or a number of contracts) are approved, followed later by the purchase order or contract documents. In this instance the financial control system would monitor both commitment levels separately. At the detailed level the committed value will need to be comprehensive. For example, in the case of imported equipment or materials the committed value will need to include all costs associated with getting the goods to site. These associated costs include elements such as freight, import duties and taxes, insurance, etc.

Although costs incurred overseas will be committed in the relevant foreign currencies (the 'source currency') they must be converted at current exchange rates to their equivalents in the common project currency. All calculations, together with any assumptions, will need to be recorded.

The purchase order or contract relating to committed costs should show the budget work package numbers against which the costs are to be allocated. Where more than one work package number applies to a single contract or purchase order, the value of the committed costs must be apportioned appropriately between those work packages.

Sunk costs

Sunk costs are the total costs, at a given time, that would be incurred should the project be cancelled. In addition to costs already expended, these would have to include any cancellation charges arising from committed purchase orders and contracts. Proceeds from the resale of any surplus equipment or materials are deducted from the sunk cost calculations. Because sunk costs are always related to a given point in time, a degree of judgement is necessary to determine the value of work done, and the likely charges that would arise in the event of cancellation. By its nature, the estimation of sunk costs is usually a special exercise, rather than information that is held as a matter of routine.

Project expenditure

Project expenditure is the total cost of work done, of goods received, and of services used, whether or not these items have actually been paid for. Expenditure therefore includes invoices paid, plus accruals and provisions (see the separate definitions for these items below).

Expenditure has to be recorded in the source currency by invoice, for each work package, to show invoices paid and accruals. Separate allowances should be made for provisions. For the purposes of cost reporting, source currency amounts should be converted into the common project currency at the exchange rates ruling when payments are made. By definition, the expenditure in source currency will never exceed the commitment value, unless incorrect payments have been made and not put right, or there is an unusual action such as selling recently purchased plant and equipment.

Accruals and provisions

Sums of money due to suppliers of goods or services at the end of a month (or other accounting period) where the invoices have not actually been paid, but where the amounts themselves are reasonably certain, are termed accruals when they are included in expenditure reports. Where the invoices have not been received, and the amounts due are less certain, the allowances made in expenditure reports are termed provisions.

Outstanding commitments

The outstanding commitments are the total costs committed minus expenditure (at any given time). The value of outstanding commitments will therefore tend to zero as work proceeds. A negative value for outstanding commitments will require scrutiny because it could indicate an accounting error or an erroneous payment.

Estimate to complete

The 'estimate to complete' costs are the estimated final costs minus expenditure (at any given time). Similar to the outstanding commitments they will tend towards zero as the project proceeds.

Estimated final cost

The estimated final cost is the best estimate which can be made at any given time, taking account of the project scope and of trends to date, of the final cost of a work package, contract or AFE.

At the start of a project, before any costs have been committed or spent, it is usual for the estimated final cost to be equal to the control budget. As the project proceeds the estimated final cost will reflect all known financial changes to the project. Such changes are likely to include:

1. Discrepancies between the estimated quantities and those currently being used.
2. Changes of project scope authorized in variation orders.
3. Changes of project scope which are apparent, but which have not yet been made the subject of variation orders.
4. Discrepancies between the estimated inflation or escalation amounts and those actually being experienced.
5. Exchange rate fluctuations occurring between the project currency and the source currencies.

By definition, forecast contingency provisions are not usually included in individual work package estimates, but are more likely to be listed separately as a lump sum provision.

Work breakdown structure (WBS)

The WBS is a way of organizing the project into an hierarchy for control purposes – for example, AFEs, contracts and work packages – so that contracts are not divided between AFEs nor work packages between contracts. Unlike the code of account convention, the work breakdown structure is unique to the particular project.

Work package

A work package is an element of work with defined scope, start and finish dates, single responsibility, estimated resources and cost. It is used to break down a contract into measurable units and facilitate project control.

Code of accounts

A code of accounts is a standard coding structure, usually hierarchical, applicable to all projects for cost estimates at work package level. The compilation of the coding structure will be designed to accommodate the needs of the company in respect of: reporting, cost estimating, cost control, planning and accounting.

PREDICTING TRENDS AND OVERSPENDS

Perhaps the most difficult and challenging aspect of cost control is in determining the estimated final cost of the project. The major strategic decisions taken at the start of the project are likely to have the most significant effect upon the final outcome. However, rigorous cost control during the life of the project will still be crucial to its success. To complete this task, there is perhaps no substitute for maintaining a detailed knowledge of the project from both a technical and commercial aspect. The cost engineer will therefore need to communicate effectively with discipline engineers, not only in respect of work that is presently being undertaken, and the likely problem areas, but also in the scope of future work not yet committed. In particular, there is a need to be aware of any scope changes that are either being contemplated or are in the approval process.

Contract conditions

Contract conditions are discussed more fully in Chapter 6. This section is intended briefly to relate the topic to cost engineering. The type of contract (lump sum, reimbursable, etc.) will influence the prediction of future cost trends.

Lump sum conditions

Under lump sum contract conditions the contractor supplies plant (or carries out certain works), the scope of which has been clearly defined in advance, for a stated price. In most cases the contract price can be cautiously regarded by the

218

owner as the final estimated cost, after correcting for any scope changes and their associated variation orders.

Measured work

Where contract terms rely upon an element of measurement, such as a schedule of rates applied to quantity values, the cost engineer will need to quantify the scope of work already completed, together with work yet to be completed. For large contracts this will mean collaborating with specialist discipline engineers and with quantity surveyors. The estimated final costs will therefore be:

expenditure to date + future work to be done.

In this instance expenditure includes invoices received to date (both approved and those not yet approved) plus provisions for work done but not yet invoiced. Future work will need to recognize:

1 The quantity of future work (cubic metres, hours, tonnes, etc.).
2 The contract rate per unit (pounds per cubic metre, hour, etc.).

As with lump sum conditions, all scope changes, both real and proposed, will need to be included in the assessment.

Reimbursable work

Under reimbursable conditions, the supplier or contractor is reimbursed his costs for work completed to specification. This may also include a fee, or alternatively the rate under which he is reimbursed may already include a profit element. As with measured conditions, the cost engineer will need to have access to the approved hours for work accomplished, plus the estimated hours content of work yet to be completed. This estimate will need to include any scope changes apparent at the time in order to establish the cost at completion.

Like-for-like comparisons

It will be remembered that the control budget comprises:

1 basic cost estimates for the original scope of project work;
2 contingency allowances; and
3 cost estimates for approved project variation orders;

and all of the above elements will be corrected for:

4 provision for cost escalation with time; and
5 allowances for currency fluctuations;

all of which together provide a control budget which is expressed in money- *219* of-the-day terms. It follows that prediction of the estimated final cost must take account of all these factors, in order that the predicted costs are directly comparable with the control budget.

Since the escalation allowances for each work package or AFE depend so much on the timing of expenditure, the cost engineer will need to be familiar with the project time schedules. He will therefore need to collaborate closely with the planning and scheduling engineers in order to be aware of the schedule details, and to understand the extent and effect of any programme changes on the phasing of costs.

The estimated final costs differ in content very slightly from those made for the control budget, since predictions have to take sensible account of changes which are expected, even though they might not have approval or authorization at the time of prediction. Thus, although the control budget only includes project variations which have received approval, the estimates of final costs should include the costs of all project variations, including those which, although apparent, have not received formal approval.

Planning and accounting function interfaces

Accurate cost predictions must depend in part upon the establishment of a close rapport between the cost engineer and the planning and accounting functions. In addition to their influence on escalation, any significant programme changes can have other effects on total costs. A substantial delay could lead to the imposition of penalty charges. The planning engineer will also be an important source of information when making assessments on the completion of measured work. These estimates of work completed (usually expressed as a percentage of the total contract) must be based on fact, and not merely an assumption based on the proportion of money, man-hours or time spent. A job might be halfway through its time and cost estimates, but only 30 per cent complete in terms of actual measured work.

The project accountant is the information source for all matters concerning the project bank accounts. This will include information on invoices paid and on the accrued value of all invoices received but not yet actually paid. Invoiced information will grow substantially in volume as the project progresses, involving perhaps thousands of detailed invoices. The accountant will help to reduce this workload mountain substantially, allowing the cost engineer to focus on the important issues to be faced by the project in the future. This is likely to include issues relating to estimated final costs, cash flow, cost trends, and dealing with contractors' claims.

Changes in project scope

By their very innovative nature, all projects are likely to undergo change during their execution. These changes can be technical, contractual, financial, or some combination of these.

Technical changes

Technical changes are concerned with the specification and design of the finished project. For example, in some projects they might be represented by changes to the process flow sheets, including changes in the processing capacity or the configuration of the plant.

Contractual changes

Contractual changes are those which alter the defined contract strategy. For example, the project contract strategy may have anticipated well-defined scope conditions with a preponderance of lump sum contracts. If in the event contract scope is ill defined, with subsequent recourse to reimbursable contracts, then there are likely to be increased cost implications.

Financial changes

Financial changes will include any alteration to project funding arrangements (especially loan funds) which could affect subsequent procurement policy.

Programme changes

Programme (or schedule) changes are those which include significant alterations to the planned construction sequence, where these do not of themselves constitute technical changes, but which will delay or shorten the programme. There may also be increased or decreased project capital costs resulting from such programme changes.

The cost engineer will need to record all changes (whether technical, contractual, etc.) that have a financial impact on the project. For simplicity these changes can be considered in two areas: defined scope changes; and apparent scope changes.

Defined scope changes

Defined scope changes are those which can be quantified in the same manner as the original project. Thus they will include a scope of work, programme and cost estimate. Defined changes occur as project variations or as contract variations.

Project variations are defined changes which alter the scope of the project and require the authorization of the owner or client. They can be formally recorded by the project manager and, when approved by the client, they will normally be included in the control budget total as authorized changes. An example of a form used to summarize and record a project variation is shown in Figure 13.4.

Contract variations are defined changes in the scope of work agreed between the project manager and a contractor or supplier of equipment. After approval, contract variations should be recorded as formal contractual documents. In the *221*

PROJECT VARIATION   SUMMARY

COST DATA

Total increase/decrease in cost =

PROGRAMME DATA

LIST of RELEVANT DOCUMENTS and DRAWINGS

DESCRIPTION of CHANGE (Use continuation sheet if necessary)

APPROVALS

Originator	Project Manager			
Date	Date	Date	Date	Date

PROJECT TITLE	AFE No
	PV No P V
	Rev No
VARIATION TITLE	Sheet of
	Date

Figure 13.4   Project variation summary form

Example of a form used to summarize details and approval – or rejection – of a change in the defined project scope.

case of purchase orders, these kind of variations will probably require the issue of contract/purchase order amendment documents.

Apparent scope changes

Apparent scope changes are those where, although a change is foreseen, the implications have not been formally recorded or approved as a project variation. For example, a project might require the sinking of a mine shaft in ground which is judged to be dry, and the contract established on this basis. If water is hit during the works, this situation will have to be recognized in the contract conditions existing between the project team (representing the owner) and the shaft sinker. However, it could be difficult, in such a case, to prepare a well-defined project variation request. The rate of water ingress into the shaft could be speculative, and the total amount of water present in the shaft might not be known. The cost engineer has to quantify the financial implications by the best means available, and make a provision in the future cost forecast for the apparent change of scope.

Other changes falling into this category of apparent changes are those where additional work is completed, with the formal variation being agreed later. They could also include changes of a politically sensitive nature where formal documentation would not always be appropriate.

Earned value concepts

An earned value system makes use of measured actual progress to apportion the budgeted man-hours, in order to arrive at an 'earned value' of the work completed. Thus, when a job is finished, its earned value is equal to its apportioned share of the control budget. If a job were to be measured at (say) 30 per cent complete, its earned value would be 30 per cent of the relevant portion of the control budget. These earned values are not derived from the actual man-hours or time expended. They are an attempt at expressing the true value of work done, related to the control budget, in order that the remaining work and future costs can be accurately evaluated so that the project manager is able to advise the owner, at any time during the life of the project, on the likelihood of all work being completed within the constraints of the control budget.

By deriving ratios of the actual cost of work performed to the earned values (or budget cost of work performed) a measure of productivity is established. The productivity factor can then be applied, where relevant, to all budgeted work not completed or started, in order to reassess the estimates for that work, and to help in the calculation of the final project cost predictions. The technique needs careful application insofar as it needs to recognize the different types of contract conditions. Earned value methods are particularly relevant for contracts subject to a measurement process. They may not be quite so valid in the case of lump sum or turnkey type of contracts.

Forecast contingency

In addition to all the other elements of final cost prediction and cost trend observations, it will be necessary to include an overall provision to cover future contingencies on the costs which are not yet committed. By its nature the sum provided is usually a proportion of the original contingency sum based upon:

original contingency × [estimate to complete costs/estimated final costs]

Therefore as the project proceeds, the unknown element (reflected by the estimate to complete cost) diminishes, and as a consequence so does the forecast contingency.

COLLECTING PROJECT COSTS

While the more difficult and challenging aspects of cost control are concerned with the prediction of future trends, it is obviously important that committed costs and expenditures are monitored and recorded. Detailed records will be essential for project audit purposes.

Committed costs

To ensure that financial commitments are identified promptly, the cost engineer will need to be a party to the approval process before commitments become contractually binding. In particular, the estimated committed cost will need to be known and compared with the relevant part of the control budget before approval. Any potential cost overrun implications are therefore highlighted and weighed at the time of approval, and not afterwards when it is too late to exercise control.

Expended costs

The final authority for the approval and payment of invoices often rests with the accounts function, but the time lag between the work being done and the resulting payments is usually too long for the purposes of cost control. The project manager and, more particularly, the cost engineer, will therefore need to be party to the auditing of suppliers' and contractors' invoices as early as possible. In this way the implications for expenditure (the value of work done) becomes known well in advance of the actual payments.

In cases where payments are dependent upon the actual hours worked (e.g. day-work rates) it is necessary to have comprehensive details of hours worked by individual people. With current state-of-the-art computing technology this is usually a straightforward exercise with the information being passed electronically from the contractor/supplier system to the project team. After approval, these records can then be used by the cost engineer to calculate expenditure in advance of the invoices being received.

CASH FLOW

Cash flow can be defined as an estimate of the amount of cash flowing into the project (earnings – usually nil before the project becomes operational), and the cash outflows (expenditures) divided into convenient control periods (monthly, quarterly or yearly) throughout the life of the project. Each element of forecast income or expenditure is assigned to the period when money is expected to be received or spent. Thus, a cash flow statement becomes a time-related schedule of receipts and payments. Within each period, receipts and payments are taken together to arrive at a net overall inflow or outflow of cash for the period. An accurate cash flow forecast of this type is crucial to the organization that has to provide funds for the project. The provider of funds will require advance notice of the amounts of funds needed and the timing.

There may be circumstances where project funds are to be supplied from a number of loan sources, possibly in more than one currency. The cost engineer will need to be aware of such arrangements in order to be able to advise the owner accordingly.

In the development stage of the project, the cost engineer will be primarily concerned with the capital costs of the project. Other cash flow studies relating to the project during its operational phase (operating, maintenance, income from sales, working capital and so forth) would need to be considered separately from the mainstream project control activities,

Forecast cash flow calculations for the capital costs of a project will need to include:

1   The estimated value of work done over the project timescale, expressed in terms of the base cost.
2   Calculated provisions for escalation and any exchange rate changes, based on the estimated value of work done, in order that the value of work done is expressed in money-of-the-day terms over the project timescale.

The forecast cash flow is then calculated by:

1   Estimating when invoices are likely to be received in relation to the value of work done (in money-of-the-day values).
2   Estimating when invoices are likely to be paid. This is usually taken as the date approved for payment.

The forecast cash flow will need to take account of the estimated value of work done, expressed in money-of-the-day terms. In the absence of information to the contrary, it may sometimes be necessary to assume the receipt of invoices in accordance with the projected value of work done. In some companies the projected value of work done is lagged by (say) two months, to allow time for invoices to be 'approved for payment'. The actual cash outflows (invoices paid) would normally be recorded by the project accountant. An example of a cumulative cash flow report is shown in Figure 13.5.

225

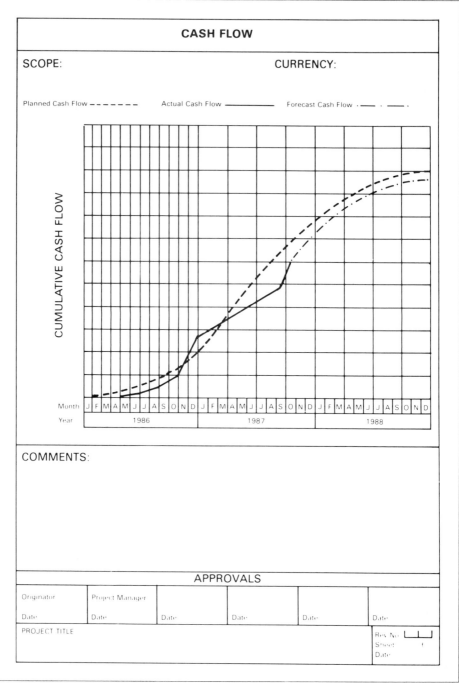

Figure 13.5   Cash flow graph

This is an example of a cash flow forecast in graphical form. It is usually necessary also to provide this information in tabular format, with the columns representing the months, quarters or other control periods spanning the project life, and with the amount of cash outflow or inflow expected entered for each period.

CAPITAL SANCTION STATEMENT

PROJECT

Company
Currency
Date of report
Cut off date
Date printed

FINANCIAL SANCTION

Date	Memo No.	Amount £.000	Adjustments

COST REPORT

1	2	3	4	5	6	7
AFE Budget No	Description	Approved control budget Estimate class	Authorised for expenditure	Commitment as at	Estimated final cost (EFC)	Over (under) budget
		Dated				6 - 3

Sub Total
Contingency
Total

EXPENDITURE

8	9	10	11
Current year		Previous years	Cumulative to date
Estimate for year	Actual as at		
			9 - 10

Notes

Accruals & Provisions Included above

Figure 13.6 Cost tabulation used for reporting

This form is an example of a report used to show the status of capital sanctions at a given report date.

227

COST REPORTING

The content and frequency of project cost reports will clearly depend upon the requirements of management, and the nature of the project, or projects, being undertaken. Where a considerable number of small projects are being undertaken, each of which is of relatively short duration, weekly reporting might be appropriate. Larger projects, particularly international projects and/or those involving partners, would normally be reported monthly.

Cost reports will typically include data summarized in tabular form, supported by trend graphs. Ideally the reports will be 'rolled-up' from details held in a computer database. In this way, summarized information can always be scrutinized at detail level if needed.

Figure 13.6 illustrates a monthly report format which has been used for large international projects. Of particular importance is the relationship between the estimated final cost and the control budget. In addition to the commitment and expenditure profiles, there might be cases where the sunk costs need to be plotted in the early stages of the project. Cash flow statements will also be important to show the estimated value of work done, invoices received, and invoices paid.

Using a computer-based system, the cost engineer should be able to produce a variety of control reports very economically. These would include:

1   Summary tabular and graphical reports for management review.
2   Budget, commitment and expenditure listings.
3   Analysis-type reports, which enable comparison of the budget and committed and expended reports, highlighting potential cost-related problems.
4   Movement reports which identify movements in cost totals within a given reporting period.

COMPUTER-AIDED TECHNIQUES

Under the rigorous financial constraints within which projects are now completed, it is virtually mandatory to use computer-based systems. The continuing and rapid development of desktop microcomputers now affords very powerful computing aids at very low cost.

Well-designed computer systems allow detailed information to be gathered, analysed, stored and quickly summarized for management reporting. Unlike planning systems, where there is a veritable plethora of quality packages available in the market place, it is more difficult to purchase off-the-shelf cost control applications. The user can either build a cost management system in a standard database, or purchase a standard product and have it tailored to meet specific needs. The former solution could prove expensive and may inevitably involve 're-inventing the wheel'. Tailoring an existing system can usually provide a more economic solution. Unlike estimating systems (which tend to hold one set of data), cost systems will need to have substantial storage capabilities. A large project can involve thousands of invoices. For this reason a database system may be preferable to a spreadsheet approach.

When selecting a system there are a number of factors to be considered. These include the following:

1 Existing company policy on hardware/software selection.
2 Existing company systems that would need to be accessed to avoid duplication of data.
3 Operating environment of the system, that is, single user, multiple user/viewer, in-house or remote site, etc.
4 The needs of the project, perhaps a large international project requiring overseas data links down through a single small project operating in a local environment.
5 The needs of the user (cost engineer), that is, a system that is simple to operate with minimum systems support, or a large complex system requiring more substantial systems support staff.

With the explosive development of desktop hardware, it is now perhaps preferable to adopt low cost microcomputer-based technology. Machines can be either stand-alone or linked via a local area network (LAN) or wide area networked applications (WAN).

A quality computer-based cost control system will allow the cost engineer to sort, select and subtotal data rapidly from a common, single source of information. When pressed to substantiate summarized data, the system can be interrogated rapidly for solutions. Quality-based systems will also alert the cost engineer to potential areas of concern, such as potential overspends, negative trending and so forth.

To reduce the risk of duplication, it is best to produce all the key control documentation on the computer system. This means that indents, purchase orders, variation orders, etc., can be produced on the same system being used for cost control. The advantage is that as (say) an indent is prepared on the computer system, the key financial data is carried forward automatically into the cost control/purchasing module. This ultimately saves time and money and removes further opportunities for error.

Low cost systems technology

The advent of desktop technology now provides low cost computer-based system applications to meet a variety of needs for the cost engineer and small company environment alike. Using a single desktop portable it is now possible to meet virtually all cost engineering and business needs including:

- Word processing for reporting.
- Spreadsheet applications for business planning.
- Desktop publishing for presentations.
- Database for high volume work (e.g. cost control, time writing, accounting, document control, etc.).

- Modem technology to establish data links with external groups.
- Imaging technology to store and retrieve documents electronically.

Quality systems technology of this type will enable the cost engineer to be more productive and simultaneously improve the quality of his/her information sources.

HISTORICAL COSTS AND LESSONS LEARNED

At the end of the project, the actual cost details should be carefully recorded for future reference. In many companies this is achieved through the discipline of writing a project 'close-out' report. The important lessons to be learned from the project may then in turn be passed into a central 'lessons learned' database for the benefit of future projects.

In any event the cost engineer should ensure the electronic filing of a comprehensive set of project cost reports. For future project needs it is useful if these reports can be related to the project work breakdown structure, together with the company standard code of accounts convention.

In summary, historical project records could include the following:

1 Brief technical scope statement.
2 Key project personnel.
3 Project/contract strategy.
4 Project work breakdown structure and code of accounts convention.
5 Project programme.
6 Summary and detailed cost and man-hour reports.
7 Lessons learned.

For future estimating needs, it is important that such details as the scope of the project and relevant dates are clearly associated with the cost records for each project or contract. Since cost escalation can quickly render historical cost information less useful with the passage of time, the records should ideally include the man-hours associated with the costs.

FURTHER READING

Kharbanda, O. P., Stallworthy, E. A. and Williams, L. F., *Project Cost Control in Action*, 2nd edn, Gower, Aldershot, 1987.

14 Controlling Cash and Credit

John Butterworth

Profit is measured in money. All forms of industrial or commercial performance are perforce measured in or reduced to money terms. Every successful industrial project has therefore to be measured in money as well as in the time taken to completion and its technical excellence. For project managers with a financial background this will be obvious. If a project manager's training and discipline is non-financial he has nevertheless to understand and control the financial elements of the project if it is to be concluded successfully.

The amount of time taken to complete a project has a direct relationship with the money invested or otherwise tied up in the project. Quite apart from the completion of all work within estimated man-hour durations, and estimated material costs, a project will generally cost more than another with the same work content if it takes longer to finish. This is simply due to the employment of resources such as space, plant and management for the longer time. These are resources which have to be paid for. Money is also a resource, and money costs money to employ for as long as it is tied up in the work in progress. Time is money.

If the project manager's employers have access to all reasonable funds, then efficient resource management, including the management of funds, will simply maximize project success and demonstrate that it has been professionally managed. If the contractor's funds are limited, then inefficient fund management could produce a crisis – even a disaster – owing to lack of finance at crucial stages in the project. For example, supplies vital to project completion might be witheld by the vendors if there is doubt concerning the contractor's ability to meet his bills promptly through lack of cash. This chapter, therefore, deals with the management of funds from the planning aspects of cash receipts from customers, of scheduling and providing for cash outgoings, and in the collection of overdue amounts from customers.

THE IMPACT OF INTEREST CHARGES ON THE COST OF MONEY

Developing the foregoing arguments further, just as money saved means interest   *231* earned, so money spent means interest forgone. This is true regardless of whether the contractor is a net borrower or has money on deposit, because even to spend less of the money which would otherwise be on deposit would produce higher deposit account interest.

The interest element also means that money spent at the beginning of a long project will effectively cost more than money spent much later, towards the end of the project. Efficient use of money is an essential part of project management.

FORECASTING RECEIPTS

As with most other things in life, financial management becomes easier with practice, so that with successive projects planning the finances becomes more and more a matter of routine.

The fundamental point to note about cash flow management is fairly obvious but is nevertheless worth stating. The cash impact of a project is not necessarily the same as the physical implementation but is usually subject to leads and lags in time. Assuming the project involves the commissioning of a new production line it will be readily appreciated that sales of products from this production line, if sold on 30 days' credit terms, will produce cash only after 30 days following date of sale. In other words cash receipts lag behind physical sales. (Note that in the examples in this chapter all accounting is assumed to be on a calendar monthly basis, with holidays ignored, and with every month comprising 30 days unless otherwise stated – for simplicity.) In a perfect world the new production line results might look as follows, given an arrangement which allows the customer 30 days' credit:

Table 14.1

	Month 1 £'000s	Month 2 £'000s	Month 3 £'000	Month 4 £'000s
Invoiced sales	50	75	100	100
Cash receipts	Nil	50	75	100

However, it is an unfortunate fact that customers rarely pay on the due date. Suppose that the average amount of credit taken by customers is 45 days (quite normal in practice), the table of receipts, or *cash inflows*, is further distorted, as follows:

Table 14.2

	Month 1 £'000s	Month 2 £'000s	Month 3 £'000	Month 4 £'000s
Invoiced sales	50	75	100	100
Cash receipts	Nil	25	62.5	87.5

If the customers are allowed to deduct a discount for prompt settlement the cash receipts will be reduced by the amount of discount granted. Assuming, for example, that customers all deduct 2½ per cent discount, the position for 45-day credit payments becomes:

Table 14.3

	Month 1 £'000s	Month 2 £'000s	Month 3 £'000	Month 4 £'000s
Invoiced sales	50	75	100	100
Cash receipts	Nil	24.38	60.49	85.31

This table is not entirely realistic, as it assumes that all customers deduct 2½ per cent discount, whereas it has been assumed that some customers are paying late. The principle is, however, clear. The management will have to estimate the proportion of customers who will avail themselves of the discount offer, and then forecast the effective level of discount averaged over all customers (possibly 1.8 or 1.9 per cent of turnover, or as the case may be).

Offering a cash discount to speed up customers' payments is not always cost effective. A 2½ per cent cash discount to speed up payments by 30 days is equivalent to a rate of interest of 30 per cent per annum. And some customers may deduct the discount and still pay late, giving rise to even more hassle.

A further consideration may be the length of time goods are held, on average, in stock. This would be highly relevant for a production or distribution unit forecast. Ignoring the discount shown in Table 14.3, but using the example in Table 14.2, consider the cash inflow time lag after output on the additional assumption that all goods are held in stock for an average of 30 days before they are sold. The result is as follows:

Table 14.4

	Month 1 £'000s	Month 2 £'000s	Month 3 £'000	Month 4 £'000s
Invoiced sales	50	75	100	100
Cash receipts	Nil	Nil	25	62.5

Further complications can be added. For example, 10 per cent of the turnover might be over the counter for cash. Or there could be (say) two products, one of which is held in stock for 30 days and the other for 60 days. If the cash flow is to be accurate the forecast sale volumes of each product must be established with some degree of accuracy, and also the proportion of each product (if any) that is sold for cash.

Remember also if turnover is subject to value added tax (VAT) that this is added to the value of the goods or services when these are invoiced. The VAT *233* becomes a cash receipt when the invoices in question are paid but is subsequently accounted for separately to the VAT authorities.

The conventional way to show these aspects in a cash flow forecast is to list cash sales separately from credit sales and to provide a third line for other cash receipts (such as rent receivable, proceeds of sale of a capital asset, new capital paid into the project or the proceeds of loan received from head office or from a bank). Where the characteristics of the products differ, as with the two different stocking periods suggested above, or possibly due to longer terms of sale to a different market, it is recommended that separate subsidiary schedules are drawn up for each product or market, etc. The totals of these subsidiary schedules can then be combined into the monthly cash flow forecast, with the format similar to that of Table 14.5.

Table 14.5

	Month 1 £'000s	Month 2 £'000s	Month 3 £'000	Month 4 £'000s
Receipts				
Cash sales				
From credit customers				
Other receipts				
Total receipts				

FORECASTING PAYMENTS

Just as receipts are subject to leads and lags relative to the physical movement of goods, etc., the same is true of payments. Obviously every project is different, but the following notes should be of help to the reader drawing up a cash flow forecast for the first time.

Cash purchases, like cash receipts, have immediate impact. If the project involves a new venture it may be necessary to pay cash for a higher proportion of purchases than if it is part of an established operation. Indeed on a new project it may be necessary to pay for certain requirements in advance. The project manager may be wise to take a conservative view of the proportion of purchases paid for on a cash basis. Obviously cash in this context would include immediate payment by cheque and not merely petty cash disbursements.

Where cash purchases are significant it may be necessary to split them into those subject to VAT and those not so subject, remembering that the VAT is paid with the invoice.

Goods and services not purchased for immediate cash payment result in an element of credit received from the creditors. This period of credit gives rise to a time lag before these purchases impact on the cash flow, exactly in the same way as do sales made on credit terms – except that this time the time lag delays the
234 cash outflow and thereby reduces the project's cash needs. As in the sales

forecast, in so far as cash settlement discounts are available to the project, then cash needs are reduced still further. Beware of planning to take longer than usual credit from suppliers, however. The suppliers do not always cooperate, and may retaliate by cutting off supplies. On a project with tight time constraints the project manager will need the maximum cooperation and goodwill from suppliers.

Capital expenditure may or may not be significant, but in many projects substantial payments for large capital items will be required. The project manager must estimate this expenditure, possibly with the assistance of his technical management. He should be aware that for many capital items cash is required in advance of delivery. The sums of money required may be significant, even for head office.

Where capital expenditure is sizeable, a complete schedule of capital expenditure should be prepared and agreed with the relevant technical departments and with the organization responsible for providing the funds (head office, the client, the bank, or other source of finance). It is also worth mentioning that any sizeable capital expenditure needs to be sanctioned before all the other work involved in the cash flow forecast is carried out, since a decision by the funding source (e.g. head office or client) to phase such expenditure over a different period must affect all aspects of the project and might mean re-scheduling all activities and producing a complete new cash flow forecast.

Value added tax (VAT) must be calculated wherever it is involved in either purchases or sales. The UK procedure is to complete the VAT return quarterly, showing the amounts of VAT charged to customers or clients and the amounts paid out to suppliers of goods and services. The resulting balance becomes payable 30 days from the date of the return. Failure to complete returns on time will incur the wrath of the authorities.

Liability to VAT runs from the date it is invoiced – not from the date it is paid by customers. If customers or clients pay very slowly, it is possible that the contractor will become liable to pay VAT to the authorities before he has collected it from his customers. This is one important reason for maintaining good credit control.

VAT payable on goods imported into the United Kingdom becomes due when the goods are cleared through the customs. It can only be delayed if the importer provides a formal bank guarantee to the authorities.

Where the product or service provided by the contractor does not carry VAT, but where the goods and services bought for the project do, then the VAT becomes a net receivable item and a credit. In these circumstances VAT may be shown under the receipts section of the cash flow forecast.

Corporation tax is normally paid annually. Few projects will have to provide for this charge, but some kind of tax may be payable for overseas projects.

Labour costs comprise wages or salaries plus other elements such as employee tax and social security payments. Wages are usually (but not invariably) paid weekly. If the cash flow forecast is made on a monthly basis, then some months will have four pay days and others five. This will distort the cash flow, and payments must be scheduled accordingly. Salaries, on the other hand, *235* are almost always paid at the end of each month, with no month to month variation. Income tax (pay as you earn) and National Insurance elements of wages and salaries become due 14 days from the end of the month in which the wages or salaries were paid. Other points to bear in mind when scheduling the costs of labour are:

1 Any bonus payments which may arise.
2 Holiday pay, which is often paid in advance.
3 The impact of periodic pay reviews which could increase pay rates, reflecting the rate of inflation.

Rent, rates and water may be payable monthly, quarterly or half-yearly. There may be a degree of payment in advance demanded for some of these items. Light, heat and power are normally payable quarterly in arrears, and their due dates may not fall at the end of a calendar month. These payments for public utility services have to be made promptly to avoid danger of the service being withdrawn.

Costs and timing of payments for transport and packing will vary enormously in their impact on the cash flow schedule. It is sometimes possible to establish an arithmetic relationship between these items and, say, the value of goods being despatched.

Among the many other payments to be considered are the charges levied by the bank or other financing authority providing funds for the project. If funding is from head office on an interest-free basis, only the current account commission of the administering bank will have to be provided.

FORECASTING NET CASH FLOW

The format of a typical cash flow schedule is shown in Figure 14.1. This brings together, spaced according to their appropriate timings, all the receipts (inflows) and payments (outflows) discussed in the two previous sections of this chapter to arrive at a net monthly inflow or outflow figure, and uses these results to predict the level of the current account bank balance each month.

If receipts are greater than payments the resulting credit to the bank balance will increase any credit balance or reduce the debit balance as the case may be.

If payments are greater than receipts the converse will be the case. Obviously the closing bank balance for Month 1 becomes the opening bank balance for Month 2.

Most managers make a point of preparing a separate schedule for each line in the cash flow forecast to show how each month's figure has been calculated. This is worth doing even if the forecast expenditure for an item is the same, regular, small amount every month (simply note on the relevant schedule sheet, for example, 'Repairs and renewals estimated at £50 per month'). These schedule sheets can be kept in a loose leaf folder behind the master schedule, where they are easily available for reference.

CASH FLOW FORECAST FROM _____ 19   TO _____ 19

RECEIPTS	Jan	Feb	Mar	Apr	May	Jun	Jul	Aug	Sep	Etc →
Cash sales										
From credit customers										
Other receipts										
Total receipts (A)										
PAYMENTS										
Cash purchases										
Creditors for goods and services										
Wages and salaries										
Rent, rates, water										
Light, heat, power										
Transport and packing										
Repairs and renewals										
Bank and finance charges										
Capital expenditure										
Value added tax (net)										
Corporation tax										
Other payments										
Total payments (B)										
Net inflow (A − B) or										
Net outflow (B − A)										
± opening bank balance										
= closing bank balance										

Figure 14.1   A typical cash flow format

The list of payments shown is not exhaustive. Other relevant items may include, for example, advertising, royalty payments, audit fees and other professional charges.

Reviewing cash flow forecasts

Cash flow preparation can be a daunting task at first, but it becomes increasingly straightforward with practice, provided the manager subjects himself to the vital discipline of examining the variances. This means writing in, as month succeeds month, the actual figure on each line against the forecast. Any fool can write down a forecast but it may be wildly inaccurate. It is only by comparing the actual with the forecast figures that the relationships become apparent.

To do anything successfully in business the manager needs to carry out three separate activities:

1 Plan.
2 Do.
3 Review.

This is the review phase. It may be late, extremely hot, and the boys may be having a party next door, but this review must be carried out if the manager is to exercise control of current and future projects. It is what he learns from the current review that will improve his control in the future.

Finally, cash flow forecasts should be regularly revised if the project is to last much more than say three months or so. Variances are bound to arise. The review process will highlight them. If they are not to reverse themselves, they need to be built into a revised forecast. Head office will prefer to be warned in good time if the original forecast was too optimistic rather than be faced with a mini cash crisis.

A second reason for regular revisions is that in any forecast the error factor must increase with time. It is quite reasonable to expect a high degree of accuracy for three months or so and then an increasing $\pm$ error factor for succeeding quarters as the variances build up and compound.

It is not usual to prepare detailed cash flow forecasts more than twelve months ahead but the business may require a 'rolling' forecast, that is, a forecast for the next 12 months to be reviewed after six months with a view to producing another 12-month forecast as at the date of the review.

SPEEDING UP THE CASH FLOW

The remainder of this chapter deals with collections. A better description might be 'safeguarding and speeding up the cash flow'. Once a project manager has worked out his cash flow forecast he has two basic tasks:

1 To implement the project in accordance with the timetable.
2 To ensure that the client or customer pays for it, and that the budgeted profit duly accrues to the project in cash.

Of course the major part of the project is the implementation. Successful
238 achievement of this will produce the flow of product or services (or in some

projects will eliminate the costs), which is the ultimate objective of the project in the first place. Successful implementation on time will help to ensure that the budgeted costs do not overrun. This aspect therefore is quite vital.

However, the project will not be successful – indeed it may break down completely – if implementation does not result in the anticipated cash receipts. If these are not achieved on time the project manager will be running up bills and paying out money with the risk of running out of cash funds. If head office or higher management are not aware of the bills being accumulated without funds with which to pay them, when the day of reckoning arrives the situation could be at the least awkward, at the worst a crisis. Every possible step has to be taken to ensure that money due is paid promptly by the customer.

The contract

The first consideration of the project manager must be the contract with the customer or client. This contract may have been written by the contractor (in consultation with his legal advisers) or may be a contract imposed upon the contractor by the customer (in consultation with *his* legal advisers). On the other hand, the contract could be a standard, general purpose contract. The subject of contracts generally is dealt with in Chapters 5, 6 and 7.

The experienced project manager will have a good idea of the payment stipulations he requires and will, if at all possible, have tried to be present personally at any negotiations with the customer on this point. If it is (say) a construction project, and the manager is an engineer he should not simply concentrate on the engineering aspects and leave the payment clauses to someone else. These are vital to the successful completion on budget of the project. If the manager is responsible for the project, he is also responsible for getting paid, as this is the real object of the whole operation.

But mention must be made of lawyers. Assuming the project manager is using his own lawyers, they will put in as tough a set of payment conditions as they can draw up. Make sure from actual experience that these are reasonably enforceable in the field or in the market concerned. Otherwise they become at best pointless and at worst a future stumbling block. The lawyer needs to have a clear understanding of the nature of the work and the sorts of problem likely to be encountered. The project manager may need to prepare a detailed briefing for his lawyer. This may seem unnecessary or tedious but time spent on these points will pay dividends when it comes to getting the money in later. Of course most projects follow, in broad terms, a previous job and the conditions of the last job can be used for the new one, provided that the manager learns from any problems experienced previously.

It might be appropriate to include a provision for payment of interest by the customer in respect of any late payment. The lawyer will cheerfully draft a paragraph to this effect but only the project manager will know how best to implement this condition. For example, it must be clearly seen what are the due dates of the payments. If this kind of detail cannot be established beyond reasonable doubt, the best lawyer's contract will not be enforceable in the matter *239* of interest on late payments. This is an example of how the project manager needs to work closely with his lawyers.

In many cases the manager will be faced with the customer's own set form contract. Here the boot is on the other foot and the customer's lawyers have been at work in strictly the customer's interest. In such a case read the contract carefully and check the provisions for payment and those covering arbitration over disputes. Make sure that they are workable and reasonably fair. Discuss with the customer if necessary how he implements these conditions in practice. If the contract says payment 30 days from an event find out if the customer's own accounts department is efficient. If dealing with, say, the customer's engineering department, they will probably be very happy to say (for example) 'Should you experience payment delays, which is unlikely, contact our Mr White who can sort them out very quickly'. Make a note of Mr White's name and his telephone number.

Consider any foreseeable snags arising out of the customer's contract. What are the critical conditions? In certain construction contracts certification of work done will be critical. Consider how to obtain this promptly when required. The customer's contract may (for example) say that payment will be made so many days from certification or measurement of work done by the customer's architect or surveyor or engineer, etc. Make sure that the person who is to certify the work will be available to do this when required. If considered appropriate, obtain written confirmation that this work will be done promptly. A letter along the following lines could be used:

> In consideration of our carrying out the work/building/providing the services covered by your contract No.00101 dated ... and for which payment will be made following certification of work done by your nominated architect/surveyor/engineer please confirm our discussion of yesterday (by signing and returning the enclosed copy of this letter) that your nominated architect/surveyor/engineer will attend the site to carry out the necessary certification work within 7 days of being requested by us to do so.

Such a letter could prove very useful at a later date if payments are delayed through no fault of the project manager, who might be instructed by his superiors to claim interest for the late payment. Even if interest is not shown in the contract as payable on late payments, a letter such as that shown above will help to safeguard prompt payments.

If the project is large, the contract will probably have a clause setting out arrangements for settling disputes. This clause should be read carefully to ensure that it is workable and, it is to be hoped, in line with previous similar projects undertaken. If it is not considered workable, the project manager should endeavour to have it changed to a practicable arrangement which is agreed as fair by both parties. It always has to be remembered that the work has got to be performed correctly in the first place for payment to be due: this is fundamental.

In the writer's experience, set form contracts drawn up by engineering-oriented companies tend to be fairly straightforward. After all the company in question simply wants the work to be done to the required specification within the timescale agreed and at the stipulated price. Set form contracts drawn up by financial organizations tend to be a lot tougher in the conditions they contain.

Consider also in the light of the main contract what implications there may be for the project manager if he, in turn, is proposing to subcontract part of the work to a third party or parties. It is difficult to be specific here because of the wide range of work and conditions for carrying it out. But subcontractors have to be paid, sometimes extremely promptly, and this fact may need to be reflected in some way in the project manager's own contract with the end customer.

Terms of payment

Careful consideration must be given to the terms of payment in the contract. These affect not only the cash flow, but also the endemic risk of the work. As a general rule, the greater the risk in the project, the greater the need for a mobilization or 'up-front' payment by the customer. The manager's objective in this case should be to arrange matters so that the customer has a clear financial interest in the completion of the work because he has already paid in advance for a proportion of it.

Perhaps the most extreme need for up-front payments is in foreign markets where there is the possibility of political problems or even of a revolution. In Iraq in the 1950s and again in Iran in the 1970s, following their respective revolutions there was widespread abrogation of commercial contracts by the new rulers. A number of companies suffered severe losses or went bankrupt. It is, of course, easy to be wise after the event, but the lesson is clear. Contracting companies which have been paid up-front, even if only in part, will:

1 be able to save at least something from the situation; and
2 have a valuable bargaining counter if the contract has to be renegotiated.

In most normal commercial situations it is the second point which is most important. If the contractor has been paid partly in advance he is in a far better position to negotiate with the customer when something unforeseen occurs. He can actually threaten to lay off his men or slow down the completion rate. If he has no money in hand such threats will have far less effect. The customer may regard them with disdain, inviting the project manager to go ahead and carry out his threatened action if he dares – in which case the customer will simply replace the present contractor with another.

Every project manager, wherever he is operating, needs to take this point into his calculations. If he cannot reduce the risk by means of a down payment by the customer, he needs something else as a bargaining counter. This might be the withholding of part of the technical know-how from the customer's operatives, for example.

Length of credit terms

Terms of credit also contribute to the risk. The longer the terms the greater the *241* risk and vice versa. Quite apart from the question of cash flow, if the customer is to pay on 90-day terms rather than 30-day terms there are two effects:

1 Three times as much money is owed by the customer. If the customer is a poor credit risk, the project manager has three times as much money at risk. In the absence of any down payment, if the customer fails, the resulting bad debt will be three times as great.
2 The manager will have far less warning of deteriorating payments. If, for example, the payment terms are 30 days and payment is not forthcoming, the project manager is put on notice that something is wrong and can take steps to remedy the situation before any more time is lost. If, however, the payment terms are the 90 days of our example the project manager cannot react until much later and this delay could turn out to be a serious matter.

It will be appreciated that the greater the credit risk is considered to be, the lower should be the maximum amount of credit to be granted to the customer and, accordingly, the shorter the terms of settlement. If the work involves payment by the customer of £5 000 per week and if we do not want to grant to the customer more than £10 000 credit outstanding at any moment of time then the terms have got to stipulate 7-day payment. This permits 1 week's work in progress prior to invoice plus 1 week's credit to the customer. If he does not pay on the due date the workforce must down tools or the credit exposure will rise above £10 000. Of course, things are never quite as simple as this, but the principle is clear – short terms mean less risk.

Retentions and guarantees

For many contracts it is usual for the customer to withold payment (typically 10 per cent) of the total amount invoiced. This 'retention' amount becomes payable after an agreed period, which might be six months or even a year. Payment of the retention amount might be related to an event, such as the commissioning of a machine or production process. If retentions are applicable to the project in question, there is little that the project manager can do about them except to:

1 Remember to include them in the cash flow schedule.
2 Recognize that they increase the credit risk (if the customer becomes insolvent before they are paid they become a bad debt).
3 Arrange for these retentions to be accounted for properly and ensure that they are followed up for payment as soon as they become due.

Another way in which risk may be reduced is by incorporating in the contract a guarantee by a third party such as a bank. Where there is a significant risk the project manager should always bear in mind the desirability of obtaining such a guarantee, particularly since he may have considerably more at risk than the amount invoiced and outstanding. There may be considerable work in progress awaiting certification. He may have liabilities to subcontractors. He may have run up other bills himself, not yet due, or entered into firm purchase contracts which he must fulfil regardless of whether he is paid by his customer. In these circumstances he may be wise to have the contract guaranteed by a substantial third party such as a bank or other financial insititution.

A limited amount of security can be obtained by specifying payment under a letter of credit. This is a document issued by a bank in which the bank undertakes either to pay cash or to accept a bill of exchange (which in turn can be discounted for cash) up to a specified maximum amount against receipt of specific documentation. This documentation is usually evidence of shipment of goods such as invoices and bills of lading but can include certificates of work done by a nominated authority.

The very fact that the customer has provided a letter of credit is evidence that he has the funds to pay for the project. The project manager has to be extremely careful, however, that the documentation which he lodges with the bank in order to obtain payment complies in every way with the terms of the letter of credit. Letters of credit carry expiry dates for completion of the work or shipment of goods and for the presentation of the claim documents. Late completions or late submissions will not be eligible for payment, which will have to be renegotiated with the customer.

COLLECTION OF ACCOUNTS WHEN DUE

Having done as much preparatory work as possible in the way of examining the contract, ensuring that all paper work required is in order and obtaining the most secure or risk-free terms as possible (not to mention implementing the actual project) the time will come when the customer is due to pay. What steps should the project manager take to ensure that payment is received promptly?

Of the many different types of project, the following sections of this chapter will consider two categories for the purpose of collection of accounts. First there are the large projects, of which the contractor will only be handling a few (even only one) at any particular time. At the other end of the scale are the smaller projects, so that the contractor could be handling a larger number, involving collections from a considerable number of customers.

High cost, large projects

Projects which, by their size and value, generate the collection of substantial sums obviously deserve treatment as special cases by the accounts department. Because the sums owing are large, the impact on the cash flow (for the contractor and for the project) is great and the effects of any late payments generally more serious than for one of a series of smaller projects. For example, if the annual rate of interest is running at 12 per cent, a debt of £50 000 would cost over £16 a day, or £115 a week, in finance costs. The impact of late payments on the viability of a large project is clear.

Under the terms of the contract governing the project it may be necessary to apply for payment in a specified way. This will be either set out in the contract or *243* will be required in a form which is usual in the trade or industry concerned. In either case it is important to apply for payment by the method laid down, be it by invoice and statement or by application for stage payment, etc., as the case may be. By following this laid down procedure strictly the project manager makes it easier for the customer to process the payment through *his* own administration. For example, quoting the customer's own order or job number on the invoice may be quite vital if prompt payment is to be obtained. If the project manager has delegated this follow-up or collection activity to a subordinate, it is most important that the person in question fully understands the contract or trade requirements.

The first and obvious step to take if money is not forthcoming is to telephone the customer. When this call is made depends upon the circumstances. It might be prudent to telephone *before* the account is due and while still raising the paper work. Such a call could be used to ensure that the paper work was accurate, sufficiently comprehensive and was addressed to the right payment authority at the right address. Just one telephone call at the beginning might save great frustration and delay throughout the remainder of the project for, in the matter of collecting debts, there is absolutely no substitute for getting the paper work right first time.

Alternatively the telephone call might be made *after* the paper work has been dispatched, but before the account falls due. Here the purpose of the call will be to ensure that the customer has received the paper work and to ascertain that there are no 'problems'.

The project manager may feel that these telephone calls are unnecessary. The author would question such a view, especially if significant sums of money (for example, over £20 000) are involved, preferring to telephone after the account falls due. In such a case the call should be made within 7 days of the due date.

Many customers are simply late payers, resulting from a mixture of laziness, weak administration and poor cash flow. Obviously a customer whose administration is weak is not likely to be efficient when it comes to getting his own money in. Some customers are slow payers because they are financially weak and, therefore, bad credit risks. The assessment of credit risk is a specialized subject. If necessary, the reader should consult a specialist textbook on this subject (see Hutson and Butterworth (1984) for example). But by far the most common reason for late payments is some technical administrative problem, which the project manager or one of team can sort out quickly. So, the reasons for the early telephone call are:

1 To put pressure on the customer to pay.
2 To identify any problem and get it sorted out as quickly as possible.

If a couple of telephone calls do not clear the matter up it may be necessary for someone from the project team to visit the customer. But who should be visited? It is now that the work recommended earlier in this chapter will bear fruit. The project will have its own contact personnel in the customer's organization. If they

cannot help or do not know why payment is being withheld it is time to visit the

Mr White whom the project manager, in his early discussions, discovered was the official in charge of the customer's purse strings.

If these telephone calls and visits do not produce the required results and if the problem is not due to failure in some way by the project manager or his team, then the manager must seek to escalate the confrontation to the most senior official he can identify in the customer's organization. Here the right approach might be another telephone call or a carefully worded letter or another visit. It really depends on the manager's own personal style. Arriving at the customer's premises and politely refusing to leave until either a meeting takes place with the required official or better still a cheque is handed over is a procedure which does actually work. It is far preferable to the next step, which consists of either slowing down the work rate or complete withdrawal of labour from the project. The latter action in particular is tantamount to crossing the Rubicon. It can never be taken lightly. It may sour relations with members of the customer's own staff with whom good relations are important. It may even give rise to a counterclaim by the customer for unfinished or late work. In other words it is a step which should only be used by a project manager when he is entirely certain that he has carried out *to the very letter* his side of the contract. If he is not sure on this point he should take advice from his superiors.

Finally, the project manager can instruct a solicitor to write to the customer. Before doing so he should again be satisfied that he has completed the work he has contracted to carry out and has billed the customer for. The solicitor's letter should specify the amount owing and the contract under which it is due. If the customer does not respond to such a letter with either a cheque or a valid reason for non-payment the solicitor has the following main options open to him (at English law):

1 to obtain a court's judgement against the customer;
2 to seek to enforce this judgement by having the court's officials seize the customer's assets with a view to selling them for the benefit of the creditor; or alternatively
3 to use the existence of the judgement to petition the court at a subsequent hearing to wind up the customer compulsorily if it is a limited company or to make the customer or its partners bankrupt if it is a sole trader or firm.

There are a number of other, more specialized, remedies available to an unpaid creditor but the ones set out above are the most commonly used.

It will be appreciated that legal action will differ in detail in other countries and the project manager's local solicitor will advise on local practice. Regardless of the market, one point remains the same and that is that if the customer disputes his liability to pay, judgement is unlikely to be obtained and the dispute will have to be negotiated. Normally speaking, negotiation is better carried out before in effect the project leader crosses his Rubicon and escalates the problem out of normal day-to-day commercial relations. With a few customers escalation may be inevitable. With the majority a face-to-face meeting will solve the problem. Nevertheless the importance of the early preparatory work suggested throughout *245* this chapter will readily be appreciated since this, it is to be hoped, will prevent later crisis management.

Multi-project collections

Where a relatively large number of small value projects are being undertaken for a number of customers the collection process will need streamlining to some extent at least. Exactly how the contractor decides to do this will depend on the available resources. The following suggestions provide a guide which can be varied in the light of circumstances. For the sake of illustration, it is assumed that there are 100 customers to whom the value of goods or work provided ranges from £250 to £10 000 each month.

Obviously, bearing in mind the fact that money carries its own financing costs, more strenuous efforts must be exerted to recover overdue payments from the larger value contracts. A telephone call to collect a £10 000 debt will cost no more to make than a call to a customer owing only £250, but the payback for such a call is 40 times as great. It is suggested, therefore, that at least two collection programmes are drawn up, with one arrangement for debts exceeding (say) £1 000 and another for smaller debts. These arrangements could be organized as follows:

1 *Collection programme for debts exceeding £1 000*

Timing	Action
Every month	Send detailed statement of account
14 days after due date (if unpaid)	Telephone call
21 days after due date (if unpaid)	First letter
28 days after due date (if unpaid)	Final letter/second telephone call
35 to 40 days unpaid	Solicitor's letter

2 *Collection programme for debts under £1 000*

Timing	Action
Every month	Send detailed statement of account
14 days after due date (if unpaid)	First letter
28 days after due date (if unpaid)	Second letter
44 days after due date (if unpaid)	Final letter
60 days after due date (if unpaid)	Solicitor's letter

It will be noted that the telephone is not used in this example for chasing smaller debts. Although there is no reason why it should not be used it is more expensive in clerical time than letters, which can be standard texts produced by machine.

Examples of debt collection letters

Here are a few examples of standard collection letters which are suitable in many cases.

1 A first reminder letter designed to accompany statement of account.

> Dear Sirs,
> We enclose your statement of account giving details of an overdue balance of £   .
>   Would you kindly look into this and let us have your cheque in settlement or state your reason for withholding payment.
> Yours faithfully,

2 A first reminder letter designed for use without a statement of account.

> Dear Sirs,
> We have already sent you details of your account, on which there is now an overdue balance of £   .
>   Would you kindly look into this and let us have your cheque in settlement or state your reason for withholding payment.
> Yours faithfully,

3 Second letter, for use without a statement of account.

> Dear Sirs,
> Despite one reminder we are still carrying forward an overdue balance of £   .
>   May we therefore have your immediate payment.
> Yours faithfully,

If a statement of account is to be enclosed with this letter, the words 'as can be seen from the enclosed statement' can obviously be added after the overdue amount.

4 Letter to a customer who has paid only part of his account.

> Dear Sirs,
> We thank you for your payment of £   in reduction of this account.
>   There remains, however, a balance of £   which is extremely overdue and we must insist on receiving this sum/a further substantial payment* within the next seven days.
> Yours faithfully,

> * whichever is appropriate.

5 Example of a final demand, prior to a solicitor's letter. This may be sent by recorded delivery, for greater impact.

247

FINAL APPLICATION

Dear Sirs,

Account £

We note with regret that our previous applications for settlement of your now long overdue account appear to have been ignored.

It is with reluctance that we must inform you that unless we receive your remittance or your explanation for not making settlement within seven days of the date of this letter we shall be left with no alternative but to take whatever steps we consider necessary to secure collection.

Please help us to avoid this unpleasant step.

Yours faithfully,

Collection letters generally should be polite, firm and as short as possible. They are unlikely to be filed, let alone framed by the recipient. The final demand is a little different, being intentionally slightly high-flown in style and rather longer. It implies that the sender is about to take further action (i.e. to cross the Rubicon, as suggested earlier) without being specific. The project manager, in sending this final demand, can keep his options open – but he must do something when the seven days are up. If he does nothing then his credibility disappears, and any subsequent threat made by the project manager or his team will have less effect.

CONCLUSION

Various ways in which accounts receivable can be collected when they fall due have been discussed. As stressed continuously throughout this chapter, the three main points to be remembered remain:

1 Careful preparation will always be worthwhile and pay dividends.
2 Efficient work execution and accurate records are vital in order to establish the basis for a strong cash flow.
3 Prompt, polite but firm follow-up of overdues is most important in all circumstances.

Given these ingredients, the project manager will be less likely to suffer problems with his projects' finances.

FURTHER READING

Clarke, Brian W. (ed), *Handbook of International Credit Management*, Gower, Aldershot, 1989.

Gatenby, John, *Recovery of Money*, 7th edn, Longmans, London, 1989.

Hedges, Roy A., *How to Get Debts Paid Faster*, Gower, Aldershot, 1989.

Hutson, T.G. and Butterworth, *Management of Trade Credit*, Gower, Aldershot, 1984.

15 Project Appraisal

Dennis Lock

This chapter is concerned with decisions that have to be made before investment in a project can be authorized. All of us are familiar with investment decisions for modest domestic projects, such as home improvements or purchases. Some of us are also involved professionally, either having to make investment decisions for companies in which we are involved or being asked to give our recommendations to others.

There are several techniques which can help managers and investors to make go- or no-go decisions, or to point to one of a number of options as being the preferred choice. These techniques cannot, however, always be regarded as a means for providing definitive criteria for decision making. There may be overriding ethical, legal or environmental reasons for having to adopt a different course from the ideal. Furthermore, it is often the case that the parameters and data used in calculations have to be estimated or even guessed and will be revealed as dangerously inaccurate when the real project takes shape. Techniques, therefore, although important, are not the only ingredient in the mix of information, judgement, intuition and, yes, courage needed by investors.

The techniques outlined in this chapter start with a simple, small-scale case which has an obvious solution, and progress to more complex examples which illustrate some of the pitfalls and difficulties in making project investment decisions.

PAYBACK AND SIMPLE BREAK EVEN METHODS

A very simple payback case

The problem

A device for reading microfilms of drawings has been in use for many years in an engineering office. It has a first-class optical system, which is still in good condition. A print of any drawing can be obtained simply by pushing a button. The only problem with the machine is that its printing technolology is well out of date, so that the prints are not durable, the print paper is very expensive, and all the materials (paper and wet developer) deteriorate rapidly in storage or in the machine.

The office manager of this company has received a proposal from a sales representative for the supply and installation of a replacement machine. The new machine can be purchased, leased-purchased, leased or rented. Two of these options will now be considered.

This account is based on an actual case in an engineering company. Tax implications have been ignored in all calculations for this introductory example.

Existing cost rates

The following costs are being incurred using the old reader printer.

	£
Cost of machine (long since written off in the accounts)	Nil
Likely cost of paper and developer this year	10 000
Annual machine maintenance contract	1 000
Estimated cost this year	11 000

Future projections indicate that usage will increase by some 10 per cent per annum, at least over the next two or three years.

The rental option, compared against doing nothing

A new machine can be rented at a cost of £500 per month. This is subject to conditions typical of many rental agreements, namely, that the rental payments are fixed for the first year but can be reviewed annually (upwards) thereafter. The rental includes all maintenance and insurance costs. The user will have to buy paper, but this is plain paper, far cheaper than the silver-based light-sensitive paper and chemicals needed for the old machine. Here are the figures for the first year for the new proposal:

	£
Capital cost	Nil
First-year rentals	6 000
Cost of first-year paper supplies	2 000
Maintenance costs (included in rental)	Nil
Insurance costs (paid by renter)	Nil
Total first-year cost	8 000

250 This case is clear cut. The first-year cost will only be £8 000, against the option of

keeping the old machine (£11 000). Installing the machine will save £3 000 in the first year for no capital outlay. The only risks lie in the renter's option to increase rents in later years, or in the renter going bankrupt and the machine being recovered. Both of these risks are small and need not influence the decision to go ahead as soon as possible.

If the office manager needs higher management approval, he would probably argue the case by saying that the new machine will begin to make savings right from the start. The action taken will 'pay for itself' within the first week or so of the machine being installed.

The purchase option, compared against doing nothing

Now suppose that, for some reason, the engineering company dislikes renting or leasing agreements, and always prefers to buy new plant and office equipment outright. There are such companies. The implications for this case are that the new equipment would involve capital expenditure in its first year, but would thereafter incur no rental charges so that it should be extremely cheap to run. Expressed in project appraisal terms, one could say that the purchase option would produce lower operating costs at the expense of higher initial capital investment. The figures might look like this:

	£
Capital investment required	
(purchase price of new machine)	15 000
Cost of first-year paper supplies	2 000
(usage will increase each year by 10 per cent)	
Annual maintenance contract for first year	Nil
(covered by guarantee, but will be £2 000 in	
subsequent years)	
Insurance premium, all risks	100
(the old machine was not worth insuring)	
Total first-year costs	17 100

The machine has cost more in the first year than keeping the original machine, and it is necessary to look further ahead to find out how long it will be before the investment is at least matched by the predicted savings. The data have been set out twice in Figure 15.1, once in the table at the top and again in the form of two graphs plotted on common cost and time axes.

The breakeven point is seen to occur during the third quarter of the second year. Another way of expressing this is to say that the payback period is approximately 22 months. The biggest risk is that the company's forecast workload might not materialize. Provided that the company is confident that its workload level will not drop dramatically, buying the new machine would be better than keeping the old one.

In general terms, it is not necessary to use any more sophisticated project *251*

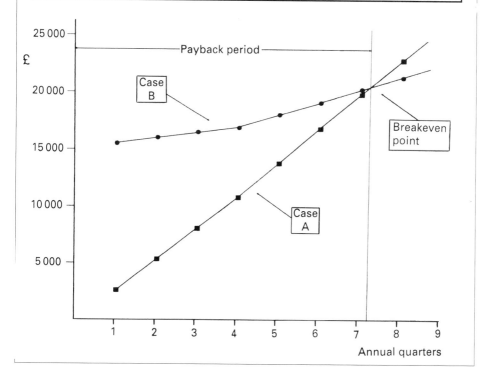

	First year				Second year			
	First quarter	Second quarter	Third quarter	Fourth quarter	First quarter	Second quarter	Third quarter	Fourth quarter
Case A (status quo):								
Paper and developer	2 500	2 500	2 500	2 500	2 750	2 750	2 750	2 750
maintenance	250	250	250	250	250	250	250	250
Cumulative totals A	2 750	5 550	8 250	11 000	14 000	17 000	20 000	23 000
Case B (buy new machine):								
Capital investment	15 000							
Paper supplies	500	500	500	500	550	550	550	550
Maintenance					500	500	500	500
Insurance premiums	100				100			
Cumulative totals B	15 600	16 100	16 600	17 100	18 250	19 300	20 350	21 400

252   Figure 15.1   A very simple example of a payback calculation

appraisal method if a simple payback calculation points to a payback period of two years or less *provided that*:

1 The estimates and forecasts are reasonably sound.
2 No significant cost factor has been omitted.

The purchase option compared against the rental option

There is one further aspect of this very simple case which needs examining before this chapter moves on to more complex examples. That is to compare the advantages of the purchase option with those of renting the new machine. Any reader who cares to carry out this arithmetic, ignoring inflation and the prospect of rental increases but allowing for paper usage to continue expanding at the rate of 10 per cent per annum, will find that the payback period has extended to about three and a half years. Purchasing would then continue to show savings over the other two options for years four, five, six and beyond.

In this case purchasing outright seems to be the best of all options, at least in the longer term. However, as later sections of this chapter will demonstrate, payback calculations which show breakeven points occurring more than two or three years ahead can be misleading and it is advisable to use a discounting method to prove the case.

The need to consider total costs

Here is another simple example, again based on an actual case, but this time illustrating what can go disastrously wrong when the starting parameters are not properly set (if the project is not properly and fully defined). The lessons to be learned from this example apply whatever method of project appraisal calculation is used.

A computer manager in an engineering company had to rely on external bureau computer facilities whenever a minicomputer or mainframe machine was needed. At that time the only computing facilities within the company were a few separate microcomputers with modest capabilities. The manager wanted to install a minicomputer with which to justify expanding his empire, but could not obtain authorization for the significant amount of capital expenditure needed because one of the directors was rigidly opposed to the idea, and also because the company's foreseen computing requirements did not seem to warrant installing such a machine on site.

The computing manager, like many of his fellows, was competent not only in computing techniques but also in company politics. Choosing a time when the hostile director was thousands of miles away, he came up with a proposal to buy a minicomputer that could double as a central word processing station for some or most of the company's secretaries and typists. The argument went something like this:

Outlay: £

    Minicomputer, with word processing software, six printers and ten
    workstations (visual display units)   60 000

Offsetting annual cost savings:

    Saving of two secretaries, owing to increased efficiency. Annual
    salaries, including high head office overheads   30 000

    Saving of professional engineers' time, by having purchase speci-
    fications and contracts stored in the machine, reducing the time
    needed to write, edit and check these documents   25 000

    Saving in external bureau costs for computing which could be
    carried out in-house in future   10 000

    Total annual offsetting savings   65 000

Faced with these promising figures, the company's board of directors authorized
the plan and asked the office services manager to implement it.

In the event, the first-year capital, installation and other 'once only' costs were
far higher than budget, because the project had not been properly thought
through and many extra items had to be paid for. The actual costs were, in round
figures:

	£
New equipment, as forecast	60 000
Allocation and redecoration of accommodation	1 500
Structural alteration (door widening, and so on)	850
Removal of all central heating radiators and pipes from the room	300
Installation of air conditioners and heaters	2 500
Installation of 60 Amp 'clean' electrical power supply and new mains wiring	1 200
Automatic Halon fire extinguishers	1 800
Installation of proprietary raised floor	2 550
Underground cable ducts across the car park (under thick concrete) between two buildings	1 500
Cabling from computer room to users' offices	3 500
New telephones	300
Purchase of six additional printers	6 000
Purchase of 12 acoustic hoods for the printers	4 200
Insurance premiums	300
Training costs of secretaries	5 000
Total first-year cost	91 500

The predicted offsetting first-year savings were not achieved because:

- Round the clock running of the machine and its air conditioners added
  £5 000 to electricity bills.
- The word processing software was peculiar to the equipment and

unfamiliar to all new or temporary secretarial staff.

- Secretarial efficiency was not increased immediately and staff cuts took longer to implement than forecast.
- It was found necessary to engage two extra people for the computer department, at salaries higher than those of the two secretaries saved.
- Computer crashes and down time for maintenance caused work loss and idle time among the secretaries and led to staff dissatisfaction.

The operating problems were overcome and the system eventually proved useful generally in the company but the computing capacity soon had to be increased, needing yet more investment. Maintenance and repair costs, totally ignored in the original cost forecasts, became heavy from the second year of operation onwards.

Before ever allowing this investment to take place, the board of directors should have demanded to see a properly argued case for the project, with total costs, proposals from suppliers of alternative equipment and an assessment of the possible risks. Another essential point that was missed was that the end users (secretaries with experience of word processing systems in their previous companies) were not asked for their views beforehand.

The forecast payback period for this project had been about thirteen months. In fact, in spite of very hard work from the computing staff to overcome all the problems, this project never paid for itself.

THE SIGNIFICANCE OF CASH FLOW AND TIMING OF PAYMENTS

In all financial project appraisals, the timing of payments and receipts is crucial. It is most important, therefore, that all the data are carefully tabulated, with each item shown in the period when it is expected to occur. It may not be possible to forecast these data with accuracy, but at least the analyst should be clear on how they ought to be presented. The table in Figure 15.1 was a simple example. In most projects many more items have to be considered.

A few definitions

Cash outflows

A cash outflow is any item of expenditure for, or resulting from, the project. Cash outflows for a typical project could include:

- All salaries, expenses, purchases, overheads, payments to contractors, suppliers and agents, professional fees, rental and hire charges, interest payable on loans, and anything else which contributes to the total project investment cost.
- Operating costs or the costs of using the completed project.
- Tax payments in respect of liabilities incurred through cash inflows generated by the project.

255

Cash inflows

Any item of income or cost saving resulting from the project is a cash inflow. Typical cash inflows include:

- Sales revenue.
- Royalties or licensing fees expected to be earned.
- Reductions in taxation through allowances, incentives or concessions.
- Proceeds of disposal sales for plant, buildings or materials rendered obsolete by the project.
- Proceeds expected from the disposal of the project itself when it reaches the end of its planned life.

Net cash flow

Sometimes simply called the cash flow, the net cash flow is the difference between cash outflows and cash inflows during a specified period or for the whole project. The result, obviously, might be either a net cash inflow or a net cash outflow.

Schedule periods

A cash flow schedule will always be divided into rows or columns that correspond to consecutive, equal periods in the overall timescale. The periods chosen will depend on the overall period covered by the appraisal (which might extend beyond the initial project manufacture or construction to include several years of use or operation). Calendar months or quarters are often appropriate for payback calculations for short-term projects. Half-years, whole years or even longer periods are more likely to be chosen for assessing larger projects. It is usual to align the periods chosen with one of the following:

- The contractor's accounting periods.
- The client's accounting periods.
- Fiscal periods (government or tax accounting periods).

Discounting

Whenever a financial analysis extends over a period which exceeds two or, at the most, three years, straightforward addition and subtraction of cash inflows and outflows (used in the simple payback method) is likely to produce a misleading result. This is because the value of any given sum of money depends on the date when it is to be received or paid out. The argument often used is that £1 today is worth more than £1 in the future because today's £1 can be invested immediately to increase its value.

Suppose, for example, that a person receives £1 000 now, and is due to receive a further £1 000 in one year's time. That person can invest the first £1 000 immediately, let us say (for simplicity), at 10 per cent net interest. By the time the second £1 000 is received the first payment will be worth £1 100. Financial analysts would say that £1 100 is the *future* value of £1 000 in this case. Alternatively, they would say that £1 000 is the *net present value* of £1 100.

Financial analysts make allowances for this time-related value of money using a process known as discounting to find net present values. Tables have been devised and published which give factors from which future values and net present values can be calculated for a range of percentage rates over different periods. In project financial appraisal, it is the net present values which are of most relevance. A short, but useful table of net present value discounting factors is given in Figure 15.2. More extensive tables of future and net present values can be found in Franks and Broyles (1979).

Inflation

Inflation is another important case where monetary values can change significantly with time. Perhaps it is the most obvious case. However, although the effects of inflation have to be allowed for when estimating the total costs of a project for budgeting and tendering, inflation is usually ignored when calculating net present values. This is a convention that is probably based on the loose assumption that inflation will affect both sides of the equation, and will therefore tend to cancel.

NET PRESENT VALUE

The net present value of a proposed project is found from a calculation which uses the discounted cash flow technique. The results can be used to help in decisions as follows:

1 To compare the net present values of two or more project options. The highest (or least negative) net present value points to the best financial choice. This application can be used to help choose between different technological processes, logistic approaches or strategies in major projects, or to help in choosing whether to buy, lease, lease-purchase or rent plant and equipment.
2 To evaluate the likely worth of a proposed investment over a given period, which should usually include not only the period of initial investment, but also the useful working life of the project.
3 To estimate the rate of return that can be achieved on the capital invested (percentage rate of return is equal to the discounting percentage rate that gives a net present value of zero).

Net present value calculations may be required in project feasibility studies, as part of the argument to obtain financing or authorization to proceed.

Year	1%	2%	3%	4%	5%	6%	7%	8%	9%	10%	11%	12%	13%	14%	15%	16%	17%	18%	19%	20%
0	1.000	1.000	1.000	1.000	1.000	1.000	1.000	1.000	1.000	1.000	1.000	1.000	1.000	1.000	1.000	1.000	1.000	1.000	1.000	1.000
1	0.990	0.980	0.971	0.962	0.952	0.943	0.935	0.926	0.917	0.909	0.901	0.893	0.885	0.877	0.870	0.862	0.855	0.848	0.840	0.833
2	0.980	0.961	0.943	0.925	0.907	0.890	0.873	0.857	0.842	0.826	0.812	0.797	0.783	0.770	0.756	0.743	0.731	0.718	0.706	0.694
3	0.971	0.942	0.915	0.889	0.864	0.840	0.816	0.794	0.772	0.751	0.731	0.712	0.693	0.675	0.658	0.641	0.624	0.609	0.593	0.579
4	0.961	0.924	0.889	0.855	0.823	0.792	0.763	0.735	0.708	0.683	0.659	0.636	0.613	0.592	0.572	0.552	0.534	0.516	0.499	0.482
5	0.952	0.906	0.863	0.822	0.784	0.747	0.713	0.681	0.650	0.621	0.594	0.567	0.543	0.519	0.497	0.476	0.456	0.437	0.419	0.402
6	0.942	0.888	0.838	0.790	0.746	0.705	0.666	0.630	0.596	0.565	0.535	0.507	0.480	0.456	0.432	0.410	0.390	0.370	0.352	0.335
7	0.933	0.871	0.813	0.760	0.711	0.665	0.623	0.584	0.547	0.513	0.482	0.452	0.425	0.400	0.376	0.354	0.333	0.314	0.296	0.279
8	0.923	0.854	0.789	0.731	0.677	0.627	0.582	0.540	0.502	0.467	0.434	0.404	0.376	0.351	0.327	0.305	0.284	0.266	0.249	0.233
9	0.914	0.837	0.766	0.703	0.645	0.592	0.544	0.500	0.460	0.424	0.391	0.361	0.333	0.308	0.284	0.263	0.243	0.226	0.209	0.194
10	0.905	0.820	0.744	0.676	0.614	0.558	0.508	0.463	0.422	0.386	0.352	0.322	0.295	0.270	0.247	0.227	0.208	0.191	0.176	0.162
11	0.896	0.804	0.722	0.650	0.585	0.527	0.475	0.429	0.388	0.351	0.317	0.288	0.261	0.237	0.215	0.195	0.178	0.162	0.148	0.135
12	0.887	0.789	0.701	0.625	0.557	0.497	0.444	0.397	0.356	0.319	0.286	0.257	0.231	0.208	0.187	0.169	0.152	0.137	0.124	0.112
13	0.879	0.773	0.681	0.601	0.530	0.469	0.415	0.368	0.326	0.290	0.258	0.229	0.204	0.182	0.163	0.145	0.130	0.116	0.104	0.094
14	0.870	0.758	0.661	0.578	0.505	0.442	0.388	0.341	0.299	0.263	0.232	0.205	0.181	0.160	0.141	0.124	0.111	0.099	0.088	0.078
15	0.861	0.743	0.642	0.555	0.481	0.417	0.362	0.315	0.275	0.239	0.209	0.183	0.160	0.140	0.123	0.108	0.095	0.084	0.074	0.065
16	0.853	0.728	0.623	0.534	0.458	0.394	0.339	0.292	0.252	0.218	0.188	0.163	0.142	0.123	0.107	0.093	0.082	0.071	0.062	0.054
17	0.844	0.714	0.605	0.513	0.436	0.371	0.317	0.270	0.231	0.198	0.170	0.146	0.125	0.108	0.093	0.080	0.069	0.060	0.052	0.045
18	0.836	0.700	0.587	0.494	0.412	0.350	0.296	0.250	0.212	0.180	0.153	0.130	0.111	0.095	0.081	0.069	0.059	0.051	0.044	0.038
19	0.828	0.686	0.570	0.475	0.396	0.331	0.277	0.232	0.195	0.164	0.138	0.116	0.098	0.083	0.070	0.060	0.051	0.043	0.037	0.031
20	0.820	0.673	0.554	0.456	0.377	0.312	0.258	0.215	0.178	0.149	0.124	0.104	0.087	0.073	0.061	0.051	0.043	0.037	0.030	0.026

Figure 15.2 Discount factors for calculating net present values

A simple example of a rent or buy study

For this case study the project is the same as that used to demonstrate the payback method earlier in this chapter. The problem here is to choose between renting or buying a new microfilm machine. All the data are unchanged from before, but the following additional parameters have been introduced:

1 It has been decided that the useful life of the new machine would be seven years, so that costs are to be analysed over that period
2 The effects of corporation tax are to be taken into account.

Tax conditions

At the time of this project, corporation tax was chargeable at 35 per cent of profits. All the operating and rental costs for the new machine can be offset against this tax. However, the savings for any particular year would not be seen until the subsequent year or even later, when the tax would have become due for payment. In our example all tax items lag their causal events by one year, and the tax savings have been set out accordingly in the cash flow schedules.

In addition to tax saved on operating expenses, there will also be a capital allowance if the company buys the machine. This will be claimed at the maximum rate allowed, which in this case is 25 per cent of the machine's residual book value per annum. Each year, therefore, the company accountant will subtract 25 per cent from the book value of the machine and claim the amount subtracted as an allowance to set against taxable profits. In other words, the amount of money saved each year in terms of tax that does not have to be paid will be 35 per cent of 25 per cent (which is 8.75 per cent) of the machine's written down value.

The rental option

The cash flows for renting the machine over seven years are shown in Figure 15.3. A proforma has been used to ensure that all the entries are set out logically and clearly (the proforma used throughout this chapter was taken from Lock (1990). Proformas need only be very simple, but confusion and errors will occur if one is not used. Conversely, the use of a proforma greatly simplifies the whole calculation.

Notice that the case details are written at the top of the form. This may seem obvious, but it is important to remember that some project appraisal calculations may have to be repeated many times for different parameters or strategies, and it is very important to be able to distinguish each of these from its fellows.

Another point to notice is that discounted cash flow schedules always starts from year zero, and not from year one. Think of this as '0' for origin.

Figures in parentheses are negative quantities (losses or cash outflows), according to the notation beloved of accountants.

A study of Figure 15.3 will show how all the cash inflows and outflows have been set out in their respective years, to show the net cash flow before *259*

CALCULATION OF NET PRESENT VALUE

Project title: New microfilm machine   **Date:**

Case tested: Rental for seven years   **Periods used:** Years   **Discount rate** 10 %

Period	Item	Cash flow at present cost			Discount factor	Discounted cash flow £
		Cash outflow	Cash inflow	Net cash flow		
0	Rentals Supplies	6 000 2 000		(8 000)	1.000	(8 000)
1	Rentals Supplies Corporation tax savings	6 000 2 200	2 800	(5 400)	0.909	(4 909)
2	Rentals Supplies Corporation tax savings	6 000 2 420	2 870	(5 550)	0.825	(4 579)
3	Rentals Supplies Corporation tax savings	6 000 2 662	2 947	(5 715)	0.751	(4 292)
4	Rentals Supplies Corporation tax savings	6 000 2 928	3 032	(5 896)	0.683	(4 027)
5	Rentals Supplies Corporation tax savings	6 000 3 221	3 125	(6 096)	0.621	(3 786)
6	Rentals Supplies Corporation tax savings	6 000 3 543	3 227	(6 316)	0.565	(3 569)
7	Corporation tax savings		3 340	3 340	0.513	1 713
8						
9						
10						
11						
				Project net present value (NPV) >		(31 449)

Figure 15.3 Net present value calculation for microfilm machine project (rental option)

discounting (in the fifth column from the left). A discount factor of 10 per cent was chosen for this project and the corresponding discount factors for this rate (taken from Figure 15.2) have been entered in the sixth column. The final column shows the net cash flow for each year after multiplication by the appropriate discount factor to show its net present value. The total net present value for this rental option is seen to be an outflow of £31 449.

The purchase option

Figure 15.4 shows all the cash flows expected to result over seven years if the machine is purchased for £15 000. The calculations are similar to those already explained for the rental option. This time the tax savings include both the amount related to allowable operating expenditure and the capital allowances (the detailed tax calculations were carried separately and are not shown here).

The net present value of the purchase option is an outflow of £27 333. Since minus £27 333 is greater than minus £31 449, the purchase option is indicated as the better course of action. (If the tax implications had been ignored, these outflows would have been calculated as £38 240 for purchase and £46 122 for rental.)

Net present value of an industrial project

A company is considering whether or not to go ahead with a manufacturing project to make 'Magiboxes'. Initial investment is estimated at £10m. pounds. This expenditure would be spread over three years, paying for Magibox design and development, purchase of machinery, pre-production trials and marketing. The sales department have forecast a useful product life of about seven years, after which some of the machinery might be sold at virtually scrap prices.

This example has been kept simple by not showing tax payments or allowances. The sales revenues shown are the gross margins expected, calculated from separate estimates of all factory costs and predicted sales at a particular price. When set down in a simple table, the data look like this:

Year	Investment forecast £	Revenue expected £	Comment
0	2 000 000	nil	
1	6 000 000	nil	
2	2 000 000	100 000	Pilot sales launch
3		500 000	Sales picking up
4		2 000 000	Product becoming known
5		3 000 000	
6		3 500 000	Sales at peak
7		3 000 000	
8		2 000 000	Sales dropping
9		1 000 000	Product discontinued
10		20 000	Sale of scrap machinery
Totals	10 000 000	15 120 000	

CALCULATION OF NET PRESENT VALUE

Project title: New microfilm machine   **Date:**

Case tested: Purchase   **Periods used:** Years   **Discount rate** 10 %

Period	Item	Cash flow at present cost			Discount factor	Discounted cash flow £
		Cash outflow	Cash inflow	Net cash flow		
0	Purchase price Supplies Insurance premiums	15 000 2 000 100		(17 100)	1.000	(17 100)
1	Supplies Maintenance + insurance Corporation tax savings	2 200 2 100	2 048	(2 252)	0.909	(2 047)
2	Supplies Maintenance + insurance Corporation tax savings	2 420 2 100	2 489	(2 031)	0.825	(1 676)
3	Supplies Maintenance + insurance Corporation tax savings	2 662 2 100	2 321	(2 441)	0.751	(1 833)
4	Supplies Maintenance + insurance Corporation tax savings	2 928 2 100	2 220	(2 808)	0.683	(1 918)
5	Supplies Maintenance + insurance Corporation tax savings	3 221 2 100	2 175	(3 146)	0.621	(1 934)
6	Supplies Maintenance + insurance Corporation tax savings	3 543 2 100	2 174	(3 469)	0.565	(1 960)
7	Corporation tax savings		2 212	2 212	0.513	1 135
8						
9						
10						
11						
				Project net present value (NPV) >		(27 333)

Figure 15.4   Net present value calculation for microfilm machine project (purchase option)

CALCULATION OF NET PRESENT VALUE

Project title: Magibox **Date:**

Case tested: 15 per cent return   **Periods used:** Years   **Discount rate** 15 %

Period	Item	Cash flow at present cost			Discount factor	Discounted cash flow
		Cash outflow	Cash inflow	Net cash flow		
0	Initial investment in research and plant	2 000		(2 000)	1.000	(2 000)
1	Continued investment	6 000		(6 000)	0.870	(5 220)
2	Final investment Initial sales revenue	2 000	100	(1 900)	0.756	(1 436)
3	Sales revenue		500	500	0.658	(329)
4	Sales revenue		2 000	2 000	0.572	1 144
5	Sales revenue		3 000	3 000	0.497	1 491
6	Sales revenue		3 500	3 000	0.432	1 512
7	Sales revenue		3 000	3 000	0.376	1 128
8	Sales revenue		2 000	2 000	0.327	654
9	Sales revenue		1 000	1 000	0.284	284
10	Disposal of plant		20	20	0.247	5
11						

All figures £'000s   **Project net present value (NPV) >**   (2 109)

Figure 15.5 Net present value of Magibox project at 15 per cent

This company always seeks to make a return on its investment (before tax) of not less than 15 per cent. On the basis of the figures in the above table, the investment of £10m. seems set to yield a total return of £5.120m. (51.2 per cent) over the product life. However, this is spread some years into the future, and it is necessary to discount the cash flows to get somewhere nearer to the real picture.

The discounting calculation is shown in Figure 15.5, using a discount factor of 15 per cent to test whether or not the company can really expect to achieve this rate of return. A negative net present value indicates that the company cannot achieve its target rate of return on the basis of the existing data. In this case the net present value is minus £2 109 000, showing that the company must think again and alter its strategy to improve the cash flow significantly if it is to achieve a 15 per cent rate of return.

Calculating the expected rate of return on investment

Now suppose that the company proposing to make Magiboxes decides that its forecasts of cash flow are realistic and cannot be improved. The question arises, 'What rate of return could we expect?'

In order to find this notional rate it is necessary to repeat the calculation shown in Figure 15.5 several times, using different discount rates until a rate is found that produces a net present value of zero. In practice it is unlikely that an integer would produce this result. For example, in this Magibox project the following net present values were obtained in calculations (not shown) when the discount rate was stepped down progressively:

Discount rate	NPV
11	(898 000)
10	(535 000)
9	(151 000)
8	270 000
7	723 000

It is obvious from these figures that the rate which would produce a net present value of zero lies between 8 and 9 per cent. The search for the precise answer can be narrowed down by a reiterative process, using fractional percentages by trial and error until a sufficiently close result is obtained. Alternatively, and more quickly, a graph can be plotted and used to interpolate the result. Figure 15.6 shows that the forecast return on the Magibox project investment should be about 8.75 per cent.

General

The examples in this chapter had to be kept simple, but they illustrate the principles of using discounted cash flow to indicate the net present value of a
264 particular project strategy or its expected rate of return on investment. The

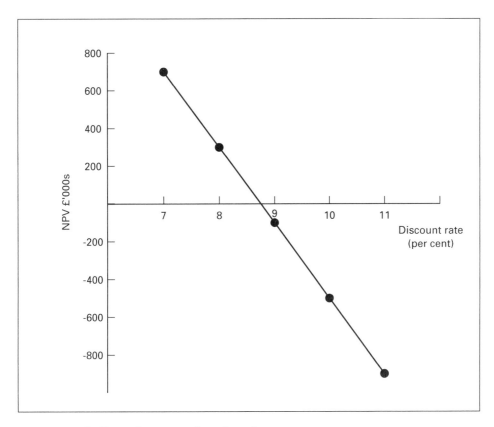

Figure 15.6   Rate of return on investment

This shows how a range of discount rates can be tested in net present value calculations for a proposed project and plotted to find the factor that would yield an NPV of zero (this factor is equivalent to the percentage rate of return on investment).

techniques are applicable to any proposed investment, whether the project is for manufacturing, construction, petrochemical processing, mining, agriculture or any other purpose. Discounting methods should always be considered for any comparisons of cash inflows and outflows where the period extends beyond two or three years. The calculations are not difficult, and will be found straightforward provided that all the data are carefully tabulated.

One difficulty could be choosing an appropriate percentage discount rate. This applies particularly when calculating the net present values of alternative expenditure options (rent or buy decisions, for instance). If there is no company accountant or other suitably qualified person willing to offer advice, no great harm should be done by pitching the discount rate somewhere between the current bank lending rate and the interest rate that could be earned by investing in a suitable deposit account.

PROJECT FEASIBILITY AND RISK ANALYSIS

Financial appraisal is a comforting process, because it produces figures that can be regarded as a way of justifying investment decisions. They are useful in helping to convince financial backers that their investments will be safe and sound. They give the analyst or investor something to grasp, even in proposals for projects that are really so complex and full of risks that accurate prediction is impossible. Financial appraisal techniques must be seen in the wider context of project feasibility study and risk analysis.

Feasibility studies

Proposals for projects requiring significant investment should obviously be subjected to some form of feasibility study before the contracts are signed. Studies for projects on the grand scale are often significant projects in their own right, taking years to complete and consuming considerable expenditure. It is, however, painfully apparent, from the number of projects which fail to meet their cost, time and performance targets, that feasibility study recommendations are not always wholly reliable.

Example

Suppose that an independent consulting engineering company has been commissioned by an international organization (the World Bank, for instance) to conduct a feasibility study for the huge investment needed to exploit a recently discovered deposit of copper ore. The project, to build a mining and metallurgical complex on a virgin site, would take many years to design and build before any useful amounts of copper could be produced and sold.

Much data would need to be collected and the study would have to investigate and quantify various possible processing methods and logistic strategies in depth. For example, one project strategy might involve having a smelter and a refinery built specially at the new site, while another case could evaluate the alternative of building only a smelter, and shipping unrefined copper to an existing refinery elsewhere. For each case considered the study report would forecast the expected return on investment, derived from a mix of estimated capital costs, output rates for the product, operating costs, all other expenses, revenue from copper sales and tax implications.

Risks

In practice many things can happen to ruin the predictions of the feasibility study report, even where considerable care has been taken in its preparation. Perhaps some of the technology to be used is advanced and unproven. There might be unsuspected flaws in the chosen contractor's performance and professional capability. All manner of climatic, geological or other environmental problems could arise. Political unrest might erupt. One of the project organizations might not be financially sound. There are well-known cases of projects that have been held up by the discovery of archaeological remains, or because steps have had to be taken to avoid disturbing wildlife (hibernating bears were allowed to hold up one project for several winter months).

Even if the copper mining project in our example had gone ahead as planned, adopting the recommended strategy, with everything well built, on time and within budget, the market price of copper could fall disastrously during the ten years or so needed to bring the project to full production. On the other hand there is always, of course, a chance that the price of copper might rise.

Similar uncertainties can be cited for many large projects. An industry in which feasibility studies have a habit of proving wrong is property development, particularly where industrial and office property is built speculatively. A proposal to build a prestigious office tower might seem to be a very attractive investment because of the high rents which are currently obtainable in a particular locality. The project could, however, be held up for a number of reasons, possibly starting with a difficult public planning inquiry, then through all manner of site difficulties and labour problems. As in the mining example, property market values could change significantly during the construction programme. The property might have to be let or sold at a loss, or have to remain unoccupied for many months or even years.

All of this does not mean that the initial feasibility studies are unnecessary, or that the studies are necessarily flawed. It does demonstrate, however, that all the possible risks – technical, environmental, political and commercial – should be listed and, where possible, tested in mathematical models for their possible significance.

Some risks can be covered by insurance (Chapter 8), but many more can not. Some commercial risks can be avoided or at least minimized by reading the small print in contracts carefully and by gathering information about the financial standing and technical competence of those who are to take part in the project (including the client). Other risks must be considered carefully, to try and establish the effect that they could have on the project outcome.

Sensitivity analysis

Sensitivity analysis is a technique for testing the possible effects of risk on the net present value of a proposed project by varying one or more of the parameters in steps according to the analyst's perception of possible risk. For example, if there is doubt about the timing or amount of revenue that a project is expected to produce, the analyst can repeat the initial discounted cash flow calculation several times, changing the revenue predictions in small percentage steps each time to test the resulting effect on net present value or rate of return.

Simulation

It may be possible to specify the upper and lower limits of one or more parameters thought to be at risk. Best and worst market prices, highest and least   *267* possible capital costs, longest and shortest project duration, and many other parameters can be considered in this way.

Using a computer, it is possible to repeat a discounted cash flow calculation many times, with one of the parameters being varied within its specified worst-to-best range. The actual value used in each reiteration is chosen by the computer, by pure chance, governed by random number selection. Provided that enough reiterations are carried out, the use of random numbers should ensure that the spread of net present value variations follows a normal distribution. The analyst or investor is thus provided with a probability graph or statement, giving the mean and standard variation for net present value according to the perceived risk of the parameter tested.

A similar technique can be used to test the timescale risks, but with the calculations based on network analysis rather than cash flows (see Chapter 25).

FURTHER READING

Franks, J. R., and Broyles, J. E., *Modern Managerial Finance*, Wiley, Chichester, 1979. (Cloth bound, this book is reasonably priced, deals at length with many aspects of financial appraisal and risk assessment, and is very well written.)

Kharbanda, O. P. and Stallworthy, E. A., *How to Learn from Project Disasters*, Gower, Aldershot, 1983. (This book is aptly subtitled 'True-life stories with a moral for management'.)

Lock, Dennis, *Project Planner*, Gower, Aldershot, 1990. (This is a collection of 50 forms in a loose leaf binder, together with an explanatory book. The examples in this chapter were all calculated with the aid of forms from this collection.)

Part Four
PLANNING AND SCHEDULING

16 Planning with Charts

A. G. Simms

The human eye is very good at recognizing patterns. Management science makes good use of this attribute by presenting complicated facts in the best visual form. Charts and diagrams can be made to convey a good deal of such information. In verbal descriptions or written text, where words have necessarily to follow one after another, cross-connections cannot be shown clearly by the words alone. This is where charts are most powerful. If a chart models reality really well, then all sorts of connections and comparisons are made evident.

BAR CHARTS

One of the oldest and most familiar management aids is the bar chart. This shows all relevant jobs, operations, activities, processes, etc., in the form of bars. The length of each bar is proportional to the duration of the activity being represented, and it is shown against the same timescale as all other activities. Such a chart illustrates at a glance what jobs are to take place at any one time, how starts and ends of different jobs are related, and so on. A Gantt chart, named after Henry Gantt who introduced it in the 1900s, is basically a horizontal time bar chart.

Item	Start date	Finish date
Prepare brief	1 March 1995	30 April 1995
Design	1 May 1995	30 September 1995
Bills of quantities	15 August 1995	30 September 1995
Await return of bids	1 October 1995	31 October 1995
Examine tender bids	1 November 1995	15 November 1995
Demolition	20 November 1995	4 December 1995
Building construction	5 December 1995	5 October 1996
External works	5 June 1996	5 October 1996
Move in furniture and equipment	6 October 1996	31 October 1996

Timescale for new office building

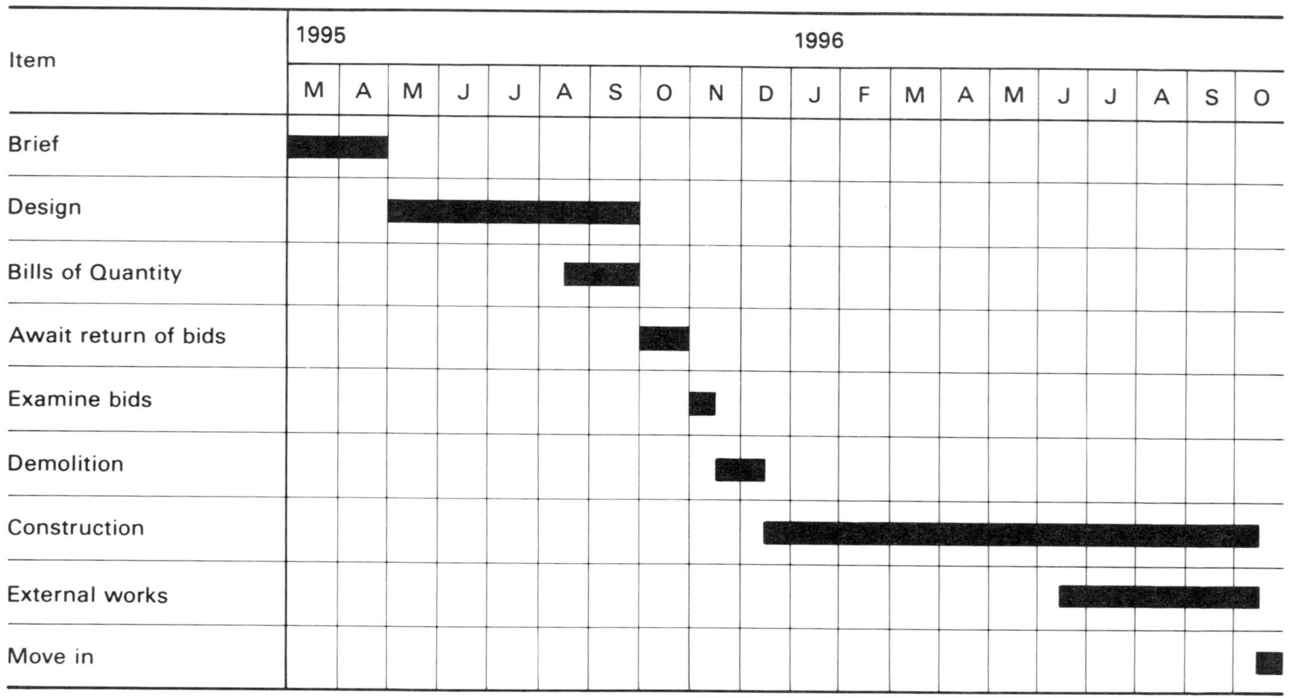

Figure 16.1 A project plan in bar chart form

To appreciate the immediacy of understanding which a bar chart can give, compare the listing of jobs to be done when developing a new office building (including their start and end dates) with the corresponding bar chart (Figure 16.1):

The bar chart (Figure 16.1) has a horizontal timescale, in this case a calendar, and each of the nine items is shown against the listed dates. Note that one of the items does not represent any action by members of the project team, namely, waiting for the return of the bids.

This form of a bar chart is quite typical in that it gives an outline plan of the timescale of a project broken down into a relatively small number of project components, some of which represent a collection of many activities. If necessary, any large component can be broken down into suitably detailed jobs to provide a guide for supervision at a lower level. For instance, the supervisor in charge of external works would be given a plan in the form of a bar chart of all the separate jobs summarized here as 'external works'. Long experience on the working site has proved that such a chart is more easily used than a list of start and end dates of activities and their durations.

It may often be convenient to give the timescale relative to the start date of the project (whenever that may be) starting with zero, so that there would be no need to change all the dates if the project start is changed.

Bar chart for project control

The progress actually achieved can easily be entered on the bar chart. For example, the bar showing the plan of the job can be in the form of an open bar or box, which can be filled in for the time during which work is being carried out. Alternatively, the bar representing work reporting back from the working site can be shown in parallel. Figure 16.2 shows the position of the project described above on 5 December 1995. We note that there has been a change in the time-table, as the go-ahead for the project was given on 1 May instead of 1 March 1995. This means that all dates are 2 months later than planned, unless there has also been a change to the plan itself. It might have been easier for the planners to use a timescale relative to the start date – whenever that took place – but at working level it is much better to show actual dates or week numbers.

No changes of plan (other than the start date) have been made to the first jobs of the project, and both the design and the preparation of the bills of quantities should have been finished by 25 November. Figure 16.2 records the reports from the work and this shows that the drawings have been completed on time, but the bills of quantities are not yet to hand. On the other hand, demolitions were not expected to start until well into 1996, but in fact they were reported to have started on 1 December 1995. The bar chart in itself is quite incapable of showing what has happened, or indeed of indicating what actions are open to the planners to make such a change. In this case, when the project was planned demolitions were intended to be part of the main contract, and that was the reason for their start to be planned immediately after the contract had been awarded (at the end of the activity: 'examine bids'). Instead of this the project team decided to award a *273*

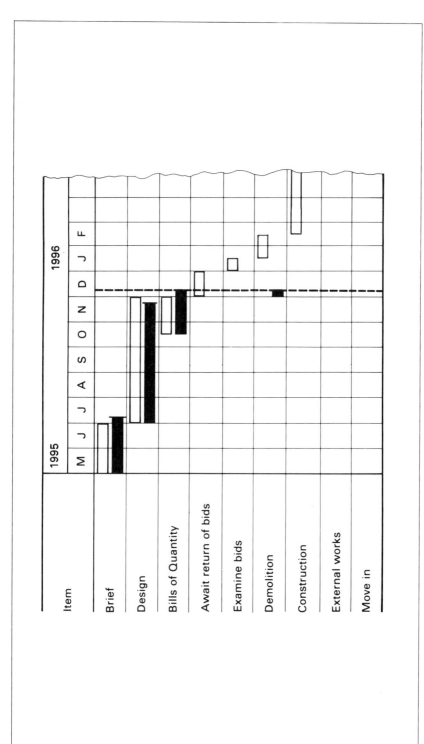

Figure 16.2 Bar chart used for project control

The chart shows the state of the project on 5 December 1995. Open bars are the planned operations – revised if necessary to accommodate programme changes. The filled-in bars show dates actually achieved, with the completion of each phase indicated by a vertical line at the right-hand end of the appropriate bar.

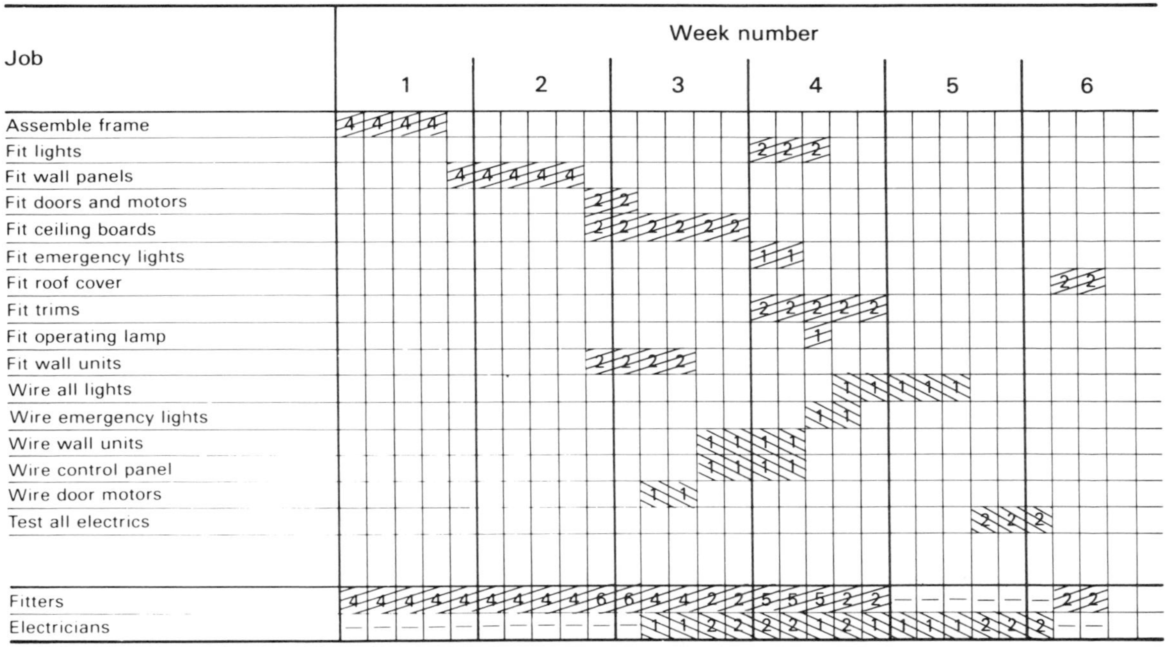

Figure 16.3 Bar chart with resource scheduling

The total number of men in each trade needed for each day are shown at the foot of each column. If the chart is constructed on an adjustable board, so that the bars can be moved or slid horizontally, when it is possible to adjust the planned timing of jobs to achieve a sensible and practicable rule of usage for each resource.

separate contract for the demolitions. As a matter of fact these could have been done at any time, but the bar chart cannot show which jobs, if any, must precede demolitions. Figure 16.2 does not show either whether the plan has been changed in other ways: it seems likely that construction of the building could start sooner; at least one can assume that that was the reason for the early start on the demolitions.

Adding information on the bar chart

The information on a bar chart can be enhanced in a number of ways. For example, the bar symbol itself can be labelled. Such a label could be used to indicate who is to carry out the job, or the responsible department. On manually drawn charts a colour code can be helpful, but for reproduction it is better to use shading. A further refinement is an indication of the resource loading. For example, the number of tradesmen needed for an activity can be shown on the bar symbol. Figure 16.3 shows two different grades by their shading, and it gives the number of each that is needed. The manager can see how many tradesmen are needed day by day from the totals shown on the bottom lines. In this way the chart makes it simple to allocate resources efficiently.

It is most important, however, never to lose sight of the greatest advantage of the bar chart, namely the directness and power of its message. Any secondary information that is added should never obscure the main point, namely, the timing and duration of the depicted activities. 'If in doubt, leave out'.

Uses and limitations of bar charts

The purpose of the bar chart is to aid the timescale planning and sequencing of tasks, and to present timing information to the manager in a form that is grasped easily. Too much detail can be a hindrance. Thus a bar chart with more than 50 activities or so becomes little more than a list, and it loses its point of clarifying the structure of the project. This does not mean that bar charts cannot be used on projects consisting of many activities. For such projects one could simply use single bars for groups of jobs or processes. That would enhance its use at the top level, that of project supervision, wherever an overview is needed with sufficient (but not too much) detail.

It is at the work level that the bar chart is the most useful management tool. Supervisors in charge of jobs actually being carried out need to see precisely the timing of that part of the whole project for which they are responsible.

The main drawback of the bar chart is that it does not show directly how the jobs are connected, in particular how far the start of any job is constrained by the completion of one or more other jobs. For instance the activity: 'move in' in Figure 16.1 is planned to start when two other jobs have finished. It is not possible to tell from the chart alone whether there is any connection between the end of one or both of these jobs, and the start of the subsequent one. While such connections may seem obvious to the person who drew up the plan, or to anyone familiar with

such building projects, they are simply not represented on the bar chart. It would

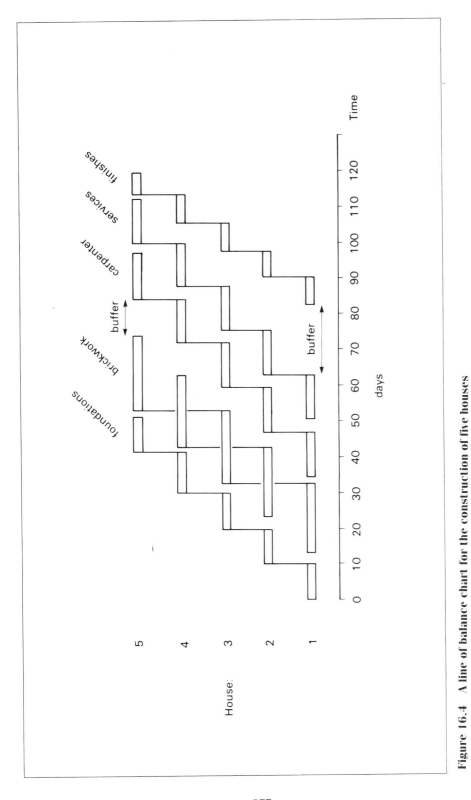

Figure 16.4 A line of balance chart for the construction of five houses

Each horizontal bar represents an operation on a house. The vertical lines show how a gang of tradesmen moves from one house to the next as the jobs progress.

be possible to enhance bar charts by showing connections, but they were not devised for that: it is much better to use diagrams designed for that purpose. These are discussed in Chapter 17.

To sum up, it is not so much the size of the project that limits the use of bar charts, as the amount of detail that can usefully be shown. For the beginner, bar charts with more than 20 or 30 bars are not so easy to handle, and even experienced practitioners rarely employ such charts with more than 50 bars (except possibly as a form of list). Provided that bars represent appropriate sections or components of a project, a bar chart can be a useful and productive aid to management of large and small projects.

THE LINE OF BALANCE CHART

The bar chart concept has been extended to deal with some kinds of repetitive projects, for instance the manufacture of a number of units, or the construction of identical houses on a housing estate, or floors of multi-storey buildings. Successive units go through the same stage, and after one unit has passed through a stage, the next one can start to go through it. The bar charts for each unit are the same, and all of them can be drawn on the same figure. Conventionally one draws them one on top of another, with the first unit at the bottom.

There is a time lag between the start of one unit and that of the next, and at the end of the process units are completed and handed over at a similar rate. Figure 16.4 shows, on the same figure, the five bar charts for building five houses in succession. For each house the construction process is broken down into a simple succession of jobs. As an illustration, the whole process is broken down into: foundations, brickwork, carpentry, services and finishes. Each of these stages is done by a different gang, so that any one of them can only start its work on one of the houses when the previous gang has finished its work there. A brief interval of time is allowed on the plan between one gang finishing its task and the next starting. This arrangement can deal with minor hold-ups as well as the planned change-over between gangs. These periods of no activity are called buffers. It is quite economic to be reasonably generous in allocating buffers, as it is much cheaper to have a unit not being worked on than to have to pay people employed on the next for unproductive idle time after small hold-ups.

A brief look at Figure 16.4 shows that four of the five operations take about the same time, and that the brickwork takes about twice as long. By having two gangs of bricklayers it is then possible to plan the work in such a way that all gangs work at about the same rate, namely about 12 days per house; some more and some less. The second bricklayer gang starts working on the second house as soon as the foundations are finished, and while the first gang is still working on the first house. When the first has finished the brickwork on the first house, it starts on the third, the other gang goes from the second to the fourth house. The carpenters take a little longer than the bricklayers with their work, so that the gap between them increases with each house. On the other hand, the finishes take less time than the services, and they must therefore not be planned to follow on immediately, otherwise they would have to stand idle each time. Instead, a correct gap is

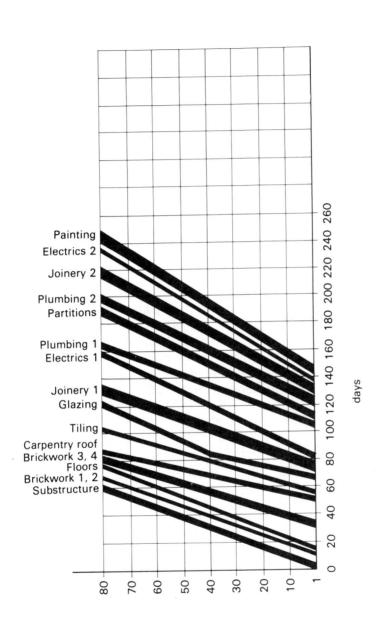

Figure 16.5   A line of balance chart for building 80 houses

calculated for the first house, and the finishing gang is not scheduled to start until day 83. However, they catch up with the previous gang until the fifth house when the gap has disappeared.

For schemes with a large number of units, for broad-brush planning and discussions, it is sufficient to draw straight lines instead of the stepped ones of Figure 16.4. The term 'line of balance charts' is used. Thus, in Figure 16.5, the strategy for a housing estate of 80 houses is shown. At this level of discussion, one can immediately appreciate with the help of the chart that ideally all lines should be parallel. If they are not precisely aligned, one can assess the effect, and make adjustments to the size of some of the gangs, for example. One such adjustment is shown in connection with glazing. For the first 40 houses, two glaziers are used, rapidly making the working site available for the following gangs. At that rate they get nearer and nearer to the previous operation, roof tiling, until they have caught up. This is shown in Figure 16.5 by the minimum buffer that has to be allowed. At this stage, one of the glaziers is released (to another project), and the other one completes all the remaining houses. This means that glazing now falls behind roof tiling, and joinery first fix gets closer and closer but does not catch up until the last house.

The line of balance chart in use

The examples in this chapter illustrate the use of line of balance charting for the planning stages of multiple construction projects. The method is, however, equally useful in many other types of project. It can be used, for example, in administration projects such as reorganizing a number of branch shops or offices, introducing new procedures into a number of different departments, and so on.

Occasions for using line of balance as a *planning* tool may not arise frequently: they really come into their own when they are used as a *management* tool for projects such as those mentioned above. The method is quite simple, yet surprisingly powerful. A chart like the background grid of Figure 16.5 is prepared for the project. Actual progress is then measured or assessed as the project proceeds and entered on the same chart. It is convenient to use a different symbol (a coloured pencil mark, for example) for each of the trades working on units of the project.

Entering the progress information need only take a few minutes each day, but the annotated chart will give a surprisingly clear picture of the actual progress in relation to the original plan. In particular, it highlights small delays at a very early stage, well before the more traditional 'seat of the pants' danger signals appear.

An early application of such line-of-balance progress charting took place on a 170-unit housing estate. It turned out that one of the trade gangs, the electricians, was slightly undermanned. Although the electrical jobs seemed to be progressing more or less as planned, delays accumulated gradually. The line-of-balance chart clearly showed the blue dots (representing the electricians) crowding back against the other tradesmen that were supposed to follow them, long before this was noticed by site supervisors.

280   Unfortunately, in that instance the chart had only been introduced as an experiment. The site manager did not react to the early warnings. The result was that delays were allowed to accumulate until other trades became affected seriously, so that additional electricians eventually had to be employed in difficult and expensive remedial action. The project finished three weeks late whereas, if the early warnings shown so simply and graphically by the line-of-balance chart had been heeded, earlier action would almost certainly have allowed completion on time and within budget.

Like the bar chart, the line-of-balance chart is most useful as a control tool on the working site. It allows actual performance to be monitored, so that deviations from the plan can be detected as quickly as the information feedback allows. This enables the supervisor to judge whether such a deviation is likely to have serious effects, or can be dealt with routinely (that is: within the buffers of the line-of-balance chart). If the deviations shown by the review threaten to encroach on other operations (i.e. if the buffer is not large enough), then the chart can be used for replanning, and for taking the most suitable action.

Line of balance in general

The technique originated in the manufacturing industries for controlling the manufacture of components in repetitive production (see, for example, Chapter 10 in Lock, 1992). As a graphical technique, such as that outlined above, it has been used in multi-project situations, particularly in construction.

The techniques in these two situations are similar but not identical and terms may be used in slightly different ways. It may be necessary to consult a reference such as British Standard BS 4335:1985 (Appendix C) to avoid any possible confusion.

REFERENCES AND FURTHER READING

Lock, Dennis, *Project Management*, 5th edn, Gower, Aldershot, 1992.

17 Critical Path Methods

A. G. Simms

Methods for planning project activities were, at one time, limited by the notation available. Visual representation in the form of bar charts afforded a useful scheduling and control tool, but (except in the very simplest cases) it was never possible to indicate all the complex relationships and sequence dependencies between activities. The introduction of network diagrams overcame this problem, and introduced a powerful notation which allows all activities to be displayed in charts which clearly indicate all the interrelationships.

Basic ideas of project network techniques were formulated at about the same time in the 1950s by a number of managers in different, independent organizations. Two of these were in the United Kingdom, at ICI and the Central Electricity Generating Board. One was in France, and another group was in the United States. The US group published a full account of their method and of their experience with major projects in 1958. By 1960 project network methods had spread to many of the larger public and private organizations. In the United Kingdom, many of those working in this field came together in the Network Study Group of the Operational Research Society.

It was found that a proliferation of symbols and terms had been developed by different groups. Efforts to rationalize practices resulted in the first British Standard *Glossary of Terms used in Project Network Techniques* in 1968. The notation used in this chapter is that recommended in the 1985 edition, which bears the reference number BS 4335:1985.

PHASES OF PROJECT NETWORK PLANNING AND CONTROL

Project network analysis can be seen as divisible into four phases. A typical project network will undergo development through each of these phases, which are as follows:

1 *Project planning*, in which the network is drawn to show all the activities necessary for project completion, together with their logical interrelationships.

2 *Project timing*, when estimates of durations are made for all activities, and calculations determine likely project duration and identify those activities which are likely to prove critical to the programme.

3 *Resource allocation*, in which the information derived from the planning phase is used to produce a practical schedule of resource usage (techniques for resource allocation are described in Chapter 18).

4 *Project control*, where progress is measured against the network plan and deviations noted and used for corrective action. During this phase the network will almost certainly need to be updated in order that the schedule for all activities in progress or not yet started remains valid and acceptable.

ACTIVITIES AND EVENTS

An activity

An activity is an operation or process which consumes time and possibly other resources. In order to build up a picture of the project in terms of its activities and their relationships to one another, it is convenient to symbolize an activity by an arrow. Since in the planning phase it is only connections that matter, the direction, length and shape of the arrow have no significance, although conventionally it is always drawn from left to right.

An event

An event is a state in project progress after the completion of all preceding

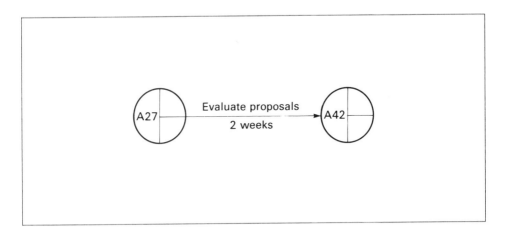

Figure 17.1 An activity with its start and end event

The estimated duration of this activity, which is to evaluate proposals, is two weeks. The start event has been numbered A27 for reference, and the end event A42. Event numbering becomes significant when a computer is used for network analysis, and this activity would be known as activity A27, A42.

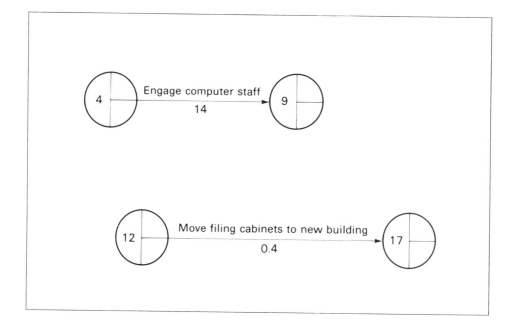

Figure 17.2   Two independent activities

activities but before the start of any succeeding activity. The event symbol used to show the connection between activities is a circle. Each event has to have a unique label which is shown in the left half of the symbol. The two pieces of information that go into the right half will be discussed later.

Figure 17.1 shows an activity, symbolized by the arrow, with the direction of the arrow showing the flow of time as the activity is being carried out. It also shows the start event of the job (labelled A27) and the end event (labelled A42). The nature of the job is briefly described on the diagram. Each activity is identified uniquely by its start and end event labels, so that the activity: 'Evaluate proposals' would be called 'activity A27, A42'.

RELATIONSHIPS BETWEEN ACTIVITIES

There are only a few kinds of relationships and these suffice to circumscribe completely the most complex project.

1   *Independence.* Two activities are not related to one another. For example, in Figure 17.2, the activity 'engage computer staff' is not directly related to the activity 'move filing cabinets to the new building': neither the start nor the end time of each job is affected by what happens to the other.

2   *Sequence.* One job cannot start before another is finished. For example, a wall cannot be built until its foundation is finished. The end event of the earlier activity is the start event of the later one (see Figure 17.3)

3   *Burst.* As soon as one activity is finished, two or more others can start. In

Figure 17.4, for example, as soon as the board has decided to go ahead with building a new office the design team can be engaged and the building plot can be bought

4 *Merge.* An activity cannot start until two or more immediately preceding activities have been completed. This is illustrated by the example in Figure 17.5. The motor car assembly cannot start until the body and the engine are made

5 *Combined burst and merge.* Several activities cannot start until two or more immediately preceding activities have been finished. This situation has to be examined carefully. Consider, for instance, the example in Figure 17.7. The first two activities 'Dismantle machine' and 'Fetch new component' must evidently take place before the jobs 'Repair old component' and 'Fit spare and reassemble machine'. It would be quite wrong, however, to picture the situation as in Figure 17.6, since the completion of all the earlier jobs is not necessary to start at least one of the later jobs. D can be started as soon as A is finished, regardless of what happens to B, whereas C requires that both A and B have finished. In other words, while it is true that job D follows job A (so that the start event of D is the end event of A) it is not enough to allow C to start when B is completed. The logical link from the end of A to the start of C is also necessary. The end of B is then shown correctly as the start of C. Figure 17.7 shows the situation correctly, including the additional dotted link. This dotted link is called a dummy activity.

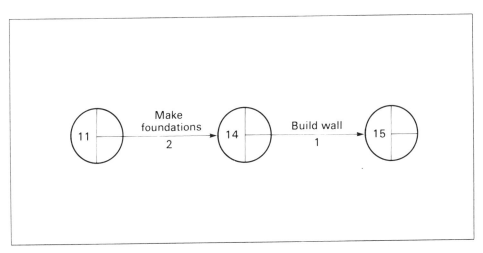

Figure 17.3   Simple sequence of two activities

Activity 14, 15 cannot begin until activity 11, 14 has been finished or, in other words, until event 14 has been achieved.

Dummy activities

Dummy activities (usually called, simply, dummies) are activities which do not in themselves represent time or work. They are put in the network to show logical   *285*

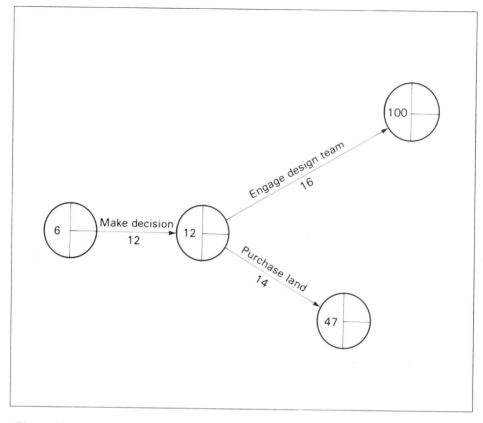

Figure 17.4 Dependent activities – 1

Neither activity 12, 100 nor activity 12, 47 can begin until activity 6, 12 has been finished.

links between other (real) activities. Dummies are shown as dotted arrows. As with any other activity arrow, they are not drawn to a timescale (if they were they would have zero length!) but their direction is important. Figure 17.7 illustrates the use of a dummy to show a logical link, and there is another such example in Figure 17.12.

Another use of dummies is to ensure that two or more activities which share the same start and end events (known as parallel activities) can be isolated and given their own unique start and end event numbers. This is illustrated in Figure 17.8. If it were not for the dummy 33, 34, both activities would be in parallel and both would be labelled 33, 40. This becomes very important when a computer is used to list and analyse network activities, since the computer uses the event numbers (not the descriptions) to identify activities uniquely.

In cases where it is necessary to show a time lag between the end of one activity and the start of the next, this could be indicated by the use of a dummy to which a duration has been added. However, it is not advisable to use dummies for this purpose: it is better to use a full activity arrow, and either put in the description the reason for the delay or, simply, write 'Delay' for the description.

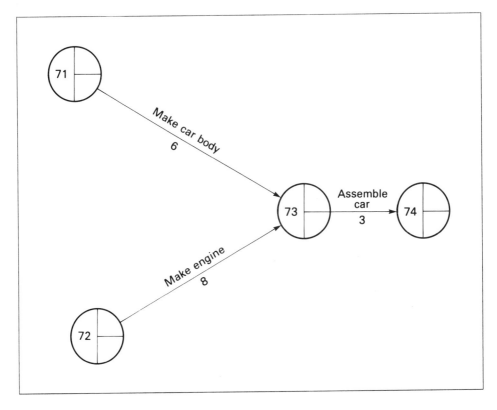

Figure 17.5 Dependent activities – 2

Activity 73, 74 cannot logically start before both preceding activities (71, 73 and 72, 73) have been finished.

THE ARROW DIAGRAM

The project network that shows all the activity arrows and event circles is called the arrow diagram. It pictures the interrelationships explicitly, and this is essential at the planning stage. Every project has a definable start, and this is shown by the existence of the project start event, the only event symbol with outgoing but no incoming arrows. The definable project completion is shown by the finish event which has arrows entering it but no outgoing ones.

The arrow diagram is the project team's first complete project document. As such it forms the basis for informed discussion of strategic methods for carrying out the project. It can point the way to improvements, for instance by changes so that more activities are done in parallel rather than in sequence.

Detail and complexity

In small projects, all activities may be under the direct control of a single person. The supervision of larger ones often involves several levels of management, or indeed several independent organizations. The manager in charge of the whole *287*

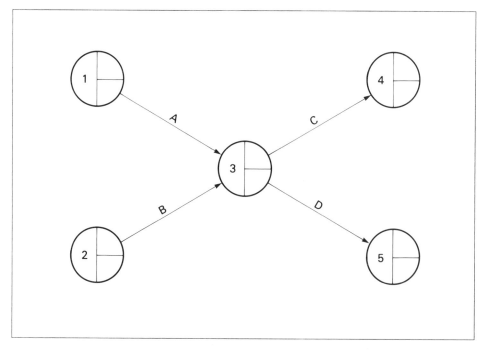

Figure 17.6 Dependent activities – 3

In this example, both activities 1, 3 and 2,3 must be finished before either activity 2, 4 or activity 3, 5 can start.

project needs to know its overall shape and the relation of major parts to one another without having to go into the kind of detail appropriate for a subordinate in charge of a small portion. If all the detail needed by everyone were to be shown in a single network, there would be the danger of not seeing the wood for the trees. The problem of not obscuring the structure and yet showing adequate detail can be solved by using the concept of a hierarchy of networks. When planning a large project, a master network showing a relatively small number of major activity groups or subprojects gives a level of detail or subdivision appropriate for the level of control exercised by the project manager. Each activity group under the control of an immediate subordinate is then prepared in greater detail, breaking up a single arrow (or just a few arrows) on the master network into a whole subnetwork. Such a second-level subnetwork could be further subdivided into third-level networks and so on.

This way of planning reflects levels of responsibility, draws attention to the correct level of detail and highlights interactions between activity groups under different supervisors, or between different organizations taking part in a large project. Communications between different levels are facilitated, since interface events (events common to two or more subnetworks) are a firm guide.

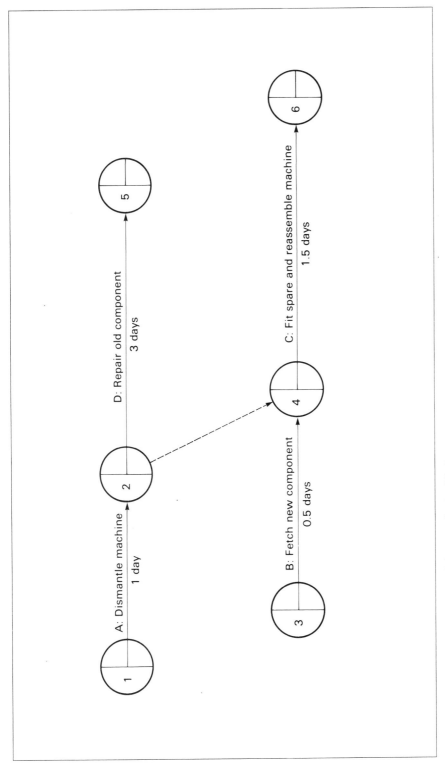

Figure 17.7   Use of a dummy activity as a logical link

The dummy activity does not represent any work and has no duration, but is used to show a logical link. In this case the dummy denotes that activity 4, 6 is dependent not only on activity 3, 4 but also on the completion of activity 1, 2.

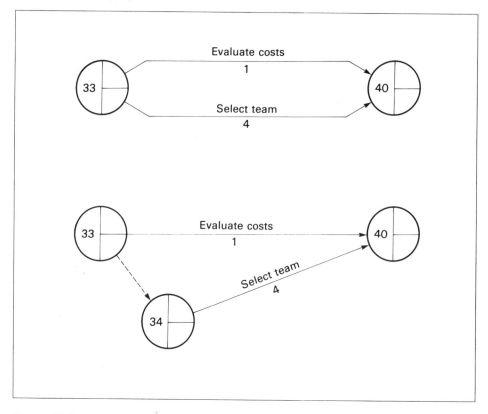

Figure 17.8 Dummy activity used to ensure unique activity numbering

Without the dummy, two activities would both be numbered 33, 40. This would confuse any computer used to process the network, and the dummy avoids this situation, without affecting the logical intention depicted in the top diagram.

PROJECT TIMING

The timing phase of project planning produces the project programme, namely, start and end times for all activities. Its basis is the project plan, as pictured by the arrow diagram, together with estimates of the duration of every activity.

The timescale

There are projects with a timescale running to many years, while on the other hand project planning has been applied to special small projects, such as the evacuation of a building on receipt of an alarm, where the timescale is minutes. For most usual projects the most convenient units for activity durations are weeks, days, shifts or hours. A convenient rule is that the basic unit should be of the order of 1 per cent to 2 per cent of the timescale for the whole project (e.g. weeks for projects lasting up to 2 to 5 years). The unit used should relate to the time span of routine control: there is no point in using hours when the reviews are only once a week.

It is essential that the same unit is used for all activity durations, and this unit is then also the unit for the event times.

Estimating the durations

Duration estimates should be free from bias and have the smallest possible estimating errors. The smallest errors are likely to be made by those closest to the job to be estimated, namely those who will carry it out when the project gets under way. They are the ones, however, who could easily misunderstand such estimates to be promises. It is only human nature that they would try to ensure being able to keep each 'promise' by over-estimating the time that job would take. Such a bias would defeat the objective of realistic timing, in which over-estimates and under-estimates should average out.

Many jobs are relatively easy to estimate with acceptable error margin, but others are more difficult. For instance innovative or exploratory projects, such as search, research or development, basic changes of existing systems and the like, often have a few activities which are difficult to envisage fully beforehand in sufficient detail to allow reasonable duration estimates.

Difficult estimates

When dealing with activities that are difficult to estimate, it has been found that it is often easier to give three estimates than to commit oneself to a single one. For example it may be quite easy to find a minimum time for the job, a time that cannot be undercut even if everything goes well: the optimistic estimate. Similarly, the longest time for the job, a duration that can be guaranteed not to be exceeded even if things go wrong, namely, the pessimistic estimate, can usually be agreed without too much difficulty. Having guarded his reputation by these two values, the estimator is much happier to estimate a most likely duration. A weighted average of the three estimates gives the expected duration, which is then used in time analysis. A weighting of optimistic: most likely: pessimistic in the ratio 1:4:1 is the most popular, but 1:3:1 or 1:5:1 could be used equally well. One of the first projects for which project network techniques were developed contained several innovative activities which were troublesome to estimate and the psychological advantage of the three estimates was incorporated into the project network technique known as PERT (Program Evaluation and Review Technique). It does not otherwise differ from other activity-on-arrow techniques.

Consider the example of a task where 600 files have to be checked in a records section. The total activity time must depend upon how many queries arise, and on how long each takes to sort out. The supervisor reckons that it takes about 5 minutes to go through a file if no queries result. This would give a total time for the job of 50 hours for one clerk working continuously. But clerks do not work continuously. They are not robots. They need to sleep, eat, take breaks. Their hours in the office may amount to 40 (say) in a week, of which only a proportion are used effectively. However, in its simplest interpretation, at the most optimistic estimate of 50 man-hours, the activity duration would come out at 1.25 weeks (assuming a 40-hour week).

A better guess in this example (perhaps made after looking through a small sample of files) might be that some 100 files are likely to contain queries or problems needing half an hour each to sort out. This would give a total time, in man-hours, of 50 hours' basic work plus another 50 sorting out the problems: 100 man-hours total. Again assuming a 40-hour working week, this is 2.5 weeks. If the supervisor is trying to be realistic, he will add on a factor for lost time (short breaks, mistakes, and other causes).

A pessimistic estimate would assume that half the files were going to prove troublesome, adding an hour each to the work. This would make a total estimate, in man-hours, of $(50 + 300) = 350$. At 40 hours per week, and with the clerk possibly being the only one available, and with a record of time off for illness (or feigned illness), this job might run to a duration of 12 weeks.

Using the PERT formula, with a weighting of 4 given to the most likely estimate, we have:

$$t_e = \frac{t_o + 4t_m + t_p}{6}$$

where:

t_e is the expected time
t_m is the most likely time
t_o is the optimistic time
t_p is the pessimistic time

Substituting the values from this example we get:

$$t_e = \frac{1.25 + (4 \times 2.5) + 12}{6}$$

which is 3.875 (4 weeks for practical purposes).

This example illustrates one important aspect of time estimates for activity durations. The concern is with *elapsed time* and not simply with the man-hour content of the job.

Calculating event times

The earliest possible time for each event

Two sets of calculations are needed in order to determine the timing of all the network events (and consequently their associated activities). By working from left to right through a network, adding the durations of activities leading to an event will give the earliest possible time at which the event can be achieved. Where more than one path is possible through to the event, then the longest path, in duration terms, will provide the answer. In other words, an event does not take place until the last of the incoming arrows completes it. The earliest event time, therefore, is the last of the end times of all activities going into that event.

The result, for each event, is written in the top right-hand quadrant of the circle (see Figures 17.9 and 17.10). An illustration of earliest event time calculations is given in the (very simple) network of Figure 17.12. This network starts on day 8, so that if this is considered to be 8 May, then taking event 6 as an example, it is seen that the longest path to this event lies through events 1, 2, 4 and (through the

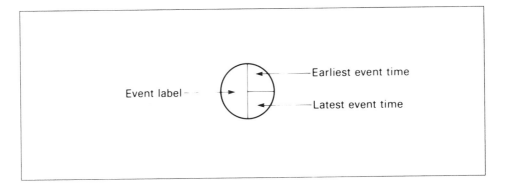

Figure 17.9   The event symbol

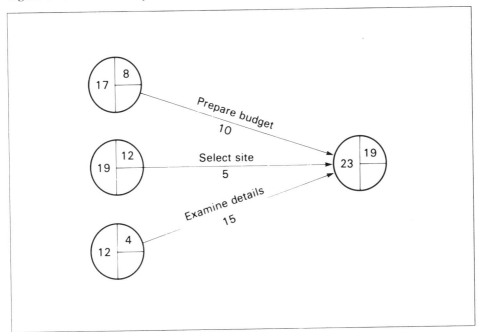

Figure 17.10   Convention for earliest event times

The earliest possible completion time for each event is written in the upper right-hand quadrant.

dummy) to 6 itself. The durations are $1 + 8 + 0$ (dummy) $= 9$, which added to the 8 May gives 17 May. The path through 1, 2, 3 and 6 is shorter by one day, and does not count in this calculation.

The latest permissible time for each event

The latest permissible time for each event is found by using a process which is exactly opposite to that used to find the earliest time. It is necessary to work back along each path through the network, subtracting activity durations from the earliest time of the final event (that is, from the earliest time when the project can be completed). The result for each event is the latest permissible time for that event to be completed if the final event (project finish) is to be achieved at the earliest possible time. This, again, can be examined by looking at Figure 17.12. The notation conventions are illustrated in Figures 17.9 and 17.11.

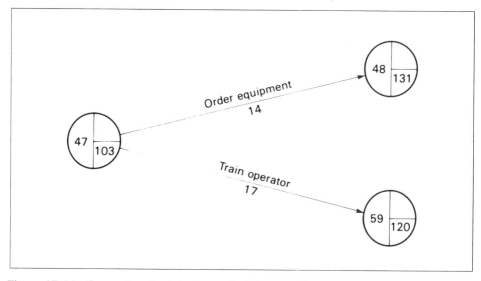

Figure 17.11 Convention for latest permissible event times

The latest permissible event times are written in the lower right-hand quadrant.

If two or more activities emerge from an event, a choice has to be made as to which of the backward paths determines the latest permissible time for the event. In all cases it is the earliest of the calculated activity start dates or, in other words, the date determined by the backward path with longest estimated duration. This can be examined by looking at Figure 17.12.

Whichever pass is done first, the forward or the backward, depends upon circumstances. In most cases, where the final end date is not known, but the start date is, then a forward pass is done first, followed by the backward pass. This yields the earliest possible time for project completion which, because it is normal to want to finish a project as soon as possible, is also taken as the latest permissible time for the final event. Conversely, if the backward pass is done first from a specified completion time dictated by external circumstances, then the latest time at which the project may be allowed to start is discovered (this could be the case, for example, where a school refurbishment programme has to be finished before the first day of the next term).

Event times can be given and calculated in one of two ways. Either they can be specified in units (hours, days, weeks, etc.) from the start event (usually at zero) or (as in Figure 17.12) dates or times can be used. The former method is used when the start (or finish) date is not known. The latter method can be used to work ahead from a known start date or time.

The critical path

When the forward and backward passes have been carried out through the network diagram, and the earliest and latest dates are known for every event, then the initial part of programming the project is complete. This process is called, for obvious reasons, time analysis. The most important result is that the total project duration becomes known, namely, the difference between the times for the project start and finish events.

Note that a study of the network in Figure 17.12 reveals a number of events which each have identical earliest and latest times. These are called critical events, since at least one following activity must take place immediately after completion of each critical event if the total project time is not to be extended. The project start and finish events are always critical events. In the example of Figure 17.12 events 1, 2, 4, 6 and 7 are critical. Events 3 and 5 are not.

Critical activities can also be identified. These are important in project management because, if they are delayed or exceed their estimated durations, the whole project will be delayed by that amount. A critical activity is an activity which:

1   Joins two critical events.
2   Has a duration which equals the difference between the times of these critical events.

For example, in Figure 17.12 activity F is not critical because only its end event is critical. Job G is not critical either, even though it joins two critical events, because its duration (4 days) is less than the difference between the times of its two critical events ($23 - 17 = 6$). On the other hand C is critical, as it joins the two critical events 2 and 4 and its duration is equal to the difference between the times of these events. Similarly A and H are critical activities. It is also clear that the dummy is critical, since it joins two critical events, and the difference between their times is zero, which equals the duration of the dummy.

While there is usually no need to mark critical events, it is very useful to highlight critical activities and dummies on the diagram. Figure 17.13 shows preferred ways of doing that.

Every critical activity (except a final one) has at least one critical successor, and it also has at least one critical predecessor (except for initial activities).   *295*

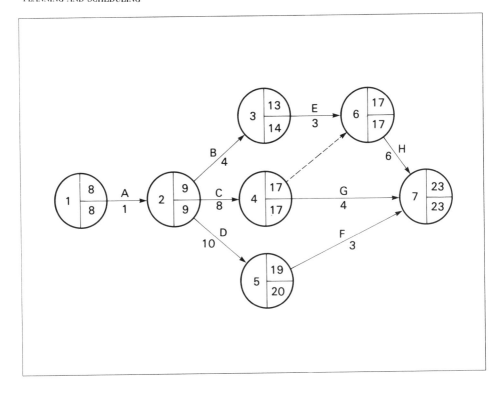

Figure 17.12   A simple critical path diagram

In this very simple network diagram, the 'project' is shown as starting on day 8, with the earliest possible finish time at day 23. The critical path flows through events 1, 2, 4, 6 (via the dummy) and 7.

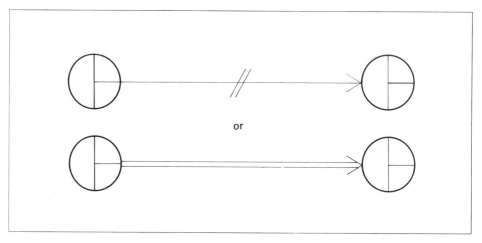

Figure 17.13   Depicting critical activities

The two methods shown here can each be used to mark critical activities in order to
highlight the critical path on the network diagram.

In a network, an arrow or unbroken sequence of arrows is called a path; the most important paths are those which join the project start to the project finish. Examples of such paths are 1, 2, 3, 6, 7 or 1, 2, 4, 7 in Figure 17.12. A critical path consists of critical activities only. Every project has at least one critical path. If it has more than one, they all have the same duration. In the example there is a single critical path, namely 1, 2, 4, 6, 7. Its duration is 15 days, the total duration of the project.

The arrow diagram obtained from the timing phase and showing the critical path is usually known as the critical path diagram. Other timing information, such as event times, is also usually shown.

Float and slack

An event that is not critical is said to have slack. Slack is the calculated time span within which the event must occur. The term 'slack' is used only in referring to events.

Of greater practical importance is the concept of float, the time available for an activity in addition to its duration. Non-critical activities have float. There are different kinds of float, and their measure has the form:

$$\text{Float} = \text{end time} - \text{start time} - \text{duration}$$

Since both the start and end events of an activity have earliest and latest times, there are four kinds of float possible. In practice only three of these are used, as follows.

Total float

This is the time by which an activity may be delayed or extended without affecting the total project duration.

$$\text{Total float} = \text{latest end} - \text{earliest start} - \text{duration}$$

Free float

This is the time by which an activity may be delayed or extended without delaying the start of any succeeding activity.

$$\text{Free float} = \text{earliest end} - \text{earliest start} - \text{duration}$$

Independent float

This is the time by which an activity may be delayed or extended without affecting preceding or succeeding activities in any way.

$$\text{Independent float} = \text{earliest end} - \text{latest start} - \text{duration}$$

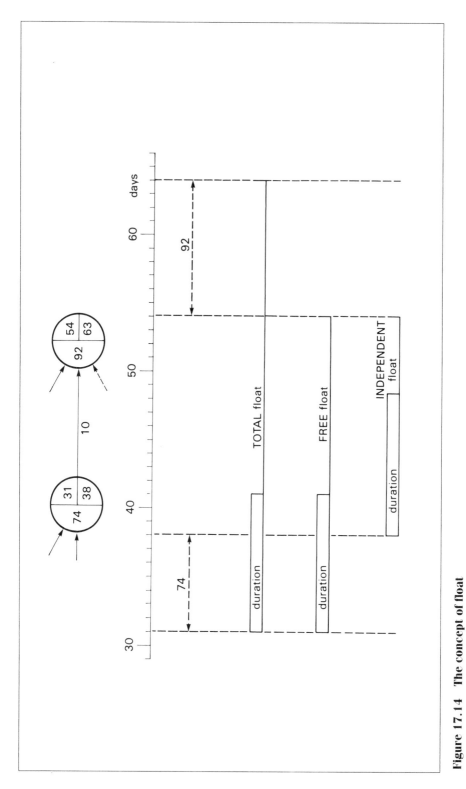

Figure 17.14 The concept of float

If the activity shown here is part of a network, and has the early late event times shown, then there are three different kinds of float as shown in the time-scaled diagram.

Calculation of floats

Figure 17.14 illustrates the different kinds of float and their calculation. It shows just one activity and its two events against a timescale.

The slack of event 74 is 7 days: that is the meaning of the time interval marked 74. Similarly the slack of event 92 is $63 - 54 = 9$ days. The total float is $63 - 31 - 10 = 22$ days. The (early) free float is $54 - 31 - 10 = 13$ days. The late free float is of little use, its value is $63 - 38 - 10 = 15$ days. The independent float is $54 - 38 - 10 = 6$ days.

The importance of the float for project management decisions is considerable. For example, the person in direct charge of one activity can (usually) be allowed to make use of any independent float, since it would not affect anyone else if he used it all up. Total float, on the other hand, is shared with other jobs, and it should not be used by one activity at the expense of others. It is quite usual to leave the allocation of total float to a higher level of management than that of single activities.

Another important application is using float to achieve a more economic allocation of resources. This is discussed in Chapter 18.

More than one imposed date

Sometimes both the start date and the completion date are fixed for a project before the planning phase. During the planning and timing phases more information becomes available, and it is often found that the time allowed by the imposed dates (the difference between the completion and the start) differs from that found with better information. Usually more time is needed than was first thought necessary.

In such a case, the forward pass is based on the imposed start date, and the backward pass on the imposed completion date. It may then happen that when the slack of every event is calculated, the smallest value found is not zero but some negative number. In such a case, the definitions of criticality need to be slightly modified: a critical event is one with the smallest difference between earliest and latest time. This difference may be negative. The start event and the finish event of the project are always critical events. All events having the same slack as these two are critical events. In such a case, all critical activities will have the same float, namely a negative one rather than zero.

The managerial implication of such a situation is that it cannot be resolved at the level of the management of the project. A higher level of management has to make suitable decisions: to relax one or both of the imposed dates or to allocate more resources so that some of the critical job durations can be reduced, or a combination of both.

THE TIME-SCALED DIAGRAM

While the project is being carried out, the task of project management is that of control. A powerful aid for that purpose is a modified form of the critical path diagram.

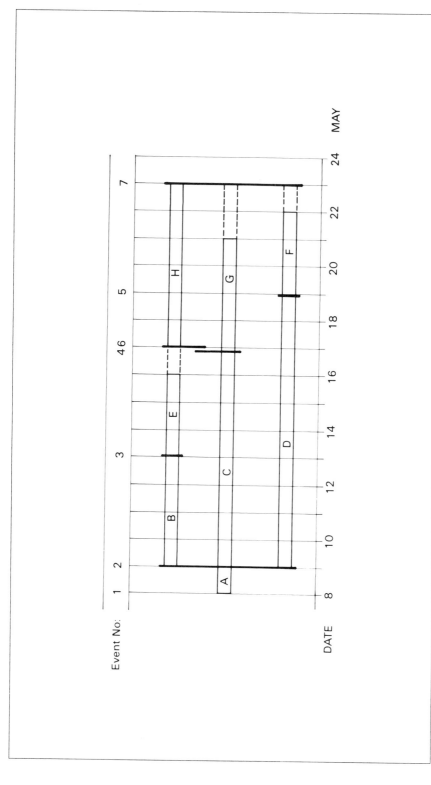

Figure 17.15 Time-scaled network diagram

Although not normally drawn to any timescale, it is possible to redraw a network to a timescale. It then resembles a linked bar chart. The dotted bars indicate float. This example is derived from the simple network of Figure 17.12.

Whereas previously the length of the arrow symbol in arrow diagrams or critical path diagrams had no significance, the critical path diagram can now be modified by making the length of each arrow proportional to its duration, with all arrows horizontal, and events indicated by vertical lines (the middle line of the event symbol). This form of the project network is a time-scaled diagram. At the same time it can be regarded as a bar chart, but a bar chart showing the way activities are linked to one another: a linked bar chart.

Figure 17.15 is the time-scaled diagram, the linked bar chart of the project whose critical path diagram was shown as Figure 17.12. Events with slack are normally shown as occurring at their earliest event times, but critical events and critical jobs can only be placed in one position. Non-critical activities however have float, which is shown on the time-scaled diagram in the form of a dotted line.

Note that the critical path is a solid line from project start to finish, while non-critical paths have float. The critical dummy is represented by the way events 4 and 6 are connected. If the paths were railway lines, and the activities were wagons, it is apparent immediately that a small push from either end would be transmitted to the other only by wagons on the critical path.

Being a bar chart, the time-scaled diagram is immediately understood at the working site where the project activities are being carried out. In effect it shows the project programme directly in the kind of graphical form that has been in use for many years.

The time-scaled diagram as a control tool

Contrary to superstition, projects will not automatically finish on time just because they have been networked! But networks are indeed a powerful aid for project management, enabling those in charge to identify actions most needed for success.

Two kinds of input form the essential basis for any effective project control:

1 A sufficiently detailed programme has to be shown in a convenient form.
2 Information about the progress achieved to date has to be acquired, transmitted and presented reliably, timely and completely.

These two elements are the essence of project monitoring, the comparison of the current project status with the programme, to identify and explain any deviations.

The time-scaled diagram shows the programme as a whole, and a vertical line corresponds to a given date. Such a vertical line can be used as a cursor; it cuts the bars corresponding to all activities in progress on that date. The role of the progress information is then to report on the status of each activity in progress on that particular review date, and all activities that were programmed to be completed since the previous review.

In its simplest form, the progress record is the time-scaled diagram with a movable cursor marking the current review date. The most reliable and incontrovertible information about any activity is whether it has started or not, and whether it is completed or not. Such a report can then be marked visibly on *301* the diagram and compared with the cursor: any unmarked event to the left of the cursor is a danger signal showing that the event has not yet occurred although it was supposed to. It is more difficult to measure jobs in progress. In practice it has been found that estimates of what percentage of the job has been completed tend to be unreliable. A slightly better measure is to estimate what percentage of the job still remains to be done.

Another way of picturing progress is to stick pins into achieved event symbols on the chart and to use a thread to mark all the pins furthest to the right: ideally that thread should lie on the current cursor line, and any parts of it on the left indicate delays.

There is a more detailed and general account of progress management in Chapter 28.

PRECEDENCE NOTATION

There are two fundamentally different ways of representing activities on a network. One is the activity-on-arrow method, which is the system that has been described so far in this chapter. The alternative approach is the activity-on-node method, in which the activities are placed at the nodes, and the network logic is completed by drawing lines that simply link the nodes to show their sequence and interdependencies.

The most common form of activity-on-node networks is the precedence system. This has found increasing popularity in recent years, and some computer programs will only accept input in this notation. (There is a short section in Chapter 23 about the choice between arrow and precedence networks.)

The activity-on-node network

In the basic form of the activity-on-node network, each job is represented by a rectangular box. A descriptive label and the duration of the activity is written into the box, the left edge of which represents the start and the right edge the completion of the activity. Sequence arrows represent the relationship between the completion of preceding activities and the starts of succeeding ones. Figure 17.16 shows the project of Figure 17.12 in this alternative representation.

The time analysis of a project shown in this form is identical with that of the activity-on-arrow diagram. The only slight difference is that instead of event times, it is the job start and end times that are calculated. The total float of each activity can also be derived immediately, and all jobs with zero float are critical. Critical sequence arrows are those which join critical activities, and they can be marked to show up the critical path clearly on the diagram.

The precedence diagram

A slightly more elaborate form is the precedence diagram, also known as the multi-dependency network. It is an activity-on-node network in which a sequence arrow represents one of four precedence relationships, depending on the positioning of the head and the tail of the sequence arrow.

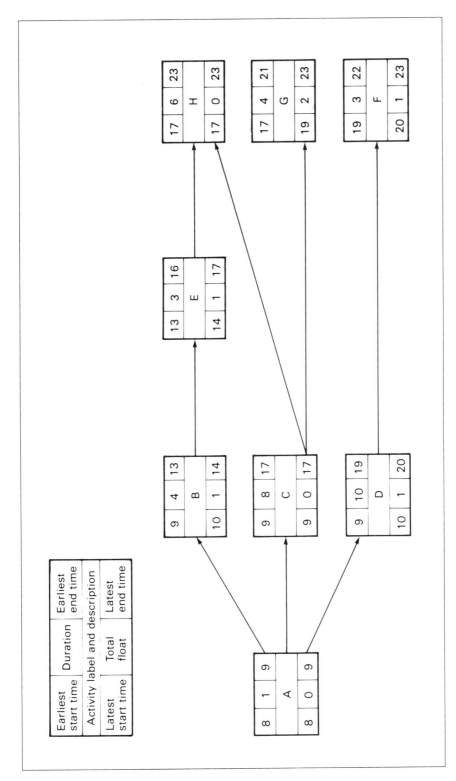

Figure 17.16 An activity-on-note network

An alternative to the activity-on-arrow network. Each box represents an activity and the arrows are merely logical links. The notation is the basis of the precedence method.

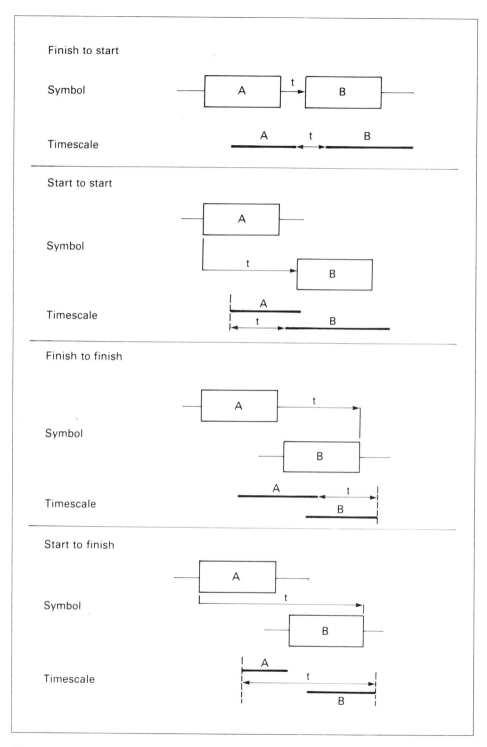

Figure 17.17 Precedence logic roation

The four kinds of precedence dependence are illustrated here.

The precedence relationships

1 *Finish-to-start.* The start of an activity depends on the finish of the preceding one. The notation is able to specify if the second activity can start immediately after the predecessor, or if there must be a delay.
2 *Start-to-start.* The start of an activity cannot take place until a stated lapse of time after the start of a preceding one.
3 *Finish-to-finish.* An activity cannot finish until a given time after the finish of the preceding activity.
4 *Start-to-finish.* An activity cannot finish until a given time after the start of the preceding activity.

Figure 17.17 shows the symbols for these four precedence relationships, with a time lapse t in each case. An explanatory bar chart (because it is drawn to a timescale) shows the real time equivalent. The time value t of the dependency arrow must be equal to or greater than zero. It cannot be negative. It is possible to use different kinds of dependencies in combinations.

When obtaining rules for calculating start and finish times of activities, note that the first relationship (finish-to-start) is the one discussed so far in this chapter in the arrow diagrams (but with t always equal to zero).

To find the earliest possible activity times in a precedence network, a forward pass is made (from left to right, as in the arrow diagram). The general rule for calculating the early start and early finish times during the *forward pass* is:

> To the activity time at the tail of the sequence arrow add the time lag t and enter this value at the activity time to which the arrow head points. The other time of the activity is obtained by adding the duration if the arrow head points to the start, or subtracting if the arrow head points to the finish of the activity. If there is more than one preceding activity, calculate the start time from each of the arrows but enter the highest value as the actual start time on the symbol.

The corresponding form for the *backward pass* is:

> Each latest activity time is found by subtracting the time lag from the latest time of the succeeding activity on the arrow head. This gives the latest time of the preceding activity at the arrow tail. The other time of that activity is found by adding or subtracting the job duration. If there is more than one succeeding activity, calculate the latest start time from each of these outgoing arrows, but enter on the symbol the lowest of the calculated latest start times.

PROJECT NETWORK ANALYSIS AS AN AID TO PROJECT MANAGEMENT

Advantages over the bar chart

The various forms of the project network are well suited to the phases of project *305* management. The arrow diagram brings out one of the aspects that a bar chart fails to picture, namely that of the interrelationships between activities. This important aspect is fundamental during planning, when alternative methods of proceeding are discussed and the best choice refined and amended. Since bar charts do not show relationships, they are not suitable for the planning phase of any but the simplest projects.

As originally conceived, the bar chart was used on well-known types of project only, such as the manufacture of products, building projects and the like, where most jobs follow one another in sequence with little paralleling. This inability to show connections makes it quite difficult to handle large numbers of jobs within a project. Very few pre-network planners were able to deal with projects that were broken down into more than 30 to 50 jobs. This in turn shows that, even for projects of moderate size, each 'activity' represents a fairly large work package rather than a well-defined job sufficiently small for work on it to proceed without interruption from other tasks.

The bar chart clearly shows the timescale of jobs, but the lack of connections makes all the difference, since it is impossible to identify critical jobs or the critical path. On a bar chart there is no means of indicating whether or not a job can be started earlier than planned (other than from knowledge of the nature of the job) and, conversely, there is no means for showing what would be the effect on subsequent activities of a delay.

The bar chart in its long history has proved invaluable as a control tool, as a means of indicating start dates of jobs and showing durations, even though the scheduling of dates was done by other methods. The time-scaled network diagram is in the form of a bar chart and therefore it can be used wherever bar charts have been well established. This avoids the complication of introducing unfamiliar innovations. The additional facility of showing connections brings more benefits; for example in helping coordination and in assessing the likely consequences of delays.

Disadvantages of project networks

Project networks methods were first developed in environments where time was of overriding importance (a complex routine maintenance operation during which a highly productive oil refinery had to be shut down, and a large military project to develop and deploy a new missile system vital for defence). The primary objective of the management of projects where the value of time is very much greater than that of the resources involved is to reduce the total project duration as much as possible. This includes dealing with emergencies, interruptions of costly processes, reorganizations and introduction of new administrative procedures. For these, project network techniques based on time analysis alone are adequate.

In a commercial environment, however, the economic use of resources is at least as important for the management of the project as the need to complete it quickly. The methods described above are not directly capable of scheduling more than one resource in the best possible way, though the network diagram of all activities and their interrelationships can, after time analysis, provide the information on criticality and float upon which effective resource scheduling can be based.

USING NETWORKS IN PROJECT MANAGEMENT

Having presented the methods of project networks, a few practical guidelines will now be given to help those who have not used networks before. The British Standards Institution has published a four-part guide to the use of network techniques in project management, BS 6046:1992. Its first part, *Guide to the use of management, planning, review and reporting procedures*, is particularly relevant at this point. Only points referring to networking will be discussed here; more general aspects of project management are dealt with in other chapters.

Starting to plan a project using a network

At the start of project planning, one or more meetings are necessary to produce the first network diagram. The initial planning meeting should not be too large, six to ten people usually being enough to allow discussion while avoiding speechmaking. All aspects of the project need to be represented by experienced managers who have sufficient seniority to make decisions and accept commitments.

The job list

This is often the starting point at such meetings. All members contribute to this list, which must eventually include every significant activity of the project.

At first very little is known about the sequence of the various activities, and they can be written down in any order as they are mentioned. A useful method for ensuring that the discussion is conducted at a suitable level of detail is to identify a few key operations, after which it is quite easy to find a level of detail that appears correct in relation to the project as a whole and to the degree of supervision and control envisaged. The jobs listed should not be too small (making the list too long, and obscuring the overall shape of the project plan). On the other hand the jobs must not be so large that significant details of co-ordination or opportunities for rationalizing progress are hidden. Such a key forms an obvious start for formulating a planning strategy for the project. By writing down jobs connected with those already mentioned, each member of the meeting can satisfy himself that he has covered all aspects for which he is going to be responsible.

The rough first draft will probably consist of some 50 to 100 jobs, and it forms a good basis for more detailed probing. During discussion, the list is refined. Particular attention should be given to completeness and to the boundary areas between different responsibilities (for example between cooperating departments or organizations). The discussion is made more effective if, for each job, a note is made of other jobs which must immediately precede it. This can help to *307* highlight omissions and clarifies the relationships between activities to assist in drawing the network logic.

The network diagram

This can now be drawn. For the first draft, pencil and eraser are the best tools, as there will be plenty of changes. The starting point will be the event common to all activities for which no predecessor is needed: the start event. The rest follows in succession.

Drawing up the diagram could be a simple routine if all the activities had been listed with their precedences correctly and completely noted. However, such perfection rarely happens, and the first attempt at the diagram gives all the main participants their first opportunity of seeing an outline of the whole project. This joint effort usually gives considerable and valuable insights. In the first place it allows amendments and revisions of the job list but, most importantly, it points to improvements in methods of execution and of co-operation in boundary areas.

Another function of such a draft is the detection and avoidance of logical inconsistencies. There are two kinds of such logical faults that must be dealt with. The first is the 'dangle', an activity represented in the network where its head or tail does not connect either with any other activity or to a start or finish event. The second kind is a 'loop', an error in a network which results in a later activity imposing a logical constraint on an earlier activity. Loops can be detected if a simple numbering rule for events is followed: the end event of any activity must have a higher number or label than that of its start event. If it is found impossible to label at least one of the events, even after attempts to renumber the events of the network, then the network contains a loop.

Dangles can usually be rectified by finding the missing relationship, but loops often require a thorough re-examination of the whole project plan.

All good computer programs have error detection routines that are capable of identifying and reporting network logic errors (which may have been caused either by mistakes in constructing and numbering the network itself or through data input errors). There is more on this subject at the end of Chapter 23.

It is good practice not to allocate consecutive numbers to all nodes, but to leave gaps in case renumbering is made necessary by insertions or logic changes. One method is to use only even numbers at first. Another, common, method is to start by allocating node numbers in the series 1, 5, 10, 15, 20 and so on.

Hierarchies of networks

These can be discussed at any stage, for instance at the outset of planning large projects. For smaller projects the first diagram may suggest the convenience of subnetworks, but sometimes that need is not felt until a later stage. It may be convenient to use as event numbers for the top level network only multiples of 1 000, and multiples of 100 for the second level, and so on.

Time estimates

Time estimates for the durations of all activities are the next task. The project manager may wish to arrive at the more important ones in a project meeting, but more specialized subordinate jobs, and those in subnetworks, will normally be estimated at a lower level. All duration estimates are then collated for the purpose of the time analysis. Those experienced in the use of networks for project management usually do not need the three-times estimates of PERT. These have been found quite useful, however, for the inexperienced. Involvement with two or three projects provides sufficient experience to enable unbiased duration estimates to be made.

The time analysis

The time analysis of smaller networks is straightforward, and even a beginner can handle projects with 50 or so activities. Before computer methods became widespread, experienced project engineers had no difficulty with much larger networks of 1 000 or more jobs. Such large projects are almost invariably broken down into subnetworks of more manageable size, making it quite feasible to do time analysis by hand. One great advantage of hand analysis is that it gives a better and deeper understanding than looking at a computer print-out. The flexibility of computers (for instance in coping with changes) is one of their main advantages. In recent years there has been a dramatic improvement in the availability of 'user friendly' project management programs and packages (even on personal computers) in parallel with the fall in price and increase in power of computing. It is probably true that a large number of project networks, particularly those needing regular updating, will be on computers. It is equally true that a rough draft network is best analysed by hand at some early stage, not only providing a check on the computer but also because it is often quicker than keying in and checking all the data.

Resource allocation

This is not recommended to project teams inexperienced in the use of project network techniques. Project management using networks requires a substantial degree of discipline which has to be acquired through experience with a few projects networked for time-only analysis. Only when such discipline is firmly established should resource allocation be attempted.

Reviews of plan and programme

These, whether in response to instructions by the controlling authority (for instance, changes in specification or imposed dates) or because of a need to shorten the programme, can be made at any time before the execution of the project. Small changes may have relatively few consequences, but should significant time savings be required, changes may be needed in the basic *309* method. For instance, jobs hitherto shown as single arrows may have to be broken down into several components so that some of them can be carried out in parallel. In any case, a minute checking of relationships may reveal refinements in the logic; for example, a job could possibly be started when the preceding one has reached some intermediate stage rather than waiting for its completion.

Checking the durations is not a paper exercise. It might seem quite simple for higher management to shorten some duration arbitrarily, but this should never be done without a careful examination of the implications at the workplace and on the number and quality of the available resources. A change in plan means the recalculation of the programme.

Completion of planning and timing

This is signalled by the preparation of the time-based network. This can be broken down conveniently by workstation, so that each of these has its own bar chart. A list of all activities in earliest start-date order is an essential document for the management of the whole project and of subprojects, activity groups and single activities. Rules for the disposal of float need to be made.

Arrangements for information collection

These arrangements are central to any project control. To this end the length of the project review cycle has to be decided and arrangements have to be made to ensure that project information is collected rapidly and accurately and transmitted regularly and reliably to the monitoring centre. Unless this link is dependable, control is lost, and it is well worth checking all data collection points and links and rehearsing the operation of the system before the project gets under way.

FURTHER READING

Battersby, A., *Network Analysis*, 3rd edn, Macmillan, London, 1970.

BS4335: 1987 *Glossary of Terms and Symbols used in Project Network Techniques*, British Standards Institution, Milton Keynes.

BS6046: Parts 1 to 4: 1992 *Use of Network Techniques in Project Management*, British Standards Institution, Milton Keynes.

Lester, A., *Project Planning and Control*, 2nd edn, Butterworth-Heinemann, Oxford, 1991.

Lock, D., *Project Management*, 5th edn, Gower, Aldershot, 1992.

Lock, D., *Project Planner*, Gower, Aldershot, 1990 (includes looseleaf pack of planning forms).

Lockyer, K., *Critical Path Analysis*, 5th edn, Pitman, London, 1991.

18 Resource Scheduling

Dennis Lock

Project planning, whatever the techniques used, can never be considered complete until both the sequence and the timing of jobs have been scheduled to make the best use of the available resources. The aim must be to plan work so that neither impossible overload peaks nor wasteful idle periods occur, and to achieve this without any overall time penalty for the project. Of course, this will not always be possible, but this chapter sets out a few rules and techniques that can help at least to schedule resources sensibly.

WHO NEEDS TO SCHEDULE RESOURCES?

In addition to time, the resources used in most projects include materials, accommodation, cash, plant and labour. Responsibility for scheduling one or more of these resources may be that of the project manager, or it could be a problem for someone else along the management chain. It all depends on the type of project and its organization.

The project manager who acts only as a consultant or adviser may be able to leave all resource scheduling except cash flow to the contractors and sub-contractors employing the labour to do the work. In many cases, a main contractor for a construction project will have to schedule work in detail for his head office engineering staff but, again, can leave the scheduling of most direct labour to the relevant subcontractors.

The companies most likely to benefit from detailed project resource scheduling are those which employ direct labour in significant numbers. If temporary staff can be engaged readily at short notice with the requisite skills, the resource scheduling required may simply be aimed at assessing future numbers, a crude form of manpower planning. The most complex and difficult resource allocation problems are likely to be found in those organizations where the labour force is largely permanent (and, therefore, relatively stable and inflexible) and where the people have valuable skills, training and experience that are peculiar to the company and its work.

THE SMOOTH OBJECTIVE OF RESOURCE SCHEDULING

Figure 18.1(a) shows the type of resource usage pattern that might be expected if no resource scheduling were to be attempted. Imagine, for example, that the histogram represents the number of pipefitters needed each day in an instrumentation assembly bay. The horizontal line indicates the number of pipefitters actually available in the bay. What has happened is that the person responsible for planning has simply (and unreasonably) expected every task to be performed at its earliest possible time, as calculated from the project network diagram. Adding up the number of pipefitters needed to do all the tasks in each day (a calculation known as *resource aggregation*) reveals the unsatisfactory pattern of Figure 18.1(a), where there are overloads on some days and people are idle on others.

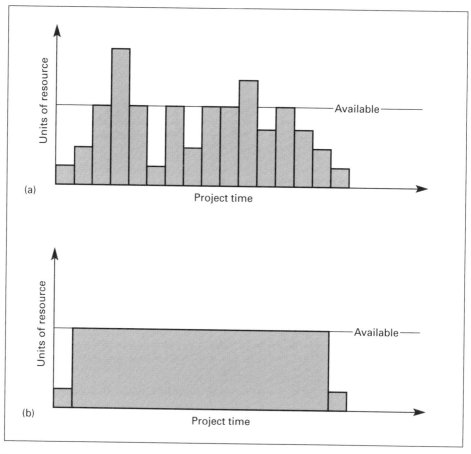

Figure 18.1   Planned resource usage patterns – before and after resource allocation

The histogram in (a) is the sort of unacceptable resource usage that would be needed if every activity were to be scheduled to start at its earliest possible time. The purpose of resource allocation is to achieve a more practicable planned use of resources, aiming for a usage pattern which approaches the ideal sort of picture shown at (b).

Figure 18.1(b) shows the type of resource usage pattern that scheduling should attempt to achieve. Whatever the method used, the principle of this scheduling (known as *resource allocation*) is to delay the start of non-urgent (non-critical) activities to help reduce the height of work peaks and fill the troughs. The perfectly smooth pattern shown in Figure 18.1(b) may may not always be possible to attain in practice, but sensible resource scheduling will at least remove the worst and most uneconomic fluctuations.

CONFLICT BETWEEN TIME AND OTHER RESOURCE LIMITS

During the resource allocation process it is often found that the resources normally available will not allow work to take place fast enough to complete the project within its target timescale (assume, for simplicity, that this target timescale is equivalent to the duration of the network critical path, the shortest possible time in which the project can logically be finished given ample resources).

Figure 18.2 illustrates the problem. The total work content of the project is depicted as a volume of an incompressible liquid contained within a balloon. This volume is a constant, but the balloon is bounded by two variable limits, the resources that can be made available and the permissible project completion

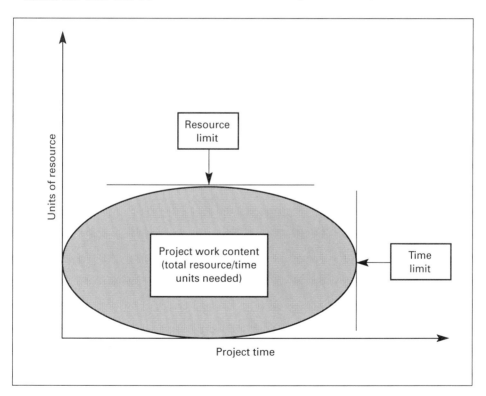

Figure 18.2 The conflict between time and resource limits

time. If the available timescale is reduced (for example, if the client wants his project finished earlier) the time limit can be moved to the left until it hits the earliest possible time indicated by the network, but the balloon will be squeezed upwards to require a greater number of resources. If the amount of resources available has to be reduced for any reason, then the balloon must be squashed flatter, and the project timescale has to be extended to arrive at a later project completion date.

This gives rise to the terms 'resource-limited schedule' and 'time-limited schedule'. The planner often has to decide or be told which option is the more important: keeping within available resources at the risk of running late, or running to time at the possible expense of having to hire extra labour. Computer systems with resource scheduling facilities will almost certainly require the planner to state whether time-limited or resource-limited rules apply before running the program.

RESOURCES THAT CAN BE SCHEDULED USING PROJECT MANAGEMENT TECHNIQUES

Techniques which have evolved specifically for project resource scheduling tend to be used mostly for skilled trades, but are also used to schedule costs and cash flows. Most of the cases quoted in this chapter are illustrated using direct labour examples, but the same techniques can be applied to any other type of resource that is quantifiable in terms of simple units or numbers. The techniques can therefore be used to schedule hire plant, bulk materials, some types of accommodation, process plant capacities and so on.

Accommodation is often a very difficult resource to plan. It is not a resource than can always be described and calculated adequately in terms of simple units of area, such as square metres. Area shape, height, means of access, lighting, power supplies and other services, materials handling facilities, floor loading, may have to be taken into account. In planning the use of assembly bays for the assembly and test of large machines, for example, one machine can sometimes be allowed to overhang another. This is just one example of circumstances where different projects may be able to share common floor space. Such problems cannot be solved by simple arithmetic, but may need three-dimensional drawings, physical scale models or a sophisticated dynamic computer-aided design system.

RESOURCES THAT SHOULD BE SCHEDULED USING PROJECT MANAGEMENT TECHNIQUES

It is usually a mistake to attempt to schedule every possible kind of resource that is going to be used on a project. That leads to unnecessary complication, and one attempt at the monumental amount of work needed will probably be enough to deter the planners from ever trying the exercise again.

Consider, for example, an engineering department which designs special purpose machinery. The department is handling a continuous work flow for several projects. The engineering manager knows, from experience, that for every ten engineers working on mechanical design, one instrumentation engineer is needed to design the supporting pipework and lubrication systems. In this case, it may only be necessary to schedule the mainstream engineers. If 100 engineers are going to be needed, the manager knows that 10 instrumentation engineers must be provided to support them. This approach, which has been proved by the writer in practice, can be extended to many other types of resources (for example, inspection personnel in relation to machine operators, paint oven capacity in relation to sheet metal machine capacity, and so on).

Similar arguments usually apply to most indirect staff, such as print room operators, purchasing clerks, and those involved in the more general administrative and management activities.

The old expression KISS – Keep It Simple, Stupid – applies. Do not attempt to schedule everything, but concentrate on the scarce or key resources and let their dependent resources fall into place.

PROJECT RESOURCE SCHEDULING IN RELATION TO OTHER SCHEDULING SYSTEMS

Project resource planning has to be seen as the backbone of a total planning system (Figure 18.3 illustrates this concept in the manufacturing projects context). The project schedule governs the general rate at which work will reach various departments by providing achievable 'work-to-lists'. Each of these work-to lists will correspond to the network activity level of detail and will establish priorities at this level.

Project scheduling cannot be expected to cope with the fine level of detail needed for production operations in a manufacturing project, for example. That must rely on production control methods. But the project schedule will provide the framework within which production control schedules must work, by recommending the start and finish date and quantifying the priority for each network activity. Project scheduling can ensure that work is loaded to the production facility at a rate which is in line with its overall capacity. This should enable the separate production control system to plan all the detailed machining and assembly operations within the overall project target dates.

The allocation of work to skilled individuals according to their particular experience or aptitudes (for example, an engineer with a special flair for gear design) must be left to departmental managers and supervisors. Project resource scheduling does not, therefore, remove or dilute the responsibility of supervisors and managers for work allocation within their departments. It is left to these managers to decide which of their staff should be assigned to each job on their work-to lists. The purpose of the project schedule in this case is to see that no department is expected to work beyond its capacity.

SIMPLE SCHEDULING USING BAR CHARTS

Charting methods (see Chapter 16) can be used to schedule resources for very *315*

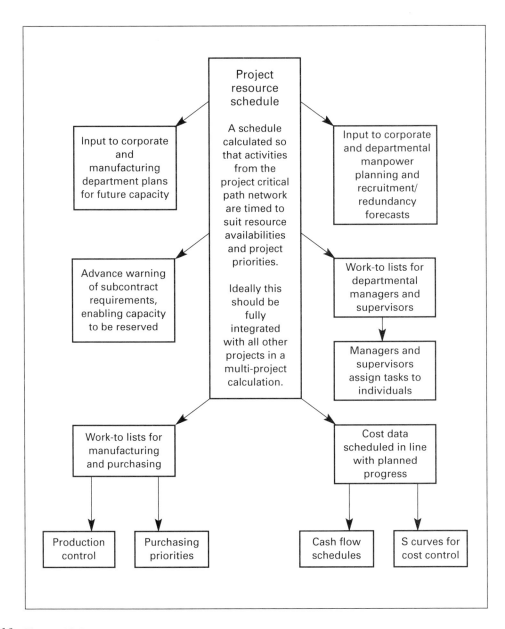

316 **Figure 18.3 Project resource scheduling in the manufacturing context**

small projects. Figure 16.3 (p. 275) showed how an adjustable bar chart can be used for this purpose. Bar charts and tabular charts (known as Gantt charts) are very useful for planning human and machinery resources within departments and for personnel duty rosters. They can often be used to plan local departmental resources even in large projects that are being planned using the most advanced methods.

Charts can be drawn on paper, card or blackboards. They can also be set up on proprietary wall-mounted boards. By using different colours or patterns, bars can be coded to indicate different types of resources, so that it is possible to schedule several different types of resource on one chart. Charts are ideal (and may be preferable to computer systems) for very simple cases. In fact the human brain can sometimes achieve a perfect result (a completely smooth, 'optimized' schedule) where the typical computer system would only produce a suboptimal result.

Charting methods cease to be of value, however, when the amount of data to be considered is too great. Once the planner attempts to use more than a few different colours for coding, or tries to plan more that about 50 different jobs, the whole thing becomes difficult to interpret. Unlike a critical path network, it is not usually possible to show all (if any) of the logic constraints between jobs on a chart and this can give rise to scheduling errors.

Worse still, a complex or very detailed chart is inflexible, and very difficult and tedious to change in line with project progress or modifications. In the remainder of this chapter it is assumed that the planner has access to a computer system that can handle critical path networks and resource allocation.

THE ROLE OF CRITICAL PATH NETWORKS IN RESOURCE SCHEDULING

Consideration of resource constraints when the network is drawn

When a network is first drawn, the planner will have plenty to do in identifying all the activities needed, specifying the logical constraints between them, estimating durations and then carrying out time analysis. It is not usually possible to consider potential resource constraints at that time, owing to the complexity of the task and the unsuitability of critical path networks for this purpose.

If the planner happens to know that a particular resource is scarce, he might be tempted to introduce special constraints in the network logic. For example, suppose that the project organization only employed one instrument fitter, and that the network contained ten instrument fitting activities, the planner could ensure that no two of these activities could be scheduled in parallel by the simple expedient of linking them all in series using dummies. But that would indeed be a foolish approach. How can the planner know the best sequence in which those activities, from different parts of the network, should take place? What would all those extra dummies do to the main body of the network logic? How would the planner be able to remember all those resource constraints if the network had to be changed?

The critical path network is not the place for dealing with constraints arising from resource limitations.

Estimating resources needed for each activity

A preliminary step in resource allocation is to consider each network activity in turn and estimate not only its duration, but also the number of units of each resource type that should be used to complete the activity within that duration. As an example, the planner might decide that a bricklaying activity will have a duration of one week, and will require two bricklayers and two labourers throughout that week. This information can be assembled as part of the initial network preparation.

It is usual to use short codes for each resource type, which helps in writing the information on the network and will be essential when it comes to enter data into the computer. In this bricklaying example, the planner may decide to identify bricklayers with the code BL and labourers as LB. If the project duration units are weekdays, with five days per week, the bricklaying activity needing two bricklayers and two labourers would have the following written along the activity arrow (arrow diagram) or within the box (for a precedence network):

$$5 \quad 2BL \quad 2LB$$

Although the planner cannot consider resource constraints at this planning stage, and must keep resource scheduling and critical path network analysis apart as two different (but related) techniques, there is one exception to the rule. This is best explained by returning to the pipefitting activities example from the previous section.

Suppose that the planner is considering a pipefitting activity on which one, two, three or even more fitters could work without falling over each other. In simplistic terms, if the activity was estimated to need three man-weeks of effort, this might be regarded as one pipefitter for three weeks, three for one week, or two pipefitters for one and a half weeks. If the planner knows, or even suspects that the company only employs one pipefitter, then it would be foolish to schedule any activity as requiring more than one. Here is the exceptional case in which early knowledge of resource limitations can and should be allowed to influence network preparation.

Float

Critical path analysis will determine how much float each activity has at the start of the project. It is this float information that is vital to the subsequent resource scheduling process. Those activities with float can be delayed, until their latest permissible dates if necessary, if resources are not available for them. Critical activities must obviously be started at their earliest possible dates if the project is to be finished at its earliest possible time.

RESOURCE SCHEDULING USING A COMPUTER

For practical purposes, and in simplified terms, the sequence of scheduling by which a computer system works from a critical path network can be seen in terms of the following stages.

Initial data processing

The computer digests network data and checks for logic or other obvious input data errors and omissions.

Time analysis

The computer makes forward and backward passes through the network to calculate float for every activity. This, incidentally, identifies the critical path or paths.

Resource allocation

The machine attempts to start each activity at its earliest possible date but checks, in each case, whether or not sufficient resources are available. If not, the scheduled activity start will be delayed until a time is found when resources are available. This process will be affected by the various priority rules that the planner is allowed to assign, according to the characteristics of the particular program used.

Reports

Work-to lists

The computer will sort activities into lists by department or other specified need and print out a list for each designated department or manager. Each of these work-to lists will contain some or all of the following data for each activity:

1 Activity number.
2 Activity description.
3 Estimated activity duration.
4 Earliest possible starting date.
5 Scheduled start date.
6 Scheduled finish date.
7 Latest permissible finish date.
8 Resources required (resource type codes and quantities).
9 Remaining float. This is the amount of float still remaining from the original total float after the scheduling program has had to delay the planned start of the activity because of resource limitations. Remaining float will be a negative quantity if the computer is unable to meet program requirements *319*

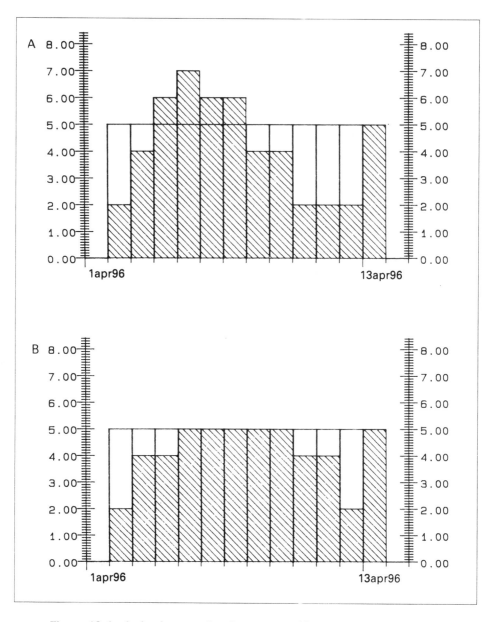

Figure 18.4 A simple example of a resource histogram

These histograms were plotted using KeH Project Systems' Cresta software. The upper chart is a resource aggregation histogram. The lower figure shows the smoothing effect which resource allocation has produced. Compare these with the hand-drawn examples in Figure 18.1(a).

using the priority rules that have been set (negative remaining float is often seen, for example, in a resource limited schedule where there are insufficient resources).

Other report possibilities

Many other reports, tabular and graphic, can be obtained from a resource scheduling program, especially if cost rates are given for each resource, and where estimated costs are specified for activities such as purchasing materials. These can include:

- A tabular statement of the quantity of each type of resource needed for the project, spelled out day by day, week by week, or for whichever duration units apply. The report can include day-by-day and cumulative scheduled project costs
- Resource histograms (see Figure 18.4)
- Cash flow schedules
- Bar charts, converted from the work-to lists.

These are just a few of many possibilities, some of which can be plotted using multiple colours.

Parallel and serial scheduling

Considerable effort has been expended in the search for mathematically ideal project scheduling methods. Theoreticians have tried to apply many of the popular techniques of operational research to resource allocation, with some success. Linear programming approaches exist which will find the optimum solution to networks of up to five activities. Mathematical optimization algorithms tend to over-kill the problem, and use more computational resources than is practical.

In any case, even if one could slot activities into the resource schedule with watch-maker precision, this has certain disadvantages. The estimates of activity durations are approximate. Reality varies from the estimate, the beautifully fitted pieces turn out to be a different size from that imagined.

For most practical systems the goal is to provide a good, usable schedule – not necessarily the mathematical optimum – without using vast amounts of time or computer resources. There are two main approaches which have been popular. Nearly all resource-levelling methods are based on either a 'parallel' or a 'serial' approach. Both are 'heuristic', common-sense techniques.

Parallel scheduling

This can be visualized as follows. Imagine a network with several possible start points. This network is to be scheduled on a day-by-day basis through the *321* project. First, we consider day one. Take all the start activities of the network. Those are all the activities which could start at day one. Build an 'eligibility list' consisting of those activities. Take the activity with the highest priority from the eligibility list. Can it start yet? Is its earliest start less than or equal to the day we are considering? If so, compare its resource requirements for its next day with the resource availability on day one of the project. If all relevant resources are available in sufficient quantity, schedule the first day of that activity to occur on the first day of the project. If that completes the activity, then include all successor activities into the eligibility list. Repeat the process for the activity with the next highest priority from the eligibility list, and so on until all eligible activities have been considered for that day.

Then move to the next day of the project. Any amounts remaining of 'pool' resources are rolled over to day two. The actions described in the above paragraph are repeated for day two ... and so on until all activities in the project have been scheduled.

Notice that this process works more naturally when the resources available to a project are limited, and the time available to complete it can be extended indefinitely.

Serial scheduling

This considers each activity in turn, rather than each day of the project in turn. It can be visualized as follows. Consider a two-dimensional table of resource availabilities. It will have an amount available for every resource for every day of the project. Against this, there is a pre-sequenced list of activities which comprise the project. In addition to its time analysis results, each activity will have an 'earliest feasible start' figure, which will initially be the same as its earliest start.

Each activity is taken from the list of activities in turn. The section of the resource tables between the activity's earliest feasible start and the activity's late finish is scanned to see if the activity can be scheduled as a whole. If so, it is scheduled at the first available point. If not, then if the activity is splittable, an attempt is made to fit the activity in between its earliest feasible start and latest finish in sections. If this is impossible, an extra layer of resource availability is called in and the process is repeated for the activity, until it can be fitted in. If an activity is scheduled at a point later than its early start, the earliest feasible starts of all successive activities are updated to be greater than the finish of the activity that has just been scheduled. When all this has been done for every activity in the network, the project has been scheduled.

Notice that this process works more naturally if there is a fixed end date to the project, but the resources can be exceeded if necessary.

Serial methods are now more popular than parallel methods, for a number of reasons. Parallel scheduling tends to split activities rather more than serial. Ideally, a parallel scheduling algorithm would like to be able to split any activity into one-day sections, particularly if activities have complex resource require-
322 ments, or if resource availability changes during the project. Parallel schemes

are typically heavy users of computer resources, both in the time taken to carry out a schedule, and in the amount of computer memory required per activity (which can limit the size of network that can be calculated on a given computer).

Special features in resource levelling

The above descriptions of the parallel and serial techniques show the basic method involved in each case. There are many refinements and special features which can be added to both processes.

A 'threshold' amount can be associated with each resource, as mentioned above. This is an additional emergency allocation of the resource which can be used if the project is about to run behind time. The threshold resource level cuts in when activities would otherwise be delayed past their latest finish.

Serial levelling schemes sometimes have a feature whereby two project end dates are specified – a desired project end and a maximum project end. Resources are classified into two sections – 'important' and 'exceedable'. If the scheduling system would have exceeded the availability of an 'important' resource (and its threshold level, if there was one), then the activity is allowed to delay itself past its latest finish. It is not allowed to delay past its secondary latest finish – that is, the latest finish relative to the maximum project end date.

Alternative and summary resources

In practice in project management, resources in short supply can be compensated for by substituting other resources.

For example, in a project using both senior and junior engineers, senior engineers might well be substituted for junior engineers to ease a temporary overload.

One can attach an 'expansion factor' to the use of alternative resources. The expansion factor is multiplied into the resource requirement of the primary resource to determine how many of the alternative resources are required to complete the task. Two different kinds of tool may be capable of carrying out a given process. One type may be less efficient than another for this purpose, so that larger numbers of that particular type may be required if it is used as an alternative.

Summary resources act in a similar way. If a given resource is used, a corresponding amount of the associated summary resource must be available too. For example, if there is a limited pool of machine operators, each capable of operating any of three types of machine, then the operator might be specified as a summary resource associated with each machine. Using expansion factors, money can also be treated as a summary resource associated with any or all other resources in a project.

MULTI-PROJECT SCHEDULING

Most organizations work on several projects simultaneously. The projects may be *323*

at different locations and may be represented by logically independent networks.

They frequently require some of their resources to be provided from a
common pool. Engineers, draughtsmen, laboratory facilities, corporate resources
are all examples of this.

Multi-project scheduling has to allow for scheduling some or all of the projects
based on the resource availabilities in the common resource pool, and also on the
resource availabilities assigned to specific projects. When several projects are
being scheduled against resources which are common, one has to consider the
question of the relative priority of these projects.

It may be enough to consider the total float of the individual activities in the
projects as being the criterion upon which they are scheduled. This is adequate
if the projects are of roughly equivalent importance, so that a critical item in
project A is 'worth' the same as a critical item in project B. If this is not so, a
process known as 'residual scheduling' may be appropriate.

In residual scheduling, the projects to be scheduled are taken one by one. All
of the highest priority project is scheduled before any of the second priority
project. The second priority project uses those resources remaining after the first
project has finished, and so on down the list. This tends to produce a resource
utilization pattern like that shown in Figure 18.5

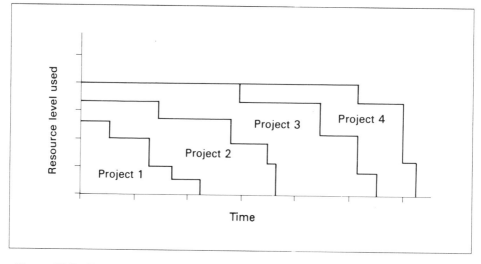

Figure 18.5   Resource usage pattern typical of residual scheduling

This pattern results from considering projects one at a time in a multi-project resource
scheduling calculation.

This is the opposite extreme from the first strategy of giving each project
essentially equal weight. The ideal situation often lies in between these two
extremes. Compromise solutions can be obtained by allocating only part of the
total resource pool to the highest priority project or group of projects. When they
have scheduled themselves against their allocation, an additional allowance of

resources can be added before the second priority projects are considered. Strategies of this kind tend to spread out the projects considered earlier in the sequence more or less in inverse proportion to the size of the resource share allocated to the earlier projects. It may be necessary to try a few experiments. One possible approach is to carry out two calculations, one of which mixes all the projects together with the same priority, the second of which treats the projects in strict priority sequence with no secondary allocation. The comparison between these two extremes may suggest what compromise answer will give the most acceptable solution for the particular case under consideration.

FURTHER INFORMATION

Project resource scheduling by computer is not well supported in the literature, at least not in books which deal with the subject in sufficient depth of detail and offer a lot of practical advice. Users of scheduling programs will find that they learn by experience, and will adapt the facilities provided to suit their own particular requirements, possibly inventing a few tricks in the process.

Many questions will arise, such as:

- How do we deal with scheduling when we know people are going to be off sick, or taking holidays?
- There are twenty design engineers in the department. How many should we show in the computer as being available for allocation in total across all our projects?
- How do we deal with people who are working on several projects at the same time and cannot be scheduled full-time for any project activity as a whole resource unit?
- What about a project which has some resources working for eight hours a day, but others operating two or even three shifts in each twenty-four-hour period?
- How can we schedule resources where some departments work five days a week and others six or seven days?
- Our UK head office has different national holidays from the overseas project site, and both are on the common network and schedule.

Readers who need answers to these and similar questions can refer to the planning and scheduling chapters in *Project Management*.

The more reputable software houses have very experienced and enthusiastic people on hand who can give practical advice on the application of their systems.

Finally, an essential step for anyone who needs to take this subject seriously is to join the Association of Project Managers, through which they will be able to meet others with whom they can discuss their problems and share their experiences.

FURTHER READING

Lock, D., *Project Management*, 5th edn, Gower, Aldershot, 1992.

Part Five

MANAGING PROJECT MATERIALS

19 Materials Planning and Control

Kim Godwin

Materials planning is an important element in any industrial project. Expenditure on materials will often constitute a large proportion of the total project costs. The availability of materials is also likely to have a big impact on the overall project timescale; installation and assembly work cannot start until the first materials are received and, likewise, project completion can be conditional on receipt of the last items. Identifying those materials which require a long lead time is crucial (particularly if they are required for early or other critical activities), and consideration may also have to be given to special handling or storage requirements. All these aspects mean that the cost and availability of materials are often the determining factors for performance against the whole project budget and schedule.

INTRODUCTION

The range of possible projects is obviously very wide, from development programmes (such as the manufacture and testing of prototypes) to large engineering and construction projects. It is therefore not surprising that the range of techniques used for materials planning is similarly wide. Which technique is chosen is clearly dependent upon the characteristics of the particular project, but one common theme is that no activity should ever be considered in isolation. All aspects need to be coordinated, from the original contract or authorization to proceed, the materials planning and purchasing, the receipt of the goods, and on to their issue and installation. It is not sensible to make a decision regarding the purchase of materials, for example, in isolation from storage considerations. It would clearly be foolhardy to negotiate a low purchase price and take delivery of all the materials at one time if the storage space was insufficient.

Efficient materials planning, purchasing and handling, ensuring that excesses, losses and damages are minimized, are all essential in achieving a satisfactory outcome for a project. This chapter (the first of four consecutive chapters in this handbook which deal with project materials) examines concepts and techniques *329* used in materials planning, determining what materials are necessary to make or build a project, when they are required, and what factors should be considered when receiving and storing the goods. The chapter considers these topics under four main headings:

- The make or buy decision
- Determining requirements
- Scheduling and monitoring
- Storage and issue.

MAKE OR BUY?

With every item that is to be used in the project, a decision needs to be made whether the work is to be done by the main project contractor, or whether it is to be purchased or subcontracted. In the manufacturing sector this is often referred to as the 'make or buy decision'.

In some situations, the decision is a very easy one to make. If the main contractor does not have the technological know-how or the necessary equipment, then clearly the work will have to be purchased or contracted out. For example, obtaining large turbine generators or, at the other extreme, specialist integrated circuits would usually mean that these items are to be purchased, unless their development and manufacture actually happens to lie within the core business activity of the project contractor.

Similarly, the decision not to subcontract work is very clear for goods where the main contractor has the necessary resources or expertise.

However, there will often be cases which are not so clear cut, where the contractor could undertake the work but has to decide whether or not subcontracting would be the better option. Many factors need to be taken into account, but primarily these will fall into two main categories:

1 Where the goods can be purchased more cheaply than they could be manufactured.
2 Where the main contractor has the equipment and know-how but not enough capacity to do the work or complete it on time.

Figure 19.1 lists some of the main factors involved in 'make or buy' decisions. One overriding issue will almost certainly be the consequences for industrial relations. Several years ago it was not possible for some companies to subcontract any work because of the power wielded by the trades unions. For some, this situation might still exist. For many, it does not, but even here the decision to contract out will be influenced (and rightly so) by the impact upon the workforce. If the contractor has the resources in people and equipment but has decided to purchase the materials because they are cheaper, then there are two possible courses of action:

1 Leave the equipment and workforce idle and so further increase costs in the short term; or

Make	Buy
• Lower overall costs than purchasing	• Cheaper than in-house manufacture
• No suitable supplier exists	• Commodity item (for example, fasteners)
• Surplus internal capacity	• Lack of internal capacity
• Need to absorb overheads	• Flexibility – avoiding additional overhead costs and adapting easily to fluctuations in demand
• Need to maintain design secrecy	
• Direct control over manufacturing and quality	
• Technological knowledge and the need to retain core skills	• Technical expertise of the supplier
• Industrial relations	• Small quantity requirement
• Control of changes during development phases	• Development of multiple sources
	• Strategic partnerships

Figure 19.1 Factors that influence the 'make or buy' decision

2 Dispose of the equipment and make some of the employees redundant.

This would clearly be a significant and strategic decision and one which, if contemplated, would require far more detail and consideration than can be provided here.

DETERMINING MATERIALS REQUIREMENTS

The main stage in any materials planning activity is to determine what materials are required, and when and where they will be needed. This stage will often be started before a contract or other authorization to proceed has been signed. Materials must be considered when an original proposal is being prepared; detailed needs may not be known at this stage, but an estimate will have been made regarding the likely amount and cost of the materials. All items that are likely to be critical because of their cost or lead time should certainly have been investigated in detail before a final project proposal is submitted.

However, it is when the project is given authorization to proceed (which usually means the award of a contract) that most of the materials planning work starts in earnest. The overall schedule for receipt and installation has to be determined and preparations for purchasing put in hand. The source document in almost every case is the drawing or original design created by the engineers, designers, or architects. The design will often be evolving, with changes occurring throughout the development period regarding the type and amount of materials specified. Monitoring, controlling and reacting to these changes is very important, and will be considered in greater detail later.

The first task is to identify what goods are required to start work on the project and also to list the long lead-time materials (for it is these that will determine major phases of the project). There are three main techniques for determining materials requirements. These are:

1   Quantitative surveying.
2   Parts lists (sometimes called equipment lists).
3   Materials Requirements Planning (MRP).

Quantitative surveying

Quantitative surveying is a technique used in the construction industry to estimate the amount of materials that will be required for the project (and also, later, to measure and certify the actual amount of work in progress achieved). The source documents are the architect's design drawings and a 'project special document' that gives all the necessary materials specifications. The quantity surveyor is able to use the drawings to find the quantities of materials that will be needed to build the project, using reference tables to convert from drawing dimensions to actual quantities. The resulting list is referred to as the 'bill of quantities'.

In the very simple example of a brick wall, the architect's drawings will give the thickness, length and height. Conversion tables can then be used to translate these dimensions into the number of bricks needed. The actual specification (defining the type of bricks to be used) will come from the project special document.

Information needed to determine the timing of deliveries will again be derived initially from the original architect's drawings. The quantity surveyor will assess the sequence and amount of work involved in the construction, and this information can then be used by the planners who draw up the project bar chart or critical path network. The precise delivery time at site will often be left to the discretion of the site managers and clerks, who will call-off deliveries against a blanket purchase order as and when they are needed. A good example of this procedure would be the delivery of ready-mix concrete. This will set within a matter of hours, and it is clearly impossible for the quantity surveyor and materials planners to decide the actual delivery many months earlier when the project is being planned. Better that they calculate the total amount of material that is required, and give a rough schedule to the purchasing department so that the contracts can be negotiated and orders placed, while leaving the site personnel free to control individual deliveries.

The main point to stress with the construction sector is that the sourcing and pricing decisions will nearly always have been made at the pre-tender stage. The proportion of material costs is so great that this essential work has to be completed before the tender can be submitted to the potential customer. After the award of the contract, purchase orders are placed with the suppliers, and materials called-off for delivery as described above.

Parts lists

Parts lists are typically used in one-off engineering projects. These documents are sometimes known as equipment lists, although the term 'equipment list' is commonly used in mining and petrochemical projects to describe a different

ITEM NO.	PART NUMBER	DESCRIPTION	QTY	REMARKS
1	F13A	13 AMP fuse	1	
2	A9002	Live pin assembly	1	
3	A9003	Neutral pin assembly	1	
4	A9004	Terminal post assembly	1	
5	5006	Earth pin	1	
6	5010	Terminal screws	3	Brass M3 × 6 mm cheese-head screws
7	9005	Plug cover	1	
8	9006	Plug body	1	
9	5012	Plug housing screws	2	Brass M3 × 10 mm cheese-head screws
10	9007	Plastic cable grip	1	
11	5013	Cable grip screws	2	

Iss	Mod No.	Date	Sig	Iss	Mod No.	Date	Sig
1	First	27.12.92					

Drawn by: KRG	Checked: AMC	Approved: D. L. Lock	Date: 7.1.93

Title: HOUSEHOLD 3-PIN PLUG	Sheet 1 of 1	Assembly number: A9001

Figure 19.2 Parts list for a 13A 3-pin electrical plug

document used for listing installed equipment for the purposes of operational control and plant maintenance.

At its very basic level, the parts list is a shopping list of the type and amount of goods required for the project. There is not necessarily any structure to the list, indicating which items should be purchased first or the order in which they are to be assembled, but the list is often broken down into main modules. Figure 19.2 shows a simple example for a UK pattern 13A 3-pin electrical mains plug.

The parts list is usually determined from the engineering drawing, which can take the form of a circuit diagram for electrical or electronic assemblies, or a technical drawing of the item itself. These used to be drawn by hand by the engineer or designer but, increasingly with the use of CAD/CAM systems (computer aided-drawing/design and computer-aided manufacture), this output can take the form of a magnetic tape or other form of software transfer.

In addition to the amount and type of materials that are shown on the drawing or design documents, the specification of the individual parts also needs to be determined. In the case of an electronic circuit for example, the circuit diagram will show what type of integrated circuits are required, but it might not show their specification (ceramic or plastic packaging? MIL spec. or commercial release?). This specification is usually decided by the original design engineer, the components engineer or a quality/reliability engineer.

The engineering department will normally issue and control parts lists but, in some industries or businesses, the materials controllers or planners may have to work from the engineering drawings themselves. Their task will be easier where the parts being specified are commodity items (such as fasteners) or where the parts have been used or considered in previous designs. In these cases, standard specifications can be used to specify each item.

When acting upon a parts list the first priority is to establish the source and lead time for every item listed. Stock items can be requisitioned from the stores. Remaining items need to be purchased, remembering that it is the long lead time items, or those required for the first phases of the assembly or manufacture, that need to be handled first.

Materials Requirements Planning (MRP)

MRP is a technique that is used in manufacturing for:

1 Repetitive projects, where many similar products are required.
2 Prototype projects, where the prototype is to be followed by a production phase.
3 Projects where there is a high degree of parts commonality throughout the project, so that the same item will be used in many different assemblies. In these circumstances parts lists can be very difficult to manage.

MRP uses a bill of materials, which at first sight can appear similar to a parts list. The primary difference, however, is that the bill of materials is structured, and each bill is normally a single level assembly. Figure 19.3 shows the example of

LEVEL	PART NUMBER	DESCRIPTION	QTY	REMARKS
1	A9001	Plug assembly	1	
2	. 9005	Plug cover moulding	1	
3	. . X6003	Plastic granules (white)	0.012	
3	. . B2007	Brass insert	2	
2	. A9000	Plug body assembly	1	
3	. . 9007	Plastic cable grip	1	
3	. . 5013	Cable grip screws	2	
3	. . 5012	Plug housing screws	2	
3	. . A9008	Main pin assembly	1	
4	. . . F13A	13 AMP fuse	1	
4	. . . A9004	Terminal post assembly	1	
5	. . . . A9050	Fuse clip	1	
5	 5010	Terminal screw	1	
5	. . . . T6010	Terminal post	1	
6	. . . . . X9007	Brass bar	0.037	
4	. . . A9002	Live pin assembly	1	
5	. . . . A9050	Fuse clip	1	
5	. . . . A9051	Live pin (shrouded)	1	
6	. . . . . X6006	Plastic granules (black)	0.007	
6	. . . . . X9020	Machined brass pin	1	
3	. . A9003	Neutral pin assembly	1	
4	. . . 5010	Terminal screw	1	
4	. . . A9052	Neutral pin (shrouded)	1	
5	. . . . X6006	Plastic granules (black)	0.007	
5	. . . . X9021	Machined brass pin	1	
3	. . 5008	Earth pin assembly	1	
4	. . . 5006	Earth pin	1	
4	. . . 5010	Terminal screw	1	
3	. . 9006	Plug body moulding	1	
4	. . . X6003	Plastic granules (white)	0.023	

Figure 19.3 Bill of materials for a 13A 3-pin electrical plug

the 3-pin electrical plug (in practice this would be more complex, with effectivity dates and other data but these have been omitted for simplicity).

MRP is a process of breaking down the finished item, using the bill of materials, assembly by assembly, down through all the subassemblies to the constituent components and raw materials (the 'family tree' approach). This process is best explained by the example of the electrical plug. If 11 plugs are to be manufactured and the amount of plastic needed to make this batch has to be determined, then this can be done level by level. In this example, 11 plugs require 11 cover assemblies and 11 body assemblies. By moving down one level on the bill of materials, it can be seen that 0.012 kg of plastic (part number X6003 in Figure 19.3) is needed to make each cover, and 0.023 kg for each plug body. For 11 plugs, 0.132 kg will be required for the covers (11 × 0.012) and 0.253 kg for the bodies (11 × 0.023), so that 0.385 kg will be needed in total.

Lead times for purchase, manufacture and assembly can be used to offset each stage, so that the total lead time for the whole product can be determined. Again using the example of the electrical plug, consider the live pin assembly (Figure 19.4) for which, even in this simple example, there are quite a few sequential machining and assembly operations before the whole plug can be fitted together. This live pin assembly is one of the basic parts required for the final plug assembly. It consists of a machined brass pin, with a moulded plastic shroud and a copper clip swaged to the top of the pin. Assume that the pin is first machined from stock brass bar and then sent out to a moulding supplier to mould on the plastic shroud. When the pin is received back from the moulding company, the copper clip (purchased from another company) is swaged to the pin top.

This process might need two days to machine the pin, followed by two weeks for the moulding supplier to add the plastic shroud, before another two days for the final swaging operation. The supplier of the copper clip might also require two weeks to make this component after the order has been placed.

All this is shown diagrammatically in Figure 19.4, from which it is clear that the total manufacturing and assembly time is two weeks and four days. Moving from left to right across the diagram shows the sequence of operations; when each must start and how long each will take. If the final assembly of the pin into the plug takes a further day, then it can be seen that the very first operation of machining the pin from the brass bar needs to start three weeks before the plug is required. Two days later, two activities take place:

1 A purchase order has to be placed with the supplier of the copper clip.
2 The machined pin has to be sent to the moulding supplier to add the plastic shroud to the pin.

This very simple example has been used to illustrate the MRP process, but it rapidly becomes far more complex when common items (such as terminal post screws) are used in several different assemblies, or when items do not have a one-to-one relationship. The situation obviously becomes far more demanding when assemblies such as aircraft flight computers are considered, where the number of component parts can number several thousand, and where there can

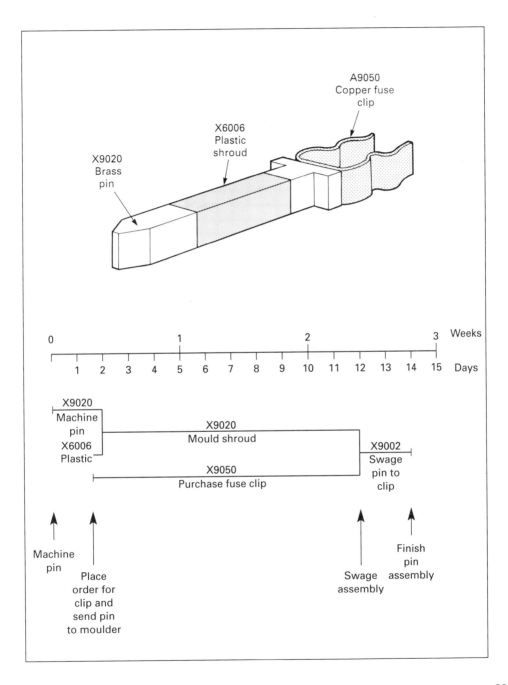

Figure 19.4 Lead times for live pin subassembly

be quite a lot of commonality between parts on different assemblies, or between different models.

MRP is therefore a very powerful technique for breaking down the materials required for a particular manufactured product, and in time phasing these so that a schedule is developed of when each activity should be started and finished. The critical path, shown by the longest cumulative lead time, is easily determined. The downside to MRP is that it will invariably require a computer to do the calculations. There is therefore an overhead expense associated with entering the bill of materials, lead times, and other product data. Unless there are several similar products to be made as part of the project, or the application is particularly complex, this data overhead may be unnecessary and inappropriate for a one-off project.

One version of the older line of balance technique charting technique (different from the application shown in Chapter 16) requires calculations that are virtually the same as those used in MRP. An example is given in Chapter 10 of *Project Management* (Lock, 1992) which illustrates the bill of materials structure and shows the calculations needed for a small manufacturing project with varying batch sizes spread over a range of delivery dates.

SCHEDULING AND MONITORING

Once the materials requirements have been determined, and purchase orders placed, it is necessary to monitor the procurement plans, and to reschedule if necessary. Many factors can change, the most likely being the design or specification. Losses and damage can also result in unforeseen demands. In the worst case the whole project may be suspended. The general guideline is to determine the materials requirements and plans as early as possible, commit these to fixed purchase orders as late as possible, and then monitor the plans closely and take urgent corrective action when necessary.

Progress monitoring is considered in Chapter 28, which also deals with the control of changes in some detail. It will be convenient here, however, to examine how changes affecting materials can be identified, and how the materials schedules can be monitored.

From the materials planning point of view, changes can be conveniently categorized into two types:

1 Materials required earlier or later than originally planned.
2 Changes in the quantity or specification of materials.

Considering the first category, it is common in any project to make changes to the dates when materials are required. The main reason for this is that when the materials schedules are first prepared, estimates are made of how long each of the project stages will take. Because they are only estimates, they will frequently prove to be wrong in practice, and stages will be completed earlier or later than originally planned. Minor variations can be handled within the contingencies included when the original schedule was prepared, but more significant differences will have an impact on the call-off of materials.

In the construction industry changes often arise as a result of technical considerations (such as how easy or difficult the foundations are to prepare) and from changes in design. These matters can obviously have an impact on all subsequent construction phases. The weather can also affect schedules, with good weather meaning that work will progress faster than originally planned, so that materials are needed sooner. Similar risks exist in the engineering industry, where timing differences will often arise from design changes or technical difficulties.

When changes in timing requirements occur, they first need to be recognized and then dealt with. Clearly, project monitoring techniques (using critical path networks, for example) will highlight when project stages are ahead or behind schedule. Other necessary approaches might be:

- Discussion of changes with suppliers, perhaps as part of the established inspection and expediting procedures (see Chapter 21). Significant changes might require the issue of a purchase order amendment.
- MRP, where changes in the schedule or design can be broken down level by level, product by product. Using the lead times already built into the product database, a completely new schedule can be calculated and all cases where there is a change in the requirement date can be highlighted.
- Line of balance (the materials supply version described briefly earlier in this chapter and demonstrated more fully in Lock, 1992). Introduction of this technique, or recalculation of an existing line of balance, will highlight the lead times and priorities and identify the risk of shortages resulting from the change.

Changes in the specification of the project will frequently occur as a result of unforeseen circumstances, or because the customer has changed the contract specification. In the latter case these changes need to be carefully recorded, and included in amendments to the project contract so that the additional costs can be recovered from the customer. The proper control of specification or design changes is vital, not only to the materials planning of a project, but also to the project itself.

The actual system used to control changes will depend on the type of project. The administration of variation orders (used particularly in the construction industry) is described in Chapter 7 and Figure 13.4 (p. 222) is also relevant. In construction projects, each architect's design change is converted into a bill of quantity by the quantity surveyor, who then authorizes a bill or invoice which is passed to the owners of the building.

In manufacturing projects, engineering change notes are used to control design modifications. An example is shown in Figure 19.5. These documents are numbered serially and are fully traceable, so that all details of the changes are recorded together with the necessary authorizations, and are used to update the design drawings and parts lists. The parts lists in turn are used to modify the bills of materials used in the MRP system. Please also refer to Chapter 28, where *339*

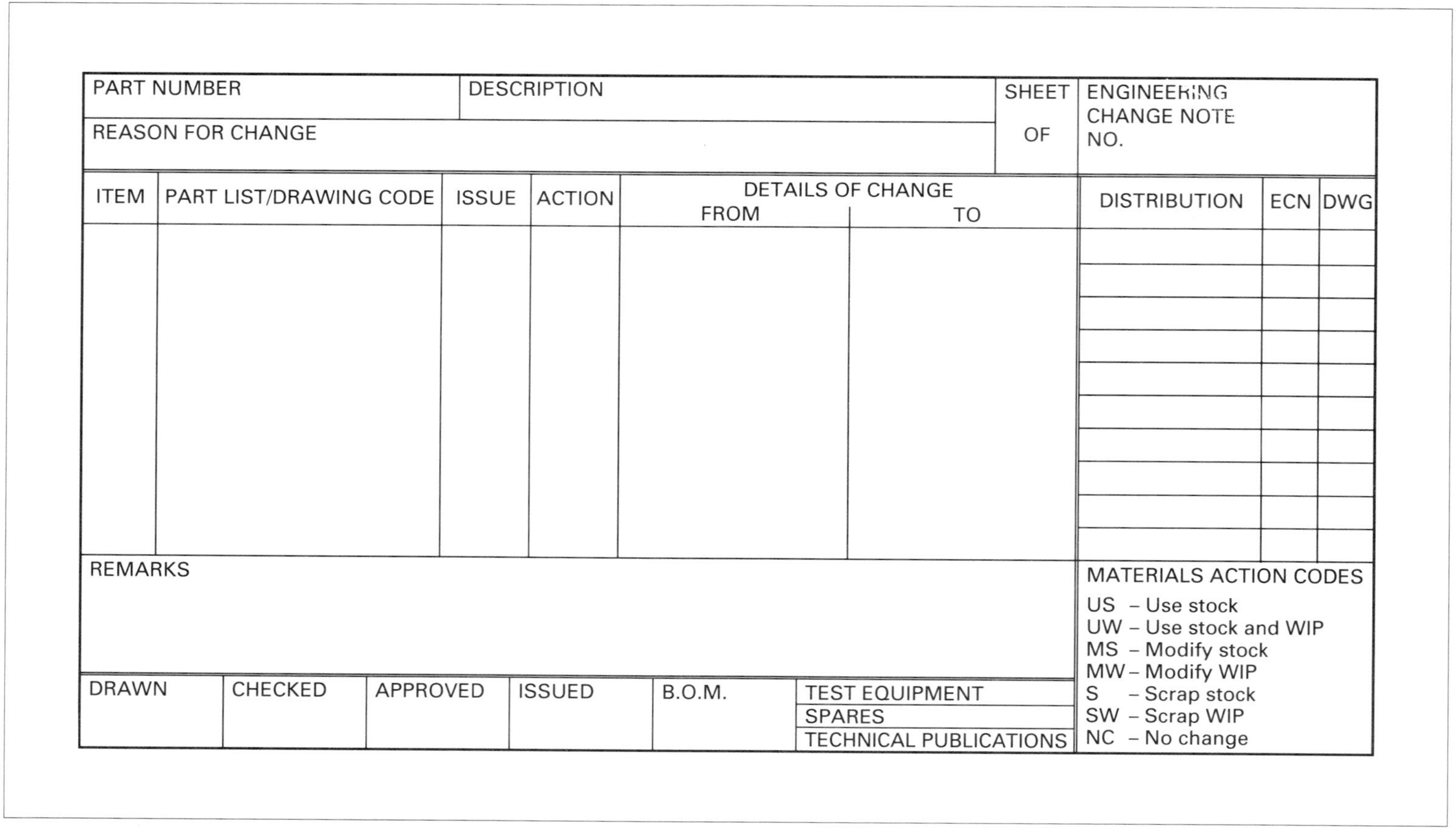

PART NUMBER	DESCRIPTION		SHEET	ENGINEERING CHANGE NOTE NO.
REASON FOR CHANGE			OF	

ITEM	PART LIST/DRAWING CODE	ISSUE	ACTION	DETAILS OF CHANGE FROM	DETAILS OF CHANGE TO	DISTRIBUTION	ECN DWG

REMARKS

MATERIALS ACTION CODES

US – Use stock
UW – Use stock and WIP
MS – Modify stock
MW – Modify WIP
S – Scrap stock
SW – Scrap WIP
NC – No change

DRAWN	CHECKED	APPROVED	ISSUED	B.O.M.	TEST EQUIPMENT
					SPARES
					TECHNICAL PUBLICATIONS

Figure 19.5 An engineering change note

requirements and procedures for change control in engineering projects are described in more detail.

The impact of a design change might simply involve the change in quantity of an item, in which case additional quantities need to be purchased or manufactured. This would be handled in very much the same way as the original materials are sourced. Of greater complexity is the situation where the specification of the item changes, so that it has to be replaced by another. Decisions then need to be made about the work in progress and outstanding purchase orders. Can these be modified to the new design? Is a concession possible? What are the additional costs? Figure 19.6 shows a checklist of some of the factors to be considered when handling design changes.

- What products will be affected by the change?
- Are the affected products manufactured in-house or are they purchased?
- Is the change to be effective immediately, or has some time in the future been specified?
- Can existing stocks be used, or will they have to be modified?
- Will the change affect work in progress and, if so, how?
- Will outstanding purchase orders be affected? If so, can they be amended?
- Can alternative materials, components or products be used under concession?
- What is to happen to items made obsolete or surplus by the change? Can they be used elsewhere or returned to the manufacturers?
- Do tools, jigs and test equipment have to be modified?
- Can additional costs created by the change be recovered? How?
- What is the likely impact of the change on the overall project timescale?
- Who is responsible for authorizing the change?
- Who has overall responsibility for ensuring that the change is fully implemented?

Figure 19.6 Materials planning issues to be considered when design changes are made

The final type of change that needs to be considered is the 'unplanned issue'. As the name suggests, these are demands for additional supplies that were not foreseeable by the designer. They affect the materials planning and control process by introducing a requirement for additional materials, which are usually required at short notice. Causes include, for example, stock losses, scrap or damage. In all these cases it is only when the materials are required or are being used that the problem becomes known, and these situations can therefore cause significant delays to the project, particularly if the items have to be reordered.   *341*

RECEIPT, STORAGE AND ISSUE

The storage and handling of materials is a vital element in any project, bearing in mind both the financial value of the materials and the need to have them available, in good condition, when they are required for building, assembly or installation.

Physical storage

The first task is to establish a safe and secure area in which to store the project materials. For manufacturing situations a suitable stores area is already likely to be established for other production applications. The decision then has to be made whether the project materials are to be physically segregated or can be stored along with other materials. Figure 19.7 compares the merits of each approach.

Segregated	Integrated
• Substandard or items subject to concession are physically separated • Items can easily be allocated to a specific project • Kits of parts can be issued quickly • Status of the project can easily be assessed • Relies upon simple stores procedures	• More efficient utilization of space • Special storage conditions do not need to be replicated • Stock transfers are minimized • Wholly dependent upon well-run stores operations • Usually needs a computerized stores system • Easy reallocation of parts between kits

Figure 19.7   Factors to consider when deciding whether or not project materials should be separately stored

If a storage facility has to be built specifically for the project, this can become a specialist and quite large exercise. The references at the end of this chapter list some books that can be consulted, but a number of factors are common to all stores applications.

The storage area has to be physically secure, so that the risks of losses, damage and theft are all minimized. The stores area must be segregated and contained within walling or fencing (depending on the application). Locks are obviously necessary on all entrances and exits, and the premises might have to be be guarded and controlled by security cameras and other devices.

The goods themselves must be stored securely and safely, to minimize accidental damage or loss. Storage and handling equipment has to be chosen that is suitable for the type of goods to be stored. Large equipment will require fork-lift trucks, pallet racking and perhaps hoists and cranes. If the materials are flammable or corrosive, then separate secure storage will be necessary.

In all cases steps will have to be taken to protect against fire, with smoke detectors and fire extinguishers specified as the absolute minimum.

Consideration also has to be given to the environmental storage conditions. Most goods require protection from rain and extremes of temperature. Some types of goods require very specific storage and handling conditions: for example, many electronic devices can be damaged by electrostatic discharges.

In the stores it is not only the goods that need to be protected. The staff too have to be able to work in a safe environment, and laws exist in most countries that attempt to guarantee this. The hazards are many. In addition to the establishment of storage conditions, layout and facilities that do not present foreseeable safety risks, staff have to be trained to avoid unsafe working practices and to be aware of possible dangers.

Records and administrative procedures

Besides the physical conditions, all stores must have good records and clear procedures. Stock records are required which show the location and quantity of all the materials. For many existing stores the stock records will be kept on a computer, but the disciplines are the same as for any manual system (systems based on indexed cards, for example).

By carefully logging goods in and out, the stores staff should always know exactly how much material is being held and where it is. It is not just the expensive items that need to be protected: a cheap item that has been purchased specifically for a project can be just as critical to the delivery programme if its purchasing or manufacturing lead time is long. Many a project has been held up awaiting a small and apparently insignificant part.

Receiving materials

Accurate records are vital in any stores operation to ensure that all materials can be quickly and easily accounted for. This record keeping starts with the receipt of goods, when the goods inwards or storekeeping staff must check the materials being delivered against both the original purchase order and the supplier's documents:

- Is the description of the goods correct? Does it match what has actually been delivered?
- Is the quantity correct?
- Is the packaging damaged or stained with moisture?
- Are any items damaged?
- Is any supporting documentation required, such as a certificate of conformity?

Any discrepancies must be clearly marked on both the supplier's documentation and internal documents so that the purchasing, accounts and project management departments can be informed. Staff must be trained and provided with suitable *343* procedures so that proper action is taken to ensure that the supplier rectifies discrepancies quickly and thoroughly. These procedures will also ensure that the supplier is not paid until delivery has been completed satisfactorily.

Goods which are accepted as satisfactory then need to be safely stored, first ensuring that they are clearly identifiable for easy subsequent location. Internal stores records need to be updated, showing the description and part number of the goods, quantity received, supplier, date received, stores location, document reference numbers, and so forth.

Besides the maintenance of accurate records, consideration has to be given to the physical handling arrangements for unloading and moving materials on receipt. This might not be an issue if a general stores facility already exists, as in a factory. Receiving of goods will in that case follow the usual company procedures, apart from perhaps separate storage of the project materials, or special handling conditions.

For an on-site stores, exactly the same factors need to be considered for the receiving area as for the main stores itself. It must be secure, and provide for the safe unloading and examination of the materials being delivered. Protection from the elements might also be necessary – both for the goods and for the staff!

One of the main differences between on-site storage of the project materials and an established stores operation concerns the delivery of heavy or bulky items. This requires very close coordination between stores, purchasing and project management staff to plan and arrange:

- Special unloading equipment.
- Adequate storage space.
- Suspension of other deliveries.
- On-site testing of goods.

Issuing materials

Many of the storekeeping activities involved with issuing materials correspond with those associated with receipts. Similar materials handling equipment will often be required, and there is the same need to maintain accurate and up-to-date records. Failure to heed these requirements will lead to avoidable losses and damage which, in turn, will lead to project delays and higher costs as replacement materials have to be obtained.

Two activities unique to the issuing of materials are allocation (often called pre-allocation) and kitting.

Allocation

Allocation involves the reservation of items for a particular assembly or stage in the project. It is usually undertaken to give priority to that stage so that a complete set of parts can be collected as quickly as possible and then retained safely to ensure that they are not issued for other, less urgent work. The risk of such issues applies particularly where parts are common to a number of different production assemblies or other projects.

Another important reason for allocation can be that the goods have been accepted as fit for use only on a particular assembly (possibly authorized by a concession document or production permit) and must not be used in other applications. This would happen often in prototype stages where, for example, laboratory evaluation models used in the aerospace industry might be assembled with commercial parts having no certificate of conformity.

Allocation might be mandatory for projects where all materials must be covered by certificates of conformity, which again includes the aerospace industry and will also apply to many projects for the defence industry. The requirement can be so strict that a separate secure storage area (a bonded store) has to be established for a particular project.

The allocation process can be controlled using handwritten records with a manufacturing computer software package. However, bitter experience has taught some managers that the only certain way of ensuring that allocated stocks will actually be found intact when they are needed for kitting and issue for their specified project activity is to separate them physically and lock them away from the main body of stocks.

Kitting

Kitting involves physically collecting or 'picking' the components from their various stores locations and assembling them into a kit of parts that can be issued for each assembly or subassembly.

Materials should only be issued from stores when they are actually required for assembly or construction, and certainly not if any appreciable period is expected to elapse before they are actually worked on. In this way security is assured right up until the items are required. Should an engineering change be issued before assembly has started, it will be far easier to amend the affected kit of parts before it is exposed to the assembly environment, and also far easier to amend the relevant stores records accurately.

When the materials are issued, the normal transaction records such as part number, quantity issued, job reference, date, will need to be completed. In addition, document, batch or lot references will often have to be specified in order to provide a method for subsequent traceability.

The demands of the project or the desire to avoid idle time in the production departments can mean that incomplete kits of materials have to be issued, but this action should only be taken if it is authorized by the site or project management. Once the incomplete kits have been issued there is the problem of reconciling what materials are still required for the job and of ensuring that when these are received they are automatically routed to the correct assembly or construction area for completion. Retaining incomplete kits in store can have the advantage that shortages might be cleared by transferring parts between kits – but this will give rise to problems if those parts have already been allocated for other jobs.

REFERENCES AND FURTHER READING

Baily, Peter and Farmer, David, *Materials Management Handbook*, Gower, Aldershot, 1982.

Compton, H. K., *Storehouse and Stockyard Management*, 2nd edn, Pitman, London, 1981.

Dilworth, J. B., *Operations Management: Design, Planning and Control for Manufacturing and Services*, McGraw-Hill, Maidenhead, 1992.

Dobler, D. W., Burt, D. N. and Lee, jun., L., *Purchasing and Materials Management*, 5th edn, McGraw-Hill, Maidenhead, 1990.

Jessop, D. and Morrison, A., *Storage and Supply of Materials*, 5th edn, Pitman (in association with the Chartered Institute of Purchasing and Supply), London, 1991.

Lock, Dennis, *Project Management*, 5th edn, Gower, Aldershot, 1992.

Vollmann, P. E., Berry, W. L. and Whybark, D. C., *Manufacturing, Planning and Control Systems*, 2nd edn, Irwin, Homewood, Ill., 1988.

20 Project Purchasing

Peter Baily

Purchasing for projects differs in some ways from other kinds of purchasing, but certainly also it has a great deal in common with purchasing generally for productive organizations.

Purchasing has been defined as 'the process by which organizations define their needs for goods and services, identify and compare the suppliers and supplies available to them, negotiate with sources of supply or in some other way arrive at agreed terms of trading, make contracts and place orders, and finally receive the goods and services and pay for them' (from Baily, 1987). It is in the details of this process that project purchasing differs from purchasing for batch production or continuous production, rather than in the aims and objectives.

Aims and objectives at their most basic are to arrange for the supply of goods and services of the required quality at the time required from satisfactory suppliers at an appropriate price; but to achieve these basic aims, purchasing departments may need to engage in a variety of activities aimed at subsidiary objectives, including purchase research, supplier development, and so on.

Project purchasing has two main subdivisions: buying parts and materials, and placing subcontracts. Closely associated with these buying activities are the related activities of expediting (or progressing), which is intended to ensure delivery on time, and inspection and quality control, which is intended to ensure delivery to specification, together with stores management and stock control.

SOME SPECIAL CHARACTERISTICS OF PROJECT PURCHASING

Differences between project purchasing and purchasing for other types of production are most noticeable in the case of very large projects. Very small projects do not differ so much in their purchasing requirements from jobbing production or (if they are undertaken on a regular and frequent basis) from batch production. Batch production, with most batch sizes in the 6–6 000 region, accounts for about two-thirds of UK manufacturing output. As far as printers and binders are concerned, this *Project Management Handbook* is itself part of batch production, although for the editor and publisher it is more an example of project production.

Differences exist in the way specifications are arrived at (with a single client playing a dominant role); in the way suppliers are identified and compared (with the client often involved and sometimes insisting on the use of particular sources of supply) and in the often complicated details of cash flow and payments in and out.

Project production is essentially discontinuous, in comparison with batch production and continuous production. Even though the company concerned may expect to undertake a series of projects of similar type, nevertheless each project stands on its own. It is therefore very important to devise and negotiate terms and conditions of contract which are appropriate for the individual project and which so far as possible cover all eventualities.

Differences also exist in the way the purchasing people, and those on associated activities, are slotted into the organization structure. For large projects, the project manager may have full-time staff, including a purchase manager, attached to him for several years. Much has been written about matrix organizations, which do not comply with classical organization theories because senior people answer to at least two bosses. The project purchasing manager for instance would be responsible both to the project manager and to the purchasing director in the permanent organization structure. He would in principle have line responsibility to the senior project manager and functional responsibility to the purchasing director: one would be concerned with *what* is to be done, and *when*, while the other would be concerned with *how* it should be done. In practice things are not always quite so clear cut, which is why people in matrix organization structures have to be able to cope successfully with fluid situations, political pressures, uncertainty and conflicts of interest.

An important responsibility of such a project purchasing chief for a very large project would be manpower planning, which would, of course, be done in consultation with his two immediate bosses. Some purchasing staff would be seconded to the project for the whole of its duration, or at any rate the greater part of it. Others would be attached to the project for a shorter period. It might be necessary to cope with peak work loads by hiring outside personnel on short contracts. At the other extreme, some of the purchasing work could no doubt be dealt with by permanent staff who had not been attached to the project full-time, as part of their normal work.

THE PROJECT PURCHASING MANAGER

A sample job description for a project purchasing manager on a very large project taking years to complete follows.

The project purchasing manager:

1   Reports directly to the project manager and liaises with all other managers in the project team.

2 Provides a procurement service to the project manager. This includes subcontracting, ordering equipment and materials, expediting, inspection and shipping.

3 Represents the project manager in meetings with the client on all procurement matters.

4 Prepares procurement procedures for the project in agreement with the project manager, corporate procurement management and the client.

5 Ensures that the project procurement procedures are adhered to.

6 Directly supervises the chief subcontracts buyer, chief buyer, senior project expediter and the senior project purchasing inspector.

7 Reviews and agrees regularly with the project manager and with corporate procurement management the manpower needs of the project procurement department.

8 Maintains close liaison with corporate procurement management on all project procurement activities.

9 Supervises the preparation of:

(a) conditions of contract and subcontract;
(b) list of approved suppliers and subcontractors;
(c) detailed inspection procedures;
(d) shipping documentation; and
(e) all other documentation required for project procurement.

10 Agrees the names of firms to be invited to tender, in conjunction with the client.

11 Attends at the opening of tenders when sealed tender procedures apply.

12 Monitors and reviews procurement progress on a continuous basis and prepares monthly status reports. Attends and reports to project progress meetings whenever the progress of purchases and subcontracts is being considered.

13 Signs bid summaries before their submission to the project manager and the client, after ensuring that the correct procedures have been followed.

14 Supervises the placement of all procurement commitments, whether these are by letter of intent, purchase order, contract, or any other form.

15 Ensures that copies of purchase orders, correspondence, and all relevant documents including drawings, specifications, test certificates, operating and maintenance manuals, are correctly distributed to the client, the project manager, or elsewhere as laid down in the project purchasing procedures.

16 Obtains from suppliers and subcontractors schedules of work compatible with the project programme.

17 Ensures that negotiations concerning orders and subcontracts are properly conducted, and takes personal responsibility if they are critical.

18 Ensures that invoice queries from the invoice checking section are promptly dealt with by procurement staff.

SUBCONTRACTING

Large projects are usually the subject of one main contract between the client (or customer, purchaser, or employer if these terms are preferred) and the main contractor. The main contractor will then place a number of subcontracts, which themselves constitute contracts between him and the subcontractors. The client is not legally a party to these subcontracts, but will usually take part in the process of awarding them, deciding on the subcontractors, approving the terms and conditions, etc. In effect the client is subcontracting part of his purchasing activity to the main contractor, and will naturally want to keep an eye on things (except in turnkey contracts) and perhaps also to stipulate that certain preferred firms should be used as subcontractors. This can be seen from the paragraphs numbered 3, 4, 10 and 15 in the project purchasing manager's job description example given above.

Computerized databases are being used increasingly to assist in finding the names of possible subcontractors and suppliers. One such database, launched in 1985, was aimed particularly at the offshore oil and gas industries. Suppliers paid £300 a year for being listed in the appropriate subsection of the fifty product groups covered. The information listed included each supplier's name and address, the five most recent contracts, and details of the parent company and any associates, etc.

Suppliers have a long way to go between bringing their name to the notice of a possible customer, and actually getting the business. Quality capability is important. Track record is very important. A few years ago when the whole British offshore oil and gas industry was getting under way, the government set up the Offshore Supplies Office, mainly to ensure that available business was not pre-empted by overseas-based organizations which had built up track records in offshore work in South America, North America and in other parts of the world to the exclusion of home-based organizations which were trying to break into new market opportunities. A voluntary agreement between the Offshore Supplies Office (OSO) and the operators includes such clauses as:

1 All potential suppliers selected to bid are given an equal and adequate period in which to tender, such period to take into account the need to meet demonstrably unavoidable critical construction or production schedules of the operator.

2 Any special conditions attached to the materials, the source of supply of components and materials, and the inspection of goods are stated in the specification or enquiry documents.

3 Stated delivery requirements are not more stringent than is necessary to meet the construction and/or production schedules of the operator.

4 Where the requirement includes the need to develop equipment or proposals in conjunction with the operator, all bidders are given equal information at the same time.

5 When the operator is unable to identify a reasonable number of suitably qualified UK suppliers for his invitation to tender, he will consult the OSO before issuing enquiries.

6 The enquiry documents require the potential bidders to estimate the value of the UK content of the goods and/or services to be supplied.

and:

7 When the operator has determined his decision for the award of contract, in the case of non-UK award, he will inform the OSO prior to notifying selected suppliers and will give the OSO a reasonable time, in the circumstances applying, for representation and clarification. This procedure will be followed in the case of subcontracts referred by main or subcontractors to the operator for approval. Where the operator does not intend to call for prior approval of subcontracts, the procedure for adherence to the Memorandum of Understanding and this Code of Practice will be agreed between the operator and the OSO. Where this gives the OSO access to the operator's contractors and subcontractors this procedure will not diminish the direct and normal contractual relationship between the operator and his suppliers. The principle shall be adopted that following disclosure of prior information to the OSO on intended awards no subsequent representation to the operator by a potential supplier, other than at the express request of the operator, shall be entertained.

8 To satisfy the OSO that full and fair opportunity is being given to UK suppliers operators will, on request, make available to officers of the OSO such information as they may reasonably require about:

(a) the programme of intended enquiries to industry necessary to implement the anticipated overall programme of exploration and/or development to the extent that this information has not already been made available to the Department of Energy. (The operators may supply this information in any format convenient to themselves provided it is sufficiently comprehensive to enable the OSO to assess the potential opportunity for UK industry.) etc.

How long such agreements should last, and indeed whether or not there is still any justification for them, are matters outside the scope of this chapter.

THE PURCHASING CYCLE

Conventional notions of the purchasing cycle which apply in batch production, mass production or in merchandising are less appropriate to the realm of the complex project.

Large complex projects, such as the construction of complete factories, fully equipped hospitals, and offshore oil rigs, are carried out all over the world. Purchase departments are involved on both sides of the contract: on the client's side, in obtaining and helping to analyse tenders and in contract negotiation, and on the contractor's side, in obtaining information from subcontractors and suppliers which is needed in preparing the bid or tender. Once the contract is *351* settled, a large number of orders and subcontracts need to be placed by the contractor's purchase department, usually with the approval of the client.

It is often desirable to use the expert knowledge and experience of contractors in converting the preliminary functional specification into the final build specification. Two-stage tendering is sometimes used for this purpose. There are several versions of this. The World Bank, in its booklet *Guidelines for procurement under World Bank loans*, suggests that the first stage could be to invite unpriced technical bids. Based on these, a technical specification would be prepared and used for the second stage, in which complete priced bids are invited.

It is admittedly difficult to reconcile the public accountability requirement that all tenderers have equality of information and are bidding for the same specification, with the common sense purchasing principle that exceptional expertise on the part of a supplier should be used in preparing the specification. To expect a contractor with unique design and construction ability to tell the

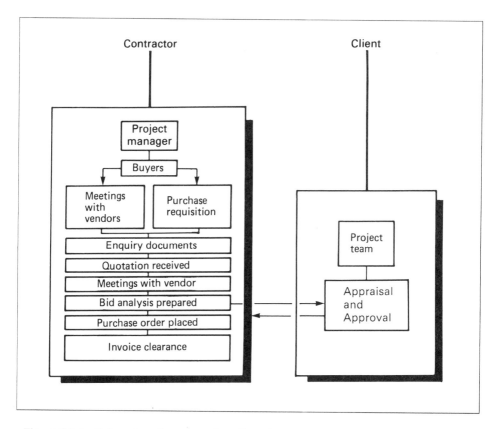

Figure 20.1 Subcontracting procedure for a large contract

This diagram illustrates the respective roles of project manager and client, when it comes to order placement (adapted from E. A. Stallworthy and O. P. Kharbanda, *Total Project Management*, Gower, Aldershot, 1983).

	(1)	(2)	(3)	(4)	(5)	(6)	Budget
Vendors asked –							
Exchange rate used							
Date							

Bid analysis for: **Client:**   **Job no:**   **Requisition no:**

All costs are tabulated in the currency indicated in the job procedure, namely:

Selected vendor

Reasons

Questionnaire on selected vendor

- Is past record satisfactory?
- If no past record has shop been surveyed or investigated?
- Are shop facilities adequate?
- Is experience adequate?
- Is test equipment adequate?
- Are subcontractors or subvendors involved?
- If so is abnormal expediting/ inspection effort required?
- Are extra exped/inspection costs expected due to shop location performance or sub-contracting?
- Do prices represent a good deal under present market conditions?

Escalation / Duties / Taxes — Percentages included in above price calculations

Total percentage applied to quoted prices

Freight, packing, handling, etc. amount

Total price delivered site

Estimated extras

Above normal procurement cost

Total comparative cost for selection

Quoted delivery time

Estimated delivery on site (including shipping time & slippage)

Schedule:

	Signature	Date
Compiled by		
Procurement recommendation		
Technical review & recommendation		
Project approval		
Construction approval		
Management approval		
Client approval		

Figure 20.2 Example of a bid analysis form

This form is designed to make sure that all the relevant aspects of vendor selection are reviewed, and compares the bid, or tender price, with that in the budget, or control estimate (from E.A. Stallworthy and O.P. Kharbanda, *Total Project Management*, Gower, Aldershot, 1983).

353

client the best way to do a job, without payment, and then in the second stage to lose the contract to a low bidder with less design capability, seems unlikely to work out. Such firms sometimes insist on some version of the cost-plus contract or on negotiated contracts.

Once the contract has been signed, purchasing work goes ahead on placing the subcontracts. Very often this has to be done in conjunction with the client, as shown in Figure 20.1. Specifications are prepared, possibly in consultation with vendors and incorporated in the Request for Quotation documents. Normal practice is to allow a month for quotations to be submitted, although on the bigger subcontracts running into millions of pounds' worth of work more time may be necessary. Further discussion with suppliers may take place after receipt of tenders, to clarify things, before the bid analysis is prepared for discussion with the client.

An example of a bid analysis form is shown in Figure 20.2. This provides columns in which to list the bids received, allowing comparisons with budget, freight and duty, escalation and other extras. The form also includes a questionnaire on the vendor selected, in which explicit reference must be made to his past record, experience, shop facilities, test equipment and other important aspects of vendor selection.

Whatever procedure is adopted, it is unusual for a bid for a major subcontract to be accepted exactly as made, despite the parity of tender principle. Several meetings between the buyer and the preferred bidder (or bidders) may be required to discuss and negotiate aspects of the specification and commercial terms and conditions. After all bids have been received and appraised, with perhaps only one bidder still in the running, detailed negotiations still continue to establish identity of view between the parties. This should not be seen as an attempt by the buyer to squeeze more concessions out of a supplier who has already put in his final price. Given the timescale, bidders have to concentrate their effort on specification, price, and completion date. Selection of a sub-contractor can be made on this basis, but buyers will still want to hammer out the commercial terms and technical people may still want to tinker with the design.

Delay in finalizing contract terms or specification details leads to the use of *letters of intent*. These simply say 'we intend to place the contract with you' and in English law they are not binding on either party. Consequently they may not have the desired effect of enabling work to start unless the contractor is able to trust the purchaser.

An unconditional *letter of acceptance* on the other hand sets up a binding contract between the parties. Somewhere between the two is the *instruction to proceed* which authorizes the contractor to start work on specified parts of the contract and possibly states an upper limit to the expenditure which the contractor can make on the authority of the letter.

Purchasers usually follow up or accompany the letter of acceptance with an official order form, in order to get the contract into normal administrative and accounting procedures.

PURCHASED MATERIALS AND EQUIPMENT

Projects vary enormously in size, complexity, duration and the nature of their location (a factory in Russia, a hospital in the Middle East, a bridge over the Bristol Channel, a tunnel joining two islands, etc.). Some are far less innovative and more routine than others. But most require the procurement of materials and equipment such as pipe, valves, cables, explosives, none of which was designed specially for the project and the acquisition of which falls more into line with routine purchasing. All must be available on time if delays to the project are to be avoided. All must meet specification. All must be suitably priced if the project costs are to stay within budget.

Even in large projects such purchases may be handled in the purchase department by staff not attached to the project, but who handle these purchases as part of their normal work (although it may be better to second such staff to the project team if the work involved occupies them full-time for significant periods). Getting deliveries in on time, product guarantees, and fixed prices, together with the legal, commercial and financial complications of operating on a world scale, can provide a variety of challenges to the purchasing staff affected.

Price analysis and cost analysis

In the consideration of quotations, some form of *price analysis* is always used. Sometimes a more specialized technique is brought into play to support, for example, negotiations about cost-based pricing. This technique is *cost analysis.*

Price analysis attempts, without delving into cost details, to determine if the price offered is appropriate. It may be compared with other price offers, with prices previously paid, with the going rate (if applicable) and with the prices charged for alternatives which could be substituted for what is offered. Expert buyers deal with prices daily and, like their opposite numbers on the other side of the counter, they acquire a ready knowledge of what is appropriate. When considering something like a building contract which does not come up daily they refer back to prices recently quoted for comparable buildings.

When several quotations are received, some will usually be above the average and some below it. Any prices well below the norm should be examined with care. If a supplier is short of work, a price may be quoted which covers direct labour and materials cost without making the normal contribution to overheads and profit. Accepting such an offer can be beneficial both to supplier and purchaser, but it may be prudent to ask why the supplier is short of work. It can happen to anyone, of course, but in this instance have customers been 'voting with their feet' because the supplier's work is not satisfactory?

Low prices may be the result of a totally different position: a seller may have enough work on hand to cover overheads (i.e. expected sales revenue already exceeds breakeven point) and is consequently able to make a profit on any price which is above direct cost. Such offers are not necessarily repeatable; next time round the price quoted may be higher to cover full costs.

Low prices may also be quoted as special introductory offers in order to attract *355* new customers, giving them in effect a fair trial of the goods or services. This can be regarded as a form of compensation to the purchaser for the risk which he incurs in switching to an untried source. Some buyers do not like accepting such offers, regarding the arrangement as opportunism. Building long-term working relationships with proven suppliers matters, of course, more than a single purchase at a cheap price – but this does not exclude acceptance of special offers in all cases.

Management may be pleased with the immediate cost reduction resulting from a one-off low price purchase, but there is a danger that they will expect the buyer to do even better next time. This can be overcome if it is made clear that special offers are, as their name implies, special to the particular occasion: they cannot be made the basis for standard price expectations.

Low prices can also be quoted simply through a mistake of the supplier, or through his incompetence. Suppliers should be given the opportunity to correct such mistakes or withdraw their offers if the price appears to be suspiciously low (say more than 25 per cent below the price which would normally have been expected). Insistence on a contract at low quoted prices has led to bankrupt suppliers and unfinished contracts, and thus to additional costs for the purchaser, when this point has been ignored.

High prices may be quoted as a polite alternative to refusing to make any offer by sellers with full order books. Buyers should not write off such suppliers as too expensive since next time round they could well submit the lowest bid if conditions have changed. High prices may also be quoted because a better specification, more service, prompter delivery, etc., is offered. Obviously such offers should be considered with care. The best buy, not the cheapest price, is the buyer's objective.

Cost analysis examines prices in quite a different way from price analysis. It concentrates only on one aspect, namely, how the quoted price relates to the cost of production. When large sums are involved, and a considerable amount of cost analysis needs to be done, full-time estimating staff or cost analysts may be employed for the purpose by the purchasing department. These people are as well qualified to estimate a purchase price as their opposite numbers in suppliers' sales departments are to estimate a selling price; they have the same qualifications, engineering experience and costing knowledge plus specialist knowledge of sheet metal processing, light fabrication, electronics or whatever is relevant.

Usually suppliers are asked to include detailed cost breakdowns with their price quotations. Some are reluctant to comply, but if one supplier does, others find it hard not to follow suit. Differences between a supplier's cost breakdown and the purchaser's cost analysis can then be examined one by one to arrive at a mutually agreed figure. Cost analysis is also used by purchasing management to set negotiating targets for their buyers.

Cost analysis is a useful technique for keeping prices realistic in the absence of effective competition. It concentrates attention on what costs ought to be incurred before the work is done, instead of looking at what costs were actually incurred after the work is completed. This seems more likely to keep costs down (as well as less expensive to operate) than the alternative of wading through a supplier's accounting records after contract completion, probably employing professional auditors to do it.

AMENDMENTS TO PURCHASE ORDERS

It is sometimes unfortunately necessary to amend or even cancel purchase orders.

This should of course be avoided if possible. Good practice is for buyer and seller to agree on all details of specification, price, terms and delivery when the order is placed, and for both parties to comply with the agreement as it affects them. Buyers do not always seem to be aware that if their purchase order constitutes a contract, they have no legal right to amend or cancel it without the seller's consent, since a contract is equally binding on both parties. In the interests of goodwill, however, suppliers are usually willing to accept amendments. Changes to specification, programme changes, increases or reductions in the quantity required, and changes emanating from the buyer's own customers are some of the reasons why buyers may seek to amend purchase orders.

Any amendment incurs the risk of delay and confusion. To avoid confusion it is necessary to ensure that an amendment is notified not only to the seller, but also to each internal department that received copies of the original order. One way to do this is to give details of the amendment on the same form as is normally used for purchase orders. If the original purchase order was numbered 7300, for example, the amendment form could be numbered 7300A. Some firms prefer to use a specially printed form. This should have the same number of copies as the purchase order form and should be distributed in the same way. Even if these methods are not used, and the amendment is notified to the supplier by letter, it is important to ensure that every person who received one or more copies of the original purchase order also receives copies of all subsequent amendment letters, and files these with the order copies.

ELECTRONIC DATA INTERCHANGE (EDI)

Increasingly, routine communications between trading partners, such as orders, delivery schedules and invoices, go direct from computer to computer, rather than by typed documents sent by post which may then have to be typed yet again into a computer. EDI has been defined as 'the transfer of structured data, by agreed message standards, from one computer system to another, by electronic means' (International Data Exchange Association).

A considerable saving in paperwork, postage and administrative time is claimed for EDI. Further savings may result from shorter lead times, which make possible lower stocks. Against this, fees have to be paid for access to networks, plus annual subscriptions and possibly the cost of the hardware and the software.

EDIFACT (Electronic data interchange for administration, commerce and transport) is being developed as a general message standard. Specialized standards include EDICON (electronic data interchange construction), devised *357* by the construction industry to cover electronic trading in the construction industry from design, quotation and tendering through to invoicing.

Trade data such as request for quotation, the quotation itself, purchase order, acknowledgement, delivery instructions, dispatch note, invoice, statement and credit note can be sent by electronic means via EDI. Technical data such as specifications, CAD/CAM data, and so on, can also be sent, and there is increasing use of systems for electronic funds transfer, computer to computer, rather than making payment by cheque or other paper delivered by post.

Paperless trading systems of this kind are increasingly used by large purchasers both in retailing and in manufacturing, and can make a significant contribution to project purchasing.

FURTHER READING

Baily, P., *Purchasing and Supply Management*, 5th edn, Chapman & Hall, London, 1987.

Baily, P., *Purchasing Systems and Records*, 3rd edn, Gower, Aldershot, 1991.

Baily, P. and Farmer, D. H., *Purchasing Principles and Management*, 6th edn, Pitman, London, 1990.

Farmer, D. H., *Purchasing Management Handbook*, Gower, Aldershot, 1985.

Lester, A. and Benning, A., *Procurement in the Process Industry*, Butterworth, 1989.

Stallworthy, E. A. and Kharbanda, O. P., *Total Project Management*, Gower, Aldershot, 1983.

21 Inspection and Expediting

Bob Chilton

The procurement of materials and equipment for a project is, obviously, not simply a matter which ends when all the purchase orders have been placed. If that careless approach were to be adopted, vital items might arrive late, and other consignments could be received with undiscovered damage, specification faults or shortages. The twin processes of inspection and expediting are carried out in order to limit the likelihood of such failures.

ORGANIZATION

At first sight, expediting and inspection appear to be two different functions. The project management novice might well be justified in asking why they deserve places in the same chapter. The answer lies in the practical approach to carrying out the expediting function. Very often this involves close cooperation with suppliers and manufacturers, to the extent of visiting their premises to view progress and verify claims for progress payments. Since quality is also of paramount importance, it is sensible to arrange that visits to monitor progress are combined with a physical examination of the goods in order that any possible deviation from the specification can be identified as early as possible, rather than waiting until the goods have been delivered. Thus it is common for visiting expediters to be technically qualified personnel who can also carry out basic inspections. Where the nature of equipment is such that a highly specialized engineer should carry out inspection (or witness tests), the expediter should be supported by the project engineering team, in the shape of a suitable engineer to accompany the expediter on relevant visits.

Expediting is customarily seen as part of the function of the purchasing department, and it is here that the expediters usually have their base. Sometimes, owing to the international nature of projects, a company will employ a specialist organization to carry out expediting and inspection for them, either by virtue of the expertise which can be brought to bear, or by the fact that the specialist organization chosen resides in the same geographical region as the *359* suppliers (which would otherwise be too remote from the contractor's own home base to allow regular visits to take place). In fact, there are many ways in which the functions of purchasing, inspection and expediting can be arranged for a project. In some cases the client's own purchasing department might act as purchasing agent. The matter can be complicated further by the insistence of the client for third party inspections to take place, either to verify conformance with quality and performance standards or to certify that progress achieved is in line with progress payment claims.

For the purposes of this chapter there are three main parts of the organization, and it is not particularly relevant to be concerned about their corporate positions in the organization. Wherever they are, the functional arguments and principles are the same. The three main roles (in addition to the project manager) are:

1   *The engineering authority*. This is responsible to the client and to the project manager for quality and performance as defined in the engineering standards and project specification.
2   *The purchasing organization*. This function might exist within the contracting company, within the client's organization, as an independent organization, or as a combination of these.
3   *The inspecting authority*. Again, this role might be within the client's organization, could include the independent specialists, and would certainly involve the contracting company's own quality control staff.

See Figure 21.1 for an amplification of these arguments.

PROGRESSING AND EXPEDITING

Expediting and its closely allied progressing function (on which it depends for direction) have no internationally agreed definitions. Clients often place different interpretations on these processes and the two aspects therefore tend to be confused.

Progressing should be regarded as obtaining and verifying information on the procurement position of equipment. This may include the position of ordering equipment from subcontractors and progress on design. The position should be presented to the client in a 'status report', which is an integrated report that summarizes the information determined by the progressing activity related to the project programme.

Expediting is action taken with the manufacturer with the objective of restoring the procurement and manufacturing programme whenever the status report indicates that progress is in danger of being late, or has already failed to achieve the requirements of the programme.

The progressing and expediting activities should be started immediately the contract has been awarded. Of equal importance to the checks on the manufacturer's output are the checks during the initial stages to ensure that the manufacturer has sufficient information to proceed and that the requirements of the contract in respect of the provision of a procurement and manufacturing

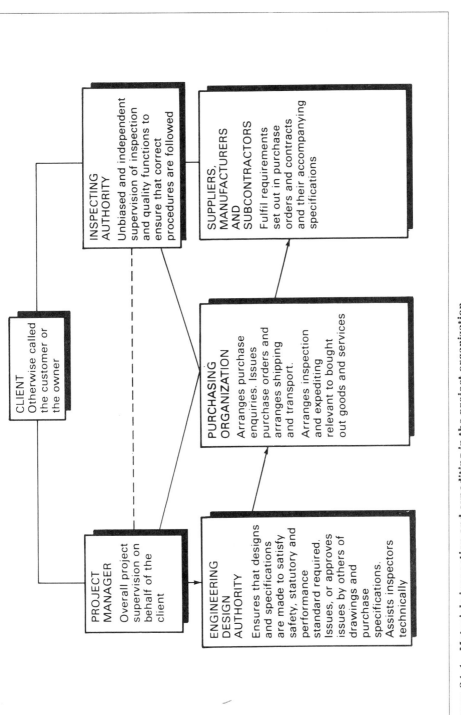

Figure 21.1 Materials inspection and expediting in the project organization

It is not possible to be specific about what constitutes a typical organization. There are simply too many possible variations. Apart from the client, any of the roles shown above could be found within the contractor's own corporate group – even including suppliers and subcontractors – or all the organizations could be independent firms linked only for the purposes of one project.

361

programme are met. The manufacturer's programme should be examined critically to ascertain that:

- It has been planned to meet the requirements of the overall project programme.
- It is in a form that will allow progress to be monitored and compared objectively against measurable targets, quantities or events.
- The periods shown are realistic and achievable.

In addition to the manufacturing activities, the preceding design and drawing work should also be monitored. Margins built into the manufacturer's overall programme to cater for unforeseen circumstances are all too often taken up during the design stages, so that the construction period is under pressure from the outset.

As each contract progresses, checks should be made to verify that:

- The often overlooked – but vitally important – design interface information involving other suppliers is available on time.
- Orders and requisitions are placed by the due dates.
- Necessary materials and components are received as required.
- Manufacture is proceeding according to programme.

To safeguard progress, availability of production and test facilities should be considered, and programmes established for any special or type tests that may be required. Checks should also be made to ensure that adequate and timely arrangements have been put in hand for packing and despatch.

Where the inspecting engineer has discovered that the manufacturing programme is in danger of slipping, or has slipped, and has established with the programmes controller that the overall programme is likely to be in jeopardy, expediting action should be pursued vigorously with the object of restoring the position. This action will vary with the circumstances but would involve a review with the manufacturer to ensure that all possible steps are considered with the aim of optimizing recovery of the programme. Such matters as the establishment of additional check points, resolving priorities, overtime working, additional facilities and/or subcontracting work and the possibility of air freighting would be considered in this review.

It is considered that, following guidance from the programmes controller, the inspecting engineer is the best person to initiate such a review as he knows the manufacturer's works and is familiar with the processes involved and the facilities available. If the inspecting engineer fails to get the required results he will escalate the action, firstly by involving his own supervisor or the project engineer. This escalation may well then be taken further to project manager and executive management level, particularly if a solution to the problem is seen by the inspecting engineer but not accepted by the manufacturer. In these circumstances pressure may be brought upon the manufacturer by the inspection authority until a senior member of the project executive management may have discussions with senior executives of the manufacturing company. While such escalation in expediting may not always be certain to succeed, progress on a project is better assured with it than without. It is clearly true that results are obtained only by the adoption of vigorous and active channels of communication.

The client would be given information arising out of the progressing and expediting activities by the status report, which would also give a summary of the position of the assignment as a whole, highlighting important matters. Many clients require regular status reports to give them a proper understanding of progress on their projects and thus enable them to exercise control as may be necessary. In providing status reports the attempt is made not only to state clearly the actual position as it is found to exist, but also to give an estimate of the likely despatch date based on the assessment at the time when the report is prepared and knowledge of the processes to be completed. Status reports should normally be provided at regular intervals (usually monthly at the height of an assignment) and issued to ensure that they are in the client's hands in time for such regular progress meetings as may be held on the project as a whole.

Spares lists and operating and maintenance instructions should be monitored and expedited as vigorously as the procurement and manufacture of the plant itself. Delay in the production of these documents can seriously jeopardize the initial start-up and operational intentions for the project.

Recommended spares lists should be established early enough to ensure availability of spares on site in time to meet operational requirements. Instructions for the guidance of operating and maintenance personnel should be available at least six months before commissioning activities begin at site. For multi-contract projects it is often necessary to prepare overall project manuals particularly directed towards separate groups in the client's organization. (For example, control room operators are interested in the overall systems and operational regimes rather than in the detailed maintenance aspects.)

There is one aspect of progressing and expediting which is not allowed to wait until the routine date for reporting. If in the course of inspection work an item is rejected or the inspecting engineer becomes aware of any other reason why the overall programme may be in doubt, the client should be notified by fax or telex. Thus, with routine status reporting at regular intervals and immediate reporting of situations critical to the programme the client can be kept fully informed as to the progress of procurement and manufacture.

Payment verification

Payment verification is another function which relies on a sound progressing procedure. For large capital cost projects the terms of payment provide for contractors to obtain regular payments at monthly intervals. These payments are related to progress achieved and it is necessary, for financial control purposes, to ensure that appropriate checks are carried out. Several methods are adopted.

For measured work contracts (such as civil works and cabling contracts), where unit rates are predetermined, physical measurement of the work achieved determines the value of each payment.

For other firm lump sum contracts one of the most popular methods is to break down the contract price to identify the value of each of the principal items of equipment. These values are further segregated to show the separate amounts for design, procurement, manufacture and erection. Either financial values or percentage weighting values are used, and the payment due is verified by assessing the progress achieved each month against each element of each item.

Another method is to establish predetermined payment values which are released when specific key stages in the individual contract programmes have been achieved.

INSPECTION

Inspection work demands a very logical and systematic approach. Assignments to inspect equipment and plant during manufacture require the preparation of product verification plans. Each of these should be compiled from three inputs:

1 The client's operational concern with the proposed design and with the relevant licensing and other mandatory requirements.
2 The inspection authority's design assessment of the equipment and its susceptibility to failure in relation to highly loaded or stressed areas.
3 The inspecting engineer's knowledge of the particular manufacturer's works and of any weaknesses which may exist in them.

Where appropriate, project verification plans should take into account the type of quality programme and the extent of quality systems surveillance required (for example, the surveillance of series production standard stock-item components). The plans define in detail any inspections and tests which the inspection authority proposes to witness fully, those of which it is proposed to witness a proportion, and other inspections and tests to be carried out by the manufacturer where it is proposed to accept his test certificates.

During preparation, the product verification plan should be discussed with the client to ensure that his requirements are satisfied. The plan must also (obviously) be discussed with the manufacturer to ensure that it complies with his proposed method of manufacture and to determine that he will be providing adequate facilities for quality control. Once agreed, the product verification plan is used throughout the inspection assignment to cover all aspects of the contract from the inspection of raw materials to the final inspection of packing and shipping (as required by the client).

The overall advantage of a carefully prepared product verification plan is that all parties are agreed on the proposed procedures, and on who will be responsible for the various activities. It often happens that the finished plant or equipment is assembled from components originating from subcontractors or from other factories of the main contractor (sometimes involving overseas manufacture). The product verification plan ensures that, wherever they take place, all inspections and tests are treated similarly. At the end of the purchase contract, the plan forms an index to the inspection reports and certificates produced during manufacture.

The extent of the inspection authority's involvement with any assignment should be adjusted according to knowledge of the contractor's standards and the opinions held of his quality assurance systems. In cases where vendor assessment or vendor rating has been undertaken before the issue of the purchase order, the evidence available has to be considered. Such assessments should be carried out by engineers with particular knowledge of the type of product and manufacturing activities concerned. Visits to the manufacturer should evaluate:

1 The existence and maturity of a quality programme appropriate to that considered necessary for the product.
2 The manufacturer's experience relative to the anticipated order.
3 The manufacturer's history of achievement in quality and delivery.

If the opinion of any manufacturer is low, suggesting poor performance, comprehensive and rigorous (or, at least, additional) cover should be proposed in the areas suspected of weakness. The proposed inspection activity should also be arranged to suit the operational importance of the plant items concerned. The plan can be varied to meet a particular client's requirements: it should always be the intention that the client is clear from the outset on the extent of surveillance to be carried out.

The frequency of inspection visits should not necessarily be related to specific intervals, but should rather be set to correspond with the manufacturing status. As work on an assignment proceeds, surveillance should include periodic checking to ensure that the manufacturer is following the agreed procedures, and that the certificates he is required to provide are always valid.

Design approval

Design approval activities should not be undertaken until the jurisdictional requirement of the country in which the equipment is to be installed is fully understood. Many jurisdictions require the equipment to be inspected during manufacture by an authorized inspection agency appointed by the jurisdiction but themselves retain the right to approve the design calculations. Others permit the authorized inspection agency to perform both the design approval and perform the inspections. In both cases any inspection agency must seek the approval of the jurisdiction as an authorized inspection agency.

Approval by a jurisdiction

On the award, or indeed in many cases prior to the award, of a contract where design approval is required, the manufacturer or design agency should ensure that all information concerning design approval is obtained and fully understood. This is particularly important in countries where English is not the official language, since the requirements for submission may have to be translated from *365* the official language. Also the methods of calculation may be defined by law and if this is the case alternative methods of performing design calculations may have to be determined and proved.

In many cases the submission to the jurisdiction may have to be in the official language and this can cause problems particularly when translating technical terms. One solution to this problem is to employ, if possible, the services of a firm in the country to which the equipment is being sent, who have experience in the requirements and format of the design submission.

If an inspection agency is appointed (normally by the purchaser or his agent) the manufacturer should ensure that the agency has been appointed as an authorized inspection agency by the jurisdiction. Failure to check on this will unnecessarily cause problems during the latter part of the manufacturing process and could prove extremely costly if fabricated equipment has to be dismantled for reinspection.

Approval by an authorized inspection agency

Approval follows a comparatively simple procedure, the agency having been authorized by the jurisdiction both to approve designs and to inspect the equipment in accordance with jurisdictional requirements. Normally this is termed third party inspection and the manufacturer is responsible for employing the agency. However, the manufacturer must ensure that the agency is authorized by the jurisdiction.

In general design submissions are made to the agency, who prove the design calculations (generally using a different method of calculation from that used by the manufacturer). When satisfied, the agency approves the design for manufacture and performs the inspection according to jurisdictional requirements.

Reports

Reports should be prepared after each inspection and these should be produced on standard inspection report forms with significant rejection reports clearly identified as such. All reports should be sent to the client at monthly intervals, each batch covering the manufacturing activities of the preceding month. This procedure may vary depending on the particular requirements of the client. Figure 21.2 is an example of a summary inspection and expediting report used by the purchasing organization of a contracting company.

Contrary to what is sometimes argued, experience does not lead to the belief that the use of the same person for inspection and expediting produces any conflict of interest in respect of, say, an item of equipment found unsatisfactory in test but known to be urgently required on site. Indeed, it is felt that the reverse is true and that the problems being basically technical, the fact that the inspecting engineer works closely with the manufacturer and is kept fully informed of the programme requirements leads to a good and satisfactory solution in respect of both quality and delivery in the best interests of the project.

CHILTON PROJECTS: Purchasing Department					INSPECTION EXPEDITING REPORT	

This Report No.	Last Report No.	Date of this visit	Sheet		DISTRIBUTION	NO. OF COPIES
			of	sheets	CLIENT	
					PROJ. MGR.	
					ACTION FILE	

ORDER DETAILS

CLIENT ....

PROJECT NO. ....

ORDER NO. .... DATE OF ORDER ....

EQUIPMENT ....

REQUESTED DELIVERY

Wk No ....

Date ....

MAIN SUPPLIER DETAILS

SUPPLIER ....

LOCATION ....

SUPPLIER'S REF. ....

PERSONNEL CONTACTED ....

TELEPHONE NO. .... FAX .... TELEX ....

EQUIPMENT ....

DRAWING DETAILS WHERE APPLICABLE TO BE GIVEN IN TEXT OF REPORT

QUOTED DELIVERY

Wk No ....

Date ....

LATEST DELIVERY

Week No ....

Date ....

NEXT VISIT

Wk No ....

Date ....

SUB-SUPPLIER DETAILS

SUPPLIER'S ORDER NO. .... DATE OF ORDER ....

SUB-SUPPLIER ....

LOCATION ....

SUB-SUPPLIER'S REF. ....

TELEPHONE NO. .... FAX .... TELEX ....

EQUIPMENT ....

DRAWING DETAILS WHERE APPLICABLE TO BE GIVEN IN TEXT OF REPORT

QUOTED DELIVERY TO MAIN SUPPLIER

Wk No ....

Date ....

LATEST DELIVERY

Wk No ....

Date ....

NEXT VISIT

Wk No ....

Date ....

Specification complies	Tests or Certificates	Shipping Released	Ahead Target	Action by:
YES/NO	YES/NO	YES/NO	On Target	
			Slippage .... Wk.	Date Inspecting Engineer

Figure 21.2   Inspection and expediting report summary

An example of a form used by the purchasing department of a contractor to summarize the results of visits by its inspecting engineers to the premises of manufacturers.

GOODS INWARDS INSPECTION

So far, this chapter has been concerned with the activities of manufacturers before delivery of the goods. The functions of inspection and expediting are not finished, however, until the goods are safely in stores, fit for use on the project. Goods inwards inspection is the last link in this chain. Unlike the other activities so far described, goods inwards inspection is more likely to come under the direct supervision of the works or site inspecting team, rather than that of the purchasing organization.

Material being received on a site (manufacturing or construction) is normally delivered to the stores receiving bay. An exception to this general rule is when the material is large or heavy and requires handling equipment outside the range of the stores equipment. When this occurs the material should be clearly labelled 'HOLD FOR INSPECTION' and stored in a suitable environment.

The storeman should normally sign the delivery note and relate it to the corresponding purchase order copy before requesting inspection of the material. The receiving inspector (on receipt of the delivery note and copy purchase order) should check through the documents to determine what attributes are to be inspected and obtain the necessary documentation and equipment. Any certification of materials that is required should be requested from the supplier via the purchasing office if it has not already been received. In this case the material may be physically inspected and, if satisfactory, should be held in a bonded area of the stores labelled 'HELD FOR CERTIFICATION' and not released for use. When necessary, assistance should be requested from specialist services (chemical, electrical, electronic, metallurgical laboratories, etc., as appropriate).

Conforming material

Acceptable goods can be released for further operations to be carried out and a material release note (MRN) should be drawn up. The top copy should be sent to the purchasing office to enable payment to be made to the supplier, two copies plus the delivery note and copy order to the storekeeper and one copy for file. If supplier history records are kept, these should be completed by the inspector.

The storekeeper should then allocate storage space in the stores, mark up both copies of the MRN with the location and forward one copy to the quality assurance/control department, retaining the other copy with the returned delivery note and copy order on file.

Non-conformances

Non-conformances found during goods inwards inspection are covered by a non-conformance report (NCR) which must be drawn up immediately giving full details of the supplier, purchase order number, material description and non-conformance, etc. Since a minimum of four copies is required these NCRs may be of self-copying carbon paper or a single sheet which will be copied. In the former case the sets of copies should utilize a different coloured sheet to enable the top original to be identified. In the latter case a single sheet is used and this should have a coloured identification strip to distinguish the original from any copies. The distribution of these copies should be two to the purchasing office (original for transmission to supplier, copy for file), one to the quality assurance/control department and the final copy for the receiving inspector's files. The non-conforming item should be placed, where possible, within a quarantine section of the bonded area and, in any case, the item should be clearly labelled as non-conforming.

Resolution of non-conforming items

Action to resolve each problem of non-conformance should be pursued unless it can be determined that the material cannot be used. The supplier should be requested to indicate on the NCR his proposed method of resolving the non-conformance. This could be 'return to supplier', 'repair at site' (manufacturing or construction) or a concession to 'use as is' and to return the NCR. Whatever the resolution is, provided that it is acceptable, the original of the NCR should be completed and copied. The original is sent to the quality assurance/control department, two copies to the purchasing office (one for the supplier, one for file) and a copy retained for the receiving inspector's files, the previous copies of the incomplete NCR being discarded.

Damage in transit

Details of any damage suffered by the goods in transit should be recorded by the storekeeper, who should annotate the carrier's copy of the delivery note indicating that the goods were received in a damaged condition. The receiving inspector should be advised and requested to make an immediate appraisal of the damage. For raw material (bar stock, tubing, plates, etc.), providing the damage is superficial and can be removed during subsequent operations, a transit damage report (TDR) should be made out and submitted to the quality assurance/control department for approval.

Excessive damage to raw materials or damage to proprietary goods (valves, fabrications, etc.) or machined items should be handled in accordance with the procedures for non-conforming items. When crates containing delicate or intricate items are received with excessive damage, an initial TDR should be drawn up and copies sent to the purchasing office (one for the supplier, one for file), the quality assurance/control department and one for the receiving inspector's file. The crate should not be opened but stored in a bonded area. The purchasing office should immediately advise the supplier to ascertain whether he wishes to be present when the crate is opened. Following a decision on the parties to be present, the case may be opened paying attention to ensure that no further damage occurs. In certain cases it may be advisable to make a photographic record of the procedure for future reference. If, after examination, the goods are found to be unfit for project use, a non-conformance report should be prepared in the usual way as the first step towards getting the faulty goods rectified or replaced.

369

22 Shipping Project Equipment and Materials

Colin Beaumont

Project shipping is a multifunctional discipline involving the management of a complex supply chain aimed at ensuring safe delivery to site of all equipment and materials needed to complete the project. There are, of course, many examples of projects which require international shipping: they might include, for instance, the building of a large facility such as a power station or a desalination plant. Alternatively, however, a project could be for the delivery of supplies to a designated disaster area in the wake of an earthquake or famine, or in some other case where international aid needs to be mobilized on a large scale at short notice.

While each of these examples might require a different approach, there will be many common factors and principles. Often the site for delivery will be in the developing world, where local conditions and lack of communications could pose severe difficulties. Such is the complexity that the opportunities for failure in one or more aspects of the project could threaten complete failure of the whole venture. Modern commercial projects require sophisticated logistical techniques. This chapter deals with the process that collectively ensures successful completion within an agreed timescale.

FEASIBILITY

The delivery of equipment and material according to a planned timetable is the basic responsibility of the freight forwarder appointed to the task. However, this work will be the culmination of months, even years, of work evaluating feasibility. It is vital, therefore, that the freight forwarder is involved from the very beginning of the project to take part in the evaluation of site access, and transportation methods to the location. Port facilities, bridge loadings, rail gauges and equipment must be able to handle the largest items destined for the site if they form part of the transport infrastructure. A substantial amount of local knowledge must be gathered as part of the feasibility study and a freight forwarder, through his local office or agent, can make an invaluable contribution – not least in holding down the project contractor's time, travel and accommodation costs spent on this aspect.

The choice of a freight forwarder with sufficient specialist knowledge is clearly important, and will depend on the level of commitment expected from him. Inviting competitive bids is the normal way of evaluating the forwarder's potential: not only must he be able to handle the volume of cargo, but he must demonstrate financial standing, professional competence and technical expertise, supported by evidence that these meet the requirements of the project.

Apart from the handling and delivery of materials and equipment to site, the feasibility study might also have to consider availability of labour, accommodation requirements, local materials, as well as local attitudes and customs, licensing requirements, and the degree of cooperation which can be expected from the administrative authorities who will impact upon the quality of local services.

PLANNING AND ORGANIZING

Moving from the feasibility stage, and based on the results of that study, a detailed plan will have to be developed. Responsibility for preparing the plan would normally rest with the project manager or project team. Those involved would usually include experts from the various disciplines, such as purchasing staff, engineers, freight forwarders and representatives from subcontractors. The plan must take account of the following factors:

1 Construction completion date.
2 Procurement lead times for plant equipment and material.
3 Pre-shipment inspection requirements.
4 Shipping and transportation to destination country.
5 Clearance and delivery of materials to site.

FREIGHT FORWARDING

The freight forwarder included in the team (presumably the successful bidder) will have a multifunctional role, liaising with all the other discipines to ensure that lines of communication are maintained and that timely information is delivered to those who need it. The forwarder's role might extend to purchasing, and it will almost certainly be part of his job to call the consignments forward at appropriate times according to the shipping schedule.

Transport and delivery of materials

Clearly the freight forwarder's core responsibility is the efficient transport and delivery of materials in line with the shipping schedule. This will involve a number of tasks.

Booking cargo space

In order to carry out his tasks effectively, the freight forwarder must have access *371* to a full specification of all cargoes for each order. This must be provided by the suppliers in time to enable the forwarder to book space or plan vessel and aircraft requirements ahead of the delivery schedule:

1   *Sea cargo bookings.* The choice of vessels lies between two main alternatives:

(a)   conference lines (which offer scheduled services at published rates in cooperation with other lines in the conference); or

(b)   independent lines (non-conference).

The sailings of independent lines might be less frequent that those of conference lines, but this might be balanced by cheaper negotiated rates The freight forwarder must bear in mind the requirements of the project schedule, and must also be aware of cargo specifications, to ensure that outsized cargoes, heavy lifts, deck stowage and so forth can be catered for by the chosen vessel. The forwarder's role might also extend to negotiation with the carrier to agree freight rates and rebates.

2   *Air cargo bookings.* Normally used for time-sensitive deliveries or for small parcels of cargo, the principles of air cargo booking are similar to those for sea freight (although the choice of available carriers might not be as wide).

Calling forward

Maintaining contact with all suppliers and ensuring that they are given clear instructions for delivery is another vital role played by the forwarder. Often material for a particular phase of the project will be produced by a variety of different suppliers. Getting these items to the right place, at the right time, requires planning, timing, and persistence on the part of the project forwarder, who will have developed these skills over many years of experience. This stage of the project will also involve the need to coordinate pre-shipment inspection and the issuing of particular packing or marking instructions to clearly identify the cargo in transit, and also for the engineers at destination.

Terms of sale

In the context of transport and shipping, the terms of sale of a contract or purchase order should define clearly the respective responsibilities of the supplier and the buyer. Internationally recognized terms, known as 'Incoterms', have been devised and published by the International Chamber of Commerce (see ICC, 1990). These Incoterms provide a concise formula which enable a buyer and seller to specify and agree their contractual relationship. Examples of commonly used Incoterms are as follows:

- EXW. This stands for 'ex-works'. Under this arrangement, the supplier's responsibility ends when the goods are ready to leave his warehouse or manufacturing plant. The main project contractor must arrange and pay for loading and collection and for all subsequent actions and risks involved in getting the goods to the project site.

- FOB. This Incoterm means 'free on board' at a named port, defined literally as when the goods pass over the ship's rail. The supplier's responsibility ends at the point when the goods pass into the hands of the carrier or the carrier's agent. An FOB supplier will often ask the project freight forwarder to provide the FOB services for the sake of continuity.

In a project which involves a number of different suppliers it could be that the terms agreed will vary from one supplier to another. It is always important that the agreed terms of sale for each particular order are clearly indicated on all the relevant contract documents.

Documentation

The preparation, organization and administration of project documentation is another vital part of any project which has to be accommodated in the planning process. Although overall control would normally rest with the project manager, the freight forwarder has a significant contribution to make in the production and presentation of all documents associated with transport and shipping. The most important elements in this context are the shipping instructions for each supplier and the various shipping documents needed to control movements, satisfy port and customs authorities, and provide a means for reporting and controlling progress.

Delivering these documents between the various parties to contracts is an important facet of document administration. Freight forwarders operate their own courier services for this purpose. Hard copy (paper) documents remain a vital part of project administration, but the use of electronic data interchange (EDI) or 'paperless trading' is coming to be recognized as providing a faster, more accurate method of transferring information between the relevant parties.

Packing

The packing of goods for shipment overseas has three main objectives:

1   To protect the goods against loss, deterioration or damage.
2   To facilitate handling.
3   To provide proper marking for identification.

Packing methods vary widely and will largely, but not exclusively, depend upon the intended mode of transport. Goods going by air, where weight is a crucial factor and handling less rigorous, will not normally require to be packed as substantially as, for example, goods having to be loaded into and shipped in the hold of an ocean-going vessel. Cartons, rather than crates, are more likely to be used for airfreight consignments. However, the choice of packing method must also take into consideration all the elements of a journey, including handling facilities and any localized transport risks (such as poor roads to the project site). The need to limit packing costs must be weighed against the need to protect the goods and, also, against any special requirements of insurance companies (whose premiums might reflect the method of packing).   *373*

Liaison between the supplier, the packer and the project manager is vital, to ensure that the proper instructions are issued, that they are understood, and that they are correctly carried out.

The use of ISO containers where sea shipments are concerned can solve many problems for the project manager. Containers can reduce the need for expensive packaging, cut down pilferage, and make consignment consolidation and handling much easier. Containers can also provide a short-term storage facility at remote sites where goods cannot be used immediately upon their arrival or stored elsewhere. The limitations of containers include cargo size restrictions and, in some cases, difficulties on site if there is no equipment suitable for discharging the containers.

Packing a variety of goods into a container is a specialized skill, which the project freight forwarder will have. Stowing a safe and balanced load, which will remain stable and level during lifting and avoid risk to the contents, takes experience and planning. Containers can be placed at suppliers' premises, allowing the cargo to be loaded directly into the container and then transported to its final destination without being disturbed *en route*. Highly delicate equipment can be loaded, and subsequently unloaded at its destination, by specialists provided by the manufacturer.

If door-to-door container services are not possible, different packing criteria are required to take account of additional handling activity and exposure.

Projects often involve the transportation of large fabrications that are impracticable to pack. These will need timber ties and bracings to facilitate handling. Safe lifting points must be provided and clearly indicated in such cases.

Dangerous goods, such as some chemicals, corrosive substances, or items with flammable or explosive characteristics, are all subject to international transport regulations. These define acceptable package design in accordance with United Nations regulations and limit the quantities that may be carried in the same unit. Separate regulations apply according to the mode of transport (IMDG for sea, ADR for road and ICAO for air). Specialized knowledge is required in understanding and applying these regulations. This expertise is particularly important when a shipment will involve more than one mode of transport during its journey from supplier to final destination.

Airfreight

Generally speaking it will be mainly lightweight goods or those of a particularly fragile nature that will be intentionally programmed for airfreight despatch. The tare weight of the packaging has to be kept to a minimum in order to avoid unnecessarily increasing the total weight on which the freight costs are calculated. At the same time, the packaging has to be consistent with safety and able to withstand the handling to which the package will be subjected throughout transit.

To this end many types of standard size cartons are marketed. These are constructed of two- or three-ply corrugated cardboard and have immense integral strength but remain vulnerable to an external blow such as an ineptly operated fork-lift. Lightweight plywood panel cases built on to a strong base are a

374

more expensive alternative with a higher survival rate, particularly on the final leg from airport of discharge to the project site, and are more likely to deter the pilferer than a carton which can easily be opened up with a knife.

Care should be taken to ensure that case dimensions are acceptable to the air carrier. On most international routes there are freighter aircraft operating, but occasionally there will be a requirement to move a consignment at a time, or to a place, served only by passenger aircraft where cargo has to be stowed in the belly-hold. Even with freighter aircraft, the loading of a large case can present problems. The door size may permit access but the other case dimensions have to be within the limits dictated by the curved fuselage, otherwise it would not be possible to turn and manoeuvre the case down inside the cabin to the required stowage position.

Case markings

Cases can be specially marked for a variety of reasons but markings are essentially used to identify:

1 The port of offloading together with the final destination.
2 The contents of the case through the medium of an order number with project prefix reference. For goods which may be potentially attractive to villains there is merit in avoiding declaring the contents on the exterior of packages.
3 The hazardous nature of the contents, supplemented by obligatory warning labels.
4 Dimensions, and gross and net weights: not always shown but nevertheless very useful for checking packages against a written specification, and also to indicate the appropriate capacity of handling gear to be used.

In a project shipping programme, where goods are being despatched to a destination already used by the same company, it is advisable to instruct suppliers and forwarders to give prominence to the project reference and to apply an additional distinguishing mark which will be unique and immediately recognized by port workers, transport contractors and all others concerned. This mark would usually be in colour in the form of a diamond, square, circle or cross, and the project reference is frequently shown within this symbol.

Specially printed labels, bearing the project reference prefix with space to insert the purchase order number, are also recommended and these can be colour-coded in agreement with the project manager to provide for segregated delivery of varying categories of materials to the required locations on the construction site. Such labels are always useful to have for dealing with the occasional case which is found to be insufficiently or incorrectly marked prior to shipment.

Those persons involved in handling freight also appreciate an indication of unusual centre of gravity. The wording 'Heavy This End' can help to avoid accidents, quite apart from damage to goods.

Transport arrangements

Upon being told by the purchasing or shipping department that a particular order is ready at the supplier's premises, the freight forwarder initiates one of the following processes, depending upon the terms of purchase:

1 *Ex works (EXW)*. He arranges for transport to collect the goods for delivery to the port of loading, inland container depot (ICD) or forwarder's warehouse for grouping with other goods for the same project.
2 *Free on board (FOB)*. He instructs the supplier to deliver the goods to the port or depot (having first obtained confirmation of space booking on the required sailing) or to the warehouse for groupage.

For goods delivered direct to the port or ICD the supplier is given a booking reference to include in his own delivery documentation. This is normally a standard shipping note, the format of which is multipurpose and contains many details which will be repeated on the bill of lading.

Goods received into the forwarder's warehouse would generally be relatively small items for repacking into larger containers prior to redelivery to the port or ICD, or for airfreight despatch, or to be held for examination by an inspecting agency. It is quite common for such inspection to be made a precondition of shipment by overseas parties who require to be satisfied as to the quality and/or quantity of goods, and this is particularly the case where a government has some interest in the enterprise.

On delivery of goods to the ocean or air carrier, the forwarder completes a bill of lading or an airwaybill. This shows the names and addresses of the exporter, final consignee and (usually) the clearing agent at the port or airport of discharge. Also shown are the description, weight and measurements of the consignment and the case markings. These would include the project order numbers and such other item references which may be required by the shipper or consignee to ensure correct identification of specific packages or crates. These documents constitute a contract of carriage, when signed on behalf of the carrier as confirmation that the shipment has been duly loaded on the nominated vessel or flight. The documents therefore give title to the goods when presented to the carrier's agent at the destination.

In liaison with his principals, the forwarder is frequently required to transmit shipping documents to the consignee or his clearing agent. A typical set of such documents would comprise:

1 Original bill of lading or airwaybill
2 Original supplier's invoice, plus copies.
3 Packing specifications.
4 Certificates of origin, as required by the customs authorities at the port of discharge. (These certificates can be prepared by the freight forwarder from particulars given in the supplier's invoice. Depending on the statutory requirements of the destination country these particulars are certified by an approved chamber of commerce, and then 'legalized' by the appropriate consulate or embassy.)

5   Insurance certificates, or other acceptable evidence that the goods have been covered, together with the premiums paid.

Alternatively, these documents may be required for negotiation through a bank, where a Letter of Credit facility exists to guarantee payment for the goods.

On discharge of the consignment at the port or aiport of destination declared on the bill of lading or airwaybill, delivery will be given to the carrier's agent against presentation of the bill of lading or airwaybill and payment of any landing charges. Release of the goods from the port area, however, would normally be subject to approval of the customs clearance document. This document is usually prepared by the consignee's clearing agent, who probably also has the responsibility for forwarding the goods by road or rail to the project site.

Customs formalities vary considerably and many countries have complicated entry and clearance procedures. These are best delegated to an import broker or to the import clearance department of the consignee's agent.

On taking delivery, the clearing agent must satisfy himself that the goods covered by the bill of lading or airwaybill are correct in all respects and undamaged. If not, he must qualify the receipt given to the carrier with details of any visual damage and notify the local insurance interests. In the case of severe damage, it may be prudent to have the goods surveyed by a local insurance surveyor nominated by the insurance company. The operation of taking delivery, examination and transfer to the customs area for clearance may be observed and reported on by a shore superintendent. Details of the materials received would be sent to the project site in preparation for their subsequent arrival.

Onforwarding to final destination is undertaken either by project site management, using their own or hired transport, or is delegated to the clearing and forwarding agent at the port of entry to organize. If onforwarding is by rail a series of additional handlings may be involved in transferring goods from the port area to railway depot, with subsequent handling from rail wagons to vehicles for eventual site delivery. At all handling stages goods will be at risk of damage or pilferage. Maximum supervision is necessary to ensure that correct receipts are given so that the appropriate party can be held responsible in case of need. The forwarding agent's duties would be to:

* Arrange for transport to remove goods or containers from the quay or the carrier's depot.
* Prepare on-carriage documentation.
* Supervise the loading of vehicles or rail wagons.
* Prepare transit customs documents and manifests (if the project site is across an international border).
* Defray inland freight charges.
* Advise project site management in advance of the delivery, with full details of the goods.

In undertaking these duties the freight forwarder is at all times acting on behalf of his principal, who is ultimately responsible for paying charges. The freight   *377* forwarder's liability is limited by his terms of trading. These include provisions to protect himself from the consequences of actions by carriers, subcontractors or others involved in the transit of goods over which he does not have direct physical control. Frequently the freight forwarder finds himself caught up in disputes between the cargo interest and the carrier, but his allegiance must be to his principal.

The freight forwarder can be remunerated through varying arrangements. He can make agreed charges for the specific services provided (for example, booking cargo space, compiling shipping documents, and so on). Under arrangements which are possibly more suited to project shipping he could negotiate a lump sum payment, or a fixed charge for each individual purchase order handled (with disbursements recovered at cost). The laws of fair trading prevent the operation of any cartel regulating charges made by UK freight forwarders, and as a consequence this section of the business community has become highly competitive.

In the case of very large projects, involving the discharge of substantial quantities of cargo from ocean going vessels, it used to be the practice to appoint a 'shore superintendent'. Acting on behalf of the project manager, he provided an independent interface between the carrier, the forwarder and local services. This practice has become less frequent, the role now more commonly being split between the various parties. However, there remains an argument for keeping such a person in place on large projects to safeguard the interests of all those involved.

COMMUNICATIONS

Communications are vital to the whole process of project shipping, not simply during the passing of messages between the forwarders and their opposite numbers at the destination, but over the whole programme of events from the initial ordering of goods to their arrival on site.

The freight forwarder plays the vital role of 'information broker'. In this he is helped by the use of EDI (electronic data interchange, a system of passing messages and instructions through the supply chain using digital datalinks). An integrated communication system, to which all parties are linked, substantially reduces the risk of errors and speeds up the process of passing information. In less sophisticated environments, the fax machine has become an indispensable tool for enabling information to be communicated to all those who need it.

For messages received from suppliers or manufacturers it is usually preferable to use telex or facsimile, so that written proof is generated. In the world of shipping and forwarding it is paramount that the written word is kept on file.

At all levels of the production, packing, shipping and final delivery stages good communications can speed the flow of work, minimize delays and allow corrective action to be taken when necessary. The aim must be to keep all parties fully informed, even when the news is bad. It is better to be advised of a production delay, short shipment of a piece of equipment with a critical delivery deadline, or the dropping of a crate into the waters of the harbour, rather than have everyone find out the hard way.

CONTINGENCY

Regardless of planning and the best professional control throughout the operation, there will be occasions when one or more points in the delivery cycle are interrupted, usually with minimal warning. Industrial disputes at source of supply or at the construction site, or misadventure in transit, can have a serious effect with imponderable knock-on consequences. Although the circumstances are generally outside the control of the project management, the heavy commitment in terms of finance and manpower dictates that a contingency plan should be agreed in basic form in advance, be it additional storage space for goods supplied ex works, or alternative means of export shipment.

The decision to put a contingency plan into operation is never easy, as invariably it attracts higher costs. The tendency is therefore to sit out the dispute for a while and wait on developments. Unfortunately such a policy can aggravate matters and the freight forwarder finds himself seeking shipping alternatives in a carrier's market at inflated rates.

Airfreight is an obvious alternative as means of delivery if the dispute affects ports or deep-sea shipping services and, from the wide selection of freighter aircraft employed across the world, an air broker can obtain price indications and take out options on whatever availability may be on offer. The aircraft finally 'fixed' must, of course, be suitable for the task which the freight forwarder and air broker can evaluate between them. The weights and dimensions of pieces, their 'stowability' within the aircraft, equipment necessary to load and offload the cargo, and the availability of suitable handling equipment at the airport of destination are all elements requiring detailed examination before commitment to an air charter. The project forwarder, either directly to the air carrier or through an air charter broker, can establish the availability of aircraft in a matter of minutes via modern communications systems. A fax or telex confirmation by the carrier and the cargo interest forms the basis of an Air Charter Agreement which, by universal custom, calls for payment prior to flight departure.

The short notice at which a flight or series is arranged in support of an emergency normally dictates that the project managers resign themselves to paying for the round trip. But occasionally there are opportunities to broke the return 'empty leg', subject to there being no objection raised by the national carrier of the country concerned, thus facilitating the granting of traffic rights. However, generally speaking, revenue derived from an empty leg makes only a small contribution. The organizational effort is regarded by many as disproportionate to the benefit and possibly jeopardizing the performance of the succeeding flight.

Contingency planning should also take into account the otherwise orderly processes that stand to be disrupted. If goods are being supplied by the manufacturer on FOB terms and he has elected to arrange his own delivery to the port, the shipping departments of the manufacturer and the project manager must be able to pre-empt the situation and implement alternative delivery instructions. These may call for diversion to a different port of loading, to an inland container depot for movement to the continent, to an international airport, or to the freight *379* forwarder's storage facility depending on the decision taken and success of alternative fixtures. For goods supplied on ex works terms, the project forwarder may find himself required to organize additional storage space, regardless of the overseas despatch method, because the manufacturer is unwilling to allow the goods to remain on his premises in space needed for other purposes, or because he wants to realize payment for the goods against their delivery.

There are, of course, endless permutations of the circumstances and of the remedial actions which can be taken. As with planning, the essential feature is close liaison between all the parties concerned coupled with a clear mandate from the principal defining areas of responsibility and lines of communication. An emergency air charter might be organized in exemplary fashion but, if the freight controller in charge of final delivery at the destination has not been properly advised in advance, time will be lost while road transport and materials handling equipment is moved to the arrival airport. If such delays hold up unloading of the aircraft high demurrage charges could be incurred.

INSURANCE

Marine insurance is a vast and complex subject. The following account describes its application to project shipping.

Responsibility to insure

For goods purchased on ex works or free-on-board (FOB) terms the buyer arranges transit insurance of the goods. Goods supplied on CIF terms (cost of goods, insurance and freight) are insured by the seller unless otherwise agreed.

There is an anomaly with FOB sales because legal title to the goods does not pass to the buyer until they are loaded on to the vessel or delivered to the carrier's shore-based facility. The supplier should, therefore, insure the goods fully up to the point at which the risk technically passes to the buyer.

Many foreign governments are able to insist that the insurance of goods delivered to their countries is placed with locally registered insurance companies (usually state controlled). This frequently dictates that purchases are made on ex works terms, as a supplier would not accept the risk of insuring outside his own country.

In Chapter 8 the subject of insurance is treated in its wider application to project work, and we repeat here the advice that there is an advantage in placing transit insurance with the same insurer who covers the risks of construction and erection at the project site. Should any damage be discovered to equipment during erection, it may not be possible to determine exactly when the damage occurred. The project manager will want to avoid a situation where two insurance companies, one responsible for shipping and the other for erection, each refuse to meet a claim on the grounds that the damage cannot be proven to have taken place while the goods were covered by their policy.

Scope of insurance

For most project accounts, an 'all risks – warehouse to warehouse' cover is contracted through an insurance broker who places the risk with an underwriter at Lloyd's. The total amount held covered must not be less that the insurable value of goods destined for the project on board any one vessel, or aircraft. Otherwise only a proportional settlement can be obtained in the event of total loss.

The contract of insurance will be given a reference specifically identifying the cover with the project, and will probably have an agreed schedule of percentage rates regulated to the nature of the various commodities to be shipped. High-risk goods such as fragile electronics will be charged at top rate, steel girders at a low rate, and (depending on the location of the project and the route) the underwriter may encourage specialist packing in exchange for a reduced level of rates.

The 'warehouse to warehouse' scope is intended to cover every aspect of transit through to the project site, including retention of cover while goods are held in a forwarder's warehouse or carrier's depot. There is normally a time limit placed beyond which the cover would expire unless the insurers were notified. Declarations of individual consignments despatched against such 'all risks' cover are usually made in summary form 'per vessel' or 'per flight', detailing:

1 Purchase order number.
2 Class of goods, as defined in the contract of insurance (for example, 'fragile' or 'hazardous').
3 A brief description of the packing method.
4 Value for insurance purposes.
5 Name of the vessel.
6 Sailing date.
7 Intended port of discharge.

Inaccuracies in particulars given on the declaration could lead to a disputed claim in the event of loss or damage. Care must be taken to make a full and correct entry for each consignment. Responsibility for lodging declarations with the insurer could be assumed by the project contractor, acting as overall exporter, or it could be delegated to the freight forwarder. The forwarder already has the necessary information from the documents in his possession and from the shipping or flight arrangements which he makes.

For some overseas destinations the customs at the port of discharge require a declaration of the CIF (cost of goods, insurance and freight) value to supplement the import entry. This declaration can be in the form of a CIF certified invoice, which the exporter (or forwarder) would compile. The insurance element would be calculated from the agreed schedule of rates. This system is often required when the insurance cover is contracted abroad, and under these conditions the insurance declarations themselves have to be filed abroad. Here again is a service which can be performed by the freight forwarder's office or agency in the destination country.

The current cargo insurance policy is known as the 'MAR' policy. This *381* incorporates the findings of the technical and clauses committee of the Institute of London Underwriters, following the *Report on Marine Insurance*, United Nations Conference on Trade and Development, 1978. The MAR policy became obligatory in 1983.

Cargo insurance claims

There are three distinct aspects of cargo claims. These are:

1 Total loss.
2 Partial loss.
3 Damage in transit.

Settlement of a total loss claim is the insured value of the goods, while partial loss claims are dealt with on a proportional basis. Claims for damage in transit can be time consuming and require that precise attention is paid to the collation of supporting documents as the onus to prove damage rests with the claimant.

If there is visible evidence of damage when the goods arrive at the clearing agent or final destination, the receipt for the goods given to the carrier must be qualified by a written statement to the effect that the goods are damaged. A copy of the receipt must be retained by the recipient of the goods. Unless this is done, the carrier can maintain that a 'clean receipt' was given, which would limit his liability and impede the settlement process in the event of a claim.

If goods are found to be damaged on receipt they should be surveyed as prescribed in the terms of the insurance cover or policy and a report obtained. The consignee must concurrently address letters of reserves to the carrier (or carriers, if ocean and inland transport were employed to achieve delivery). These letters hold the carriers responsible for the damage caused, and reserve the right to claim from them in due time. The carrier, in order to protect his position as required by the insurers, will probably reply repudiating any liability.

A typical claim for damage to goods against a cargo insurance policy would require the following documents:

1 The insurance policy or copy of memorandum.
2 The invoice relevant to the damaged goods.
3 The original bill of lading, consignment note, airwaybill or other document of carriage.
4 The survey report (described above).
5 A copy of the claim sent to the carrier, together with his reply.

The insurance underwriter will settle the insured value (or a negotiated proportion if there is a discrepancy in the proof supplied) through the broker's claims department. Most project managers will elect to stipulate 'claims payable in the United Kingdom' (or in their own country) as this simplifies the reordering process. A 'claims payable abroad' basis is obviously undesirable but this occasionally has to be accepted if the insurance cover is held (by decree) in the destination country. Technically the reordering or replacement of damaged goods would have to proceed regardless of the prospects for settlement by overseas insurers in order to get the project finished. Another difficulty in using overseas insurers is the possibility that fluctuations in exchange rates could put true settlement figures at risk.

CONCLUSION

Packing and shipping form the last links in a chain of procurement activities which begin with the specification of goods and equipment needed for the project and end with their safe arrival on site. Being at the end of the procurement chain, shipping dates are subject to the cumulative delays and programme slippages of all preceding activities. There is often a degree of urgency needed to get the goods transported as quickly as possible to their destination. And yet any haste in packaging, or in the preparation of vital shipping documents can, if carried out wrongly, put the safety of goods at risk and lead to avoidable delays at ports, airports and frontiers. International shipping has to be a team effort, and the project manager will want to be reassured that the members of that team, wherever they are, are properly experienced and competent.

As part of the project shipping team, a freight forwarder in the exporting country, complemented by his counterpart at the destination, can make a very important contribution to the efficient delivery of goods and materials. The freight forwarder therefore makes a positive contribution to project progress and efficiency. There are over 3 000 freight forwarding companies in the United Kingdom, many of whom are equipped to handle complex shipping programmes through worldwide connections. Many are specialists in their own fields, or in the range of commodities which they handle. One thing which they all share is enthusiasm for their chosen profession, which is (without doubt) one of the most absorbing possible.

FURTHER READING

Croner's Reference Book for Exporters, Croner Publications, New Malden, Surrey, UK (by subscription, updated monthly).

Croner's Reference Book for Importers, Croner Publications, New Malden Surrey, UK.

Croner's World Directory of Freight Conferences, Croner Publications, New Malden, Surrey, UK (by subscription, updated monthly).

Export Education Packages, Formecon Services Ltd, Crewe, CW1 1YN, UK.

ICC, INCOTERMS 1990, ICC Publication 460, International Chamber of Commerce, Paris.

ORGANIZATIONS

British International Freight Association, Redfern House, Browells Lane, Feltham, Middlesex, TW13 7EP.

Export departments of the major clearing banks.

Technical Help to Exporters, British Standards Institution, Linford Wood, Milton Keynes, Buckinghamshire, MK14 6LE.

Part Six

COMPUTERS IN PROJECT MANAGEMENT

23 Computer Programs for Network Analysis – 1

K&H Project Systems Ltd

It is not easy to carry out the amount of calculation implied by the resource allocation techniques described in Chapter 18 without enlisting the aid of a computer. If one is going to use a computer, one might as well make full use of it and allow it to suggest a complete resource schedule.

The time analysis of networks above a certain size and complexity can be handled faster by computer equipment. The results will tend to be more reliable. They will be free of calculation errors (although the planner will still have to watch out for data errors). A computer program will apply a consistent set of rules to a project network. Providing that the planner can predict how his program will react to any given combination of circumstances, he can use it as a precise tool for evaluating initial network plans. More importantly, it can be used to show the effect of progress when the project is under way, and the effect of variations and additions when the project scope changes.

There is a wide range of computer programs on the market capable of carrying out these kinds of calculation. The programs vary enormously in price and in usefulness. These two aspects are not necessarily co-related.

Programs vary as to which computer equipment they require. Such machinery itself varies dramatically in price and capacity. It is possible to obtain a computer program for a few hundred pounds to carry out critical path analysis; at the other extreme, products exist which are marketed at prices of more than £1 million.

Computers capable of carrying out the necessary calculations have an even greater price range, starting at about £100 pounds, with practically no upper limit to the price that could be paid.

Such vast price ranges imply great differences in the characteristics of the products in question.

COMPUTER HARDWARE

Factors affecting hardware costs

The main factors affecting the cost of the computer equipment will be:

1 How many simultaneous users can be handled.
2 Memory size – possibly affecting the maximum network size which can be computed.
3 Speed of peripheral devices. Disk storage access speed will affect calculation speed. Printer speed will affect report production speed.
4 Number of specialized display devices available: automatic drawing equipment, colour screen displays.
5 Size of disk storage. This affects the amount of information available 'on-line' with minimal delay.
6 Communication capability with other computers.
7 Hardware maintenance costs and reliability.

Hardware performance per unit cost is increasing all the time. It is, however, possible to use up additional hardware capability by careless or inefficient software design much faster than engineers can produce faster computers. Do not believe the 'just get a bigger machine' line, particularly if it is the hardware manufacturer who is persuading you to use inefficient software. He may have an ulterior motive.

Every company has a different view of the relative advantages of central and of local computing. At one extreme there is the gigantic number-cruncher buried beneath a mountain in Wales, with large numbers of wires leading from it to hundreds of users scattered over the country or, via satellite links, the world. At the other extreme is the microcomputer sitting on the desk of every user.

A single central computer makes integration of information and systems easier. Individual machines give each user control of his own facilities, and avoid conflicts in the assignment of priorities for the use of machine time. Various compromise solutions are possible. Local machines may be able to handle a few simultaneous users, and so allow more than one person to access the same body of information at one time. The local machines may be able to pass information down a wire to the central facility.

The larger the memory of a computer, the larger the network a given piece of software will be able to handle, up to a certain limit determined by the software itself and by the addressing structure of the computer. Memory comes in two popular flavours, 'real' and 'virtual'. The more of the computer's memory that is real and the less that is virtual, the faster will be the computation speed of the machine. Some machines provide memory to multiple simultaneous users by using virtual instead of real memory, others do not have the possibility of using virtual memory, and need enough real memory to be able to service the maximum number of users envisaged at any one time. Different computer programs need different amounts of memory when they are in use, so that both the number of users and the efficiency of the software as regards the use of memory must be considered when deciding how much memory is required by a particular installation.

Disks

Disk speed has a strong influence on the time necessary to perform a calculation. In the terms used in this chapter, the word 'disk' refers to 'hard' disks, which are used for the storage of online information rather than to 'floppy' disks, which should only be used for information transfer between computers, or to hold information copied from a hard disk for security purposes.

The speed of the disks seems to be one of the important dividing points at the moment between so-called mini- and microcomputers. The time taken to fetch a piece of information from the disk, which is used to store network information, and also for intermediate working storage during computation, directly affects the time elapsed for computer operations. In addition to this effect, virtual memory (mentioned earlier) is implemented by rolling information in and out of main memory from and to disk. The disk speed therefore affects the processing speed if virtual memory is being used. The number of reading mechanisms on the disk equipment can be critical when many users are active on the computer at the same time. These arms can be constantly in motion from the areas of interest to one user to the areas of interest to another. Such 'thrashing' of disk arms can slow down processing for all users dramatically.

Printers

Printers vary greatly in speed and in price. The speed of slower models is generally measured in characters per second. Faster printers are often quoted in lines per minute. The very fast laser printers now available usually have their print speed quoted in feet per second of output.

Amongst the slower printers, the most popular printing methods are by 'dot matrix', whose quality tends to be inversely proportional to its speed, and by 'daisy wheel' which tends to produce slow but high quality output. Ink-jet printers can combine reasonable speed with good quality output.

The speed of printing can be a significant factor in the delay between a planner ordering a recalculation of a network, and his receiving the results. One user, having switched from K&H Project Systems' IBM mainframe program PREMIS to the K&H CRESTA system on a super-microcomputer complained about the relatively slower speed of the second system. Upon investigation, it turned out to be the slower speed of the printer on the small computer, compared with the very fast printer on the mainframe that was the cause of the problem. The answer was to find a faster printer for the super-micro and attach two of them to the machine, so that two reports could be produced simultaneously.

Screens

Visual display units (VDUs) used for the input and display of information have a *389* range of capabilities and features. Very simple screens may not be capable of graphical output. Others may or may not have the capability for reverse video display, making fields blink, and the like. Some screens have colour capability. Both the screens themselves and the program driving them must have the particular feature for it to be usable by the planner. Some of the most powerful terminals are almost small computers in themselves, and can for example accept a network drawing, and from that point onwards carry out automatic panning, zooming and windowing to display parts of the network on request without further troubling the main computer, until a new network or network section is requested.

After allowance has been made for the operating system of the computer, any virtual memory paging areas that may be necessary, and for the project management programs themselves, enough disk space must remain to be able to store the network information.

Different project management programs use very different amounts of disk storage to hold each activity. Database systems also vary considerably in the amount of disk space taken up for a given amount of data. One must allow room for the maximum likely amount of network data, and should bear in mind what must be C. Northcote Parkinson's nth law . . . that information grows to fill and overflow the disk space allocated to it.

It is not always easy to transmit information from one computer to another, especially if they come from different manufacturers. Even the 'standard' interfaces such as RS232 are less standard than one would wish, and the programs which are used at each end of the connecting wire to send and to receive information often use different protocols. If one program passes some information and says 'After you, Cecil' where the receiving program is expecting 'After you, Claude' an uncomfortable silence will ensue.

The speed of passing information down a wire from one computer to another is measured as a 'baud rate'. The faster the rate, the greater probability of error. The greater the amount of error checking that is carried out by the computers at each end of the wire, the slower the transmission process. Satisfactory error-free transmission procedures can make the passing of data a very slow and painful process.

If the two computers in question have removable disks, tapes or cassettes which are compatible in their data recording methods, it may be more satisfactory to send such media through the post rather than to attempt direct transmission.

Plotters

Automatic drawing equipment also varies tremendously in speed and price. Electrostatic plotters are much faster than other models, but their quality is not always as good. They do not produce coloured output, and may need special paper. Pen plotters may have multiple pens of different colours; they vary in speed and in precision. Precision is not generally an important factor in project management outputs, which are generally not drawn to scale.

The drawing area of cheaper plotters may be limited, so that a network has to be drawn in several sections and glued together afterwards.

Hardware maintenance

The costs of maintaining the chosen computer should not be forgotten. Typical rates vary around 10 per cent per annum of the list price of the equipment. It is worth checking with existing users of the equipment what speed of response is provided by the agent or manufacturer in case of operational failures, and how often such problems occur.

Is it blue?

Some companies suffer from centrally decided policies which dictate that computing hardware should only be purchased from one particular manufacturer. This will obviously subject the user's choice of equipment to very constrained limits.

SOFTWARE

General software factors

Practical considerations can short-cut the software selection process. If computer facilities already exist, and are easily accessible, it may just be a matter of discovering whether a program has already been acquired. If not, or if that program is inadequate, the first step might be to find out what programs are available for the computer equipment which is currently installed.

Computer manufacturers maintain catalogues of programs which have been made commercially available for their equipment. Organizations such as INTER-NET in Europe or PMI in America can advise on what may be available, or point out the main companies who supply software for project management. The names and addresses of some relevant software companies are given at the end of Chapter 24.

Even if the planner does have access to a large company computer with an appropriate program, he should consider that he will be sharing a facility with other users. He will not necessarily have the highest priority among them. Before committing himself to use the locally available facilities, he should experiment to see whether delays in computer access or in calculation time when using this equipment are acceptable in the context of the project he is controlling.

It may be better to acquire a small computer completely under his own control, rather than to rely upon a large shared facility. The wider range of possible machines under these circumstances will imply a wider selection of computer programs. Many programs are only available for a restricted range of computer equipment. The planner will wish to choose a combination of hardware and software appropriate to his situation.

Consider in a little more detail some of the factors which affect the choice of *391* software package. Many of the categories already summarized will overlap a little. Capacity and speed, for example, are interrelated in that a theoretical ability to handle networks of many activities may in fact be unusable because long calculation times make the analysis of large networks undesirable.

Program capability related to network size

The maximum network size which a computer program can handle may vary from a few tens of activities to millions. The limitation almost always applies to a single network. The user is allowed to have many independent networks, but no one of them may exceed (say) 2 000 activities. The limit on the number of activities per network is generally determined by the computational algorithm used in the program and by the memory capacity of the computer. The larger the memory, generally, the larger the network which can be handled with a given computational method.

Sometimes, programs with a relatively low limit of network size will calculate network sections independently and then combine the results. Taking a very crude example, consider a network which divides itself into two distinct halves – say phase I and phase II of a project – whereby the connections between one part and the next run entirely through a single activity (perhaps a decision point as to whether or not to commence the second part at all). Then it is very easy to compute part I first, and then use the earliest finish of the end of part I as the project start of part II.

If there is a definite required end date to the project, as is so often the case, then that end date can be applied to part II of the project. The latest start of the first activity of part II can then be applied to part I as a required finish date. To express the computation of the network in critical path terms, please refer to Figure 23.1. Notice that three computational passes are required to calculate the two networks.

If a program must resort to this kind of 'subnetting' or 'interfacing' in order to be able to calculate a network of the required size, it will probably not be operationally efficient.

The number of passes of the data tends to grow rapidly as the number of independent network sections increases, and as the number of points of contact between them increases too. In general it is unwise to attempt to stretch the capacity of a program in this way. Better use a tool that will be adequate for the maximum network size envisaged. Allow an appropriate safety margin for the fact that networks tend to grow, particularly if there is a computer available to solve them (yet another of the countless corollaries of Parkinson's first law).

The above comments should not be taken as advice to avoid subnets and interfaces in general – only in those cases where they are forced upon the user by computer-related limitations. It may well be convenient to divide a project into subnets, provided that the computer program being used can take them in a single mouthful for calculation purposes. Generally, subnets can be numbered independently, so that the same activity number or event number can be used in two separate subnets without fear of confusion. This is particularly helpful when

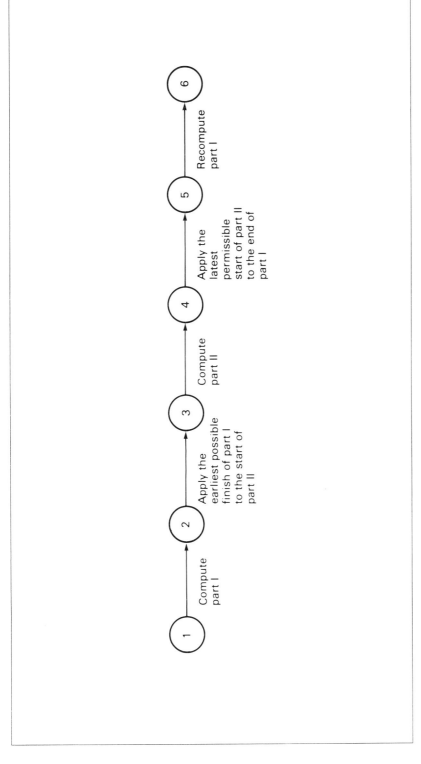

Figure 23.1 Network representation of computing stages required to calculate two subnetworks

By splitting a network up into a series of separate subnetworks it is possible (given a suitable divisibility of the main network) to overcome limitations of a computer program which can only cope with a relatively small number of activities in any one network or subnetwork. But this arrangement increases the amount of computational work for the computer, as shown in this example of just two subnetworks. I and II, which together form one larger network.

the same general pattern is repeated in different parts of an overall network – for example, the installation of pumps occurs many times in networks describing the construction of an oil refinery. It may be possible to duplicate one network and include it in many different places.

It may be convenient to assign responsibility for different network sections to different individuals, particularly if the network is large. Normally one will allocate a different range of possible activity numbers to each person responsible for a network section, but such schemes have been known to go awry. When they do, the logic is sometimes difficult to disentangle.

Where subnets are used, they must be able to connect at one or more points into the main network. These connection points are commonly called 'interfaces'. The activities which are identified as interfaces do share a common numbering system with the overall network, and so provide connections with it.

The fewer connection points for each subnet, the simpler will be the evaluation of paths which cross several subnets and hence perhaps more than one area of responsibility. If each planner working on a project has activities separated into his own individual subnet or subnets, he can more easily update the tasks under his control with progress information, without needing close coordination with his colleagues.

Many computer programs have a quoted limit of 32 000 events for activity-on-arrow networks, or 32 000 activities for precedence networks.

This particular figure is a common one because it arises as a consequence of a popular type of computer design. This design tends to group the fundamental 'binary bits' of which computer memory is constructed into sets of eight at a time. Two sets of eight make a conveniently sized storage medium for holding a sequential activity counter. Such a counter can count up to 32 767 easily, and with some difficulty can be persuaded to count up to double that figure. This is why many programs quote a theoretical limit of 32 000 or 64 000 activities. Nevertheless, the practical maximum network size may be well below this figure, either because a very large computer memory could be needed for the program in question to attain such a maximum, or because calculation time might be unacceptably long.

There may well be several capacity limitations to a given computer program. There may be different limitations on the network size which can be handled in resource analysis as opposed to time analysis. This is because different computational methods will be used for these two functions. There may be limits to the number of resources which can be processed per project, and limits to the number of resources which any one activity can be specified as using.

Software price factors

The main factors affecting the prices of computer programs are:

1 The maximum network size which can be computed.
2 The kind of data which can be handled (arrow, precedence, arrow and precedence, resources, costs, materials and other associated data).

3 The calculation features (time analysis, resource aggregation, resource smoothing, probabilistic analysis, cost performance analysis, and so on).
4 Flexibility of output reports, graphical presentation of results, and the like.
5 Ease of use (screen input, menus, special updating methods).
6 Speed (calculation speed, updating speed, report production speed).
7 Level of support provided to the user (documentation, training, 'hotlines').
8 Software maintenance costs and enhancement schemes.

Arrangements for numbering activities or events

One should look for possible limitations in the numbering schemes that the program allows for either precedence activities or for arrow events. Some programs will accept only numeric input for these fields. There are even still some programs which demand that a succeeding event has a higher number than its preceding events, so that a network must be numbered from left to right sequentially. This requirement produces less than ideal results when it is necessary to insert a new network section, or to expand an existing activity into more detail. It may also be relevant to look for limits to the number of characters which a program will allow the planner to use for an activity number. If this is small compared to the network size contemplated, then there will be a danger of using the same number twice inadvertently. If it is necessary to match the activity number with any existing numbering scheme – say, cost coding structures, work breakdown structures, or work-order numbers – then the activity numbering scheme must allow enough characters of information to accomplish this.

CHOICE BETWEEN ACTIVITY-ON-ARROW AND PRECEDENCE NETWORKS

When planners get together, a favourite topic for discussion is 'Which is the better technique – arrow or precedence?' Despite the many man-hours spent arguing this question no clear answer has emerged. An analogy could be drawn with different systems of religious belief. It is rare for a believer in one system to convert a believer from another system to his own faith.

If there is a clearly defined policy in an organization as to which planning technique must be used, then the computer program must be able to compute networks of this kind. Some programs are able to compute either precedence or arrow networks, at the user's option. A few programs are capable of calculating arrow and precedence networks simultaneously, or of computing 'mixed' networks, which may become more popular in the future. If a company contains strong believers in precedence networks, and also contains strong believers in arrow networks, it may avoid bloodshed to acquire a program capable of handling mixed networks. A main contractor may be able to accept all the different forms of network diagram used by his subcontractors if he can process mixed networks.

395

RESOURCE SCHEDULING FEATURES OF PROGRAMS

Resource aggregation

Resource aggregation is the accumulation of resource usage based on the results of time scheduling. It may be interesting to see what resources would be used if every activity were started at its earliest start (incidentally, beware of programs which claim to be capable of resource scheduling but which, in fact, can only carry out resource aggregation without being able to perform levelling).

A resource aggregation can show the amount of each resource required on each day of the project. Sometimes this will be best expressed cumulatively, particularly if the resource in question is money. The results should be available either in the form of a table, a series of printed, or plotted histograms, or a plotted curve.

It is sometimes a good idea, before carrying out the resource analysis of a project, to do a resource aggregation based on the earliest start of each activity, followed by another aggregation of resources used based on the latest starts. If it is anticipated that lack of resources will delay the project, these latest starts should be based on an estimate of the project completion date. The comparison of these two graphs will show the two extremes of probable resource usage. If they are close together, there is not much room for improvement by resource analysis.

Once the resource calculations have been done, the resulting resource schedule should lie somewhere in between the earliest and latest time aggregations. It should look much smoother than the time analysis-based results. The improvement over the earliest/latest case should show the amount of effective work the resource analysis process has carried out.

In cases where resources are effectively unlimited, and the goal is to produce a smooth utilization of resources, then one should look at the results of a resource aggregation based on earliest and latest starts to decide where to set the initial availabilities. Most resource smoothing programs will work reasonably well if the availability of every resource is specified as being zero for the entire project, but they work better if a positive but tight availability is allocated initially. This availability can be estimated by inspection of the resource aggregation tables.

Resource levelling features

If the planner wants to use automatic resource levelling, then the program chosen should be able to do this. Look for limits on the size of the resource code. Is it large enough to be meaningful, and instantly identifiable amongst the set of resources that might be used? Some programs insist that the amount of a resource used by an activity be expressed as a 'rate constant'. This implies that the amount of a resource used is broken down into a daily rate, and associated with the activity in this form. This is ideal for skilled trades, labour, machinery and the like, where it is easy and natural to say that a given activity requires 10 carpenters or 3 labourers or 1 crane throughout its duration. It is less natural to express a need for 1 000 cubic yards of concrete, or 100 man-hours of effort in these terms. Other programs demand that resource requirements be expressed as 'work-content' – that is, a total amount used by the activity. This is excellent for volumes of material, for example, but not a natural form for labour and machinery. The planner should be able to express the resource requirements in either way for each resource for each activity. Some computer programs allow for this.

Fractional resource amounts

Fractional resource amounts can be used when scheduling individual people who have different skills. A particular person may be required to attend to a given task which will only take up a certain percentage of his time. One way of dealing with this is for the different tasks needing the person's attention each to ask for a fraction of his time – his initial availability will be either one or zero at any one time unit. The same technique can be extended to handle a number of individuals with similar skills included under the same resource code. If the computer program will not accept fractional or decimal resource requirements, one can always scale up by a factor of (say) 100, so that the resource requirement is in terms of 1 per cent of a person per day (or time unit). Approximate planning for overtime can be carried out in this way – in the case of an individual, if he ends up being used at the level of 1.1 in a day, this can be interpreted as a need for about one hour's overtime on that day.

Complex resources

Activities are described as complex when they do not require a constant rate of resource usage throughout their durations. For example, an activity could need two bricklayers for 7 days, and then only one bricklayer for a further 3 days, so that the resource requirement throughout its 10-day duration is not constant. The planner may wish to plan in great detail, so that any change of resource usage during a process is taken care of by ending each activity and starting another every time there is a change in the resource usage. In such a case there is no need to be able to tell the program at what point in an activity a resource is required, or for how long. This kind of detailed planning tends to increase the number of activities in the network, but it keeps each activity much simpler.

Splittable activities

It is preferable to be able to define a process as one complex activity, rather than a series of sequential operations. One reason for this is associated with whether an activity can be discontinuous. If a complex task is expressed as a series of sequential operations, each of which uses resources, then an automatic scheduling system might well schedule one section of the task to start long after the end of the preceding section, if resources were not available in the mean time. The planner may wish the process to be carried out as a continuous sequence, either to avoid moving labour from one location to another, to avoid the loss of *397* concentration involved in the workers starting a task, stopping it, and restarting later, to minimize the amount of work or investment in-process, or for a variety of job-dependent reasons. Some programs allow an activity to be 'tied' to its predecessor as a way of producing this effect. Such features have drawbacks in that the sequence is not considered as a whole for scheduling. The tying of activities will sometimes cause resources to be used badly.

Many computer programs allow the user to mark each activity as 'splittable' or 'non-splittable'. A process to be carried out as a continuous sequence would therefore be coded as non-splittable, and its use of resources might well need to be specified in a complex manner; that is, for each resource used by the activity the planner would specify not only the code and the amount required, but also the number of days for which the resource was required and at what point within the activity duration.

It is valuable to be able to specify that activities can be split into sections if there is no significant penalty involved in so doing. Some programs contain facilities for the planner to control such splitting by specifying a minimum size section into which the activity may be divided, a maximum elapsed interval between the end of one section and the start of the next, a minimum size for the first section and/or for the last section. In general, 'serial' resource scheduling handles activity splitting better than 'parallel' methods, which work best if every activity can be split into single time units if necessary. If this capability is important to the project, it might be as well to know which candidate programs use the parallel and which the serial method.

In the early days of resource scheduling, activity splitting was the only way in which complex working shift situations could be expressed. In cases where, for example, three 8-hour shifts per day were available to carry out the project, some activities could be worked 24 hours per day, some 16 per day, and some only eight hours per day ... in prime shift. A resource levelling program with the capability of splitting activities could be persuaded to deal with this kind of situation. A 'prime shift' resource would be defined. The availability of this resource would be very large – say, the largest number the program would accept as an availability – during the eight hours of prime shift, but would be zero at other times. Any activity which had to be operated during prime shift only would have a requirement of one unit of this resource throughout its duration, and would be marked as being 'splittable'.

This technique produced reasonable results, but was not entirely satisfactory. Activities marked as being splittable in order to work the correct shifts tended to get split for other reasons too – the temporary lack of other resources – and jobs would become fragmented over time for no good reason. The time analysis float of such activities would be hard to interpret, as it would include large quantities of unusable second-and third-shift time. A number of inadequacies in reporting were experienced – computer programs were capable of showing each split section of an activity separately in a report. An activity working prime shift only would tend to appear in reports as many times as there were days covered by its duration unless special action was taken to prevent this.

Multiple calendars

Multiple calendars are used to overcome the problem of a project in which the workforce includes groups of people who work shifts in addition to others working a normal day. When the planner specifies the activity data, he states not only the duration, but also the calendar on which that duration is based. To illustrate and explain this point, a schedule could be prepared using three calendars as follows:

1   A calendar based on a 24-hour round-the-clock day of 3 shifts.
2   A calendar using two shifts, totalling 16 hours each day.
3   A calendar incorporating only one 8-hour shift each day.

In this example, an activity using people only working the single 8-hour shift would be coded as using calendar 3.

Activity float is expressed according to the calendar relevant to the activity, and so the time analysis float of such activities would be meaningful. The activity could still be coded splittable or not, relative to its own calendar. It would not be necessary for the program to generate a printable result for each day of the activity.

Multiple calendars are of use in many different situations – not only that of shift work. Working weeks of different lengths may affect a project. Some activities may be carried out in offices where a five-day week is worked, and others on-site where a six-day week is worked; a seven-day week may be appropriate for such activities as allowing concrete to cure.

In international projects, activities may have weekends located around Saturday rather than Sunday, or around Friday rather than Sunday (though rarely both, in the present political climate). Different countries have different patterns of national holiday. Some companies shut down altogether for two or three weeks in the year. Large projects involving consortia can involve the use of thirty or forty different calendars to account for all the different combinations.

Other practical considerations can be approximated by multiple calendars. Activities will be more or less affected by weather conditions. It is common to set up several 'weather' calendars one of which might show a six-day week in the summer, five-day weeks in spring and autumn, and four-day weeks in the winter, to approximate the effect of weather conditions on a certain type of activity. In extreme cases, the calendar might show a complete gap in the winter. Activities showing planned operations on oil-rigs in the North Sea are sometimes of this type, as certain tasks cannot be scheduled for times when the wave-height is likely to be above a certain threshold.

Totally irregular 'calendars' are sometimes worthwhile. Consider a network where progress has to be reviewed by a committee before certain tasks are undertaken. This can occur in local government work, where networks are used to express the procedures that must be undertaken before a section of new road is to be constructed, for example. If the committee meets on an irregular, but known, schedule, a calendar can be constructed which consists of only the dates *399* in that schedule. Activities requiring a decision from the committee are preceded by short activities based on the committee calendar, so that if all the other preceding necessary items have been completed just after a meeting, nevertheless the next step will be delayed until the next meeting occurs. It might even be possible to estimate the maximum number of decisions such a committee could take in one session, and express that as a resource availability – each activity requiring a decision could use up one unit of that resource! To enter further into the realms of fantasy, the resource availability could express the number of useful minutes of meeting time in each session, and the resource requirement of each activity might be the estimated time required to discuss it.

An additional example of an irregular calendar might occur in building work, where an architect has to inspect certain phases of the construction before they are covered up and become inaccessible. If the architect has a defined inspection schedule, then a job which misses one of those days will have to wait until the next before it can be continued. The architect's inspection schedule could be specified to the system as an irregular calendar in this case.

It can be dangerous to mix weekly time units with daily time units in a multi-calendar network when resource levelling is used. Depending on the procedure used by the computer program, a week on a weekly timescale may not be a full week, but may just cover the Monday. This will not matter greatly in the case of time analysis, but if the same resource is used by activities with both weekly and daily time units, one should take care that the weekly activity really uses the resource during the whole week. It may be necessary to multiply the durations of the weekly activities by the number of days per week, and treat them on a daily calendar. The same consideration can apply to mixing activities whose durations are expressed in terms of whole days with activities whose time units are in shifts or in hours.

One objection to the use of multiple calendars in networks is that float does not always remain consistent down a chain. Planners have been accustomed to selecting all the activities with zero float (or the maximum negative float, if targets have been used) for concentrated analysis in order to reduce the network duration. With a single calendar, this will isolate the entire critical path or paths in coherent chains. With multiple calendars this is not necessarily so.

It should be noted that an activity on the critical path can quite genuinely show a float greater than zero. The simplest example occurs when one considers a mixture of activities, some of which work a seven-day week, and others of which work a five-day week, say. If there is a sequence of three activities:

> A = pour concrete
> B = allow concrete to set
> C = lay railway lines

and C must follow B which must follow A, it is possible that activities A and C might use labour which works a five-day week, but B can occur on a seven-day week. If the project starts on a Monday, and the durations are: A = 6: B = 5: C = 6, then the project will end on the Monday of the fourth week. Activity A will start on the first Monday and finish at the end of the second Monday, and will have zero float. Activity B will start on the second Tuesday and finish at the end of the second Saturday. It will have a float of one day. Activity C will start on the third Monday, and will finish at the end of the fourth Monday.

In this example, if activity B happened to take six days instead of five, this would make no difference to the project duration. If activity B had a duration of four days, this would leave the project duration the same, but activity B would have a float of two days. It would also have a free float of two days. This gives a clue to one technique which can be used to complete the chains for float analysis purposes – the selection is done not on total float, but on a figure produced by subtracting the free float from the total float. This tends to include all necessary activities in the maximum float chain, but it will associate the activity at the end of each subchain with the activity it enters, rather than with the subchain to which it belongs. The analysis may have to be done separately for subcritical chains, if these are to be analysed at the same time as the critical chain.

It is helpful to have a key logic analysis feature when making extensive use of multiple calendars, where the float may change from activity to activity. In this feature, activities or events are picked out as key points of the network, and the computer is asked to select out all those chains which connect the events or activities in question. In the simplest case, chains connecting two points of the network which are on the critical path(s) can be selected out for examination.

It is, then, a good thing if one can define a complex activity, whose resource requirements change during its duration – either requiring different resources or different amounts of the same resources. If a complex activity is used to define a series of tasks which the planner wishes to schedule together as a coherent whole, then the amount of descriptive information that the program allows to be associated with an activity should be adequate for this purpose.

Pool resources

Pool resources differ from normal resources in that their availability is cumulative. If an amount of the resource is left unused at the end of one day, it becomes available for use on the following day. Resources available in this way are expressed as a series of lump amounts on particular dates. Pool resources are normally used either for consumable materials, like cement or bricks, or for money. For example, if there is a limited budget for a job, the available money can be made available in 'lumps' whenever the budget allows, and the activities will use up this money until none is left, at which point any further work will have to be delayed until the next cash inflow. Similarly, bricks are used up in construction, and any activity needing bricks may have to wait until the next delivery.

Pool resources generally feature in 'parallel' rather than 'serial' resource levelling schemes. This is one of the few advantages of parallel over serial levelling. Most of the effects of a pool resource can be simulated by using a normal resource, whose availability is specified in the same way as a pool resource, with individual 'deliveries' at specific times. The activities which would *401* normally need to use the pool resource do not mention this resource in their requirements. Instead, an extra activity with a duration of one time unit is inserted before the activity needing that resource, and the requirement is associated with the extra activity. The extra activity normally has no pre-decessors, so that it can occur at any time before its successor. It will then make sure that there is an allocation of the necessary money or materials before the succeeding activity begins. Sometimes activities are allowed to have negative availability, so that they can add in to the availability of a pool resource. This can be applied if deliveries of a consumable material are scheduled as activities in the network.

Delay start constant

A delay start constant is the maximum time that an activity can be delayed during the resource analysis process. Once this delay limit is reached, then the resource levels will have to be exceeded if necessary to meet the schedule. It is normally applied to activities that occur early in a project, in order to prevent them from using up all the project float during scheduling. This leaves some float for activities occurring later in the project. For example, in a project consisting of two phases, design and construction, if the design phase must be completed with very limited resources, it could use up much of the available float, causing scheduling problems in the construction phase. Delay start constants applied to the design activities will tend to limit this effect.

Imposed dates

Imposed dates have a variety of subtle differences. Most network analysis programs will contain a facility for ensuring that an activity's earliest start is not before a given fixed date. Similarly, one can usually specify that an activity's late finish must not be after a given fixed date.

A number of variations on this are possible. Simple and obvious variations that fix an activity's earliest finish as not being before a given date, or its late start as not being after a given date occur in some programs. More dangerous are features such as 'mandatory finish' dates. These occur when the project controller has determined that a particular key date in a network is going to be met. Such key events are sometimes known as: 'The sun will not rise tomorrow unless ...' events. In this case, the planner instructs the computer that the activity on which the mandatory finish is placed will happen on or before the specified date, even although the chain leading up to it contains negative float. The earliest start of the activity coming out of the mandatory finish will start at or before the mandatory finish date, even though the earliest finish of the preceding activity may be greater than the mandatory finish.

In some programs the 'Time now' date acts as an imposed start date on all uncompleted activities. One should be able to specify different 'Time now' dates for different sections of the network, or even individual activities if required.

When a planner is updating his network, it will probably take more than one day to extract progress reports for all the in-progress activities. In this case, the planner might choose an 'as of' date which is the notional date at which he is updating the network. All progress reports are related to that date. The updating process involves a certain amount of mental strain on the planner who has to consider not only how much time is required to finish the in-progress activity, but also how much time will be required to finish the activity on the 'as of' date chosen (or how much was required at that date, if it happens to be in the past). It is simpler to be able to give a date to the progress information which is the date at which it was current.

Some programs allow the user to place 'expected finish' dates on activities. After they have been reported as started, such activities automatically adjust their remaining duration so as to finish at the date specified. There is a temptation to forget about such activities altogether, and to sit back and let the computer carry on blindly reducing their remaining duration. However, used with sufficient caution, this feature can help to avoid the constant updating of durations on activities involving the delivery of materials, for example.

ORDER AND DELIVERY ACTIVITIES

Order and delivery activities are mainly concerned with the ordering and delivery of materials. Such activities may be associated with fairly large capital expenditure, or they could refer to bulky items. It is prudent, therefore, not to have these activities scheduled at their earliest start for two reasons:

1　The equipment could arrive on site long before it is needed, giving rise to storage and security problems.
2　Money is spent earlier than necessary, to the detriment of project cash flow.

Some systems allow the planner to mark delivery activities with a suitable code so that they 'slip' along their free float (i.e. towards the earliest start of the activity needing the equipment) during the time analysis calculations (see Figure 23.2).

In the calculation of arrow diagrams, one should mark dummy activities with the 'order and delivery' code, so that any dummy activity will pass its free float back to the preceding activity, where it is of more practical use, and where it should appear for reporting purposes.

ERROR DIAGNOSIS

No matter how sophisticated the program, the output produced will be meaning-less if the input data contains any significant error. Many of the program features described in this chapter are indeed sophisticated, and even more advanced techniques are discussed in Chapter 24. Among the most important features of any network analysis and resource scheduling program are its ability to detect and report input errors, in order that the planner can correct them. Of course, not all input errors can be recognized as such. If the planner inputs 100 weeks for an activity instead of 10 weeks, for example, the computer will not be able to tell him *403*

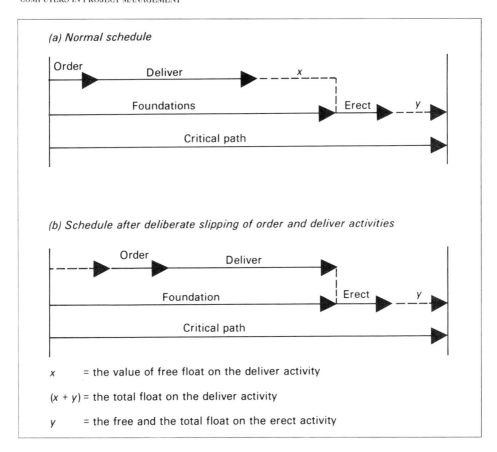

Figure 23.2 Scheduling of order and delivery activities

In the upper diagram the order and delivery activities have been scheduled at their earliest possible start dates, in the normal way. In the lower diagram, the computer has been informed by special input coding that these are order and delivery activities and it has slipped them as late as possible without affecting the float of their following activity (erect) in order that purchasing funds shall not be committed too early and that the goods or equipment is not scheduled for delivery to site until it is required.

why his critical path has come out almost two years longer than expected! What the computer is able to do is analyse the network logic, to ensure that there are no unexplained discontinuities or feedback loops caused by mistakes in the input. The function of error detection is carried out just before time analysis. Until the errors have been corrected by the planner the subsequent phases of time analysis, resource scheduling and reporting cannot proceed.

Dangles

If an activity is left out of the input data by mistake, then it can give rise to an end dangle for its predecessor and a start dangle for its successor. This is explained in Figure 23.3. It is necessary for the planner to inform the computer of the

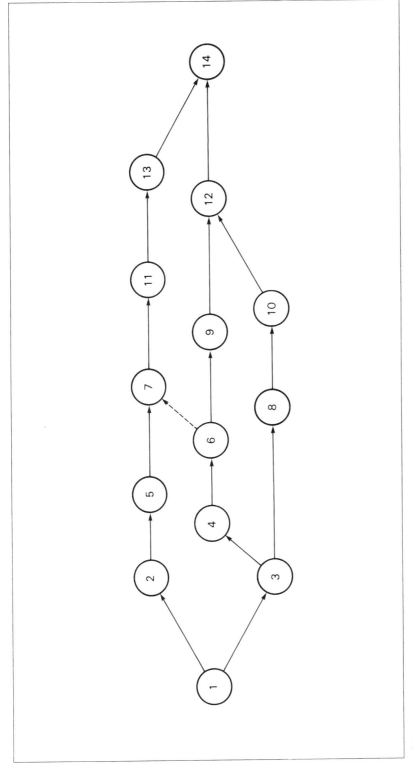

Figure 23.3   Start and end dangles

In error detection routines, critical path analysis programs should identify and report any unintentional start and end dangle. In the example above, the planner should report event 1 as a start event and event 14 as an end event. If these are not so reported, they will be printed out as logic errors. Now suppose that, by mistake, activity 8, 10 is left out of the input. The computer will identify event 8 as an end dangle and event 10 as a start dangle. Identification of these dangles by the computer tells the planner which activity is missing from the data.

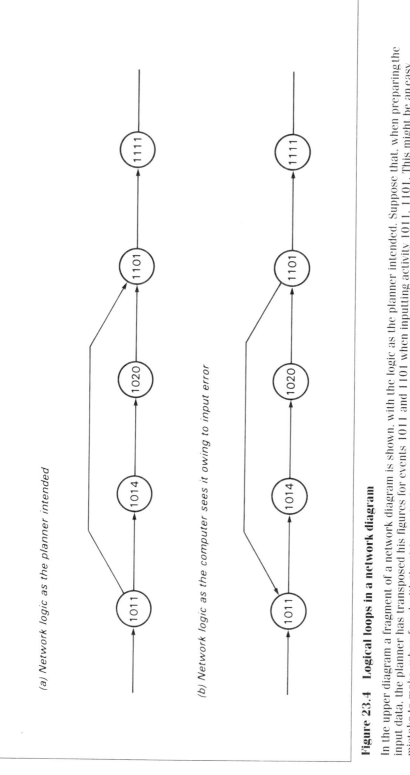

(a) Network logic as the planner intended

(b) Network logic as the computer sees it owing to input error

Figure 23.4   Logical loops in a network diagram

In the upper diagram a fragment of a network diagram is shown, with the logic as the planner intended. Suppose that, when preparing the input data, the planner has transposed his figures for events 1011 and 1101 when inputting activity 1011, 1101. This might be an easy mistake to make, when faced with the tiring task of inputting a large number of activities, and with numbers looking very similar. In this case, the computer would therefore be given, and would read the activity as 1101, 1011, thus effectively reversing its direction. The result is to create an endless loop, as shown in the lower diagram. The program's error detection routine should print out all the activities comprising the loop, in order to lead the planner to his mistake. Here, the activities in the loop are 1011, 1014; 1014, 1020; 1020, 1101 and the culprit reported as 1101, 1011.

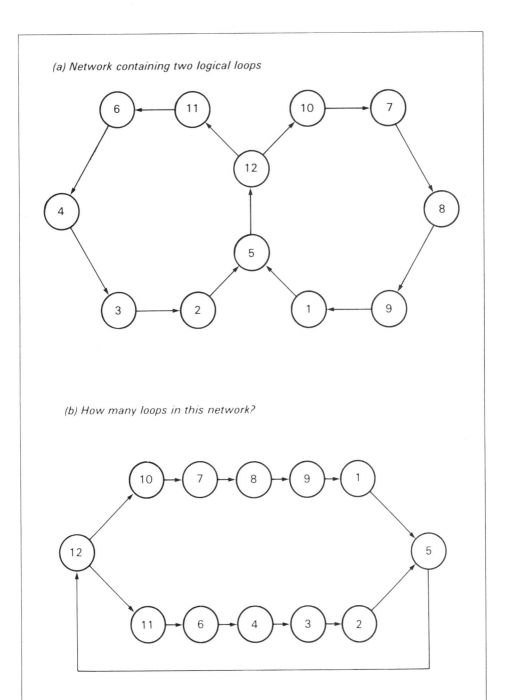

(a) Network containing two logical loops

(b) How many loops in this network?

Figure 23.5   Multiple loops

Here are examples of multiple loops. In fact, the lower diagram is the same network as that in the upper diagram and both contain the same two loops, no doubt caused by the planner making the mistake of calling activity 12, 5 activity 5,12 when he prepared the input data. *407* intentional start and end dangles; otherwise the computer will identify these as errors. The program should be able to handle multiple starts and ends, and should believe its own analysis of the start and end points if there is any conflict between that and the planner's expectation (after giving the appropriate warning messages).

Loops

Probably the most important error detection facility in a time analysis program is the detection of logical loops in a network.

Most programs contain a facility for detecting whether a network contains logical loops. They can print out all those activities or relations involved in such loops. But, for large networks this may not be enough. Anyone who has seen a group of planning engineers faced with a network of 15 000 activities containing loops involving 5 000 of those activities will realize that the more help the computer program can give in a such a situation, the better.

Figure 23.4 shows how a very simple loop can be created through an error in the input data. This is the simplest case, and the error print-out showing all activities contained in the loop gives the planner all he needs to know to put matters right by deleting the incorrect activity and replacing it with correct data.

One very necessary feature in loop detection is for the computer program to be capable of separating a number of loops from each other. These can be individually identified and solved by the planners. It should be able to recognize

```
           K & H   CRESTA LOOP ANALYSIS

        Analysing Loops

        Following are not a loop, but link to other loops
          1              events  5           events
          7              events  8           events
          8              events  9           events
          9              events  1           events
         10              events  7           events
         12              events 10           events
        Following are Loop Number      1
          2              events  5               events
          3              events  2               events
          4              events  3               events
          5              events 12               events
          6              events  4               events
         11              events  6               events
         12              events 11               events
```

Figure 23.6   Error detection report – loop analysis

Produced by the K&H Project Systems' CRESTA system from the network loop shown in Figure 23.5.

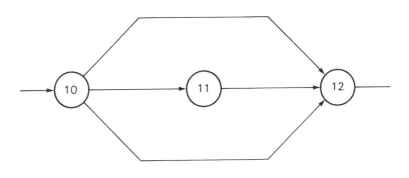

(a) Duplicate activities created by network logic inappropriate to computer applications

(b) Fragment of network to illustrate creation of duplicate activities through input error

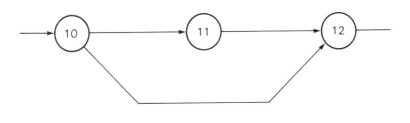

Figure 23.7   Duplicate activities

Duplicate activities can be created in several ways. In diagram (a) there are two activities which can be labelled as 10, 12. While the human brain can perceive the logical intention and calculate the network, the computer simply sees both activities as the same: it is necessary to insert a dummy in one of the activities to provide separate identification. In (b), if the planner should make an error in his input, describing activity 10, 12 wrongly as 10, 11 (it's easily done at the end of a long day), then the computer will see and report duplicate activities 10,11.

loops connected by a single directional chain, and separate those from each other.

Complex loops involving several connected cycles are more difficult to identify. For example, how many loops are there in Figure 23.5(a)? The usual answer, after a rapid inspection, is two. How many loops are there in Figure 23.5(b)? The usual quick answer is one. But a closer inspection reveals that both diagrams actually represent the same network.

Most computer programs capable of detailed loop analysis would take the view that the activities in Figure 23.5(a) and (b) form only one loop. The more sophisticated loop analysis programs are able to suggest that the activity 5, 12 is the most likely to have caused the problem, or of breaking the loop into a main chain and subchains of activities. See Figure 23.6.

Duplicated activities

To conclude this section on error diagnosis, having discussed the heady subjects of dangles and loops there remains one other, simple yet important error category. This concerns the problem of putting two or more activities into the computer file which have the same start and finish event numbers. This may be done intentionally by an inexperienced planner, or unintentionally by a person with more experience.

The intentional source of duplicated activities arises from planners who have been accustomed to mental network analysis, and who fail to realize that while the human brain can cope with two activities drawn parallel to each other in the network diagram, the computer will recognize these as twins. This point is explained in Figure 23.7(a). The inexperienced planner must learn that it is necessary to identify each activity separately, if necessary adding dummies to provide new event numbers.

Unintentionally duplicated activities occur when the planner makes a mistake in his input data, perhaps when he breaks off his input session for a cup of coffee, and repeats some of the input upon his return to the computer because he has forgotten where he left off, and failed to tick off all the activities already entered. Another cause is a simple numerical mistake in entering event numbers; this is illustrated in Figure 23.7(b).

Detection of duplicated activities is a simple matter for the program, and this can be done during the merging of file data before time analysis begins.

24 Computer Programs for Network Analysis – 2

K&H Project Systems Ltd

This chapter continues the discussions of Chapter 23 with a more detailed examination of some complex ways in which the starts and finishes of activities can be related. Time analysis is taken a step further in the context of probabilistic and risk analysis. Progress reporting is included next, where procedures are described for updating networks according to progress made on a project. The chapter continues with a collection of more advanced techniques, with sections on automatic network generation and plotting, treatment of cost data, and some database applications. The concluding section is concerned with the user, and his 'interface' with the computer input and output.

COMPLEX RELATIONSHIPS FOR ACTIVITY STARTS AND FINISHES

Precedence network relationships

It is quite common that network logic has to be arranged to indicate that one activity must occur completely within the duration of another, longer, activity. In precedence diagrams it is natural to attempt to express this by giving a start-to-start relationship from the beginning of the longer activity to the beginning of the shorter one. In order to ensure that the shorter activity does not drift past the end of the longer one, it is natural to add a finish-to-finish relationship from the end of the short activity to the end of the longer one. This is illustrated in Figure 24.1. Many computer programs will consider this specification to be a logical loop. Some allow an extra type of relationship – a parallel relationship – to deal with this situation.

Other than the parallel relationship, the more common ones are:

SS	=	start-to-start
FF	=	finish-to-finish
N or FS	=	normal, finish-to-start
SF	=	start-to-finish

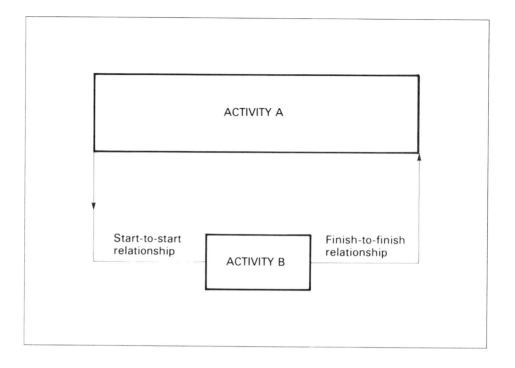

Figure 24.1   Parallel activities – precedence system

In some programs this arrangement might be interpreted as a logical loop.

The SF relationship is less necessary than the others in practice, and is omitted from some computer programs.

Most computer programs will use a mathematical definition of finish-to-finish relationships which is slightly different from the intuitive view of them. An FF relationship is usually considered to condition the earliest start of the activity which follows it. If, for example, activity B follows activity A with an FF relationship lag of two days, then the earliest start of activity B must be at least:

$$[\text{earliest start of A}] + [\text{duration of A}]$$
$$+[\text{lag(2 days)}] - [\text{duration of B}]$$

This is not quite the same as saying 'Activity B must finish at least two days after the finish of activity A'.

Most programs will not allow precedence relationships between activities to stretch out the durations of activities or to break them into discontinuous segments. The network shown in Figure 24.2 could have two different project durations, depending upon how the effects of its SS and FF relationships are viewed.

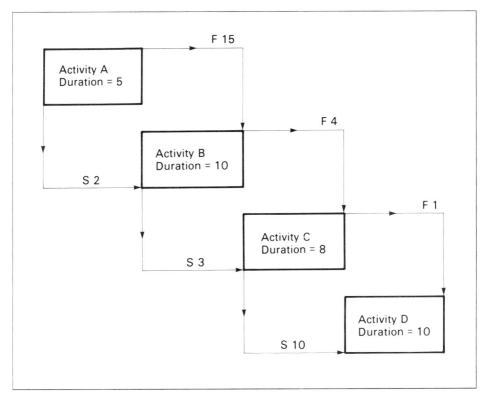

Figure 24.2 Interpretation of precedence network duration

As explained in the text, the project duration of this network might be understood as 25 days intuitively, but a computer program (using a mathematical approach) could arrive at an answer of 34 days.

The intuitive approach

This approach, looking first at the SS relationships in Figure 24.2, would indicate that activity B can start on day 3, so activity C can start on day 6, and activity D can start on day 16. As the duration of activity D is 10 the project could end on day 25. Considering the FF relationships, activity B must not end before day 20, activity C must not end before day 24, activity D must not end before day 25. It would seem that the project duration is 25 days.

The computer approach

This approach to this question might run as follows. Because of the relationship A to B SS 2, the earliest start of activity B must be at least the morning of day 3. Because of the relationship A to B FF 4, the earliest start of activity B must be greater than 1 (earliest start of A) + 5 (duration of A) + 15 (FF lag) − (duration of B). The answer is 11. The earliest start of activity B is 11.

413

Because of the relationship B to C SS 2, the earliest start of activity C must be at least day 13 (earliest start of B + lag of 2). Because of the relationship B to C FF 4, the earliest start of activity C must be greater than 11 (earliest start of B) + 10 (duration of B) + 4 (FF lag) − 8 (duration of C). This gives the earliest start of activity C as day 15.

Because of the relationship C to D SS 10, the earliest start of activity D must be at least day 25 (earliest start of C + SS lag). Because of the relationship C to D FF 1, the earliest start of C must be greater than 15 (the earliest start of C) + 8 (duration of C) + 1 (FF lag) − 10 (duration of D), which is 14 days. The earliest start of activity D is day 25, and the project ends on day 34.

The reason there is such a difference between the intuitive approach and the mathematical approach in this case, is that the intuitive approach would split activity B into two sections, one having an earliest start of day 3, because of the SS relationship from activity A, the other having an earliest finish of day 20 because of the FF relationship from activity A. However, the duration of activity B is only 10 days, and so will not stretch from day 3 to day 20. We can arrive at the ironical situation where, for certain activities, the longer they are, the shorter is the overall project. This effect is illustrated in Figure 24.3.

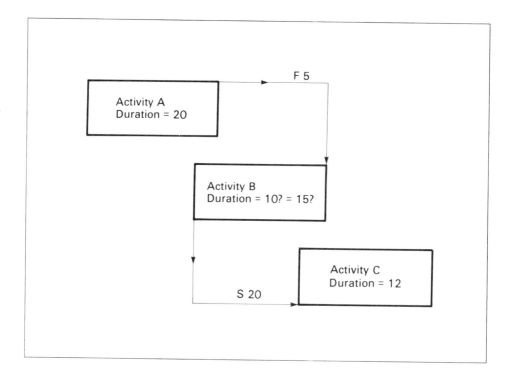

Figure 24.3   A paradox in precedence logic

When this network is subjected to time analysis by a computer, the strange result is produced
that the longer the duration of activity B, the shorter the project duration.

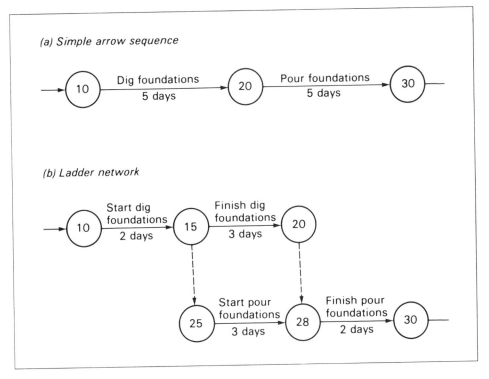

Figure 24.4   Ladder networks and transit times

The upper network, as it stands, does not reflect true life. It is not necessary for the whole length of the foundation trench to be dug before pouring can begin. It is possible to use a ladder network, such as that shown in diagram (b) to reflect planning intentions more accurately but, as explained in the text, the use of a computer program having the feature of transit times allows diagram (a) to be used without the unwelcome complications of ladder notation. The dummies in (b) have zero duration in this example, but durations are sometimes used in these circumstances.

Relationships in arrow diagrams

Some relationships which can be programmed into arrow diagrams (otherwise known as IJ networks) were described in the program features listed in Chapter 23. These included slippage of order and delivery activities and tied activities.

The rules of IJ network logic imply that, for two activities in sequence, the first must be 100 per cent complete before the second can start. In practice, many situations arise where this ruling does not apply to the real-life project. The conventional way of expressing this in the network diagram was to break the activity into two or more sections such as 'start activity', 'continue activity' and 'finish activity'. This is illustrated in Figure 24.4 There are two main disadvantages with this approach.

1   The number of activities in the network is increased (from two to six even in this very simple example, which omits the 'continue activity' option).

2   During resource allocation, because of possible resource availability restrictions, the completion part of each operation could be scheduled later than the start – in effect splitting a single operation into two parts scheduled at different times, even although the whole operation might not be strictly splittable.

The 'transit time' concept overcomes both of these disadvantages. A *transit time* is a number associated with any arrow, which can be negative or positive, and can refer to the beginning or to the end of an activity. Transits which refer to the starts of activities are called 'transits before' (TB). Transit times which refer to the end of activities are called 'transits after' (TA).

A positive TB is the delay between the predecessor event of an activity and the activity's start.

A positive TA is the delay between the end of an activity and its successor event.

A negative TB is the amount by which an activity can overlap its predecessor event.

A negative TA is the amount by which an activity can overlap its successor event.

In the practical example above, the overlap can be achieved by coding the activity for 'pouring foundations' with a negative TB of 3.

One of the main advantages quoted for precedence diagramming over IJ is that precedence allows for the overlap of sequential activities, by the use of SS and FF relations. An IJ system with transit times has the same capabilities, so that particular advantage disappears.

Not all IJ diagramming programs have transit time features in them. One reason for this is that it is technically difficult to combine parallel resource analysis with transit times, so that systems which use one tend not to have the other.

PROGRESS REPORTING

When all the techniques so far discussed have been used to produce a schedule, the job of planning has only just begun. Obviously the network and its resulting schedule need to be updated with sufficient frequency to ensure that the schedule remains valid as the project proceeds and, almost invariably, is subject to changes.

Progress reporting techniques vary considerably between programs. It is quite common for a planner to wish to report progress on activities which should theoretically not have been started, according to the network logic. If one is not to plan at a very low level of detail, the network will correspond only approximately to the possible sequence of tasks in reality, particularly if an attempt is being made to catch up on the schedule. Overlaps between operations may be possible, although not planned.

416   Many computer programs act in a bewildered fashion when confronted by updates that are out of sequence according to the logic of the network. They remark 'That's not logical, Captain!' and wiggle their ears. The easiest answer for a programmer is to assume that the input must be in error, and to not allow the situation at all. A network is a tool not a prison, and should not involve the planner in unnecessary work making the sequence of what has already happened look logical to the program he is using.

It makes sense to force the earliest start of any activity which has been started or completed to be 'time now' (the date relevant to the update in progress, from which the computer will recalculate the remaining schedule) even though it is preceded by items which have not yet been completed. Sometimes one may wish to ask the program to maintain the sequence, so that the earliest start of the in-progress activity drifts away from time now to allow room for the non-completed chain preceding it.

The situation as regards the calculation of the latest times of activities preceding the out-of-sequence progress is more complex than the action as regards earliest times. The answer is less intuitively obvious. One might require the following options:

1 The backward pass is unaffected. The latest times of the activities preceding the out-of-sequence progress follow on logically from the out-of-sequence activities. This implies that these preceding activities will suddenly have much lower float as one reads back along the chain which includes the out-of-sequence progress; they may even develop negative float that is difficult to justify objectively and which looks bad on progress reports.

2 The chain of logic is completely broken at the point of out-of-sequence progress. Activities followed only by in-progress or completed activities act as if they were disconnected ends. Activities followed by a mixture of in-progress and not started activities take their results from the activities which have not yet been started. This can be awkward if the following chain is in fact critical, and it is still necessary to complete some of the preceding logic before continuing with the network.

3 The latest finish of the activity preceding the out-of-sequence progress is 'adjusted' so that the float of that activity is equal to or less than the float of the in-progress or complete following activity. This is somewhat artificial, but may be the best compromise.

Some programs allow the planner to mark particular events or activities in a special way, so that they do not follow the normal logic of network analysis. The usual convention is that an activity cannot start until all preceding activities are complete. The 'or-node' or 'short path activity' does not follow this rule. Instead, such an activity can start as soon as ANY of its predecessors is complete.

Practical uses for this kind of feature are fairly rare, but they do exist. In particular, two alternative sources of supply for a certain material for a task could exist in a network, and the one which arrived first would be used in preference to the one which arrived later.

417

In the network analysis of such items it is by no means clear what action should be taken by the computer program on the backward pass through the network, when latest finishes are being computed. If an activity C can start as soon as either activity B or activity A has finished, and the durations of the activities are A = 2 days, B = 4 days and C = 6 days, then, supposing the project starts on 1 January, working seven days per week, activities A and B can both start on 1 January. Activity A will finish on 2 January, and so activity C can start on 3 January. The project will then finish on 8 January, at the end of activity C. Working the late times backwards, the latest start of activity C will be the same as its earliest start – 3 January. Therefore it would seem that the latest finish of activity B would be 2 January. Its earliest finish is 4 January. It will therefore appear to have a negative float of 2 days.

COMPUTER-AIDED NETWORK CONSTRUCTION

Library networks

In many projects, certain groups of activities are repeated several times throughout the network with perhaps only the duration, part of the description, and the identifying area or work breakdown codes being different. For example, in petrochemical construction, the network logic for the design, procurement and installation of a pump is identical for the majority of pumps. Only the durations and identifications tend to change.

It is possible to generate large networks rapidly in this way. One uses a computer to generate them, needs a computer to analyse them, and may well need a computer to display the resulting network, particularly if there are extensive local changes to the library modules once called – so one cannot just use many prints of the library network drawing.

If a library of standard subnetworks has been established, it can be valuable not only as a method of creating networks rapidly for new projects, but also as a repository for a history of activity durations. If the spread of durations is recorded, together with some appropriate measure of the size of the job, if appropriate, better estimates can be produced in the future, together with some idea of the possible variation that can be encountered. If the estimate is associated with a job size, then the new estimate for a given use of the library network can be automatically made to be a function of the size factor.

When networks are not drawn by the planner initially, but are generated in this way, it is helpful to have automatic plotting equipment available to draw out the network once it has been created.

Graphic displays and plotters

It is not easy to program a computer to design a diagram of a network, and programs which do this vary greatly in the elegance of the network which is produced. The more clumsy the layout, and the greater number of crossed lines and linkages, the harder the network will be to follow.

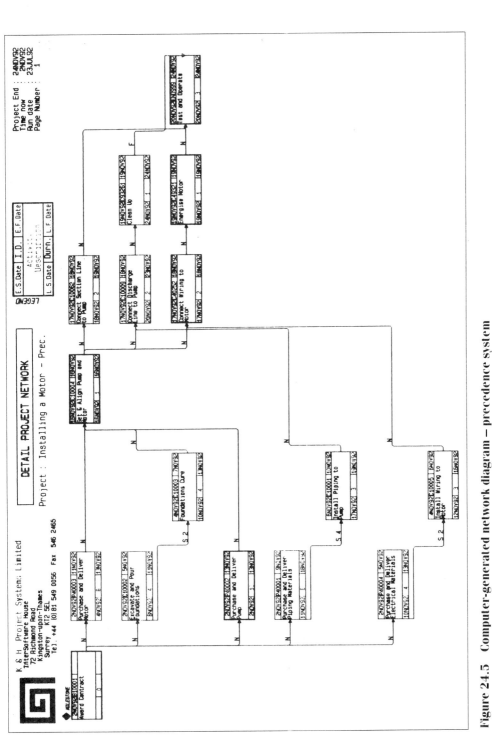

Figure 24.5 Computer-generated network diagram – precedence system

Compare this with the same project network plotted in arrow notation in Figure 24.6.

419

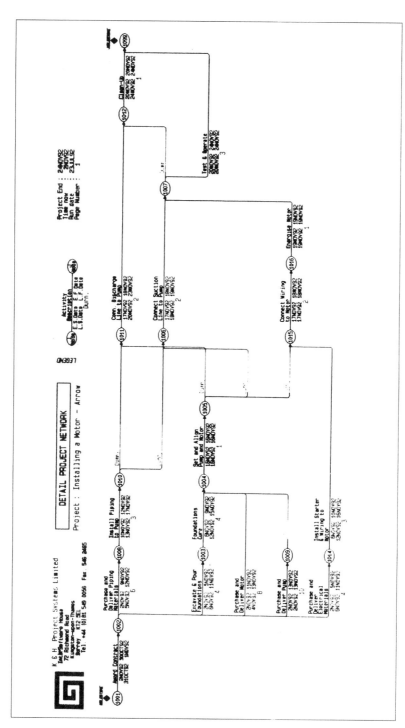

Figure 24.6 Computer-generated network diagram – activity-on-arrow method

This shows that the arrow diagrams allow more detail in a given space than their precedence counterparts – the precedence version of this network is in Figure 24.5. (Both diagrams produced by K & H Project Systems CRESTA system).

More information can be drawn on a page for arrow networks than for precedence networks, where the boxes tend to get in the way of the relationship lines. See Figures 24.5 and 24.6.

A good design algorithm will react to a change in the connectivity of a network caused perhaps by adding or deleting a single activity, and will produce a new, perhaps different, layout. Planners sometimes find this frustrating because they have become familiar with a particular layout, and have learned where to find particular activities. If the computer has redesigned the layout and moved activities about, they can no longer find them in their accustomed places.

In some plotting software it is possible to define 'zones' in a network layout. These are horizontal bands which can be associated with particular activity codes. If this feature is used, then all activities of a particular area or responsibility can be confined within the same general area. This can make it easier to find activities after a redesign has been carried out.

One useful capability is that of being able to 'fix' a design and to determine manually where any new activities are to be fitted in to the drawing.

Online updating

Given computer-designed graphic representation of a network, and a terminal capable of displaying reasonably large sections of the network, it may be possible to update the project directly in network form. The planner picks out the activity he wishes to alter, zooms in for a detailed display of the information associated with the activity, and alters it *in situ*. New relationships and connections can be drawn in on the screen, and activities can be moved about by 'connecting' them to the screen cursor and moving them about until they are 'dropped' at the appropriate point in the display.

Not all project management software is capable of doing this.

COST FEATURES

Early attempts to integrate cost factors with the time analysis and resource analysis of critical path networks met with little success in general. When dealing with costs, it would seem logical to unify the cost reporting schemes of planners and of accountants who are working on the same project, so that costs have to be estimated only once, and reported only once, However, the working methods of planners, and their goals, differ from those of the accounting staff.

A planner will tend to break a project down into functional units. An accountant will tend to use a cost-centre breakdown. Thus, the elements against which a planner will report progress for time and resources will be different from those which an accountant will naturally use. One compromise has been to use a work breakdown structure which can codify the lowest level of detail used by either the planner or the accountant in each individual case, or which can assign the percentage contribution to each cost centre item of each task defined by the planner. Although this adds complexity to the coding structures used by both the planner and the accountant, it does have the merit of being a 'database' approach, *421* where each piece of information is reported and recorded in one place only.

Planners operate with rough estimates, and are pleased if they come within 10 per cent of the eventual reality. Accountants strive for precision. Normally therefore, the cost estimates used by planners are recorded separately from the accountant's information in the data structure – although both can benefit from the other's information. The planner can eventually integrate more precise estimates, and then actual figures, into his reports. It is most important (and more rare than it should be) for the planner to compare his initial estimates with the actual figures eventually reported through the accounting procedures. The single most essential factor to improve the quality of estimates or forecasts in general is feedback. The estimator must be able to discover how close his estimates were, so that he can improve his future guesses. The accountant too can make use of the planner's estimates in the early stages as a cross-check to look for gross errors in his data.

The timescale of reporting is usually quite different for cost and for time. This is probably the principal reason for failure to integrate costing and scheduling. The planner will know which activities are complete, and (for those that are in-progress) roughly how far along they are, quite quickly. Depending on the kind of project being carried out, he might know hours, days, or a few weeks after the progress has in fact occurred. The accountant might not know for several months what the costs have been. Thus, the evaluation of in-progress work items is very difficult. Interim estimates have to be made of the value of work done, before the full accounting procedures have returned their final result. In cases where interim progress payments are important, delay in reporting work done means delay in receiving money, and possible cash-flow problems. In this sort of environment, the planner is still looking to the future. His priority is to know what work remains to be done, so that he can schedule it properly. The accountant is looking to the past. His priority is to know what work has been done, and how much he can charge for it as an interim payment, and how much it cost to accomplish.

The planner looking forward and the accountant looking back sometimes end up with an eyeball-to-eyeball confrontation.

It may be important for project costing that the computer program chosen is sufficiently flexible in its method of coding what activities are associated with which cost packages. In general, an activity may involve several cost items, and a cost item may involve several activities. An activity may include part of several cost elements. It must also be possible to summarize costs at different levels of the pyramid of the work breakdown structure. There can be a limit to the number of such levels which a program will allow.

The method of evaluating activities which are in progress, or which have received partial reporting information, can be critical. It is desirable to have a wide range of methods available for this purpose. It may be appropriate to compute the value of work done according to:

1 A 50 per cent rule, where half the job price is released on commencement and the rest on completion.

2 A progress rule, where the proportion of time completed on the job is applied directly to the value of work done.
3 A 100 per cent completion only rule, where the job only contributes to the value of work done when it is complete.
4 A 'started' rule, where the job is added in as soon as it has been started.
5 An 'equivalent units' rule, where some independent measure is taken and work done is evaluated according to the proportion completed (e.g. cubic yards of concrete poured, and the like).
6 A 'level of effort' rule, based on elapsed time in the activity.
7 An 'apportioned effort' rule, where the progress of the cost element is proportional to the progress of a number of other cost elements or activities, perhaps weighted by value or work content.

And many others; the wider the range of possible methods offered by a program, the better.

For cost performance analysis it is important to determine whether or not the program being considered can be integrated with the company's cost accounting procedures. This may indeed be totally unacceptable to the accounting department, which in many cases is reluctant to accept what they term 'unfiltered' data from a planning process. Can the system easily accept files produced by the current accounting programs now, or will additional programs have to be written? Can it produce files in the form which the accounting programs will accept, or will some kind of translation have to take place? Can the program being considered replace some of the reporting functions of the current accounting system altogether?

Some programs rely upon fixed input formats. Others can accept guidance as to what information is to be provided, and in what form. It is sometimes necessary to extract data from existing computer files, to enter the project planning system. If the computer system selected can only accept data from a fixed screen panel, which is built into the system, it will not be able automatically to 'steal' data from files created by other programs. If it can accept information as a file, it is important to know whether this file must be in a given fixed form, or whether data can be captured directly from other files. If the data must be in a given fixed form, some programmer familiar with the system from which data is to be accepted will have to write a program to produce the information in the form required.

A planning system should ideally be able to accept data other than that envisaged by the suppliers of the program. Additional data can then be input to the system and associated with the activity records, and can eventually be output in reports. All kinds of data may be required to be associated with activities in the network, in which case one might need a facility for defining any kind of information, and printing it out in any way. There may be a use in particular situations for associating:

1 Material lists, quantities, prices and so on.
2 Drawing number lists, version numbers.
3 Work breakdown structure codes.

423

4 Purchase order numbers, delivery times.
5 Job numbers.
6 Electrical conduit routing codes.
7 Area, responsibility, department codes.

There are many other kinds of information, with activities.

If one adds to this the ability to carry out computations on any numbers stored, and place results on computer files or on output reports as listings or as tables, the result can be a system which can carry out most data processing functions. Once planning engineers have mastered such a system, they can carry out a great variety of computer processing without needing to have recourse to computer specialists. Planners using K&H Project Systems' CRESTA system, for example, have been known to establish supplementary data processing departments within their own organizations.

DATABASE APPLICATIONS

Rational database capabilities can be valuable when attaching a list of items to each activity, rather than a single value. This can be difficult to specify and manipulate, using the control instructions provided by the software supplier. If large quantities of information are associated with each activity, the network computation process is bound to become more clumsy, with gigantic lists of data rumbling around inside the machine, contributing little to the pure critical path analysis or resource levelling calculations.

The most quoted advantage of a 'database' approach to information handling is that it reduces duplication of data. This has some truth in it, but perhaps more important is its effect in simplifying the processing of lists of information.

A database structure will enable the planner to store any lists of information, or indeed any information not essential to the time analysis calculation, separately from the activities themselves. Each set of information that is associated with an activity will have a pointer to that activity. When computations involving the network are to be carried out, they do not need to refer to the associated lists in any way. When reports are to be produced for (say) materials, then relevant activity information (perhaps the activity early starts or scheduled starts) can be picked off from the activity file from the pointers on the materials file.

The nature of these pointers determines whether the database in question should be termed 'relational' or 'hierarchical'. After the invention of the relational approach, it gradually became more popular than the older hierarchical systems. Relational systems tend to be more flexible; hierarchical systems are usually more efficient in their use of computer resources. The pointers in relational systems tend to refer to the content of the records being pointed to. The pointers in hierarchical systems refer to the physical location within the computer of the records being pointed to.

The salient differences between the systems can be visualized by comparing the processes that have to be carried out when an activity number is changed, and there is a materials file with several records for materials which are required

by that activity.

In a hierarchical system, there would be no change required, other than altering the activity number itself. The pointers would still be pointing to the correct place.

In a relational system, the current activity number would have to be removed from the 'index' being used to relate materials to activities. The new activity number would have to be added to the index, and associated with the correct physical location of the altered record. All the materials records referring to the activity would have to have the activity number on them altered. Note that the relational system does involve some duplication of data – namely, the data on which the matching process from one file to another takes place.

Once a hierarchical structure has been established, it is difficult to add new pathways to it. *Ad hoc* enquiries on bases which have not been planned for right from the beginning cannot easily be made. On the whole, it is probably better to pay the performance penalty and use a relational system; though it is perhaps wise to use the most efficient relational system possible so as not to lose more than absolutely necessary in response speed.

INPUT, OUTPUT REPORTS AND THE USER INTERFACE

Fourth generation languages (known as '4GLs') are usually, but not necessarily, associated with particular database systems. They are intended to enable personnel not trained in computer work to take advantage of the potential flexibility of modern computer systems without needing to rely upon computer experts.

Failure of communication between people is by far the greatest cause of problems in data processing. The application specialist who wants the computer to carry out some particular kind of processing has to explain what he wants to a systems analyst, who then explains it to a programmer or programmers who then 'explain' it to the computer. 4GLs try to 'cut out the middle man', so that the application specialist talks directly to the computer system.

If a prewritten program is to be acquired for project planning, it is not ideal if the operations of the company acquiring the program have to be distorted to fit the pre-set reporting formats of that program. A program may have a sufficiently well-chosen variety of standard reports that current and future conceivable needs are covered by them. Alternatively, it may contain a 'report generator' facility whereby the planner can specify his own reports.

The best situation is probably a mixture of these two solutions, where the planner may:

1 Choose a standard report.
2 Ask for simple variations in that standard report such as different sort sequence, activity selection, or control-break field for totalling.
3 Make temporary or permanent changes to the standard report and create new standards of his own from it.
4 Build his own reports from scratch.

Where a report generator language is used, it should be designed for use by *425* personnel not trained in computer work. Some generators have several levels of use, where the program predefines more or less of any given report, giving correspondingly greater or less ease of use and increasing flexibility with greater complexity.

A program should be capable of producing:

1 Listings in almost any form, sequence, or selection, with totals and page changes as chosen by the planner.
2 Bar charts on computer printers (even if automatic plotting equipment is available, a computer-printed bar chart is produced much faster and more cheaply).
3 Tables, especially of resource usage, resources remaining, cost by time, cumulative cost curves, and so on.
4 Histograms of the above. (Again, computer-printed histograms are more efficient than plotted histograms, and should be used unless quality present-ation is the overriding factor.)

The reporting system should be capable of handling lists of information, and, in particular, of expanding any of the codes used in the activities – resource codes, department codes, area codes, etc. – for reporting purposes. It should be possible to direct reports to other systems or back into the input phase of the planning program as well as to the printer. This is useful if one wishes to 'print' an update candidate list containing all those activities likely to show progress during the next update cycle, to use as a basis for the inputting of progress information.

Opinions vary as to which method of inputting and updating information is the easiest to use. Some prefer to be able to select from a number of options displayed on a menu. Some prefer a question-and-answer method of working. Others prefer a 'command' language structure, consisting of a keyword followed by options.

It is common for a user to prefer the use of menus when he first starts to use a system. He knows where he is and what is expected of him at any time. After he has become familiar with the menu structure and options, they can become irritating, and he may begin to prefer a command-oriented system. By the same token, inexperienced users will prefer to carry out updating one activity at a time, editing a screen-full of information, with the maximum amount of online error checking from the computer system. More experienced users will become impatient with this, and may graduate towards the preparation of update lists, with many activities on the screen simultaneously, with minimal delay produced by the computer system.

Ideally, a computer program should have a wide variety of possible input methods, to suit users with different tastes and different amounts of experience with the system.

As an extreme case, there is one system which attempts to judge the competence of each user, who is identified by his/her log-on code. It adjusts the degree of 'user-friendliness' downwards as the number of user mistakes decreases. Eventually it allows short-cut methods and rapid bulk input.

There are many special updating operations which are useful in practice, but are not included in all computer programs. It is worthwhile to have a transaction to change activity numbers or node numbers in arrow networks. In precedence networks such an operation should automatically alter any relationships pointing to the activity whose number is being changed.

It is important to determine how long the program will take to handle networks of the size normally used by the planner, using the computer equipment which has been chosen.

Times to carry out updating, time analysis, resource analysis, and produce reports are all important. When updating activities or other data, how long will the user have to wait while the computer finds the appropriate record, and paints the appropriate screen to be filled in, if a full-screen approach is to be employed?

Older systems are mostly based on 'batch' processing. Newer systems tend to be more 'interactive'. There are advantages and disadvantages to both approaches. With a batch approach, the planner makes all the alterations he is going to make to the network, and submits them to the computer to be analysed. With an interactive approach, the computer makes each change as it is typed in, and may produce error diagnostics at any stage. The added convenience of immediate error detection has to be balanced against any additional delays between updates as the planner sits at the screen and waits for the error checks to be performed and against the larger amount of computer time used by an interactive system. If the planner is using his own dedicated microcomputer, there is no advantage in operating in batch mode, providing that the micro-computer is fast enough to carry out all the updating functions he requires without appreciable delay.

It is important to know how much help and assistance the producer of the program, or his local agent, will provide in the implementation process. How much will this assistance cost?

The quality of the program documentation is important. Possibly the perfect program, perfectly documented, might need no support from the supplier – especially for the perfect user. Most systems do not aspire to these heights.

Any training offered by the program supplier should be gratefully accepted. It should produce more rapid learning than that obtained by trial and error from the use of the system itself and from its associated manuals; but more important, it will give a feeling for the emphasis provided by the supplier on the different features of his system, and for the particular interpretation made of some of the claims in the publicity literature for the product.

Some software suppliers offer a telephone support service, sometimes called a 'hotline', whereby users can ask questions of experienced personnel. This is an important advantage, where it is available, and if the service is reasonably priced (sometimes it is free).

It is advisable to have a definite procedure to follow when the computer system appears to have gone wrong. Most software suppliers do not find it helpful to receive a fax or telephone call stating that 'the program does not work'. Greater detail is preferred. One good procedure is to build up a standard test network *427* containing examples of most of the features of the program that one uses. Whenever an error appears in the results, this standard network should be run to see if it still comes to a successful conclusion, and produce the same results as before. This procedure should also be carried out whenever a new version of a programme is received from the supplier. Any changes in results from the standard network should be investigated to determine whether they are really improvements to the system.

In this way, it may be possible to give the supplier a clue as to whether the problem lies with his software or with the computer hardware being used, and to locate and correct any error with maximum dispatch. Sometimes, the problem may be caused by an intentional software 'time-bomb', and may be a tactful way of saying 'Have you paid your rental for this year?' Some suppliers arrange for their software to degrade gracefully (or, according to some of their clients, disgracefully) if payments are not made where appropriate, in order to defeat the processes of software piracy.

It is not ideal to introduce intentional errors into software, which suffers quite enough from unintentional ones. Such anti-piracy measures, although being more complex, are still fairly easy to defeat, for the most part. Those that are based on dates can be circumvented by the user lying to the computer as to what is today's date. They can be brought into action unintentionally by an operator who mistypes today's date into his machine, and thereby perhaps destroys copies of such intentionally sabotaged software.

An additional advantage can be derived from making a standard test network in the initial stages of using a program. It is important to learn how the program reacts to different situations.

Make a test network and try out typical practical operations. For any special features which look interesting, try to produce the situation in which you would use them, and see if the results indeed correspond to what one would expect from the manual.

A good way of judging the support offered for a given product is to speak to as many as possible of the existing users. Try not to talk exclusively to those clients recommended by the supplier as good contact points, nor exclusively to those who have just got out of bed with a bad hangover after celebrating the successful conclusion of their latest project. The worth of any individual opinion should be weighted by the length of time the organization in question has been using the software.

SOFTWARE SOURCES IN THE UNITED KINGDOM

This list gives brief details of some of the companies which market project management software in the United Kingdom either direct or under licence from others. In each case the name of a typical program or family of programs is given. Several of these companies market products in addition to those mentioned here.

Asta Development Corporation, 5 St Andrews Court,
   Wellington Street, Thame, Oxon, OX9 3WT
   Telephone: 0844 261700
   Product: PowerProject

Claremont Controls Ltd, Albert House, Rothbury,
   Northumberland, NE65 7SR
   Telephone: 0669 21081
   Product: HORNET

Computerline Ltd, Tavistock House, 319 Woodham Lane,
   Weybridge, Surrey, KT15 3PB
   Telephone: 0932 351022
   Product: PLANTRAC

Cosar Project Management Ltd, Dovetail House,
   Wycombe Road, Stokenchurch, Near High Wycombe,
   Bucks, HP14 3RQ
   Telephone: 0494 482359
   Product: TrackStar

Deepak Sareen Associates, Bydell House, Sudbury Hill,
   Harrow on the Hill, Middx, HA1 3NJ
   Telephone: 081 423 8855
   Product: InstaPlan

Forge Track Ltd, 27 Old Cross, Hertford, SG14 1RE.
   Telephone: 0992 587059
   Product: PRIMAVERA

K&H Project Systems UK Ltd, InterSoftware,
   1 Canbury Business Park,
   Elm Crescent, Kingston, Surrey, KT2 6HJ
   Telephone: 081 547 1133
   Product: CRESTA

Hoskyns Group, 95 Wandsworth Road, Vauxhall Cross,
   London, SW8 2LX
   Telephone: 071 735 0800
   Product: PMW

Lucas Management Systems Ltd, Metier House,
   23 Clayton Road, Hayes, Middx, UB3 1AN
   Telephone: 081 848 3400
   Product: ARTEMIS

Mantix Systems Ltd, Mantix House, London Road,
   Bracknell, Berks, RG12 2XH
   Telephone: 0344 301505
   Product: CASCADE

Micro Planning International Ltd, 34 High Street,
Westbury on Trym, Bristol, BS9 3DZ
Telephone: 0272 509417
Product: MICRO PLANNER

Panorama Software Corporation, Chatsworth House,
59 London Road, Twickenham, Middx, TW1 3SZ
Telephone: 081 891 0202
Product: PANORAMA

PSDI (UK) Ltd, Unit 5, Forsyth Road, Woking,
Surrey, GU21 5SB
Telephone: 0483 727000
Products: PROJECT/2; QWIKNET

Symantec (UK) Ltd, MKA House, 36 King Street, Maidenhead,
Berks, SL6 1EF
Telephone: 0628 77634
Product: TimeLine

Tekware Ltd, The Barclay Centre, Worcester Road,
Hagley, West Midlands, DY9 0NW
Telephone: 0562 88212
Product: PROJECT SCHEDULER

Transaction Point Ltd, 41 London Street, Reading,
Berks, RG1 4PS
Telephone: 0734 560846
Product: KERNEL-PMS

Welcom Software Technology International,
South Bank Technopark, 90 London Road, London, SE1 6LN
Telephone: 071 401 2626
Main product: OPEN PLAN

25 Project Risk Management

Chris Chapman

Uncertainty (lack of certainty) is inherent in most aspects of most projects. Risk (interpreted as undesirable or desirable implications of uncertainty) might or might not be associated with some of this uncertainty. When risk is significant, it is important to be able to recognize why and manage it. Understanding the nature of risk properly in order to manage it effectively is a subtle business. This chapter provides a broad understanding of the key issues. Further reading is suggested at the end of the chapter for those who wish to implement the processes recommended.

INTRODUCTION

Risk can permeate all aspects of project management. The simplest starting point for considering risk implications is in planning a project when time or schedule risk is the central concern (cost and performance issues being largely time-risk dependent, along with resource and materials management, contractual, financial, insurance and organizational issues).

The body of this chapter focuses on time or schedule risk associated with project planning. The subject is developed and various processes are described in sections that follow each other logically, and this chapter is therefore intended to be read in continuous sequence. The concluding section links this discussion to some of the wider issues.

THE NATURE OF RISK AND UNCERTAINTY

Suppose that Fred offers a gamble to Gill, as follows. Fred will roll a single die. If Fred throws a six, Gill must pay Fred £24. If Fred rolls anything else, Fred pays Gill £6. Assuming that the die is 'fair', with a 1:6 probability of a six, the expected outcome for Gill is a profit of:

$$£[(6 \times 5/6) - (24 \times 1/6)] = £1$$

(The 'expected' value here and elsewhere in this chapter means 'mathematical expectation', defined as all possible outcomes weighted by their probabilities – our best estimate of what will happen on average – although it may be that any specific outcome cannot have the 'expected' value.)

If Gill can afford to lose £24 and can trust Fred not to cheat, this looks a reasonable gamble for Gill. If Fred is prepared to keep playing and Gill has a few hundred pounds available she could afford to lose; there is no real downside risk for Gill, and an expected profit of £1 per game. There is *uncertainty*, because Gill will win or lose each game. The game might be a little tedious, but there is no significant *risk*.

Now suppose that Fred wants to play for £6 000 and £24 000, on only one toss. The upside risk of £6 000 on a single toss is now very attractive. If Gill happened to be a millionaire the downside risk of a £24 000 loss might be bearable, but this would be too great for most people. The *uncertainty* is essentially the same as for the £6-for-£24 gamble but the *risk* is now significant.

Gill could turn down Fred's offer. But she could accept it and manage the risk. For example, she could transfer all or part of the risk to other punters who are prepared to pay a premium to take on the upside and downside of the gamble with Fred. This is what bookmakers do. They manipulate the odds to obtain a set of bets that should make a constant profit. Skilful bookmakers do not gamble. This is also similar to what insurance companies do; they take lots of independent risks if they can and then try to reinsure when they cannot achieve independence. Sound insurance companies do not specialize in earthquake risk in San Francisco.

This is also what sensible project managers do. They take the uncertainty of £6-for-£24 gambles in their stride; they recognize the risk inherent in £6 000-for-£24 000 gambles and manage that risk; and they recognize the risk inherent in £6 000 000-for-£24 000 000 gambles which may need to be avoided.

THE CENTRAL PURPOSE OF RISK MANAGEMENT

The central purpose of risk management is risk efficiency and balance.

Risk efficiency

Consider the meaning of risk efficiency in a project planning context. An offshore project in the North Sea involved a hook-up between a platform and a pipeline. Risk analysis indicated that:

- The proposed August target date was sensible.
- The intention of using a barge with 1.6m waveheight capability would be appropriate for August.
- There were many preceding activities with much scope for slippage and the chances were that the hook-up would be in September, October or later.
- There was a chance that winter weather could delay hook-up until spring, which would mean a consequential loss of the order of £100 million.

Risk analysis had identified a gamble which needed to be managed (at the very least) and perhaps avoided altogether.

Reworking the analysis assuming use of a 3m waveheight barge indicated that the chance of delay until spring was effectively eliminated. The best estimate of average cost was decreased by £1 million. This was a risk-efficient improvement in the base plan, because it reduced the expected cost and the associated risk. This more than paid for the risk analysis and persuaded the company involved to use this kind of analysis for all subsequent important or sensitive projects worldwide.

In more formal terms, 'risk efficiency' means:

- The minimum level of risk for any given level of expected cost.
- The minimum level of expected cost for any given level of risk.

Risk balance

Now consider the implications of 'risk balance' in the same context of the North Sea project. If the probabilities had been different, the 3m waveheight barge might have avoided the delay until spring but increased the expected cost (say, by £500 000). In this case the 3m barge would not increase risk efficiency, but it would offer a trade-off between risk and expected cost which might be a wise choice.

In more general terms:

- We can usually decrease risk if we increase expected cost.
- We can usually decrease expected cost if we increase risk (assuming risk efficiency).

Recognizing the need to make choices which get the balance right is central to effective risk management.

PERT (PROGRAM EVALUATION AND REVIEW TECHNIQUE)

CPA (critical path analysis) and PERT (program evaluation and review technique) models were introduced at about the same time in the 1950s, and common use of the joint term CPA/PERT tends to blur the historical distinctions. These techniques are described in some detail in Chapter 17, but the key distinction for present purposes is that CPA models used single value deterministic estimates for each activity duration where PERT used three-point probability estimates. PERT explicitly considered uncertainty in probabilistic terms: CPA did not.

Early PERT models assumed that three duration estimates for each activity (optimistic, pessimistic and most likely) provided the maximum and minimum of a probability distribution approximated by the Beta distribution. It was later realized that associating the optimistic value with a 5 per cent chance of doing better, and the pessimistic value with a 5 per cent chance of doing worse, provided a more practical model, avoiding consideration of extreme events which could be confusing in this framework.

433

Like early CPA models, early PERT models used an activity-on-arrow representation of network logic in which all constraints were finish-start relationships. For example, activity C cannot start until activities B and C have been completed. Activity-on-node representation of the same model is possible.

Computation procedures

The original PERT computation procedures used a 'method of moments' ('mean-variance') approach. Expected values for each activity were considered first, using a standard CPA algorithm to identify the longest path through the network based on these values. Variances (a measure of spread) of the probability distributions for activities on the critical path were then added and assumed to define the variance of the project duration. A normal (Gaussian) distribution was associated with the project's expected duration and variance, to yield a probability of completing the project by the relevant range of dates.

An obvious shortcoming of this approach is that it ignores all paths through the network which are subcritical in terms of the expected value approach. Modern PERT software avoids this shortcoming by using Monte Carlo (sampling) methods. The Monte Carlo solution of a network involves taking a sample from the probability distribution for each activity in the network such that the value observed is as defined by the probability distribution for that activity. A standard CPA algorithm is used to compute the associated sample project distribution, and this process is repeated many times (500, for example) to obtain a histogram that approximates to the project duration probability distribution. Sampling error associated with this approach reduces as the sample size is increased.

Reasonably unbiased expected project durations, given the PERT model assumptions, are possible with fewer than 500 samples. Reasonably smooth project duration probability distribution approximations require more than 500 samples or smoothing curve-fitting approximations. Even modest network sizes mean that computation time and/or sampling error is an issue with this approach, but not a critical one.

Early research on computation procedures for PERT also considered discrete probability methods. These approaches avoid the sampling errors associated with Monte Carlo based approaches. But they involve a systematic error associated with discrete approximations of continuous distributions. More important, they become difficult to use if irreducible networks are involved.

Monte Carlo procedures are the industry standard, with some software offering various ways to reduce or control sampling errors and computation times.

Methods

Methods for CPA/PERT, procedures which provide an effective manner of using CPA/PERT models, are part of the notion of CPA/PERT as a technique developed in most textbooks on the subject. Like scientific methods and many other formalized procedures or systems, they may be associated with a distillation of successful practice. In broad terms, most follow the sequence outlined below, used in a highly iterative manner, looping back to earlier steps.

1   Decompose the project into activities.
2   Identify precedence relationships.
3   Produce a diagram of the activities.
4   Estimate activity durations (or duration distributions).
5   Compute (to identify earliest start times, float, and so on).
6   Adjust for timetable restrictions (and seek to optimize project duration).
7   Adjust for resource restrictions (and seek to optimize resource utilization).
8   Implement the project.
9   Update the plan as a basis for control.

The rationale for this sequence is efficiency and effectiveness. For example, there is no point in trying to identify precedence relationships before the activity structure is fairly well established.

Software for CPA/PERT

Software packages for CPA/PERT models must obviously be capable of performing the necessary computations. They should also provide a database structure (which most modern software does). There are substantial differences between the features of the different packages available, but they are all designed as generic to projects based on a single form of basic CPA or PERT model or, in some cases, a PERT addition or insertion to a CPA model.

GENERALIZING PERT MODELS

The basic PERT model, even using modern Monte Carlo based PERT software, involves a number of important assumptions. Many of these assumptions were clearly identified in the early 1960s. Collectively (in my view) they render the basic PERT model useless in most circumstances, dangerous in many circumstances. Some other writers will disagree, and individuals will have to make up their own minds. This section provides a basis for that judgement, and subsequent sections will develop the argument further.

Generalized PERT

Generalized PERT is the label applied to a model which provided the first key generalization of the basic PERT model. The basic PERT assumption in question is:

> For any activity A followed by activity B, activity B is statistically and causally independent of A. Whatever the outcome of A, the probability distribution for B is unchanged.

In generalized PERT, decision trees are embedded in the basic PERT network. For any activity B following activity A, different outcomes for A can condition different definitions of B. Usually these different definitions of B are used to reflect different responses to early or late completion of A – negative causal depend-   *435* ence. That is to say, if A takes longer than expected, B will take less time than expected, because we will try to 'buy back time' (for example, by allocating additional resources or effort to B).

Positive statistical dependence could be modelled, however. In that case, if A were to take longer than expected we might then expect B also to take longer that originally expected. A reason for this condition might be that both activities depend on the same project staff and equipment, with no way possible for changing our plans.

GERT

GERT (graphical evaluation and review technique) is a generalization of generalized PERT. The basic PERT assumption of relevance here is:

Activity duration uncertainty can always be modelled directly.

GERT allows indirect modelling of activity duration via a Markovian process. This is best explained by an example.

Suppose that, instead of asking how long it might take to lay 220km of pipeline in the North Sea, we were to ask 'How much cable can we lay in April, how much in June, and so on?', using the associated probability distributions to compute how long the whole pipeline might take. Decision trees modelling causal and statistical dependence can be embedded in these Markov processes. For example, should the equipment not work properly in the first month, it might be likely that it would continue to work badly, but we might be able to replace it.

Repetitive processes such as laying pipework are much more effectively modelled in this framework. This is especially true if weather windows make rate-of-progress probability distributions different in different months.

SCERT

SCERT (synergistic contingency evaluation and response technique) is a generalization of GERT. The basic PERT assumption of relevance here is:

Activity duration uncertainty can be considered without explicit reference to the reason for variations.

The basic GERT assumption of relevance here is:

Responses and statistical dependence can be considered without explicit reference to the reasons for variations.

SCERT requires formal identification and documentation of sources of risk before going on to consider responses to those sources of risk. For example, offshore pipelaying might have to be delayed because equipment is not available when planned, equipment does not operate at the expected speed, the weather is bad, the pipe develops a 'buckle' (fracturing, filling with water, ripping itself off the lay barge and sinking), and so on.

Responses may be general, but most will be specific to a source of risk.

Responses may be purely after-the-fact contingency responses. For example, if a pipe buckle is experienced it can be repaired. Divers are sent down to cut off the damaged pipe and put a cap on the good pipe (with valves in it). A 'pig' (torpedo-like object) is then sent through the pipe under air pressure from the other end to 'dewater' it by forcing the water forward and out through the valves in the cap.

Responses may require prior action. For example, if a pipe buckle occurs close to shore, time and money can be saved by abandoning the pipe and starting again. But this might mean ordering enough pipe to facilitate this option in the first place. When a buckle occurs it may be too late to obtain more pipe.

Responses may be preventive. For example, a larger and more capable barge could be used to reduce the risk of a buckle in the first place.

SCERT requires formal consideration of possible secondary risk and responses. For example, when the pig is sent through the pipe to dewater it, it might run over a rock or some other debris and stick. This might be resolved by cutting the pipe behind the pig, putting the cap on again and trying again with another pig. Alternatively, the air pressure could be turned up in an attempt to pop the pig through, risking damage to the pipeline over its whole laid length. It is important to understand the implications of these secondary risks and responses when considering the choices between repair, starting again, and using a more capable lay barge.

SCERT requires formal consideration of formal links between risks and responses. For example, if a more capable barge is used to reduce the risk of a pipe buckle, it will also speed up the repair of a pipe buckle and the basic pipelaying operation.

SCERT also requires formal consideration of which risks should be quantified and which should be treated as conditions for which purposes. For example, one pipelaying operation involved crossing three other pipelines. The probability of a lay barge anchor damaging one of the pipelines was assessed as high, and the consequences extremely serious. At a corporate level this risk was quantified and provision made. At a project level a quantified provision was not made, because the expected delay would not be an adequate provision if a pipeline was damaged, and such a provision should not be given to the project manager if a pipeline was not damaged.

SCERT also requires careful attention to precedence relationships between activities. These may be simple finish-to-start relationships. But they could be start-to-start or finish-to-finish. They might involve overlaps, including probabilistic overlaps. In formal modelling terms, event trees or fault trees (as used in safety and reliability studies for some time) are embedded in the decision trees, which may be embedded in the Markovian processes of GERT models. Precedent relationships are also generalized.

CURRENT VIEWS ON THE NATURE OF FORMAL RISK MANAGE-MENT PROCESSES

SCERT was developed for a major British oil company during the late 1970s and early 1980s. The complex nature of the models, relative to the basic PERT model, required a designed and pre-tested method, to allow effective and efficient implementation for the first 'live' study. Later, software was developed using a discrete probability basis, with no specific model form.

Variants of SCERT have been developed for a number of other organizations since the late 1970s, most simplifying the models to some extent but preserving a concern for identifying where the risk is coming from and how it can be managed (based on an understanding of complex relationships, if those relationships are important).

Without any direct reference to SCERT, a number of organizations and individuals have argued for some of the features of a SCERT type of approach, coming to the same key conclusions via different routes. It is now widely recognized that there is no best model for project planning, and different aspects of any one project might require a range of treatments. However, modelling choices can be made within a process which has a formal framework analogous to the method developed for SCERT, with short cuts where simpler models are deemed appropriate. This approach is widely accepted, with or without an association with SCERT.

For example, the Procurement Executive Risk Analysis Group of the UK Ministry of Defence (PERAG) do not endorse any specific modelling choice or any specific named method, but they do endorse such a process. The description which follows and some of the earlier comments are based on a paper presented as part of a PERAG one-day seminar on risk management (and provided as documentation for the seminar). The structure of this description follows the outline of the structure of such methods (see Figure 25.1). In practice, the process is iterative to a considerable extent, and quantitative analysis might not be appropriate in some cases.

Qualitative analysis: the identification or scope phase

The identification or scope phase begins the qualitative analysis process. It is concerned with documenting what is involved in a form which provides some initial structuring of this information.

Activity list

The first step in the scope phase involves decomposing the project into a set of component activities, documenting what is involved in each, and indicating precedence and time relationships.

The key to successful risk management lies in keeping this breakdown as simple as possible to ensure that the 'wood is not lost sight of because of the trees'. Even a £1 billion offshore project might only involve 20 to 50 activities for

Qualitative analysis	Identification or scope phase	Activity list
		Risk lists
		Response lists
		Secondary risks and responses
	Structure phase	Risk and response links
		Minor and major risks
		Specific and general responses
		Simple and complex decisions
		Ordering responses
		Diagramming the risk/response structure

Quantitative analysis	Parameter phase	Where and when to quantify
		Quantification of uncertainty
	Computation phase	Combination of risks in a nested manner

| Risk management | Interpretation of results and development of alternative approaches as appropriate, for initial planning and subsequent control/ planning revisions |

Figure 25.1   An outline structure of risk management methods   *439*

comprehensive risk management purposes. For example, fabrication of a plat-form might be one activity, laying a 220km pipeline from the platform to shore another. Half a dozen activities might be appropriate for a £20 000 000 computer replacement project.

Separating components of the project into activities allows for the separation of sources of risk which are largely different and unrelated, the responsibility of different people, amenable to different responses or solutions and other rules of thumb of this nature.

Risk lists

The second step in the scope phase involves identifying sources of risk associated with each activity and with the project as a whole, and documenting what is involved. For example, in the case of laying the offshore pipeline the list of risk sources identified might include:

- Arrival of the barge on site later than planned.
- The barge not operating as quickly as planned.
- Encountering bad weather.
- Experiencing a pipe buckle.

and so on.

One key to successful risk management lies in not overlooking any important source of risk. In the pipelaying context this might lead to some forty or so risks needing separate identification and documentation. Some activities, and some projects, might justify attention to only a few key risks.

Response lists

The third step in the scope phase involves identifying responses for each source of risk and documenting what is involved. The previous case descriptions gave examples of the possible kinds of response.

Another key to successful risk management lies in not overlooking any realistic response for any critical source of risk.

Secondary risks and responses

The final step in the identification or scope phase involves identifying secondary risks and responses as appropriate, as indicated earlier, and documenting what is involved. The extent to which it is worth identifying these higher order risks and responses is very much a matter of judgement, necessarily dependent on a variety of issues. Once again, the key lies in not overlooking any important issue.

Qualitative analysis – the structure phase

The format of the information gathered in the identification or scope phase provides the initial structure. Further structuring is the purpose of the second phase of this project planning process and other risk management processes. This additional structure is initially sought while maintaining a qualitative approach.

Risk and response links

Many risks and responses involve important interdependencies which need to be identified. For example, a response to one risk might affect the chances of another risk. If the analysis cannot be structured to avoid such links, it is important to consider where the effects might be significant. Some links might already have been identified, as with the use of a more capable barge in the pipelaying example given earlier, but, at this stage, a systematic search is appropriate.

Minor and major risks

At some stage in any analysis there is a need to decide what is and what is not important in terms of the project. A related (but different) issue is deciding what needs care and attention in terms of analysis and what does not. There is a natural tendency to make these judgements as quickly as possible, failing to note potential difficulties or dismissing them as unimportant. The discipline associated with leaving such judgements until this stage is useful. Once primary responses and secondary risks and responses are clear, and when risk and response links have been identified, it is easier to dismiss some risks as minor because effective responses will be listed. Major risks are identified as a residual.

It is also possible to distinguish between significant problems that have only one simple and effective solution (requiring no further attention in terms of analysis) and those for which appropriate responses do not involve obvious choices (where further analysis would be useful).

Specific and general responses

Some responses are specific to particular risks. Examples from the pipelaying project in relation to a pipeline buckle were 'repair' or 'abandon and start again'. Others might be identified in the context of a particular risk, but offer a solution to a wide range of other risks. For example, the delay associated with a pipeline buckle could be recovered by using a second lay barge working from the other end, with a submarine connection to join the two parts of pipeline (this response would be provisional on having an option in place to obtain the second barge if needed). This response will also recover time lost due to bad weather, equipment failures, delayed start to pipelaying, and a wide range of other difficulties – including some which might not have been identified in the first place. The key lies in being aware of any particularly useful general responses and ensuring that these can be implemented if necessary.

441

Simple and complex decisions

An efficient and effective risk management process does not involve gathering all the facts and defining all the options in order to make all the necessary decisions simultaneously. Instead, the analysis and management process has to start with relatively simple decisions and then move towards the relatively complex decisions.

The process starts with strategic level planning and then moves towards the tactical. But some tactical decisions will have to be considered before the strategic issues can be fully understood. For example, assessing how much extra pipe should be ordered to allow implementation of the 'abandon and start again' response to a pipe buckle is a simple decision relative to whether or not to take out an option on a second lay barge, and its possible use will affect the value of taking the barge option, so they should be considered in that logical order.

More generally, there is a need to plan the planning process, a level of planning which is above the project planning level.

Ordering responses

Part of the structuring process is to arrange responses in the preferred sequence.

Diagramming the risk response structure

Preparing a diagram to provide a basis for discussion of this structuring of risks and responses could be an integral and useful part of the process. The purpose served is analogous to that served by an activity-on-arrow diagram portrayal of precedence structure, providing a basis for discussion by the project team of the nature of the risks and responses to be managed.

Quantitative analysis: the parameter phase

Quantitative analysis, using probability distributions to help further our under-standing of uncertainty and how best to manage it, may be the third phase of this project planning process, if appropriate.

Where and when to quantify

Formal risk management procedures do not necessarily require quantification of uncertainty. If an organization is not able or not prepared to take any significant risks, the risk management process will be concerned with avoiding or transfer-ring risks and measurement will not be appropriate. Usually some degree of quantification is useful, but quantification of any aspect should be in response to a considered view that it would be useful to do so.

For example, when considering an offshore pipeline, sources of risk like weather, equipment breakdowns, pipe buckle and so on all lend themselves to useful quantitative analysis. However, suppose that the proposed pipeline route might be changed should drilling for oil in a nearby field prove successful. Keeping to the proposed route might then be best identified as a *condition* upon which current plans depend (as opposed to its being an uncertainty within those plans) without attempting to embed the possible changes in route in the current plan. Similarly, if a pipeline has to be laid across other pipelines, involving a significant chance that lay barge anchors might damage those other pipelines with very serious consequences, it might be best to identify preventative and contingency responses in detail but keep this issue separate from the 'base plan' (as indicated earlier). In particular, it would not be appropriate to give the project manager 'contingency time' or money based on such an incident, to be used whether or not such an incident occurred.

Quantification of uncertainty

Separate consideration of different sources of risk as part of a formal process allows analysis to integrate data from those sources, and enables judgements to be made by different people according to who is best able to make those judgements.

Some uncertainty is relatively easy to quantify using very appropriate data. For example, North Sea average wave heights have been recorded by sea area by month for many years. This makes estimating the effect of weather-related uncertainty on equipment whose operational limitations are defined in terms of wave height conditions relatively straightforward.

Some uncertainty requires important subjective adjustments to data-based estimates. For example, in the late 1970s the number of kilometres of pipe laid in the North Sea was known, and so was the number of pipe buckles. This provided a simple estimate of the probability of a buckle per kilometre of pipelaying. However, it was also known that equipment was improving rapidly, and that the operators were becoming much more experienced. In this case a very important subjective adjustment was needed to adjust the historically based estimate.

The most important case is where uncertainty is very important, but appropriate data are not available. Some people argue that formal analysis is a waste of time if good data are not available. I believe that, although lack of data certainly makes analysis more difficult, it also makes it more important, as there is no other way to deal effectively with uncertainty. This is a fundamental issue in the overall process of risk management.

Consider an extreme case. A few years ago I was asked to advise on the risk of sabotage associated with a water supply pipeline which had already suffered one unsuccessful attack. The client did not know what he would say should he decide that it was not worth spending money to protect the pipeline and it were then to be attacked successfully. The client anticipated that, in that event, an explanation might be required that would stand up in court. Such a situation requires turning the issue round – avoiding the question 'What is the chance of a successful sabotage attack?' (almost impossible to answer). The question that should be asked instead is 'What does the chance of a successful sabotage attack have to be in order to make it worth spending money on protection?' In this case, the most likely point of attack was identified, the most effective response to such an attack was identified, and both the response and the consequences of a successful attack were costed. The resulting analysis suggested that a successful attack every two years would be necessary to justify the expenditure. The case for *not* spending the money was therefore clear and defensible.

Computation phase

A range of software is available to combine quantified risks (whatever their structure) based on method-of-moments, discrete probability methods and Monte Carlo simulation. A key to successful project risk management is avoiding gathering up all the numbers and running one big model directly. It is important to develop a feel for where the problems might come from, and what can be done about them, by building up an understanding of the quantified risks and their associated responses in a nested manner. For example, to consider pipelaying in terms of weather risk might be the starting point, then the effects of pipe buckles could be added, and so on. I prefer discrete probability methods, because they force a careful build up. Monte Carlo based software is, however, the industry standard and it will do the same job. Method-of-moment software is less flexible.

Interpretation of results and risk management

The final phase of this formal project duration risk management method is directly concerned with the management of risk given the insights provided by the earlier phases. At this stage, the iterative nature of the process becomes more pronounced. Interpretation of results based on all the assumptions inherent in the base plans and contingency plans will generally leave us uncomfortable in some areas, and lead us to revise our plans.

At this stage the bottom-up approach to building up an understanding of the risks and responses is used in a top-down manner. Where final consequences at the project duration level are unacceptable ('We can't afford to build it if it will take that long', for example), the analysis must be examined to deduce the best way to improve the situation. Understanding the relationships developed earlier between risks and responses is essential to allow effective and efficient management of risk at this stage.

It is at this stage in the overall process that the benefits of such a comprehensive formal risk management process are realized. The nature of these benefits will be discussed in the next section.

CURRENT VIEWS ON THE BENEFITS OF FORMAL RISK MANAGEMENT PROCESSES

The rationale for comprehensive formal risk management processes is not well understood, even among managers in some organizations where those processes are in frequent use. This is because the benefits are many and diverse. But it is important to appreciate all of these benefits in order to realize them fully. This section outlines the main benefits.

Risk efficiency

Doing things better in terms of risk efficiency is the central role of formal risk management (as pointed out earlier). Most projects might not present such dramatic opportunities for improving risk efficiency as the offshore pipeline example cited earlier (where a 1.6m barge and a 3m barge were compared for a hook-up activity) but chances are there for those who look for them.

Risk balance

Reducing risk or reducing expected cost where appropriate, and making such trade-offs, is another central role for formal risk management procedures (again, as pointed out earlier).

Formalizing risk analysis enables managers to make decisions on risk – whether to be more risk-averse, for example – with full knowledge of the implications. Knowing which risks to take and which to avoid is critical to good corporate risk management at *all* levels.

Distinguishing different types of estimates

It is important to set targets which can be achieved provided no significant difficulties are encountered, but which are 'lean' (as free as possible of the 'fat' associated with allowances for unspecified contingencies). If people are given allowances against unspecified contingencies they will tend to use them, whether or not this is necessary.

It is also important to identify contingency allowances associated with all significant individual risks, plus a residual allowance for other unidentified risks, to allow for controlled adjustments from target figures to realized figures. As part of this process it is important to relate these contingency sums in an appropriate manner to expected outcomes, to commitment outcomes which have an appropriate chance of being achieved, and to outcomes which will or will not happen.

For instance, the numbers in the example hook-up activity used earlier to illustrate risk efficiency and balance might have been significantly different. The use of a 1.6m barge might have involved a considerable expected cost saving, but a significant risk of additional cost and time. In such a case the company's board might have authorized the use of the 1.6m barge, with a target completion date and budget which assumed completion that season, while putting aside a contingency provision that would be made available to the project manager in case an additional season of operations were required. This provision would have been related to the overall corporate position. It would involve an expected value component based on the extra season, and a component providing a contribution to the risk associated with all such provisions for the organization's portfolio of large expenditures on projects.

Suitable expected and commitment values are usually very much higher than target values. Very different numbers are involved. Formal risk management procedures clarify what is involved. Without such procedures, there is considerable scope for confusion. This issue is important in all projects, large or small.   *445*

Culture change

Controlled adjustments from target figures to realized figures (as just discussed) have important corporate culture implications, as does the explicit understanding of risk efficiency and risk/expected cost trade-offs discussed earlier. They allow a clear distinction between good management and good luck (and between bad management and bad luck). For example, the hook-up activity just discussed and used earlier in this chapter actually took place in late October during a period of good weather. Had the project manager argued for a 3m barge on quite sound intuitive grounds, his career might have looked quite different (he 'wasted' the additional cost) than it did in the light of the formal analysis (which justified the 3m barge decision and also made it very clear that he had done very well to achieve the hook-up by October).

If people have reason to believe that they will be punished for being unlucky, they will not take calculated risks early in the planning process. This will lead to higher expected and average costs than might be appropriate. Formal risk management processes ought to facilitate greater risk taking at this stage, to reduce expected costs and increase expected profits. This aspect alone can prove to be the most important benefit of formal risk management, and it has a linked benefit which is also of great importance. If formal risk management processes have not been used early in the planning process, project managers will tend to gamble in the later planning and implementation stages, taking greater risks than warranted from an organizational perspective in order to preserve their credibility in the face of adverse events (which might, or might not have been within their control).

Clarifying the 'big picture'

It can be very important to relate analysis of a specific choice to the broader concerns of an organization. The important of such relationships might not be recognized if formal risk management procedures are not adopted.

For example, I was once asked to assess construction cost risk associated with one method of recovering offshore oil (method A) with a view to comparing this with an alternative approach (method B). Method B had a relatively low capital cost, but the operating costs were higher, with reduced revenue. It soon became clear that the cost risk for method A in itself was not an insurmountable problem. However, method A, with a cost in the upper end of the likely range, in conjunction with both oil reserves and an oil price at the lower end of their likely ranges, could mean disaster for the whole organization. A disaster of this extent was not a reasonable possibility for method B. Without the analysis, the company would not have been aware of the extent to which choosing method A could involve 'betting the company' on that choice.

Opportunities as well as threats

Some common reactions to the possibility of imposed formal risk management
procedures are:

- 'We will be overcome by doom and gloom.'
- 'We will suffer paralysis by analysis.'
- 'We will frighten ourselves to death and never do anything.'

Properly conducted, formal risk management procedures should not produce such responses. They should be very much concerned with identifying and managing opportunities as well as threats, upside risk as well as downside risk. This is not just a question of taking more risk. It is also a question of identifying opportunities more effectively and more efficiently.

Creativity and lateral thinking

An important concern about the possibility of imposed formal risk management procedures that people are often reluctant to state directly is based on a wish to avoid being involved in a mechanistic process which is perceived as boring and lacking in interest. Again, if properly conducted, formal risk management procedures should not produce such concerns. Rather, they should allow scope for creative and lateral thinking, the searching out of more effective ways of avoiding risks well in advance of such risks actually being realized. They should allow the proper management of *risk* rather than the later management of *crisis*. If a formal management process is not stimulating, it is probably not being done properly.

Valuable documentation

Documentation developed as part of a comprehensive formal risk management process is not a central benefit in the sense of those benefits discussed above. But it does have five very useful functions:

1 People tend to think more clearly if they commit their thoughts to paper.
2 Communication is greatly enhanced if all activities, risks, responses, and relationships between them are described at length in words and in summary graphical forms.
3 The effects of staff turnover are usually a substantial source of risk for projects. Documentation of the kind associated with comprehensive formal risk management processes greatly reduces this risk.
4 Even those who initiate the documentation often find it useful to return to it, to refresh their memories with what they had in mind when making a judgement some time earlier.
5 The value of this documentation can extend across projects, in effect capturing important corporate knowledge, making that knowledge portable and therefore more valuable.

CHOOSING THE MOST EFFECTIVE LEVEL OF ANALYSIS

Choosing the most effective level of activity detail for critical path analysis is a matter of judgement with which most experienced project staff feel comfortable *447* (although beginners will obviously need guidance). Choosing the most effective level of activity–risk–response structure involves the same kind of judgement, but in different dimensions and for different reasons. This judgement is driven by the need to manage risk effectively, in a manner appropriate to where the project is in its life cycle, and the costs of failing to understand the risks. For example, early in a project's life the key issue may be an unbiased estimate of its expected cost – not how the project will be implemented – but who is going to bear the risks might also be important.

In my view most organizations start too late and do not go as deep as they should. The later this kind of risk management process is started the easier it becomes, because the project is then better defined. However, the potential gains are then less, because there is less scope for significant improvements in risk efficiency.

Taken together, the above points suggest starting down the learning curve at the point when a go/no-go decision is about to be taken, the easiest place to start, and taking the analysis further than might be thought appropriate. As experience is gained, analysis short cuts can be used (with an understanding of what is lost by taking the short cuts, as well as the savings in effort). Analysis can be moved upstream in the flow of a project's life cycle into early feasibility studies. It can also be carried downstream, to develop detailed project implementation plans, as well as updating the strategic position.

Once a risk management process of this nature is in place, data acquisition to service it can begin. As databases are developed the process will become simpler. Experience gained with this style of analysis will also sharpen people's intuitive judgements, because learning is more effective if people have a conceptual framework within which they can structure the implications of their experience. This allows formal treatment at a simpler level. Not only is there no best single model for all activities in any project; the most appropriate models for formal analysis will evolve as experience is gained and data are acquired.

ISSUES BEYOND PROJECT DURATION RISK MANAGEMENT

Project duration risk analysis is the easiest and most appropriate place to start if a project is sensitive to duration risk (as is the case with offshore oil and gas projects). The process of managing duration risk involves cost trade-offs, and cost risk trade-offs (as illustrated by the 1.6m/3m barge examples used earlier).

When a satisfactory base plan and contingency plans have been developed in terms of duration risk and associated cost risk trade-offs, cost risk analysis can be completed. That is to say:

- Duration uncertainty can be considered in conjunction with uncertainty about the cost per unit time of the resources associated with each activity.
- Further uncertainty associated with the costs of materials can be associated with the costs per unit of those materials.
- Still further uncertainty associated with any further lump sum or overhead apportionment costs can be considered.

If duration risk is not an issue, cost risk can be approached in a (quantity × rate + lump sum and apportionment) structure, without the (duration × rate) structure.

As a general rule, an exhaustive source of risk structure is harder to define in terms of rates, lump sums and apportionments than it is for durations, and levels of statistical dependence between risks and between cost items are far higher and much more important. For example, cost items in North Sea projects often average a 70 per cent level of positive dependence, equivalent to a 0.7 coefficient of correlation – a very strong tendency to go up and down in unison. This arises because of market pressure effects. It is very important, because it means that the risk associated with different cost items does not cancel out rapidly as items are added.

Offshore projects offer relatively little chance to trade off duration or cost with performance. This is not true of military projects or computer software projects, for example. If the project is very sensitive to duration risk, duration risk analysis could be the best place to start, but in managing duration risk, cost and cost-risk trade-offs plus performance and performance-risk trade-offs might have to be considered. Performance can have a number of dimensions. The performance parameters of a military aircraft, for example, can include speed, range, firepower, manoeuvrability, reliability, maintainability and so on.

As a general rule it is too difficult to work directly with more than one of the three dimensions (duration, cost and performance). One has to be selected as a working dimension, and the others treated in terms of trade-offs. Duration is a convenient choice, and a good one if the project is highly sensitive to duration risk, but cost or performance could be chosen instead.

The notion of managing risk in terms of its sources was probably first used in a formal way by insurance companies and those interested in safety and other performance issues. All the risk management process issues discussed earlier in terms of project duration risk can be carried back into these areas. There can be considerable benefit in doing so. For example, the use of fault trees and event trees is standard practice in safety analysis, but many safety studies based on these models do not exploit the notion of associated decision trees and a direct concern for risk efficiency and balance, as set out here.

The sequence in which duration, cost and performance risks are considered is a method issue. Simultaneous modelling of all these issues is not feasible. It is necessary to use models which focus on one part of the issues at a time. And the sequence chosen has to be that which is the most effective and efficient in practice.

Cost risk assessment using this sort of risk management process can be linked to cost estimates prepared in a conventional deterministic manner (as described in Chapter 12). In the same way, duration risk management processes can be linked to a base plan initiated using basic critical path analysis techniques (Chapter 17). In this context the risk management processes serve as an audit or check. Usually this is a sensible way to start. However, most organizations find it useful to move towards an embedding of these processes in each other. Risk management becomes an integral part of all other kinds of estimation, planning and management (including resources, materials, purchasing, and so on). As a *449* separate 'add-on' its potential is not fully exploited.

As indicated in the previous section, the nature of the risk management process adopted needs to reflect the purpose of the analysis. Project appraisal, as described in Chapter 15, is concerned with go/no-go decisions and straight comparisons which do not necessarily require detailed understanding of how best to execute a project. The essential input required is simply an unbiased estimate of expected cash inflows, outflows, and associated uncertainty. Appropriate choices in relation to important strategic issues which will affect cost and cost uncertainty need to be understood, but not tactical detail. This modification of the risk management process to suit its purpose or role has to be considered carefully.

Insurance is a very powerful way of managing risks, but its use involves risk balance decisions needing careful attention. It is vital to insure some risks and not insure other risks. Knowing which is which is a central risk management issue. The identification of risk and responses as described in this chapter is a sound basis for considering insurance responses to risks (as discussed in Chapter 8). But if risk management via insurance is a key issue, the risk management process will need to be modified to reflect the concerns of those responsible for dealing with insurance issues.

Contractual clauses and, more generally, contracting strategy, is another way to manage risks (and sometimes a source of risks). From a client's perspective, knowing which risks to take and which to pass on to contractors is a crucial issue – often managed with a conspicuous lack of success. Contractors need to manage risks too. A client's risks are often a contractor's opportunities, and what appears to be a contractor's risk might become an unexpected client's risk. For both parties to manage their risks effectively, it may be important to move towards a cooperative shared information approach to project management, recognizing that once trust is lost (and both sides become confrontational) the project and both main parties could be in serious trouble. An understanding of the risk/response structure as discussed in this chapter also has relevance to other contractual issues discussed in Part 2 of this book. But a risk management process designed to deal with contractual issues will have to reflect this purpose explicitly.

All aspects of project management can to some extent be embedded in a process which is concerned with the management of risk, or vice versa. This does not mean that all these issues can be dealt with simultaneously. They will have to be dealt with in an orderly sequence, often by different people with different skills. But managing the links can be vital. For example, a political risk associated with obtaining or not obtaining a vital permission might be managed by political activity, technical changes to the project, contractual arrangements, insurance arrangements, financial arrangements, or some combination of these that is more effective than any single dimension response.

FURTHER READING

For a useful discussion of the evolution of PERT, generalized PERT and GERT models and computation procedures:

Moder, J. J. and Philips, C. R., *Project Management with CPM and PERT*, 3rd edn (or other editions), Van Nostrand, New York, 1970.

For SCERT, start with one or more of:

Chapman, C. B., 'A risk engineering approach to project risk management', in *International Journal of Project Management*, **8**, (1), 1990.

Chapman, C. B., Cooper, D. F., and Page, M. J, 'Risk engineering' in *Management for Engineers*, Wiley, Chichester, 1987.

Cooper, D. F. and Chapman, C. B., *Risk Analysis for Large Projects: Models, Methods and Cases*, Wiley, Chichester, 1987.

For further discussion of the benefits of formal risk management processes see:

Newland, K. E., 'Benefits of risk analysis and management', in *Project*, The Bulletin of the Association of Project Managers, November, 1992.

For an introductory guide to project risk analysis and management, and for a project risk management software directory, contact the Association of Project Managers, whose Special Interest Group on Project Risk Management compiled both documents.

ACKNOWLEDGEMENTS

The examples used in this chapter were first used in this way in a presentation developed for IBM UK senior management as part of their 1989–90 Forum 2 programme. This presentation was further developed for one-day seminars on risk management held by PERAG (Project Estimating and Risk Analysis Group) for the UK Ministry of Defence Procurement Executive project managers and Treasury officers. Some of this material was first published in 'Risk' in *Investment, Procurement and Performance in Construction*, edited by P. Venmore-Rowland *et al.*, published by The Royal Institute of Chartered Surveyors, E. and F. N. Spon, Chapman & Hall, London, 1991.

26 Integrated Systems for Planning and Control

Lucas Management Systems*
(formerly Metier Management Systems)

A typical project includes a number of areas and disciplines which often operate as separate, autonomous units. Great benefits can be reaped from bringing them together. This approach is termed 'integration'. Integration is the key to effective project management and yet, until recently, the whole concept of integrated systems had been almost impossible to apply in practice. Several key developments during the past five to ten years have created a situation where not only are integrated systems possible, but they are now viewed as an essential element of successful project management. A major factor in making integrated systems available to the project team has been the revolution in computer technology. Not only have computers become faster, smaller and more easily available, but there have been fundamental changes in the nature of computer programs. Just ten years ago, using a computer required expert assistance. Nowadays, comprehensive project control systems are available that can be operated directly by the project team itself. Areas such as planning, resource scheduling, costing, design management, procurement, commissioning, in fact every aspect of project control, can now be effectively managed by the project team.

THE PROJECT MANAGEMENT PROCESS

In its broadest sense, project management can be considered as a combination of the tasks of planning, coordinating and controlling resources such as men, machines, materials and money in order to meet the objectives of a project.

The time-tested approach begins with the formal process of planning the work and then deciding when each part of the work will take place, what resources it will require, what it will cost, and so on. In short, creating a yardstick against

---

*Updated from an original chapter by Ray Palmer.

which the steps required to achieve the objectives can be measured. But, the problem with plans is that they cannot always be adhered to. Bad weather, low productivity, design changes, and a thousand and one other factors continually undermine the validity of the original plan. In an attempt to minimize the effect of these changes, an almost continual replanning of the project is required to incorporate new information affecting the project.

This process of constantly replanning ranges from day-to-day changes in the sequence of work, the allocation of equipment, materials, and manpower to meet local conditions, to formal reviews where the whole plan is revised. This process is often described as the control cycle, although this tends to suggest a far more formalized and considered process than the complex mixture of formal and informal changes that actually occurs in practice.

Decision making

The fundamental element in controlling a project is decision making. To make reasonable and rational decisions a number of conditions must be met. Information relevant to the problem in hand must first be isolated. Often this is the most difficult part of the process and, in practice, most decisions are made in the knowledge that much relevant information is submerged in the mass of project related data, and is not available on demand. When as much relevant information as possible has been gathered, the process of deciding the most appropriate course of action can begin. In most cases there will be several options and the usual process is to evaluate each one in turn and then choose the most appropriate. This is in fact the approach we intuitively use in the solving of all kinds of day-to-day problems. We automatically build a mental 'model' of the situation and test various alternatives against it, forecast the outcome for each possible combination of circumstances, and then choose the most appropriate. A simple everyday illustration of this is in choosing a holiday. It is usual to examine the alternatives in terms of cost, convenience, likely enjoyment, and so on, and then to choose the option that most closely meets the objectives. The 'model' in this case is the mental image of how all these factors combine to make a good holiday.

The project model

A project is, of course, a much more complex undertaking than choosing a holiday. It may well require thousands of material items, drawings, and individual tasks, combined with many different types of resources and complicated cost/time relationships. A mental model is not adequate to evaluate the astronomic number of possible ways of carrying out the job. Indeed, to encompass every eventuality, the project model would need to incorporate all the factors that could possibly have an impact upon the project management process.

To be of practical use it also has to cope with the many subobjectives that are the realities of project work, such as the need to minimize overtime, increase productivity, reduce plant movement, and so on. In real life each and every aspect of a project is interrelated and interdependent. A delayed material *453* delivery, for example, may well require a section of a project to be rescheduled. This in turn changes the required delivery dates for other materials, which can in turn affect the procurement process and, ultimately, priorities in the design office. In an extreme case, the overall timing of much of the rest of the work can be affected, along with the associated cash flow, borrowing requirements and profit margin.

With an *integrated* system the project information is interrelated and inter-dependent in *exactly* the same way as in real life. This can have a dramatic impact on the effectiveness of the project team. In decision making, for example, several options can be run through and tested to see the effect on each aspect of the project and examine the cost effectiveness of alternative approaches in detail before any action is taken.

The decision reached may on the basis of a clear-cut cost benefit or a complex trade-off between a number of conflicting factors. Without an integrated system, the decision can only be based on limited information, rudimentary costings, and virtually no evaluation of alternatives. With an integrated system the project team can be confident in the knowledge that they are making well informed, rational and cost justified decisions across all relevant aspects of their project.

An integrated system is essential for effective decision making. It also provides a project or even company-wide communication medium: this is (or should be) consistent in each area of application. The day-to-day work of collecting time-sheet data, or details of material deliveries is all part of the project and as such is an essential element of the integrated system. The ability to incorporate such detailed information means that the process of managing the project is based on real information that is directly available to the project team. This information should be available not just in its detailed form, but 'rolled-up' and summarized in the appropriate form for the task at hand.

The scope and complexity of integrated systems varies considerably. At one extreme, companies limit themselves to integrating cost and schedule data and at the other, there are systems that incorporate almost every aspect of a company's work. Integration can be applied to individual projects or to a number of projects running concurrently and can include central, head office work such as buying and accounts. Integration can also be viewed as extending throughout the life of a project. Information generated at the design stage is subsequently used for construction, commissioning and eventually for maintaining the resulting product.

THE REQUIREMENTS FOR INTEGRATION

Until recent years, computer assistance was not directly available to the project team. A number of computerized project management tools existed such as 'critical path analysis' and 'cost control', but these were stand-alone applications, each designed to meet *one* need in *isolation*. Integration of these techniques varied from being 'impossible' to 'possible with difficulty'. Often too, it was difficult to enhance individual applications. For example, adding an extra cost code or producing a non-standard report, could involve weeks of a computer programmer's time. Now, with computers becoming more easily available, more powerful and with dramatic software advances, a fully integrated system dealing with every aspect of project management can be achieved. Although a fully integrated project control system was theoretically possible by manual methods, advances in computing now make it a reality.

Merely having a computer and a range of application packages is not, however, enough in itself. A successful integrated system requires a number of essential additional features. There are a number of systems which meet these requirements to a greater or lesser extent. The author's experience is of one of these systems, ARTEMIS (by Lucas Management Systems), from which the following examples are drawn.

Man–machine interface

The concept of integrated systems would have remained an academic exercise had it not been for developments in the so-called man–machine interface – broadly the way in which we understand and communicate with computers. In this respect, it is vital that the system has the support, involvement, and commitment of the project team. *Any* obstacle presented by the system will adversely affect this situation. Lucas's early research, now confirmed by their clients, is that acceptance and use of a computer system is related to several key factors:

1 The system must be based on a simple concept, and must be easy to understand and to use. This is especially necessary if staff other than computing personnel are to use it.
2 The language used to communicate with the computer system should be simple, and as much like everyday language as possible. Once again, this is necessary if the system is to be available for use by project staff rather than by computing experts.
3 It should be possible to produce and to amend reports rapidly and easily, so that project managers can react to the changing requirements for information.
4 The system should enable information from all project areas to be brought together as and when required by the changing needs of the project environment.
5 There must be a rapid method for implementing project control applications, and for their subsequent modification or enhancement to meet changing requirements.

Each of these man–machine factors is essential for successful integration. The absence of any one factor will inhibit the successful adoption and use of the system. The examples given later are based upon this understanding and it is worth looking at the practical implications in more detail.

A simple concept

In practice it has been found that the simple analogy of a filing system is an ideal *455* method for understanding the fundamental principles of database systems. Surprisingly, the analogy holds up well in a project environment, only being replaced by more sophisticated concepts for complex and extensive systems.

If the storage of information about, say, drawings is considered using purely manual methods, one would maintain a record of all relevant information on cards – one for each drawing – which would be kept in a filing cabinet drawer or drawers. Each card might list: drawing number; drawing description or title; date drawn; date first issued; subsequent revision numbers and issue dates, and so on. For a complete project records system there would probably be a considerable number of other filing cabinet drawers, containing information on subjects such as materials, costs and the project schedule.

With an integrated computer system, the storage of information can be viewed in exactly the same way. This is illustrated in Figure 26.1, in which:

1 There is a 'card' for each drawing (called a 'record').
2 Each individual item of information on the record is called a 'field'.

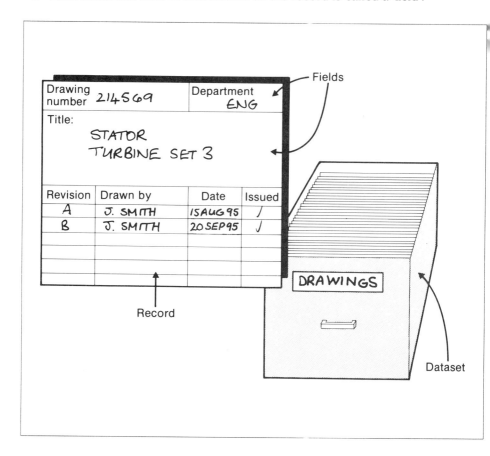

Figure 26.1   Dataset principles

3 The 'filing drawer or drawers' containing each set of records is called a 'dataset'.

4 The complete collection of all the 'filing cabinets' is called the 'database'.

With a manual system there is more or less total freedom to decide what information should be kept for each drawing and the number of cards in the file. The number of different sets of information is limited only by the amount of space available in which to store them. The ARTEMIS system enables the user to design his own record cards, and create a virtually unlimited number of 'datasets' in which to store his information. The above example uses drawings but, of course each element of the project – materials, manpower, money, and so on – can be held in datasets in exactly the same way.

Thus, as a basic concept, ARTEMIS mirrors manual methods and enables users to develop systems that reflect the 'natural' organization of information.

An extension of this analogy is to think of the computer system as a 'super-clerk', with unlimited ability to store, recall and combine information and present it as printed or graphical reports – all in response to the 'conversation-like' commands of the user.

Communicating with the system

A number of approaches are possible in communicating with the system.

Historically, using 'batch' processing computers, it was necessary to prepare a list of instructions on punch cards and then feed them to the computer. These cards would typically tell the machine which programs were needed, which data to use and which reports to produce. Preparing the data, having the cards punched and then submitting the job to the computer centre could often take anything from several hours to several days. The frustration of then discovering that a vital instruction had been omitted, causing the 'run' to fail, caused many project people to look for alternatives that could produce more immediate results.

The breakthrough came with 'interactive' computing, where the user carries on a conversation with the computer. The nature of this 'conversation' can vary from the computer acting on a spoken instruction, (an approach still being developed), to the now familiar arcade game method of using a joy-stick. Somewhere between these two extremes are the more usual 'menu' and 'command' driven systems, both of which are appropriate to the project environment.

The so-called menu approach is where the system offers a list of options on the VDU screen. The user indicates his choice, usually by typing the appropriate number or letter. In the following example, the system is giving the user a choice of three report types. By entering the number '2' after the command 'GIVE NUMBER' the user has requested the 'COST THIS MONTH' report, which the computer proceeds to print.

WHICH REPORT DO YOU WANT?
1   CRITICAL ACTIVITIES

2   COST THIS MONTH
3   RESOURCE FORECAST
GIVE NUMBER 2
REPORT BEING PRINTED

This can be useful where the overall extent of the system is limited. Problems occur when there are many options available or a non-standard report is required. For a limited application, used infrequently, the menu approach can be the ideal means of conversing with the computer.

The alternative approach of using a command language enables the user to converse in English-like phrases. Typical ARTEMIS commands include:

PRINT REPORT FRED
    which produces a printed report that the user has previously specified, in this case report Fred.
DISPLAY IF RESOURCE IS FITTER
    which displays on the terminal screen all the activities involving fitters.
DISPLAY TITLE IF START AFTER 1 JUNE 95
    an enquiry asking for the title of, in this case, drawings where the production starts after a particular date.

The command language approach allows the user to specify exactly what is required without having to pass through several menus.

The ideal arrangement is perhaps a combination of both approaches: a menu system for simple repetitive tasks and a command language for those aspects of the system that require fast response to a variety of changing circumstances.

In an integrated system the approach should be consistent across all the applications, all the system facilities such as producing printed reports, plotting graphic reports, carrying out calculations, and even in communicating to other systems. This brings benefits in that the users can use any part of the system without the need for additional training – the method of operation and the commands required are all predictable and consequently reassuring to the user.

Producing reports

Reports are the primary means of communicating information. A general rule for designing reports is that they should contain *just* the information for the task in hand. In the fast-moving projects world, it is also essential that the reports can be easily and quickly modified to keep pace with changing requirements.

An effective project system will include a comprehensive and flexible 'report generator'. This will be used by the project team members themselves and should take into account the need for simple and direct operation. Using the ARTEMIS system, for example, existing reports can be comprehensively modified within a few minutes using simple commands. Take a situation where, because of problems on-site, a specific report is required which identifies all the pipework related drawings. Supposing the 'standard' report, report DRAW, is the drawings register, containing information on 1 000 drawings, the pipework drawings can be quickly isolated as follows:

LUCAS

Client : LUCAS MANAGEMENT SYSTEMS
Location : METIER HOUSE, LONDON
Project name: ARTEMIS DEMO

DRAWING LISTING

ARTEMIS

Project start : 1-JAN-94
Time now : 1-JAN-94
Project complete : 24-JUL-95

DRAWING NUMBER	DRAWING DESCRIPTION	ACTIVITY CODE	DATE REQUIRED	FORECAST ISSUE	DRAWN BY	DATE DRAWN	DATE SUBMITTED	DATE APPROVED	DATE ISSUED
E261	PIPING & INSTRUMENTS AREA E06	9798	5-JAN-94						
E262	AREA E06 PIPEWORK LAYOUT	9798	5-JAN-94						
E271	PIPING & INSTRUMENTS AREA E04	6162	6-JAN-94	6-JAN-94	TRJ	20-DEC-93	22-DEC-93	1-JAN-94	6-JAN-94
E302	M.ENG. COOLING PIPEWORK	E4E7	28-JAN-94	28-JAN-94	JMcD	7-JAN-94	10-JAN-94	20-JAN-94	

Figure 26.2 Selective drawings report

PRINT REPORT DRAW
SELECT IF TITLE CONTAINS 'PIPE'

The standard report DRAW is now printed but with only the piping drawings (see Figure 26.2).

In practice, there are several other commands that could be used:

ORDER
to put the items on the report in a particular sequence, perhaps by date or drawing number, as required.

DIVIDE
to divide the report, page by page, into a particular grouping, perhaps by department or by approval status and so on.

BAR
to add a printed bar chart to each page, illustrating the dates in the drawing production cycle.

HISTOGRAM
to add a printed histogram to each page. This could show the drawing production rate or the number of draughtsmen required at particular times.

Indeed, all the fields of information in the drawings dataset can be included or excluded as required.

Integrating information

The situation could of course be more complex and require us to discover when

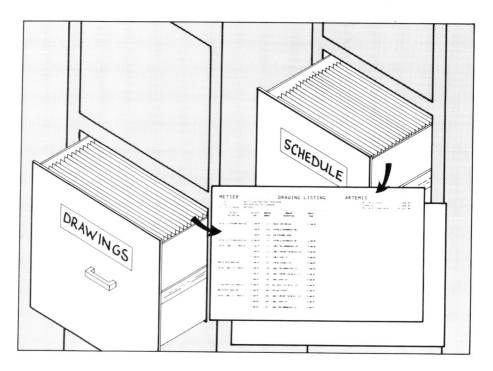

Figure 26.3   Integration of information

LUCAS

DRAWING LISTING

ARTEMIS

Client   : LUCAS MANAGEMENT SYSTEMS
Location   : METIER HOUSE, LONDON
Project name: ARTEMIS DEMO

Project start   : 1-JAN-94
Time now   : 1-JAN-94
Project complete : 24-JUL-95

ACTIVITY DESCRIPTION	ACTIVITY START	DRAWING NUMBER	DRAWING DESCRIPTION	FORECAST ISSUE
INSTALL SYSTEM PIPEWK AREA E06	7-JAN-94	E231	VALVE LOCATION AREA E06	5-JAN-94
	7-JAN-94	E261	PIPING & INSTRUMENTS AREA E06	5-JAN-94
	7-JAN-94	E262	AREA E06 PIPEWORK LAYOUT	5-JAN-94
INSTALL SYSTEM PIPEWK AREA E04	8-JAN-94	E271	PIPING & INSTRUMENTS AREA E04	6-JAN-94
INSTALL CABLES ETC AREA E01	11-JAN-94	E321	CABLE TRAY ARRANGEMENT E01	9-JAN-94
	11-JAN-94	E322	CABLE TERMINATION DETAILS E01	9-JAN-94
	11-JAN-94	E323	CABLE LAYOUT AREA E01	9-JAN-94
PRELIM PAINT AREA E04	11-JAN-94	E331	FINISH SCHEDULE AREA E04	9-JAN-94
FIT AUX MACHINE SEATS AREA E02	4-JAN-94	E391	AUX MACHINE SEAT DETAILS E02	4-JAN-94

From the project schedule

From the drawings dataset

Figure 26.4   Combined report from integrated information

each of these pipework drawings is required on-site for assembly. This requires the integration of information held in two separate datasets. The drawing information is, as we know, in the drawings dataset, but the pipework installation dates are held in the overall construction schedule. In order to integrate these separate sets of information we need an additional ARTEMIS command:

```
PRINT REPORT DRAW
USE SCHEDULE
SELECT IF TITLE CONTAINS 'PIPE'
```

The second line (the USE line) joins the two datasets together and links the drawings to their corresponding site activities. All that remains is to specify which fields of information the user would like to see in the combined report. These steps are illustrated in Figures 26.3 and 26.4.

Rapid implementation and modification

The approach of using an all-encompassing command language coupled with the ability to create new datasets as required are the basic building blocks for producing or extending project systems. The approach, broadly termed 'fourth generation', is many times faster than using more traditional, 'third generation' languages such as COBOL and FORTRAN. With a system such as ARTEMIS, the approach is further enhanced by the use of in-built project management facilities such as network analysis scheduling, and cost calculations. In practice a fully integrated cost/scheduling system can be created from scratch in a matter of weeks. In fact, by using pre-built applications, even this time can be reduced.

This pre-built applications approach can be very effective. With sufficient experience the supplier can design-in 80 per cent of the users' needs in (say) an application such as cost control. When the system is installed either the supplier or the project team can quickly finalize the application, modifying it to meet the exact needs of the project. In the case of cost control this could include adding company cost codes, modifying report formats and adjusting calculation routines to match the existing company practices. In the case of an ARTEMIS application not only can the project team carry out the final 'tailoring' but the experience of doing this means they are ideally placed to modify the system should it become necessary.

INTEGRATING THE REQUIREMENTS OF PROJECT STAFF

To be effective, information must reach all those who need it in a form which they can easily interpret. Failure to meet this fundamental requirement nullifies the purpose of the whole system. In the past, systems were viewed as tools for processing information. The question of tailoring the output to meet the users' needs was rarely considered. A common experience was that of receiving a stack of computer print-out, without being able to discover why it had been produced.

In an integrated system the storage of data is designed around each user's view of the system. This means that the information he receives reflects this structure and, as it were, speaks to him in his own language, using *his* perception of the project.

Take, for example, a materials expediter in a typical project environment. His primary concerns are the materials required, the dates when they are required and the manufacturing location for each item. The expediter's view of the world could be considered to be that shown in Figure 26.5.

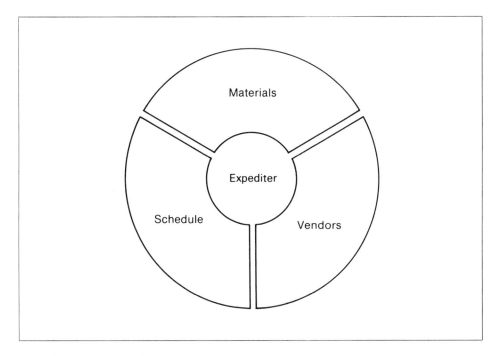

Figure 26.5 A user's view

The expediter sees only particular aspects of the database content as having relevance to him and it is necessary to arrange that the reports can select the appropriate data and combine it for his application.

In dataset terms, therefore, it is possible to visualize the information being pulled together to generate the appropriate reports. Typical reports for the expediter could include:

1 Materials required on site in the next four weeks.
2 Late materials only, grouped by vendor or manufacturer.
3 All materials expected ex-works this week.

A typical report is shown in Figure 26.6.

The advantage to the expediter is obvious. The information he receives is tailored for his specific needs and, what is more, is drawn from the up-to-date *463*

LUCAS

PURCHASE ORDER SCHEDULE

ARTEMIS

Client : LUCAS MANAGEMENT SYSTEMS
Location : METIER HOUSE, LONDON
Project name : ARTEMIS DEMO

Project start : 1-JAN-94
Time now : 1-JAN-94
Project complete : 24-JUL-95

MATERIAL CODE	MATERIAL DESCRIPTION	JOB NUMBER	VENDOR CODE	REQ'N NUMBER	REQ'N LINE ITEM	LEAD TIME (DAYS)	REQUIRED DELIVERY DATE	EXPECTED DELIVERY DATE	REQUIRED PURCHASE DATE	PURCHASE ORDER DATE
MT101	50CM BOLTS	EN1869	19054	101	1	20	4-JAN-94	11-JAN-95	8-DEC-94	16-DEC-94
MT104	2CM * 12CM OAK	EN1869	09189	104	2	58	4-JAN-94	28-DEC-94	31-OCT-94	25-OCT-94
MT121	LIGHTBULBS	EN1869	25006	161	2	78	4-JAN-94	28-DEC-94	11-OCT-94	5-OCT-94
MT124	COPPER WIRING	EN1889	25006	104	1	30	4-JAN-94	11-JAN-95	28-NOV-94	6-DEC-94
MT151	ELECTRICAL WIRING	EN1889	25006	151	2	98	4-JAN-94	28-DEC-94	21-SEP-94	15-SEP-94
MT152	ELECTRICAL JOINERS	EN1889	25006	152	1	101	4-JAN-94	11-JAN-95	16-SEP-94	26-SEP-94
MT153	CROCODILE CLIPS	EN1889	25006	153	1	47	4-JAN-94	11-JAN-95	11-NOV-94	18-NOV-94
MT101	50CM BOLTS	EN1854	19054	101	2	20	5-JAN-94	29-DEC-94	9-DEC-94	3-DEC-94
MT104	2CM * 12CM OAK	EN1854	09189	104	4	58	5-JAN-94	4-JAN-95	1-NOV-94	1-NOV-94
MT121	LIGHTBULBS	EN1854	25006	161	3	78	5-JAN-94	5-JAN-95	12-OCT-94	13-OCT-94
MT124	COPPER WIRING	EN1894	25006	104	3	30	5-JAN-94	5-JAN-95	29-NOV-94	30-NOV-94
MT151	ELECTRICAL WIRING	EN1894	25006	151	3	98	5-JAN-94	5-JAN-95	22-SEP-94	23-SEP-94
MT152	ELECTRICAL JOINERS	EN1894	25006	152	2	101	5-JAN-94	29-DEC-94	19-SEP-94	13-SEP-94
MT153	CROCODILE CLIPS	EN1894	02458	153	2	47	5-JAN-94	29-DEC-94	12-NOV-94	4-NOV-94
MT163	5CM PIPING	EN1934	01110	161	5	21	5-JAN-94	22-DEC-94	8-DEC-94	27-NOV-94
MT165	STEEL PIPES	EN1934	02458	165	1	15	5-JAN-94	12-JAN-95	14-DEC-94	22-DEC-94
MT169	2CM PIPING	EN1934	19054	999	23	60	5-JAN-94	22-DEC-94	30-OCT-94	19-OCT-94

Figure 26.6 Typical expediter's report

This combines information from the materials, schedule and vendor's datasets.

situation in all the appropriate parts of the project. And, because the system can pin-point problem areas, each report contains only the items requiring action. Typical ARTEMIS selection commands could include:

SELECT IF DELIVERY AFTER 20 JUN 95
SELECT IF DELIVERY AFTER 15 SEP 95 AND
SUPPLIER IS SMITHS AND DELAY > 10 (The > 10
is a shorthand way of indicating 'greater-than 10 weeks'.)

Graphical reports

A picture is worth a thousand words. The ability to use graphics to communicate project information is invaluable. In some circumstances, examining a chart for a few seconds can give a complete understanding of what could otherwise be thousands of pieces of data. Take, for example, the traditional activity lists produced from a simple, project planning system. Written out as a list of activity descriptions, start dates, finish dates, floats, and so on, it becomes difficult to interpret. As a diagram, though, the sequence of work is obvious, the relative timing of the work can be seen at a glance, and colour can be used to highlight critical work and show progress. As a means of communication it is excellent.

In an integrated system, however, the opportunities for using graphics are enormously increased. Almost every area of the system can benefit from the increased clarity that using project graphics brings.

Take for example cost forecasting, which is effectively the complex combination of cost and schedule information. As a chart, the position can be summarized on one piece of paper, as illustrated in Figure 26.7.

Quite sophisticated concepts can be used in conjunction with graphical output. In Figure 26.8 a report is shown which combines the results from progress monitoring, the schedule, and costs to give the overall status of a project in summary form.

Vertical integration

Another feature of a fully integrated system is what could be termed 'vertical integration'. Many of the available project planning systems fall down at this crucial stage. Stated simply: without the ability to *implement* the carefully considered decision of the project team, the whole system is reduced to a conceptual exercise. An effective system must convert plans to actions *and* provide an effective means of monitoring and controlling progress. In fact this whole process can be viewed as a hierarchy of project control, as illustrated in Figure 26.9.

Referring to Figure 26.9, a number of stand-alone computer systems are capable of dealing with the top part of the triangle, the decision making and modelling part of the process. Many systems are available for the varieties of tasks which compose the lower levels of control.

Again, without a complete, integrated system, each level in the hierarchy is effectively isolated from the other. Summarized information cannot be auto- *465*

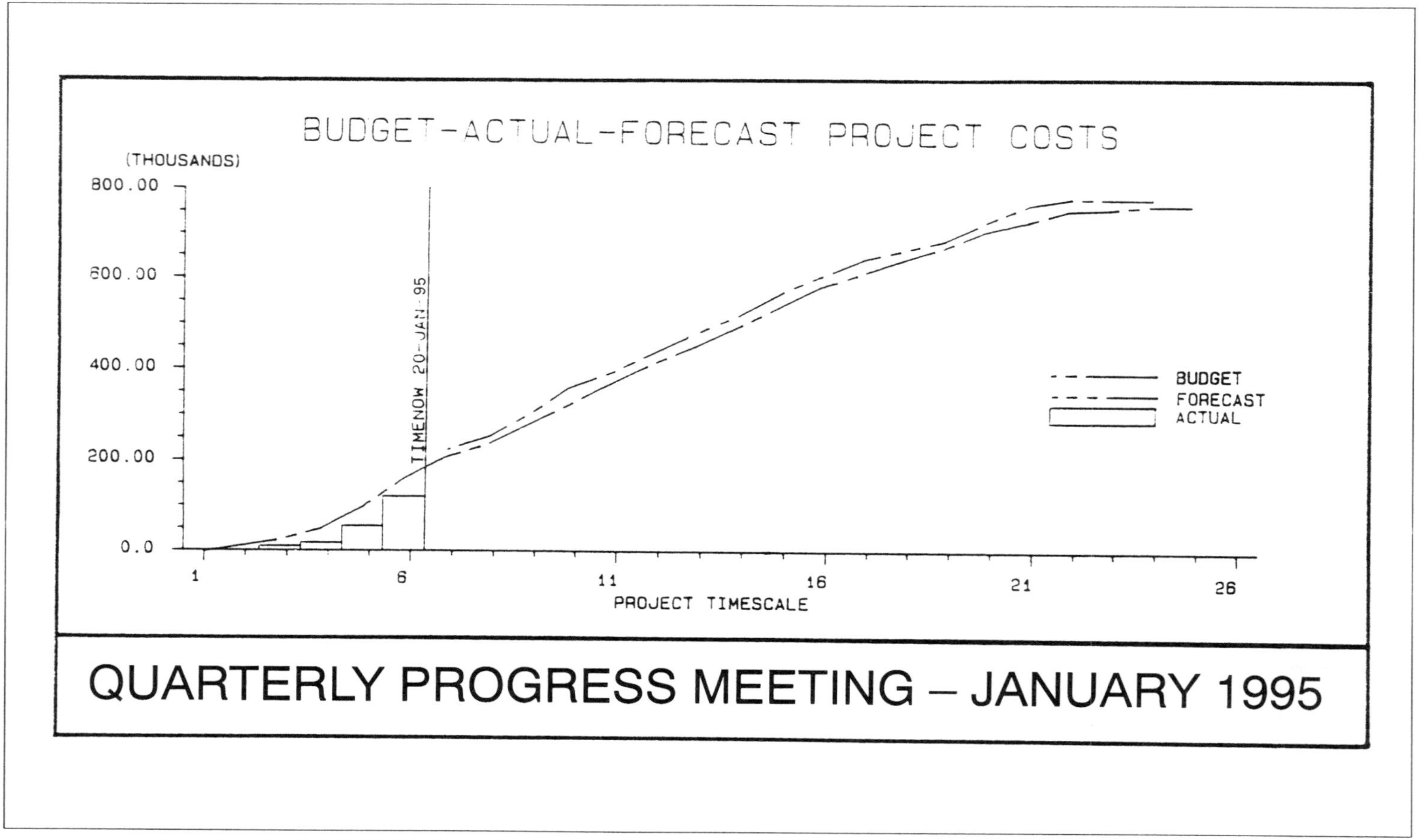

Figure 26.7 A cost forecast in graphical form

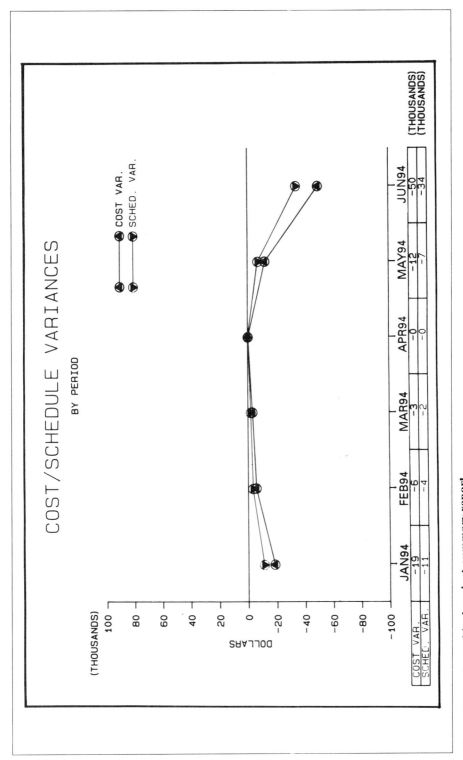

Figure 26.8   A graphical project summary report

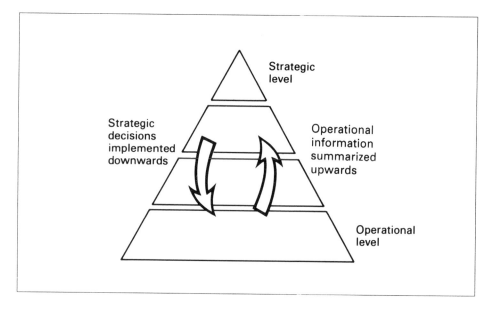

Figure 26.9 Vertical integration

matically generated and so the manager finds himself without a solid basis for his decisions. He could, of course, demand that the information of a particular type be collected and summarized as required, but the variety and quantity of information needed would soon render this approach impractical. What is required is an automated means of producing the necessary summaries on a routine on an *ad hoc* basis.

These gaps in the information hierarchy also mean that management decisions cannot be directly implemented at the working level. Complex instructions, requiring, for example, the quality assurance testing of particular types of components for a specific area of a large project by a team of QA staff, could require considerable manual effort in simply identifying the appropriate components. An integrated system can identify the components, the suppliers, the appropriate QA persons, and reference the documentation, delivery dates, and relevant specifications! Not just that, but it can also produce the information in the form of reports: an inspection schedule, a delivery schedule highlighting potential delays, a purchase order summary showing each supplier's details and delivery commitments, and so on.

In other words a fully integrated system operates at all levels in the project hierarchy and facilitates effective communications both up and down.

INTEGRATING THE COMPUTER HARDWARE

Concerned with the cost of a new system, many new computer users limit their risk by buying the cheapest possible option to address their most pressing need. This will often be a micro-based system. This is relatively successful, so they buy another to handle a second application. Eventually there are several micros dotted around the project. Having now spent the equivalent of the cost of a full function project management system, it seems an obvious step to bring all these micros into one integrated system. This is where the problems start. The individual micros were not designed to communicate with each other. Even if they could, the applications are written by different software vendors in different languages. At this stage everyone falls back on manual methods to try to integrate the separate components. Reports are prepared by each independent discipline and passed up the project hierarchy, leaving the all-essential integration to be carried out in the minds of the middle and senior managers. Horizontal integration between disciplines also suffers. Cost/schedule integration, for example, is almost meaningless when the 'cost' and 'schedule' programs are written in different languages on different machines.

It is not just the reporting aspects of the system that fall down; all the advantages of the 'project model' are lost. The crucial function of decision making is impaired. Testing alternative courses of action by asking 'What if...?' just cannot operate when the individual components of the project do not form part of a 'well oiled' project system.

Reluctantly, the project team is then forced into the conclusion that the only way to achieve real integration is to scrap the existing collection of micros and start again. Sadly, they are probably right.

How then is the project team to avoid this trap? Well, there are a couple of alternatives.

Mini-based systems

The second approach requires some degree of forward thinking. A similar result to the multiple micro approach can be achieved by installing a *mini*computer with multiple terminals. This has the advantage that all the users are using the same database and consequently integration between applications and up and down the project hierarchy is immediately available: given care in choosing appropriate software, of course.

The cost of a mini system with perhaps half a dozen terminals may well be comparable to the equivalent number of independent micros. The big advantages of course are the direct integration of the system and the potential for sharing facilities such as a graphics plotter and a high-speed printer.

Micro, mini and mainframe

An all-encompassing project system will operate on micros, minis and, of course, mainframe computers. A sophisticated system, particularly a company wide, multi-project system, may well use all three (see Figure 26.10).

The final choice of a computer system

For a company new to computers and with a very limited budget, an integrated *469*

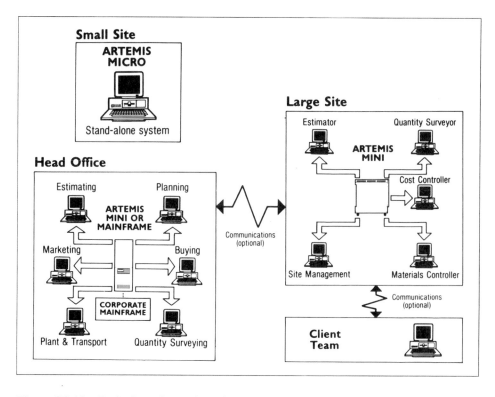

Figure 26.10 Typical configuration of computer hardware for a company using the ARTEMIS system for project management at head office and at remote sites

system can be built up starting from a single micro. For a company with a clear idea of how their integrated system should look, then the mini or mainframe approach is the most effective. This may well involve micros as terminals into the main system, and these can also provide some element of 'local processing'. (For example, an IBM PC can operate either as a complete stand alone ARTEMIS system, or double-up as a terminal to a larger computer also running ARTEMIS).

The choice will be to a large extent dependent on the size, number and complexity of the projects and, of course, the number of applications required. There is no simple answer to this and there is no substitute for working through the available configurations with a knowledgeable supplier, who will be able to advise on the most appropriate hardware and software combinations. A few general guidelines, however, may be useful:

1 Buy one piece of software that has the potential to meet *all* anticipated application needs (e.g. cost, planning, materials, plant, maintenance).
2 Buy software that can be genuinely integrated horizontally, to other applications.
3 Buy software that can be integrated vertically, to the *same* software running on mini or mainframe computers.

4 Make sure the appropriate computer for the software is readily available, well supported, and comes from a reputable manufacturer.

To start with, particularly when buying a system for just one application, this may seem to be somewhat over-cautious. Not really. Bear in mind that the reason why this first system is being bought is to improve business performance. If it does just that, then repeating the exercise for other disciplines will be viewed as essential.

27 An Integrated Project Management System in Action

Lucas Management Systems*
(formerly Metier Management Systems)

An effective way of seeing the impact that an integrated system can make is to examine the way in which it can be applied to a real-life project. This chapter, as in Chapter 26, is based on experience gained by project managers using the ARTEMIS system.

THE PROJECT INFORMATION STRUCTURE

Figure 27.1 is a diagrammatic representation of a complete project system. Each of the individual boxes in the chart represents a dataset that will, in practice, contain many thousands of information items.

The network dataset

The network dataset is the project plan. Typically, each project will contain from several hundred to several thousand activities. The network is constructed from library subsets which are derived from previous projects and are structured to reflect the physical construction and the resources required. Deadlines are highlighted using key events or milestones. Phases of work are identified using 'hammocks' (basically descriptive activities which span groups of more detailed activities).

The drawings dataset

The drawings dataset is effectively a drawings register. It contains details of every drawing including its number, its description, its status (submitted for approval, approved, issued) and the dates for each of these events. It will also have revision details, the draughtsman's name and department, the date of revision and perhaps notes on the nature of the revision.

*Updated from an original chapter by Ray Palmer

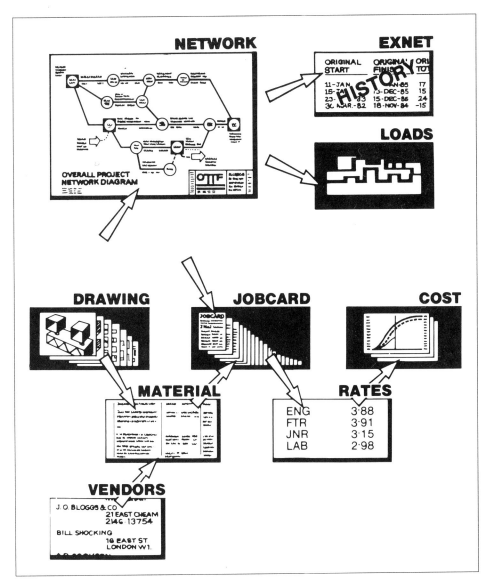

Figure 27.1   A typical project information structure

The materials dataset

Details of each material requisition are contained in the materials dataset. This also includes purchase order details and, in practice, will often carry progress information showing the status of deliveries against each item on order.

The vendor dataset

This provides a record for each supplier, his name, address, telephone and telex   *473* numbers, the name of the usual person to contact, and the principal line of business. Often, details of past performance will be included for use in vendor rating and the initial choice of vendor.

The job cards dataset

Job card records carry details of each job to be performed on the project. Typically the cards will contain a job description, the budget or target man-hours, and the planned start and finish dates. Often they are printed out as task lists for departments or trades. A full job card system will include facilities for progress control and, effectively, provides the mechanism for allocating work, collecting progress information and (via the relational database) updating the rest of the project systems.

The rates dataset

Each type of resource can be held in the rates dataset with its appropriate cost rates. Usually this will include a standard rate, the appropriate overtime rates and bonus details. The information is, of course, held only once in the system as any change in the rates can be communicated directly to other parts of the system, as required.

The cost dataset

This dataset contains details of each project cost account. This is usually based on a defined piece of work with an identified manager, and reflects the physical structure of the project. The basic information is generated when bidding for the work and is shown as a budget amount for each account. A large project could contain several hundred records, usually structured so that the costs can be 'rolled up' to show the position on each section of the project, and the overall position. As the work progresses actual costs are collected against each account along with an assessment of the value of the work completed to date. This enables the cost performance to be accurately monitored, and variances quickly pin-pointed. It is usual to include a forecast of the cost of future work taking into account 'change orders', or variations, which can also form part of the system.

The resources dataset

All the resource types used on the project are detailed in this dataset. The information includes the times when they are needed, the quantities involved, and details of periods when they are expected to be scarce or unavailable. This dataset is closely related to the network dataset and reflects the total resource requirements of the current project plan.

The history dataset

474 Usually, the history dataset will contain 'snapshots' of the project taken at different

times. For example, it is usual to store the details of the project as originally defined and contracted, plus subsequent updates whenever a significant change has occurred to the scope of work. These snapshots can be called up as required, and incorporated in reports to show progress compared with the original plan, slippage and so on. In fact, it is an easy matter to set up a history dataset for any aspect of the project, plans and costs being favourite subjects.

HOW THE SYSTEM OPERATES IN PRACTICE

Broadly, the system operates in the following manner.

The drawing office produces information from which the materials and equipment requirements can be calculated. This is passed to the buyer in the form of requisitions which he categorizes and pulls together into orders against particular suppliers. The supplier then manufactures or procures the materials and eventually delivers to site. Once on site, the material is checked off against the orders, and allocated to a store prior to consumption.

Meanwhile the planners decide the overall approach to the work and this is converted into job cards, against which work the materials are subsequently consumed.

The cost system is set up once the scope of the project is known and this is then used to track all expenditures on every aspect of the work.

Against this backcloth we can now see how an integrated system can provide not only a high level control of the project, but can also provide a complete and comprehensive method for turning plans into actions and then coordinating the work of all the project participants.

DESIGN MANAGEMENT

Now consider some of the situations in design management where the integration of information is important. Reports are produced directly from the drawings dataset to provide a variety of information. Reports can range from a comprehensive drawings register, for example, to more specific reports identifying all drawings which are not yet approved, due for issue in the next four weeks, or perhaps listing drawings for a specific area of the project. In practice though the on-site priorities can change from day to day. At the same time, the ability of the drawing office to produce specific drawings by a particular date can be drastically modified by conflicting priorities and the availability of staff. In other words, the drawing office should be modifying its targets in line with progress on site but in reality is often working to priorities which were set before the start of the project. What is needed is the ability to continually draw together the *current* project plan with the *current* drawing office workload.

Using the ability to link datasets we can quickly draw information from the required areas of the system. Figures 26.3 and 26.4 in the previous chapter illustrate this process and the resulting report compares the on-site requirements with the drawing office's anticipated issue dates. The difference between these two dates is effectively the 'float' on the production of each drawing. This *475* may well be sufficient information to enable the design manager to plan the workload. If, however, he requires a somewhat more sophisticated approach, then the 'on-site required' dates can form the 'target completion' dates, against which he can then reschedule his workload.

With an integrated system, the user can choose the degree of sophistication to suit his requirements. A full scheduling system, itemizing each drawing through each stage of production, could be called for. Or, this could be simplified by handling drawings in 'packages' for scheduling purposes, on the basis that only a complete package is of use to the on-site team.

In the earlier stages of a project where there is more latitude for solving problems, then rescheduling the drawing office to meet on site changes is a feasible approach. At the other extreme, usually later in the project when other options such as buying in additional designers and so on have been exhausted, it becomes necessary to integrate fully the design and construction process and schedule it *en masse*. This can result in design delays causing on-site work to be rescheduled, perhaps causing overall delays to the project.

A straightforward way of testing the seriousness of the situation would be to link the drawings dataset to the plan and transfer the anticipated drawing issue dates to the activities for which they are required and then reschedule using the new dates. The late drawings, we may find, only affect a small number of activities and (with luck) only activities with substantial amounts of float. If, however, this reveals unacceptable delays to the work, then we are immediately able to identify the drawings in question and take steps towards resolving the situation.

On a small project of course, it may well be possible to keep track of on-site priorities and drawing office schedules without a computer based system. On larger projects (perhaps with design and manufacture being carried out in several countries and shipments being required to a central project site) an effective system becomes an essential requirement for remaining in control of the project.

MATERIALS MANAGEMENT

Project materials fall into two main types. There are discrete components such as pumps, valves, motors and so on, and consumables such as cement and nuts and bolts. The first category in some industries will be non-interchangeable, specific components and as such will carry unique 'tag' numbers. Under these circumstances very close control is required and the facility to tailor the control system to the requirements of each different project is paramount. Consumables on the other hand are usually treated as bulk items with the emphasis being on the forecast rate of consumption and related storage requirements. In both cases, of course, the need to plan the manufacture and delivery and then to track the stages through which each material passes is important.

Components however must be treated as an integrated part of the whole project system for effective planning and close control. Take, for example, a situation where a number of material delivery dates are slipping. The serious-

LUCAS	LATE MATERIALS BY VENDOR				ARTEMIS

Client : LUCAS MANAGEMENT SYSTEMS
Location : METIER HOUSE, LONDON
Project name : ARTEMIS DEMO

Project start : 1-JAN-94
Time now : 1-JAN-94
Project complete : 24-JUL-95

VENDOR'S CODE: 099854   NAME: R.J. WILKINTHORPE

KEY CONTACT: JOHN MARSHALL

ADDRESS: HIGH STREET   WATFORD   HERTS

LINE OF BUSINESS:

TELEPHONE: 0923-6544   FAX: 0923-6545   TELEX: 09883

MATERIAL CODE	MATERIAL DESCRIPTION	REQUIRED UNITS	DATE REQUIRED	DATE EXPECTED	
MT109	WATER PUMP VALVE	5S	15-JUN-94	1-MAY-94	
MT162	COCK STOP	25S	15-JUN-94		
MT163	5CM PIPING	METRES	5-JAN-94	14-FEB-94	Late
MT169	2CM PIPING	METRES	5-JAN-94	14-FEB-94	Late
MT205	BALLAST PUMP MANUAL	QUIRE	25-APR-95	2-MAY-94	Late
MT401	PUMP SYSTEM	QUIRE	25-APR-95	2-MAY-94	Late
MT404	WATER PUMP MANUAL	QUIRE	25-APR-95		
MT405	WATER PUMP	UNITS	15-JUN-94	2-MAY-94	Late
MT549	PRECISION PUMP	10S	15-JUN-94	2-MAY-94	Late

Figure 27.2 Integrated system report for use by an expediter

ness of this can be judged by linking the material dataset to the schedule and checking the latest acceptable delivery dates against the required on-site dates. In practice a report selecting only late items would be produced, probably sorted so that the largest delay is shown first, with the responsible engineers flagged for appropriate action.

Conversely, the material dataset could be linked to the schedule *and* to the supplier datasets, and reports produced which not only flag the late items, but identify each late material by purchase order number, forecast delay, and so on. This has the advantage that the report can be sorted so that the expediter is given, *on the same report*, the supplier's name, the purchase orders placed that are now late, the name of the contact person within the company, his telephone, fax and telex numbers – in fact all the information required to pin-point and expedite the late items. This is useful for a small project, essential for a large project, and very difficult to achieve without an integrated system. Figure 27.2 shows such a report.

Other materials-related information that could be produced may include forecasts of material to be delivered during the next four weeks (for planning storage, etc.), required delivery dates for specific items based on the current site priorities (as a guide for the buyer in placing orders), and even inspection schedules arranged to focus the quality assurance team on the current critical items.

PLANNING AND SCHEDULING

The ability to operate as part of an integrated system has transformed the work of the project planner. Large, cumbersome networks have been replaced with smaller networks designed to facilitate decision making. The detailed tasks which bogged down earlier systems are now held in the appropriate datasets and called into use only when required. The whole approach to networking is now much more that of fast-moving decision making, using the network plan to help choose the most cost-effective alternative.

Much more than before, the planner is seen as the central figure coordinating the effort of the whole project. The ability to integrate material deliveries, design team activities, plant movements, documentation, task lists, costs and other related items directly with the plan, enormously increases the confidence of the project team.

Network analysis and integration

In their simpler forms network analysis techniques are currently available on a large number of computer systems and, indeed, have been available since the mid-1960s. The systems vary, of course, in their ease of use but they nevertheless operate using the same principles. In the days when the only computerized project application available was network analysis, a great deal of effort was expended in 'cheating' the systems to make them behave as though they were capable of rudimentary integration, usually in conjunction with costs. This involved adding cost information to activities and then trying to produce summary reports using the resource processing facilities. By and large these efforts were not particularly effective, especially as the resulting system became totally inflexible and often unwieldy.

With an appropriate integrated system, an almost unlimited amount of extra information can be added to each activity directly or (probably more conveniently) the additional information can be held elsewhere in the system and linked to the network as and when required. So, for example, the cost information can be managed by the cost department and linked to the current plan to produce cash flow forecasts. A benefit of this arrangement is that it does not require special cost estimates to be made for each activity on the network (a disadvantage of the old cost-on-activity approach).

Integration has also enabled the planning team to structure their networks in more sophisticated ways. One approach is to use 'hierarchical networks', where the top level network (management network) contains perhaps fifty to one hundred activities and this is driven by a second level of network with perhaps several thousand activities. The usual arrangement is for a group of second level activities to correspond to one top level activity. Progress information on the second level is then 'rolled-up' and summarized to the management level network. This ability to summarize data for consumption by higher levels of management is a key benefit of an integrated system. Large projects may have many levels which correspond with, and provide information to, appropriate levels within the company structure. The following paragraphs deal with reports which are typically used for these levels.

Key event, or milestone reports

These reports highlight significant events (such as the beginning and end of a project), significant dates throughout the project (such as the beginnings and ends of phases) and achievements (such as 'building watertight'; 'dc control systems functional' etc.). This type of report is most useful for reporting to senior managers (see Figure 27.3).

Summary bar chart

These charts show overall sections of the work in a graphical form. In this case it is produced using 'hammock' or summary activities which span large sections of work. This is useful for reporting at high level, but includes sufficient detail to be useful as a working document for senior project staff, team leaders, area engineers, and so on. An example is given in Figure 27.4. In this illustration comparison is possible between the 'before' and 'after' project dates following resource scheduling. This illustrates its use in quickly highlighting the overall effects of change on the project. Variances in a particular area can be quickly identified and more detailed reports produced to examine further the causes.

479

LUCAS

KEY EVENT PROGRESS REPORT

ARTEMIS

Client : LUCAS MANAGEMENT SYSTEMS
Location : METIER HOUSE, LONDON
Project name: ARTEMIS DEMO

Project start : 1-JAN-94
Time now : 1-JAN-94
Project complete : 24-JUL-95

EVENT	DESCRIPTION	EARLY FINISH	ACTUAL FINISH	TARGET COMPLETE	TOTAL FLOAT	STATUS
STA	PROJECT STARTED	31-DEC-93			0	* CRITICAL *
E1	READY TO INSTALL HEAVY LIFTS	27-MAY-94			200	
T2	READY TO COMMISSION BOILERS	24-JUN-94			258	
44	READY TO TEST WATER BALLAST SYSTEM	14-OCT-94			7	
T1	READY TO TEST INSTRUMENTATION	22-APR-95			66	
FIN	PROJECT FINISHED	24-JUL-95		24-JUL-95	0	* CRITICAL *

Figure 27.3 A milestone report

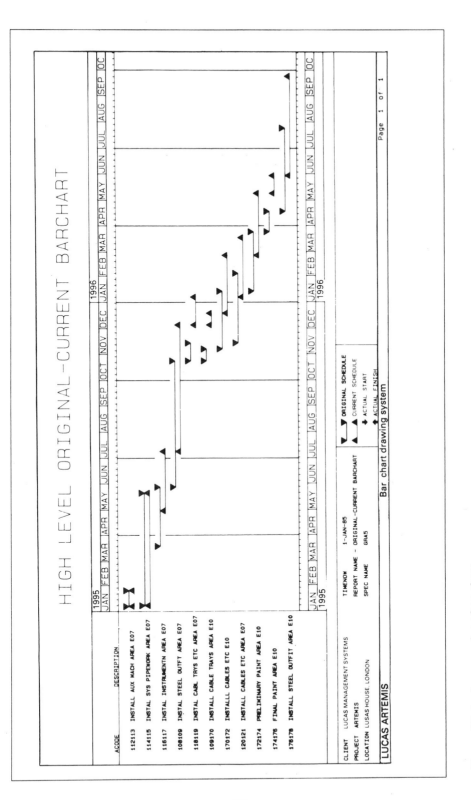

Figure 27.4 A comparison bar chart

This computer-produced report compares original and current schedule information.

LUCAS

ACTIVITY LISTING

ARTEMIS

Client : LUCAS MANAGEMENT SYSTEMS
Location : METIER HOUSE, LONDON
Project name : ARTEMIS DEMO

Project start : 1-JAN-94
Time now : 1-JAN-94
Project complete : 24-JUL-95

PREC EVENT	SUCC EVENT	DESCRIPTION	DUR	EARLY START	EARLY FINISH	TOTAL FLOAT	TRADE	NO MEN
128	110	PREPARE SEATS AREA E08	2	4-JAN-94	7-JAN-94	217	LABOURERS	1
110	111	FIT AUX MACHINE SEATS AREA E07	15	4-JAN-94	24-JAN-94	5	LABOURERS	2
11	12	INSTALL CABLE TRAYS AREA E01	15	4-JAN-94	24-JAN-94	66	ELECTRICIANS	2
136	137	INSTALL CABLE TRAYS AREA E08	15	4-JAN-94	24-JAN-94	144	ELECTRICIANS	2
140	141	PRELIM PAINT AREA E08	40	4-JAN-94	28-FEB-94	326	PAINTERS	2
19	20	INSTALL STEEL OUTFIT AREA E02	80	4-JAN-94	25-APR-94	7	LABOURERS	2
112	113	INSTALL AUX MACHINE AREA E07	15	7-JAN-94	25-JAN-94	5	FITTERS	2
114	117	INSTALL SYSTEM PIPEWORK AREA E07	95	8-JAN-94	20-MAY-94	5	PLUMBERS	3
							FITTERS	3
138	139	INSTALL CABLES ETC AREA E08	15	11-JAN-94	31-JAN-94	144	ELECTRICIANS	2
13	14	INSTALL CABLES ETC AREA E01	40	11-JAN-94	7-MAR-94	66	ELECTRICIANS	2
132	133	INSTALL SYSTEM PIPEWORK AREA E08	80	4-FEB-94	24-MAY-94	200	FITTERS	1
14	15	PRELIM PAINT AREA E01	60	8-MAR-94	30-MAY-94	66	PAINTERS	1
116	117	INSTALL INSTRUMENTATION AREA E07	50	19-MAR-94	27-MAY-94	0	ELECTRICIANS	3
							FITTERS	4
							LABOURERS	4
134	135	INSTALL INSTRUMENTATION AREA E08	35	15-APR-94	31-MAY-94	275	ELECTRICIANS	2
							FITTERS	2

Figure 27.5 A detailed activity report

This example is based on part of a much larger schedule produced by Lucas Management Systems using ARTEMIS (redrawn and slightly simplified here for clarity of reproduction in this smaller size).

Detailed activity report

This is a typical report for what could be termed the 'working level' of the hierarchy. The report gives details of individual activities, their start and finish dates, float, resources and so on, and as such is probably too detailed to be used successfully by workmen themselves. A simplified version with only the activity description, start and finish dates, and (perhaps) float, would be more easily assimilated (see Figure 27.5).

Integrated checks and tests

A feature of the ARTEMIS system is the ability to generate new reports as required. For the planner starting a project from scratch, the process of setting up the network, checking the logic, allocating resources, and so on, can be quite time consuming. Producing special reports as required can considerably reduce this time. Conventional reports such as critical activity listings can be produced in minutes. However, the real power of an integrated system is demonstrated when the resources on the network can be linked to the original estimate to verify the man-hours, or perhaps linked to the cost information to confirm the cash flow forecasts. In short, the planner using an integrated system substantially increases his ability to cross-check information and dramatically reduces the time taken for the system to go 'live'.

ALLOCATING WORK AND MEASURING PROGRESS

In simplistic project systems the 'grass-roots' level is often overlooked. Management may well use a system for overall planning, yet for day-to-day planning they are forced to fall back on entirely manual methods. With an integrated system, however, the control of detailed work forms a cornerstone of the project management process.

Allocating work

In many industries, the users of integrated systems have adopted the traditional job card, or task list, and have made it an essential part of their project control process. The job card now though, rather than being pre-prepared and issued manually, is produced by the system on demand. It incorporates all the appropriate information for the job in hand. Not only that, but because the information is held in the system, it provides an ideal basis against which progress can be measured. Typically, the job card level is directly below network planning in the project hierarchy. The hierarchy of control is illustrated in Figure 27.6.

Each network activity may contain several hundred job cards and could involve several types of resources (fitters, welders, electricians, and so on). In effect, therefore, job cards are the most detailed level of project planning.

Before issue, the latest activity dates are transferred from the network to the *483*

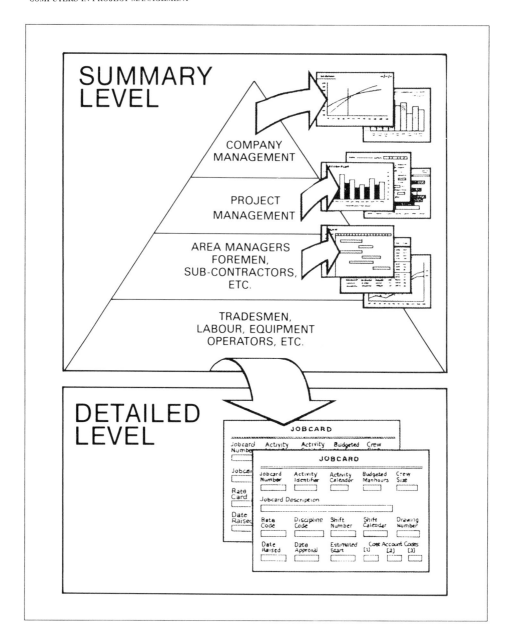

Figure 27.6 The hierarchy of project control levels

job cards required in, say, the coming week. Using the filing cabinet analogy, the process can be represented as shown in Figure 27.7.

In practice, the system can also hold details of any special equipment needed to carry out the work, the relevant drawings and the materials required (together with their stores locations). The job cards can then be issued as part of a

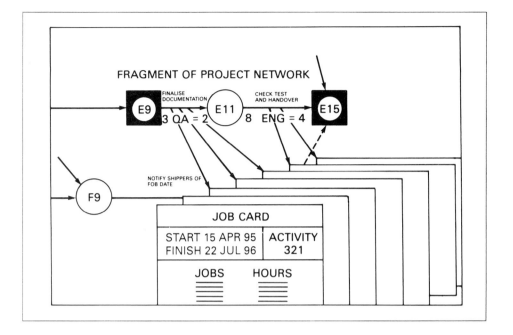

Figure 27.7 Updating job cards

complete pack of information, giving the workman all the information needed for the work in hand.

Measuring progress

There are many approaches to measuring progress. They range from simple assessments based on the quantities of time or resources consumed, to more sophisticated calculations involving the value of work completed, forecasts of work outstanding, anticipated completion dates and so on. The level at which the progress is measured is also important. At a sufficiently detailed level it is only necessary to know that work is either not started or completed.

The method of operation used here is to collect the progress of each 'live' job card as a 'percentage complete' figure. This is done using a 'turnround' report, a report produced from the system listing all the 'issued' but 'incomplete' job cards, with a blank column for each trade foreman to give his estimate of the 'percentage complete'.

Once the progress information has been collected, each appropriate job card record is updated to reflect the current situation. Because we are using an integrated system, we can now summarize the progress from the job cards to the relevant activities on the network (see Figure 27.8).

In practice this process involves several thousand 'live' job cards and perhaps several hundred associated activities. Although the physical process of collecting the data can take several hours, the steps of updating the system and then   *485*

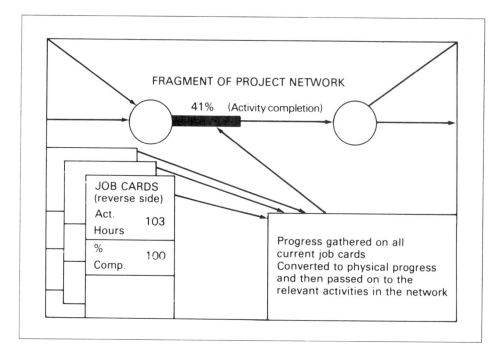

Figure 27.8 Updating the project network from job cards

being able to see the results in terms of progress on the overall project plan, is completed with little additional work.

Again, because of the ability to link information together, the progress position on the individual job cards is quickly turned into progress on the project network. This then enables the whole project to be re-examined in terms of overall cash flow, material delivery requirements, resources, information and completion dates. Problems can be quickly isolated and decisions made as to the appropriate course of action.

COST MANAGEMENT

It is probably true to say that every action taken on a project has a cost implication. Often though the *true* cost of an action is often just not visible to the project team. Take for example the situation where an area of a project is falling behind schedule. To speed it up the decision is made to bring in a larger piece of plant. The only cost analysis that is carried out is whether the additional cost of the machine is likely to offset the cost of finishing the project behind time. On a large project, decisions of this type are taken continually.

With an integrated system a much more comprehensive view can be taken: the extent to which the accelerated work will reschedule activities further down the line, how this will affect their resource usage, how these resource changes will cause otherwise unrelated activities to be rescheduled, the effect this will have on material and equipment deliveries, the effect on the design office and (perhaps most importantly) how all these various changes affect the cost of the project.

In the first instance the changes to all these items may influence the overall cost. But the sum total of all the rescheduling may well affect the project cash flow. For an individual project this could mean that the amount of money 'locked-up' is increased or that the agreed borrowing limit is exceeded. For a company with several projects in hand the aggregate result of these individual changes could even prevent the financing of an additional project. With the integrated approach, the 'dynamics' of a proposed action can be thoroughly examined before any decision is made and the overall implications assessed against the overall objectives.

COST FORECASTING

Traditionally, cost forecasting has been a somewhat laborious and inexact process. Two factors have contributed to this: the cost estimate or cost accounts do not necessarily reflect the components of a project in a way that can be directly related to the construction process; and the network is usually drawn without reference to the cost structure. So, to produce a cash flow forecast, the project team have to work through the programme to pick out dates where recognizable expenditures occur and then tie these back to the appropriate costs, a time consuming task.

Over recent years the whole approach to this problem has gradually changed. Due to developments in the defence industries, particularly in the United States, there is increasing emphasis on the ability to operate integrated cost/shedule systems.

A basic requirement of the approach is that the project should be viewed as a number of packages with defined scope, responsibility and costs. A common method of arriving at this arrangement is by employing a work breakdown structure which divides the project into a hierarchy of work. Work breakdown structures are described elsewhere in this book, particularly in Chapter 13. An illustration of the concept is also given in Figure 27.9.

Once such a work breakdown exists, each item can be treated as a package of work, with the account codes being structured or 'nested' so that the total costs can be 'rolled up' to ascertain the overall position whenever required.

In the ARTEMIS system, each account is usually treated as an individual record within a cost dataset. The fields of information usually include:

1   The account code or cost code.
2   The description.
3   The person responsible.
4   The budget.
5   Actual costs to date.
6   Forecast remaining cost.
7   Percentage completed.

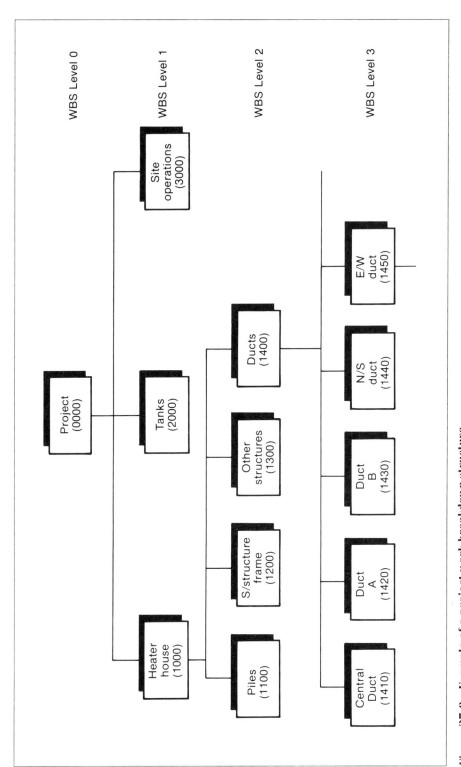

Figure 27.9 Example of a project work breakdown structure

This example might be found in part of a civil construction project work breakdown.

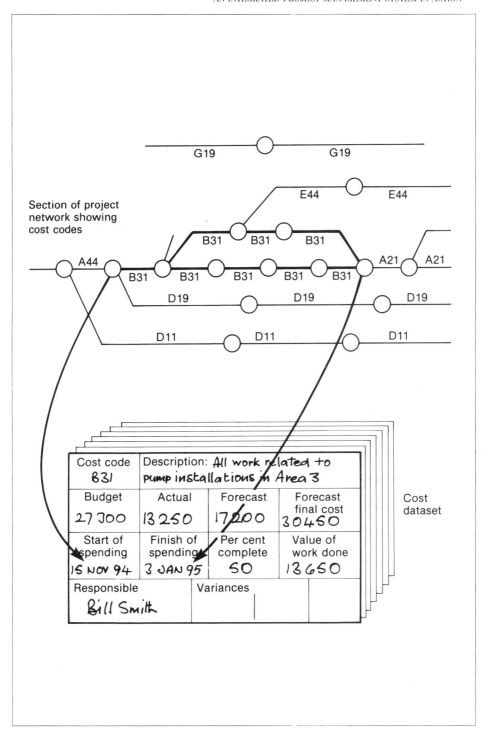

Figure 27.10 Linking the project network to the cost dataset

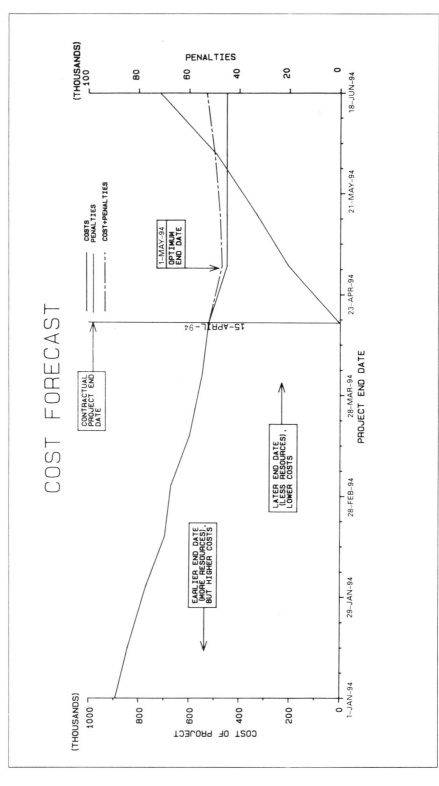

Figure 27.11 Analysis of economic completion date

The computer has taken all relevant facts to produce this calculation of the minimum-cost project completion date.

8   Forecast final cost.
9   The value of work completed.
10 Several variances.

The last four of these items are calculated by the system.

Additionally, the individual network records can be coded, to show the account to which each belongs. Any one account could well have several dozen related network activities. For the cost forecasting exercise it is necessary to bring the cost dataset and the current schedule together. This can be considered diagrammatically as shown in Figure 27.10.

Using ARTEMIS, the two datasets can be linked and the earliest and latest expenditure dates for each found. Practically, this could require combining several thousand activities with a similar number of account records. The result of this is that we now have the appropriate dates for each account which is sufficient information to generate the appropriate cost curves.

Again, in practice, the cost record is often more complex. There are often several versions of the 'budget', for example, and there is usually a requirement to identify 'commitments' separately. Some users of ARTEMIS also split the figures into manpower, plant, materials and overheads. Additional fields can be added to the records, as required, to accommodate these needs.

The example above assumes a linear distribution of costs. Some users define 'spend profiles' for various cost types, which means they can produce much more accurate expenditure forecasts. Another approach to this is just to use smaller cost code items, which in turn enables the real expenditures to be allocated to shorter and more specific periods of time. Using a sophisticated project system the possible number of approaches is quite extensive.

The improvement that integration brings transforms the whole process, from one of accounting for historic costs to that of dynamically modelling the whole process.

Figure 27.11 illustrates a perhaps surprising result from the integration of project cost and schedule information, with penalties for late completion. The 'minimum cost' finish date is shown as two weeks after the contractual completion date! Again, a calculation that is possible by manual methods. In an integrated system, however, it is just one of the many ways of analysing information and presenting the results for management action. The manual approach could take days of investigation and calculation. With an appropriate integrated system the analysis and the production of the graphical output could be completed in minutes, and could even form part of a regular monthly analysis of the project status.

CONCLUSION

During the relatively short time in which integrated systems have been available, the whole approach to project management has been transformed. Disciplines that were once viewed as 'stand-alone' and even secondary (planning for example) have jumped to the forefront with the extra leverage brought   *491* to bear by integration. Clients are now aware of the benefits, and are starting to insist that their contractors manage projects using integrated systems. In consequence, contractors who still use older methods find that they are in danger of losing their competitive edge.

The breadth of the project system is also expanding. In this chapter the more 'traditional' areas of planning, materials, costs and the control of work have been discussed, but the leading project management systems now have far wider horizons. ARTEMIS, for example, is used for dozens of applications which in the mid-1970s would not have been considered as part of a project management system. Estimating, plant management, maintenance, accounting, personnel administration, claims management and many other functions now form part of successful integrated systems.

After years of being constrained by manual methods, information technology (in the form of improved computer hardware and software) has provided responsive systems which are appropriate to the needs of project managers and their teams. An obvious direction for development is to combine computer-aided design with the management system of the associated project. Increased integration of company administration systems is also likely, with management accounting (particularly in a project-oriented company) a potential area for inclusion.

Fully integrated, interactive project management systems have always been possible, but they have been limited in scope and flexibility by the cumbersome nature of the manual methods that were required. Dramatic advances in the power and availability of computer facilities have now changed the emphasis completely, so that even small projects are able to gain practical benefit from truly integrated systems.

Part Seven

MANAGING PROGRESS AND PERFORMANCE

28 Managing Progress

Dennis Lock

This chapter starts with a crop of assumptions, the first of which is that progress needs managing. The importance of carrying out all project commitments on or before the promised dates should be obvious to all. A project is not successful if its late completion results in delayed start-up of a process or production plant, causing lost revenue for the owner. A project is an obvious failure if the exhibits being prepared for a trade exhibition are ready two weeks after the exhibition has closed. It is a general rule that any extension of a project beyond its agreed timescale must lead to extra expenditure or losses, simply through the cost of the money and other resources (accommodation, people, materials) which are locked into the programme. No one should, therefore, argue with the assumption that project time is itself a vital and expensive resource. Just as all other project resources have to be managed, so does time.

THE FRAMEWORK OF PROGRESS MANAGEMENT

In order to give a project some chance of being carried out according to the client's delivery wishes, the management methods and structure have to be suitable. The following assumptions are made: if any of these is not met in a particular project, progress management will be made more difficult, if not impossible.

Organization

It is assumed that the project organization is appropriate to the size and nature of the work, and that all members of the organization are clear on their roles.

Project definition

Another assumption is that the project is clearly defined, so that the project manager knows exactly what has to be achieved.

Supportive management

The project manager cannot operate in a vacuum, without the support and encouragement of his superiors. It is assumed that this exists, both in the provision of facilities and in backing up any requests for action that demand intervention at senior level, either within or outside the contractor's own organization.

A reasonable client

The client (or customer, or owner) must act responsibly by providing funds when they are required, by avoiding unnecessary requests for changes, by approving designs and authorizations for expenditure when asked without undue delays, and generally by appreciating the problems which face his contractor and acting to cooperate rather than hinder progress. A reasonable client is assumed.

Competent people

A lot of people are involved in a large project. They will be spread throughout the contractor's own company, the organizations of subcontractors and suppliers, in the firms responsible for moving materials by rail, road, sea and air, in government and other official functions, and in the client's own management. Some of these people will be competent. Others might be less so. We have to assume that the majority are capable of performing their jobs properly if project progress is to be assured.

Good communications

Good progress is dependent upon good communications. It must be possible to pass information and instructions quickly and clearly down all lines of management and to receive feedback of problems or progress just as quickly in the reverse direction.

A workable schedule

It is not enough to plan a project by simply drawing a few lines on a piece of paper, calling it a bar chart, and then attempting to use it as a working programme. Schedules have to be thought through carefully, taking into account all task interdependencies, resource constraints, and so on. A workable schedule is one which does not expect impossible things of the resources employed. Scheduling is dealt with fully elsewhere in this book, but it is assumed that the project manager has the benefit of a schedule which exists in sufficient detail to highlight the dates when measurable events should take place if the programme is to be met. Given a set of targets at which control can be aimed, there is some basis for control. A good schedule is to progress management what a properly authorized budget is to cost control.

Control of changes

Uncontrolled introduction of changes can play havoc with progress and project costs. Procedures for controlling changes are discussed later in this chapter.

With all these assumptions, perhaps it is a wonder that any project ever gets finished on time. And, so far, we have not even thought about all the other things which can go wrong accidentally, as seen in any insurance company's catalogue of policy disasters (fire, storm, tempest, civil commotion, riot, war (civil or otherwise), strikes, lockouts, objects dropped from aircraft, other natural disasters, unnatural disasters – you know the sort of thing. What chance does any project ever have of being finished on time? The truth is that many do finish late.

Efficient progress management seeks to plan the project effectively, to foresee possible risks to the programme, to monitor work in progress and identify any current problems, to assess priorities for using scarce resources, and (above all) to take action whenever problems do arise which, if left alone, would threaten the programme.

COMMUNICATING THE WORK PROGRAMME

Consider a contracting organization into which is received a prized order for a new project. Possibly over one hundred of this contractor's staff are going to be working on the new project for a prolonged period. All good news. But how do they know when to start and what to do?

Project authorization

The first official document used in many companies to start up a new project is a works order. This sets out the most important dates, is accompanied by budget instructions, summarizes the technical details, and notifies everyone of the cost codes and project number to be used. Much of the works order content is derived from the sales engineers who worked with the client when the project negotiations took place, so that the works order should be seen as part of a detailed project specification. If the engineer who headed up the sales team can take over as project manager, so much the better.

Apart from containing information about the project, the other important function of a works order is that it authorizes work to start: in other words the start of project expenditure is approved.

Limited pre-contract authorization

No work should ever be allowed to start on a commercial or industrial project until a firm contract exists between contractor and client. This is an inviolate rule that should be ground into every self-respecting project manager almost from birth. Or so we are told. As with all rules, there is an exception to this one.

In most, if not all, projects, the rate of working and (therefore) the rate of *497* expenditure follows a well-known pattern which, when plotted cumulatively against time, produces a characteristic *S* curve. A simple example is shown in Figure 28.1. The rate of expenditure is slow at first, while preliminary preparations are made and the project resources are gradually mobilized. During the middle part of the total time span, the rate of expenditure is at its highest. Finally, work and expenditure tail off, until the curve becomes asymptotic with the final project costs.

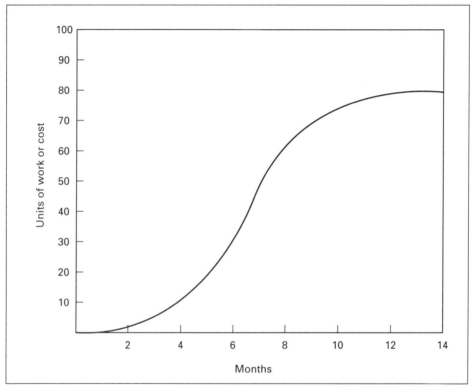

Figure 28.1 Typical relationship between time and cumulative project costs

Each division along the timescale in Figure 28.1 represents two calendar months. Activity during the first few weeks of this project would be taken up in planning the project, gathering information on technical standards, specifying the project procedures that should apply, and so on. Many companies use check lists for controlling these preliminary activities, and at least one company uses a standard network diagram for the purpose.

All these preliminary activities are likely to need only one or two people and it is easy to see from Figure 28.1 that work during the first two, three or four weeks of the project is unlikely to form a very significant part of the total project expenditure. Yet this early work must be performed before the main project can start. If the completion date for this project is seen as tight, or if the company wants the project completed and out of the way as soon as possible for any other reason, it may be advantageous to allow some or all of these preliminary activities to go ahead (in other words, to incur some costs) before the contract has been signed.

Obviously such a procedure needs to be undertaken with caution. Negotiations with the customer or client must be near completion, with a high probability that the contract will be won. The company must limit the risk by issuing a preliminary internal works order. This must allow only a very small budget, specify what work may be done, name the individuals authorized to carry out the work and give a cut-off date, after which no further expenditure can take place until a main works order is issued for the fully live project.

Where such pre-contract preparations involve discussion with the customer's engineers to gather or clarify information, these should be conducted as if they are part of the final stage of sales engineering: if the customer is led to believe that work has already been committed for his project, the contractor's bargaining position in final contract negotiations will be weakened.

Nonetheless, in spite of the risks, a contractor can gain a useful time advantage by bringing preparatory work forward in this way.

Kick-off meetings

When the contract has been won, the kick-off meeting is a good way to get things started. The project manager, having digested all the requirements from the sales specification and the contract, must call together all the key participants, explain the project's technical and commercial requirements, quantify the targets, get everyone's agreement to the targets and encourage all concerned to mobilize their resources.

The kick-off meeting gives the project manager the opportunity to explain the particular project organization, outline the procedures that will apply, and answer questions about these issues.

Task lists

While the works order or other project authorization document gives instructions in broad management outline, it does not carry enough detail from which to issue work down to the level of separate jobs.

Before the days of computers, the project manager could arrange for the project schedule to be broken down into a series of tasks, each of which was sufficiently small to be handled by an individual member of staff, or by a small department. Task lists would be handed out as a means for authorizing work on the tasks, and to tell the working staff exactly what had to be done.

Computerized schedules, derived from network analysis and subsequent resource scheduling, have opened up a new dimension in progress management. Such schedules can be 'personalized' for each departmental manager or specialist chief engineer by editing, so that these departmental schedules only contain activities for which each particular department is responsible. From the point of view of progress management, the individual schedules become *499* invaluable when the activities are listed in order of their scheduled start dates. Thus, each manager has what is known in production management terms as a 'work-to' list. The lists are also useful checklists, since (provided the schedules are complete) they help to ensure that no essential task is forgotten. Another condition for success is that the resource scheduling has been properly carried out, based on reasonable estimates and realistic levels of resource availability. Examples of these edited schedules are given in Figures 28.2 and 28.3.

Please refer to the work-to list in Figure 28.2. This is adapted (for clarity) from an actual project for the design and manufacture of a special purpose heavy boring machine. The manager of the engineering department can see all the activities needed from his department, when they should take place, and how critical each job is (from the amount of float left after the computer has scheduled the resources). Consider activity 1002, 1003 for example. The duration is eight working days, the job can start on 10 March 1993 according to the network logic (earliest start). The computer has scheduled the job, in fact, to start on the earliest date because, presumably, resources are shown to be available (i.e. not all engineers have been committed to other work on that date). The job is scheduled to finish on 19 March 1993. If, for any reason, this job ran into difficulties, it would not matter to the programme if the finish were to be delayed until 1 April 1993. All jobs in the department are seen to require the employment of one engineer, except the design review activities, which are carried out by the manager. Several jobs are seen to have zero remaining float, with their scheduled finish dates equal to their latest permissible finish dates. These jobs are critical, either as a result of the network logic analysis or as a subsequent result of the computer delaying the jobs until resources have become free to work on them.

Figure 28.3 shows the two other lists which, together, complete all the design engineering and drawing activities needed for this machine project. Note, for example, that detailing and checking the machine assembly (which follows 1014, 1018 review machine layout by engineering design) will take an estimated ten working days to finish and requires one draughtsman. The computer has delayed the start of this activity from the earliest date of 23 March 1993 (no draughtsmen free) until 1 April 1993. The job still has two days' float left.

The report for the administration department which is shown in the lower half of Figure 28.3 shows the vital dates when drawings should be issued for production (although, in the case of this simple example, only one batch of drawings is involved). It is excellent practice to arrange that schedules highlight such important events, which are worthy of vigorous progress monitoring.

Similar work-to lists can be produced for production departments. These would be unlikely to contain sufficient detail for the day-to-day loading of machines and shop-floor facilities, but they ensure that work packages are loaded to production engineers and production control at a rate consistent with the total production capacity available. All this assumes that the computer has scheduled the total company workload together in a multi-project calculation, which was the case in the example shown in Figures 28.2 and 28.3. This was only one of several projects being undertaken, and all project networks were indeed

DEPARTMENT — ENGINEERING   ALL ACTIVITIES BY SCHEDULED START   SINGLE TRANSFER MACHINE

PREC EVENT	SUCC EVENT	DURN DAYS	WORKS ORDER	..ACTIVITY DESCRIPTION..	EARLIEST START	SCHED START	SCHED FINISH	LATEST FINISH	REM.G FLOAT	RESOURCES
1001	1002	12	75001	DESIGN TRANSFER LAYOUT	22FEB93	22FEB93	09MAR93	22MAR93	9	1E
1012	1020	15	75001	DESIGN BORE HEAD LAYOUT	22FEB93	22FEB93	12MAR93	25MAR93	9	1E
1004	1009	15	75001	DESIGN FIXTURE LAYOUT	22FEB93	03MAR93	23MAR93	23MAR93	0	1E
1002	1003	8	75001	DESIGN TURNOVER LAYOUT	10MAR93	10MAR93	19MAR93	01APR93	9	1E
1002	1006	1	75001	REVIEW TRANSFER DESIGN	10MAR93	10MAR93	10MAR93	26MAR93	12	
1020	1023	2	75001	REVIEW BORE HEAD LAYOUT	15MAR93	15MAR93	16MAR93	29MAR93	9	
1003	1007	1	75001	REVIEW TURNOVER DESIGN	22MAR93	22MAR93	22MAR93	02APR93	9	
1019	1025	2	75001	CHECK TOOL LAYOUT	22MAR93	22MAR93	23MAR93	20APR93	18	1E
1009	1013	2	75001	REVIEW FIXTURE LAYOUT	15MAR93	24MAR93	25MAR93	25MAR93	0	
1010	1014	5	75001	DESIGN MACHINE LAYOUT	15MAR93	24MAR93	30MAR93	30MAR93	0	1E
1014	1018	1	75001	REVIEW MACHINE LAYOUT	22MAR93	31MAR93	31MAR93	02APR93	2	
1015	1021	10	75001	MAKE FOUNDATIONS DRAWING	22MAR93	31MAR93	15APR93	15APR93	0	1E 1D
1016	1026	2	75001	PRE-ISSUE CHECK TRANSFER	01APR93	01APR93	02APR93	22APR93	12	1E
1017	1026	2	75001	PRE-ISSUE CHECK TURNOVER	06APR93	06APR93	07APR93	22APR93	9	1E
1025	1026	2	75001	PRE-ISSUE CHECK HEAD	06APR93	08APR93	13APR93	22APR93	7	1E
1021	1026	5	75001	CHECK FOUNDATION DRAWING	05APR93	16APR93	22APR93	22APR93	0	1E
1024	1026	2	75001	PRE-ISSUE CHECK ASSEMBLY	06APR93	19APR93	20APR93	22APR93	2	1E
1027	1026	2	75001	PRE-ISSUE CHECK FIXTURE	08APR93	21APR93	22APR93	22APR93	0	1E

Figure 28.2 Example of a work-to list produced from a computer-based resource schedule

The computer has analysed the project network diagram, scheduled the activity times according to available resources, edited the activities into separate departmental lists (engineering in this case) and printed out the activities in sequence of their scheduled start dates. This gives the department manager a valuable checklist and a schedule from which to issue work to individual engineers in line with the project programme requirements.

501

DEPARTMENT — DRAWING OFFICE   ALL ACTIVITIES BY SCHEDULED START   SINGLE TRANSFER MACHINE

PREC EVENT	SUCC EVENT	DURN DAYS	WORKS ORDER	..ACTIVITY DESCRIPTION..	EARLIEST START	SCHED START	SCHED FINISH	LATEST FINISH	REM.G FLOAT	RESOURCES
1006	1016	15	75001	DETAIL+CHECK TRANSFER	11MAR93	11MAR93	31MAR93	20APR93	12	3D
1023	1025	14	75001	DETAIL+CHECK BORE HEAD	17MAR93	17MAR93	05APR93	20APR93	9	2D
1007	1009	10	75001	DETAIL+CHECK TURNOVER	23MAR93	23MAR93	05APR93	20APR93	0	2D
1013	1003	16	75001	DETAIL+CHECK FIXTURE	17MAR93	26MAR93	20APR93	20APR93	9	2D
1018	1006	10	75001	DETAIL+CHECK GEN. ASSY	23MAR93	01APR93	16APR93	20APR93	12	1D

DEPARTMENT — ADMINISTRATION   ALL ACTIVITIES BY SCHEDULED START   SINGLE TRANSFER MACHINE

PREC EVENT	SUCC EVENT	DURN DAYS	WORKS ORDER	..ACTIVITY DESCRIPTION..	EARLIEST START	SCHED START	SCHED FINISH	LATEST FINISH	REM.G FLOAT	RESOURCES
1026	1027	3	75001	PRINT+ISSUE TO PRODUCTN	14APR93	23APR93	27APR93	27APR93	0	

Figure 28.3 More examples of work-to lists

The above examples are complementary to that shown in Figure 28.2 and complete all design engineering activities for the machine design project up to the issue of a complete set of drawings to the production department. This issue would include all the associated bills of material for the purchasing department.

put into the same computer resource allocation run. Detailed shop-floor loading is a separate function, to be carried out by the usual production control methods.

For large-scale construction projects, although design and drawing schedules could be produced in the same way, the practical approach is usually somewhat different. Here, the workload is set out in the form of drawing and purchase control schedules.

Drawing schedules are prepared at the start of the project and attempt to list every drawing needed for construction. They are typically set out in sections according to different parts of the plant to be built, and the drawing numbers are determined at this stage. They can be converted into work-to lists by the computer, taking either single drawings or groups of drawings as network activities, depending upon the amount of time and work needed for each drawing. At one time target start and completion dates were written by hand on the schedules, which was a tedious and unsatisfactory exercise from the progress point of view, especially when a change in programme requirements demanded that all dates had to be rescheduled. With the computer-based network techniques, such problems become far easier to manage.

Purchasing activities

Since every respectable network diagram for a project must show purchase order activities and material lead times, it is a simple matter to sort out work-to lists for the purchasing department in the same way as for other departments, although it may not be necessary to attempt resource scheduling of buyers. For the purposes of expediting and inspection of suppliers, the expediting section of the purchase department can be given the list of order activities sorted by completion dates, so that the expediters can plan their letters, telephone calls, telexes or visits accordingly when monitoring progress. Of course, the instruction to start actual work in a supplier's organization is contained in the purchase order and its attached specification, so there should be no ambiguity there.

In large construction contracts, the individual purchases are probably going to contain some high-value orders. This is especially true for projects such as mining or petrochemical plants, where some of the purchase orders are for the supply of large items of capital equipment, or for the employment of sub-contractors on site. Purchase control schedules list all the purchases which can be foreseen at the start of the project. Like the drawing schedules used to control the preparation of project drawings, the purchase schedules are used to carry scheduled target dates for the various stages leading to the issue of purchase orders. Again, this was a tedious practice, difficult to change with changing project needs. Modern practice links such schedules to the project network, and the computer can produce the schedules and, if necessary, reschedule all the dates.

Since each major purchase activity starts with the preparation of a purchase specification, the purchase schedules are intended to cover the issue of work to engineers who will have to write these specifications, then the subsequent stages of purchase enquiries (invitations to suppliers to bid), the preparation of *503* final specifications and requisitions, and the issue of the purchase orders themselves.

On a large project, it will also be necessary to list as network activities the purchase lead times, and some principal shipping activities (at least to allow for the time required for goods to be shipped from supplier to project site).

All of this information, appropriately edited, sorted and listed by the computer, gives the progress engineers and progress chasers valuable control checklists for the purpose of monitoring progress.

Subcontracted services

Companies providing manufacturing services as subcontractors (e.g. heat treatment, plating, special gear cutting, etc.) can be instructed through the official purchase order system.

When engineers and draughtsmen are supplied for work on a project by external agencies the issue and control of work can become a little complicated, especially when these people are going to work away from the project home office in the offices of the agency companies. One way around this problem is to give each subcontractor a self-contained piece of design work that starts with engineering design and layout, and then proceeds through detailing and checking to arrive at a batch of drawings which are issued to production (or to construction, depending on the type of project) as a discrete part of the works. The main contractor arranges for the subcontractor to provide a senior design engineer to work in the main engineering offices for as long as it is necessary for him to learn the engineering standards required, and to produce the first layout drawing. This engineer then returns to his own company, and supervises the day-to-day work of the draughtsmen and checkers needed to finish the drawings. The completed parcel of drawings must be rechecked by a responsible engineer in the main contractor's organization, naturally. Once this process has been carried out, it should be possible to place further work with the subcontractor without the need for the design engineer to work in-house. Then, the following procedure can be followed to ensure that the work commitments are made known and followed up.

The main contractor appoints a subcontract liaison engineer. This person should be of sufficient technical competence, and have enough knowledge of the main contractor's standard engineering practices, to be able to answer queries raised from the outside offices. This liaison engineer carries out the functions of issuing work, and progressing it. It is unlikely that a purchase order will be issued for each piece of design: rather the work would be carried out at agreed hourly rates against timesheet control. The simple job sheet shown in Figure 28.4 has been used to good effect in issuing work of this type.

Note that the example given in Figure 28.4 does not indicate how much float is available, and it does not show the budget estimates or the number of draughtsmen required. The company from which this example was taken took the view that subcontractors must finish within the dates given, regardless of float and that to give details of cost estimates in advance would preclude any possible savings. (Suppose, for example, that a job was estimated to take two weeks for three men, and that the subcontractor was given this information. If in fact he managed to complete the job in less time, this company argued that the subcontractor might be tempted to submit his invoice for the full estimate.) Readers will hold different views on these points, but the principle of using small engineering subcontract orders of this type, printed on handy cards, is a useful aid to progress control. The subcontract liaison engineer retains copies of all orders issued and in progress, and uses these to follow up progress.

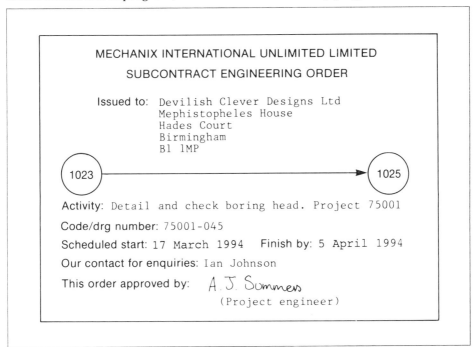

Figure 28.4   A simple subcontract engineering order

The idea of showing each subcontractor's assignment as its corresponding network activity may appear at first sight to be a gimmick, but it does highlight the fact that the job is part of a larger schedule, and that the timescale commitments are important. These little orders are printed on cards, a copy of which is kept in the subcontract liaison engineer's files, from which he monitors and expedites progress.

MONITORING AND CONTROLLING PROGRESS

This chapter began with a series of assumptions. Here is another. It must be assumed that the project organization contains a sufficient number of individuals whose task is to ensure that progress is watched, measured and controlled. The subcontract liaison engineer discussed in the last section of this chapter is one example of such a person. The expediters in the purchasing department and the progress chasers in the factory are others. On site, quantity surveyors work with *505* site management to ensure that work is progressing at the planned rate, measured in terms of tonnes of earth moved, the number of bricks laid, and all the many other quantities involved. Back in the home office, it is usual to appoint a project coordinator responsible to the project manager for monitoring and following up the progress of many of the routine, yet vital, office tasks. The project planners may also be assigned to following up progress: in some organizations this job will be left to the coordinator and to the discipline managers, with the planners simply using the progress information to update their network schedules.

In addition to the obvious need to keep the programme on schedule, progress measuring has another important function. This concerns the establishment of equitable charges for work done which each contractor can invoice (subject to the contract terms). Thus the work of subcontractors has to be measured to establish how much they can bill the main contractor (or the client, depending on the payment structures agreed in the contract) and the main contractor's own work should be measured for similar reasons. Even where the contract does not allow for such progress payments, it is still necessary to know, at any stage in a project, the actual value of work done by measurement in order that expenditure trends are known by comparison with cost estimates and budgets. This subject is dealt with more extensively in the chapter on cost control.

Engineering design and project administration

It is common practice to measure engineering and drawing progress in terms of percentage completion. Thus, if a particular design job were to be estimated as taking four weeks, the progress might be reported as (say) 75 per cent complete, from which the project manager and any other interested person would conclude that one week's work remained. It is, unfortunately, true that most people tend to be optimists when making assessments of their achievements. Thus, the project manager with several years' experience should not be surprised when this particular job is finished not one week later, but after two weeks, and then with questions still to be answered on some finer engineering point or other.

Another problem facing the manager trying to get a project designed on time is the frequency with which engineers and draughtsmen report their work as 90 or 95 per cent complete, leaving that last tantalising 10 or 5 per cent just out of reach.

The shrewd manager will quickly learn to apply a few simple rules that should get progress back on course. The first requirement is for a set of milestones, key events, happenings (call them what you will) that allow no compromise in interpreting whether or not they have been achieved. These events, which should appear on the project network (and therefore have the benefit of scheduled dates) must be chosen at intervals which are not too far apart. Two or three weeks is about the limit. This reduces the risk of being deceived by optimistic promises. A good general rule when setting targets is to choose events where jobs pass from person to person, or from department to department. Thus, the handover of a drawing from draughtsman to checker, or the number of isometric piping drawings completed as a proportion of the total might be firm indications of real progress.

Design activities very often depend on information from outside sources. In the case of a large construction project, this information can include considerable correspondence from suppliers, and from the client. Engineering can be held up while the client approves (or rejects) design layout drawings, and the project coordinator's job should include close monitoring of all such correspondence against the target dates. Another function of the project coordinator is to ensure that every letter, telex and fax, both outgoing and incoming, is answered within a reasonable time. This is important for keeping progress on the move, and for checking against the possibility that messages have gone astray – which often happens on very large international projects. Where regular correspondence, telexes and faxes exist between participating organizations (the client, contractors, site management, purchasing agent, etc.) all messages should be numbered serially so that any gap in the series is seen as a lost message.

Another check on engineering (or indeed any other) departmental progress is to compare the number of people engaged in any discipline with the resource schedule. The author remembers one occasion when he carried out such a check himself on an engineering project and discovered that instead of about 30 agency draughtsmen, only about six could be found actually working on the project under review. Yet engineering appeared to be in step with schedule. The reason was found to be that the engineering designers were declaring that their layouts were 100 per cent complete, but were not releasing them for detailing because, in fact, they were simply reluctant to let their work go. The engineers were, perhaps, a little uncertain. They wanted to give a few last-minute tweaks to their designs to arrive nearer perfection. This was a case where an appeal to the engineering director soon put things right, and got the show back on the road.

Engineers must be encouraged to release information ahead of drawings when it comes to purchasing items with long delivery times. These include such things as special bearings, weldments and castings, flameproof motors, and so on. It is not good enough to await the final parts list, bill of materials or purchase schedules to get such equipment on order.

Production progress

A factory organization is used to controlling progress, and it should be equipped with an established production control system which ensures the efficient scheduling of work. Progress chasers see that work is moved from each work station to the next without undue delay.

The physical movement of machined parts, subassemblies and other production jobs between work stations is all important to progress. If a job requires, say, 10 operations from raw material to completed part, including inspections, and if it takes a day to move the part between each work station, then that part will spend two weeks of its time in the factory sitting on racks or trolleys. There *507* are methods used to overcome such delay possibilities in factories. A project manager who has access to the production facilities employed on his project can spend profitable time walking through the factory regularly (perhaps once a day). Just ten minutes is often sufficient for the project manager to note whether any job is held up. A stack of steel piled in a corner for a few days might be an indication that the production management have downgraded the priority on the project work to the advantage of some other project manager who is able to shout louder. One project manager once became frustrated that his work did not move as it should through the factory, and his protests had no effect on the production manager. During one lunch hour, when the factory was deserted, this project manager collected some stalwarts from the engineering office and, together, they lifted a heavy steel workpiece from the factory floor (where it had lain neglected for a week) and laid it across the production manager's desk. Of course there was a terrible row, and the production manager felt embarrassed because he had to get his own labourers to move the offending workpiece. But he never ignored that project manager again.

Special priority cases in manufacturing

It is generally not good management practice to attempt the allocation of priorities to production work outside the normal scheduling sequence. The procedure, seen in some companies, of allocating 'Priority A', 'Priority B' and 'Priority C' to jobs can lead to great difficulties. If a factory is heavily loaded, the chances are that all project managers calling on the common production resources will label their jobs as 'Priority A', and any job unfortunate enough to carry a 'Priority C' tag will probably never get done at all.

There are occasions, however, where special action is needed to accelerate production. One obvious situation is a job held up for shortages, caused by the failure of suppliers to deliver materials (or by the failure of the purchasing department to order them on time) or by the inadvertent scrapping of materials or components through manufacturing errors. The progress chasers will usually follow up such delays vigorously, informing the managers of the relevant production departments to ensure that prompt corrective action is taken.

The cost to a project of a delay in the production of one small item can be out of all proportion to the production cost of that item. This is especially true for any specially manufactured item which lies on the project network critical path. Particularly disastrous is the case of an assembly, possibly containing complex electronic or electro-mechanical gadgetry, which fails catastrophically on its final test. Possibly some single component has broken down, causing other components to be lost. Situations such as this are even more serious when it transpires that the failures were caused by fundamental design errors, so that the dud components were destroyed by overloading. When such calamities arise they demand urgent action. Here is real cause for allocating top priority – covering not only the production facilities, but also going right back to the office where the design errors occurred. There is a procedure which copes with such problems very well. It depends upon the issue of immediate action orders.

The usual documents seen in the factory or engineering offices are printed on ordinary white paper, so that one document looks very like another. The first thing which strikes the observer about an immediate action order is that it is anything but an ordinary piece of white paper. These top priority documents are printed on paper with brilliant diagonal stripes. They cannot fail to be seen on a desk or worktop. Another feature of such orders is that, because they are so special, they have to be authorized at general manager or managing director level. Once so authorized, there is no limit placed on the expenditure authorized to get the job done. If the factory has to keep open all night, or over Christmas, then so be it. If materials are only available in Scotland, and the factory is in Cornwall, then those materials must be obtained by the quickest route regardless of cost. The immediate action order commits all project departments, so that in any case where a design fault existed the engineering department would be expected to modify the appropriate drawings without delay. So important is the emphasis placed on these special immediate action orders that only one is allowed to be in existence at a given time. The order is hand-carried from department to department by a progress chaser, and it is date- and time-stamped when it arrives at and leaves each departmental manager's desk. In companies where this system operates, managers actually learn to fear immediate action orders. They are a nuisance. They command priority over all other work – even to the extent of stopping a machine in mid-cut, removing the workpiece, and resetting the machine to take the immediate job. The logic in this approach is seen when by spending, perhaps, £5 000 to finish a job which should only have cost £500 the project programme is retrieved by several weeks, equivalent (say) to a saving of £50 000 in penalties and lost reputation.

As an example of what can be achieved by an immediate action order, a special high-voltage, high-frequency transformer was produced for a prototype piece of military defence equipment. The transformer took six weeks to make, being mounted in special screening, and with an aluminium frame, all encapsulated in epoxy resin. The transformer had to be subjected to rigorous inspection routines at each stage. It failed on overload test. The replacement, including modified design, was produced against an immediate action order in only three days.

Construction site progress

At a production site, which may be thousands of miles removed from the project manager and the home office, it is customary to establish a management team which controls progress on the spot. But the size and organization of that team can vary, from just two or three individuals on a small project to a semi-permanent management group for a large job. Progress measurements and actions depend very much on the contractual arrangements, so that a managing contractor would leave day-to-day progress to the many subcontractors employed, satisfying himself through site quantity surveyors and quality control engineers that work was being performed on schedule and to the required standards of materials and workmanship.

The contract conditions existing have a marked effect on the degree of management control that the site manager must exercise on the individual subcontractors. This point is amplified in the chapter on cost control, where the same arguments apply.

In order that site progress can be maintained according to schedule, it is obviously essential that all materials are delivered to site at the right time and in good condition. Thus the project purchasing organization has a prime responsibility to the project site progress.

No less important than the flow of materials and equipment to site is the supply of construction information. This exists in the form of drawings, suppliers' installation instructions (for equipment), take-off lists, engineering standards, and similar specifications and erection instructions. It is usual for construction to start while engineering design is still in progress, albeit in the later stages of completion. Thus there is real danger of construction work outstripping the supply of drawings and other engineering information. The project organization must provide a channel of communication, preferably using telex, fax or some other electronic means, by which the site management can make known any engineering problems or deficiencies in information. The project coordinator in the home office would be expected to monitor the progress of the home office engineers in responding to such requests, so that no undue delays are allowed.

Drawings sent to site for use in construction are usually stamped to show that they have received all the necessary checking and approval stages. 'Released for construction' is a typical rubber stamp legend used for this purpose. It often happens on large projects that the design engineers are not able to release complete drawings for construction, although they have the drawings nearly ready. Possibly they await details of holding-down bolt positions for some item of equipment, or the exact location of a hole for pipes cannot be shown in a floor slab. In these circumstances drawings may be released for construction as incomplete, a rubber-stamped legend reading 'Released for construction with holds'. Although a drawing released with holds is probably better than no drawing at all, since it allows some site calculations and planning to take place, project management in the home office must not be complacent about such issues, and all steps have to be taken to get the missing information needed to complete the drawings and allow construction to proceed unhindered.

The use of network float is another point worthy of consideration. It is too easy to allow all float to be taken up in the design phase, so that the construction site team are left with no remaining float, and therefore find themselves squeezed for time. One way out of this difficulty is to include a special final activity in the network which does not represent work, but which adds an artificial delay of, perhaps, four weeks to the end of the construction programme. This has the effect of removing float from the front (engineering) end of the network, and emphasizes the need to get design finished. This is not unfair to the engineers. Most project difficulties, at least most of the excusable ones, occur on site. The engineers are not likely to be affected by ice, snow, floods, running sand, strikes, fights, thefts, or any of the other myriad unforeseen problems which the site

manager has in store.

CHANGES

Any change to a project during progress is likely to pose a threat to progress and to cost control. It is true that some contractors on construction projects (and other projects) welcome requests from their clients to make changes, since such requests can provide an excuse for levying additional charges and for extending the programme with the client's permission and funding. Project managers, however, usually view all changes as nuisances.

Changes which need control procedures

Changes can obviously occur at any stage in a project and some are insignificant, because they happen early, cause little wasted effort, and do not affect the project as it is defined in the sales specification and contract. For example, a designer may have to make several attempts at a difficult design problem before a drawing can be produced which is suitable for issue to the production or construction organization. It would not be reasonable or practicable to expect the designer to seek formal approval through a change procedure every time he wiped the computer screen and started again.

There is a way to decide whether or not a change ranks as a modification or variation needing formal management approval. This is to ask whether or not the proposed change would alter any information on a document that has already been issued to authorize work. This definition means that a formal procedure should be applied whenever a change would affect:

- The contract document or any of its attachments (in which case the change document would be called a contract variation).
- An issued purchase order (the change would probably be called a purchase order amendment).
- Any drawing or specification issued for manufacture, purchasing or construction (which will be referred to in this chapter as a modification).

These changes can be interactive, so that a contract variation originated by the client (for instance) might result in a series of engineering modifications and purchase order amendments.

Terminology varies from one organization to another. Contract variations are often called variation orders. In Chapter 13, for example, the writer distinguishes between 'project variations' and 'contract variations', using definitions based on his particular experience.

See Chapter 7 for a detailed account of contract variations and their administration. Purchase order amendments, as part of the purchasing function, are explained in Chapter 20. This chapter continues by describing procedures by which many companies deal with the problem of engineering changes.

Control procedures for engineering changes

Before a proposed engineering change is allowed to go ahead, it is usual to assess *511* its risks, examining the possible effects carefully in all respects (technical, manufacturing or construction methods, commercial, safety, reliability, timescale and costs). Because no one person can usually be found in the organization who is capable of assessing all these factors, a committee of departmental managers or other experts, which will probably be called the change committee, is usually formed for the purpose.

All requests for engineering changes should be submitted to the change committee on suitable standard forms. These, and the procedure for their use, are necessary to ensure that change requests are dealt with properly, with no undue delays, and that the actions recommended by the committee are followed up (including the reissue of all affected documents). The procedure should be centred upon a technical clerk or project coordinator, who will serial number and register all change requests, and use the register to control the progress of each change right through until it is either rejected by the committee or implemented in the project.

The coordinator must keep those who are likely to be affected by each change (including the request originator) informed of the committee decisions. This is usually done by distributing copies of the change form after it has been approved or rejected by the committee.

In a typical arrangement, the change committee will meet at regular intervals (perhaps weekly or every two weeks) to consider change requests in batches. Very urgent change requests can be dealt with more quickly by the coordinator carrying the change request form to the various committee members (or their deputies) in turn, without waiting for the next change meeting date to come round.

The committee will consider each change on its merits and potential risks. In one company the view was taken that, unless requested by the client (and therefore to be paid for), all changes would initially be classified as either 'essential' or 'desirable'. Essential changes would include those necessary to guarantee safe and reliable operation of plant, or to correct errors. These might be approved without comment, sent back to the originator for more information or an alternative proposal, given approval in a modified or limited form, or rejected altogether. Desirable changes would always be rejected. The slogan was 'If it's essential we do it, if not we don't'.

Updating engineering documents in line with changes

Management and supervision of drawings and engineering documents has to be carried out strictly to ensure that drawings are, in fact, modified when they should be and, also, that the revision numbers are correctly updated and recorded in all the appropriate places. At one time it was possible to enforce this rule by insisting that every original drawing was placed in central files as soon as it was checked and finished. Only prints could then be issued, unless the drawing were needed for modification or redrawing, in which case the drawings clerk or registrar could keep an eye on the modification process to make certain that a revised issue number did appear.

The control situation became somewhat complicated when 35mm microfilm aperture cards were introduced as the source of prints, with the original drawings kept locked in files. Old microfilms, possibly existing in duplicate or triplicate, might be used as masters for obtaining new prints after the original drawings had been modified and refilmed. This danger was overcome by insisting that only one set of centrally filed aperture cards could be used to print drawings for production or construction. When any original drawing was removed for modification, the master microfilm aperture card was taken out also, and used as a loan card in a separate file from which printing was prohibited.

With the advent of computer-aided engineering, the situation has become perilous indeed. At one time an original drawing was easily recognized as such, and copies were easily identifiable as prints (even when they were printed on translucent paper or polyester film). Now it is a simple matter to call-off prints from the computer plotter, each of which can be on clear film or tracing paper, and each of which becomes an apparent original. Great care is needed to ensure that revision numbers are in fact added as changes are made, and that the original is clearly identifiable as such.

It is often possible to arrange for the coordinator to follow up the document-ation of all approved changes. The coordinator will only close off each change entry in the register when the change has been rejected or (if it has been approved) when all the relevant documents listed on the change request form have been updated and reissued.

Design freeze

Sometimes project organizations recognize that there is a point in the design and implementation of a project after which any engineering change would be either very inconvenient or unacceptably damaging to costs and progress. This leads the organization to announce a 'design freeze', which is intended to deter anyone from having the temerity to suggest further engineering changes.

The change committee will refuse approval for any change request once design has been frozen, unless the originator can convince the committee that there are compelling reasons such as safety or a funded customer request. Ideally the customer should also be bound by the design freeze, or at least should be made to pay heavily for the privilege of breaching it.

PROCEDURES RELATED TO ENGINEERING CHANGES

There are at least three procedural systems that are similar in many respects to engineering change procedures, especially in manufacturing companies. These are all intended to keep manufacturing delays to the minimum, while ensuring that quality, performance, safety, reliability and proper documentation of the project are not compromised. All can be administered and progressed by the same clerk or coordinator chosen to deal with engineering change requests.

Engineering query procedure

Manufacturing projects, with their new designs and untried drawings, often lead to queries from the production staff, directed to the engineers, asking for help in interpreting the drawings and specifications, or highlighting problems. Perhaps a hole position has been incorrectly dimensioned on a drawing, or it might be that a specified adhesive process does not produce a bond of sufficient strength.

Any person with a design-related manufacturing problem is expected to refer it to the engineering department using an engineering query form. The procedure for handling engineering queries is very similar to that for change requests, with an administrator (project coordinator or engineering clerk) responsible for accepting, numbering and registering each query before taking it to the relevant engineer. As with change requests, the clerk will follow up each query to see that it is answered without undue delay.

If the query has revealed a design weakness or drawing error, it may be necessary for the engineer to originate an engineering change request to authorize the necessary drawing changes.

Production permits and manufacturing concessions

There are sometimes occasions when the manufacturing departments are held up and cannot follow instructions on a drawing or process specification exactly, not because the documents are wrong but as a result of materials shortages or lack of the required production facilities.

Requests for production permits or concessions seek permission to disobey one or more aspects of the written instruction. For example, a drawing may specify screws to be chromium plated on brass, where only zinc-plated steel screws can be obtained in the time available.

The procedure, apart from the title of the form, is almost the same as that for engineering queries. Indeed, one form can easily be designed to do both jobs. There are only two significant differences from the engineering query procedure:

1 Because permits or concessions seek permission to ignore one or more aspects of an approved design, they could be seen as a downgrading of quality, or as introducing an element of risk. Requests might, therefore, have to be referred to someone more senior than the responsible design engineer, possibly to the chief engineer (acting as the design authority for the project) or to the change committee.

2 For the same reasons of quality and reliability, every concession or permit that is granted becomes part of the project documentation, to be retained in records to assist in any subsequent investigation should the relevant project component fail in service.

Inspection and test reports

514 It sometimes happens that a manufactured component or assembly fails either inspection or test or both, but to a degree which does not appear serious to the production team or inspector responsible. Under those circumstances the production manager might consider using the relevant inspection report as a request for concession or a production permit, in which case the inspection report is passed to the coordinator, who will deal with it just as if it were a request for concession or production permit.

PROGRESS MEETINGS

Progress meetings usually serve two purposes. They provide a forum in which progress difficulties and risks can be discussed, and actions are agreed. The other function of progress meetings is secondary to the main project management theme of this book, being concerned with the inevitable technical discussions that arise. It would be unrealistic to expect that a gathering of project technical and management staff would not raise technical problems when they had the opportunity provided by a progress meeting, but such discussions should be limited strictly to those technical problems which are a danger to progress. A progress meeting should be managed efficiently by the chairman, with the aid of a sensible agenda, so that it concentrates on matters related to keeping the project on schedule. Progress meetings should also be kept as short as possible, given that those attending are probably busy, short of spare time, highly paid, and needed back at their own departments for actually doing work rather than simply discussing it. It is not a bad plan to arrange that progress meetings, at least those which only contain in-house staff, are started at a fairly late hour in the working day. Then there is a real incentive to get on with the business. Of course, this argument would not apply to a project where the client had travelled thousands of miles to attend the meeting.

The frequency of progress meetings depends on the duration and complexity of the project. For a highly intensive project carried out at feverish speed over just a few weeks or months it might be deemed appropriate to hold short progress meetings every week. Monthly is a more usual interval for most projects. But progress meetings can be avoided altogether if (a very big 'if') the planning, scheduling and project management are perfect. Why hold progress meetings when everyone on the project has been told exactly what to do, when those instructions are carefully planned to be achievable, and when the follow-up by supervisors and managers ensures that any difficulty is immediately corrected? One company did, in fact, abolish regular progress meetings by the successful establishment of effective day-to-day control. These arguments apart, a project manager has no alternative to the calling of a progress meeting, or series of meetings, when the participants come from different departments or organizations and either cannot agree with their planned commitments, or have to meet to agree joint actions needed to overcome genuine difficulties and get the programme back on course.

During progress meetings it is common for individuals to be asked to make estimates, or to give promises of fresh dates by which late or additional jobs can be finished. The chairman will ensure that promises with vague wordings such as *515* 'the end of the week', or 'sometime next month' or (worst of all) 'as soon as possible' are not allowed. The chairman must insist on firm, measurable commitments. If any member of the meeting feels that the promises being made by others are unrealistic, he should (politely) say so, in order that all possible consideration is given in advance to the likely problems. All promises and commitments must be as realistic as possible. How many readers have attended progress meetings where, from one meeting to the next, the same item keeps cropping up with the only result being that a new, later, promise is given each time?

Progress meetings are a waste of time when the agreements reached are not followed up by the relevant project management personnel to ensure that promises are kept. The control document for this purpose is that containing the meeting minutes. It is most important that such documents are:

1 Concise, using short statements of actions required.
2 Annotated to show clearly those persons who are required to perform or manage the agreed actions.
3 Issued promptly, as soon after the meeting ends as possible.
4 Distributed to all those present plus any person not present but to whom action had been delegated by the meeting.

PROGRESS REPORTING

Progress reporting takes place at many levels, formally and informally, on any large project. At the simplest level reporting is person to person when, for example, a supervisor performs the daily rounds and asks how individual jobs are progressing. Then follows an ascending hierarchical structure of reporting, involving other departments, subcontractors, purchasing and shipping organizations, finally reaching the level of regular, comprehensive cost and progress reports to the client.

Progress reporting for network updates

As a project proceeds, those responsible for planning and scheduling have to ensure that their carefully laid plans are not rendered useless by events or activities which deviate from the network logic. It may be necessary to update the network from time to time, and rerun the computer schedules. For this purpose, the computer has to be given at least the following information:

1 A list of activities which have been completed since the first run and all previous updates.
2 A 'time now' date. The computer will use this date as a new zero time from which to start the scheduling of all remaining work. Occasionally, the 'time now' date used might be slightly in the future. This would be done where the time taken to produce a revised schedule was significant (perhaps a week or more) in which case a small risk is taken by forecasting results, to gain the benefit of a new schedule with an issue date that looks reasonably fresh.

3 If 'time now' is in the future, activities expected to be finished by 'time now' must be reported as actually complete.
4 All activities which are started at 'time now', together with their percentage completions, or the durations remaining after 'time now' (the actual method depending on the program used).

It will be appreciated that this kind of detailed progress information requires a good deal of effort to collect, especially where some of the activities are concerned with shipments of materials in remote places, and in the activities of those on a far away project site. Although good management practice should concentrate only on those aspects of progress which are likely to go wrong (management by exception) the computer does not understand management principles, and demands that simply everything is fed in. Thus, here is a level of progress reporting that must be set up to gather and use facts on the progress of every activity on the network.

Exception reporting

Strictly speaking, the more senior the person in the management structure of the project organization, the less detail should be given about progress. Those managers responsible for taking action when things look like going wrong should not just be given a long list of jobs which are on course, with the few problems hidden among them. It is necessary to edit out the problems and highlight them. Then managers' time can be focused on the problems. When a computer is used for scheduling, it is possible to edit lists so that only critical activities are shown, and there are several techniques for reducing the number of activities in reports for individual managers still further, so that each only receives information on critical activities within his area of responsibility.

Although material shortage lists produced by stores staff are a good example of exception reporting, the control of material movements for overseas work may demand complete reporting in great detail, at least to the purchasing staff concerned. This is one example where exception reporting may not be enough, it being essential to know for each purchase order where the materials are at any given time. There is usually some difficulty in getting information together from all the various organizations involved in supplying and shipping equipment and materials, which is unfortunate because the data is essential.

An example of exception reporting might be that the general manager receives a simple statement that the project is either on course or expected to finish at some other (early or late) date. He may be given an overall reason. The general manager would also expect a cost performance summary, in terms of total sums involved. A manager of a department engaged on the project, however, needs to be told clearly and quickly about any activity under his control which is not running to plan, together with the forecast consequences to the project if the departmental manager is not able to put more effort into getting the job finished on time. This departmental manager would also expect to receive regular statements of his department's project expenditure against the *517* set budgets. He should also be given advance information about any jobs running late in other departments, where such delays are going to have a direct effect on the start of work in his department.

Progress reports to the client

If the project is large in terms of timescale and overall cost, then the client will want to know how well the project is progressing at any time, and he will need this information in the form of an official progress report (usually issued monthly).

It is usual to combine progress reports to the client with cost reports and statements showing how project funds are being used. When a large project starts, most of the activity takes place in the contractor's home office. It is obviously from that office that the first series of monthly reports to the client will be issued. When a site office is established, and work emphasis shifts from the home office to the site, most of the information contained in the report will be generated from site. However, facilities for typing, printing and binding the report to the presentation standard which the client of a large and expensive project should expect may require that the home office continues to produce and issue the monthly reports. Where the site is new, and remote from the client's own headquarters, then the home office will probably continue to be the source of all bound reports throughout the life of the project. Where, however, the site is at or close by the client's existing plant, then it often falls to the site manager to have the responsibility of taking reports to the client each month, and being prepared to explain the contents.

The main contractor of a large international project might include the following items in his regular reports to the client:

1　A written account of progress achieved to date, with special emphasis on progress achieved since the previous report.
2　Photographs showing the current state of progress at the project site.
3　Some form of quantified evidence to back up the achievements claimed. This might include a table of drawing achievement showing:

　(a)　total drawings required for the project;
　(b)　number of drawings issued this reporting period;
　(c)　total number of drawings issued to date;
　(d)　number of drawings in progress and not started; and
　(e)　percentage of total engineering design and drawing finished;

and for purchasing, a statement of engineering progress showing:

　(a)　total number of purchase specifications required for the project;
　(b)　number of purchase specifications completed and issued as enquiries during the period reported;
　(c)　total number of purchase enquiries issued to date;
　(d)　number of enquiries remaining to be prepared and issued; and
　(e)　percentage of engineering work completed on purchasing tasks.

These tables might be divided into rows, each row representing a major area of the plant or work package, with the total figures given at the foot of each column.

4 A statement of the position regarding purchased equipment, possibly in the form of purchase and order schedules

5 A cost report, showing in tabular and graphical form the expenditure to date on main areas of the project, and the totals. The cost report would include the latest predictions of total final project expenditure, and would also give the client up-to-date cash flow forecasts

6 A summary of the work planned for the next reporting period.

7 A list of any problems caused by the client in holding up the supply of information, approvals or funds. In other words, a schedule of actions which the contractor requires from the client.

8 A summary of project variations, separated into those which have been approved and those which are undergoing appraisal.

9 Where projects involve complex communications, and especially where the clerical facilities at one or more project locations cannot be adequately staffed, lists of all communications sent and received during the reporting period. These would show the serial numbers of all telexes, faxes and letters sent, highlighting any gaps in the series. Strictly, such reports should be unnecessary, since any gap in any series should automatically cause action to get the missing document or message traced, but some clients, especially in Third World countries, have been known to insist on this 'belt and braces' procedure.

Project managers or their superiors should edit reports for clients carefully to ensure that the contents represent a true picture of the project progress. It is not necessary, obviously, to tell the client of every silly mistake made during design or manufacturing, provided that such mistakes are correctable within the time and cost constraints of the contract. The client must, however, never be misled or intentionally misinformed. If a problem is foreseen which poses a real threat to the timescale, to the budget, or to the technical performance of the finished project, then the client must be told. If the client is left to find out for himself, much later in the project, he will not feel that the project manager has acted to protect his interests, and should feel justified in asking how the contractor felt able to ask a fee for managing the project when, at best, there appears to have been no awareness of the problem and, at worst, the project manager has practised deception.

FURTHER READING

Harrison, F. L., *Advanced Project Management*, 3rd edn, Gower, Aldershot, 1992.

Lock, Dennis, *Project Planner*, Gower, Aldershot, 1990. (A looseleaf pack of 50 forms for photocopying and use in project planning and control, with explanatory book.)

Lock, Dennis, *Project Management*, 5th edn, Gower, Aldershot, 1992.

Lock, Dennis (ed.), *Handbook of Engineering Management*, 2nd edn, Butterworth-Heinemann, Oxford, 1993.

O'Neil, J. J., *Management of Industrial Projects*, Heinemann Newnes, Oxford, 1989.

Stallworthy, E. A. and Kharbanda, O. P., *Total Project Management*, Gower, Aldershot, 1983.

29 Fast Tracking

Edmund J. Young

'Time is money.' 'Time is the essence of the contract.' How often these words apply in project management! Another phrase is 'time to market', which means the overall time needed from the start of a new product development to the time when the product can be supplied in quantity to the market for profitable sale. No one concerned with projects can ever ignore the important factor of time. The need to shorten project delivery times and to counter delays and overruns on many projects was stressed in the NEDO report (1983).

Fast tracking is a technique which can be used to shorten the overall duration of many large-scale projects which have long construction times. Originally developed in the United States, the technique is increasingly being applied in various parts of the world. This chapter outlines the principles and method, with particular reference to construction projects.

DEFINITIONS

Kolesar (1989) defined fast tracking as:

> A method of reducing the overall project time, from the day the client makes his decision to build, to the moment the building can be put to use, by overlapping certain operations, while keeping a firm grip on the scheme.

Kwkakye (1991) gave a more comprehensive definition by stating it as:

> A managerial approach to the achievement of early delivery, involving the application of innovations in the management of construction procurement and recent advances in the industrialization of the construction process, bringing into play:
> * the integration of design and construction phases;
> * the involvement of the contractor in both design and construction phases;
> * work packaging: that is, the arrangement which breaks down works into trades or skills, or to a group of closely related trades or skills;
> * overlapping the work packages to enable construction of sections of the

project to proceed while the design for other sections is being considered or progressed;

- the employment of the expertise of works contractors and the recognition of their active participation in both design and construction.

Ashworth (1991) viewed fast tracking as the letting and administration of multiple construction contracts for a single project that results in the overlapping of the various design and construction operations.

PRINCIPLES

Fast tracking depends on a radical approach to planning. In the 'traditional' approach to planning and work management, activities are listed and placed in a logical start–finish sequence, either using bar charts or some form of critical path method. With fast tracking, the plan has to be analysed critically, from a fresh viewpoint, with the following questions asked:

1   Is every activity necessary or could one or more be omitted? For example, does a contract have to be put out to competitive tender, with all the delays which that will cause? Do we really need to build a prototype of this product, or could we instead launch straight into a pilot production batch?
2   Is it really necessary for the start of each new activity to await the full completion of its predecessor, or can overlap or concurrent working be planned? This approach has long been recognized by planners, who have used ladder networks in arrow diagrams, complex constraints in pre-cedence networks, or other features of particular computer programs that allow overlapping of individual activities. However, fast tracking takes a braver look at this approach, and considers the possible overlapping of whole work packages.

For example, consider the traditional working sequence for a typical con-struction project. After the preparation of an outline project specification and site surveys, design takes place. This is followed by the issue of drawings and specifications, and the soliciting of tenders from suppliers and subcontractors. Although there might be some slight blurring of the boundaries between these activities (perhaps by the early ordering of materials with very long lead times, for instance) it is only when all these stages are complete that construction begins.

The fast tracking approach recognizes that the appointment of a management contractor at the outset to undertake both design and construction would eliminate some or all of the delays associated with tendering. Further, overlapping certain activities can be considered, so that initial construction can be started before all the design has been finalized. Thus, instead of the strictly sequential series of operations under the traditional method, there are now overlapping or concurrent operations that result in a shorter overall project time. This technique of fast track construction has also been called 'phased construction' and 'concurrent con-struction'. The principles are illustrated in Figure 29.1.

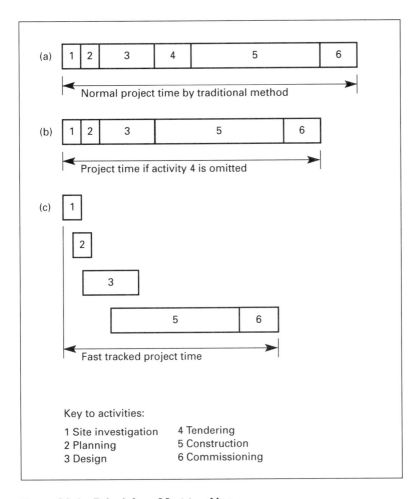

(a) Normal project time by traditional method

(b) Project time if activity 4 is omitted

(c) Fast tracked project time

Key to activities:

1 Site investigation 4 Tendering
2 Planning   5 Construction
3 Design   6 Commissioning

Figure 29.1   Principles of fast tracking

Figure 29.1(a) shows the traditional situation. All the activities are in strict finish–start relationships and all lie on the critical path. The project cannot be fast tracked.

The plan shown in Figure 29.1(b) demonstrates how project time can be saved by eliminating the tendering activity. This can be achieved if a single management contractor is engaged to undertake all the other five activities, or alternatively, using a construction management system suggested by Colgate (1991). Another option is to adopt multiple tendering, advocated by Kolesar (1989).

Figure 29.1(c) shows how the project time can be reduced further by overlapping. In practice this has to be arranged by breaking the project down into discrete work packages, and by identifying which activities can be overlapped and by how much (some might be allowed to run in parallel). The plan in Figure 29.1(c) shows the project time reduced as far as possible.

523

The most obvious advantage of successful fast tracking is the saving possible in overall project time. Most of the other benefits follow from this time reduction.

One advantage claimed, relating to cases where a management contractor is not used, is that the contractor (or contractors) can work with the client and the consulting engineer in the planning and design stages (not possible where the traditional tendering stage means arm's length communications). This close co-operation even allows the contractor to advise the designers and engineers on better and more economical construction methods, with the prospect of cost savings in both design and construction. Closer cooperation and better team-work are claimed to be possible.

FAST TRACKING OR CRASHING?

It has long been recognized that it is possible to shorten a project time by crashing activities which lie on the critical path of a network. Money can be spent on critical activities to shorten them, perhaps by allowing the use of overtime or by employing more expensive methods or resources. (One example might be the installation of floodlighting to allow working to proceed round the clock.) As planning proceeds along these lines, critical activities can be crashed to the point where they acquire float, so that other activities then become critical instead, and can themselves be considered for crashing. Taken to its limit, a project might be crashed to the point where there are many critical paths through the network (which thus has a greatly reduced overall time) but at the expense of increased costs (the costs of crashing).

There is a minimum theoretical possible project time that can be planned by crashing, below which no further shortening of time can reasonably be achieved no matter how much extra money is made available. A characteristic curve of total project costs against total project time for a crashed project is shown in Figure 29.2(a). It is seen that the penalty of extra costs rises steeply as attempts are made to crash the time from the 'normal' time N to the shortest possible crash time at C. (The slow rise in costs as the project completion time extends later than time N is explained by such things as the continued use of project resources, fixed costs and so on).

The cost versus project time relationship is quite different for fast tracking. The important difference claimed for fast tracking is that the time savings are achievable without incurring additional expenditure. This is depicted in Figure 29.2(b), where it can be seen that there is no rise in costs as the project is shortened from the normal time N to the fast tracked time FT.

While it is true that fast tracking removes the need for the cost excesses associated with crashing, fast tracking tends to favour the use of a management contractor and cost-plus contracts and can, therefore, be more expensive to the client than a fixed price project whose duration is allowed to take the traditional course (see the 'Cost considerations' section on p. 527).

Fast track success depends on the ability to break the project down into suitable work packages and on knowing how and where to overlap them to achieve maximum benefit for minimum risk. This requires a high degree of

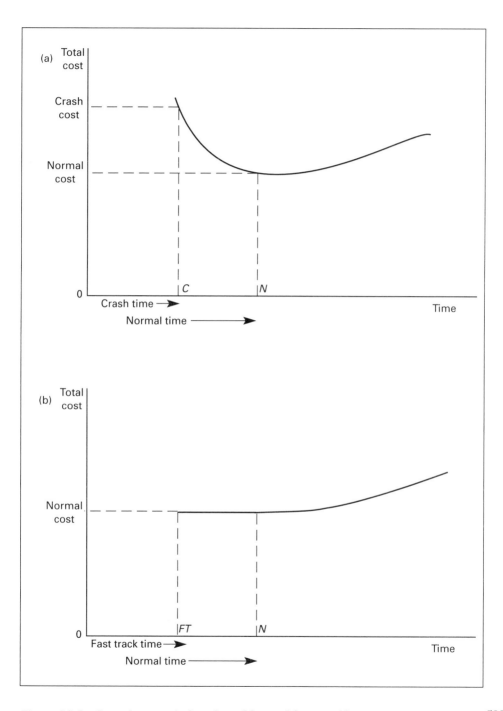

Figure 29.2   Cost characteristics of crashing and fast tracking

planning, knowledge of all the operations involved, and a flexible but decisive mental approach. When the project is implemented, very close coordination, direction and control are essential ingredients. Fast tracking therefore demands a higher degree of management skill than the alternative of planning and spending to crash through a project.

PRACTICAL CONDITIONS AND CONSTRAINTS

Before embarking on fast tracking for a project it is important to consider a number of conditions and constraints that might influence the success of a fast tracking attempt.

Project suitability

Fast tracking is generally applicable to large-scale projects with an expected time span of more than one year (preferably much longer). It is seldom applied to projects of less than six months' duration. Terpak (1989) writes that the best candidates for fast tracking are projects with long construction times and costs estimated at over $15 000 000.

Fast tracking should never be considered for a project which has a continuous sequence of activities along a critical path where the start of each activity really does depend on full completion of its predecessor. It will probably be better to accept that crashing is the only way to speed up such a project. In that case, the penalty of increased costs will have to be accepted.

A limitation stressed by Kwakye (1991) is that, for the fast tracking system to work well, there must be a management contractor standing ready and available to start work on site immediately while negotiations and designs are in progress.

The suitability of a project for fast tracking will be limited if activities cannot readily be broken down into discrete work packages (to enable effective overlapping and concurrent working to be planned and implemented) or where the durations of certain operations are so short that concurrent scheduling saves little.

Fazio *et al.* (1988) write that, for efficient use of the fast track technique, special attention must be paid to:

1 Formation and overlapping of work packages.
2 Coordination between design and construction.
3 Planning and scheduling.

Work packages

The project must be capable of being split into suitable work packages, and this breakdown must be carried out with thoroughness. The aim should be to identify discrete work packages which have some degree of independence from others, allowing them to be started early without being dependent on the completion of others. The ideal objective is to dovetail all the work packages properly so that the maximum possible amount of concurrent working is planned.

Flexibility

A flexible approach to planning and work management is essential. This must be sufficient to allow rapid replanning of operations or other measures to cater for unforeseen delays and contingencies.

Organization and communications

Effective cooperation and teamwork between all project parties is another essential ingredient of fast tracking, and this aspect has to be considered when determining the contractual and organizational arrangements for the project. If a project involves a mix of the client, consulting engineers, various suppliers, a principal contractor, and other contractors who are not responsible to a main contractor as subcontractors, then the problems of coordination and of enlisting cooperation will be more difficult.

In practice, it is possible to see many variations in the methods for overlapping activities. These might include the appointment of various contractors for undertaking design, supply of materials and components, for example. There might be several different ways in which design and the start of construction could be overlapped, some being more extreme than others. Whatever the approach, however, one person or a single planning authority must have the power to:

- plan;
- programme or schedule;
- issue designs;
- initiate action for certain activities or work packages to start; and
- coordinate and exercise total control over the whole project.

This managerial aspect generally points to the need to use a management contractor for fast track projects (although some clients might be capable of undertaking this role themselves). The management contractor chosen must have sufficient resources to be able to carry out both design and construction. Small-scale contractors without such capabilities are less likely to undertake or be suitable for fast track projects.

Terpak (1989) maintains that, for fast tracking to be successful in real estate development, the contract with the developer should include a guaranteed maximum price, a supervising general contractor and a construction manager.

COST CONSIDERATIONS

Kwakye (1991) claims that fast tracking should be cheaper for building project clients in the long term because the client:

- saves money on land charges;
- is not subjected to inflationary pressures;
- faces smaller cost increases through price fluctuations; and

527

- gains earlier return on the investment, or earlier use of the facilities provided by the completed project.

Tighe (1991), on the other hand, argues that claimed savings in the costs of financing, reduced inflationary pressures and time and money savings in land acquisition are illusory. However, see the story of the medical science building project, University of Toronto, which is outlined in the following section of this chapter.

The cost savings shown in Figure 29.2(b) assume the use of a management contractor who can undertake both design and construction for the client. This arrangement is preferred for fast tracking, but it usually implies the use of a cost-plus form of contract rather than fixed or lump sum. Fast tracking can therefore mean higher costs to the client than those associated with the traditional sequential progression through design, tendering and construction under fixed price contracts. The client must weigh the benefits of shortening the project time (which might include balancing cost benefits) against the likelihood of increased costs associated with cost-plus contracts.

SOME PROJECTS WHICH HAVE BEEN FAST TRACKED

Many projects have been fast tracked around the world, particularly in the United States and Canada. Some lessons can be learned by mentioning a few of these projects. Significantly, all were undertaken using the management contractor system.

Slepaw and Mendelssohn (1989) describe how the Florida Power and Light Company fast tracked their coal-oil machine demonstration project. The company chose an engineering management contractor with total capability: he was able to provide engineering, personnel, computing, installation and operating services. All bidding and associated contract phases were therefore eliminated. It was found that close-knit teamwork, timely decision making (particularly), being able to adapt readily to sudden changes in conditions, a flexible budget and top management support were essential to the successful fast tracking of this project.

Fast tracked construction of the medical science building project at the University of Toronto in Canada was described by Sek (1981) as:

- enabling earlier start of medical education and care of the community;
- reducing the chance of obsolescence for the new building; and
- avoidance of increased costs over the long period.

The project duration from conception to the end of commissioning was 60 months. Fast tracking reduced the planned duration by 25 per cent. The cost estimate for this project, based on traditional planning and using the conventional method of lump sum tendering, was $22 000 000. Surprisingly, the actual total cost with fast tracking and using a management contractor was reduced to $20 000 000.

Antill and Woodhead (1990) describe the design and construction of the entertainment centre in Sydney, Australia, for which the management contractor was John Holland (Constructions) Pty Ltd. The closest coordination was required between the architects, the structural, mechanical and electrical design engineers, the construction team, and all the suppliers and off-site fabricators. The project was planned and controlled using a 1 000-activity critical path network, which was analysed by computer and updated monthly. Particular attention was given to earliest start dates, total floats and short-term planning reports.

Vargas (1991) tells how fast tracking of a compressor and pipeline installation at Sylvan Lake, Alberta in Canada saved six months of project time. Once again it was demonstrated that fast tracking required close coordination of all project activities and assurance that the shortest possible times were achieved on critical activities.

CONCLUSION

Fast tracking has become something of a fad in recent years but it is not a panacea that can be used to shorten the duration of every project. Many projects can prove more costly to the client when they are fast tracked. Fast tracking must be used with caution, with a full understanding of the principles, constraints, advantages and limitations of the technique. The key to effective fast tracking lies in proper planning, programming and coordination of the various activities. Far-sighted and effective project management is essential if such a system is to work well.

REFERENCES AND FURTHER READING

Antill, J. M. and Woodhead, R. W., *Critical Path Methods in Construction Practice*, 4th edn, Wiley, New York, 1990.

Ashworth, A., *Contractual Procedures in the Construction Industry*, 2nd edn, Longman, London, 1991.

Colgate, M., *Fast Track Concrete Construction*, The Institution of Civil Engineers, London, 1991.

Fazio, P., Moselhi, O., Theberge, P. and Revay, S., 'Design impact of construction fast track', *Construction Management and Economics*, **6**, (3), autumn, 1988.

Kolesar, S., 'Fast track speeds build', *Professional Engineering*, December, 1989.

Kwakye, A. A., *Fast Track Construction*, occasional paper no. 46, The Chartered Institute of Building, 1991.

National Economic Development Office (NEDO), *Faster Building for Industry*, HMSO, London, 1983.

Sek, R. H., 'Project management in construction: fast tracking' in Alans, J. R. and Kirchof, N. S. (eds), *A Decade of Project Management*, Project Management Institute, Drexel Hill, Penn., 1981.

529

Slepaw, J. L. D. and Mendelssohn, K. S., 'Fast track projects: a case history' in Kimmons, R. L. and Lowerz, J. H. (eds), *Project Management – a Reference for Professionals*, Marcel Dekker, New York, 1989.

Terpak, M. T., 'The fast track construction alternative', *Real Estate Finance Journal*, **4**, (3), winter, 1989.

Tighe, J. J., 'Benefits of fast tracking are a myth', *Project Management*, **9**, (1), February, 1991.

Vargas, K. J., 'Fast track production cuts installation time in half', *Oil and Gas Journal*, **89**, (6), 11 February, 1991.

30 Motivation in the Project Setting
F. L. Harrison

The bulk of this book up to now has been concerned with the organization of projects and with project management systems. There is one system that has not yet been covered but, unless it is effective, all the other systems will not work. That system is the 'people system'.

INTRODUCTION

Management is about obtaining results 'through people'. How the project manager deals with people, and how these people deal with each other can make a big difference to project performance. Effective project organization, a structured methodology of project planning and control, and good human relations are all necessary for good performance, but none of these is sufficient on its own. In addition to professional skills in organizing, planning and controlling a project, the project manager must develop skills in managing people. These are critical to project performance which, in reality, is 'people performance'. This people performance is, of course, dependent on their ability but it is also a function of their motivation, which can influence a person's performance both positively and negatively.

So how does a project manager motivate the people working on a project to perform at a high level? In looking for guidance the project manager might attend a course, or read a text on organizational behaviour, and one segment or chapter will cover theories of motivation. In the twentieth century there have been many theories advanced on motivation in the organizational setting. Some of these are basically philosophies, a few of them are very popular, and most are very moralistic. If the project manager goes beyond a first course on organizational behaviour, it will become apparent that there is much controversy over these theories. Furthermore, when they are applied in real-life situations, he will find that they often give very varying results.

The project manager may then turn to the pre-eminent, politically correct approach of the 1980s, in which the behaviourial consultants advocated open- *531* ness, consideration and participation as *the* only way of motivating people. Unfortunately, many of the assumptions underlying this approach do not represent the reality of people, managers and organizations and, on its own, this approach has been found to be not necessarily effective in achieving goals or stimulating people to a high level of performance. This is partly because the objectives, values and cultures of the advocates of this behavioural approach tend to give priority to the 'needs, aspirations, satisfaction and personal growth of people', rather than to making a profit, winning, success, performance or completing a project to its time, cost and technical objectives.

Unfortunately for the people involved, a high goal orientation is a necessity for effective management. Results count; not making people happy and satisfied at work, except in so far as this contributes to the achievement of goals. As Belbin (1981) says:

> Is the best leader the one who is most acceptable to the group, with the personal behaviour and image that most fits what people look for in a leader? Or is the best leader the one most likely, during the tenure of his office, to enable the team to reach its goals? ...
>
> If a choice is to be made between these two types of leader, then from a management standpoint there is only one option: the effective leader has to be chosen. A more popular but less effective leader creates a fool's paradise with long term benefits being sacrificed for short term gain. The very essence of a manager is that he achieves the goals he sets himself or which belong to the corporate body of which he is part.

Thus, surprisingly, it can sometimes be difficult for the project manager to obtain positive, realistic guidance in how to motivate people to a high level of performance in the harsh reality of the project setting. Yet there is much to learn from the various theories of motivation, and some of these do give guidance in how to motivate some people in some situations, if you know where to look. Thus this chapter takes an applied human behaviour approach which combines theory and practice to show how a project manager can motivate the people involved in a project to a high level of performance. In particular it emphasizes how the organization structure and the control systems can be combined to enhance motivation.

SOURCES OF MOTIVATION

Many people have contributed theories about what motivates individuals. Those listed in Figure 30.1 are merely some of the principal theories described in most textbooks and which could be considered as milestones along the way. One way of looking at these theories of motivation is to consider them as simply identifying the sources of motivation that a project manager can tap to influence people to perform at a high level. However, as there are a large number of sources, it is worthwhile to group them in relation to the type, style or dimension of management behaviour with which they are associated.

Most managers are aware of the two dimensions of management behaviour or style popularized in the managerial grid (Blake and Mouton, 1964). This contrasts

Date	Theory	Reference (where given at the end of this chapter)
1943	Maslow: The hierarchy of needs	
1955	Maslow: Deficiency motivation and growth motivation	
1957	Vroom *et al.*: Expectancy theory	
1960	McGregor: Theory *X* and Theory *Y*	McGregor (1960)
1961	Likert: New patterns of management	Likert (1961)
1961	McClelland: Achievement motivation	McClelland (1975)
1966	Herzberg: Motivation, hygiene theory	
1972	Alderfer: Existence, relatedness and growth (ERG)	Alderfer (1972)

Figure 30.1   Some motivation theories

'concern for people' with 'concern for production' or, to give these wider scope, 'supportive' and 'directive' behaviour. Leadership theory also identifies a third dimension of management behaviour which is important in motivation, namely goal-oriented or leadership behaviour. In addition to these three dimensions of management behaviour which influence motivation, people are internally motivated to varying extents to perform without any external stimulus, although this can be influenced by managerial action and organizational climate. This is termed 'intrinsic' motivation, and forms a fourth group of sources of motivation.

Figure 30.2 shows a summary of these sources of motivation, identified by the principal motivational theories and grouped into these four broad categories:

1   Supportive or 'people-oriented'
2   Directive or 'task-oriented'
3   Leadership or 'goal-directed'
4   Intrinsic.

In Figure 30.3 these motivation sources are consolidated in a more useful manner. All these factors are motivators, but not all apply to every individual. Some lead to satisfaction rather than to increased performance and, in practice, *533* very variable results are obtained when they are applied. Which sources of motivation are most effective, and which dimension or dimensions of managerial behaviour should be used to motivate people, are actually very much determined by the 'situation'. Thus motivational sources, management behaviour and the situational determinants must all be considered together for effective motivation.

Theory	Supportive	Directive	Goal	Intrinsic
Maslow[a]	Love Belonging Esteem	Physical safety	Self-actualization	Aesthetic
Maslow[b]		Deficiency reduction	Growth aspiration	
Vroom et al.[c]	Extrinsic rewards			Intrinsic rewards
McGregor	Theory Y Consideration	Theory X Control	Theory Y Goals	
McClelland	Affiliation		Achievement Power	
Likert	Consideration Participation			
Herzberg	Recognition	Advancement Hygiene needs	Achievement Responsibility	The task itself
Alderfer ERG[d]	Relatedness	Existence	Growth	

[a]The hierarchy of needs (1943)
[b]Deficiency motivation and growth motivation (1955)
[c]Expectancy theory (1957)
[d]Existence, relatedness and growth (see Alderfer, 1972)

Figure 30.2 Motivation theories and sources

Situational determinants

There are two situational factors that mainly determine the effectiveness, or indeed the applicability, of any action aimed at motivating people. These are:

1 The characteristics of the people involved.
2 The characteristics of their environment (see House and Mitchell, 1974).

The organizational person is a complex being and no single sterotype or motivational source, method or theory will apply to all of the people for all of the time. People differ in many ways, not least of which has been termed 'subordinate maturity'. This is defined as 'the capacity to set high but attainable goals, willingness and ability to take responsibility, and education and/or experience' (Hersey and Blanchard, 1977). People of differing maturity will tend to react differently to any particular source of motivation.

People will also vary in their need for, or response to, the following (see
534 Miner, 1980):

Supportive	Directive	Leadership	Intrinsic
Consideration: Supportiveness Affiliation Praise Recognition	Production: Emphasis on performance Planning, organization and control	Goals: Leadership Objectives Achievement Sense of mission Goal setting	Task Professionalism Commitment Aesthetics Creativity
Participation	Self-interest: Rewards Advancement Survival, security and safety Criticism Discipline	Managerial: Autonomy Power Responsibility Competition Conflict	Loyalty Conscientiousness
Emotions: Love Hate Envy Friendship and so on.			

Figure 30.3   Sources of motivation

1   Consideration.
2   Achievement opportunities.
3   Extrinsic rewards (such as pay and promotion).
4   Autonomy.
5   Authoritarianism.

Thus individuals can vary in their response to each of the motivational sources shown in Figure 30.3. For instance, some will be motivated by the opportunity for achievement, while others will not. Some will need supportive behaviour to perform but others will be indifferent to it.

People will also react differently to sources of motivation in different environments, for example whether:

1   The task is structured or unstructured.
2   The degree of formalization is high or low.
3   The work is interesting, stressful, boring, tedious or routine.
4   The work is difficult.
5   The organization structure is mechanistic/bureaucratic or organic/loose–tight.
6   Organization morale is high or low.
7   Relationships approach teamwork or conflict.

535

Behaviour	Effective		Ineffective or negative	
Supportive	1	Subordinate maturity is moderate: that is, neither high nor low.	1	The person has a high maturity, confidence or ability.
	2	The task is routine.	2	The task is stimulating, enjoyable or interesting.
	3	The task is difficult.		
	4	The person has a high need for affiliation.		
Participative	1	The individual's maturity is high, and the individual has a high need or desire for autonomy and achievement	1	The task is structured, formalized or routine.
	2	The task is unstructured.	2	There is conflict.
Directive	1	The individual's maturity is low.	1	The individual's maturity is high.
	2	There is a high role ambiguity: for example, the task is unstructured, there is low formalization, the individual lacks confidence.		
	3	The individual is motivated by extrinsic rewards; the manager has control of these rewards and they are linked to performance.		
	4	The individual has a high respect for authority.		
Leadership	1	The individual has a high need for achievement, growth and maturity.	1	There is a static situation.
	2	The task is unstructured or ambiguous.		
	3	There is change, and an opportunity to perform.		

Figure 30.4   Effectiveness of management behaviour (Yukl, 1981)

8   There is change or a static situation.

Thus, to be able to motivate those involved in a project successfully, the project manager must vary or adapt the methods of motivation according to the characteristics of the people and their work environment. In addition, the project manager must be aware of how he can change the situation to enhance the effectiveness of motivation (which is sometimes called 'situational engineering'). This may involve job enrichment, as described later, or simply training.

The project manager must, therefore, be able to use any or all of the motivational sources as appropriate. He must also be aware of which sources are more effective with which people and which environment. Figure 30.4 shows some of the guidelines which have been generated by applied research.

Thus, for example, in a situation involving change, mature individuals and a fluid organization, consideration and directive behaviour would be ineffective or counter-productive. Participation and goal-oriented behaviour would be the favoured motivation approach. On the other hand, if people lacked confidence in such a situation, then consideration may get the best results. However, if the work is routine and the organization formalized, then directive behaviour would be more appropriate with these less mature individuals.

THE PROJECT ENVIRONMENT

The project environment is unique and has the following characteristics.

1　The work is unstructured.
2　There is considerable ambiguity.
3　The project manager's authority is limited, and he often lacks the normal manager's control over rewards.
4　There is a high level of professionalism.
5　There are clear-cut goals.
6　Change is endemic.
7　There are many managers, groups, departments and companies involved.

In such a situation, the project manager must be particularly aware of the following motivational problems, sources of motivation and methods of situational engineering if he is to motivate people effectively in the project setting:

1　The motivation of effective managers.
2　Participation.
3　Extrinsic rewards.
4　Goal setting.
5　Job enrichment.

MANAGERIAL MOTIVATION

In the project situation, the project manager must manage senior managers from the various functions within his own company, and those from the other companies involved in the project. Not only has the project manager little control over the normal positional sources of motivation of these managers, but in addition the motivation of effective managers can be somewhat different from the conventional assumptions in most courses or textbooks. For example, in a survey carried out by Management Centre Europe (Brussels) in 1988, European managers were questioned about their superiors. The general consensus was that 'He [or she] is ambitious' and, in many cases, 'is motivated by power' or 'is motivated by money'. More specifically, those questioned gave the following opinions of their superiors:

- 40 per cent were motivated by money.
- 60 per cent were motivated by power.
- 28 per cent were ruthless.

These results were not surprising. Previous research into the motivation of effective managers (see McClelland, 1975) identified their motivations as being based on:

1 A high need for power.
2 A desire to win in competition with their peers.
3 A high need for achievement.
4 A low to moderate need for affiliation, generally subordinate to their need for power.

If the project manager is to manage these senior, mature managers effectively he must understand their motivation.

Power motivation

The simplest definition of management is 'Getting results through people'. In a similar vein, the simplest definition of power is 'The ability to get people to do what you want them to do'. Management can therefore be defined as 'The use of power to get results'.

Power is thus essential to management – the power to:

- Take decisions.
- Commit resources.
- Control.
- Take action.
- Reward.
- Punish.
- Sway minds.
- Generate enthusiasm.
- Get others to follow.
- Change the course of events.

Such power is essential for leadership and all achievements.

The behavioural theorists identify two sides to power motivation, a dark side and a light side; or to give them their theoretical text book names, *personalized power motivation* and *socialized power motivation*. The senior manager with personalized power motivation tends to operate as a bully, has a strong detrimental effect on individual motivation, and conflict within and between groups is the norm. Personalized power motivation is characterized by a desire to dominate others, win over competition, keep subordinates weak and dependent, practise 'divide and rule' politics to maintain dominance, and to use power for personal gain. He often employs classical bully-type methods, that is, encouraging toadies and spies, rewarding favourites, and punishing those who resist those methods. He generally motivates people by the use of 'force, fear and favour', but motivation is considerably reduced, as fear is a poor motivator. Participation and teamwork are non-existent within the manager's group. It is only because of the subordinates' inherent acceptance of positional power, their commitment to the organization's goals, their desire to survive, and admittedly the ability and energy of the superior manager that the organization achieves any results. In addition, such managers are normally expert in the use of their reward and coercive power to motivate subordinates.

On the other hand, socialized power motivation can enhance the effectiveness of an organization, in that the senior manager uses his power to achieve results for the benefit of others and the objectives of the organization. Social norms restrain the negative use of power and it is still possible to have participation and teamwork. It is the manner in which power is used that largely determines whether it results in enthusiastic commitment, passive compliance or resistance by those concerned. Strong leadership, the exercise of authority and power, autocratic management, and firm control need not be contradictory to partici-pative management, motivation and teamwork, but can actually be complement-ary to them. It is the combination of all these factors which leads to effective project management. Power should be exercised in a manner that is more implicit than explicit, and which recognizes respect for the individual, to get the best results.

Winning in competition

Linked to power motivation is the desire to win in competition with peers. As Miner (1978) says:

> There is a strong competitive element built into managerial work. Managers must strive to win for themselves and their subordinates and accept such challenges as other managers may offer. In order to meet this role requirement a person should be favourably disposed towards engaging in competition. If he is unwilling to compete for position, status, advancement and his ideas, he is unlikely to succeed.

People vary as to how strongly they are motivated by the 'desire to win' (competition). Cultures and traditions differ too: the English may stress the virtues of 'good losers', while Americans might emphasize the need to win at all costs. Whether these stereotyped images represent reality or not, the desire to win (or perhaps, in some people, the desire 'not to lose') is generally a strong motivator for most managers.

Belbin (1981) describes such competitive managers as 'shapers' and com-ments on their proneness to aggression, which produces reciprocal reactions from other group members. These managers have no hesitation in pursuing their goals by illicit means. In business, management and organizations, winning is everything for many managers: to come second is to fail, so that beating competitors is the name of the game. All too often, coming second means not surviving very long in that organization.

Competition is an important stimulus to performance, both in athletics and in management, but it is also a significant source of conflict. Competition with others does spur individuals, groups and organizations to higher performance and greater teamwork. Thus competition between groups will lead to greater teamwork within the group and (if the groups are independent and do not interact with each other) higher organizational performance. On the other hand, if groups are interdependent and do interact with each other, then competition between groups will be likely to lead to conflict and lower organizational performance.

Achievement

The need for achievement has been identified as a strong motivator for many people, and in particular for the effective manager. Belbin (1981) found that:

> The general impression of the proven top men to which the evidence both of their test profiles and behaviour in the exercise contributed was that of extroverts abounding in nervous energy and actuated by the need for achievement.

Given an opportunity to perform, people who have a high achievement motivation will exert a high level of energy and commitment to the achievement of their goals. They will prefer a moderate level of challenge, to be in control of events and to receive feedback on how well they are performing.

Although research emphasizes achievement motivation for the entrepreneur, it also applies particularly to the manager who is in charge of a business within a business. Thus achievement motivation applies to the project manager and to the managers of discrete elements within a project, such as organization units, work packages, cost accounts, work and organization breakdown structure elements and contract/consignee pseudo-contracts for functional managers in the matrix set-up.

Affiliation

In general, the need for affiliation in effective managers – that is, a concern for establishing close friendly relationships, being liked and accepted by others – is only low to moderate and is subordinate to their need for achievement and power. This is because the person with a high need for affiliation is generally unwilling to take decisions with unpleasant personal consequences, unwilling to allow work to interfere with harmonious relationships, tends to show favouritism and bends rules and procedures to keep people happy. However, affiliation is still important because managers must deal with people and establish effective interpersonal relationships. In the project setting (where the project manager often has little positional power) the need for affiliation is more important, but still tends to be subordinate to the need for achievement and power.

Managerial motivation: a conclusion

The project manager is thus faced with a particular problem in motivating these senior managers. Motivational theory indicates that participation and goal-oriented behaviour are the most effective sources of motivation to use with mature individuals. The project manager must then exercise leadership to establish the project as a superordinate objective (as discussed next) to give a common sense of mission and purpose, and to gain the loyalty and commitment of these managers to the project. He must ensure that the objectives of individual managers are aligned so that they are complementary and not conflicting: for example, by avoiding the use of forms of contract designed to create conflict (such as the basic reimbursable contract).

The motivation of these managers can be increased by structuring the project and its organization in discrete organizational units that give them their own sphere of activities, autonomy, responsibility, their own goals and the opportunity to achieve. This also ensures that any ensuing competition is between semi-independent units and not interdependent groups.

PARTICIPATION

During the 1960s and 1970s participative management, based on organizational behaviour concepts, was very much the fashion and was considered to represent good practice. Those who did not adopt these concepts were looked down upon pityingly and were considered to be old fashioned or even immoral.

The participative approach to management and motivation could be said to have evolved as a reaction to the adverse effects of scientific management. The scientific approach to management, which involves an emphasis on planning, direction, control and work study, could be said to incorporate Theory X concepts of human behaviour, and it has been found wanting over the years.

As is implicit in the name, participative management involves the participation of the subordinate in the decision making and a reduction in the use of direct authority. Subordinates or groups would set, or largely contribute to the setting of their own objectives. The senior manager would not take decisions unilaterally or autocratically, but would meet with the group, share the problem with them and encourage them to participate with him in determining the solutions. It emphasizes the role of the senior manager as being less of an autocratic boss and more of a teacher, professional helper, colleague or consultant. In turn it assumes that the individual can then derive satisfaction from doing an effective job and have a high level of motivation.

The concept of a manager's role in relation to the other managers as being a teacher, professional helper, colleague and consultant on the lines of a professional to his clients, does hold some validity. In intergroup and intercompany relationships, authoritative management is often difficult, if not impossible, and therefore there must always be a substantial element of participative management in project work.

However, in the late 1970s and 1980s doubts began to be raised about the *541* validity of this human behaviour approach as an all embracing philosophy of management. Although it was recognized that these concepts can and do represent relationships between some individuals and groups, it began to be questioned whether the fully participative approach:

- Leads to high performance.
- Is really applicable in its basic form to the reality of man, and of life in the typical hierarchic organization.

Among the comments at this time were:

> In discussion of this concept, two of its propositions should be clearly distinguished. One, of a factual – that is, testable – nature is that participation leads to increased productivity: 'Involve your employees and they will produce more', management has been told by a generation of industrial psychologists.
> ... it is interesting that the factual proposition has not held up in much of the research. Studies by Fiedler and others have indicated that participation is not necessarily correlated with satisfaction or productivity. These relationships depend on the work situations in question. (Mintzberg, 1983)

If the human behaviour, participative approach is implemented on its own, results in terms of task achievement are not guaranteed, and it is results that count. There is a danger that implementing this approach to management can result in a well-adjusted, happy and contented organization, but not necessarily one which will produce the best results. Thus, unfortunately, the participative human behaviour approach has also been found wanting. Nevertheless, participation can increase employee creativity, initiative, morale and satisfaction, and can generate commitment to the project and its goals.

Commitment can be defined as:

> A strongly held attachment to, personal association with or belief in something, such as values, a cause, a person, or a project and its objectives.

Commitment is an emotional state and can motivate people to extreme self-sacrifice. Although participation on its own does not necessarily increase performance, it is a motivating factor that the project manager should use to achieve his objectives.

People need meaning in their organizational life, to feel they are part of events and to have some influence over them. If you treat people like children, they will certainly behave like naughty children; if you treat people as adults, they might behave like responsible adults. Generally, people do work better if they are given respect, are involved with important decisions affecting their life and work, and are treated in a participative manner – though not everybody and not all the time. Participation when combined with a task-oriented approach is an effective motivator. This is not the weak, 'Charlie Brown' style of management, which was sometimes the result of the participative movement, but a combination of leadership, the scientific and the human sides of management.

542   Participation can be used to build a strong commitment to a project, so that it almost becomes a living entity to which people owe loyalty and are committed. Many professionals and supervisory people feel alienated by the nature of their work and their failure to see how it fits into the overall company or project picture. The many layers of management in a large organization leave those at the lower and middle levels feeling a sense of powerlessness and remoteness from decision making, and it is difficult for them to equate their own personal needs with those of the organization. This leads to a loss of involvement and commitment to the project and its objectives.

Participation can overcome these problems and lead to a high level of personal commitment and satisfaction, when combined with the delegation of accountability and responsibility to a defined cost account, work breakdown package, or contractual element, and with a structured approach to project control. Everyone on a project can become associated with its success or failure. They can see how their individual contribution fits into the overall picture and, if they work a little harder, they can see what effect it has on the progress of the job.

This commitment to the project can lead to the development of what could be termed a project attitude of mind, in which people's interests are subordinated to the overall project. This project attitude of mind is a way of thinking that penetrates throughout the organization and unites all involved towards the accomplishment of the project's objectives. There is an acceptance that it is no longer enough to say 'Our department's effort was satisfactory but the project was delayed because of someone else.' The efforts of individuals or of the group are not satisfactory unless the project is a success, and every effort is made to assist other organizational elements to carry out their tasks successfully. It involves taking off departmental blinkers and cooperating by helping one another to complete the project successfully in terms of all its objectives. Thus participation can generate commitment to the project and the project itself can become a strong motivator.

EXPECTANCY THEORY AND THE REWARD SYSTEM

Behavioural theorists tend to assume that all managers are 'social beings who are totally unselfish and primarily concerned with the organization's interests'. It would be nice if such a paragon of virtue could be called the 'normal' manager, but it is highly debatable whether this is so. Nonetheless, it would probably also be wrong to accept totally the cynical opposite approach that all managers are cold, calculating beings, concerned solely with self-interest.

However, most managers are at least partially motivated by their own self-interest, and it would be foolish to imagine otherwise. There is nothing intrinsically immoral with this, particularly if these self-interests are, or can be, aligned with the organization's interests. Even if they are not aligned and they are purely selfish, this is still understandable and very human. Yet when the self-interests of managers differ, there can be conflicts of interests, or in-compatible objectives, and they in turn lead to conflict.

Most managers in the project setting have personal goals and are ambitious: *543* that is, they want to advance their careers. As a result, they will exert considerable effort if they think that these efforts will lead to promotion, more money, power, recognition, praise, more scope, or a better assignment. This applies to all levels of management, junior, middle and senior managers, although the actual personal goals may vary with the individual and the level of management.

This essentially describes what the theorists call *expectancy theory*, in which the individual is motivated by the belief that increased effort will result in higher performance, which in turn will be rewarded by the fulfilment of personal goals. This expectancy theory of motivation does not apply to all individuals in all types of organizations, and is subject to several constraints. Nevertheless, applied research on expectancy theory, as expressed by the reward system, has confirmed it is an effective motivator for some of the people, some of the time. In general, the reward system can motivate individuals to higher performance when:

- The individual values highly such rewards as advancement, more money, more scope, power, a good assignment and a good assessment.
- He believes that a high level of personal or team performance will be recognized, produce results and will bring him these rewards.
- He has an opportunity to perform.

Expectancy theory can therefore be made to work through the reward system, particularly when it is linked to clear-cut individual objectives and performance measurement. This motivational factor can be combined with the emphasis on individual accountability and responsibility as expressed in the contractor/ consignee principle, and for cost account, or work breakdown element managers, in structured and personalized project planning and control. However, as shown in Figure 30.4, unless the reward system is linked to performance and the project manager has some control over it, this source of motivation will not be directly available to the project manager.

The equity of the reward system is also important, as nothing demotivates people faster than inequity. If promotions and pay rises are seen to be fair and just, then motivation is increased. If they are based on nepotism, fawning and favouritism, then all but the chosen few are demotivated.

ACHIEVEMENT, GOAL THEORY AND TARGET SETTING

McClelland's achievement motivation theory is a well-established concept which states that the need to achieve is a strong motivator. It is generally accepted that this applies to most of the kind of people engaged in project work. Indeed, project work is designed for achievement: 'I built that!' In addition, it has been established that setting people specific, difficult, but achievable targets can motivate many people to a higher level of performance than a simple admonition to 'Do your best' (Locke, 1986). Achievement and target setting can be combined with the project planning and control system to give an extremely

effective motivator in project work.

A large amount of research has shown that people will exert themselves to achieve difficult targets. Acceptance of the reasonableness of targets plus feedback on actual performance are critical factors in making such motivation effective. Whether or not these targets are set participatively or autocratically does not appear to be critical, as long as the targets are accepted by the individual. Participative target setting facilitates acceptance, of course, but tends to result in easier targets being set. Targets that are set autocratically will neither be accepted nor achieved if they are perceived as being too difficult.

In effect this describes the planning process, where involvement of those who are to carry out the work is vital to the acceptance of (and commitment) to the plan. One objective of the project manager, therefore, is to use planning as an important motivating tool. The contractor/consignee principle, cost account, work breakdown structure, and the structured and personalized planning and control system can be used to create personal targets for each manager and group, helping to motivate them to a high level of performance.

Research has also shown that knowledge of how a person is performing can enhance the motivational effects of target setting. For this reason, feedback on performance is essential. In other words, project control information is another motivator, but it must be related to the individual and to personal targets. At this stage the recognition of achievement is important: that is, praise, rewards and positive reinforcement – expectancy theory.

One danger inherent in the use of target setting for motivation is that of the individual focusing completely on his own targets to the detriment of co-operation with others and the overall project targets. Thus it is essential that the individual's target must be a building block in the overall project organization's targets and joint responsibilities must be defined and targeted. This is in essence what planning is all about. The matrix of responsibilities also defines individual and joint responsibilities, and the overall structured plan integrates the individual's plans and targets.

JOB ENRICHMENT

The method of situational engineering applicable to motivation is termed 'job enrichment'. This involves adding motivators to the job, or designing the job and the organization so that intrinsic motivation is increased and the use of other sources of motivation – particularly achievement, goal setting and the reward system – are facilitated. Job enrichment owes its development to two sources, namely Herzberg (1959) and Hackman and Lawler (1971) who developed their theories from different approaches, but arrived at similar action guidelines.

Orthodox job enrichment originated from Herzberg's motivation hygiene theory and involved adding some of the motivators identified in this theory to the job. This meant making the work itself more attractive, increasing responsibility, giving people the opportunity to grow and linking it to advancement. Orthodox job enrichment has been shown to increase motivation and performance, but care must be taken in its application for it to be successful.

Applied research has indicated that orthodox job enrichment:

can work with some people, under certain circumstances, for some period of time. . . . Even in the best of circumstances, 10–15 per cent of the participants do not respond to job enrichment and in some contexts, particularly those of a blue collar nature, the result is frequently nil. (Miner, 1980)

An alternative theory of job enrichment was developed by Hackman and others under the name of job characteristics theory (Hackman and Lawler, 1971). They identified what they termed the core characteristics motivating jobs, namely:

- Autonomy, leading to a feeling of responsibility.
- Task identity.
- Task significance.
- Skill variety.
- Feedback.

Jobs with those characteristics generated a feeling of meaningfulness and responsibility, and gave a knowledge of results, and these psychological states generated high intrinsic motivation. However, for this to occur, Hackman and others identified three situational determinants that were necessary; these are as follows:

1 The individual has a high growth need (i.e. a desire for self-actualization, self-fulfilment and/or achievement).
2 The job context has to be viewed as satisfactory (i.e. pay, job security, personal relationships with colleagues and supervisors).
3 The organization structure has to be more organic than mechanistic. An organic organization emphasizes informality, flexibility and adaptation between individuals. A mechanistic organization is the opposite of this and tends to be formalized and bureaucratic.

Job enrichment is only effective as a way of increasing motivation and performance with some people in some situations. When the conditions are favourable, as is often the case in the project situation, the lines of action advocated by both Herzberg and Hackman are very similar, as shown in Figure 30.5. These guidelines should be familiar to many project managers as this is the approach actually followed in the modern project organization and the structured methodology of project planning and control (Harrison, 1992).

The modern approach to the project organization emphasizes the delegation of accountability to every manager, right down the line to individual work elements and group managers. There is discrete responsibility for individual project tasks, not only for the efficient completion of these tasks, but also to motivate individuals and encourage teamwork. Each manager and group knows what is expected of him and his group and what they have to do to achieve high performance.

The structuring of the project using the single-dimension work breakdown structure (WBS) approach or the two-dimensional WBS and organization *546* structure (OBS) approach facilitates this delegation of accountability and

Herzberg	Hackman and Lawler
Direct feedback of performance.	Increase feedback, especially direct feedback from the job itself.
Existence of an internal or external client.	Client relationships should be established with the ultimate user.
The opportunity for individuals to feel that they are growing psychologically through new learning.	Tasks combined to increase skills variety and task identity.
	Natural work groups formed to increase task identity and task significance.
Scheduling one's own work and carrying it out in one's own way.	The job should be vertically loaded with responsibilities and controls that were previously reserved for management, in order to increase autonomy.
Having one's own mini-budgets, being directly responsible for costs and accountable for results.	
Communicating directly with individuals needed to get the job done, regardless of hierarchical constraints.	

Figure 30.5 Job enrichment guidelines (see Miner, 1980 and Hackman and Lawler, 1971)

responsibility. The individual manager, group, contractor/consignee and organizational unit responsibilities are then discrete entities with their own deliverable, clear objectives, and performance and output criteria; they act as cost, performance and profit centres in their own right, and have a degree of autonomy with responsibility and accountability for results. This delegation enables the organization structure to have wider spans of control, and thus a flatter and less hierarchial structure with fewer levels of management.

The pyschological impact of adopting this approach cannot be overrated. The consequences include:

- Individuals and groups can identify themselves with the smaller unit and internal solidarity and unit loyalty are increased.
- Team development and teamwork are facilitated.
- It creates shared values, common clear-cut objectives and aligns self-interests.
- Integration is improved.

- Hierarchial steering and control are minimized, and replaced by self-control within the overall agreed plans and budgets.
- Dysfunctional conflict and politics are reduced.
- Individual, group and unit motivation are increased.

The modern structured methodology of planning and control also reinforces this job enrichment and motivation by ensuring that planning and control are participative and personalized and that:

- Each individual manager and group has specified their own unique goals, objectives, and planned base lines of schedule, cost and resources.
- They each receive their own reports on progress and performance measured against these base lines.
- They have participated in the setting of these goals and base lines.
- They know what they have to do to achieve good performance and they get feedback on their own and their colleagues' performance.

These factors are used to:

- Encourage commitment to the project and the development of a project attitude.
- Give meaning to individual contributors to the project.
- Facilitate motivation through achievement, goal theory and target setting.
- Give a basis for the supporting reward system.

CONCLUSION

The purpose of motivation in project management is to stimulate people to achieve the project's objectives through high performance. The theories of motivation identify many sources of motivation in four broad categories, which, except for intrinsic motivation, correspond to the three dimensions of management behaviour – supportive, directive and leadership.

Which dimensions of management behaviour and which sources of motivation are the most effective depend on the characteristics of the people involved and of the environment they work in. Thus in order successfully to motivate the people involved in a project, the project manager must be adaptive in his behaviour, contingent on these situational determinants, and prepared to change them to facilitate the effectiveness of motivation.

However in project work, achievement can be a powerful motivator, particularly when it is combined with goal setting and the reward system. The structured approach to project management can therefore combine: the project organization; a structured methodology of project planning and control; and these sources of motivation to enrich jobs in order to create a high level of motivation and performance – providing that the project manager knows how to use it as such.

REFERENCES AND FURTHER READING

Alderfer, C. P., *Existence, Relatedness and Growth: Human Needs in Organisational Settings*, The Free Press, New York, 1972.

Belbin, R. M., *Management Teams: Why They Succeed or Fail*, Heinemann, London, 1981.

Blake, R. R. and Mouton, J. S., *The Managerial Grid*, Gulf Publishing Company, Houston, 1964.

Hackman, R. J. and Lawler, E. E., 'Employee reactions to job characteristics', *Journal of Applied Psychology*, **55**, 1971.

Harrison, F. L., *Advanced Project Management: A Structured Approach*, 3rd edn, Gower, Aldershot, 1992.

Herzberg, F. J., *The Motivation to Work*, Wiley, New York, 1959.

Hersey, P. and Blanchard, K. H., *Management of Organizational Behavior*, 3rd edn, Prentice Hall, Englewood Cliffs, NJ, 1977.

House, R. J. and Mitchell, 'Path goal theory of leadership', *Contemporary Business*, **3**, autumn, 1974.

Likert, R., *New Patterns of Management*, McGraw-Hill, New York, 1961.

Locke, E. A., 'The relationship of intentions to level of performance', *Journal of Applied Psychology*, **50**, 1966.

Maslow, A., *Motivation and Personality*, 2nd edn, Harper & Row, New York, 1970.

McClelland, D., *Power: The Inner Experience*, Irvington, New York, 1975.

McGregor, D., *The Human Side of Enterprise*, McGraw-Hill, New York, 1960.

Miner, J. B., 'Twenty years of research in role motivation and managerial effectiveness', *Personnel Psychology*, **31**, 1978.

Miner, J. B., *Theories of Organizational Behavior*, The Dryden Press, San Diego, 1980.

Mintzberg, H., *Structure in Fives: Designing Effective Organizations*, Prentice Hall, Englewood Cliffs, NJ, 1983.

Vroom, V. H., *Work and Motivation*, Wiley, New York, 1964.

Vroom, V. H. and Deci, E. L. (eds), *Management and Motivation*, Penguin, Harmondsworth, 1970.

Yukl, G. A., *Leadership in Organizations*, Prentice Hall, Englewood Cliffs, NJ, 1981.

31 Project Quality Management
Lionel Stebbing

Quality management is the managing of all functions and activities necessary to determine and achieve quality. As such, it probably offers more scope for achieving and maintaining an organization's competitive advantage than many other management techniques. In pragmatic terms this means providing a product or service which is 'fit for purpose' at a price commensurate with that purpose (value for money) in the most cost effective and efficient manner.

With today's highly demanding environment of quality, together with the concern by customers and cost restraints within the organization, the emphasis must be proactive rather than reactive. The question 'Have we got it right?' must give way to 'Are we doing it right?'

Pressures on companies to be price and quality competitive continue to increase. These pressures, together with a requirement by many large purchasers that their suppliers demonstrate the existence of quality systems, are causing problems for manufacturing and service organizations alike.

THE COST OF POOR QUALITY

Inherent in the cost of operating any business or project is an element of expenditure relating to avoidable mistakes, waste, inefficiencies and poor performance in conforming to requirements. This expenditure can be described as the *cost of poor quality* or the *price of non-conformance*. What is often not appreciated by many company executives and project managers is the scale of these costs.

Surveys have shown that the cost of poor quality can vary from 5 to 45 per cent of turnover. It is now generally accepted that the range for most organizations is between 15 and 30 per cent of turnover. This means that in many cases the costs of poor quality can be greater than the overall profits (see Figure 31.1). We have to ask ourselves:

- What are these costs, as far as our own organizations are concerned?
- Do we have the means for measuring them?

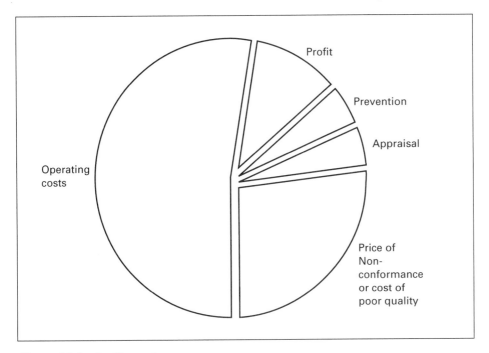

Figure 31.1 Quality costs

QUALITY COSTS

Quality costs can be divided into the following elements:

1 *Prevention costs* (quality assurance). These are the costs of any action taken to prevent or reduce defects and failures. Typically these cover the costs of planning and managing the quality systems and the preventive elements of such systems.
2 *Appraisal costs* (inspection). These are the costs of assessing the quality achieved. They include such aspects as:

   (a) process validation;
   (b) checking documents;
   (c) checking specifications;
   (d) vendor control;
   (e) product sampling; and
   (f) inspection and testing.

3 *Non-conformance costs*, which are the resultant costs of getting things wrong. These would include:

   (a) investigating the causes of defects;
   (b) downgrading of materials;
   (c) repairs and rework;
   (d) replacement costs of failed equipment or materials;

(e)   damage to project economics (time and cost overrun);
(f)   damage to the environment (and compensation payable);
(g)   liability costs;
(h)   increased insurance premiums or claims accruals;
(i)   loss of production;
(j)   loss of customers; and
(k)   loss of life!

4   In addition to the three clearly defined elements listed above, there are
     other less tangible costs that accrue outside the organization as a result of
     failure to achieve quality requirements. These costs can be substantial, but
     rarely is any attempt made to evaluate them. Examples are:

   •   poor public image for the company and its products or services;
   •   difficulty in attracting suitable recruits, as a result of the organization's
        low professional reputation; and
   •   penalties arising from contract conditions of supply.

INCREASE PREVENTION: REDUCE APPRAISAL

The basic economic principle of the application of quality management is that by
increasing prevention, a large percentage of non-conformances can be avoided
as everyone will be operating in a controlled and regularly monitored environment (see Figure 31.2). This, in turn, reduces the need for inspection.

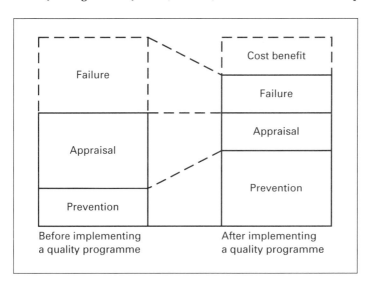

Figure 31.2   Quality programme cost benefit (Source: CSA Z299:0)

This, however, does not imply that there will be no need for inspection. The
prime objective should be to reduce inspection to the absolute minimum. Many
552   industries, by the very nature of their business, have become very reliant on

inspection which, besides being very expensive, has not been totally effective. In spite of frequent inspection not all defects have been detected, resulting in the in-service failures with which we are all too familiar.

By increasing preventative measures the scale of reduction in the price of non-conformance can be quite dramatic. With very little investment a 50 per cent reduction is not uncommon. The return on investment should be at least ten-fold and can be substantially higher in the early stages (see Figure 31.3). The achievement of such reductions will require a balanced mixture of effective quality systems and progressive quality improvement techniques.

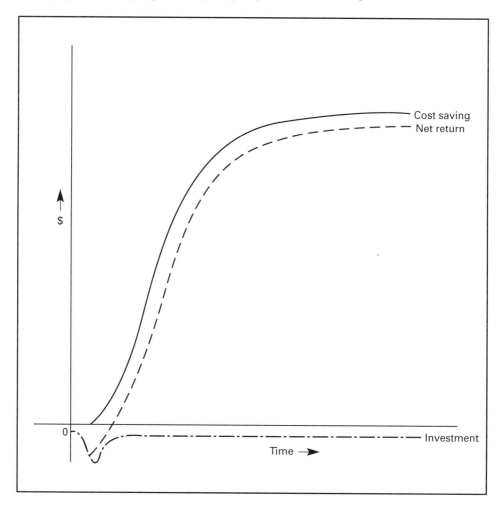

Figure 31.3   Return on investment in quality

In an environment where turnover is reducing, active quality management offers the only scope for reducing problems and for significantly improving profits.

QUALITY MANAGEMENT PRINCIPLES AND PRACTICES

Quality management is a company-wide philosophy which works upon the basis that activities are most likely to be performed to meet requirements if they are undertaken in a controlled and regularly monitored environment. This requires that those activities which are judged by management to have a significant impact upon the performance of an organization are identified and systematically controlled by means of documented procedures.

Quality management principles

To be effective, quality management must be applied in a manner that embraces three principles:

1 *Quality is everybody's business.* Each management function and activity carries a specific quality related responsibility.
2 *Do it right first time every time.* Prevention is better than cure (plan and anticipate problems).
3 *Communicate and cooperate.* Everybody knows what to do, where they fit within the organization and with whom they interface.

These principles are achieved by the development of documented quality systems.

Quality management practices

To apply the principles of quality management will require that senior management examines the organization and identifies its critical activities. Procedures are then developed to control these activities. The procedures will relate to the management of the interfaces and not detailed job instructions. In order to prove their effectiveness the procedures must be regularly audited.

To achieve a positive reduction in quality related costs there must be, in addition to the documented systems, a complete awareness throughout the entire organization of the need to manage quality. Each individual must understand this and the role they will play.

Quality systems can be effective only if the documentation and people are developed together (see Figure 31.4).

Quality system documentation

Quality documentation is normally divided into two parts, namely, the quality manual and the detailed procedures.

The quality manual is a top-level document that translates the business objectives of the company into a quality policy, the objectives of such a policy, organization and practices.

The detailed procedures are either written, or drawn as flow charts. They describe how an activity is performed, by whom and the controls placed upon it.

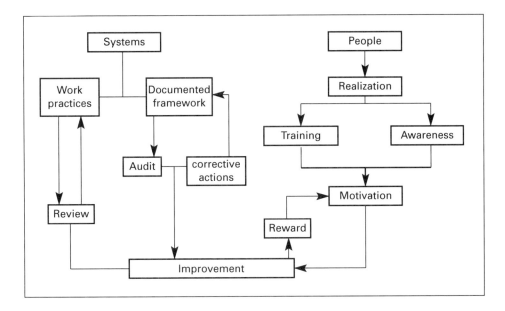

Figure 31.4   Quality assurance practices

In most instances the prime function of a procedure is to control the interfaces between departments or individuals. Detailed procedures will provide a basis for auditing. They should only be developed for critical activities. The following section indicates the types of activities which fall into this category.

Definition of criticality

The criteria for determining criticality of an activity may be seen as those actions that impact on the ability to achieve conformance to requirements in terms of:

- Primary characteristics of the product or service.
- Cost with which this is achieved.
- Safety implications.
- Environmental impact.
- Image both external and internal.

Audit

It is necessary to audit the procedures to ensure they are in place and being effectively implemented. The effectiveness of a procedure cannot be determined unless it is regularly monitored. Audits may identify the need for corrective action and such should be further audited to ensure effectiveness. Audit is a central part of active quality management; without it improvements cannot be sustained.

APPLICATION OF QUALITY MANAGEMENT

Many large organizations have, for some time, required their suppliers to implement quality systems and it has been found that both suppliers and customers have obtained internal benefits from so doing. Suppliers and customers have developed these systems to meet the requirements of quality system standards such as ISO9001/3.

Many industries are involved in a much broader range of activities than those specified in quality system standards. Thus the benefit which can be derived from implementing the philosophy of quality management across a wide range of activities must clearly be in terms of the improvement in overall business efficiency. This philosophy requires, at departmental level, the establishment of appropriate controls over all critical activities. The objective should be to achieve the required quality in the most cost effective and efficient manner.

Internal customer concept

The main strength of many companies is the competence of their departments. However, as these departments develop into strong and cohesive units, inter-face problems occur between them. Most of the quality problems of an organization arise from lack of interface control between departments or disciplines. Departments cannot exist in isolation; there must be a continual process of communication and cooperation. In this way one department or discipline may be seen as the internal customer of, or supplier to, another. In simple terms, the company could be considered to have a range of internal products from processes, proposals, new projects, planning, design, etc. Hence the main thrust of quality management is in ensuring efficient control of the internal products across all functional boundaries.

The benefits of quality management in engineering and production activities are already well recognized. These in turn, however, interface with other activities and functions within a company which are no less important in terms of overall business efficiency.

Scope and objectives

The business objectives of a company will determine initially the scope of its activities. The quality system should be developed to encompass all those activities which are considered critical to the achievement of such objectives.

This will involve the review of all activities within the company against predetermined criteria to evaluate their criticality. Quality system standards form a good basis for the identification of such criteria.

Quality systems standards

The basic principles and practices of quality management are documented in
556 the form of quality system standards. These standards have been developed

over the years essentially as tools for procurement. They represent, in general terms, those activities that most buyers consider important for their suppliers to control. As a result they well cover those controls necessary to achieve the required specification but the standards do not address the cost or profit aspects of so doing.

Most quality system standards were developed to cover generally the activities of design, manufacture and installation and hence there is a high degree of similarity between them. Many companies are now tending towards the use of the international series of standards IS09001/3, but national standards are still very much in evidence.

These quality system standards are useful guides only and no attempt should be made to apply them rigidly.

DEVELOPING A QUALITY SYSTEM

Any company implementing a quality system can experience problems with respect to the degree of detail with which the principles and practices of quality management are adopted.

On the one extreme it is very easy to pay lip-service to the whole concept, misleading customers, employees and partners into believing that the quality systems are functional. In such instances, the systems exist only on paper and bear little resemblance to actual practices.

At the opposite extreme, a company can strive mindlessly to apply the principles and practices to everything.

Both approaches are equally destructive in terms of:

- Adhering to the conformance to requirements concept.
- Employee motivation (and thus productivity).
- Effective use of resources.
- Economic feasibility of the quality systems.

Consequently any company, once having decided to establish and implement a quality system, should consider very carefully such criteria as:

- Corporate and regulatory requirements.
- Available resources.
- Eventual improvement in business efficiency.

It takes considerable time, effort and ability to devise and implement a quality system and the task should be given the appropriate status and support. Both corporate commitment and the allocation of appropriate resources are essential if the task is to succeed. It will be necessary, therefore, to review the existence and adequacy of the current system. This may identify the need for additional procedures to cover existing functions or activities not previously documented or controlled. And it will also be essential to identify the human, financial and equipment resources appropriate to the activities involved in the development and implementation of quality systems (see Figure 31.5). *557*

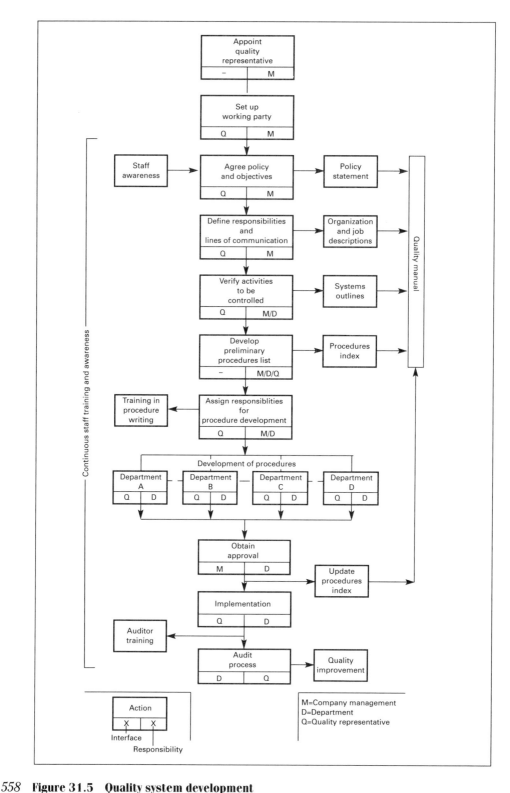

558 **Figure 31.5　Quality system development**

Experience has shown that in order to plan, develop and implement effective quality systems, every company should take the following 12 basic steps:

1 *Appoint a person to be responsible for the implementation of the quality system.* This person should be appointed for his/her management abilities and knowledge of the company's operations. The individual concerned should report or have direct access to the chief executive.

2 *Set up a steering committee.* The objective of this committee will be to establish the appropriate quality system framework.

3 *Establish the objectives for the implementation of the system.* Such objectives could be:

   (a) to meet the requirements of an appropriate quality system standard; and/or
   (b) to improve overall business efficiency.

4 *Create quality awareness within the organization.* From the very start it is essential that everyone in the company understands the concepts and benefits of quality management and their personal role in a company-wide programme.

5 *Establish organization and responsibility structures.* It may be necessary to revise organization charts at company and department level. These charts will enable each grade or level of employee to understand and accept their position within the hierarchy. The charts will also identify reporting and interfacing routes. To secure the required organizational freedom and independence it is necessary for the quality representative to report to senior management (project management) and not to any specific lower level (see organization charts in Figures 31.6 and 31.7).

6 *Review job descriptions.* In many organizations a person's responsibilities are not clearly defined. There is a tendency to appoint someone to a given position and then to delegate additional responsibilities to that person as he becomes more proficient and experienced. As time goes on, this person reaches supervisory or management status purely by taking on these additional responsibilities and then, when things go wrong, it becomes exceedingly difficult to identify the cause or the source of the problem.

7 *Agree the functions which are to be procedurally controlled.* This step will determine those functions for which documented and interfacing procedures must be developed. This will include a review of all functions undertaken by the organization and reflect the scope of activities and business objectives.

8 *Develop the quality manual.* Having established the functions to be controlled, the next step will be to prepare and assemble the quality manual. Typically this will involve preparation of the following:

   (a) policy statement;
   (b) authority and responsibilities;
   (c) organization;
   (d) outline of the functions to be controlled; and

559

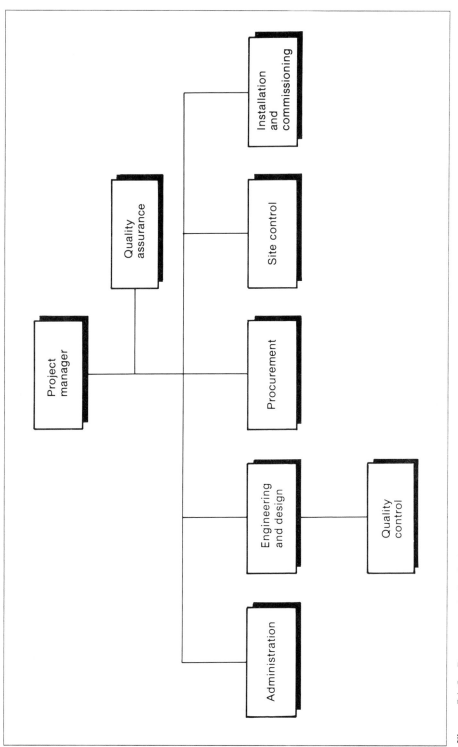

Figure 31.6 Recommended relationship of quality assurance in a project organization

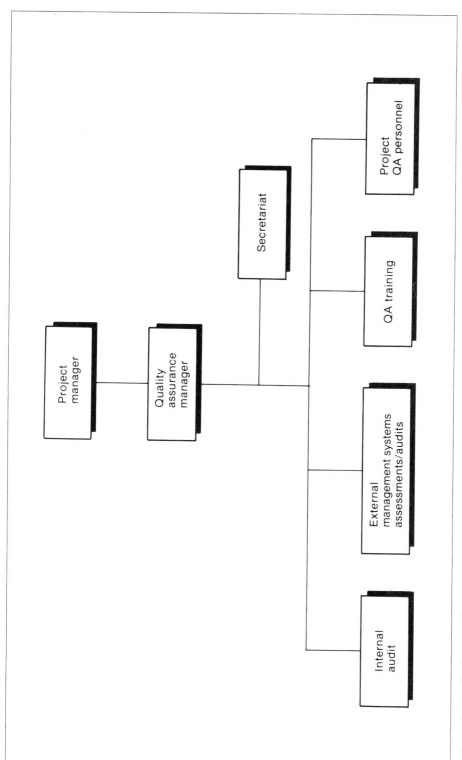

Figure 31.7 Project quality assurance department organization

(e) list or schedule of procedures.

9 *Establish employee participation.* At this point in establishing the frame-work for quality systems, the involvement and cooperation of the work-force is particularly critical. Cooperation is far more easily gained if employees understand the need for documenting the activities for which they are responsible. This will also provide them with the opportunity to highlight problem areas, and to query areas of ill-defined responsibility and possible duplications.

10 *Prepare procedures and job instructions.* Procedures should detail *what* is required or is to be controlled, *who* is responsible for ensuring the requirement is met or the control carried out, and *how*, *when*, *where* and possibly *why* it is controlled. In addition, the procedures will describe how quality and safety requirements will be accounted for. Job instruc-tions would direct personnel in a single activity and are subordinate to procedures.

11 *Implementation.* The penultimate step is the implementation of the procedures. This will involve the cooperation of all concerned. In order to obtain this cooperation, all employees must have understood the reasons for implementation and the benefits to be derived from it.

12 *Audit and review.* In order to obtain the objective evidence that the procedures are working successfully, they must be regularly monitored by formal audit. This will confirm whether the procedures put in place are appropriate and effective and are being applied.

MEASURING THE BENEFITS

When developing and implementing quality systems, the potential benefits can be viewed simply as either financial or non-financial.

Financial benefits

These can be considered as those areas where potential for measurement and reporting through formal cost systems is considered viable. Areas considered as feasible are as follows.

Total operating costs

The inability of an organization to get things right first time, every time, leads to a high price of non-conformance. The development of a quality system across all critical activities will help to reduce the price of non-conformance and hence reflect in total operating costs. The system will bring in the periodic review of operating philosophy and policies in light of the information made available.

Rework and delays

Most of the unnecessary costs incurred by many organizations result from the inability to achieve consistently a right-first-time approach for all activities. Performance indicators such as the number of change orders or rework sheets issued gives a measurement of trends in this area. In addition, the consequential cost of unproductive time is often higher than the cost of detailed planning at the start.

Safety and the environment

Many industries operate in environments where health and safety are important considerations. The consequence of failure is, therefore, potentially high in terms of:

- risk to human life;
- reputation; and
- liability costs.

A quality system will reduce the risk of consequential failure by identifying critical activities.

Supplier performance

By assessing suppliers and contractors prior to order placement the risk of poor performance, or even non-performance, is reduced and the probability of achieving the specified requirements is higher. This approach, together with the operation of detailed procedures for procurement activities, can lead to fewer specification errors and a reduction in the costs needed to verify the performance of suppliers and contractors.

A supplier evaluation system assists in measuring the overall supplier-base performance.

Non-financial benefits

Non-financial benefits are those which are impracticable or impossible to measure and report in cost terms. They include:

- Improved customer satisfaction.
- Improved employee morale and motivation.
- Reduced labour turnover.
- Enhanced company image – internally/externally.
- Improvements in coordination and communication
- Better professional performance.
- Easier training and identification of training needs.
- Greater use of creative skills by more effective control of routine activities.

All the above benefits (financial and non-financial) are interrelated and can *563* contribute to the business efficiency of any organization. They can be described as the benefits of working in a controlled and regularly monitored environment. Such benefits cannot be achieved overnight. They can only result from the investment of money, time and hard work but the dividends will be tremendous if one keeps at it.

DEVELOPING A QUALITY SYSTEM FOR A PROJECT (THE QUALITY PLAN)

Development of the quality system for any given project will depend largely on the total project work scope. In most large projects the work will involve design, procurement, manufacture and installation, in which cases procedures would be needed to control every one of these activities.

Before a quality system can be finalized, the system objectives have to be decided – what is the system intended to achieve? A design contractor, for example, would place the emphasis on different in-house controls from those applicable to, say, an installation site. The company's requirements should therefore be established from the start, taking into account requirements imposed by relevant regulations. The total control scope of work will be taken into account, and an outline of each function must be established and documented. These outlines will assist in formulating a project quality manual and in the eventual development of the detailed procedures.

Quality manual

British Standard 4778 defines a quality manual as: 'A document stating the quality policy, quality system and quality practices of an organization'. A quality manual is usually the first indication which a prospective client gets of a company's approach to quality. The manual should set out the company's intentions. It should not, however, contain detailed procedures since these would increase the production costs of the manual and their updating would present a continuous problem. By keeping the detailed procedures separate, and made available at their point of use, they can be updated independently without affecting the outlines contained in the manual. Contents of a quality manual would typically include as a minimum:

1   Policy statement.
2   Authority and responsibilities.
3   Organization.
4   System element outlines.
5   List of procedures.

Quality system

A quality system is defined in BS 4778: Part 1 as: 'The organizational structure, responsibilities, procedures, processes and resources for implementing quality management'.

It is seen (above) that the quality manual describes the intent – that is, *what* is to be done. The separate, detailed procedures not only describe *what* is to be done, but spell out *by whom, how, when, where* and *why*. Thus the quality system comprises all these documents; the quality manual together with all the supporting procedures.

Quality plan

Referring to BS 4778: Part 2, a quality plan is described as: 'A document setting out the specific quality practices, resources and activities relevant to a particular product, service, contract or project'.

A company's quality system invariably needs modification to suit each project. Such modifications can take the form of additions to or reduction of the company system. For example, a project management contractor with involvement in all project activities must develop a system covering all functions from design through to installation. If this contractor, however, were to be engaged for design only, he would need only those detailed procedures applicable to design, 'fronted' with a quality manual produced specially for that contract. The unique manual, together with its supporting procedures, comprises the set of documents called the project quality plan (see Figure 31.8).

Project organization and the project plan

It is worth commenting here on responsibilities for defining project quality and developing the project plan. This will obviously depend to a very large extent on the type of project organization and the way in which the project management task force (PMTF) is arranged.

Client PMTF   This is where the client will manage the project with his own staff and resources. In this case project quality requirements will probably be established by the client and imposed upon all the main contractors who will each, in turn, develop a quality plan in accordance with their scope of work.

Integrated PMTF   This is where the client and a main contractor manage the project with staff and resources from both organizations. In other words, they pool their resources and assign the best person for each given job. Here, the project quality requirements will be established jointly by the client and contractor although, in all probability, the emphasis will be given to the client's philosophies. Again, main contractors will be expected to develop quality plans in accordance with the quality requirements applicable to the tasks within their scope of work.

Contractor PMTF   This is where a contractor is employed to manage a project. The quality requirements will be identified by the client, and the contractor will develop a project plan. Such project plans will be reviewed by and, possibly, approved by the client before implementation.

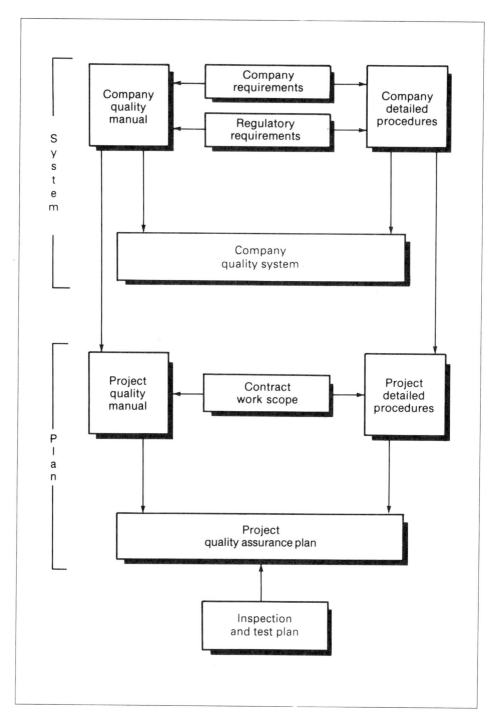

Figure 31.8   Quality system and quality plan relationship

Detail design contractor with project management responsibilities This is where a contractor is engaged to undertake the design of a given structure, and to manage the procurement, manufacture, site fabrication and installation. This design contractor will develop the project quality plan and implement it throughout all phases of the project.

Detailed procedures

As quality management should be a company-wide philosophy, so the procedures must cover all activities and functions. Thus every department should organize itself so that the work produced is not only correct but, more importantly, correct first time. This will obviously promote efficiency, improve productivity and reduce costs. The establishment and implementation of procedures should be undertaken only by personnel familiar with the particular activities and functions and, to be effective, each procedure will define the purpose and scope of the relevant activity and specify how it is to be properly carried out. Unfortunately, the quality assurance department is generally given the task of procedure writing, whereas it could be argued that the only procedures which should really be written by the QA staff are those confined to auditing, corrective action, and to auditor qualification and training.

The concept of QA could be depicted as an umbrella for protection against problems (Figure 31.9). Within the umbrella are the various QA standards which assist in establishing quality systems (although no single one of these can itself fulfil all requirements). Each of the six elements beneath the umbrella needs procedures to cover all of its activities and functions. What has to be determined is who is responsible for controlling and checking the quality of work for each element. In every case, this responsibility must lie with personnel familiar with that work if the checks are to be effective; yet, in order to ensure unbiased results, the checks must be carried out independently by people not actually engaged in the relevant activities. Checking is an activity in itself and, as such, it too must be procedurally controlled.

Thus, design documentation can be properly checked for technical detail and accuracy only by design engineers; procurement activities only by personnel familiar with those activities; manufacturing work only by manufacturing personnel (in-house inspectors) and so on. Even those engaged in simple unskilled tasks (such as housekeeping) contribute indirectly to the quality of the finished item, and their activities and functions should be similarly controlled and checked.

Referring again to Figure 31.9, the quality assurance department would be located within the umbrella. It would be responsible for:

1 Verifying, by audit, that the QA philosophy is being followed throughout the organization and that procedures and work instructions are implemented by all departments.
2 Verifying that those responsible for controlling and checking an activity have done so in a systematic manner and that objective evidence is available to confirm such.

567

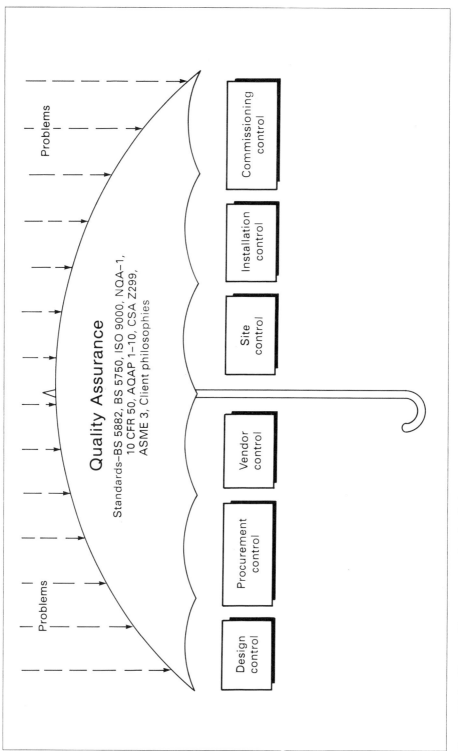

Figure 31.9 The quality assurance 'umbrella'

3 Ensuring that all procedural non-conformances are resolved.
4 Ensuring that fundamental working methods are identified and that fully approved procedures are raised to cover them and that all departments are in possession of current versions.
5 Verifying that all procedures are regularly reviewed and updated as necessary.

As all these activities are under the control of the project manager, he is responsible for the ultimate quality of the project on completion.

The assurance that each activity is right first time can be verified by audit and it is the responsibility of the quality assurance department to undertake these audits and report the findings back to the project manager.

Where difficulties are encountered in resolving problems the project manager will be the final authority. Hence the requirement within all quality system standards that a management representative, preferably independent of other functions, shall be appointed, who has the necessary authority and the responsibility for ensuring that the requirements of the quality system are implemented and maintained.

DESIGN QUALITY

It is regrettable that most expertise in quality management currently lies in controlling the quality of manufacture, and a great deal of time and effort is spent in assessing manufacturers' ability to control their own quality.

Manufacturers can be assessed and audited regularly and indeed they often are. In fact, it is not unknown for a single manufacturer to be audited or assessed a dozen times in as many months. But what do such activities tell the customer? Only how good this manufacturer's system and controls are. Yet, if the design is in error, this manufacturer, even though his system and controls are more than adequate, will present the customer with hardware which is unsuitable for the service requirements.

At the risk of stating the obvious, it is therefore essential for the design to be right before placing the specification with a manufacturer. This means that not only has the design got to be right, but it has to be right first time. In order for this to be achieved it is necessary to put quality assurance controls on a formal basis, and to develop a design control plan which meets the needs of the contract scope of work. It is worthwhile considering how an engineering contractor can use quality management as a means of controlling his design.

Design procedures and instructions

The project procedures, methods and instructions will probably comprise corporate documents, amended where necessary to suit specific contract requirements. In all cases the project procedures should be approved by the project manager, the project quality assurance manager and the relevant discipline or department manager. The client will very probably wish to see and review them also and give his agreement before they are released.

569

Each manager of an engineering discipline or department should be responsible for maintaining up-to-date procedure manuals for his area of management, including procedures for:

1 The checking of drawings, data, calculations, specifications, and so on.
2 The control of design or construction work by the use of philosophies, procedures and standards.
3 Standard preparation methods for specifications, data sheets, drawings, work packages, and so on.

Each lead discipline engineer or supervisor should ensure that all significant activities are properly conducted and documented throughout a project, verifying that:

1 All necessary data, specifications and other documents are available before the start of any activity.
2 All the required work, drawings, reports, calculations, and so on, are in fact produced during each activity.
3 All the required checks, reviews, audits, and so on, are carried out on completion of each activity.
4 Any deviation from the above requirements is properly documented.
5 All documents are systematically numbered or otherwise identified, filed, updated as required, and held securely in a system which ensures that they are readily available upon request to assist reviews or audits by the project team, the corporate discipline manager, quality assurance staff or the client's representative.

DESIGN CONTROLS

The most important design controls are: contract review; document preparation; discipline check; inter-discipline check; internal design review; design interface control; change control; external design reviews; and audits and corrective action. These are summarized in Figure 31.10.

Contract review

This is a most important activity. Before any work starts, it is important that all concerned are aware of their responsibilities within the design contract, and that they have the right tools with which to perform their job. A review team must therefore be pulled together comprising project management, discipline lead engineers and quality assurance representatives.

Work scope

The review team considers in detail the scope of work and establishes that this is fully understood and that the quality plan identifies the true scope.

Design control activity	Scope	Performed by	Action by QA
Contract review	Review: 　Work scope 　Specifications 　Philosophies 　Design criteria 　Regulatory 　requirements 　Organization	Project management Discipline engineers Quality assurance	Verify that missing or ambiguous information has been followed up and satisfactorily closed out by the responsible person.
Document preparation, control and retention	Ensure correct and uniform presentation of documents. Ensure formal preparation, identification, checking, approval and distribution including amendments. Verify retention, retrieval, storage and handover requirements.	Project management Discipline engineers (Client)	Audit adherence to procedure.
Discipline check	Verify content and accuracy of documents originating from own discipline.	Relevant discipline	Audit adherence to procedure.
Inter-discipline check	Assure compatibility of design between design disciplines. Accuracy of content.	Project management Discipline engineers	Audit distribution and approval. Verify as necessary that comments have been closed out by the originating engineer.
Internal design review	Review of design activities in progress or completed.	Project management Discipline engineers QA	Verify that comments have been closed out.
Design interface control (see also Inter-discipline check)	Check physical interfaces between systems/contractors/authorities.		Audit distribution and approval. Verify that comments have been closed out.
Change control	Check changes in design criteria.	Project management Discipline engineers	Monitor changes as required, to close out and approval.
External design reviews	Detailed design audit: 　Adequacy of design 　Adherence to 　contract 　Account taken of 　studies	Independent teams of discipline engineers (in-house or client)	Project management also involved. Audit to verify that any non-conformances have been closed out.
Corrective action	Ensure non-conformances promptly identified and corrective action taken to prevent recurrence.	Project management Discipline engineers QA	Coordinate and verify that corrective action completed and that action has been taken to prevent recurrence.

Figure 31.10　Matrix summarizing the most important design controls　　*571*

Specifications and standards

It has to be ensured that all applicable specifications and standards, of correct issue, are readily available at all activity locations.

Philosophies

These can cover studies, design philosophies – even QA philosophies (where these could be interpreted in different ways). Are these philosophies agreed upon and understood?

Design criteria

Are they all available and understood?

Regulatory requirements

If any regulatory authority is involved regarding safety and/or environmental requirements, then the project team should be aware of all parties involved and the exact nature of the statutory requirements in their current form.

Organization

Who does what in the project task force? Who reports to whom, and what are each individual's terms of reference? If the organization is defined and made generally known immediately, then there can be no misconception about reporting responsibilities. A considerable amount of time and misunderstandings can be avoided when the right person to approach concerning any given issue is known.

Document preparation

Document preparation is another important activity not given sufficient emphasis in QA standards. Documents in this context covers drawings, specifications, data sheets, and so on. These must be presented in a correct and uniform manner. On many occasions project personnel have different ideas on how documents should be formulated. Sometimes ideas developed for previous projects may not be compatible with current projects, and the rules need to be overhauled. A uniform approach should be agreed, defined and made known to all before work starts. The client should be brought into these discussions, since he may have his own ideas and requirements. For example, the client may have standard drawing files based on A1 sized drawings: he will be very concerned to find that at the end of a project the design for which he has paid is presented to him as a large number of A0 sized drawings which are too large for his existing files, and which cause him the expense of purchasing new filing equipment for which he

has no suitable accommodation.

Uniform document presentation helps to avoid errors and facilitates checking, allowing more use of standard checking routines. It is far easier to handle documents when, for example, the project number can always be found in the same corner. It is difficult and time consuming to check documents whose contents are distributed in different patterns or sequences.

Document identification

Identification of documents should be standardized and controlled using logical procedures. Complex numbering systems should be avoided, as these tend to confuse rather than assist in identification and retrieval of documents. The simpler the system, the easier it is to operate and control. Numbering systems should, as a minimum, contain the following:

1   Contract or project number.
2   Document type (denoting whether it is a specification, purchase requisition, design brief, data sheet, drawing, and so forth).
3   Document serial number.
4   Document revision status.

The following is a typical arrangement for document identification:

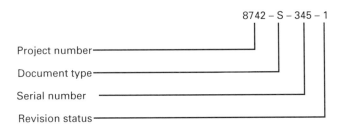

Whatever the identification system to be used, the client will probably require some input and he should be consulted before the system is put to use on his project.

Document approval

Document approval procedures need to be formalized, and all those carrying the authority to give approval at each stage (including the client's representatives) need to be named. It is desirable that specimen sets of signatures or initials should be registered in project records.

Document distribution

Document distribution procedures must be established to identify who gets what. More importantly, the procedures need to be based upon the principle of who really needs what. Many people may wish to be included on the distribution *573* list, whether they need to be there or not. Involvement by those who have no need to get involved creates confusion. A matrix chart, which lists document types along the left-hand vertical column, and has the remaining columns headed with all potential recipients is a useful and concise method for denoting the standard distribution arrangements for project documents. In the matrix, each box will link a document type with a possible addressee, and the matrix will automatically cover all possible permutations. It is simply necessary to leave blank boxes where there is to be no distribution. In each case where documents need to be sent to an addressee, the number of sets to be sent is written in the relevant box. It is stressed again that this must be arranged strictly on a 'need to know' rather than a 'want to know' basis.

A formalized procedure for distribution is also essential to ensure not only that each person needing documents appears on the list, so that he gets them in the first place, but also to ensure that they are in the right quantities (number of sets), of the correct form (e.g. full-sized drawings or microfilms), and that the initial issues are backed up by all revisions.

Discipline check

A discipline check is carried out to verify the content and accuracy of a document originating from a single engineering discipline. Such checks should be performed by engineers of the appropriate discipline, but the checking engineer must not be the same person who carried out the original work. The checker must be of at least the same grade of seniority as the originating engineer. In the case of a one-person discipline (which often occurs on small projects), it will be necessary to appoint the checker from outside the project, either from a corporate department or from another project team.

Inter-discipline check

Inter-discipline checking assesses not only the content and accuracy of a document but assures compatibility between all the design disciplines involved. Here, the document distribution list (previously described) would be important, and it would need to list all those required to comment on a document. There are various ways of distributing documents for inter-discipline checks (see Figure 31.11).

Parallel issue

This issue, although expeditious, entails considerable copying of documents and requires strict control. The document to be reviewed is issued simultaneously to all interfacing disciplines for their review and comment. The latest date for the return of comments should be indicated, and every involved discipline should make comment, even where this means writing 'no comment'. The department responsible for document control should issue the review copies on behalf of the *574* originating discipline, and should control and expedite progress to ensure the

Documents produced by Mechanical Discipline	Architectural	Electrical	Fire & safety	H V A C	Instrumentation	Mechanical	Process	Structural	Quality assurance	Project manager	
General Specifications		√	A			O					
Unique Specifications		√	A			O					
Philosophies		√				O				√	
Reports		√	A			O				√	
Studies		√	A			O				√	
Calculations	Not given an IDC										
Drawings	√	√	A					√	√		
Data Sheets	√	√	A					√			
Requisitions	Not given an IDC										
Mechanical Equipment		√	√			O	A				

IDC Matrix Minimum Distribution
O = Originator
√
A = Review as applicable

Figure 31.11 Example of a document distribution matrix chart

return of all copies within the latest completion date. Parallel issue is obviously the method best suited where a fast turnround of documents is required.

Circular issue

As its name implies, this depends upon the circulation of a single issue of the document to all interfacing disciplines on a 'round robin' basis. This type of distribution is used where urgency is not the first priority. Care has to be taken in arranging the circulation list to include the disciplines required to make comment in order of priority. Here, again, the department responsible for document control, after issuing the document on behalf of the originating engineer, must expedite and control its progress around the circuit. As with parallel issues, all involved disciplines should make comment.

Flood issue, in conjunction with a review meeting

This is similar to a parallel issue but, instead of inviting comments through the distribution circuit, a meeting is called to review and coordinate any such comments. As for any meeting, minutes will be tabled, and these will list the comments made for the subsequent attention of the originating discipline. Minutes of meetings are objective evidence of quality and can be used by QA engineers as checklists for audit purposes.

Internal design review

At important stages throughout design activities, internal design review meetings will be called to review progress. These meetings will consider all aspects of project activities to date. There may be areas of concern, perhaps even updated information from the client, or new legislation concerning safety, certification, and so on. All meetings of this kind will be minuted, and actions placed on individuals.

Design interface control

Although the design interface control could be linked to the inter-discipline check, it goes far deeper. Design interface control sets out to control the interfaces between systems, contractors, and even regulatory bodies. There are many instances where projects use more than one design contractor, creating not only interfaces between disciplines within one organization but complex interfaces between different contractors. The problems encountered in persuading all parties to liaise with one another are enormous, but not insurmountable. Providing that each of the participating organizations has a compatible design programme, the interface control can work smoothly. A strong client is needed to set the rules and to get all concerned to keep to them. If different philosophies are allowed to prevail, then interface control can be a great

problem.

Change control

The control of changes is another very important activity and, in many instances, is dealt with much too lightly. It is generally accepted that many of the significant project problems arise through the lack of change control, with changes being made to a design without reference to the original design source.

Design changes can emanate from many areas: changes in client requirements, updated information from external sources, new legislation from government bodies relating to safety and so forth, and internally from departments within the contracting organization. All must be documented, and they must be subjected to consideration and review in the same systematic manner as the original documents. In addition to aspects of quality, these reviews have to take into account the likely effect of each proposed change on the project costs and progress. Formal procedures for controlling engineering changes will ensure that the client is always consulted where this is relevant, and a suitably qualified group of people will be selected to give approval to or reject each change considered (typically known as a change committee). See Figures 31.12, 31.13 and 31.14 for examples of change control documents. Chapter 28 includes an account of relevant clerical and control procedures.

External design reviews

External design reviews can be carried out either by the contracting company, using its own corporate disciplines, or by the client. The reviews amount to a detailed design audit, verifying such items as design adequacy, adherence to contract and the account taken of studies. The timing of these reviews is usually identified in the project schedule, so they should come as a surprise to no one.

Adequacy of design

Does this accord with the scope of work? This corresponds with the first listed design control, 'contract review'.

Adherence to contract

Has due consideration been given to all contract clauses?

Studies

Has due consideration been given to the results of all field studies which may have been carried out by others?

Audits and corrective action

It is most unlikely that a project will be completed without some corrective action becoming necessary. This is where the QA department needs the support of   *577*

XYZ Company	Design Modification Proposal	Project Title Project No. DMP No.

Part 1.
Activity
Originator   Discipline   Date
Source of Modification Proposal — Indicate
☐ Client   ☐ XYZ Company   ☐ Other

Description of Modification (sketch, description, general information
e.g. Affected documents)

Part 2.
This modification proposal is rejected/accepted for further processing
Reason/affected discipline

Signed
Project Manager

Part 3.
discipline. Please estimate the effect of the
above proposed modification on your discipline
Documents affected

☐ Flow Diagrams	☐ Fire Protection	☐ Certification
☐ P & I.D.	☐ Telecoms	☐ Commissioning
☐ GA/Layout	☐ Operations	☐ Maintenance
☐ Struct. DRG	☐ Studies	☐ Fabrication
☐ Piping DRG	☐ Requisition	☐ Installation
☐ Instr. DRG	☐ Specification	☐ Hook-Up
☐ Elect. DRG	☐ Interface	☐ Histograms
☐ Other DRG	☐ Weight	☐ Schedule
☐ Vendor DRG	☐	☐

Part 4.
Summary of Modification Impact.

Signed
Project Planning Engineer

Part 5.
This modification proposal is accepted/rejected.   Prepare   DMR Yes/No

Signed
Project Manager

Figure 31.12   Example of a change control form

XYZ Company	Design Modification Request	Project Title
		Project No.

To:	Date:	Initiator ☐ Client ☐ Contractor
Title:	Payment ☐ Reimbursible	☐ Lump Sum ☐ Unit Rate

Contractor is hereby instructed to proceed with the work described hereunder:

Applicable Correspondence

Adjustment to Contract:
Total Estimated Manhours   Total Estimated Cost

Documents Affected

Estimated Impact on Programme

Work to Commence by: Effect on Contract Schedule:

Planned Completion Date: Effect on Manning

Accepted by Contractor	Approved by Client
Name;	Name:
Signature:	Signature:
Date:	Date:

Figure 31.13   Example of a change form for external issue to a contractor   *579*

| XYZ Company | Summary of Additional Manhours & Costs | Project Title |
| | | DMR No. |

Engineering & Draughting Hours

Discipline \ Position	Director/ Project Manager	Senior Engineer	Engineer	Interface Engineer	Weight Control Engineer	Senior Designer/ Checker	Draughts- Person	Planning Engineer	Document Controller	Quality Assurance
Architectural										
Electrical										
Fire & Safety										
Instrumentation										
Interface Control										
Loss Control										
Mechanical/HVAC										
Process/Piping										
Structural										
Quality Assurance										
Weight Control										
Estimated Totals										
Project Control										
Purchasing Expediting										
Estimated Totals										
Estimated Overall Manpower Costs										

Summary of Modification Costs

Manpower Costs		
Communications		
Printing & Computer		
Travel & Subsistence		
Other		
Overall Total Costs		

580 **Figure 31.14 Form suitable for summarizing the estimated costs of a change**

senior management. Without it, they would not have the authority to carry through their job. All non-conformances identified during the checks and audits already described, whether discovered by the QA staff or by the engineers themselves, should be dealt with immediately and steps taken to preclude their recurrence. Where a non-conformance is identified, but the corrective action taken by the department responsible is considered to be insufficient to prevent repetition, then the QA engineer must be able to call upon support from management in order that the problem can be resolved effectively. The intention of design control is to ensure that the eventual design meets all client and regulatory requirements. At the end of this activity, the design will result in the commitment of expensive resources to produce the hardware. So, it is essential that the audits carried out by the QA engineer are taken seriously and their results acted upon.

QUALITY CONTROL OF PROCUREMENT AND VENDORS

The activities considered to be the most significant in controlling procurement and vendors are: the inspection and test plan; supplier assessment; tender package development; bid package review; pre-award meeting; contract award; post-award meeting; and quality control;

The inspection and test plan

During the design activity the QA function should be working with the design engineers not only in an auditing capacity, but also to determine that the criticality and traceability requirements for equipment and materials have been evaluated. These factors decide respectively: the importance attaching to inspection of the items; and the need or otherwise to be able to trace the origin of the particular consignment in order to verify the quality from source, or to trace back the supply path in the event of subsequent failure in order that the remainder of the batch can be identified and withdrawn from production or service. To determine such criticality and traceability, the following factors have to be taken into consideration:

1   Design complexity.
2   Design maturity.
3   Service characteristics.
4   Manufacturing complexity.
5   Safety.
6   Environmental requirements.

The Canadian standard CSA.CAN3.Z299.1, section B2 (Evaluation and selection) can be used as a guide to establishing a criticality and traceability procedure. The results of any such determination should be compiled into an inspection and test plan.

The inspection and test plan will identify all inspection check points relevant   *581* to the criticality of the equipment. It will also identify requirements for non-destructive testing, acceptance testing, certification and documentation. It is basically a schedule of inspection points which the design engineer would expect the potential supplier to include in his own controls. It becomes a guideline that sets the minimum requirements for control and surveillance.

The inspection and test plan is not considered to be a mandatory exercise, but it is recommended if only to place the criticality of the material or equipment at the right level. Too many times materials and equipment have been subjected to unnecessary inspection, and other items have not been inspected when they should have been.

Responsibility for inspection should lie with the supplier. His own in-house system should identify the areas of quality control.

Supplier assessment

A supplier in this context is taken to mean an organization which supplies materials and/or equipment, either as a manufacturer or as a vendor. A fabricator is an organization which uses materials and equipment to assemble or build a structure. For the purposes of this section, the term 'supplier' also refers to fabricators.

When choosing a supplier, particularly when the firm is unknown, it is necessary to examine critically a number of factors in order to assess his suitability. These are: engineering capability; quality; price and delivery; and financial stability.

Engineering capability

Does the supplier have the capabilities to manufacture or supply the materials or equipment in accordance with the required specification? What is his track record, from a study of his fulfilment of recent orders of comparable size and complexity?

Quality

Does the intended supplier have an effective quality system which operates well in practice with full management support? At this stage, with no contract made, there is nothing binding upon a potential supplier to conform to any given requirement. It is only possible to review the quality system and to make observations on any apparent deficiency, perhaps advising the supplier that this deficiency could have an adverse effect on contract award if it not rectified.

Price and delivery

Are the prices right? Can the supplier show proven ability to deliver goods on time? Is the delivery date actually promised acceptable?

Financial stability

Are the supplier's finances in order? Nothing would be worse than to place an order, only to have the supplier go bankrupt during production (possibly after considerable advance progress payments have been committed – and lost for ever). It is often prudent to examine supplier's published accounts, or to seek a report from an agency such as Dun and Bradstreet.

Tender package development

During the assessment period – possibly even earlier – tender packages will have been assembled. These will comprise the specifications, drawings, data sheets, delivery requirements, inspection and test plans and so on which, together, define the commitment that the supplier is being invited to undertake. Although the purchasing department should compile and issue the tender package, both the engineering and quality assurance departments should be involved. The tender package is, in effect, subjected to an inter-discipline check, as in design control. Thus the tender package receives a review for completeness and accuracy. The tender package will then be issued to approved potential suppliers.

Bid package review

When all tenders from suppliers have been received, they will be reviewed for engineering content, quality, price and delivery.

Engineering department

This department will review the tenderers' proposals for supply. There may be cases where a supplier proposes alternative methods, materials or equipment from those listed in the specification, and the engineering department will comment on this, stating whether or not the changes represent improvements or otherwise, and whether or not they are acceptable.

Purchasing department

This department will consider the price and delivery proposals. When the potential sources of supply are remote from the sites where goods are to be delivered, especially where overseas transport and international boundaries are involved, it is necessary to consider not just the ex-works price quoted, but the total cost of purchase, transport, insurance, duties and taxes payable to obtain an on-site cost.

Quality assurance department

This reviews the package for compliance with the quality system level, quality acceptance criteria, inspection and test plan, and certification.   *583*

Bid summary

When a choice has to be made between a number of suppliers, it is of benefit to tabulate the main points arising from the review on a bid summary sheet. This is arranged to display the various price and delivery promises, all translated to a common set of units for easy and meaningful comparison (e.g. all the costs converted to pounds sterling). Tabulations are less useful for technical and quality comments, being too limited in space, but they can be used for brief comments, especially where such comments give a definitive preference or rejection. Final choice of supplier is often a complex affair, involving the company's technical and commercial departments and, usually, the client.

Pre-award meeting

Pre-award meetings with suppliers are held to review jointly the contract requirements, and to obtain the suppliers' understanding and agreement. Such meetings correspond to the contract review meetings discussed in design control.

Each pre-award meeting will verify the supplier's intended compliance with the contract, and will also take into account quality system deficiencies observed when the supplier was assessed, prior to bid package issue. Items identified on the inspection and test plan are reviewed against the supplier's own inspection and test plan, and this comparison will confirm whether or not the purchaser will need to exercise any quality control activities himself. Any contentious issues should be resolved at this meeting, or at least very shortly afterwards. Ambiguities and unresolved problems could result in delays or additional costs later on.

Contract award

The purchase order or contract package issue, apart from being issued only to the chosen supplier, is treated in the same way as the invitation to tender documents. Again, it involves the inter-discipline check and review to verify completeness, accuracy and compliance with any agreements arising from the pre-award meeting.

Post-award meeting

Among the scheduled dates proposed in the tender documents and firmed up in the issued contract should be the date by which the supplier is expected to present the purchaser with his quality plan. About seven days after receipt of the quality plan, it should be reviewed between purchaser and supplier in a post-award meeting. An audit schedule can be agreed at the same time, together with inspection hold points, certification and other documentation requirements, and the test programme. The audit schedule should include an internal audit to confirm quality plan awareness, with subsequent audits arranged to cover weak or possible non-compliant areas exposed during the original supplier assessment.

XYZ Company	Corrective action request	CAR No:
		Date:
		Audit number:

Company or department audited:

Basis of audit:

Auditor:	Company or department representative:	Area audited:

Non-conformance

Signed*   Signed:
    Company or department representative   Auditor
*Signature indicates understanding — not concurrence

Corrective action

Signed: Date:
    Company or department representative

Action to prevent recurrence

Date when action to prevent recurrence must be completed:

Signed: Date:
    Company or department representative

Follow-up and close out

Proposed follow-up date:

Follow-up details:

Date CAR closed out: Signed:
                                                    Auditor

Figure 31.15   Example of a corrective action form

Supplier (or fabricator) quality assurance

Quality control activities should be reviewed with the supplier, who should be made responsible for the quality of the items and/or services which he is contracted to provide. There may be, however, additional inspections and tests required by the design engineer to prove the items, in which case these will be identified on the inspection and test plan. These could well be the subject of mandatory hold points, beyond which the supplier cannot proceed until cleared by the purchaser. Such inspections and tests would come under the control of the project's own quality control department, and they would also be monitored by the project quality assurance representative to verify compliance with instructions. The project quality assurance representative will also audit the supplier's activities to confirm compliance with the agreed quality plan.

Where a non-conformance is identified the quality assurance representative should issue a corrective action request (CAR) to the appropriate party (see Figure 31.15).

In the case of a supplier non-conformance, a CAR will be issued to the supplier, with a follow-up audit scheduled to verify 'close out' – in other words, to verify that the corrective action has been taken and that action has also been taken to preclude a repetition of the non-conformance. If the action taken is not instrumental in correcting the deficiency, then another corrective action request must be issued. Should this still not produce the desired result, the project manager must be informed in order that he can lend support in resolving the problem.

The quality assurance representative should liaise at all times with the appropriate lead engineer and with the project manager.

In the case of purchaser quality control non-conformance, the quality control representative, together with his appropriate supervisor, should be advised of the non-conformance and corrective action agreed and followed up.

Products purchased for use on site

This section is concerned with the quality control of the products used on site. Two main categories of items occur and these have different implications for quality control. One category includes items bought by the contractor (and charged to the customer within the contract price). The other category covers items supplied to the contractor by the customer as free-issue.

Customer-supplied items (purchaser-supplied product)

British Standard 5750:Part 4 gives the following guidance:

> When materials, commonly described as free issue, are provided by the customer to the supplier the onus for their conformity to specified requirements is that of the customer. However, the supplier should not knowingly incorporate non-conforming parts into the production or service supplied to the customer.
> The supplier's system should include the provision for verification, proper

storage and maintenance of such materials supplied.

There should also be a formalized method for dealing with losses, damage or other problems discovered with such material.

The site management must therefore ensure that there are satisfactory arrangements for the following:

1   Examination of the items upon receipt to check quantities, identities, and to detect any damage caused during transit.
2   Periodic inspection during storage to detect any sign of deterioration, to check on any out-dating risk where storage time exceeds recommended shelf life; to ensure the maintenance of storage conditions which will not cause deterioration and to check generally the condition of stored items.
3   Compliance with any contractual requirement for reinspection.
4   Appropriate identification and safeguarding of items to prevent unauthorized use or improper disposal.

Procedures should exist which define the manner in which any shortages, damage or other factors rendering the item unfit for use are reported to the customer.

CONTROL OF ITEMS PURCHASED BY SITE

In addition to items delivered to site by the customer, the site will be purchasing other items that demand local control to ensure that they conform to contract requirements. Control of such purchased items is an essential ingredient of the site quality system. Arrangements for choosing potential suppliers for large items of equipment or for high-value items will be similar to those described for vendor control in the procurement section of this chapter. It is unlikely, however, that the quality level of any potential supplier in this area will be higher than that imposed on the main contractor.

Incoming (goods inwards) inspection

This inspection is carried out to verify that the supplier has conformed to contract quality requirements. Procedures must be established (including the provision of correct-issue drawings, specifications, purchase order copies, and so on) to ensure that the goods inwards inspectors have the means for confirming that each shipment is complete and undamaged, and that the goods are correctly identified with part numbers or purchase order number (as specified). The inspectors will also ensure that supporting documents such as test certificates, material certificates, letters of conformance, non-destructive test results, and so forth, are available. The procedures will deal not only with acceptance of incoming goods, but also with the actions to be taken when the goods do not conform.

Special processes

The site has now received the purchased items and those supplied by the customer. All have been inspected, accepted and documentation verified as correct. The next step is to translate all this into the finished product. Special processes are paramount in this operation. BS 5750: Part 4 gives the following guidance on special processes:

> Special consideration should be given to production processes in which control is particularly important to product quality. Such special consideration may be required for product characteristics that are not easily or economically measured, for special skills required in their operation or maintenance or for a product or process the results of which can not be fully verified by subsequent inspection and test. More frequent verification of special processes should be made to keep a check on the following:
>
> (a)   The accuracy and variability of equipment used to make or measure the product, including settings and adjustments;
> (b)   The skill, capability and knowledge of operators to conform to quality requirements;
> (c)   The special environments, time, temperature or other factors affecting quality;
> (d)   The certification records maintained for personnel, processes and equipment, as appropriate.

Among the processes that can be classified as special are certain applications of concrete mixing, welding, casting, forging, forming, plastics and wood fabrication, heat treatment and protective treatments.

Among the inspection and testing processes that can be classified as special are temperature and humidity cycling, vibration, radiography, magnetic particle inspection, penetrant inspection, ultrasonic inspection, pressure testing, chemical and spectrographic analysis and salt spray tests.

Note that some everyday activities are listed among these special processes – concrete mixing, welding, heat treatment and non-destructive testing. Problems arise because such activities are not regarded as special. If they are treated as special, and the necessary control procedures developed and implemented, then many of these problems can be prevented.

The quality of a special process cannot usually be verified by subsequent inspection and testing of the processed material. It will therefore be necessary to establish full conformance by evidence obtained during the process. This is achievable by:

1   Establishing documented procedures to ensure that such special processes have been carried out under controlled conditions by qualified personnel using calibrated equipment in accordance with applicable codes, specifications, standards, regulatory requirements, etc.

2   Maintaining current records of qualified personnel, equipment, processes, etc., in accordance with the requirements of the applicable codes and standards.

3   Defining the necessary qualifications of personnel, equipment, processes,

etc., not covered by existing codes or standards or when contractual clauses define stricter requirements than those already established.

Document control

The methods for determining documentation/certification requirements should be established at project start-up. The documentation which causes most problems is that related to testing and inspection of items. It is considered of great importance to identify which items require certification and then to verify that such certification is made available at the right time and in the correct format. Verification can be undertaken by the project quality control personnel at the time of their inspection. When no inspection is required, then the submission of such certification should be made a contractual requirement. A well-organized document control centre can be instrumental in achieving any requirements for mandatory fitness-for-purpose certification (such as a certificate to operate) in a timely manner.

CONCLUSION

A quality system, if well implemented and totally supported, will give confidence to the project manager that all activities and functions are right first time. This confidence can be achieved only by the cooperation of all concerned. This cooperation, together with communication, must inevitably lead to capability. Quality management can be summed up, therefore, by the 'four Cs':

Communication
  plus
Cooperation
  leading to
Capability
  which results in
Confidence – the confidence that fitness for purpose has been achieved in the most efficient and cost effective manner.

FURTHER READING

Crosby, P. B., *Quality is Free*, McGraw-Hill, New York, 1979.

Lock, Dennis (ed.), *Handbook of Quality Management*, Gower, Aldershot, 1990.

Juran, J. M. and Gryna, F. M., *Quality Planning and Analysis*, 2nd edn, McGraw- Hill, New York, 1980.

Lascelles, David, and Dale, Barry, *Total Quality Improvement*, IFS Publications, Bedford, 1990.

Oakland, John S., *Total Quality Management*, 2nd edn, Heinemann, Oxford, 1993.

Stebbing, Lionel, *Quality Assurance: the Route to Efficiency and Competitiveness*, 3rd edn, Ellis Horwood, Chichester, 1993.

Stebbing, Lionel, *Quality Management in the Service Industry*, Ellis Horwood, Chichester, 1990.

ACKNOWLEDGEMENT

This chapter includes material adapted with the publisher's permission from the two books by Lionel Stebbing listed above.

32 Project Health and Safety

Jim Pearce

This chapter is concerned with the prevention of accidents. It will be useful to start by explaining what is meant by 'an accident' for the purposes of this text. An accident can be defined as an uncontrolled or unforeseen event which is capable of causing one or more of the following:

- Damage to people.
- Damage to plant, equipment or premises.
- Damage to the project.
- Damage to the external environment.

Although other names are sometimes used for accidents that do not actually cause personal injury (such as near misses, incidents, and so on) the author prefers to use the term 'accident' to include all of these.

The objective of this chapter is to review the role of occupational health and safety in project management. It will highlight the requirements to which the project manager should work in order to achieve the necessary standards. Above all, common sense and a positive approach to OHS are needed. Remember, too, that the project manager or other persons responsible might eventually be called upon to justify his actions and omissions before a court.

AN INTRODUCTION TO OCCUPATIONAL HEALTH AND SAFETY

Acceptable standards of occupational health and safety do not happen by default. They can only be achieved by a proactive approach to all occupational activities. Where acceptable standards do exist, they will result from a process that involves:

- Identifying possible loss producing situations (looking for the causes of possible accidents before they happen).
- Evaluating the risk associated with each cause.

- Taking positive steps to implement suitable preventative and protective measures.
- Monitoring and controlling to ensure that these measures are maintained in practice.

How is occupational health and safety (OHS) perceived within an organization? The answer to this question should be regarded with at least the same degree of importance as questions of productivity and quality. This view is held not only by the safety professionals, but also by the more successful organizations. The following extract is taken (with permission) from the Institute of Management's Checklist No 91, *Managing Occupational Health and Safety*:

> Managing OHS can contribute positively to efficiency by controlling the destructive potential within an organisation which unchecked can cause accidents dangerous occurrences and ill-health. These events generate losses in physical and human resources and OHS forms one part of the larger area of 'risk management' which is concerned with the management of non-speculative risks to which the assets, personnel and income of a business are exposed.
>
> Although the emphasis of OHS is the prevention of human injury with legal requirements forming the minimum acceptable performance standard, effective OHS management can contribute to waste reduction. As such it stands alongside other business objectives, e.g. improving productivity, improving quality, as a method of cost reduction contributing to overall effectiveness and total profitability and simultaneously promoting a positive corporate image.

The viewpoint of the Health and Safety Commission and Executive is expressed in the publication *Successful Health and Safety Management* (HMSO, 1991):

> Organisations achieving high standards of health and safety spend more resources on the control of health and safety risks than the average, but consider that this expenditure is cost effective in terms of improved performance. The extent to which health and safety thinking is reflected in business activity and decision making is an important determinant of effectiveness.

THE COST OF HEALTH AND SAFETY

Health and safety can be expensive, but can the project manager afford to ignore it? To do so could prove even more expensive, perhaps not in the short term but, sooner or later, deficiencies will have their effect and losses will occur. The possible consequences include:

1 Injuries, damage, business interruption.
2 Possible shutdown as a result of prohibition notices.
3 Criminal prosecutions resulting in potentially unlimited fines or imprisonment.
4 Costly civil law claims for compensation.

The cost of failure should be a tremendous incentive to improve safety standards. A recent study of several companies, reported in *Successful Health and Safety Management* (HMSO, 1991) revealed that uninsured losses from accidents cost organizations between 6 and 27 times what they are paying in insurance premiums. From this it can be seen that, far from all the costs of failure being borne by the insurers, organizations are themselves bearing a substantial portion of the costs, in some cases making the difference between profit and loss.

Risk transfer

Can the cost of health and safety be transferred to someone else? If risk elimination is not possible, risk transfer might certainly be an acceptable way of controlling possible loss producing situations. Two methods spring to mind:

1　Subcontracting to a specialist supplier of products or services.
2　Insurance (see Chapter 8).

It is worth noting here that, for most organizations, employers' liability insurance is compulsory. In addition, although it is possible to insure against the effects of negligence it is neither legal nor possible to insure against fines that the courts might impose arising from that negligence.

Unfortunately, there have been several instances where the cost of risk transfer has been expensive for the 'innocent' party.

What if the damage was due to the negligence of a contractor? Can a claim be made against them? Unfortunately, conditions of contract are often drafted carefully to the effect that, as far as damage to the occupier's buildings, contents and plant is concerned, damage by fire (a common source of loss) is specifically excluded. Often the client is required to purchase insurance in the joint names of itself and the contractor.

The contract with subcontractors or suppliers often states that they accept no liability for loss of business or profit arising out of any damage caused by them. If liability is accepted, it may be only to replace unacceptable items, or for extremely limited sums. The claim may also have to be made within a short period after the supply of the product or service. This is often too short for the damage to be discovered. Even when the specialist contractor has been engaged to supply both specialist plant and operators, the contract can be worded so as to transfer liability for any accidental damage to the client.

Is it, therefore, worth trying to transfer the risk to someone else? Yes, of course it is: the best commercial and technical option can often be to use an external supplier. It is always necessary, however, to ensure that the external organizations used are competent. It is also advisable to consult a specialist risk manager at the earliest possible stage.

Even if no external suppliers are used, it will still be good sense to consult a specialist risk manager to ensure that the project is adequately covered for:

- Employers' liability.
- Fire and other damage.
- Product liability.
- Consequential business loss.

- Third party (public) liability.
- Environmental liability.

THE ROLE OF OCCUPATIONAL HEALTH AND SAFETY IN PROJECT MANAGEMENT

There are always a few basic questions that should be answered before starting any project. These include the obvious:

- Can it be done – is the project technically feasible?
- Are we capable of doing it technically?
- Have we got enough resources to do it?
- Is it worth doing (will it be profitable)?

But there is one other important question, namely:

- Can it be done with an acceptable degree of safety and without unacceptable risks to health?

True, the main initial objectives of most organizations who undertake projects are to get the job done, maximize efficiency, minimize costs and manage for profit. But actions to identify and reduce or prevent possible losses must include consideration of health and safety. OHS should never be regarded as an 'add on' function or an optional factor. 'Add ons' are too easy to remove or nullify. To achieve truly acceptable standards, safety must be built in from the design concept stage. If this can be done, it is more likely that an optimum mix of control measures and performance standards will be achieved for production, quality and OHS.

Project design objectives and responsibilities

The health and safety objectives of a project should aim to ensure that it is, as far as reasonably practicable, safe and free from risks to health during:

1 Development.
2 Construction or installation.
3 Commissioning.
4 Setting (for example, tool setting of machinery).
5 Use.
6 Maintenance and repair.
7 Removal or demolition.
8 Disposal.

The above should take into account not only normal conditions, but should also meet any reasonably foreseeable misuse or emergency conditions. Responsibility for this lies with senior project and user management, supported by all their employees. Within the project team, all the respective roles and levels of authority should be clearly defined.

In addition to the usual steps leading to project definition (see Chapter 9) the client should discuss health and safety matters with the project manager and ensure that safety and health considerations are an integral part of the basic design specification, and not just an 'add on' extra.

As a result, the design requirements will be clearly established as a set of performance standards. These, when implemented, should meet as many of the client's requirements as is reasonably practicable, in an economical manner. The 'product' must be of good construction, sound material and adequate strength so that it will be safe to use and without risk to health.

Project management should:

1 Identify clearly those authorized to prepare the design.
2 Establish that health and safety considerations are integral to all design stages from the concept onwards.
3 Set up adequate sources of information inside and outside the organization (with specialists or consultants where necessary) together with suitable information storage and retrieval systems.
4 Set up a technical file on the project, to include all drawings, specifications, calculations and so on.
5 Specify who should carry out design reviews and approve the design as meeting user requirements.
6 Conduct risk assessment exercises.
7 Ensure the preparation of operation and maintenance manuals.
8 Establish a formal change procedure for approving modifications both during development and as a service to the client (see Chapter 28).

THE LEGAL REQUIREMENTS

Traditional safety legislation in the United Kingdom, such as the Factories Act 1961, the Shops, Offices and Railway Premises Act 1963 and their supporting regulations, was prescriptive in nature. It was a response to persistent serious accidents and concentrated on a 'safe place/safe machine' strategy. Employers were expected to meet minimum requirements, based on what was good practice at the time when each law was introduced. Unfortunately, the requirements did not keep pace with technology, many loopholes were created, and thus many people were not protected.

Recognizing the need for a change of approach, and the fact that human factors needed to be brought into the argument, the Health and Safety at Work Act 1974 was introduced. This brought many aspects of common law into statute law. In particular, this included the need for safe systems of work (these being safe equipment, safe workplace, safe substances, plus safe person strategies linked together into safe working methods).

Common law

Common law, as far as occupational health and safety is concerned, is based upon the duty of care. Failure to take reasonable care that one's acts and omissions do not adversely affect neighbours is negligence. Such a failure could, if damage to persons, plant or property results, lead to a claim for compensation.

Negligence can be defined as doing something that the reasonable person would not do in those circumstances, or failing to do something that the reasonable person would do in those circumstances (*Blyth* v. *Birmingham Waterworks Co.*, 1856).

In occupational terms, a 'reasonable person' is a person who has sufficient theoretical and practical knowledge, skill and experience to be able to recognize faults, their significance in the particular circumstances, and is able to control the situation, i.e. a 'competent person'.

A 'neighbour' is anyone who could be so directly affected by one's acts and omissions that one ought reasonably to have them in contemplation (*Donaghue* v. *Stevenson*, 1932).

From all of this it can be seen that the doctrine of foreseeability is of paramount importance.

The Health and Safety at Work Act 1974

The Health and Safety at Work Act sets duties on all persons concerned with occupational activities. This means not only the employer, but also employees, the self-employed, manufacturers, suppliers, designers, importers and, potentially, the general public. To fail to meet these responsibilities is a criminal offence.

As is to be expected, however, the main duties lie with the employer. The basic duty is to ensure, so far as is reasonably practicable, the health, safety and welfare of his employees (s. 2.1).

This responsibility is carried further in s. 2.2, each employer having to, so far as is reasonably practicable:

1   Provide and maintain safe plant and systems of work.
2   Provide and maintain a safe place of work with safe access and egress.
3   Provide and maintain a safe and healthy working environment.
4   Provide and maintain safe arrangements for the use, handling, storage and transport of articles and substances.
5   Provide each employee with information, instruction, training and supervision as necessary.

S.9 requires the provision, maintenance and free replacement of any item specifically required to be provided by legislation.

In addition, the Act requires that each employer shall, so far as is reasonably practicable, ensure that his work activities do not adversely affect the health, safety and welfare of other persons (s. 3). He must also, in prescribed circumstances, supply information. All persons connected with non-domestic premises (s. 4) shall, so far as is reasonably practicable, ensure safe access and egress, and absence of risks to health and safety arising from the use of plant or substances to persons who are not their employees.

The meaning of 'so far as is reasonably practicable'

It will be noted that all the above duties are qualified by the phrase 'so far as is reasonably practicable'. The required standard of compliance is lower than that which is physically achievable, in the light of current 'market place' technology. It requires that a computation must be made of the potential reasonably foreseeable losses arising out of the activity. These should then be compared against the costs of control actions. (Note: it has been recently suggested that the value – if one can be put on a human life – is in the order of £2 million.)

There is no obligation to eliminate the risk, only to reduce it to an acceptable level. These computations must, however, be carried out before initiating the activity. In other words, there is an implied requirement to conduct risk assessment exercises. Failure to carry out this assessment is trusting to luck. Even if there was no actual unacceptable level of risk, and a low probability accident occurred, the employer could be considered negligent and as a result, be sued or prosecuted.

Burden of proof

The onus of proving what was reasonably practicable in the circumstances does not lie with the accuser. It is up to the accused to prove that it was not practicable or reasonably practicable to do more than was in fact done to satisfy the requirement, or that there was no better practicable means than was in fact used to satisfy the requirement. This is a change from the usual UK criminal legislative position, where it is the responsibility of the accuser to prove guilt. The accused should be able to prove that he had exercised due diligence. That is to say:

- that the hazards and risks had been identified;
- that the best available technology not entailing excessive cost had been employed;

and, as a result:

- that the residual risk was as low as was reasonably achievable (that is, the best OHS option had been implemented).

The burden of proof laid on the defendant is less onerous than that resting on the prosecutor as regards proving the offence, and may be discharged by satisfying the court of the probability of what the defendant is called upon to prove.

Thus an employer or project manager, can conduct his business in any way they wish, as long as they can justify their actions. This freedom has been termed self-regulation. It is not a soft option, but a quite demanding requirement. Judges' decisions have determined that there is a requirement:

1 To identify foreseeably dangerous items.
2 To take into account the reasonably foreseeable actions of persons.
3 To take into account circumstances that are reasonably foreseeable.

The above is based on *Walker* v. *Bletchley Flettons Limited* (1937). The judge in that case also said:

> The fact that an accident has never happened does not necessarily diminish the foreseeability of one, no more than does the occurrence of one accident yesterday increase the foreseeability of accidents in the future.

What is 'dangerous'?

The following definition of 'dangerous' should be noted. Something is dangerous:

> if in the ordinary course of human affairs danger can be reasonably anticipated from its use ... not only to the prudent, alert and skilled worker intent upon his task, but also to the careless and inattentive worker whose inadvertent or indolent conduct may expose him to risk of injury or death. (*Mitchell* v. *North British Rubber Company Limited* 1945)

Modern legislation sets objectives

The Health and Safety at Work Act (HASAWA) and its subordinate regulations are designed to set objectives, rather than specific standards that can easily be rendered redundant. These measures are often supported by dedicated approved codes of practice. These, when offered in evidence by the enforcing authority, must be accepted as setting the minimum reasonably practicable standard.

In addition, the Health and Safety Executive (HSE) has published an extensive series of guidance notes and booklets. These, although not automatically admissible in court, provide official guidance to what is 'reasonably practicable'. Other sources of information on acceptable standards are the codes of practice published by various professional institutions, the British Standards Institution and other authoritative bodies.

Interpretation

A required skill of employers and managers is to be able to interpret the requirements of legislation. Fortunately, the Acts and Regulations themselves often provide definition clauses.

A practical or 'normal meaning' approach is often required. For example, the term 'as applied' in HASAWA, s.82.2 (dealing with the general interpretation of the Act) requires the application of current technology. Common practice will be taken into account, but beware: common practice is often not good practice.

This mirrors the guidance provided in *Stokes* v. *GKN*, where it was stated that the reasonable and prudent employer:

- would use proven, safe and recognized practices;
- would keep reasonably abreast of developing knowledge; and
- would not be too slow to apply it.

Failure of self-regulation?

Unfortunately, the self-regulatory approach of HASAWA has not been as successful as was hoped. There is still a need for specific and prescriptive guidance. This will be supplied by the new Regulations produced to meet the requirements of EC Directives produced under Article 118A of the Treaty of Rome. These are the so-called Framework Directive, and the individual Directives (Daughter Directives) made under Article 16 of that Directive. These will produce an increasing body of common standards throughout the Single European Market.

UK implementation of EC directives

In the United Kingdom, the EC directives will be implemented by the Management of Health and Safety at Work Regulations (MHSW), supported by:

- Provision and Use of Work Equipment Regulations;
- Manual Handling Operations Regulations;
- Personal Protective Equipment at Work Regulations;
- Health and Safety (Display Screen Equipment) Regulations;
- Workplace (Health Safety and Welfare) Regulations;
- Construction Design and Management Regulations;

and so on.

These regulations will amend and extend previous legislation. Features common to them include:

1 The need to conduct a hazard and risk assessment.
2 The need to control identified risks by means of recognized 'protective and preventative measures'.
3 Employers are expected to introduce arrangements for meeting these protective and preventative measures (which means planning, organizing, implementing, control monitoring and management reviews).

It should be noted that the 'due diligence' defence of 'so far as is reasonably practicable' has been excluded from the requirements of these directives and hence the regulations. The requirements are absolute and therefore must be met. It is to be hoped that the standard achieved will be interpreted in the light *599* of current technology and what could be considered reasonable considering the circumstances. Only time and the courts will resolve this question.

RISK ASSESSMENT

Regulation 3 of MHSW requires every employer to conduct a suitable and sufficient assessment of the health and safety risks to which his employees are exposed during their work activities. There is also a requirement to assess the risks to the health and safety of persons not in his employment, arising out of or in connection with the conduct of his undertaking.

The purpose of this assessment is to identify the measures necessary to comply with the relevant statutory duties. Identical responsibilities are placed upon the self-employed. Each assessment must be revised if new or changed risks make the current assessment invalid. If an employer has more than five employees, the significant factors of the risk assessment must be formally recorded.

Objectives of risk assessment

A risk assessment has the following objectives:

1 To identify the foreseeable hazards that might cause harm to employees or others who could be affected by your work activities (which includes members of the general public and the employees of contractors on the project site):

   (a) during the project development;
   (b) during normal operation and maintenance activities when the project product is used by the public or by workers;
   (c) during demolition or disposal; and
   (d) during foreseeable emergencies.

   Note: a hazard is a property of a substance, equipment process or workplace environment that has the potential to harm persons, equipment or the workplace environment. In other words, it is a built-in property, an integral part of that item or situation.
2 To quantify the risks arising from those hazards identified in item 1, above.
3 To identify the control actions necessary to minimize the effect of these risks, choosing from the protective and preventative strategies outlined in recent HSE publications.

Method for risk assessment

The risk assessment should be undertaken by people who are:

- Familiar with legal and good practice requirements.
- Capable of evaluating the task, substance, persons, equipment and environmental (both workplace and external) factors.

- Able to identify the need for further information on the risks, or to recognize their own limitations and know when to call for specialist advice.
- Able to draw valid conclusions.
- Able to make a clear record of the assessment. Records are essential to prove that the assessment was carried out. It has to be borne in mind that the organization could be challenged by the enforcing authorities or the courts to prove that the assessment was adequate. Remember upon whom is placed the burden of proof.

  The principle of BS 5750 should be applied when making records, namely that formal documentation is only required for those items whose absence would adversely affect quality (or safety).

A common-sense approach will often be all that is needed. The extent to which the exercise proceeds beyond this depends on the complexity of the project and the identified risks. For complex and potentially high-risk projects, quantitative risk assessment (QRA) techniques and possibly external consultants may have to be used. Such QRA techniques could include failure, mode and effect analysis (FMEA), event tree and fault tree analysis, and various human action mode analysis techniques.

When the assessment has been completed, its findings should be communicated to those who need to take control action.

A simple risk assessment technique

The following risk assessment technique could prove useful.

Step 1 Conduct an exercise to identify all the tasks to be involved in project work. These tasks can then be organized into generic groups, so reducing the overall number of individual assessments needed.

Step 2 Small teams of trained and experienced people examine the tasks in order to identify the associated hazards. The hazards can also be classified generically (for example, as mechanical, chemical, electrical, falls, and so on). Teams should include representatives of the working groups who will supervise or perform the tasks. A representative of management should lead each team.

Step 3 It is then necessary to determine how each task is carried out, since this will affect the risk potential. A variant of the technique called hazard and operability studies can be used in which simple flow diagrams are examined to identify possible failure scenarios by asking 'what if ...' type questions. Workplace observations of established tasks is essential.

Step 4 The potential severity of loss S from each each event should be estimated and categorized as follows:

S = 1: Negligible injuries or damage.
S = 3: Minor injuries or damage.
S = 5: Moderate injuries or damage.
S = 7: Serious injuries or significant damage.
S = 10: Fatalities or major damage.

Step 5   The potential frequency F for failure or harmful exposure should then be estimated. A frequency rating scale can be used along the following lines:

F = 1: A highly unlikely event.
F = 2: A remote chance but an accident could happen, and has happened in the past.
F = 4: An occasional event.
F = 6: A fairly frequent event.
F = 8: A frequent event.
F = 10: Virtually certain to happen.

Step 6   An estimate then has to be made of the number of persons (employees and others) N who will be exposed to each hazard:

N = the number of people exposed to the hazard.

Step 7   These factors are then multiplied together to produce a risk rating R for each possible event:

$$R = F \times N \times S$$

For example, consider an event estimated to have a fairly frequent occurrence, where the number of people exposed is five, and the potential severity of injury is minor. Substituting the relevant values in the formula gives the following risk rating for this event:

$$R = 6 \times 5 \times 3 = 90$$

Had the potential severity of injury been serious, the risk rating would have been:

$$R = 6 \times 5 \times 7 = 210.$$

SAFETY PLAN

The duty to conduct a formal risk assessment is a key requirement. This should provide the basis for satisfying Regulation 4 of the MHSW Regulations. This regulation requires that every employer shall make and implement such arrangements as are appropriate for the effective planning, organizing, control, monitoring and review of the protective and safety measures – that is, to prepare a safety plan.

If there are more than five employees, these arrangements should be formally recorded. This is virtually the same requirement as that of s.2.3 of HASAWA, which required the establishment and revision as necessary of a health and safety policy.

As with the HASAWA requirement for a written satement of safety policy, a safety plan should provide practical organization and technical standards. These will help the employer or project manager to communicate requirements, ensure competency, monitor, and hence help the organization to achieve control of occupational health and safety.

Specific examples of this requirement in new legislation are:

- The safety and health plan required under Article 5 of the EC Temporary or Mobile Construction Sites Daughter Directive (implemented in the United Kingdom by the Construction [Design and Management] Regulations).
- The Offshore Installations (Safety Case) Regulations.

The requirement is not, however, entirely new. The Control of Industrial Major Accident Hazard Regulations 1984 required that:

A manufacturer who has control of an industrial activity . . . shall at any time provide evidence including documents to show that he has:
1 Identified the major accident hazards and
2 Taken adequate steps to:
    2.1 Prevent such major accident hazard and to limit their consequences to persons and the environment and
    2.2 Provide persons working on the site with the information, training and equipment necessary to ensure their safety.

Checklist of protective and preventative measures

1 If possible, avoid the risk altogether (for example, by eliminating the need to use dangerous substances, equipment or procedures.
2 Reduce the scale of the risk by substituting less hazardous substances, equipment or procedures, or by using more suitable or more experienced personnel.
3 As soon as possible, take advantage of new technology to improve working conditions and methods.
4 Further reduce the risk by lowering the number of people exposed and/or the scale of the operation.
5 Use collective measures that provide protection to the whole of the exposed population rather than to individuals by:

    (a) combating risks at source by correcting or repairing the problem instead of using risk reduction strategies;
    (b) the use of physical isolation methods; and
    (c) introducing engineering and procedural control measures (safe systems of work, supported where necessary by permit-to-work systems).

6 Provide adequate training to improve employee competence, backed up by information, instruction and supervision.

7 Only accept the use of personal protective equipment (PPE) when risks cannot be reduced to acceptable levels by other means. As far as is reasonably practicable the use of PPE should be accepted only as a temporary or emergency response measure.

When these protective and preventative measures have been assessed, a formal record should be made. The assessment should be circulated to senior management and other relevant people. The formal record will assist in management task reviews and subsequent reassessments.

SAFETY PRACTITIONER

MHSW Regulation 6, requires every employer to appoint sufficient competent persons to assist in undertaking the protective and preventative measures. There is also a requirement to ensure that they are allowed sufficient time and facilities to enable them to fulfil their functions. These would be dependent on the scale of the undertaking and the associated risks. Persons appointed can only be regarded as competent if they have sufficient training, experience, knowledge or other qualities to enable them properly to assist the employer in his duties.

These assistance functions could be carried out by appointed persons who are not in the direct employment of the employer.

Competence and duties of a safety practitioner

The following list has been adapted, with permission, from the *Criteria for a Registered Safety Practitioner*, published by the Institution of Occupational Safety and Health.

1 Assist management to identify the full range of hazards known and not previously encountered in the workplace by:

(a) helping to draw up safety inspection systems and occupational health and hygiene survey programmes; and

(b) assisting in drawing up procedures for vetting the design and commissioning of new plant and machinery and the introduction of new chemicals into the workplace.

2 Assist in the assessment of the extent of the risks to which workpeople outside the workplace are exposed by:

(a) helping to maintain and store adequate sources of information;

(b) analysing data on injuries, dangerous occurrences and near misses in the workplace;

(c) assessing the risks to third parties caused by products, services and pollutants; and

(d) Arranging for quantitative risk assessments when appropriate.

3 Assist in the development of control strategies by:

    (a)   helping the organization make judgements on what is reasonably practicable in minimizing particular risks and so ensuring legislative compliance;

    (b)   assisting in the development of a framework of safe systems of work (including permit-to-work systems);

    (c)   helping to set strategies for risk reduction in particular problems;

    (d)   assisting in setting up strategies for assessing health risks as required by, for example, the Control of Substances Hazardous to Health Regulations 1988;

    (e)   contributing to the development of strategies for eliminating or reducing risk, in cooperation with other professional staff and with line management; and

    (f)   helping to analyse training needs and develop training strategies.

4 Assist in the implementation of control programmes by:

    (a)   helping in the setting of safety objectives;

    (b)   helping to set control programmes for the use of personal protective equipment;

    (c)   participating in the organization and review of emergency and disaster planning procedures.

    (d)   providing hazard information to managers, workpeople and others; and

    (e)   assisting in the organization and running of safety education and training programmes

5 Assist in monitoring and evaluating the success of control programmes by:

    (a)   helping to set up systems for the regular collection of information on injuries, diseases and dangerous occurrences, near misses and the state of the workplace environment;

    (b)   helping to analyse such information to establish whether objectives are being met, and whether there is improvement or deterioration in performance;

    (c)   assisting in ensuring that the audit, survey and inspection procedures in the organization are carried out; and

    (d)   participating in the investigation of injuries, diseases and dangerous occurrences and near misses to see whether improvements to systems of work or equipment are needed, and to encourage prompt remedial action to be taken to prevent a recurrence.

6 Help maintain an adequate organizational framework for safety and health programmes by:

    (a)   assisting in the preparation and revision of the organization's health and safety policy;

    (b)   helping to establish effective safety committees and relations with workplace employee safety representatives.

(c) managing the work of subordinate safety and health staff in larger organizations;

(d) cooperating effectively with other professional safety and health staff;

(e) influencing engineers, architects, buyers, members of elected bodies and others in safety issues;

(f) helping to set up and maintain effective safety and health information systems, including access to outside sources; and

(g) helping to maintain satisfactory relations with safety and health enforcement agencies, and other relevant outside bodies (e.g. insurers, trade associations, and so forth)

The safety and health practitioner must be competent to advise on the action to be taken or (where so required) to implement such action.

In addition to ensuring that the safety and health advisor or practitioner has the necessary competence, the employer should ensure that the person or persons appointed have adequate resources and sufficient seniority and independence of action in the organization.

Safety coordinator for construction sites

The EC Directive on the implementation of minimum safety and health requirements at temporary or mobile construction sites is to be implemented within the United Kingdom by the Construction (Design and Management) Regulations. This requires the appointment of a health and safety coordinator for the project preparation and project execution stages, who will be a natural or legal person entrusted by the client and/or project supervisor with the performance of duties specified by the Directive.

Functions of a construction project safety coordinator

During project preparation

1 Coordinate the implementation of the general principles of prevention concerning OHS.

2 Draw up, or cause to be drawn up, an OHS plan setting out in detail the rules applicable to the construction site concerned. This plan must also take into account specific measures governing the activities falling within the categories specified in Annex II of the Temporary or Mobile Construction Sites Directive.

3 Prepare a file appropriate to the characteristics of the project, containing relevant safety and health information to be taken into account during any subsequent works.

During project execution

1 Coordinate the implementation of the general principles of prevention concerning safety and health when:

(a) ensuring technical and/or organizational aspects are decided, in order to plan the various items or stages of work which are to take place simultaneously or in succession; and

(b) assisting in estimating the period required for completing such work or work stages.

2 Coordinate implementation of the relevant provisions in order to ensure that employers and self-employed persons:

(a) apply the preventative and protective principles in a consistent manner;

(b) where required, follow the safety and health plan referred to above;

(c) make, or cause to be made, any adjustments required to the safety and health plan and file referred to above, to take into account the progress of the work and any changes which have occurred;

(d) organize cooperation between employers, including successive employers on the same site;

(e) coordinate their activities and information flow, with a view to protecting workers and preventing accidents and occupational health hazards, ensuring that self-employed persons are brought into this process as necessary;

(f) coordinate the arrangements to check that the working procedures are being implemented correctly; and

(g) take all necessary steps to ensure that only authorized persons are allowed on the construction site.

Note that the appointment of the coordinator does not relieve the client or the project manager of their legal responsibilities for safety and health. Employers are required to take directions from the coordinator into account on safety and health matters.

TECHNICAL PLAN

Among the responsibilities specified by the Construction (Design and Management) Regulations is one for the preparation of a technical file appropriate to the characteristics of the project. This should contain any relevant safety and health information to be taken into account during any subsequent work.

This duty to provide a technical file is similar to the requirements of EC directives made under Article 100A of the Treaty of Rome – the so-called Product Directives. These set various requirements that must be met before specified types of product can be marketed within the Community. In particular, these items must satisfy relevant 'essential health and safety requirements' (ESRs). ESRs have been produced to cover a number of cases, including use of machinery and hazardous substances, to name just two examples.

PRODUCT LIABILITY

Managers of projects for the purpose of introducing new products into the *607* marketplace may have to take into account the effects on health and safety of domestic, as well as occupational users. To provide for this, the EC has produced the Directive on Strict Product Liability. This was implemented in the United Kingdom by the Consumer Protection Act 1987.

Strict liability means that there is no need to prove that the producer of a defective product was negligent. What has to be proved by the claimant is that:

1   There was injury or damage.
2   The product was defective.
3   The defect caused the injury or damage.

A product is defective if the safety of the product is not to the standard that the consumer is entitled to expect, after taking into account all the circumstances (such as user instructions, accompanying warnings, and so on).

Among the possible defences open to the defendant is the 'development risk defence'. This means that the state of scientific and technical knowledge at the time of supply was not sufficient to enable the defect to be discovered. This defence reinforces the need to prepare a product technical file, to keep adequate records and to be prepared to respond in a positive manner to control any defects revealed through experience.

OTHER REQUIREMENTS OF THE MANAGEMENT OF HEALTH AND SAFETY AT WORK (MHSW) REGULATIONS

Regulation 7 requires the establishment of appropriate emergency procedures. These could range from first-aid arrangements, to full-scale disaster plans. They should be based on formal assessment, be fully documented, and would form part of the safety plan or safety policy.

It should be noted that, in the United Kingdom, to meet fire emergency situations the Home Office is expected to introduce the Fire Precautions (Places of Work) Regulations for implementation on or after 1st April 1994.

Regulation 8 reinforces the requirement of s. 2.2 of the Health and Safety at Work Act (HASAWA) to provide information to employees.

Regulation 9 emphasizes the duties of two or more employers sharing a workplace to cooperate with each other to enable them to meet their duties under the relevant statutory duties.

Regulation 10 reinforces employers' duties under s. 2.2 of HASAWA to provide training, as necessary. It specifies circumstances where training is required and emphasizes the need to provide refresher training.

Regulation 12 requires the provision of operational health and safety information to temporary workers and to any agency providing such workers.

PERSONAL RESPONSIBILITY

The Health and Safety at Work Act, Fire Precautions Act, Environmental Protection Act and the new regulations required by the EC all place responsibility not only on the employer, but also on individuals from directors to the shop floor or project site.

The intention and effect of this legislation is that the responsibility placed on any manager or individual shall not extend beyond matters which are, in practice, within his control and where authority to act has been delegated explicitly by the employer.

The employer remains responsible for ensuring that managers and others who exercise discretion and judgement are competent to do so, and have been provided with clear guidelines.

There are four sections of the Health and Safety at Work Act which deal with personal responsibilities.

S.7 sets the general duty of employees to take reasonable care to ensure the safety of themselves and others from their acts and omissions. It also requires them to cooperate with others (employer, client, and so on) to enable them to meet their legal duties.

S.8 requires all persons not to intentionally or recklessly interfere with or misuse anything provided in the interests of health and safety. MHSW Regulation 11 reinforces the employee's duty not to interfere with preventative and protective measures. It also adds a new duty: to inform the employer of health and safety problems and shortfalls in the protective arrangements.

It is under s. 7 and s. 8 (and presumably under MHSW Regulation 11) that offences committed by employees would normally be pursued.

S.36 of HASAWA provides for circumstances where someone (for example, an organization) commits an offence as the result of the acts or omissions of another person (for example an employee). That person may be charged with and convicted of the offence, even if proceedings are not taken against the first person. This allows for a range of responses by the enforcing authority. If the organization responsible has acted with due diligence by:

1   Identifying the risks.
2   Establishing suitable control procedures.
3   Assigning responsibilities to competent persons who are aware of their roles and have adequate authority and who are actively and adequately monitored by their superiors.

Under these circumstances the organization cannot be held responsible for the failure (*Tesco Stores* v. *Nattras* [1971]). If there are inadequacies on the part of the organization as well as those of the individual person, then both would face charges arising out of the failure. Several middle managers have faced charges under this section of the Act.

S. 37 of HASAWA makes it a separate offence for a breach of any statutory provision to be committed with the consent, connivance, or through the neglect of any director, manager, secretary or similar officer of an organization. There are almost identical provisions in s. 157 of the Environmental Protection Act 1990 and s. 23 of the Fire Precautions Act 1971.

A fairly recent prosecution under the Fire Precautions Act (*R.* v. *Boal*) has, on appeal, clarified the interpretation of the term 'manager'. The Court of Appeal determined that there was no intention in s. 23 to impose criminal responsibility *609* on anyone but those who were in a position of real authority within an organization. These were those who had the power and responsibility to set corporate policy; there was no intention to 'strike at underlings'. This decision confirms that these sections are designed to deal with offences committed by senior persons, who can be described as being 'of the mind of the body corporate'.

A case often quoted is that of *Armour* v. *Skeen*. A workman repairing a bridge over the River Clyde fell to his death. Mr Armour, as Director of Roads for Strathclyde Regional Council, was therefore responsible for supervising the safety of council workers while on the roads. It was alleged that he had omitted to prepare a written safety policy statement for road work and that he failed to inform his staff of the implications and requirements of the Act and of the need for adequate training and supervision. His defence, that he had no personal duty to carry out the council's statutory duty under HASAWA, s. 2.3, was rejected. Hence he was found guilty by means of s. 37. This conviction was upheld on appeal.

It is interesting to note that a director in a more recent case was not only fined £5 000 under s. 37, but was also disqualified from being a company director for two years under a provision of the Company Directors Disqualifications Act 1986. The offence was failure to follow the terms of a prohibition notice.

Only a few directors are prosecuted each year. However, it is the policy of the Health and Safety Executive to make greater use of prosecution after routine inspection, and to increase prosecution of individuals holding senior management positions.

As a result of the sections of the Act described here, those concerned with management should note that they are always accountable for the health and safety aspects. This accountability cannot be delegated. It will still exist even where the managers are not physically present. It is important to ask:

- Have the hazards been identified?
- Have the risks been evaluated?
- Have suitable protective and preventative measures been established?
- Have operational responsibilities been assigned to competent persons?
- Have proactive monitoring systems been established?
- Have necessary remedial actions been introduced promptly?
- Is the whole safety management system reviewed regularly by those responsible for its general management?

ENFORCEMENT

Health and safety requirements are enforced, in the main, by inspectors managed by the Health and Safety Executive (HSE) or by environmental health officers appointed by the relevant local authorities. The HSE inspector most likely to be encountered by project managers will belong to the Factory Inspectorate. All inspectors appointed under HASAWA have wide ranging powers to enable them to enforce the requirements of the Act. Summarized, inspectors have the power or right to:

1   Enter premises when they have reason to believe that work activities are in progress.
2   Take with them into the premises any persons authorized by the inspectors and any equipment needed to enable them to conduct routine inspections or to investigate accidents or complaints.
3   Take measurements, photographs, recordings and actual samples.
4   Direct that items are to be left undisturbed pending further examination.
5   Require articles to be dismantled, tested or substances made safe if the inspector has reason to believe they are in a dangerous condition.
6   Take items into possession for examination, to prevent tampering, or as evidence.
7   Take statements. Those interviewed by the inspectors have an obligation to provide statements as required and, if necessary, swear to their truthfulness. To refuse is an offence. These statements can be used in a court of law, but not against the provider or their spouse.
8   Provision of any reasonable facilities and assistance.
9   If the above is not sufficient, any other power that is necessary to carry out their functions.
10 Initiate prosecution. Depending on the degree of seriousness, cases will be heard either in a magistrates' court or a crown court (or their Scottish equivalents).

The most probable outcome of an inspector's visit will be a *letter* setting out various requirements. If necessary, the inspector will issue an *improvement notice*. This will require protective and preventative measures to be implemented within a specified period.

When, in the opinion of the inspector, the circumstances give rise to immediate danger or risk of serious injury, a *prohibition notice* will be issued. This will prohibit specified activities until the complaint has been remedied.

It is possible to appeal against these notices within 21 days to an industrial tribunal. Failure to meet the requirements of a letter or notice is an offence.

The Offshore Safety Act 1992 (OSA) allows magistrates (sheriffs in Scotland) to impose fines of up to £20 000 for a breach of ss. 2–6 of HASAWA or breach of an improvement notice, prohibition notice or court remedy order. Individuals may be liable for a term of imprisonment not exceeding six months.

The OSA also widens the range of health and safety offences for which a crown court (or its Scottish equivalent) can impose custodial sentences. These higher courts can imprison individuals for up to two years for breach of an improvement notice or court remedy order, as well as for offences against earlier legislation (explosives, licensing regimes or prohibition notices). Serious offences tried in the crown court will still attract a sentence of up to 2 years imprisonment and/or an unlimited fine.

Offences other than those outlined above will, under the Criminal Justice Act 1991, attract a fine of up to £5 000.

SAFETY POLICY STATEMENT

Every employer of five or more persons is required under s. 2.3 of HASAWA to prepare and issue a health and policy statement to its employees. If only because of the legal implications, it is prudent to take steps to ensure not only that every employee has received a personal copy of the statement, but also that they understand it.

The purpose of the safety policy as required by HASAWA is very similar to that of a safety plan, as required by other legislation. It must state the organization's health and safety objectives, define the responsibilities of its management and staff and set performance standards which can be used to guide and control implementation. Above all, it must be a working document, providing a safety management system that will give practical help to all people in the organization in meeting personal and corporate obligations.

A successful health and safety policy will comprise three parts:

1 A general statement of policy.
2 Definition of the organization needed to ensure implementation of the policy.
3 Specific arrangements for ensuring that adequate standards will be achieved and maintained.

The last two of these sections should be written as internal codes of practice, setting both organizational and technical performance standards. These will aid monitoring, management review activities and modification as required. The safety policy, like a project safety plan, should be specific to the site or project and not a generalized, organization-wide document.

The content of the three separate parts will now be examined more closely.

General statement of health and safety policy

The purpose of the general statement is to set out a brief but explicit declaration of the organization's commitment to health and safety. This should state:

- That health and safety issues are just as important as any other organizational objective.
- That the legal requirements are to be considered as the minimum – not the optimum – standards.
- That the organization is committed to review and upgrade standards on a continuous basis.
- That there is a commitment to involve all staff in the development and implementation of health and safety measures.
- The name of a senior executive appointed as health and safety co-ordinator, responsible to the board of directors for implementing the policy.

Defining the organization

The objective of this part of the health and safety statement is to set out the chain of responsibility from executive management through employees at every level in the organization. It should also define the role of specialist support staff – for example, the safety practitioner.

Each person should be given responsibility for planning, implementing or monitoring an established set of tasks. Note, however, that although such responsibilities can be delegated to individuals or to groups, the ultimate responsibility still resides with the employer, and cannot be transferred. Tasks should be described in sufficient detail to give positive guidance and also to aid performance monitoring and assessment by the individual's manager.

The monitoring and assessment of a person's health and safety performance should be regarded as a normal activity within the organization, to be conducted along with the monitoring and assessement of other project activities.

It is recommended that job descriptions should make reference to health and safety responsibilities.

Arrangements for implementation

The objective of this part of the health and safety declaration is to set performance standards giving positive guidance on how to meet the responsibilities assigned in the part dealing with organization. It should cover:

- Support activities such as training, purchasing and the operation of employee safety representatives and safety committees.
- Specific operational activities, such as the use of lift trucks, chemicals, noise, personal protective equipment, control of contractors, permits to work and so on.
- Proactive monitoring activities, such as planned inspections and reactive monitoring through accident investigation – in fact, all the activities that the risk management assessment has identified as requiring a formal standard to ensure that the protective and preventative measures are adequately controlled.

Within all these codes the following features should be evident:

- A statement that the code is formal organization policy and will be enforced through the normal management channels.
- Assignment to a senior manager of responsibility for the code's development and monitoring. (Such assignment of responsibility does not detract from the responsibility of those in charge of the area in which the activities are performed to ensure that standards are achieved. Their responsibilities should also be defined.)
- Codes should then detail the activities and standards needed to achieve adequate control, through consultation, communication and the competence of project personnel.

613

- The codes should also set out arrangements for performance and management reviews.

Policy audit

The formal statements of organization planning and implementation just described, as well as the performance and management review codes, will help the process of auditing the safety management system. It is strongly recommended that a regular (perhaps annual) audit of the whole safety management system is conducted by someone who is independent of the system and the organization's operational activities. This person could be from another part of the organization or from an external consultancy.

A number of in-house proprietary audit systems have been developed to facilitate appraisals. These include:

- CHASE: *The Complete Health and Safety Evaluation System*, from Health and Safety Technology Management Limited, Birmingham.
- *Five Star System*, British Safety Council, London.
- ISRS: *International Safety Rating System*, the International Loss Control Institute.
- QSA: *The Quality Safety Audit*, from the Royal Society for the Prevention of Accidents (RoSPA), Birmingham.

REFERENCES AND FURTHER READING

Bird, F. E. jun. and Germain, G. L., *Practical Loss Control Leadership*, Institute Publishing, Loganville, G., 1985.

Croner's Health and Safety at Work, Croner Publications, New Malden (with updating service).

Fife, I. and Machin, E. A., *Redgrave, Fife and Machin. Health and Safety*, Butterworths, London, 1990.

Greenburg, H. R. and Cramer, J. G. (eds), *Risk Assessment and Risk Management for the Chemical Process Industry*, Van Nostrand Reinhold, New York, 1991.

Her Majesty's Stationery Office, *Successful Health and Safety Management*, HS(G)65, HMSO, London 1991.

Managing Occupational Health and Safety, checklist no. 91, Institute of Management, Corby.

Offshore Installation (Safety Case) Regulations, HMSO, London.

Ridley, J., *Safety at Work*, 3rd edn, Butterworth–Heinemann, London, 1990.

Smith, A. J., *The Development of a Model to Incorporate Management and Organizational Influences in Quantified Risk Assessment*, HSE Contract Research Report, no. 38/1992, HMSO, London, 1992.

Stranks, J. W., *The RoSPA Health and Safety Practice Handbook*, 2nd edn, Pitman, London, 1991.

The Health and Safety Factbook, Professional Publishing, London (with updating service).

Tolley's Health and Safety at Work Handbook, 5th edn, Tolley, Croydon, 1992.

ACKNOWLEDGEMENT

Extracts from *Successful Health and Safety Management*, HS(G)65, included in this chapter are reproduced with the permission of the Controller of Her Majesty's Stationery Office.

33 Project Management and the Environment

Eric Cowell

Environmental management issues are principally concerned with what happens 'outside the fence' of the project site. They are about protecting the living world from avoidable or unacceptable damage and safeguarding natural resources.

INTRODUCTION

It is common in industry to group health and safety and the environment together (HSE). Although it might be easy to understand the administrative advantages of linking these three subjects, this approach demonstrates a fundamental misunderstanding of the practical management implications and of the nature of environmental issues.

Health and safety (barring major accidents such as explosions) are mainly 'inside the fence' concerns for project managers. The issues are generally covered by the Health and Safety at Work Act and its various regulations. The skills required for managing industrial health and safety relate principally to the design of the installed project, operating procedures and the attitude of management to the workplace and the workforce. The previous chapter covered most of this subject. This chapter, therefore, concentrates on matters that affect the environment 'outside the project fence'.

Environmental awareness has increased greatly in recent years and has become internationalized, scientifically based and politicized. Few of the environmental issues which arouse concern are actually new. What is new is the public demand for action. Hardly a day now passes without media attention on global climate warming, depletion of the ozone layer, hazardous substances, and so on.

The pursuit of environmental excellence is not an option for industry: it is a precondition for long-term business success. Increasingly, the public (and governmental agencies who are supposed to represent their interests) want to

know what projects are about, and what is being done to ensure that each development is environmentally acceptable. The developer must earn his licence to operate.

The environmental impacts of projects, whether actually experienced, scientifically predicted, or imaginary, inevitably become politically charged. These concerns can extend to local, regional, national, international or even wider boundaries. Politically charged public interest has led many industrial companies to link environmental activity to their public relations (PR) operations. This is a big mistake. The role of PR is to communicate information. This will, of course, include information about environmental matters, but PR must never itself be allowed to become the driving force in setting company environmental policy. Environmental management policy must aim to protect natural resources and the world in which we and our future generations expect to continue to live. Environmental aspects of project management must always be soundly based on a realistic evaluation and understanding of all the factors.

No two projects are ever exactly alike and each can bring its own problems. Anyone who tries to analyse the business implications of environmental issues soon learns that targets are constantly moving, with new issues emerging from time to time. Today's standards are a foretaste of tougher standards tomorrow. Yesterday's complacency has a nasty habit of becoming tomorrow's headache. It pays to build good environmental protection into a project from its earliest stages, and to incorporate good practice throughout commissioning, operation and even eventual closure. There is a growing number of businesses in which the costs of meeting environmental requirements during or following the closure of an industrial plant have exceeded the total lifetime operating profits.

THE NATURE OF ENVIRONMENTAL ISSUES

Issues might be local, regional, national or global. They can impinge on society immediately or be long term and difficult to assess in terms of cost and commercial effects.

Global issues

Global issues include the so-called greenhouse effect, in which climate warming is thought to be occurring as a result of increased carbon dioxide in the atmosphere, caused by the burning of fossil fuels, deforestation and other activities. The consequences include major changes in land use patterns and agricultural productivity, together with resultant phenomena such as melting polar ice caps, rise in sea level, and so on. The greenhouse effect could cause major political changes and markedly affect the world's commercial climate over the next 20–50 years.

By contrast, more immediate effects could be caused by changes in global stratospheric ozone. The so-called holes in the ozone layer allow greater penetration of ultraviolet (UV) light, which is associated with an increased incidence of skin cancer in man. The causes of ozone depletion are linked principally to release into the atmosphere of chlorofluorocarbons (CFCs) and *617* other gases, including halons used in firefighting. Global action to reduce the damage is already being taken. There are implications for the energy and chemical industries.

Other serious international issues include acid rain, which results from sulphur dioxide and nitrogen oxides released from the burning of fossil fuels. It has been identified in Europe, North America, India, Asia and elsewhere. Effects attributed to acid rain include damage to fish populations in lakes and rivers and alleged damage to coniferous forests. Legislative stringency on combustion emissions is tightening. Preventive costs may be significant in terms of fuel type, quality and formulation.

International concern has also been focused on toxic substances, toxic products and the disposal of toxic waste. The legislative framework is complex: compliance at all levels demands responsibility from 'cradle to grave', and liability for rectification of poor practice in the past – no matter how acceptable that was at the time. Companies can therefore find themselves exposed to litigation. There is a trend for chief executives to be made personally liable: some senior managers in the United States have suffered fines and even prison sentences resulting from unsafe products or for marketing products without adequate information to ensure that their customers could take correct action to prevent harm to the environment or health.

Regional and local issues

Regional issues include avoiding the contamination of groundwater sources, in order to safeguard current and future potable and industrial supplies. The technical problems of cleaning up contaminated aquifers are formidable and costly, particularly where restoration to drinking quality is demanded. This issue is already a problem in a number of countries, notably Britain, the United States, Canada and Australia.

Protection of native populations and their subsistence, food production, fauna and flora, avoidance of oil spills, and rehabilitation of land after mining and quarrying are all of primary regional and local importance.

There is global concern for some issues which are initially or superficially regional in character. An example is the loss of tropical rainforest and other widespread deforestation. Concerns include regional and global climatic change, local erosion, loss of resources for indigenous people, loss of potentially useful species and loss of timber supplies. The issue is founded on good science: increasing attention is being given to industrial development as a component of the problem. Future operations must be planned and conducted to minimize their impact. In 1988 the World Bank took the initiative to ensure that its funds for development would not damage the rainforest ecosystem. World pressure is growing to save what is left of the forests, and any industrial operation conducted in rainforest areas will come under close scrutiny from a variety of environmental organizations, most of which are highly skilled in communicating and lobbying.

Local environmental problems are individual in character, relating to local geography, the perception and priorities of society and the nature of the industrial operation. Satisfying local issues can be time consuming and costly.

PUBLIC AND GOVERNMENTAL ATTITUDES

Environmental issues have all become matters of public concern and attention. What might once have been regarded as an unfortunate but inevitable consequence of progress is today perceived as development that is harmful and avoidable. The evolution of this attitude towards the protection of human beings and the environment has been accelerated by major industrial accidents and by chronic happenings such as groundwater contamination, the acid rain issue and realization of the extent to which equatorial forests have been reduced.

Although environmental awareness in society is often well founded, public perceptions of risk are frequently out of step with the real risks. Political activity and legislative and regulatory regimes are often in advance of scientific understanding. 'Green' politics, 'green' consumers, 'green' products and 'green' investment are all becoming everyday catchphrases that reflect growing public demand for good industrial practice. The concept of 'sustainable growth' put forward by the United Nations Special Commission on the Environment has taken root and all of the UN agencies are modifying their programmes towards a coordinated 'sustainable growth' approach.

Environmental issues affect the legislative and regulatory climate, impose cost burdens on industry and can cause delays to projects. It has become essential for environmental issues to be recognized as an integrated component of project planning, linked to genuine efforts to meet local communities and to maintain an open dialogue.

INTERNATIONALIZATION

The trend for the environmental legislation of developed nations to be cascaded out into the developing nations continues at an accelerated rate. It is, regrettably, in part driven by political moves to remove the hidden trade barriers that are created by the cost of regulatory compliance in the developed nations. 1988 and 1989 saw international action on CFCs and the ozone layer, together with the initiation of intensive legislative preparatory work for protecting the earth from the greenhouse effect. Moves to impose differential taxes to reduce carbon dioxide emissions into the atmosphere have been tabled in the EC and are on the OECD agenda.

Furthermore, while most environmental issues are complex, political expediency often drives governments to legislate and regulate in advance of scientific understanding. For example, the EC nations are introducing legislation to control acid rain by reducing sulphur dioxide emissions, yet scientists (at the time of writing) still cannot give any assurance that the perceived damages are really due to acid precipitation, or that reduction in sulphur dioxide emissions will quantitatively reduce the problem, or that cost effective programmes have been devised.

Such countermeasures can result in increased project capital expenditure and post-commissioning operating costs. The competitive position of a company which operates within a regulated industry is therefore weakened when compared with companies in less stringently regulated regions.

Environmental zeal can erect invisible trade barriers. It can trigger political activity, regionally and internationally, to encourage the laxer nations to adopt tighter standards.

Industry cannot expect that operations in underdeveloped regions can be undertaken with laxer standards than those of the developed world. To do so exposes the risk of future penalties, heavy capital burdens, tarnished reputations and, perhaps in some cases, the need to return to a site of former project activity to clean up the mess.

In good project management the developer must participate positively in a debate with all interested sections of the community. The dialogue must be soundly based in good science, technology and industrial design. A thorough understanding of each issue, its perception by the local public, and the local, national, international and political nuances is essential. Without such understanding, any influence that can be exerted on future political events will be minimal. A high profile in the organizations influencing the resolution of issues must be established and maintained, either individually or collectively.

MANAGING ENVIRONMENTAL ASPECTS OF PROJECT DEVELOPMENT

There can be no doubt that the project developer is directly responsible for dealing with environmental issues. The chief executive of the development company is the person who must ultimately 'carry the can'.

Every company undertaking a project, whatever its nature and objectives, must have an environmental policy that is clearly stated, understood by every employee and linked to that of the parent company. This statement may be a simple document but, to ensure its implementation, it requires action programmes, organizational arrangements and carefully prepared operational procedures.

Every business is unique and the supporting programmes to ensure that policy is not merely a paper tiger require careful preparation to suit the individual operations for which they are intended. The commitment to protect the environment must be seen to be, and must actually be, sincere and adhered to.

Dealing with environmental issues requires professionalism, either in-house or contracted-in from an external consultant acting in an advisory capacity. In today's world nothing less than a professional approach is acceptable; it is as essential as budgetary control, the engineering, the construction programme and the commissioning. It remains an integral part of the management function throughout subsequent operations and even ultimate closure.

The environmental consequences of every project should be identified, both in terms of local and wider issues. The project plan should incorporate an environmental programme, and management/organizational and consultative arrangements to ensure compliance with the clearly stated policy.

Some form of daily monitoring and control is also essential. Environmental staff may have to be an integral component of site and head office project teams. For example, some big development projects, such as the oil industry construction work in Shetland and at Wytch Farm in Dorset, and the North West Shelf gas projects in Australia, have had resident environmental officers, including ecologists.

Most multinational corporations have learned that strong environmental departments supported by good environmental science are a cost effective necessity. Many small companies are only just beginning to recognize that environmental protection is a significant constraint on their development. Delegation of environmental responsibility down through business organizations must be on a formal basis, with written job descriptions that include the expected environmental roles. Every employee should be aware of the person to whom he answers for environmental matters. Feedback loops are vital, to ensure that perceived problems are communicated upwards to the level of management necessary for action.

Environmental protection management has important spin-offs in relations with employees, the public, the media and the statutory authorities. It is vital that managements inform employees and others not only about assessments, but also on the monitoring: this can help to create goodwill, which is important at all times and especially when incidents occur.

It is in the developer's interest to take an early initiative in environmental protection management in order to:

- Genuinely minimize environmental damage.
- Define baseline conditions that can be used later for comparative purposes.
- Demonstrate a capability for self-monitoring and regulation.
- Provide data which can assist in debate with regulatory authorities.
- Provide assurances to authorities and the public, thereby helping to generate trust and confidence.
- Demonstrate scientific and technical credibility when participating in local debate.
- Enhance the industry and company image.

Good environmental protection management rests upon three pillars:

1 Environmental impact assessment (EIA).
2 Environmental monitoring.
3 Environmental reviews.

These procedures, if well conducted, will ensure that the environmental impact of project development is comprehensively assessed and that appropriate technical and operational procedures are adopted to minimize any possible adverse impact. The procedures are cost effective and are aimed at integrating environmental considerations into the earliest phases of development or acquisition of new assets. Expensive delays are avoided, and exposure to the risk of environmental impairment liability is minimized.

Environmental impact assessment (EIA)

The immediate objective of an EIA is to predict or measure the environmental impacts of an industrial activity and to identify the social impacts. Its ultimate objective is to minimize those impacts. The industrial activity might be a new development, extension of an existing facility or a proposed acquisition. The process involves the implementation of sound scientific, technical and/or administrative controls.

Increasingly, an impact assessment is a prerequisite to obtaining a statutory licence to proceed with a development. Consultation with environmental advisers at the early stage of choosing locations will often save time and unnecessary costs. The development needs to be fairly well defined before the detailed assessment can start. This will allow the necessary interactive process to commence, in which the assessment identifies more desirable options for the development and begins to lay down technical, constructional and operational objectives. These will include, among other things:

- Anti-pollution measures.
- Handling of wastes.
- Aesthetic requirements.
- Site rehabilitation after construction.
- Rehabilitation of the area at the end of the useful operating life of the development.

The EIA enables management to identify the residual impacts of their development and to decide whether an acceptable balance exists between the impacts and the cost of appropriate safeguards: also, whether management believes it can maintain and improve that balance throughout the whole life of the development.

On an existing facility or a new acquisition, the assessment will seek to establish the quality of environmental protection and identify matters requiring attention (which might include liabilities arising from inadequate environmental protection management).

An early understanding of a development's likely environmental effects and of acceptable standards of performance is an important element of the location, design, construction, operational and abandonment phases. Early resolution of potential environment problems can avoid or limit:

- Undue environmental damage at all stages of the development.
- Delays that could result in significant additional costs or other penalties.
- Adverse publicity.
- Unexpected costs owing to design changes or later remedial measures.
- Burdening future management and the shareholders whom they serve with difficult social problems.

Assessment timing

Experience has shown that, to be of most benefit, the assessment should start at the development conception stage, to ensure that environmental aspects are properly considered when initial decisions are formed. Early reconnaissance of possible locations for a project site can save time and unnecessary costs later. The early identification of environmentally sensitive aspects of a development will obviously provide important guidance to management.

Development should, however, have reached a fairly well-defined state before commencing the detailed assessment appropriate to meeting regulatory requirements and self-imposed (in-house) environmental standards.

Subsequent reviews throughout the life of the project are essential.

Organizational aspects of environmental assessment

Multi-disciplined teams are required to prepare assessments for large developments, and for smaller projects where these involve high and diverse environmental senstitivity. For smaller, simpler projects, assessments can sometimes be completed by one person with specialist support.

An assessment team might comprise personnel from the project team, the competent authorities or external consultants. A coordinator should be appointed to:

- Ensure that all those from all disciplines are working to a coordinated brief, that information is exchanged, and that duplication of effort is avoided.
- Act as a contact point with the development management.
- Organize and collate team members' input to produce a document for management, the authorities and, possibly, for the public.

It is advisable to provide the team with terms of reference that set out scope and time objectives. However, it is important that the team has a brief which is sufficiently flexible to allow identification and proper consideration of all the potential environmental effects.

Assessment scope

The scope of any environmental impact assessment will obviously depend on the nature of the development, its location, and local issues and concerns. Regional, national and international factors can also be relevant. In the final analysis, the assessment scope could be influenced by the perceived needs as defined locally by the nature of the location, legislative requirements, public perception of the development, cultural activities, and so forth. Consultation with local interests is essential, and might well be a statutory requirement for planning purposes.

The composition of an assessment can only be defined in general terms, but it will usually consist of:

1 *Description of the existing environment and socio-economic conditions* This is a broad description of the existing biological, physical and human settings to provide baselines from which to identify potential effects of the development on the environment – and also of possible effects of the environment on the development. Baseline data collection and description will be limited to the environmental (including socio-economic) aspects that are likely to be significantly affected. Examples of aspects to be covered include population, fauna, flora, soil, water, air, climatic factors, landscape, land use and the cultural, architectural and archaeological heritage of the location.

2 *Description of the development* This will cover the facilities and activities that will be associated with construction, operation and eventual abandonment. It should describe the physical characteristics of the whole development together with a brief description of the industrial processes and the nature and quantities of materials used. It should also set out the measures taken or proposed to prevent, reduce and offset any significant adverse effects on the environment, including those from any discharges to air, water or land.

3 *Contingency planning* This part of the document should list and describe potential environmentally damaging incidents, with a risk analysis and the contingency plans for dealing with them.

4 *Description of the effects on the environment* This is a description of the foreseen effects of the proposed development on the environment. These effects might be listed under some combination or permutation of the following headings:

(a) Direct
(b) Indirect
(c) Secondary
(d) Cumulative
(e) Short-term
(f) Medium-term
(g) Long-term
(h) Permanent
(i) Temporary
(j) Positive (beneficial)
(k) Negative (deleterious)

and this classification should be taken further according to whether or not the effects result from:

(a) the existence of the development;
(b) the use of natural resources; or
(c) the discharge of liquid, solid or gaseous wastes.

Project and baseline information are used to identify potential effects. Their significance and magnitude are assessed using technical and scientific information and through discussions with appropriate authorities, academic institutions and public groups.

5 *Summary* This is a summary of the information provided in the EIA.

6 *Recommendation* Recommendations should be made to minimize environmental impacts for the design, construction and operational phases of the development throughout preparation of the EIA. These can be collated for inclusion in in-house EIAs. In rare instances, environmental considerations might be considered too sensitive, or otherwise sufficient to recommend that the development as proposed should not take place (for example, threat to a rare habitat or an endangered species). In most cases, however, an acceptable alternative siting or design of plant, buildings and other facilities can be found.

Environmental monitoring

Environmental monitoring is necessary to establish that the controls are achieving the set objectives. It involves regular chemical and biological procedures coupled to management and supervisory procedures.

The monitoring portfolio must be developed at the assessment stage, so as to provide management with the procedures that will apply during both construction and subsequent operations. The procedures will include, as appropriate, actions to be taken in the case of any emergency that could result in an acute impact on the environment.

In many cases the procedures will require endorsement by the statutory authorities, and some procedures will actually become requirements by the authorities. It is important that both construction and operational managements should review the monitoring portfolio regularly to ensure that it always matches their own requirements and those laid down by the authorities.

Environmental reviews

Environmental reviews are periodic checks of the effectiveness of the technical and management controls, and of the chemical and biological monitoring portfolio. It is necessary to carry out these reviews from time to time to ensure that the controls remain valid, that redundancy is removed or replaced, and that predictions made at the environmental assessment were sound and balanced.

Reviews performed in respect of an existing facility are likely to be less penetrating in detail than the original assessment of the facility.

The need for a review is always indicated when a change to the development is proposed or stipulated, and is a requirement that should be built into the organization's formal change approval procedures. The environmental effects of changes must be assessed and accepted.

The effectiveness of environmental reviews can be enhanced by introducing one or more independent members into the review team.

Because environmental reviews check the accuracy of predictions made at the assessment stage and recommend any remedial changes to procedures or actions, they effectively close a control feedback loop for the environmental management system.

LESSONS FOR INDUSTRY

- Environmental issues are growing in terms of their effects on industry.
- This growth can be expected to continue in the foreseeable future.
- Environmental issues are probably now the biggest constraint to industrial development.
- The environment must be an important consideration in any long- and short-term planning.
- Environmentalism is increasingly political, institutionalized and part of government organization.
- Industry must be prepared to be involved at all levels including scientific research, risk evaluation and education.
- Industrial response must be based on sound science and technology.
- Businesses should incorporate environmental assessment and costs into the economics of all activities from 'cradle to grave'. These considerations should take into account the short- and long-term environmental aspects, right through to ultimate closure and abandonment.
- All projects, including acquisitions and closures, should be subjected to environmental investigation.
- Some long-term issues will affect the marketplace.
- Public perception of environmental performance is likely to be an increasing factor in customer preference.
- Environmental challenges can present business opportunities, once the effort has been made to solve the main problems (for example, in renewable energy resources, forestry, alternative fuels and so forth).
- No environmental issue can be ignored.

FURTHER READING

BS 7750, *Specification for Environmental Systems*, British Standards Institution, Milton Keynes.

Collins, M. N., Sayer, A. J., and Whitmore, T. C., *The Conservation Atlas of Tropical Forests*, Macmillan, London, 1991.

Commission of the European Community, *The State of the Environment in the European Community*, Commission of the European Community, Luxembourg, 1987.

Davies, R. A. (ed.), *The Greening of Business*, Gower, Aldershot, 1991.

Holdgate, L. *et al.*, *The World Environment*, a report by the United Nations Environment Programme (UNEP), Tycooly, Dublin, 1982.

IPCC, *Reports of IPCC Working Groups I and II*, IPCC, Geneva, 1989.

Lean, Geoffrey, Hinrichsen, Don, and Markham, Adam, *WWF Atlas of the Environment*, Arrow Books, London, 1990.

Nicholson-Lord, David, *The Greening of the Cities*, Routledge & Kegan Paul, London, 1987.

Organization for Economic Cooperation and Development, *Environmental Data Compendium 1989*, OECD, Paris.

Our Common Future, Report of the World Commission on Environment and Development, Oxford University Press, Oxford, 1987.

Sadgrove, Kit, *The Green Manager's Handbook*, Gower, Aldershot, 1992.

United Nations Economic Programme, *Environmental Auditing*, UNEP Technical Report Series No 2, UNEP, Paris, 1989.

World Health Organization, *Management of Hazardous Waste*, WHO, Copenhagen, 1983.

Appendix A: Code of conduct for project managers

The following is an extract from the Code of Conduct issued by the Association of Project Managers (APM), which is the UK affiliate of INTERNET. For more information about INTERNET and the APM, see Appendix B.

CODE OF CONDUCT

A member of APM has responsibilities to his client, his employer, the project's users, colleagues, the profession and the general public. All members should recognize these responsibilities when exercising authority as a project manager and follow this code of conduct.

Personal responsibilities

A project manager shall:

- Accept responsibility for his actions.
- Act honestly and in such a manner to ensure that his client is not misled.
- Ensure that his professional skills are kept up to date by continuing personal development and education.
- Not give nor accept any gifts, payment or inducement of more than nominal value to or from people with a business relationship with employers or clients.
- Declare all matters which could be construed as a conflict of interest.
- Respect the confidentiality of his client's information.
- Act in the best interests of his client in all business and professional matters.
- Not replace another project manager without a clear written instruction from his client and prior notification to the other project manager.
- Be realistic in reporting and forecasting project progress, quality, cost and time.

Professional responsibilities

A project manager shall:

- Only accept responsibility for and undertake projects for which he believes himself to be competent.
- Not act in a manner that would injure the professional reputation, prospects or business of others and be ethical in all methods of seeking to secure and develop business.
- Encourage and assist the personal development of staff and colleagues.
- Before undertaking an assignment, ensure that the terms of engagement, including the scope of the service, limits of responsibilities, terms of remuneration and provision for termination are agreed and understood by both parties.
- Ensure that all delegated tasks are satisfactorily monitored and controlled.
- Take all possible steps to anticipate and prevent contractual disputes and, when called upon to resolve any such disputes, act equitably.
- Not subcontract any work without the prior consent of his client.
- Endeavour to ensure that resources are available when required and are efficiently used.
- In appropriate circumstances provide and maintain adequate professional indemnity, employers and third party insurances.
- Accept that in the event of a complaint regarding professional activities against any member [of the APM] the Council of the APM may nominate a person or persons to decide whether there is a case to answer. If so, the Council shall conduct an investigation.
- Accept that any member found to be in breach of this code may be disciplined by the Council by means of reprimand, suspension or termination of membership.

Note

All project managers are expected to be active members of the Association of Project Managers who will maintain and improve their knowledge and level of competence by regular attendance at meetings, seminars and similar project management training courses.

Appendix B: The International Project Management Association (INTERNET) and the Association of Project Managers (APM)

The information which follows has been adapted or summarized (with permission) from INTERNET and APM publications.

INTERNET

Developments in Europe and internationally imply an increasing need for internationalization in project management. More and more projects rely upon a pan-European cooperation due to the implementation of the open European market and to the dramatic changes in middle and eastern Europe. Worldwide there is an increasing need for skills in managing international projects, including overcoming cultural and language boundaries. This confirms a need for INTERNET itself, with its unique strength in the network of project management professionals in many countries that has been developed over several years.

INTERNET, based in Zurich, is an international non-profit network type of organization for qualified project management. The mission of INTERNET is to promote project management as the most powerful tool for management of changes, both nationally and internationally.

The means of the promotion are:

- To promote the *application* of project management.
- To support *implementation* of project management knowledge.

- To stimulate further *enhancement* and development of the topic.

Promotion at the national level is done through serving the national associations of project management and the international members of INTERNET and facilitating exchange of their experience.

Internationally INTERNET is the platform for development and implementation of skilled European and international project management – the means of which is a strong network of professionals and institutions in Europe and worldwide.

INTERNET organizes expert seminars and bi-annual world congresses which are attended by project managers from over 40 countries.

The body of INTERNET is the unified whole of national associations, international members and exclusive members.

APM

The Association of Project Managers is the only UK-based organization dedicated to the professional development of project managers in all industries. It is affiliated to INTERNET.

The Association is fast growing and committed to an energetic programme of activities to help project managers and others involved in or interested in project management to progress their personal careers and to further develop professionalism in project management.

Aims and objectives

The Association's aims and objectives are:

- To be the first point of contact for and the national authority on project management and, through INTERNET, an international authority.
- To further development of professionalism in project management.
- To represent the interests of project managers in all sections of industry, commerce, the arts and education, irrespective of professional discipline.
- To achieve recognized standards and certification for project managers, leading, in the longer term, to obtaining chartered status.
- To achieve national and international recognition for all certificated project managers.
- To establish and maintain an active national branch network to facilitate participation by all members throughout the country.
- To provide and maintain a comprehensive training programme suitable for project managers at all levels of experience and competence.

Publications and information services

The APM produces a regular news magazine *Project* for its members, which contains articles plus details of of activities at international, national and branch level.

The *International Journal of Project Management*, which contains papers and articles from constituent members of INTERNET, is also available to members.

APM headquarters staff maintain a wide-ranging database and library of publications on the project management theme.

APM will put members in touch with others in specific professions and disciplines to share information.

Membership of the APM

Details about the various grades of individual and corporate membership and on the APM's certification process for project managers are obtainable from:

The Association of Project Managers
85 Oxford Road
High Wycombe
Buckinghamshire HP11 2DX.

Index